The Common Sense Book of Baby and Child Care

By Benjamin Spock, M.D.

with illustrations by
Dorothea Fox

The Common Sense Book of Baby and Child Care

by Benjamin Spock, M. D.

 **ISHI PRESS INTERNATIONAL**

The Common Sense Book of Baby and Child Care

by Benjamin Spock, M. D.
Illustrations by Dorothea Fox

First Published in 1946
Copyright © 1945, 1946, 1957 by Benjamin Spock

This Printing in April, 2013
by Ishi Press in New York and Tokyo
with a new introduction by Sam Sloan

Copyright © 2013 by Sam Sloan

ISBN 4-87187-969-0
978-4-87187-969-9

Ishi Press International
1664 Davidson Avenue, Suite 1B
Bronx NY 10453-7877
USA
samhsloan@gmail.com
1-917-507-7226

Printed in the United States of America

Introduction by Sam Sloan

The Common Sense Book of Baby and Child Care
by Benjamin Spock, M. D.
Introduction by Sam Sloan

This is a reprint of the One and Only Original book by Dr. Benjamin Spock on Baby and Child Care. This is not one of those cheap, pocked sized revisions. Prior to this reprint, the original book had not been reprinted since 1957. Instead there have been many new books, all bearing Dr. Spock's name, but these have been considerably different books and usually much shorter.

No book published after 1957 has been a true reprint of the original book. Starting with *Baby and Child Care* (2nd ed.). New York: Pocket Books (1957), books have been coming out claiming to be new editions of the original book, but in reality they are different books, not the same book. Poor Dr. Spock has had to cater to the demands of various pressure groups who demanded revisions of his work.

For example, feminists did not like the fact that Dr. Spock referred to the baby as "he", so therefore every pronoun in the book had to be changed. When Gay Rights came along, the gays were outraged that Dr. Spock did not take into consideration Gay parents, so the gays had to be accommodated. (The last I knew, the parents of a child consisted of one man and one woman, but I am not up-to-date with the latest trends on that.)

The result is that these new and updated editions that have continued to come out long after Dr. Spock has died have gotten further and further away from the original book so that they are no longer recognizable.

I am the father of eight children and I discovered this when I decided that I wanted to buy Dr. Spock's original book. I was shocked to discover that the original book with the title "**The Common Sense Book of Baby and Child Care**" was out of print and completely unavailable for purchase anywhere and

Introduction by Sam Sloan

that books such as *Dr. Spock's Baby and Child Care for the Nineties* (5th ed.) (1985) and *Dr. Spock's Baby and Child Care* (6th ed.) (1992) were vastly different books, not the same book at all. Since Dr. Spock died on March 15, 1998 at age 94, any revision since then must have been done without his involvement.

It happens that my own mother had exactly the same background as Dr. Spock. My mother, Dr. Helen Marjorie Sloan, born in 1910, was a medical doctor who was a resident in both pediatrics and psychiatry, which are exactly the same fields as Dr. Spock. My mother was a child psychiatrist. Dr. Spock was born on May 2, 1903, so he was only slightly older. My mother met Dr. Spock several times, as every year she attended meetings of the American Academy of Child Psychiatry and the American Orthopsychiatric Association. Unfortunately, my mother is no longer with us, so I cannot ask her what she thinks of the numerous revisions of Dr. Spock's work that have been taking place ever since he died.

Dr. Spock's books are the best selling books, second only to the Holy Bible, ever since they first started coming out in 1946, published by Duell, Sloan and Pearce. Dr. Spock has also been blamed for all of the evils of modern society. Before Dr. Spock, if a child misbehaved, you spanked him (or her). However, Dr. Spock made spanking a child a "No, No". Nowadays, if you spank your child and the child welfare authorities find out about it, the police will come and haul you off to jail and your kid will be put into foster care.

So, it was entirely the fault of Dr. Spock for the permissiveness that pervades society today. By the way, my mother, Dr. Sloan, never spanked us. This the reason my brother, born in 1946, the same year that this book came out, turned out to be so evil.

Sam Sloan
San Rafael, California
USA
April 22, 2013

Contents

8 · CONTENTS

THE COMMON SENSE BOOK

OF BABY AND CHILD CARE

A Letter to the Reader of This New Edition

Most of you have a doctor you can consult. He knows your child, and therefore he is the only person in a position to advise you wisely about how you should treat him. By glancing at a rash or asking a couple of questions over the telephone, he can usually get to the solution of a problem that reading would only get you more mixed up about. This book is not meant to be used for diagnosis or treatment; it's only meant to give you a general understanding of children, their troubles and their needs. It is true that in certain sections there is emergency advice for those very few parents who are out of reach of a doctor. It's better for them to have book advice than no advice at all. But book advice is never so helpful or so safe as real medical assistance.

I want to apologize to the mother and father who have a girl and are frustrated by having the child called **him** all through this book. It's clumsy to say **him or her** every time, and I need **her** to refer to the mother.

The most important thing I have to say is that you should not take too literally what is said in this book. Every child is different, every parent is different, every illness or behavior problem is somewhat different from every other. All I can do is describe the most common developments and problems, in the most general terms. Remember that you know a lot about your child and that I don't know anything about him.

If you are an old reader of this book, you'll see that a lot has been added and changed, especially about discipline, spoiling, and the parents' part. When I was writing the first edition, between 1943 and 1946, the attitude of a majority of people toward infant feeding, toilet training, and general child management was still fairly strict and inflexible. However, the need for greater understanding of children and for flexibility in their care had been made clear by educators, psychoanalysts, and pediatricians, and I was trying to encourage this. Since then a great change in attitude has occurred, and nowadays there seems to be more chance of a conscientious parent's getting into trouble with permissiveness than with strictness. So I have tried to give a more balanced view.

The chapter on twins has been greatly enlarged, thanks to ingenious suggestions from about 200 mothers of twins. The only chapter that has been shortened is the one on formulas for emergency use. There are now 2 formulas instead of 11, on the suggestion of 100 pediatricians whom I consulted by mail. Many smaller changes have been made. I owe a lot of them to letters from parents, public-health nurses, and physicians.

The people who have given me most help on the entire manuscript are Dr. John Reinhart, Dr. William Wallace, Dr. Samuel Spector. Those who have helped with one part or another are Dr. John Kennel, Dr. Marian Putnam, Dr. Donald Jackson, Dr. John Kaster, Dr. David Friedman, Dr. John Montgomery, Dr. Charles O'Regan, Dr. Milton Levine, Dr. Abram Blau, Dr. Frederick Hunt, Dr. Irving Sunshine, Dr. Edwin Gerrish, and Mary Hamm Flumerfelt. Carol Colbert has typed and retyped thousands of pages of manuscript with unfailing cheerfulness. Jane Spock has made the most essential contribution of all in graciously giving up four evenings a week for two years while I wrote and erased and wrote again.

The Parents' Part

TRUST YOURSELF

1. You know more than you think you do. Soon you're going to have a baby. Maybe you have him already. You're happy and excited, but if you haven't had much experience, you wonder whether you are going to know how to do a good job. Lately you have been listening more carefully to your friends and relatives when they talk about bringing up a child. You've begun to read articles by experts in the magazines and newspapers. After the baby is born, the doctor and nurses will begin to give you instructions, too. Sometimes it sounds like a very complicated business. You find out all the vitamins a baby needs and all the inoculations. One mother tells you that egg should be given early because of its iron, and another says that egg should be delayed to avoid allergy. You hear that a baby is easily spoiled by being picked up too much but also that a baby must be cuddled plenty; that fairy tales make children nervous, and that fairy tales are a wholesome outlet.

Don't take too seriously all that the neighbors say. Don't be overawed by what the experts say. Don't be afraid to trust your own common sense. Bringing up your child won't be a complicated job if you take it easy, trust your own instincts, and follow the directions that your doctor gives you. We know for a fact that the natural loving care that kindly parents give their children is a hundred times more valuable than their knowing how to pin a diaper on just right or how to make a formula expertly. Every time you pick your baby up, even if you do it a little awkwardly at first, every time you change him, bathe him, feed him, smile at him, he's getting a feeling that he belongs to you and that you belong to him. Nobody else in the world, no matter how skillful, can give that to him.

It may surprise you to hear that the more people have studied different methods of bringing up children the more they have come to the conclusion that what good mothers and fathers instinctively feel like doing for their babies is usually best, after all. Furthermore, all parents do their best job when they have a natural, easy confidence in themselves. Better to make a few mistakes from being natural than to do everything letter-perfect out of a feeling of worry.

Prenatal classes for expectant mothers and fathers are provided in many communities by the Visiting Nurse Association, the Red Cross, or the city health department. They are very helpful in discussing the questions and problems that all expectant parents have concerning pregnancy, delivery, and care of the baby.

PARENTS ARE HUMAN

2. They have needs. Books about child care, like this one, put so much emphasis on all the needs that children have—for love, for understanding, for patience, for consistency, for firmness, for protection, for comradeship, for calories and vitamins—that parents sometimes feel physically and emotionally exhausted just from reading about what is expected of them. They get the impression that they are meant to have no needs themselves. They can't help feeling that an author who seems to be standing up for children all the time must be critical of parents when anything goes wrong.

It would be only fair if this book had an equal number of pages about the genuine needs of parents, the frustrations they constantly meet not only in the home but outside it, how tired they get, how much help their children could be if they were more considerate. The fact is that child rearing is a long, hard job and that parents are just as human as their children.

3. Some children are a lot more difficult than others. There is considerable evidence that different children are born with quite different temperaments. Parents can't order what they want. They take what they get. But parents have well-formed personalities, too, which they can't change overnight. One gentle couple might be ideally suited to raise a girl with a sweet, compliant nature, able to give her the freedom she needs in order to develop into an independent, capable person. They may not be nearly so ready for an energetic, assertive boy. They may find him uncomfortable, baffling, and challenging, no matter how much they love him. Another couple may handle a spunky son they call Butch with ease and joy but be quite disappointed with a quiet one. Parents do the best they know how with the kind of child they receive.

4. At best, there's lots of hard work and deprivation. There is an enormous amount of hard work in child care—preparing the proper diet, washing diapers and clothes, cleaning up messes that an infant makes with his food and that an older child makes with his play, stopping fights and drying tears, listening to stories that are hard to understand, joining in games and reading stories that aren't very exciting to an adult, trudging around zoos and museums and carnivals, responding to pleas for help with homework, being slowed down in housework, yard work, and cellar work by eager helpers, going to Parent-Teacher Association meetings on tired evenings.

Children's needs account for a good part of the family budget, from the high rent or mortgage on a large enough house to the shoes that wear out or are outgrown in no time at all.

Children keep parents from parties, trips, theaters, meetings, games, friends. The fact that you prefer having children, wouldn't trade places with a childless couple for anything, doesn't alter the fact that you still miss your freedom.

Of course, parents don't have children because they want to be martyrs, or at least they shouldn't. They have them because they love children and want some of their very own. They also love children because they remember being loved so much by their parents in their own childhood. Taking care of their children, seeing them grow and develop into fine people, gives most parents—despite the hard work—their greatest satisfaction in life. This is creation. This is our visible immortality. Pride in other worldly accomplishments is usually weak in comparison.

5. Needless self-sacrifice sours everybody. But some conscientious young people facing the new responsibility of parenthood feel inside that they are called on to give up all their freedom and all their former pleasures, not as a matter of practicality, but almost as a matter of principle. Even if they do sneak off when a good chance comes, they feel too guilty to get full enjoyment. A little of this tendency is natural enough in the first few weeks of the first baby's life—it's all so new and over-whelming. But too much self-sacrificing is not good for parents **or** child. Parents become so preoccupied and tense that they're no fun for out-siders or for each other. They chafe at the imprisonment, despite the fact that it's self-imposed. They can't help resenting the child, even though he hasn't asked for this amount of devotion. As a result, they expect too much from him in return. Everything gets lopsided. In theory, bal-ance is achieved by giving your child what he needs most but keeping for yourselves such other interests and pleasures as won't hurt him at all. In this way you'll be able to love him more and show it more easily when you're with him.

6. Parents should expect something from their children. Since having children does mean giving up so much, good parents naturally do, and should, expect something from their children in return: not spoken thanks for being born or being cared for—that's too much—but consider-ateness, affectionateness, and willingness to accept the parents' stan-dards and ideals. The parents want these qualities in their children not only selfishly, for themselves, but because they want their children to grow up to live cooperatively and happily with others.

If parents are too hesitant in asking for reasonable behavior—because they have misunderstood theories of self-expression, because they are self-sacrificing by nature, or because they are afraid of making their chil-dren dislike them—they can't help resenting the bad behavior that comes instead. They keep getting angrier underneath, without knowing what to do about it. This bothers the child, too. It makes him feel guilty and scared, but it also makes him meaner and all the more demanding. If, for example, a baby acquires a taste for staying up in the evening and his mother is afraid to deny him this pleasure, he may, over a period of several months, turn into a disagreeable tyrant who keeps her walking for hours. She's bound to dislike him for his tyranny. If she can be en-couraged to be firm, it's amazing how fast he'll sweeten up and she will, too.

In other words, parents can't feel right toward their children in the long run unless they can make them behave reasonably, and children can't be happy unless they are behaving reasonably.

7. Parents are bound to get cross. I think that idealistic young people approaching parenthood assume that if they are the right sort they will have unlimited patience and love for their innocent baby. But this is not humanly possible. When your baby has been crying angrily for hours, despite all your patient efforts to comfort him, you can't go on feeling sympathetic. He seems like a disagreeable, obstinate, unappreciative person, and you can't help feeling angry—really angry. Or your older child has done something that he knows very well he shouldn't have done. Maybe he was so fascinated with a breakable object of yours or so eager to join some children on the other side of the street that he couldn't resist the temptation. Or maybe he was cross at you for having denied him something or angry at the baby for receiving so much attention. So he misbehaved from simple spite. When a child disobeys a well-understood and reasonable rule, you can't simply be a cool statue of justice. Any good parent feels strongly about right and wrong. You were taught to feel that way back in your own childhood. It's your rule that has been broken. It's probably your possession that has been damaged. It's your child, about whose character you care a great deal, who has done wrong. It's inevitable that you feel indignant. The child naturally expects this and is not hurt by it if your reaction is fair.

Sometimes it takes you a long time to realize that you are losing your temper. The child may have been putting on a series of irritating acts from the time he appeared at breakfast—making disagreeable remarks about the food, half deliberately knocking over a glass of milk, playing with something forbidden and breaking it, picking on a younger child—all of which you have tried to ignore in a supreme effort to be patient. Then at the final act, which perhaps isn't so bad, your resentment suddenly boils over, and it shocks you a little with its vehemence. Often when you look back over such a series of exasperating actions, you can see that the child has really been asking for firmness or punishment all morning and that it was your well-intentioned efforts at overpatience that made him go from one provocation to another, looking for a check.

We all get cross with our children, also, because of the pressures and frustrations we are feeling from other directions altogether. A sort of comic-strip example that's true to life concerns the father who comes home on edge from troubles that he's having in his work; he criticizes his wife, who then snaps at the older boy for something that ordinarily brings no disapproval, and he in turn picks on his younger sister.

8. Better to admit crossness. So far we have been discussing the inevitability of parental impatience and resentment from time to time. But it's just as important to consider a related question, Can the parent comfortably accept his cross feelings? Parents who aren't excessively strict with themselves are always able to admit their irritation. A natural, outspoken good mother whose child has been bedeviling her is able to say to a friend, half jokingly, "I don't think I can stand being in the house with him for another minute," or, "I'd enjoy giving him a thorough walloping." She may not carry out any of these thoughts, but she isn't ashamed to admit them to a sympathetic friend or to herself. It relieves her feelings to recognize them so clearly and to blow them off in talk. It also helps her to see what she has been putting up with and to be firmer in putting a stop to it.

It's the parents who set impossibly high standards for themselves, the parents who have angry feelings at times but can't believe that good parents should, who really suffer from them. When they detect such emotions stirring in themselves, they either feel unbearably guilty or try strenuously to deny them. But if a person tries to bury such feelings they only pop up somewhere else—as tenseness, for example, or tiredness or headache. Another indirect expression is overprotectiveness. A mother who can't ever admit that she feels antagonism toward her child imagines instead all the awful things that could beset him from other directions; she worries excessively about germs, or traffic. She tries to ward off these dangers by hovering over the child, and this tends to make him too dependent.

I'm not pointing out the problems created by denying crossness in order merely to relieve the uncomfortable feelings of parents. In general, what makes a parent miserable makes the child miserable, too. When a parent believes that antagonistic feelings are too horrible to admit, the child absorbs the same dread of them. In child-guidance clinics, we see children who develop fears of imaginary dangers—fear of insects, fear of going to school, fear of being separated from their parents—that prove on investigation to be disguises for ordinary angry feelings toward their parents that these perfectionistic children dare not recognize.

To put it the other way around, a child is happier around parents who aren't afraid to admit their anger, because then he can be more comfortable about his own. And justified anger that's expressed tends to clear the air and leave everyone feeling better. I am talking not about being rough on children but about admitting your feelings. And I don't mean that all the antagonism expressed toward children is justified. Here and there you see a harsh, unloving parent who abuses his child all hours of the day, verbally or physically, with little excuse and no shame. What I have been discussing is the irritation of parents whose conscientiousness and devotion to their children is plain to see.

A loving parent who feels angry **most** of the time (whether it's expressed openly or not) is suffering from a real emotional strain and deserves help from a psychiatrist or a social worker (Section 570). The anger may be coming from some entirely different direction.

9. Children like to be kept good. I've probably given a false impression by focusing so much on irritation. Most of us, when family life is running with fair smoothness, get cross or angry only during occasional crises, though, as we all know, there are more of these on some days than others. The way we avoid irritation the rest of the time, whether we realize it or not, is by keeping our children under reasonable control and by being extra firm or sufficiently disapproving when things first threaten to go wrong. Such firmness is one aspect of parental love. By keeping children on the right track, firmness also keeps them lovable. And they love us for keeping them out of trouble.

PARENTAL DOUBTS ARE NORMAL

10. Mixed feelings about pregnancy. We have an ideal about motherhood that says that a woman is overjoyed when she finds that she is going to have a baby. She spends the pregnancy dreaming about him. When he arrives, she slips into the maternal role with ease and delight. This is all true to a degree—more in one case, less in another. But it is, of course, only one side of the picture. Medical studies have brought out (what wise women have known all along) that there are normal negative feelings connected with a pregnancy, too, especially the first one.

To some degree, the first pregnancy spells the end of carefree youth —very important to Americans. The maidenly figure goes gradually into eclipse, and with it goes sprightly grace. Both eclipses are temporary but very real. The woman realizes that after the baby comes there will be distinct limitations of social life and other outside pleasures. No more hopping into the car on the spur of the moment, going anywhere the heart desires and coming home at any old hour. The same budget has to be spread thinner, and her husband's attention, all of which has gone to her at home, will soon be going to two.

11. Feelings are different in every pregnancy. The changes to be expected because of the arrival of one more child do not look so drastic after you have had two or three, but medical experience shows that a good mother's spirit may rebel at times during any pregnancy. There may be obvious reasons why one pregnancy is more strained—perhaps it came unexpectedly soon, or the father is having tensions in his work, or there is serious illness on either side of the family, or there is disharmony between mother and father. On the other hand, there may be no explanation visible to the naked eye.

An obstetrician I know says he sometimes senses an inner crisis with the second or third pregnancy in parents who are genuinely looking forward to a family of five or six children. A mother who really wants more children may still be disturbed subconsciously during any one pregnancy with sudden doubts about whether she will have the time, the physical energy, or the unlimited stores of love that she imagines will be called for in taking care of another and another. Or the inner doubts may start with the father, who feels somewhat neglected as his wife becomes more and more preoccupied with the children. In either case, the blueness or grumpiness of one spouse soon has the other one feeling disappointed, too. To put it another way, each person, in order to keep on giving, must feel he is receiving something, too.

I don't want to make these reactions sound inevitable. I only want to reassure you that they do occur in the very best of parents and that in the great majority of cases they are temporary. The child when he arrives proves to be less of a challenge than the parents had anticipated subconsciously, probably because they have grown in spirit in response to the need.

12. Love for the baby comes gradually. Many a woman who is pleased and proud to be pregnant finds it hard to feel a personal love for a baby she's never seen or felt. But when he begins to move, it helps her to believe that he's a real person, after all. As the pregnancy progresses, her thoughts turn more realistically to him, to what it will mean to care for him.

A great majority of those who admit that their first reaction to pregnancy was predominantly one of dismay (and there are plenty of good people who feel this way) are reassured to find that their acceptance of the pregnancy and their fondness for the baby reaches a comfortable level before he is born.

But even when the anticipation is all that could be desired, there is often a letdown for the inexperienced mother when the baby actually arrives. She expects to recognize him immediately as her own flesh and blood, to respond to him with an overwhelming rush of maternal feeling. But in many cases this doesn't happen the first day or even the first week. Instead it is a gradual process that isn't complete until she has been home with him a little while.

Most of us have been taught that it's not fair to a coming baby to hope and expect that it will be a girl or a boy, in case it turns out to be the opposite. I wouldn't take this too seriously. We can't really begin to imagine and love a future baby without picturing it as being one sex or the other. That's the very first step. I think that all expectant parents have a preference for a boy or girl during each pregnancy, even though most of them will be quite ready to love a baby who turns out to be the opposite. So enjoy your imaginary baby and don't feel guilty if another kind arrives.

13. Why feelings are different for different children. Are parents meant to love all their children equally? This question worries a lot of conscientious parents because they suspect that in some ways they don't. When they reproach themselves about this, I think they are expecting the impossible of themselves. Good parents love their children equally in the sense that they are equally devoted to each. They want the best out of life for each and will make any necessary sacrifice to achieve this. But since all children are quite different, no parent can **feel** just the same about any two of them, either in the sense of enjoying their special charms or being displeased by their special faults.

It's the feeling of particular irritation toward one child that makes parents feel most guilty, especially if there is no clear reason for it. A mother says, "This one **always** rubs me the wrong way. Yet I'm constantly trying to be sweeter to him and to overlook his bad behavior."

14. Some causes of dissatisfaction. The reasons why parents sometimes get off on the wrong foot with one child are quite varied and are usually hidden under the surface. Two possible factors were mentioned in Section 11: the parents may not have felt ready for this pregnancy or there may have been unusual family tensions during it. The baby himself may have got the parents off to the wrong start by being completely different from what they had been secretly expecting—a boy when they were looking for a girl, or a very homely baby when they were anticipating a beauty, or a frail infant compared to their other husky children. The infant may cry for several months with colic and seem to spurn his parents' efforts to comfort him. The father may be disappointed when his son turns out to be no athlete, no scrapper; the mother because he's no student. It doesn't matter that the parents are intelligent people who well know that they can't order the kind of baby they want most. Being human, they have irrational expectations and can't help feeling let down.

As a child becomes a little older he may remind us, consciously or unconsciously, of a brother, sister, father, or mother who made life hard for us at times. A mother's son may have traits like her younger brother, who used to be always in her hair—and yet she may have no conscious realization that this is the cause of a lot of her irritation.

A father may be excessively bothered by some particular characteristic in his young son—timidity, for instance—and never connect it with the fact that as a child he himself had a terrible time in overcoming timidity. You'd think that a person who has suffered a lot in trying to overcome some fault would be more sympathetic with it in his child. Usually it doesn't work that way.

15. Impatience and approval are part of child rearing. The very human tendency to react intensely to our children's behavior works positively for us, too: we strongly foster in our children the good traits that our parents fostered in us. We do it automatically, without having to think, because we learned our ideals so thoroughly in childhood. Otherwise, rearing our children would be ten times as hard as it is.

So it's human and normal and inevitable that we should feel quite differently about each of our children, that we should be impatient with certain characteristics in certain ones of them and proud of others. All these mixed attitudes are only different aspects of our deep feeling of obligation to bring up our children properly.

But if we feel too guilty about our chronic impatience with one child or another, it may produce increasing complications in our relations with him. Our guiltiness then gets to be harder on him than our irritation. This is discussed in Section 474.

16. The blue feeling. It's possible that you will find yourself feeling discouraged for a while when you first begin taking care of your baby. It's a fairly common feeling, especially with the first. You may not be able to put your finger on anything that is definitely wrong. You just weep easily. Or you may feel very bad about certain things. One woman whose baby cries quite a bit feels sure that he has a real disease, another that her husband has become strange and distant, another that she has lost all her looks.

A feeling of depression may come on a few days after the baby is born or not till several weeks later. The commonest time is when a mother comes home from the hospital, where she has been waited on hand and foot, and abruptly takes over full care of baby and household. It isn't just the work that gets her down. She may even have someone to do all the work, for the time being. It's the feeling of being responsible for the whole household again, plus the entirely new responsibility of the baby's care and safety. Then there are all the physical and glandular changes at the time of birth, which probably upset the spirits to some degree.

The majority of mothers don't get discouraged enough in this period to ever call it depression. You may think it is a mistake to bring up unpleasant things that may never happen. The reason I mention it is that several mothers have told me afterward, "I'm sure I wouldn't have been so depressed or discouraged if I had known how common this feeling is. Why, I thought that my whole outlook on life had changed for good and all." You can face a thing much better if you know that a lot of other people have gone through it, too, and if you know that it's just temporary.

If you begin to feel at all depressed, try to get some relief from the constant care of the baby in the first month or two, especially if he cries a great deal. Go to a movie, or to the beauty parlor, or to get yourself a new hat or dress. Visit a good friend occasionally. Take the baby along if you can't find anyone to stay with him. Or get your old friends to come and see you. All of these are tonics. If you are depressed, you may not feel like doing these things. But if you make yourself, you will feel a lot better. And that's important for the baby and your husband as well as yourself. If the depression does not lift in a few days or if it is becoming worse, you should promptly get in touch with a psychiatrist, through your regular doctor. A psychiatrist can be of great assistance and comfort at such a time.

When a mother feels blue and thinks that her husband seems indifferent, there are two sides to consider. On the one hand, anyone who is depressed feels that other people are less friendly and affectionate. But on the other hand, it's natural for a father, being human, to feel left out when his wife and the rest of the household are completely wrapped up in the baby. So it's a sort of vicious circle. The mother (as if she didn't have enough to do already!) has to remember to pay some attention to her husband. And she should give him every chance to share the care of the baby.

17. Other feelings. Most women find that they are more anxious than usual the first few weeks at home. They worry about the baby's crying and fretful spells, suspecting that something is seriously wrong. They worry about every sneeze and every spot of rash. They tiptoe into the baby's room to see whether he is still breathing. It's probably instinctive for mothers to be overly protective at this period. I suppose it's Nature's way of being sure that the millions of new mothers throughout the world, some of whom may be immature and careless, take their new responsibility seriously. A little worrisomeness might be a good thing for some irresponsible types. But of course it hits hardest the very conscientious ones who need it least. Fortunately it wears off.

Another kind of mood shift sometimes occurs. At first, in the hospital, a woman may feel very dependent on the nurses and grateful for the care they give the baby. Then comes a quick change of heart: she becomes confident she can take care of the baby herself and secretly resents the fact that the nurses don't let her take over. If she has a practical nurse at home, she may go through these two stages again. It certainly is normal for a mother to want to take care of her own baby by herself. The main reason she may not have this feeling at the start is because she is convinced she is inadequate. The stronger the sense of inferiority, the stronger will be the determination to assert her competence when she gains the courage.

THE FATHER'S PART

18. Men react to their wife's pregnancy with various feelings: protectiveness of the wife, increased pride in the marriage, pride about their virility (that's one thing men always worry about to some degree), anticipatory enjoyment of the child. But there can also be, way underneath, a feeling of being left out (just as a small boy may feel rejected when he finds his mother is pregnant), which can be expressed as grumpiness toward his wife, wanting to spend more evenings with his men friends, or flirtatiousness with other women. These reactions are no help to his wife, who craves extra support at the start of this unfamiliar stage of her life.

The father is apt to feel particularly left out during the hospital period with his first baby. He helps to get his wife safely to the hospital, where there are dozens of people to take care of her. Then he's really alone, with nothing to do outside of working hours. He can sit in the waiting room with some old magazines and worry about how the labor is going, or he can go to his unbelievably lonely home. It's no wonder that a man may take this occasion to drink in company at a bar. Where he works he gets some attention, but an awful lot of it is kidding. When he goes to see his wife and baby, the hospital doesn't make him feel like the head of the family; he's just another visitor who's tolerated at certain hours. When the time comes to take the family home, the concern of the mother (and of the grandmother or other helper, if any) is all for the baby, and the father's function seems mainly to be that of porter. I don't mean by all this that a father expects the limelight or should have it at this time, but that he's apt to feel less important than usual and therefore let down.

19. The father's opportunity in the early weeks at home. A father shouldn't be surprised if he finds that he has mixed feelings at times toward his wife and toward his baby—during the pregnancy, during all the commotion of the hospital stage, and after they are all home again. Nevertheless he can remind himself that his feelings are probably not nearly so churned up as his wife's, especially after the homecoming. She has been through the equivalent of an operation. She has been through an intense glandular change. If it's her first baby, she can't help feeling

The father is apt to get the mistaken idea that he's unimportant.

anxious. Any baby will make great demands on her strength and spirits at first. In a majority of cases, a woman's feelings are nearer the surface than a man's, more keenly felt. What all this adds up to is that most women need a great deal of support and comfort from their husbands at this time. To be able to give a lot to the baby they must receive more than usual. Partly it's practical help—with the care of the baby, with the housework. Even more it's moral support: patience, understanding, appreciation, affection. The father's job may be complicated by the fact that if his wife is tired and upset she won't have the spirit to be charming and appreciative of his efforts. In fact, she may be complaining. But if he realizes how much she needs his help and love, it will encourage him to give it anyway.

20. The father and his baby. Some fathers have been brought up to think that the care of babies and children is the mother's job entirely. But a man can be a warm father and a real man at the same time.

We know that the father's closeness and friendliness to his children will have a vital effect on their spirits and characters for the rest of their lives. So the time for him to begin being a real father is right at the start. It's easiest then. The father and mother can learn together. In some cities, classes in baby care are given for fathers, too. If a father leaves it all to his wife for the first two years, she gets to be the expert and the boss as far as the children are concerned. He'll feel more bashful about pushing his way into the picture later.

Of course, I don't mean that the father has to give just as many bottles or change just as many diapers as the mother. But it's fine for him to do these things occasionally. He might make the formula on Sunday. If the baby is on a 2 A.M. bottle in the early weeks, when the mother is still pretty tired, this is a good feeding for the father to take over. It's nice for him, if he can, to go along to the doctor's office for the baby's regular visits. It gives him a chance to bring up those questions that are bothering him and that he doesn't think his wife understands the importance of. It pleases the doctor, too. Of course, there are some fathers who get goose flesh at the very idea of helping to take care of a baby, and there's no good to be gained by trying to force them. Most of them come around to enjoying their children later "when they're more like real people." But many fathers are only a little bashful. They just need encouragement. There's more on fathers in Sections 460–463, 477, 507–509.

RELATIONS WITH GRANDPARENTS

21. Grandparents can be a great help to young parents in all kinds of ways. They can also derive enormous pleasure from their grandchildren. They often ask wistfully, "Why couldn't I have enjoyed my own children the way I enjoy my grandchild? I suppose I was trying too hard and feeling only the responsibility."

In many parts of the world grandmothers are considered experts, and a young mother takes it for granted that when she has a question about her baby or needs a little help with him she'll ask her mother. When a mother has this kind of confidence in the grandmother, she can get not only advice but comfort. In our country, though, a new mother is often more inclined to turn to her doctor first, and some women don't ever think of consulting their mothers. This is partly because we are so used to consulting professional people about our personal problems—doctors, guidance counselors in school, marriage counselors, social workers, psychologists, ministers. Also, we take it for granted that knowledge advances rapidly, and so we often think that anyone who knew how to do a job twenty years ago is behind the times today. A more basic reason is that many young parents still feel too close to adolescence. They want to prove to the world and to themselves that they can manage their own lives. They may be afraid that the grandparents will want to tell them what to do, as if they were still dependent, and they don't want to put themselves back in that position.

22. Tensions are normal. In some families, all is harmony between parents and grandparents. In a few, disagreements are fierce. In others, there is a little tension, most commonly concerning the care of the first child, but it wears off with time and adjustment.

The fortunate young woman who has lots of natural, comfortable self-confidence can turn easily to her mother for help when she needs it. And when the grandmother makes a suggestion on her own, the mother finds she can accept it if it seems good, or she can tactfully let it pass and go her own way.

But most young parents don't have that amount of assurance at first. Like almost everybody else in a new job, they are sensitive about possible inadequacies, touchy about criticism.

Most grandparents remember this well from their earlier days and try hard not to interfere. On the other hand, they **have** had experience, they feel they've developed judgment, they love their grandchildren dearly, and they can't help having opinions. They see surprising changes from the time when they cared for babies—flexible feeding schedules, early feeding of solid foods, perhaps later toilet training—and these are hard to get used to. Even when they accept new methods, they may be bothered by what seems to them to be excessive zeal in carrying them out. (When you are a grandparent yourself, you'll probably understand better what I mean.)

I think that if young parents have the courage, they can keep relations most comfortable by permitting or even inviting the grandparents to speak up about their opinions. Frank discussions are usually, in the long run, more comfortable than veiled hints or uneasy silences. A mother who is pretty sure she is managing the baby properly can say, "I know that this method doesn't seem quite right to you, and I'm going to discuss it again with the doctor to be sure that I've understood his directions." This doesn't mean the mother is giving in. She certainly reserves the right to make her own decision in the end. She is only recognizing the grandmother's good intentions and evident anxiety. The young mother who shows reasonableness will reassure the grandmother not only in regard to the present problem but also in regard to the future in general.

A grandmother can help the mother do a good job by showing her confidence in her and fitting in with her methods as far as possible. This puts the mother in a mood to ask advice when she is in doubt.

When the children are left in the care of the grandparents, whether for half a day or for two weeks, there should be frank understanding and reasonable compromising. The parents must have confidence that the children will be cared for according to their beliefs in important matters (that, for instance, they won't be compelled to eat food they don't like, be shamed for bowel accidents, or be frightened about policemen). On the other hand, it's unfair to expect grandparents to carry out every step of management and discipline as if they were exact replicas of the parents. It won't hurt a child to be a little more respectful to the grandparents, if that's what they want, or to have their meals on a different schedule, or to be kept cleaner or dirtier. If the parents don't feel right about the way the grandparents care for the children, of course they shouldn't ask them to take care of them.

23. The parent who is sensitive about advice. More than average tension may arise if the young mother (or father) has felt a lot of parental criticism throughout her childhood. This inevitably leaves her inwardly unsure of herself, outwardly impatient of disapproval, and grimly determined to prove her independence. She may take to new philosophies of child rearing with unusual enthusiasm and push them hard. They seem like a wholesome change from what she remembers. They are also a way to show the grandparents how old-fashioned they are and to bother them a bit. It's really fun to battle about theory when you're mad at the opponent. The only trouble is that it's the child's upbringing that provides the ammunition on both sides. All I'm suggesting is that parents who find that they are constantly upsetting grandparents should at least ask themselves whether they might be doing some of it on purpose, without quite realizing it.

24. The managerial grandmother. Occasionally there is a grandmother so constituted that she has always been too managerial with her daughter and she can't stop now even though the daughter is now a mother. Such a young mother may have a tough time at first keeping her perspective. She dreads advice. When it comes, it makes her angry, but she dare not express her feelings. If she accepts the advice, she feels dominated. If she turns it down, she feels guilty. How, then, can the beginning mother in this situation protect herself? It sounds as if she'd have to lift herself by her bootstraps. In a way she does have to, but it **can** be done gradually, with practice. In the first place, she can keep reminding herself that she **is** the mother now and that the baby is hers to take care of as she thinks best. She should be able to get support from the doctor or the public-health nurse when she has been made to doubt her own method. She is surely entitled to the support of her husband, especially if it's his mother who is interfering. If he thinks that in a certain situation his mother is right, he should be able to say so to his wife, but at the same time he can show his mother that he stands with his wife against interference.

The young mother will come out better if she can learn gradually not to run away from the grandmother and not to be afraid to hear her out, because both these reactions reveal, in a way, that she feels too weak to stand up to her. Harder still, she can learn how not to get boiling mad inside or how not to explode outwardly in a temper. You might say she's entitled to get angry, which is true. But pent-up anger and explosions are both signs that she has already been feeling submissive for too long, out of fear of making the grandmother mad. A dominating grandmother usually senses these indirect signs of timidity and takes advantage of them. A mother shouldn't feel guilty about making her mother mad, if it must come to that. Actually, it shouldn't be necessary to blow up at the grandmother—or at least not more than once or twice. The mother can learn to speak up for herself right away, in a matter-of-fact, confident tone, **before she gets angry** ("Well, the doctor told me to feed him this way," "You see, I like to keep him as cool as possible," "I don't want him to cry for long"). This calm, assured tone is usually the most effective way to convince the grandmother that the mother has the courage of her convictions.

In these occasional situations that contain a lot of continual tension, it is often helpful for the parents, and perhaps the grandparents, to consult a professional person—wise family doctor, psychiatrist, social worker, sensible minister—preferably in separate interviews, so that each can present the picture as he sees it, even though they may all come together for a final discussion. In any case it should be understood that, in the end, the responsibility and the right to make the decision is the parents'.

CALLERS AND VISITORS

25. Limit the visitors at first. The birth of a baby is an occasion that brings relatives and friends flocking, to congratulate the parents and to see the baby. This is gratifying to the parents and fills them with pride.

However, too much of it may be exhausting to the mother. How much is too much? It's very different in different cases. Most mothers tire easily the first few weeks at home. They have just gone through the equivalent of an operation and in addition have felt the effects of some intense glandular changes. Perhaps more important still are the emotional shifts that are called for, especially with the first baby, which are discussed in Section 16.

Visitors are pure pleasure to some people—relaxing, distracting, rejuvenating. To most of us, however, only a few old friends have such a good effect. Other visitors, to a greater or lesser degree, make us somewhat tense, even when we enjoy seeing them, and leave us somewhat fatigued, especially if we aren't feeling well. When a new mother becomes tired out, it gets her off on the wrong foot at the time of the most important transition in her life, and this is too bad for everybody. I think a new mother should set strict limits for visitors right from the start, see how it goes, and then increase the number very gradually if she finds she has plenty of strength left over. It helps a mother to get the doctor's agreement to strict limits. Then she doesn't have to feel that she's being inhospitable; she's just following doctor's orders. I'd tell each person who calls up, "The doctor says I can see only one visitor a day for fifteen minutes, beginning tomorrow. Can you come Tuesday about four P.M.?" There are lots of additional reasons that can be thrown in to strengthen the point: extra-long labor, breast feeding, slowness in getting strength back.

To people who appear at the house without a telephone call, you can act pleased but guilty: "The doctor wants me to see only one visitor a day for the next week, but come in for just a minute, anyway."

One mother found it helped to tack on her front door a notice saying she didn't want life insurance for the baby, photographs of the baby, nursery equipment, or sets of books, so she would not have to answer the door for salesmen.

26. Visitors playing with the baby. Most visitors get all excited when they see a baby. They want to hold him, joggle him, tickle him, jounce him, waggle their heads at him, and keep up a blue streak of baby talk. Some babies can take a lot, some can't take any, and most are in between. A mother has to use her judgment about how much is wise and then be very firm. This is hard to carry out, though, because it's one of the great pleasures of parenthood to have people enjoy the baby. Most babies are easily tired, too, by strange places and strange happenings, as visits to the doctor's office prove.

HELP FOR THE MOTHER

27. Arranging for extra help in the beginning. If you can figure out a way to get someone to help you the first few weeks you are taking care of the baby, by all means do so. If you try to do everything by yourself and get exhausted, you may **have** to get help and have it for longer in the end. Besides, getting tired and depressed starts you and the baby off on the wrong foot.

Your mother may be the ideal helper, if you get along with her easily. If you feel she is bossy and still treats you like a child, this is not the time to have her. You will want to feel that the baby is your own and that you are doing a good job with him. It will help to have a person who has taken care of babies before, but it's most important of all to have someone that you enjoy having around.

If you can afford to hire a houseworker or a practical baby nurse for a few weeks, there will be the advantage over a relative that you can let her go if she doesn't work out right. In one way, a houseworker is best—the mother can have the satisfaction of taking complete care of her baby from the start—but a houseworker is hard to find. Next best is a practical nurse who will do part of the housework, who is willing to fit in with your way of doing things, who will let you feel that the baby is yours, and who has a relaxed, agreeable personality. If you find that you have a practical nurse who acts as if the baby were hers rather than yours and criticizes everything you do, for goodness' sake get rid of her right away and take a chance on finding a better one.

How long should you engage a helper for? It will depend, of course, on your finances, on your desire to take over, and on your strength. Each day as your strength increases, take over a little more of the work. If when two weeks are nearly up, you find that you still get tired easily, then by all means keep the helper, whether you can really afford her or not. She is not a luxury, under these circumstances, but a necessity. If you take over before you are strong enough, it will cost more in the end, financially and spiritually, than if you keep her on for another week or two.

Most expectant mothers feel a little scared at the prospect of taking sole charge of a helpless baby for the first time. If you have this feeling, it doesn't mean that you won't be able to do a good job or that you **have** to have a nurse to show you how. But if you feel **really** panicky, you will probably learn more comfortably with an agreeable practical nurse —or relative, if this can be arranged.

If you can't have regular help, you may be able to afford and find a woman to come in once or twice a week to do the cleaning, help you catch up on the housework, and watch the baby for a few hours while you go out for a visit.

Whether or not you have your own help, you should arrange to have a visiting nurse come in for a visit or two. See Section 55.

28. Practical aids. If you are going to be washing the baby's diapers yourself, now is the time to get an automatic washer and drier if you can possibly afford them. They save hours of work each week, and precious energy. They are somewhat less essential if you can get diaper service but still very worth while.

New mothers find it a great help to send out the regular laundry, at least temporarily during the early months of baby care. This is a good time to simplify housework by putting unnecessary furniture and furnishings in a store room for a couple of months or a couple of years. Learn to use more of the easily prepared foods for a while.

29. Sitters are a boon to parents and can help a child to develop independence. You and your child should know your sitter well. For night sitting with a baby who doesn't waken, it may only be necessary for her to be sensible and dependable. But for babies who waken and for children above the age of a year who might waken, it's important for the sitter to be a person they know and like while awake. It is frightening to most children to waken and find a stranger. If the sitter is to care for the child or even just put him to bed, you should be sure from seeing her in action with your child that she understands and loves children and can manage them with kindliness and firmness. So try to engage the sitter a few times while you and she will be there together for a while. Then the young child can get used to her before she has to do too much for him directly. As the child gradually accepts her, she can do more for him.

It is certainly important that you stick to one or two sitters as much as possible. You can learn about capable sitters or about a reliable agency through a friend whose judgment you trust.

Young or old? It's a matter of maturity and spirit rather than years. I've occasionally seen a girl as young as fourteen who was extremely capable and dependable, but it's unfair to expect such qualities in most girls that age. And some grown women may prove unreliable or harsh or ineffectual. One older woman has a knack with children. Another is too inflexible to adapt to a new child or is so nervous that she makes child and parents uneasy.

To keep things straight, it's sensible to have a permanent notebook for the sitter, listing the child's routine, some of the things he may ask for (in his words), the telephone numbers of the doctor and of a neighbor to call in an emergency if you can't be reached, bedtime hours, what the sitter may help herself to in the kitchen, the whereabouts of linen, night clothes, and other things that may be needed, how to turn the furnace up or down.

But most of all, know your sitter and know that your child trusts her. There is more on the qualities of a mother's substitute in Section 777.

Equipment and Clothing

EQUIPMENT YOU'LL NEED

30. Getting things ahead of time. Some women don't feel like buying anything until they have their baby. The advantage of getting and arranging everything ahead of time is that it lightens the burden later. A certain number of mothers feel tired and easily discouraged at the time they begin taking care of the baby themselves. Then a little job like buying half a dozen nipples looms as a real ordeal. Mothers who have gotten depressed have said to me afterward, "The next time, I'm going to buy everything that I need way ahead. Every pin and nightie is going to be in its place."

What do you really have to have, in the way of equipment, to take care of a new baby? There are no exact rules, but here are some suggestions:

31. A place to sleep. You may want to get a beautiful bassinet, lined with silk. But the baby doesn't care. All he needs is sides to keep him from rolling out, and something soft but firm in the bottom for a mattress. A crib, a clothes or market basket, a box or bureau drawer, will do. Mattresses made of foam rubber or hair keep their shape best, but they are more expensive. (Occasionally hair, principally pig's hair, causes allergy in a susceptible child in an allergic family. This risk can be avoided by enclosing the mattress in an airtight casing made for this purpose.) You can make a mattress by folding up an old blanket and tufting it. Don't use a soft pillow for a mattress. There's a slight risk of the baby's smothering in one. The sides of a small bassinet will probably have to be lined to keep the baby from hurting his hands. He doesn't need a pillow for his head, and it's better not to use one.

32. Something to bathe him in and dress him on. The baby can be bathed in the kitchen sink, an enamelware tub, a dishpan, or a washstand. You can bathe and dress the baby on a low table, at which you sit (a card table with steady legs is a good size), or on the top of a fairly high bureau, at which you stand. You can sit on a high stool at the sink.

A folding, fabric bathtub is a convenience if you can afford it and have room for it. The tub part is made of waterproof material hung from a frame on high legs. It is high enough so that you don't break your back bathing the baby. When the bath is finished, a flat canvas top covers the tub, and on this the baby can be dried, dressed, and changed.

33. Other equipment

Safety pins.

Rectal thermometer.

Absorbent cotton. A pound roll of sterile absorbent cotton. You make soft swabs for removing dried mucus from the nose and for cleaning the outer ear by firmly rolling a small piece of cotton between moist finger and thumb.

Vitamin drops, usually containing vitamins A, C, and D. Ask your doctor which preparation to get.

Soap. Any mild soap is satisfactory.

Diaper pail. This should hold 3 gallons, be nonrusting, and have a cover. You can use a plastic bag for a liner to prevent rusting. Some mothers like two, one for wet and another, containing soapy water, for soiled diapers. If you are going to use a diaper service, they will provide a container.

THE CLOTHES HE NEEDS

34. Nightgowns. Stockinet nightgowns are comfortable, practical, and require no ironing. The long ones make it harder for the baby to kick his coverings off. You will need 3 to 6. Get the 1-year size to start with.

35. Shirts. Most shirts nowadays are made without buttons or tapes, and these are handier. For most babies cotton shirts that do not provide too much warmth in a warm room are best. If the baby is thin and frail or if he is always in a cold house, there is more point in part-wool shirts. I'd get long-sleeved shirts, because if a baby needs any covering, he needs it on his arms, too. You will need 3 to 6 shirts, 1-year size.

36. Diapers. The most popular materials for diapers are gauze, cotton flannel, and bird's-eye. The gauze diapers are quicker drying but do not hold as much of the urine when the baby is larger. Two dozen will cover your needs if you wash them every day and don't use too many for sheets, towels, etc. Six dozen will cover all possible needs. Get the large size. If you live in a city that has a diaper service, you will probably want to subscribe to this if you can afford it. It saves time, effort, and drying space. The company supplies the diapers as well as launders them.

37. Sweaters and sacks. Get them too big rather than too small. In pull-over sweaters, the opening for the head needs to be large, so that you don't make the baby frantic getting a sweater off and on. Better a shoulder opening with buttons.

38. Other clothes. Knitted wool caps are all right for going outdoors in the kind of weather that makes grownups put on overcoats, or for sleeping in an equally cold room. For milder weather, caps are unnecessary; most babies don't like them, anyway. You don't need booties and stockings, at least until your baby is sitting up and playing around in a cold house. Dresses make a baby look pretty, but are unnecessary otherwise, and bothersome to the baby and the mother.

BEDCLOTHES

39. Waterproof sheeting of plastic or rubber. Most popular is sheeting that has a flannelette backing on both surfaces. It stays in place, and the sheet does not slip on it. It is more comfortable in case the baby happens to get in contact with it. Since it allows some circulation of air under the baby, there is usually no need to cover it with a quilted pad, and this makes a saving in laundry. However, in hot weather you may still need a pad, too. The sheeting should be washed (it will go in the machine) each day if it gets wet with urine, so you will need two.

The waterproof sheeting should preferably be large enough to tuck in around the mattress. Otherwise the edges of the mattress may get wet at times. Incidentally, the plastic cover that comes on most new mattresses is not sufficient by itself. Sooner or later enough urine gets into the air holes to make it smell.

Additional small squares of flannel-backed sheeting will save more laundry. Place one under the baby's hips. It will keep the bedsheet dry if the baby stays in one place. The mother can use one as a lap protector.

40. Pads. If you are using plain waterproof sheeting (without flannel backing), you will need to cover it with a quilted pad. This is to absorb moisture and allow some circulation of air under the baby's body; otherwise the skin stays too hot and wet. The number of pads you will need will depend on how often the laundry is done, how much the baby wets, how much he spits up. You will need 3 anyway, and 6 are more convenient.

41. Sheets. You will need 3 to 6 sheets. If you are using a small bassinet at first, you can use diapers for sheets. For anything larger, the best sheets are made of cotton stockinet. They are easy to wash, quick to dry, spread smoothly without ironing, and do not feel clammy when wet. Fitted sheets can be bought to cover the crib mattress.

42. Blankets. The number of blankets depends on climate and season. It is better to have lightweight blankets (best of all are knit shawls; next best, light flannel), because they wrap around the baby more easily when he is out of the crib and because you can adjust the amount of covering to the temperature. For cold climates, it is best to have most of the blankets made of all wool or synthetic material, so that the covering will not have to be too heavy. Cotton-flannel receiving blankets are not essential, but they are helpful for wrapping around the baby who would otherwise kick off his outer bed coverings or the baby who feels comfortable and secure only when he is very snugly bundled (Section 242).

EQUIPMENT THAT MAY OR MAY NOT BE NECESSARY

43. Scales. If a baby is doing well and is seen by his doctor regularly, there is no real need to have scales at home. On the other hand, if a baby cries a great deal and the mother can't tell whether it is from indigestion or hunger, a pair of scales will help a lot, especially if the doctor is far away. If a relative wants to give you scales or a friend offers to lend them, better take them. If you have to buy them yourself and can ill afford them, wait and see. Balance scales are **much** more accurate and helpful than spring scales.

44. A carriage is necessary if a baby is to have daily outings, unless there is some other substitute (like a car-bed) in which he can be put in the yard or on the porch. In a congested city a carriage is necessary if he is to go to the park or to market with his mother.

Families with cars usually find that a canvas car-bed for the baby, which attaches to the car securely, is a necessity.

There are contrivances for carrying a baby a few months old strapped to the mother's back or side so that her hands can be free during work, walks, and shopping.

45. Bottle warmer. The baby's bottle can, of course, be warmed in any kind of container. An electric warmer is very handy when the hot-water supply is undependable.

46. Bath thermometer. Not necessary but a comfort to the inexperienced mother.

47. Toiletries

Baby oil. Not really necessary unless the skin is dry. Mineral oil (liquid petrolatum), or a commercial preparation.

Baby powder. Helps a little to avoid chafing, but it is not necessary in most cases. (Zinc stearate powder is not considered safe for babies, because it is irritating when breathed into the lungs.) Any powder should be applied fairly carefully (shake it into your hand first), so that there isn't a cloud of it around the baby's face.

Zinc ointment. In tube or jar, to protect the skin when there is a diaper rash.

FORMULA EQUIPMENT

Before buying equipment, it's helpful to know which method of sterilization you will be using. In the "terminal" method, you sterilize the bottles after the formula is in them. In the "aseptic" method, you boil the formula in a container and then pour it into sterilized bottles.

48. Nursing bottles. If you know ahead of time that you are not going to breast-feed the baby, buy at least 9 of the 8-ounce bottles. You will use 6 to 8 a day in the beginning for the formula, and you will surely break a few eventually. If you expect to breast-feed, buy at least 3, for occasional formula feedings, water, and juice.

The most popular bottle is one with a wide mouth. The nipple fits into a plastic screw-on cap. Except when the baby is nursing, the nipple is stored upside down in the bottle and a plastic disk covers the opening.

There are also bottles with small mouths. The nipple fits over the neck. A glass or aluminum cap is used to cover the nipple.

Pyrex bottles are more expensive but don't break because of too rapid heating or chilling. In the long run they are probably an economy for most mothers. They chip easily at the mouth, so should be handled carefully.

Plastic bottles don't break when adults or babies drop them, but are not suitable for terminal sterilization because they become misshapen.

Water and juice can be given just as well from 8-ounce bottles, even though they are unnecessarily large. But some mothers prefer 4-ounce bottles for this purpose. Two or 3 of these will be enough.

There are also disposable bottles of thin flexible plastic that come in a long strip already sterilized. The mothers who use them swear by them.

49. Nipples. Buy the type to fit the bottles you will be using, a dozen if the baby will be bottle-fed, a half dozen if breast-fed. You have to have a few extra in case you drop one on the floor or are having trouble making the nipple holes the right size.

Nipples made with silicone are more expensive but don't deteriorate from boiling and milk fat.

Most people use nipples with one or more holes in the top. If you have trouble with clogged nipples, you can buy those with cross-cut openings or you can cross-cut your own (see Section 182).

50. Bottle caps or nipple caps, to fit your bottles. Buy the same number as you buy bottles.

51. A pail, kettle, or roaster with lid for sterilizing the bottles, preferably 8 inches high and 9 inches in diameter so that it will hold 8 bottles vertically in a wire bottle rack. If you have to economize, you can even use a gallon-size can in which motor oil is bought and make your own wire rack. The bottles shouldn't stand directly on the bottom; they're likely to be broken by the heat.

In terminal sterilization, the bottles already contain the formula and so must stand up.

In the aseptic method, the bottles are boiled while still empty, so they can be in any position in any pan that is large enough. It's more convenient, though, to have them standing up in a wire rack.

52. A container for mixing formula, marked in ounces. An enamelware quart measure (marked in ounces on the inside) is very convenient for both the terminal and aseptic methods. For the aseptic method, you can then measure and mix and boil the formula in the same container. A glass quart measure is satisfactory for the terminal method because it doesn't have to be heated.

If you don't want to buy a quart measure, you can use any measuring cup marked in ounces and then mix in any saucepan or pitcher that holds a quart. In a pinch you can use a nursing bottle for a measure, but it is inconvenient to pour into.

53. Funnel and strainer. In the aseptic method, you strain the scum off the boiled milk as you pour it into the bottles. You can buy a funnel with a built-in strainer.

In the terminal method, the milk is unboiled when you pour it into the bottles, so it doesn't need straining. But you will need a funnel, at least if you are using small-mouth bottles.

Bottle brush for small-mouth bottles. If you use wide-mouth bottles a **jar brush** is much more efficient.

54. The other equipment you will need for making a formula does not need to be bought specially.

Long tablespoon for stirring. (In the aseptic method, the handle should be one that will not get too hot from the boiling milk.)

Set of measuring spoons for measuring the sugar or syrup.

Knife to level the sugar in the measuring spoon. (Not necessary if you use syrup.)

Can opener for evaporated milk. A beer-can opener is easiest.

Medical and Nursing Care

THE VISITING NURSE

55. Whether or not you have help at home, you ought to try to get a visiting nurse or public-health nurse to come in once or twice in the early days. She will show you how to make the formula, bathe the baby, and follow other directions of the doctor. And you can always call her later when you have questions and problems. There are visiting nurses or public-health nurses in most cities and in many country districts. Ask the doctor or the nurse in the hospital, or telephone the Visiting Nurse Association or local health department, or write the state health department.

THE BABY'S DOCTOR

56. Regular visits. The way to be sure that your baby is doing well is to have him checked by a doctor regularly. The visits should be once a month in the early months, and at least once every 3 months during the second year. The doctor will want to weigh the baby to see how he's gaining, examine him to see that he's developing well, give him his inoculations. The mother will have five or ten questions that she wants to ask, with her first baby, anyway. It's a good idea to have a little notebook that's always handy for writing down questions when they come to your mind at home, and also for noting developments, such as teething or a rash, that you may want to know the date of later. Of course, some families live so far away from a doctor that they can't plan to visit him monthly. In some cases the mother and doctor can keep in touch by telephone. Naturally, every baby won't get into trouble just because his doctor doesn't see him regularly. But experience has shown that the monthly visit is vitally important for the occasional baby who is not doing well and a worth-while and comforting precaution for all the rest.

57. Who's to be the doctor? In many cases the family physician who has delivered the baby will go on seeing him afterward. A family doctor who is used to taking care of babies can do just as good a job as the specialist, unless some unusual problem comes up. In larger cities the mother may have been delivered by a specialist in obstetrics who doesn't take care of the baby afterward. Then she will want to find a children's specialist (known as a pediatrician or pediatrist). One mother gets along best with a doctor who is casual, not too fussy about details. Another feels right only if she gets every direction down to the last period. You may have more confidence in an older man or feel that you are imposing less on a younger man, or you may prefer a woman. If you have definite feelings about what kind of doctor you want, discuss the matter with your obstetrician. He will know the children's specialists who are available.

Sometimes a doctor who specializes in delivering babies will agree to supervise the baby's feeding for a certain number of weeks or months, as a convenience to the mother and as part of the fee arrangement, though he plans to have another doctor take over eventually, sooner if illness develops. I think it is wiser, if the parents expect to have another doctor care for their child later, to call him in to take charge when the baby is born, or at least before he leaves the hospital. Feeding is only one of many aspects of the baby's total care during the first year. There are such matters as changes in the schedule, thumb-sucking, bowel function and training, the amount of attention and sleep the baby needs, all of which are related to each other and all of which should be considered together from the beginning in arranging his program. Then, too, the doctor who is called in to treat a baby's illness will be in a much better position to do it wisely if he has known him from birth.

58. The child-health conference. A city baby whose parents can't afford regular visits to a private doctor can and should attend a "well-baby clinic" or "child-health conference" at a hospital or child-health station. These have been established in many country districts, too. If you live in the country, write ahead of time to the state health department to find where the nearest clinic is. In a city you can find the nearest clinic by telephoning the city health department or the Visiting Nurse Association. On the staff of the well-baby clinic or child-health conference are doctors and nurses who work as a team. The doctor examines the baby at regular intervals, gives inoculations, and advises the mother. The nurse helps the mother in carrying out his recommendations and in dozens of other practical child-care matters. She can make a home visit soon after the mother and baby leave the hospital and at other times when the mother has a problem that won't wait until the next clinic visit.

59. Getting along with a doctor. In most cases the parents and the doctor soon come to know and trust each other and get along fine. But occasionally, since they are all human beings, there may be misunderstandings and tensions. Most of these are avoidable or easily cleared up with frankness on both sides.

Unless expense is no concern, it's a good idea to discuss charges when first engaging a physician. It's easier at the start than later. Though this may embarrass you, remember that it's an old story with the doctor and he should be able to take it. Many physicians will lower their fees for people with less-than-average income and are glad to know of the need ahead of time.

Most new parents are bashful in the beginning about asking questions about baby care that they are afraid are too simple or silly. It's foolish to worry about this. If there's any kind of question on your mind, you're entitled to an answer—that's what doctors are for. A doctor is pleased to answer any questions that he can, the easier, the better.

Even if you feel sure that your doctor will be grumpy about something that is probably not serious but that you are nonetheless concerned about, call him anyway. Your child's health is more important than the doctor's feelings or your own feelings.

It often happens that a parent asks about a problem and the doctor explains part of it but gets sidetracked before he has answered the parent's most important question. If the mother is bashful, she may hesitate about coming back to that point and go home somewhat unsatisfied. She should encourage herself to be bold, to make clear exactly what she wants to know, so that the doctor can give her the answer or, if it is out of his line, refer her to some other professional person.

60. Asking for a consultation. If your child has some illness or condition that worries you intensely and you would like another expert opinion, it is always your right to ask freely for a consultation. Many parents are hesitant about doing so, fearing that this would express lack of confidence in the present doctor and hurt his feelings. But it is a regular procedure in the practice of medicine, and the doctor should be able to take it in his stride. Actually, a doctor, like any other human being, senses uneasiness in the people he deals with, even when it is unspoken, and it makes his job harder. A consultation usually clears the air for him as well as for the family.

61. Frankness works best. I think the main point in all these situations is that if you are unsatisfied with your doctor's advice or care, you should try to bring it out into the open right away, in the most matter-of-fact manner you can muster. An early meeting of minds is easier for him and you than allowing your tension and irritation to accumulate inside you.

Sometimes, though, a patient and doctor find that they just can't get along together, no matter how frank and cooperative they try to be, and then it's better all around to admit it openly. Every doctor, including the most successful, has learned that he doesn't suit everybody, and he takes this philosophically.

62. The time for telephone calls. Find out from your doctor what time of day he prefers phone calls, particularly about new illness that may require a home visit. A majority of illnesses in children first show definite symptoms during the afternoon, and most doctors would like to know about them as early in the afternoon as possible so that they can plan their visits efficiently. Naturally, if the symptoms that worry you don't come on till later, that's the time you have to call the doctor.

63. When to call the doctor. After you've raised a couple of babies, you'll have a good idea of which symptoms or questions require prompt contact with the doctor and which can wait till tomorrow or the next visit. But new parents often ask for a list. Even if they never consult the list, they feel more comfortable having one.

No list can be anywhere near complete. There are, of course, hundreds of different diseases and injuries. You always have to use your own common sense. The following discussion contains only a few general guides.

By far the most important rule, as I see it, is to consult the doctor promptly, at least by telephone, if a baby or child **looks different** (in general appearance) or **acts differently.** By this I mean such signs as unusual paleness, unusual tiredness, unusual drowsiness, lack of interest, unusual irritability, anxiousness, restlessness, prostration.

Fever is discussed in Section 604. How high or low it is is less important than whether the child seems really sick. A high fever often accompanies a mild infection after the age of 1 or 2 years, and a young baby can be quite sick with little or no fever. As a general rule, consult the doctor if the baby has a temperature of 101° or more. You don't have to call him in the middle of the night if the baby has only a mild cold with 101° and otherwise seems happy; call him in the morning. But if the baby looks sick or has more serious symptoms with a fever of 101°, call promptly.

Colds. In general, you call the doctor if the cold is more than mild, or if there are any new symptoms, or if the child looks sicker. What to be concerned about in **colds** is discussed in Sections 628–630; **coughs,** in Section 636; **earaches,** in Section 635.

Hoarseness of voice, difficulty in breathing (Sections 638–640, 649, 650), should always be reported immediately.

Pain or suspicion of pain should be reported when it first appears. (Colic that occurs every evening for weeks doesn't need to be reported every time, of course.) **Ear infection** is discussed in Section 635; **stomach-ache,** in Sections 690, 691; pain in the **urinary tract,** Sections 684–687; **headache** should be reported promptly in a small child.

Sudden decrease in appetite is sometimes a sign of illness. It doesn't need to be reported if it occurs only once and if the child is as comfortable and happy as ever. But if the child acts differently in other respects, the doctor should be called.

Vomiting of any unusual type should be reported promptly, especially if the child looks sick or different in any other way. This does not apply, of course, to the spitting up after meals that is so common at first. See Sections 288, 289, 690, 691.

Diarrhea of the more serious sort, in infants, which should be reported to the doctor immediately, and the milder kinds which should be reported within a few hours are discussed in Section 298. Diarrhea of children should be reported soon (Section 690).

Blood in the bowel movements (Sections 260, 298, 690), blood in the vomitus, should be reported promptly.

Inflammation of the eye or injury to the eye should be reported promptly (Section 697).

Injury to the head should be reported if the baby isn't happy and healthy-looking in 15 minutes (Section 714).

Injury to a limb should be reported if the baby is not inclined to use it normally or shows pain on using it (Sections 712, 713).

Burns should be reported if blisters appear (Section 709).

Poisons. If your child has eaten anything that **might** possibly be dangerous (Sections 719–724), you should reach your doctor or another, immediately.

Cuts are discussed in Sections 703–707.

Nosebleeds are discussed in Section 708.

Rashes. Of course, the commonest rashes in the first year are diaper rash (Section 302) and rough patches on the cheeks or a few small raised pink spots on the face (Section 303), none of which is an emergency. Babies are protected against contagious diseases like measles, German measles, and scarlet fever (but not chicken pox) for the first half year anyway, if the mother has had them. Cradle cap is very common but unimportant (Section 305). Eczema occurs occasionally (Section 652) and should be reported within a day or so. Impetigo is uncommon after a baby leaves the hospital but should be reported the first day (Section 658). If a child seems sick with a rash or if the rash is extensive, you should call the doctor right away.

64. Finding a doctor in a strange city. If you need a doctor for your child in a strange town, find the name of the best hospital. Telephone, and ask for the name of a pediatrician on the staff or a general practitioner who takes care of children. If there is any hitch, ask to speak to the physician-in-chief (who will probably not be a children's specialist). He will give you the names of one or two suitable doctors.

65. Things to have in your medicine cabinet. A box of sterile gauze squares, or "dressings," 3 inches square (each dressing remains sterile in a separate envelope). Two rolls of sterile bandage 2 inches wide, two rolls 1 inch wide. A roll of sterile absorbent cotton. A roll of adhesive plaster 1 inch wide. You can make narrower strips by cutting the end with scissors and then tearing. A box of small prepared bandages. A good pair of splinter forceps (tweezers to remove splinters).

Ask your doctor what antiseptic he recommends. A package of bicarbonate of soda (baking soda). A tube or jar of petroleum jelly or some other preparation that your doctor recommends for the emergency treatment of burns. A bottle of aspirin tablets for babies (each tablet contains 1¼ grains). If you live far away from medical help, ask your doctor if he recommends your having a bottle of syrup of ipecac to cause vomiting in a case of serious poisoning.

A thermometer, rectal for children under 6. A hot-water bottle. A rubber ear syringe, preferably with a soft rubber tip, for a baby's enema if your doctor prescribes it and for clearing out a baby's nose during a cold.

THE HOSPITAL

66. Hospital impressions. Nowadays most babies in this country are born in a hospital. There the doctor is closer at hand when needed, and he is assisted by interns, nurses, technicians, and consultants. A hospital offers all the complicated equipment, like incubators and oxygen tents, to cope with sudden emergencies. All this makes the mother feel very safe and well cared for. But it also has mild drawbacks, which are part and parcel of its virtues. The babies are usually in a nursery some distance from the mothers, where they can be efficiently watched and cared for by the nurses and won't disturb their mothers' rest. But it isn't quite natural, from the new mother's point of view, to have her baby somewhere else and taken care of so completely for a number of days. It may give her a feeling underneath of being somewhat ignorant and useless. A mother who has had several children might laugh at this and say, "It's **wonderful** to have that long rest in the hospital and not have to worry about the baby." But it's different for her; she has a lot of confidence in herself as a mother and takes the hospital in her stride.

A man, too, may get the wrong first impression of himself as a father when his baby is born in a hospital. The mother at least knows that she is the center of attention. The poor father is a complete outsider. If he wants to see his baby, he has to stand outside a nursery window and look beseechingly at the nurse. Viewing a baby through glass is a poor substitute for holding him in your arms. Of course, the hospital is right in guarding his baby and all the others from any outside germs. But it gives the father the feeling that he is not considered a suitable companion for his child.

Both parents, I know, can get the wrong idea from the masks that are worn in many maternity hospitals. It makes them think of themselves as a menace to their baby. They wonder whether they ought not to be wearing them at home. The reason the masks are worn in hospitals is that so many adults and babies are gathered there in close quarters. A new germ brought in by anyone could spread easily and cause a lot of trouble. But in a family group there is very little risk of infection unless some member has a fresh cold or sore throat.

If you have a doctor (or midwife) who delivers babies at home, you can be safe there for a normal delivery. If the doctor foresees complications, he will advise hospitalization.

The woman who has her baby at home can have him close by and feel that he is really hers right from the beginning. This is a nice start for both of them. She can nurse him at frequent intervals at first if that is necessary. She has her family and possessions around her. She doesn't have to wait for visiting hours.

67. Rooming-in. In an effort to overcome some of the unnatural drawbacks of the maternity hospital, doctors and nurses have been experimenting in recent years with what's called the rooming-in plan. The baby's bassinet, instead of being in a nursery, is close to the mother's bed. She is encouraged by the nurses to begin taking care of him as soon as she is able—holding him, feeding him, diapering him, bathing him. She has the chance to practice these things while she is among experienced people who can explain things to her and help her. She learns about her baby's hunger patterns, his sleep, his cry, his bowel movements, so that he is not a stranger when she takes him home. This is of particular advantage to the inexperienced mother. An irregular feeding schedule, governed by the baby's need, is no problem, and this favors the success of breast feeding. The father when visiting feels he is a part of the family, and he can hold the baby and practice a bit of baby care himself.

Though rooming-in has always been practiced in some other parts of the world and though it was practiced in the United States many years ago, it has only recently been revived here, in a few hospitals, in an experimental way. It is safe. Most first-time mothers who have rooming-in are very enthusiastic and many want to have subsequent babies the same way. Other experienced mothers, with no time or way to get a vacation, prefer the luxury of full rest in the hospital.

Rooming-in is not easy to establish in a hospital. It involves many changes in hospital administration and philosophy. Getting it started usually requires research funds and a long period of planning and testing. If you hoped to have rooming-in but find it unavailable, don't feel that all is lost. You'll be able to make up for the lack of it after going home, especially in these days when the hospital stay is so short.

Your Baby

ENJOY HIM

68. Don't be afraid of him. You'd think from what some people say about babies' demanding attention that they come into the world determined to get their parents under their thumb by hook or by crook. This isn't true. Your baby is born to be a reasonable, friendly human being.

Don't be afraid to feed him when you think he's really hungry. If you are mistaken, he'll merely refuse to take much.

Don't be afraid to love him and enjoy him. Every baby needs to be smiled at, talked to, played with, fondled—gently and lovingly—just as much as he needs vitamins and calories. That's what will make him a person who loves people and enjoys life. The baby who doesn't get any loving will grow up cold and unresponsive.

Don't be afraid to respond to other desires of his as long as they seem sensible to you and as long as you don't become a slave to him. When he cries in the early weeks, it's because he's uncomfortable for some reason or other—maybe it's hunger or indigestion, or fatigue, or tension. The uneasy feeling you have when you hear him cry, the feeling that you want to comfort him, is meant to be part of your nature, too. Being held, rocked, or walked may be what he needs.

Spoiling doesn't come from being good to a baby in a sensible way, and it doesn't come all of a sudden. Spoiling comes on gradually when a mother is too afraid to use her common sense or when she really wants to be a slave and encourages her baby to become a slave driver.

Everyone wants his child to turn out to be healthy in his habits and easy to live with. But each child himself wants to eat at sensible hours and later to learn good table manners. His bowels (as long as the movements don't become too hard) will move according to their own healthy pattern, which may or may not be regular; and when he's a lot older and wiser, you can show him where to sit to move them. He will develop his own pattern of sleep according to his own needs. In all these habits he will sooner or later want to fit into the family's way of doing things, with only a minimum of guidance from you. Read *Babies Are Human Beings,* by C. Anderson Aldrich and Mary M. Aldrich.[1]

69. Enjoy him as he is—that's how he'll grow up best. Every baby's face is different from every other's. In the same way, every baby's pattern of development is different. One may be very advanced in his general bodily strength and coordination, an early sitter, stander, walker—a sort of infant athlete. And yet he may be slow in doing careful, skillful things with his fingers, in talking. Even a baby who is an athlete in rolling over, standing, and creeping may turn out to be slow to learn to walk. A baby who's advanced in his physical activities may be very slow in his teething, and vice versa. A child who turns out later to be smart in his schoolwork may have been so slow in beginning to talk that his parents were afraid for a while that he was dull; and a child who has just an ordinary amount of brains is sometimes a very early talker.

I am purposely picking out examples of children with mixed rates of

[1] New York: Macmillan, 1954. $2.95.

development to give you an idea of what a jumble of different qualities and patterns of growth each individual person is composed.

One baby is born to be big-boned and square and chunky, while another will always be small-boned and delicate. One individual really seems to be born to be fat. If he loses weight during an illness, he gains it back promptly afterward. The troubles that he has in the world never take away his appetite. The opposite kind of individual stays on the thin side, even when he has the most nourishing food to eat, even though life is running smoothly for him.

Love and enjoy your child for what he is, for what he looks like, for what he does, and forget about the qualities that he doesn't have. I don't give you this advice just for sentimental reasons. There's a very important practical point here. The child who is appreciated for what he is, even if he is homely, or clumsy, or slow, will grow up with confidence in himself, happy. He will have a spirit that will make the best of all the capacities that he has, and of all the opportunities that come his way. He will make light of any handicaps. But the child who has never been quite accepted by his parents, who has always felt that he was not quite right, will grow up lacking confidence. He'll never be able to make full use of what brains, what skills, what physical attractiveness, he has. If he starts life with a handicap, physical or mental, it will be multiplied tenfold by the time he is grown-up.

70. He isn't frail. "I'm so afraid I'll hurt him if I don't handle him right," a mother often says about her first baby. You don't have to worry; you have a pretty tough baby. There are many ways to hold him. If his head drops backward by mistake, it won't hurt him. The open spot in his skull (the fontanel) is covered by a tough membrane like canvas that isn't easily injured. The system to control his body temperature is working quite well by the time he weighs 7 pounds if he's covered halfway sensibly. He has good resistance to most germs. During a family cold epidemic, he's apt to have it the mildest of all. If he gets his head tangled in anything, he has a strong instinct to struggle and yell. If he's not getting enough to eat, he will probably cry for more. If the light is too strong for his eyes, he'll blink and fuss. (You can take his picture with a flash bulb, even if it does make him jump.) He knows how much sleep he needs, and takes it. He can care for himself pretty well for a person who can't say a word and knows nothing about the world.

71. A baby at birth is usually disappointing-looking to a parent who hasn't seen one before. His skin is coated with wax, which, if left on, will be absorbed slowly and will lessen the chance of rashes during the hospital stay. His skin underneath is apt to be very red. His face tends to be puffy and lumpy, and there may be black-and-blue marks from forceps. The head is misshapen from "molding" during labor—low in the forehead, elongated at the back, and quite lopsided. Occasionally there may be, in addition, a hematoma, a localized hemorrhage under the scalp that sticks out as a distinct bump and takes weeks to go away. A couple of days after birth there may be a touch of jaundice, which is visible for about a week. (Jaundice that comes the first day or is very noticeable or lasts more than a week should be reported to the doctor.)

The baby's body is covered all over with fuzzy hair, which is usually shed in about a week. For a couple of weeks afterward there is apt to be a dry scaling of the skin, which is also shed. Some babies have black hair on the scalp at first, which may come far down on the forehead. The first hair, whatever its color or consistency, comes out, and the new hair that grows back, sooner or later, may be quite different in all respects.

STRICTNESS OR PERMISSIVENESS?

72. This looms as a big question for many new parents. A great majority of them find the right answer in a little while. For a few parents it remains a worrisome question, no matter how much experience they've had.

I may as well let the cat out of the bag right away as far as my opinion goes and say that strictness or permissiveness is not the real issue. Good-hearted parents who aren't afraid to be firm when it is necessary can get good results with either moderate strictness or moderate permissiveness. On the other hand, a strictness that comes from harsh feelings or a permissiveness that is timid or vacillating can each lead to poor results. The real issue is what spirit the parent puts into managing the child and what attitude is engendered in the child as a result.

73. We've been through a big transition. It's hard to get any perspective on this topic without taking a historical view. Styles in strictness vary from one period to another. The Victorian Age was quite strict, for instance, about manners and modesty. In the twentieth century, especially after World War I, a reaction set in. Several factors pushed it along. The great American pioneers in educational research, like John Dewey and William Kilpatrick, showed that a child learns better and faster with a method of teaching that makes allowance for his particular readiness to progress and that recognizes his eagerness to learn if the subject matter is suitable. Freud and his followers showed that harsh toilet training or frightening a child about sex can distort his personality and lead to neurosis. Studies of delinquents and criminals revealed that most of them had suffered more from lack of love in childhood than from lack of punishment. These discoveries, among others, encouraged a general relaxation in child discipline and a greater effort to give children what they seemed to need as individuals. Several wise leaders in American pediatrics, Aldrich and Powers and Gesell, began to introduce a similar philosophy into the medical care of babies and children. But physicians remained strict about infant feeding right into the 1940's, because they still feared that irregular schedules and irregular amounts of formula might bring on the severe diarrheal diseases that used to cause so many infant deaths. Then the experiments of Dr. Preston McLendon and Mrs. Frances P. Simsarian with the "self-demand" schedule, published in 1942, helped to convince doctors that most babies can do very well choosing their own feeding times and will remain healthy. Since then, there has been a rapid and widespread shift in medical practice. Today a majority of American babies are being put on more or less flexible schedules at first.

Doctors who used to conscientiously warn young parents against spoiling are now encouraging them to meet their baby's needs, not only for food, but for comforting and loving.

These discoveries and these changes of attitudes and methods have benefited most children and parents. There are fewer tense ones, more happy ones.

But it's not possible for a civilization like ours to go through such a change of philosophy—it really amounts to a revolution—without raising doubts in many parents' minds and without getting some parents thoroughly mixed up. It's basic human nature to tend to bring up your children about as you were brought up. It's easy enough to pick up new ideas about vitamins and inoculations. But if your upbringing was fairly strict in regard to obedience, manners, sex, truthfulness, it's natural, it's almost inevitable, that you will feel strongly underneath about such matters when raising your own children. You may have changed your theories because of something you've studied or read or heard, but when your child does something that would have been considered bad in your own childhood, you'll probably find yourself becoming more tense, or anxious, or angry than you imagined possible. This is nothing to be ashamed of. This is the way Nature expects human beings to learn child care—from their own childhood. This is how different civilizations have managed to remain stable and carry on their ideals from generation to generation.

The reason that most parents have been able to do a good job with their children during the past fifty years of changing theory is that they themselves had been brought up reasonably happily, were comfortable about raising their children the same way, and didn't follow any new theory to extremes. When doctors were emphasizing regularity, confident parents followed a regular schedule in general (and **most** babies adjusted to it **most** of the time), but they weren't afraid to make an occasional exception when the baby became painfully hungry ahead of time, because they felt in their bones that this was right.

When doctors more recently have been emphasizing flexibility, confident parents haven't carried this to extremes, either. They don't let a sleepy but obstinate baby refuse to be put to bed, because they know very well (mostly from their own childhood) that bedtime is bedtime and that theories of flexibility have very little to do with this situation.

74. Parents who become confused with new theories are often of two kinds. There are, first of all, those who have been brought up with too little confidence in their own judgment. If you don't dare trust yourself, you **have** to follow what someone else says, willy-nilly. A second group are those parents who feel that they were brought up too severely. They remember the resentment they felt toward their parents at times, and they don't want their children to feel that way about them. But this is a very difficult approach. If you want to raise your children the way you were raised, you have a definite pattern to follow. You know just how obedient, how helpful, how polite, you want them to be. You don't have to stop and think. But if you want to treat them quite differently than the way you were treated—more indulgently, for instance, or more as equals—you don't have any pattern of how far to carry it. If things begin to get out of hand—if, for example, your child begins to take advantage of your permissiveness—it's harder to find your way back onto the right track. The child makes you mad, all right, but the madder you get the guiltier you feel for fear you'll step into the very pattern you were determined to avoid.

Of course, I'm making all this sound too black or white. We all start out as young parents partly agreeing, partly disagreeing, with the methods our parents used. It's a matter of degree. And most of us find a compromise that works reasonably well. I have been exaggerating in order to make clear the difficulty that some parents have had.

75. Stick to your convictions. I think that good parents who naturally lean toward strictness should stick to their guns and raise their children that way. Moderate strictness—in the sense of requiring good manners, prompt obedience, orderliness—is not harmful to children so long as the parents are basically kind and so long as the children are growing up happy and friendly. But strictness **is** harmful when the parents are overbearing, harsh, chronically disapproving, and make no allowances for a child's age and individuality. This kind of severity produces children who are either meek and colorless or mean to others.

Parents who incline to an easygoing kind of management, who are satisfied with casual manners as long as the child's attitude is friendly, or who happen not to be particularly strict—for instance, about promptness or neatness—can also raise children who are considerate and cooperative, as long as the parents are not afraid to be firm about those matters that do seem important to them.

When parents get unhappy results from too much permissiveness, it is not so much because they demand too little, though this is part of it. It is more because they are timid or guilty about what they ask or because they are unconsciously encouraging the child to rule the roost.

Infant Feeding

WHAT FEEDING MEANS TO THE BABY

76. He knows a lot about diet. You might get the idea, in case the hospital has given you a formula slip, that feeding a baby is something like chemistry. You take so many ounces of milk and water, mix them this way, cook them that way, put 3½ ounces into each of 6 bottles, and feed at 6 A.M., 10 A.M., 2 P.M., 6 P.M., 10 P.M., 2 A.M. The formula slip is concerned with the details; it forgets to tell you that the food is for a human being who has strong feelings about how much he wants and when he's hungry again. It's true that you have the responsibility of making the formula carefully. The amounts have been calculated by the doctor on the basis of the baby's weight and what he seemed to want in the hospital. But the baby is the one who knows how many calories his body needs and what his digestion can handle. If he's regularly not getting enough, he'll probably cry for more. Take his word for it and get in touch with the doctor. If there's more in the bottle than he feels like, let him stop when he wants to.

Think of the baby's first year this way: He wakes up because he's hungry, cries because he wants to be fed. He is so eager when the nipple goes into his mouth that he almost shudders. When he nurses, you can see that it is an intense experience. Perhaps he breaks into perspiration. If you stop him in the middle of a nursing, he may cry furiously. When he has had as much as he wants, he is groggy with satisfaction and falls asleep. Even when he is asleep, it sometimes looks as if he were dreaming of nursing. His mouth makes sucking motions, and his whole expression looks blissful. This all adds up to the fact that feeding is his great joy. He gets his early ideas about life from the way feeding goes. He gets his first ideas about the world from the person who feeds him.

When a mother constantly urges her baby to take more than he wants, he is apt to become steadily less interested. He may try to escape from it by going to sleep earlier and earlier in the feeding, or he may rebel and become more balky. He's apt to lose some of his active, positive feeling about life. It's as though he got the idea, "Life is a struggle. Those people are always after you. You have to fight to protect yourself."

So don't urge a baby to take more than he is eager for. Let him go on enjoying his meals, feeling that you are his friend. This is one of the principal ways in which his self-confidence, his joy in life, and his love of people will be firmly established during the first year. Read *Feeding Our Old Fashioned Children,* by C. Anderson Aldrich and Mary M. Aldrich.[1]

77. The important sucking instinct. A baby nurses eagerly for two separate reasons. First, because he's hungry. Second, because he **loves** to suck. If you feed him plenty but don't give him enough chance to suck, his craving for sucking will go unsatisfied and he will try to suck something else—his fist, or his thumb, or the clothes. It's important to give him a long enough nursing period at each feeding and to have a sufficient number of feedings each day. All this is taken up in detail in Sections 319 to 332, on thumb-sucking. The thing to watch for in the beginning is not whether the baby is actually sucking his thumb, but whether he looks as if he is trying to.

78. Babies normally lose weight in the beginning. A good-sized baby who gets formula from the start usually begins to gain it back in 2 or 3 days, because he can drink and digest well. The small or premature baby loses weight longer and regains it more slowly, because he can take only small feedings at first. It may take him several weeks just to get back to birth weight. This delay doesn't handicap him. Eventually he will gain rapidly to make up for it. The breast-fed baby is naturally going to be slower than the bottle-fed baby in regaining his birth weight, because his mother won't be able to supply him with much milk until he's 4 or 5 days old, and even then the milk is apt to come in slowly.

Some parents worry unnecessarily about the initial weight loss. They can't help feeling that it's unnatural and dangerous for the weight to be

[1] New York: Macmillan. 1941. $2.75.

going down instead of up. They also may have heard that if a baby loses **excessive** amounts of weight, he may develop fever from becoming dehydrated (dried out). It's for this reason that some hospitals give water for the first few days to the babies who get no formula and whose mother's milk has not come in yet. But the chance of dehydration fever is small, and it can always be cured immediately by giving fluid.

Concern about the early weight loss not only may upset a mother needlessly but may also cause her to abandon breast feeding before it has been given a fair chance. Some hospitals, to keep the mother from worrying, don't tell her the daily weight of the baby, but this method doesn't always work. The mother who is anxious imagines the worst. It's better for the mother to realize how natural the weight loss is and to resolve to leave the whole matter in the doctor's hands.

SCHEDULES

Your doctor will talk to you about your baby's feeding schedule. It will depend on your baby's size, hungriness, wakefulness, and on what the doctor thinks will suit you and the baby best. What follows is a general discussion of the principles involved.

79. What regularity and flexibility are all about. During the first half of this century in this country, babies were usually kept on very strict, regular schedules. A newborn 7-pounder would be fed at exactly 6 A.M., 10 A.M., 2 P.M., 6 P.M., 10 P.M. and 2 A.M.—no earlier, no later, regardless of when he seemed hungry. Doctors did not know for sure the cause of the serious intestinal infections that afflicted tens of thousands of babies yearly. It was believed that these infections were caused not only by the contamination of milk (from carelessness in the dairy or in making the formula at home, or from insufficient refrigeration) but also by wrong proportions in the formula **and** by irregularity in feeding.

Strictness was preached and practiced everywhere—on the dairy farm, in the commercial dairy, and in the home. Doctors and nurses feared irregular feeding so strongly that they came to disapprove of it psychologically, too, and taught mothers that it would lead to spoiling the child. In the general enthusiasm for strictness, mothers were usually advised to ignore their baby except at feeding time. Even kissing was frowned on by a few.

Strict regularity worked well enough with a majority of babies. When they took an ample feeding at breast or bottle, it lasted them for **about** 4 hours just because that is the way a young baby's digestive system usually works. But it's also a fact that we are creatures of habit at any age, and if we are always fed at exactly the same hour we soon learn, inside, to become suddenly hungry right at that moment.

But there were always a few babies who had trouble adjusting to regularity in the first month or two—babies whose stomachs couldn't seem to hold 4 hours' worth of milk, babies who went to sleep halfway through feedings, restless babies, colicky babies. They would cry miserably for shorter or longer periods each day, but their mothers and doctors dared not feed them (or even pick them up) off schedule. It was hard enough on the babies. I think it was harder still on the mothers, who had to sit listening, biting their nails, wanting to comfort their babies but not allowed to do so. You don't know how lucky you are to be able to be natural and flexible.

Anyway, the serious diarrheal diseases almost disappeared. The chief factor was the pasteurization of milk in the commercial dairy, but care in preparing the formula and better refrigeration helped, too. But it took many more years before doctors dared to begin experimenting with flexible schedules. When they did, they found that flexibility did **not** lead to diarrhea or indigestion, nor did it lead to spoiling, as many had feared.

The first experiments were carried out by Dr. Preston McLendon and Mrs. Frances P. Simsarian, a psychologist and new mother, with Mrs. Simsarian's new baby. They wanted to find out what kind of schedule a baby would establish if he were breast-fed whenever he seemed hungry. The baby waked rather infrequently the first few days. Then, from just about the time the milk began to come in, he waked surprisingly often—about 10 times a day—in the second half of the first week. But by the age of 2 weeks he had settled down to 6 or 7 feedings a day, at rather irregular intervals. By 10 weeks he had arrived at approximately a 4-hour schedule. They called this an experiment in "self-demand" feeding, and this term has become well known. (I don't happen to like it for general use because it suggests the picture of a demanding baby, which isn't correct.) Since that experiment led the way, in 1942, there has been a general relaxation in infant feeding schedules, which has had a wholesome effect on babies and parents.

80. Misunderstandings about self-demand. I think, though, that there has been a certain amount of misunderstanding. Some young parents, eager to be progressive, have assumed that if they wanted to get away from the rigid scheduling of the past they must go all the way in the opposite direction, feed their baby **any** time he woke and **never** wake him for a feeding, just as if **they** were conducting a scientific experiment, or as if there were a fundamental superiority in irregularity.

This may work out well enough if the baby is a peaceful one with a good digestion, if the mother doesn't have to worry about her own schedule, and if she doesn't mind being waked between midnight and 6 A.M. But if the baby happens to be a restless, fretful one, it can lead to a great many feedings and very little rest for the parents, for several months. And in a few cases it encourages the baby to be still waking for a couple of night feedings even at the end of the first year.

When some mothers follow self-demand to inconvenient extremes, it makes other mothers shy away from it like the plague. In a group of mothers talking about schedules, one will say in a superior tone, **"My baby is on self-demand,"** and another will answer rather indignantly, **"Well, mine isn't!"** When parents act as if the schedule is a matter of belief, like a religious or political conviction, it seems to me that the real point has been lost.

The main purpose of any schedule is to do right by the baby. But another purpose is to enable the parents to care for him in a way that will conserve their strength and spirits. This usually means getting down to a reasonable number of feedings at predictable hours, and omitting the night feeding as soon as the baby is ready. Otherwise the parents won't be able to do as good a job with him in other respects. What's good for them will be good for him, and vice versa.

Now that it's no longer necessary to stick to a rigid schedule, you and the baby are free to start with what he seems to need and then to move toward what is convenient for all.

If a mother **prefers** to feed her baby on an irregular schedule for many months, there is certainly no harm done to his nutrition. It does no harm to the mother, either, if she's a person who just hates to do anything by the clock. But if she's fairly regular about the rest of her life and has other things to get done, I only worry that she has gotten the idea that the more she gives up for the baby the better it is for him, or that she has to prove she is a good mother by ignoring her own convenience. These attitudes tend to create difficulties in the long run.

81. General guide to scheduling. The main consideration for the baby is that he does not have to cry with hunger for long periods. He doesn't mind at all being waked up for a feeding after an interval of 3 or 4 hours.

Every baby has a tendency to develop regular habits of becoming hungry, and these will come much more rapidly if his mother guides him a bit.

Also, babies tend to gradually lengthen the interval between feedings as they grow bigger and older. A 5- or 6-pounder usually needs to be fed about every 3 hours. Most 8- or 9-pounders are happy to average 4 hours between feedings. They come to realize that they don't need the late-night feeding, and most of them give it up by 1 or 2 months of age. Somewhere between the fourth and eighth months, a majority of babies show a preference for a 5-hour interval, and during this period they become able to sleep through the evening feeding, too.

In all these tendencies—to more regular feedings and to fewer feedings—the baby can be greatly influenced by the mother's management. If she wakes him whenever he's still asleep 4 hours after the last feeding, she helps him to establish a 4-hour hunger habit. If, when he stirs and whimpers a couple of hours after the last feeding, she holds back for a few minutes and gives him a chance to go to sleep again, or if, when he gets crying steadily, she tries to comfort him with a pacifier or a bottle of water, she helps his stomach to adjust to a longer interval. If, on the other hand, she always picks him up and feeds him promptly when he stirs, even though it's only a couple of hours after the last feeding, she keeps him accustomed to short intervals and small feedings.

Individual babies differ widely in how soon they can comfortably settle down to regular schedules. A great majority of the ones who are good feeders, who are reasonably relaxed, and who are getting plenty to drink from breast or bottle, can be eased into a smooth 4-hour schedule and will give up the 2 A.M. feeding within a month after birth. On the other hand, if a baby is a listless, sleepy feeder at first, or a restless, fretful waker (Sections 127, 184–186, 273–275), or if the breast-milk supply is not yet well established, it will be more comfortable for all concerned to go more slowly. But even in these cases, there will be less perplexity on the part of the mother every day—about whether to give a feeding right away or to wait—and an earlier settling down on the part of the baby, if the mother is always working gently toward more regular feedings, as close as possible to every 4 hours.

82. Specific suggestions for working toward a regular schedule. A relaxed baby who weighed 7 or 8 pounds at birth usually is able to last 3½ to 4 hours on a full stomach and wants 6 or 7 feedings in the 24 hours at the start. The parents can keep in mind, as a rough guide, a 4-hour schedule (6 A.M., 10 A.M., 2 P.M., 6 P.M., 10 P.M., 2 A.M.), but be quite willing to feed him early if he really seems hungry—1 hour early if he is taking good amounts from the bottle; as much as 2 hours early if he is breast-fed and the supply is not yet well established.

If your baby is still asleep when one of these regular feeding hours comes around, you can wake him up. You won't have to urge him to eat. A baby who is waked up 4 hours after his last feeding will usually be starving-hungry in a few minutes. But suppose he wakes an hour early for his next feeding. You don't have to feed him the first minute he whimpers. He's not sure himself he's hungry. But if in 10 or 15 minutes he's crying hard with hunger, I wouldn't wait any longer. What happens to the 4-hour schedule? He may make up the difference and sleep long enough before the next feeding to get back on schedule. If he doesn't make up the time during the day, he may make it up at night. If he's always waking early, nearer to every 3 hours, maybe he isn't getting enough to last him 4 hours. If he is being breast-fed, let him nurse more often—even after 2 hours if he seems very hungry—expecting that the more frequent emptying of the breast will stimulate it to supply more milk in the next few days. When he gets a larger amount, he will be able to last longer. If he is on the bottle, draining every one and regularly waking early, consult the doctor about increasing the formula.

83. Just how early should you give another feeding? I have been saying that if the baby who generally can go 4 hours wakes after 3 or 3½ hours and seems really hungry, it is all right to feed him then. But suppose he wakes an hour or so after his last feeding. If he finished his usual bottle at his last feeding, the chances are against his being hungry again so soon. It is more likely that he has been waked by indigestion or colic. You can try burping him again, or see whether he will be comforted by a couple of ounces of water or a pacifier. I would not be in a rush to feed him again, though you may decide to try it in a little while if nothing else works. You can't be sure it's hunger just because a baby tries to eat his hand or starts to take the bottle eagerly. Often a baby who is having colic will do both these things. It seems the baby himself can't distinguish between colic pains and hunger pains. This is discussed in Section 275.

In other words, you don't **always** feed a baby when he cries. If he is crying at the wrong times, you have to study the situation and perhaps discuss it with your doctor.

84. Other hours for a 4-hour schedule. Can you aim for a 4-hour schedule with hours other than the usual 6 A.M., 10 A.M., 2 P.M., 6 P.M., 10 P.M., 2 A.M.? You certainly can, if the baby is willing. The commonest substitute is 7 A.M., 11 A.M., 3 P.M., 7 P.M., 11 P.M. (with or without 3 A.M.). The only hitch is that most young babies always want to start the day between 5 and 6 A.M., no matter when they were last fed during the night. Once in a while, a lucky mother gets a baby who is on the usual 10-2-6-10 schedule but is willing to wait until 7 A.M. for his first feeding, even when he is quite young. This is all right, too.

85. A 3-hour schedule. If your baby is getting all the milk he wants but usually wakes in about 3 hours in the daytime, it will probably be more convenient to stick to a 3-hour schedule for the time being.

It's mostly babies weighing under 7 pounds who need to be on a 3-hour schedule. But this is not an absolute rule. Some 6-pounders are willing and able to go 4 hours. And an occasional 8-pounder can't hold enough to last more than 3 hours for the first couple of weeks.

Most babies who need a 3-hour schedule during the daytime are able to go 4 hours at night if they weigh as much as 5 pounds. The feedings usually work out about as follows: 6 A.M., 9 A.M., 12 noon, 3 P.M., 6 P.M., 10 P.M., 2 A.M.

86. The 2 A.M. feeding. The easiest rule for the 2 A.M. feeding is not to wake the baby but to let him wake you if he wants to. A baby who still needs that feeding usually wakes surprisingly close to the hour of 2. Then some night, probably when he's between 2 and 6 weeks old, he will sleep through until 3 or 3:30 A.M. You feed him then, and count it as a 2 A.M. feeding. He'll probably be awake and hungry again between 6 and 7 A.M. The next night he may sleep till 4:30 or 5 A.M. You feed him then, but this time you count it as a 6 o'clock feeding and hope that he'll be happy until somewhere near 10 A.M. When a baby gets ready to give up the 2 A.M. feeding, he usually does it in a hurry, within two or three nights. Then you divide his total formula into 5 bottles instead of 6.

87. Omitting the 2 A.M. feeding. If a baby has reached the age of 1 month and weighs 9 pounds and still is waking for a 2 A.M. feeding, I think it's sensible for the parents to try to influence him to give it up. Instead of hurrying to him as soon as he stirs, you can let him fuss for 15 or 30 minutes and see if he won't go back to sleep. If he doesn't quiet down, try him on a couple of ounces of warm water. If he's crying furiously at the end of half an hour, it will be easier all around to give him breast or formula, but try again in another week or two. From a nutritional point of view, a 9-pounder who's eating well during the day doesn't really need a 2 A.M. feeding.

88. The 10 P.M., or evening, feeding is the one that you can probably time to your own convenience. Most babies, by the time they are a few weeks old, are perfectly willing to wait until 11 or even midnight for it. If you want to get to bed early, wake the baby at 10 or even a little before. If it is more convenient to feed him late, suit yourself, as long as he is willing to stay asleep.

If a baby is still waking for a 2 A.M. feeding, I would advise against letting him sleep through the 10 or 11 P.M. feeding, even though he's quite willing. When he's ready to give up one of them, you'll want him to give up the 2 A.M. feeding first, so that your sleep won't be interrupted.

If your baby is already off the 2 A.M. feeding but is still quite irregular about his daytime feeding hours, I'd continue to wake him at 10 or 11 P.M., provided he's willing to be fed. This at least ends the day on schedule, helps very much to avoid a feeding between midnight and 4 A.M., and tends to start him off somewhere between 5 and 6 the next morning.

Omitting the 10 P.M. feeding is discussed in Section 214.

GIVING THE FEEDING

The details of giving breast feedings are discussed in Sections 102 to 114. Some of the problems of babies who do not nurse well in the early weeks and are slow to settle into a schedule are described in Section 127.

Giving the bottle is discussed in Sections 179 to 186. This includes some of the difficulties in the early weeks.

89. Refusal to nurse in later months. Once in a while a baby between 4 and 7 months old acts queerly at his feedings. The mother will say that the he nurses hungrily at breast or bottle for a few minutes. Then he becomes frantic, lets go of the nipple, and cries as if in pain. He still seems very hungry. But each time he goes back to nursing he becomes uncomfortable sooner. He takes his solid food eagerly. I think that this distress is caused by teething. I suspect that as the baby nurses, the suction engorges his painful gums and makes them tingle unbearably. You can break each nursing period into several parts and give the solid food in the intervals, since the distress comes on only after a number of minutes of sucking. If he is on a bottle, you can enlarge the holes in a few nipples so that he gets the bottle in a shorter time. (Use these easy nipples only while the trouble lasts, since they will prevent the baby, in the long run, from getting sufficient sucking satisfaction.) If the baby's discomfort is excessive and comes on very promptly, you could, for a few days, give up the bottle altogether. Give him his milk from the cup, if he is skillful enough, or from a spoon, or mix a large amount of it with his cereal and other foods. Don't worry if he doesn't get his usual amount.

An ear infection, complicating a cold, may cause enough pain in the jaw joint so that a baby will refuse to nurse even though he may be able to eat solids pretty well.

An occasional baby will decline to take the breast during the mother's menstrual periods. He can be given formula during those days. It will be necessary for the mother to express the breast milk manually to relieve the fullness and to keep the supply going. The baby will resume the breast when the period is over and will usually be able to revive the breast-milk supply if the mother rapidly eliminates the bottles.

90. Getting up the air bubble. All babies swallow some air while they are drinking their milk. It collects as a bubble in the stomach. One baby's stomach becomes uncomfortably full before he is halfway through his feeding, and he has to stop. Another never swallows enough to interrupt his meal. There are a couple of ways to bubble a baby, and you can find which works best for you. The first is to sit him upright in your lap and gently rub his stomach. The other is to hold him up against your shoulder and massage or pat him in the middle of the back. It's a good idea to put a diaper over your shoulder in case he spits up a little. One kind of stomach lets go of the bubble very easily and promptly. The other kind seems to want to hang on to it. When the bubble doesn't come up easily, it sometimes helps to put the baby in a lying position for a second and then bring him back to your shoulder again.

You need to bubble your baby in the middle of a feeding only if he swallows so much air that it stops his nursing. But you should at least try to get the bubble up at the end of the feeding. Most babies will become uncomfortable in a little while if put to bed with the bubble still in the stomach. Some babies even get colic pains from it. On the other hand, if your baby is hard to bubble and if he always seems just as comfortable whether he has burped or not, there is no need for you to try for more than a few minutes.

This is as good a place as any to mention the fact that when a young baby has taken a full feeding, his abdomen bulges to an extent that's apt to worry the inexperienced mother. This is only because the amount he needs to drink at each feeding is much larger in comparison to the size of his abdomen than it is in an adult. You'd look full if you weighed 110 pounds and drank 2 quarts of milk at a meal.

GETTING ENOUGH AND GAINING WEIGHT

91. An infant usually knows how much food he needs. If he is outgrowing his present formula, or if his mother's breast-milk supply has decreased temporarily because of fatigue or tension, he will probably begin to wake earlier and earlier before each feeding and cry with a cry that you now recognize as one of hunger. He will be finishing all his bottles to the last drop and looking around for more. He may try to eat his hands. If you are weighing him, you may find that he is gaining less than he did before. Sometimes a baby who is getting hungry will become constipated, also. If he is getting **really** hungry, he may cry at the end of some of his feedings, too.

If your baby is showing some of these signs of dissatisfaction and if he is on a formula, it is time to get in touch with your doctor to see about an increase. If you are unable to consult a doctor and are using the formulas in this book, it is time to change to the stronger formula. In fact, you don't have to wait this long. It's reasonable to increase the formula just as soon as a baby is regularly finishing all his bottles, even before he's showing any signs of dissatisfaction. There's one caution: if you give him an increase on such slight provocation, he probably won't be ready to take it all. So be careful not to urge him.

If a baby is being breast-fed and waking early, you can nurse him early, even though this might mean an extra feeding a day. The more frequent feedings will help to satisfy him, and the more frequent emptying of the breasts will stimulate them to produce a larger supply if that is possible. If you have been nursing at only one breast a feeding, give both breasts at each feeding for a while.

92. How much weight should your baby gain? The best that you can say is that he should gain at the rate that he seems to want to gain at. Most babies know. If they are offered more food than they need, they refuse it. If they are given less, they show their hunger by waking earlier before feedings and eating their fists.

We can talk about average babies if you remember clearly that no baby is average. When a doctor talks about an average baby, he means only that he has added together the fast gainers and the slow gainers and the medium gainers. One baby is **meant** to be a slow gainer, and another is **meant** to be a fast gainer.

If a baby is gaining slowly, that doesn't mean for sure that he was meant to. If he is hungry all the time, that is a pretty good sign that he is meant to be gaining faster. Once in a while slow gaining means that a baby is sick. A slow gainer particularly needs to be seen regularly by a doctor to make sure that he is healthy. Occasionally you see an exceptionally polite baby who is gaining slowly and who doesn't seem too hungry. But if you give him more to eat, he takes it quite willingly and gains more rapidly. In other words, not every baby yells when he is being fed too little.

The average baby's weight is a little over 7 pounds at birth, and 14 pounds at 5 months. That is to say, the average baby doubles his birth weight at about 5 months. But in actual practice, babies who are small at birth are more apt to grow faster, as if trying to catch up, and babies who are born big are less apt to double their birth weight by 5 months.

The average baby gains close to 2 pounds a month (6 or 8 ounces a week) during the first 3 months. Of course, some healthy ones gain less, and others more. Then he slows down. **By 6 months the average gain is down to a pound a month** (4 ounces a week). That's quite a drop in a 3-month period. In the last quarter of the first year, the average gain is down to ⅔ pound a month (2 or 3 ounces a week), and during the second year to about ½ pound a month.

As the baby grows older, you can see that he gains more slowly. He also gains more irregularly. Teething, for instance, may take his appetite away for several weeks, and he may hardly gain at all. When he feels more comfortable, his appetite revives and his weight catches up with a rush.

You can't decide too much from how a baby's weight changes from week to week. What he weighs each time will depend on how recently he has urinated, how recently he has moved his bowels, how recently he has eaten. If you find, one morning, that he has gained only 4 ounces in the past week, whereas before he had always gained 7, don't jump to the conclusion that he is starving or that something else is wrong. If he seems perfectly happy and satisfied, wait another week to see what happens. He may make an extra large gain to make up for the small one. Always remember, though, that the older he gets, the slower he will gain.

93. How often do you need to weigh the baby? Of course, most mothers don't have scales, and most babies get weighed only when they go to see their doctor, which is plenty often. When a baby is happy and doing well, weighing more frequently than once a month serves no purpose but to satisfy curiosity. If you have scales, don't weigh more often than once a week. Once in 2 weeks is even better. If you weigh your baby every day, you encourage yourself to get too wrapped up in his weight. On the other hand, if he is crying a lot, or having indigestion, or vomiting a great deal, frequent weighing may help you and your doctor in deciding what is the matter. For instance, if he is crying excessively but gaining rapidly, it points toward colic, not hunger.

Breast Feeding

THE VALUES OF BREAST FEEDING

94. Breast feeding is natural. On general principle, it's safer to do things the natural way unless you are absolutely sure you have a better way. Breast feeding has definite advantages that we know of, and it may have others that we haven't learned yet. It helps the mother physically. When the baby nurses, the muscle wall of the uterus contracts vigorously. This hastens its return to normal size and position.

You may have heard that the baby gets some protection against disease from the colostrum (the fluid that comes in before the real milk). It may well be so, though it has not been conclusively proved. Breast-fed babies have somewhat fewer bowel upsets than bottle-fed babies. A big advantage of breast feeding is that the milk is always pure; a baby can't catch an intestinal infection from it. From a purely practical point of view, it saves hours of time every week, because there are no bottles to sterilize, no formulas to mix and cook, no refrigeration to worry about, no bottles to warm. You appreciate this particularly if you ever have to travel. Of course, breast feeding saves money, too. There is another advantage that isn't often mentioned: it's more adapted to satisfying the baby's sucking instinct. At the breast he can suck as long as he feels the need. I think that there is less thumb-sucking among breast-fed babies, for that reason.

The most convincing evidence of the value of breast feeding comes from mothers who have done it. They tell of the tremendous satisfaction they experience from knowing that they are providing the baby with something no one else can give him, from seeing his devotion to the breast, from feeling his closeness. It is too seldom mentioned that after a couple of weeks the act of nursing becomes definitely pleasurable for the mother—it's intended to be. A woman doesn't get to feel like a mother, or come to enjoy being a mother, or feel the full motherly love for her child just from the fact that a baby has been born to her. With her first infant particularly, she becomes a real mother only as she takes care of her child. The more success she has in the beginning in doing her part and the more visibly her baby is satisfied by her care, the sooner and the more enjoyably she slips into the role. In this sense breast feeding does wonders for a young mother and for her relationship with her baby. She and her baby are happy in themselves and feel more and more loving to each other.

However, fewer babies have been breast-fed in recent years, especially in cities. The chief reason is that bottle feeding has gotten to be safe and easy. Another reason is custom. If most of the women in a community use bottle feeding, it seems like the most natural thing to the new mother.

QUESTIONS ABOUT BREAST FEEDING

95. The mother's figure. Some mothers shy away from breast feeding for fear it will spoil their figure. You certainly don't have to eat excessively or get fat in order to make milk. A nursing mother needs enough extra to keep her own body from being depleted. She does not need to gain an ounce above her regular weight.

But what about the effect of nursing on the shape and size of the breasts? They enlarge during pregnancy and will stay somewhat enlarged as long as nursing continues; then they return to approximately their previous size. There is no one answer to the question whether nursing several children will cause the breasts to become flattened or to sag. There are women who have nursed babies and whose breasts have become flatter with the years, but there are others whose breasts have flattened without their ever having nursed a child. I know from my own medical experience that many women breast-feed several babies with no deleterious effect on their figures. Others end up with even better figures.

These are two precautions that are probably important. First, the mother should wear a well-fitting brassiere that supports the breasts, not only while she is nursing but also during the latter part of pregnancy, day and night, when the breasts are definitely enlarged. This is to prevent stretching of the skin and of the supporting tissues in the breast during the time the breasts are heavier. For many women it is advisable to change to a larger brassiere by the seventh month of pregnancy. It is well worth while to buy nursing brassieres that have changeable, washable pads in them to absorb any milk that may leak between feedings (of course, cotton may be used instead), and the fronts of which can be opened for nursing (get the kind that can be opened easily with one hand).

The other precaution during pregnancy and nursing is to avoid putting on excess weight. After all, the breasts may sag from obesity, quite apart from pregnancy.

96. Size of breasts is of no importance. Some women with small breasts assume that they will be less able to produce milk in sufficient quantity. There is probably little basis for this belief. When a woman is not pregnant and not nursing, the glandular tissue is quiescent and constitutes only a minor part of the breast. The greater part is composed of fat tissue, which is apparently concentrated there for purposes of beauty. The larger breast has more fat tissue; the smaller breast has less. As a woman's pregnancy progresses, secretions from the ovaries stimulate the glandular, milk-producing tissue to develop and enlarge. The arteries and veins that serve the glandular tissue enlarge, too, so that the veins become prominent on the surface of the breast. The milk, when it comes in a few days after delivery, causes further enlargement of the breasts. Doctors who have cared for nursing mothers agree that even women who have unusually small breasts before pregnancy may produce copious amounts of milk.

97. Does it tire the mother? You occasionally hear it said that breast feeding "takes a lot out of a woman." Many women do feel fatigued in the early weeks of nursing, but so do many who are feeding by bottle. They are getting their strength back after the delivery and hospitalization. The nervous tension from caring for a new baby is tiring. But it's also true that the breasts are requiring a goodly number of calories each day for the baby, and a mother must eat considerably more than usual just to keep her weight up. In the long run there is no more reason for a woman to feel exhausted from breast feeding than from a vacation on which she is taking a lot of exercise in the form of walks or swimming. Our bodies soon adapt to increasing or decreasing energy needs, and our appetites go up or down accordingly in order to keep our weight stationary. If a nursing mother is healthy and happy, her appetite will naturally take care of the need for extra calories for the baby's milk. Some nursing mothers are amazed at the amount of food they crave and can eat without gaining weight. Sometimes the appetite overdoes it, though, and then the woman has to call on her will power and the help of the doctor, public-health nurse, and perhaps nutritionist to keep from gaining too much.

A woman who feels that nursing takes too much out of her may be a worrisome person whose concern about the new baby depresses her appetite or her spirits. Or she may be an individual who has never had much confidence in her health and strength and therefore feels that any unusual demand on her system is a threat, even though her body is actually handling the situation well. Or, least likely of all, she may be in poor physical health. Needless to say, a nursing mother who is not feeling well or is losing weight should consult her doctor promptly.

Some women, usually because of the way they were brought up, feel deeply uncomfortable at the prospect of breast feeding—it may seem too immodest or too animal-like. If such a feeling is strong, I think it is preferable for the mother not to try, no matter how much she wants to do right by her baby.

Quite a few fathers, including some very good ones, object to breast feeding—they can't help feeling jealous. Then the mother has to use her best judgment.

98. The working mother. What about the woman who hesitates to nurse because she has to go back to work? The answer depends on her working hours and how soon she must get back to the job. If she has to be out of the home only 8 hours a day, she can still nurse her baby except for one feeding. Even if she can't nurse after she resumes work, it would still be worth while to breast-feed the baby temporarily if she has a month or two.

99. There are other ways to show affection, too. Suppose you want to breast-feed your baby but don't succeed. Will the baby suffer, physically or emotionally? No, you can't put it that strongly. If you make the formula carefully and if you keep in touch with the doctor, the chances are great that the baby will prosper from a bodily point of view. And if, when you give him his bottle, you cuddle him in your arms, he will be nourished spiritually, much as if he were at the breast. Mothers who have read what psychologists and psychiatrists say about the importance of breast feeding sometimes get the idea that it has been shown that bottle-fed babies turn out to be less happy than breast-fed babies. Nobody has proved that.

To put it in other words, there are hundreds of ways in which a mother shows her devotion to her baby and builds his trust in her. Breast feeding is one way, and a very good one, but certainly not essential. Giving flowers is one way a man may show his love for his wife. But no sensible wife who has other proofs of her husband's love will despair just because he's not a flower giver. You may think I'm laboring this point. I give it this emphasis because there are conscientious young women who, as a result of what they've studied or heard, set their hearts on being able to breast-feed. Then, if it doesn't work, they feel that they have deprived their babies and failed as women. This great build-up of the importance of nursing is not justified by the facts, and the reaction to lack of success is unnecessarily hard on the mother and, indirectly, on the baby. After all, he needs a cheerful mother more than he needs breast milk.

It's well to remember that the production of milk depends on the glandular secretions in the mother's body and on the hospital routines, over neither of which the mother has control, as well as on her own efforts. Therefore, failure in breast feeding should not be a matter for self-reproach.

So think of breast feeding not as a test of your devotion to the baby (plenty of undevoted mothers in past ages have nursed their babies) or as a test of your physical and emotional adequacy as a woman (which it hardly is at all), but simply as a good thing if you really enjoy it and it works, but no cause for despair if not.

A majority of women who are eager to nurse find that they do better with each succeeding child, probably as a result of increasing experience and confidence.

100. The mother can lead a normal life. Some mothers hesitate to nurse their baby because they have heard that they will have to give up too much. Generally speaking, this is not so. There is no evidence that it will harm the baby if the mother drinks coffee or tea, smokes, uses alcoholic beverages in moderation, or goes in for athletics. The nursing mother can usually continue to eat all the foods she is accustomed to. There is no reason to believe, for instance, that if she eats prunes, it will make the baby's bowels loose; or that if she eats fried food, it will give the baby indigestion. Once in a while, it is true, a baby seems to get upset every time his mother eats a certain food. Naturally, if this happens several times in succession, she can give up that particular food. Some drugs get into the milk, but usually not in large enough quantities to affect the baby. A mother can take milk of magnesia, mineral oil, aspirin, without affecting the baby.

When a nursing mother becomes nervously upset, it sometimes cuts down, for the time being, the amount of milk she can produce. Occasionally it seems to make the baby feel out of sorts, too. Some women never menstruate so long as they continue to nurse. Others menstruate regularly or irregularly. Once in a while a nursing baby will be mildly upset during his mother's menstruation or refuse to nurse.

There is no reason a nursing mother shouldn't let the baby have a bottle once in a while, even once a day, in case she wants to be away from home for longer than 4 hours.

101. The mother's diet. A nursing mother does need to be sure that her diet contains plenty of the elements that the baby is withdrawing in the milk. A large amount of calcium (lime) is excreted in the milk, to enable the baby's bones to grow rapidly. If the mother takes in too little, the breasts will withdraw it from her bones. It used to be thought that she would lose calcium from her teeth, too, but this is probably not so.

She should take as much milk as the baby is getting from her, plus a little extra for her own needs, in any beverage that she likes, or cooked into cereals, soups, puddings, or in the form of cheese (see Section 431).

Her daily diet should include the following elements (even if she has to limit her diet otherwise to keep her weight down): **Milk**—at the very least, a quart a day, and preferably a quart and a half. It can be the usual fresh milk or it can be evaporated, powdered, or skimmed, and it can be served in any form. **Fruits and vegetables**—6 servings a day. (This may sound like too much until you realize that the juice of 2 oranges, a salad, a green or yellow vegetable, and potatoes twice add up to 6 servings.) To include enough vitamin C, 2 of these servings should be raw and 2 should be oranges, grapefruit, tomatoes, raw cabbage, or berries. For the sake of vitamin A, there should be one dark-green, leafy vegetable or a deep-yellow one. Potatoes are valuable aside from their calories. Fruits and vegetables can be fresh, canned, frozen, or dried. **Meat, poultry, fish**—at least 1 generous portion, preferably 2. Liver is especially valuable and should be included occasionally. **Egg**—1 a day. **Cereal and bread**—3 servings a day, whole grain or enriched (to contain the B vitamins). **Butter or fortified margarine** for vitamin A. If your weight won't stand these, eat more green, leafy vegetables and deep-yellow ones. **A vitamin-D preparation,** prescribed by the doctor, to make sure you are utilizing the calcium in your diet.

If a nursing mother is gaining unwelcome weight, she can drink skimmed milk, hold down on butter, keep the cereal and bread portions small (but use whole-grain products to provide B vitamins), limit strictly or omit such high-calorie foods as candy, pastries, cakes, cookies, soda-fountain drinks. (It's too bad that these high-calorie sweets are the foods that weight-gainers crave most.) But she should not cut down on the milk, vegetables, fruit, meat, and vitamin D.

GETTING STARTED AT BREAST FEEDING
102. The mother's position and relaxation. Some mothers prefer, even in bed in the hospital, to nurse sitting up. Others find it easier, while still in bed, to nurse lying down. To do this, lay the baby beside you on the bed and lie on your side, facing him. Move closer until the nipple touches his lips. You may need to prop yourself up on your elbow to bring the nipple to the right position. When he feels the nipple near his mouth he will "root around" trying to get hold of it. At times you may need to put a finger on the breast to give him breathing space for his nose, though this isn't usually necessary. If you let your finger touch his face, he may go for it.

When you are able to sit up, in the hospital or later at home, you can find the position that suits you best. Some mothers prefer to nurse lying down; most sit up. Those who have used a rocking chair for nursing swear by it. The height of the arm of the chair is really important for resting your arms. A pillow or cushion there may help. Anyway, get comfortable so that you can relax and rest your muscles.

After a mother has become accustomed to nursing and is relaxed at that time, she may fall asleep if she nurses lying down, especially at 2 A.M. or 6 A.M., when she is sleepy. Then there is a slight risk of obstructing the baby's breathing with her breast or arm. For this reason it's better for her to nurse sitting up in bed or in a chair in the early-morning hours or at any other time when she feels sleepy, unless a nurse or other helper is in the room.

You'll probably notice that the state of your feelings has a lot to do with how easily the milk comes. Worries and tenseness can hold the milk back. So try to get troubles off your mind before beginning. If possible, lie down for 15 minutes before you expect the baby to wake and do what is most relaxing, whether it's shutting your eyes, or reading, or listening to the radio.

After you have been nursing for a few weeks, you may notice a distinct sensation of the milk being "let down" or "coming in" at nursing time. It may start leaking from the breasts when you hear the baby beginning to cry in the next room. This shows how much feelings have to do with the formation and release of the milk.

103. Getting the entire areola into the baby's mouth. A baby does not get the milk simply by taking the nipple into his mouth and sucking. The milk is formed in the glandular tissue throughout the breast. It then passes through small ducts toward the center of the breast, where it collects in a number of "sinuses." These sinuses, or storage spaces, are located in a circle right behind the areola, the dark area around the nipple. A short duct leads from each sinus through the nipple to the outside (there are a number of openings in each nipple). When a baby is nursing properly, most or all of the areolar area is in his mouth, and the principal action is the squeezing of the sinuses (behind the areola) by the baby's gums. This forces the milk, which has collected in the sinuses, through the nipple and into his mouth. The sucking action of the baby's tongue is not so much to draw the milk through the nipple into his mouth as to keep the areola drawn into his mouth and also to get the milk from the front of his mouth back into his throat. If a baby takes only the nipple into his mouth, he gets almost no milk. And if he chews on the nipple, he is apt to make it sore. But if he takes the entire areola into his mouth, his gums squeeze the areola and cannot hurt the nipple. It may help him get the entire areola into his mouth if the mother or nurse will compress it or flatten it a little between thumb and finger. If the baby starts to mouth and chew on the nipple alone, he should be stopped promptly. Slip your finger into the corner of his mouth to break the suction, or between his gums if necessary. (Otherwise you would have to pull him off the breast, which is hard on the nipple.) Then reinsert the areola in his mouth. If he persists in chewing the nipple, stop the feeding for good.

104. Different babies behave differently at the breast. A physician who has studied the behavior of hundreds of babies when first put to breast has, with a sense of humor, pointed out the different types. The **eager beaver** draws the areola in avidly and sucks vigorously until satisfied. The only problem is that he may be too hard on the nipple if he is allowed to chew it. The **excitable** baby may become so agitated and active that he keeps losing the breast and then, instead of trying again, he screams. He may have to be picked up and comforted for several minutes before he is calm enough to try again. After a few days he usually settles down. The **procrastinator** can't be bothered to nurse the first few days; he is waiting until the milk comes in. Prodding him only makes him balky. He does well when the time comes. The **taster** must, for a little while, mouth the nipple and smack his lips over the drop of milk he tastes, before he settles down to business. Efforts to hurry him only make him angry. The **rester** wants to nurse a few minutes and then rest a few minutes before starting again. He can't be rushed. He usually does a good job in his own way, but it takes him longer.

105. There are two things that often make a balky baby angrier. The first is to hold his head, in trying to direct it toward the breast. A baby hates to have his head held; he fights to get free. The other is to squeeze him across the cheeks to get his mouth open. A baby has an instinct to turn toward anything that touches his cheek. This is to help him find the nipple. When you squeeze him on both cheeks at the same time, you baffle and annoy him.

When a baby is refusing to take the breast and carrying on, a mother can't help feeling spurned, frustrated, and irritated. She shouldn't let her feelings be hurt by this inexperienced but apparently opinionated newcomer. If she can keep trying for a few more feedings, the chances are that he will find out what it's all about.

106. The early schedule. A baby is put to breast sometimes in the first 18 hours after birth. This interval varies a lot in different hospitals, and it doesn't make a great deal of difference. For the first 2 or 3 days no real milk is produced, only a small amount of a fluid called colostrum.

Fitting in with this lack of milk is the fact that most babies are quiet, sleepy, and unhungry for the first 2 or 3 days, so they don't mind waiting. Usually the length of time at breast is limited during this period (perhaps to 5 minutes at each feeding) so that the mother's nipples will not get too much use until they have become somewhat toughened. The 2 A.M. feeding is often omitted during these days so that the mother can catch up on her rest.

Whether the baby is then put to breast on a regular schedule or according to his own waking-and-hunger pattern depends on whether the baby is in a newborn nursery and can be brought to the mother only at specified times or whether mother and baby are in a rooming-in unit, close together, so that she can watch him and can feed him whenever he seems to need to be fed. A rooming-in arrangement and a flexible schedule are particularly handy for breast feeding, because the baby will get to breast when he is ready and eager to nurse. If the breast-milk supply has not caught up with his hunger, he wakes and empties the breasts more frequently, which is the principal means of stimulating the breasts to produce more milk.

107. When the milk comes in. There is considerable variation in the time and manner in which the milk comes in. It most often starts to come in on the third or fourth day of the baby's life. It tends to come earlier in mothers who have had a child before, later in new mothers. Sometimes it comes so suddenly that the mother can name the hour. In other cases the progress is much more gradual. And it's on about the third or fourth day that a majority of babies become distinctly more wakeful and hungry. This is one of the many examples of how smoothly Nature works things out. Studies of babies who have been breast-fed whenever they appeared hungry have shown that a majority of them want to nurse unusually often between the third and sixth days, commonly up to 10 or 12 times a day. (The stools may become frequent on these days, too.) Mothers who are particularly anxious to make a success of breast feeding are apt to feel disappointed by this frequency, assuming that it means the breast-milk supply is inadequate. This is unnecessarily pessimistic. It's more sensible to think that the baby is now settling down to the serious business of eating and growing, and that he is providing the breasts with the stimulation they must have if they are to meet his increasing needs. It is during this latter half of the first week, too, that the breasts are receiving the strongest stimulation from the hormones (the glandular secretions that make the milk come in in the first place). It is no wonder that in the first few days the breasts sometimes become too full, and that sometimes there isn't enough to satisfy the newly hungry baby. Still, the system is generally efficient, much better than you or I could design. The hormone factor calms down; the baby's hunger teaches the breast how much to produce, not in just the first, second, or third week, but on through the succeeding months. In other words, the supply may still be increasing when the baby is several months old, if he wants more.

108. Increase the nursing time gradually. To protect the nipples, the time a baby is allowed to nurse at each feeding is increased gradually: not more than a total of 5 minutes each feeding for the first 3 days; perhaps 10 minutes on the fourth day; 15 the next; then 20 minutes for several days. If after 10 days it is clear that the nipples have no tendency to become sore, the length of time the baby nurses can be left to his wishes and the mother's convenience. It may vary a lot from day to day and from feeding to feeding. Most babies are satisfied after between 20 and 30 minutes, and there is no point in going beyond 40 minutes.

109. The schedule in the hospital. In a rooming-in unit the baby is nursed whenever he is hungry. In a hospital in which all babies are in a nursery and are fed by the clock, full-sized babies are taken to the mother every 4 hours day and night (6 feedings in 24 hours) after the milk has come in. By this time the baby is hungry in the middle of the night, the mother is reasonably rested, and the nighttime stimulation of the breasts is important. A small baby may be put temporarily on a 3-hour schedule by day and probably a 4-hour at night, making 7 feedings in the 24 hours.

Back in the prewar days, when many mothers stayed in the hospital for two weeks and when practically all babies were kept in the nursery and brought in to the mother only on a 4-hour schedule, it was often a problem to satisfy a baby's hunger and give the breasts sufficient stimulation during the 3-day to 14-day period of a baby's life unless the mother was an unusually copious milk producer. Nowadays, when the lying-in period is usually less than a week, the mother who has not yet been able to supply enough milk to satisfy her baby on a strict 4-hour schedule, can shift to a flexible (self-demand) schedule just as soon as she gets home, and it will probably not be too late for the breasts to respond to the more frequent nursing.

110. One or both breasts? In very natural, "uncivilized" parts of the world, where nursing is the only way babies are fed, where mothers carry their babies around with them in slings while they work and where schedules are unknown, babies tend to wake and be put to breast frequently. They nurse relatively briefly, at one breast, and then fall asleep again. In our civilization, which runs pretty much according to the clock and in which babies are put in a crib in a quiet room after a feeding, the tendency is toward fewer and larger feedings. If a mother produces ample amounts of milk, a baby may be quite satisfied with one breast at each feeding. Each breast receives the stimulation of very complete emptying, even though this occurs only once in about 8 hours. In many cases, however, the amount in one breast does not satisfy the baby, and both breasts are given at each feeding, the left breast being offered first at one feeding, the right breast first at the next. To insure complete emptying of one breast, the baby might be kept on the first breast for 12 to 15 minutes, if he is willing, and then allowed to nurse on the second breast for as short or as long a period as he wishes. A baby who sticks to business will take the greatest part of the milk in 5 or 6 minutes and will have pretty well emptied the breast in 10 or 15 minutes. (The breasts will always be producing a little new milk, so he will always taste something.) Therefore, there is no need for a mother to prolong breast feeding beyond a total of 20 to 40 minutes, depending on how eager he is to continue and how much time she has to spare.

Bringing up the bubble is discussed in Section 90.

111. How do you know whether the baby is getting enough? This question is likely to baffle the new mother. You certainly can't tell from the length of time the baby nurses. He goes on nursing after he's already obtained most of the milk—sometimes for 10 more minutes, sometimes for 30—because he's still getting a small trickle of milk, or because he enjoys sucking, or because he's still awake and having a good time. Even if you weighed him before and after each feeding so that you knew exactly how much milk he obtained, it wouldn't tell you about his satisfaction. Careful observations of slightly older babies have shown that the same baby will appear to be entirely satisfied by 3 ounces at one feeding and by 10 ounces at another.

112. You can't tell from the appearance of breasts or milk. Most women with experience have decided that they can't tell from the apparent fullness of the breast before feeding how much milk is there. In the first week or two, the breasts are noticeably full and firm as a result of glandular changes, but after a while they normally become softer and less prominent, even though the milk supply is **increasing.** A baby can get 6 or more ounces from a breast that to the mother does not seem full at all. You can't tell anything from the color and appearance of the milk. Breast milk always looks thin and bluish compared to cow's milk, and there are no important variations in the composition of the milk from time to time in the same mother, or from one mother to another.

113. You can't tell by the baby's crying alone. You can't be sure that the baby who fusses a lot after feeding is hungry, because in the early weeks babies who are fretful or colicky or have what I call "irritable crying" characteristically cry after certain feedings, even when these feedings are unusually large.

114. The best guide is the combination of weight gain and satisfaction. Generally speaking, you and the doctor decide the question on the basis of the baby's behavior over a number of days and on the basis of his weight-gaining. Neither alone is conclusive. A baby who is happy and gaining fast is obviously getting enough. A baby who cries hard every afternoon or evening but is gaining weight at the average rate is probably getting plenty to eat but having colic. A baby who gains slowly but is quite contented is, in most cases, a baby who is meant to be a slow gainer. It's the baby who is gaining **very** slowly and acting hungry most of the time who's **probably** not getting enough.

So it's best to assume that the baby is getting enough in the long run unless the baby and the doctor definitely tell you differently. Certainly at any one feeding you should be satisfied if the baby seems satisfied.

115. Don't throw away your confidence. The doubt about sufficiency of the milk supply is natural enough in the new mother, who has had no proof yet of her adequacy. The doubt also arises in mothers who have had more experience but who have **never** had much self-confidence. Usually when the mother is worrying about the amount, the doctor finds that there is no insufficiency of milk, only an insufficiency of confidence. Worry only discourages the milk supply.

It's good to remember that throughout the largest part of the world, in which there are no scales and no doctors, the mother simply assumes that the baby is receiving plenty if he acts contented and looks well, and that this system works well in at least nine out of ten cases.

116. Care of nipples. Some doctors recommend regular massage of the nipples during the last month of pregnancy, to toughen them. After the baby is born and begins to nurse, some doctors do not suggest any particular care of the nipples, since throughout all the less civilized parts of the world there is no wiping or use of ointment with healthy nipples. Other doctors recommend either ointment after the nursing, or wiping with salt solution (half teaspoonful of salt to an 8-ounce cup of boiled water) before and after nursing. The salt solution will wipe away any milk but is otherwise mainly a gesture, since salt water has no effect on germs. It is sensible for the mother to wash her hands with soap before fingering her nipples (to massage or examine them), since infection can enter the breast through the nipple and since babies can easily pick up thrush, a mild fungus infection of the mouth. But hand-washing should not be necessary before an ordinary nursing.

Some experienced mothers believe that allowing the nipples to dry in the air for 10 or 15 minutes before closing the brassiere is most helpful. Others have observed that their nipples stay drier and healthier if there is no waterproof lining in the brassiere.

117. How to try extra hard. You hear of women who want to nurse their babies but don't succeed. People talk about how complicated our civilization is and how it makes mothers too tense to nurse. There's no doubt that nervousness works against breast feeding, but I don't think most women are nervous. Breast feeding most often fails because it isn't given a good trial.

There are three factors that make a big difference: (1) keeping away from formula, (2) not getting discouraged too early, (3) sufficient stimulation of the breasts after the milk has begun to come in.

If a baby is given formula for the first 3 or 4 days of life, the chance of successful breast feeding is diminished. The baby who is satisfied by plenty of formula doesn't try so hard at breast. (Water, which is sometimes given during this period to make sure he doesn't become too dried out, is not likely to interfere with his hunger at breast.) After the mother's milk has begun to come in, it's wise to avoid formula, too, if the baby can be kept fairly well satisfied and is not continuing to lose weight.

Sometimes a mother becomes discouraged just at the moment when her milk is coming in, or a day or two later because she isn't producing very much. This is no time for her to quit. She hasn't given herself half a chance. It is certainly worth continuing if she is producing as much as 1 ounce at any feeding on about the fifth day. If a mother has a practical or trained nurse at this stage, it's a great help to have one who is encouraging and cooperative.

The night nursings, which will probably come at about 10 P.M. and 2 A.M., are as important as the daytime nursings in giving the breasts regular stimulation at first. If the breasts are not supplying a sufficient amount of milk to keep the baby satisfied for 3 or 4 hours, it helps to let him empty them more frequently, as often as every 2 hours (including both breasts at each feeding), provided the nipples aren't sore. This is the way the baby and the breasts would adjust to each other in a faraway spot where there was no cow's milk. The frequent emptying of the breasts stimulates them to produce more milk. Then the baby is able to go for longer periods again. Of course, a baby cannot be kept off formula indefinitely if he remains miserably hungry for many days, or continues to lose weight, or develops fever from insufficient fluid. Frequent nursing shouldn't be carried to the point where the nipples become cracked or the mother is exhausted from having no time to rest.

If a mother is able to keep in frequent touch with the doctor, he will help her decide at each step such questions as how many days the baby can go on an insufficient amount of breast milk without resorting to formula, how much nursing the mother's nipples can stand, how frequently to nurse. The point is, though, that the doctor is influenced in many of these decisions by the mother's attitude toward nursing. If she makes it clear that she is eager to succeed, it helps him in giving the directions that will make it possible.

WHEN THE BREAST MILK SEEMS INSUFFICIENT

118. Trying to increase it after getting home (if you cannot consult the doctor regularly). Suppose that in the hospital your baby was nursed as frequently as possible and received both breasts at each feeding, but still did not get enough. The doctor decided that he had to have some formula, too. Let's say that the baby was averaging less than 2 ounces from both breasts and required a 2-ounce bottle in addition at each nursing. You decided after talking it over with the doctor that you wanted to continue the breast feeding after going home, with the hope of eventually getting the baby entirely breast-fed.

Sometimes the mother feels so much more relaxed and natural after a couple of days at home that the breast-milk supply increases without any other encouragement, and the baby is so satisfied that he isn't particularly interested in the bottle. In that case the mother should stop offering the bottle right away. Usually, however, the baby enjoys the bottle so much that he continues to take it and so has less appetite for the breast. Therefore, in most cases the mother must deliberately cut down on the formula and count on the baby's increasing hunger to give more stimulation to the breasts. Here is one method: For the first couple of days at home continue to give the formula after nursing, as in the hospital, but don't give a drop more than the baby demands. (The breast-milk supply often does not increase the first day or two at home, and it sometimes decreases temporarily because of the mother's fatigue.) After 2 days, begin to reduce the amount in each bottle by ¼ ounce each day until you are down to no bottle at all. What will happen? As you cut down the formula, the baby will probably get hungry earlier. You nurse him when he becomes hungry, whether it's after 4, or 3, or even 2 hours. This sounds like an awful lot of work, but it won't be forever. You are hoping that the frequent emptying of the breasts will stimulate them to produce more and more milk. When this happens, the baby will begin to sleep for longer and longer periods again. In a week or two he may work himself back onto approximately a 4-hour schedule. (I remember one baby who never got more than an ounce at a time from the breast in the hospital, and who worked up to 5 ounces in 2 weeks at home. Of course, this won't happen in every case.) If you try it for 5 or 6 days and the baby gets hungrier all the time and fails to gain weight, then you may have to go back to the formula temporarily. But even then, if you want to keep on trying, you can offer only 2 ounces of formula after each breast feeding, and in a few days, when you feel more rested, try gradually reducing this amount again.

Some doctors recommend manual expression of any milk that remains in the breast after the baby has finished nursing as an excellent temporary method of increasing the supply (Sections 137, 138).

119. Fluids for the mother. It's most important during this trial period that the mother take wonderful care of herself, avoid getting tired at all costs, let the housework go, forget about outside worries and obligations, keep visitors down to 1 or 2 comfortable friends, eat and drink well. A good time to drink something is 10 or 15 minutes before you expect a nursing. Some women who enjoy beer find it a very pleasant means of taking extra fluid and achieving relaxation.

There are two sides to the matter of fluids. There's no good to be gained from drinking more fluid than feels comfortable, because the body promptly gets rid of excess water through the urine. On the other hand, a new, excited, busy mother may forget to drink as much as she needs and go thirsty through absent-mindedness. This will cut down the milk supply.

120. Don't let friends discourage you. Perhaps this is as good a time as any to mention that in these days when breast feeding is the exception rather than the rule, a mother who is attempting it may occasionally be subjected to a surprising amount of skepticism on the part of friends and relatives who are otherwise quite sympathetic. There are remarks like "You aren't going to breast-feed, are you?", "Very few can make the grade," "Why in the world are you trying to do that?", "With breasts like yours, you'll never succeed," "Your poor baby is hungry. Are you trying to starve him to prove a point?" The milder remarks can perhaps be blamed on surprise, but the meaner ones strongly suggest jealousy. Later on, if there is any question about continuing to nurse, you'll find several friends who'll urge you to stop.

121. When the breast milk seems to decrease later. A good percentage of mothers who are eager to breast-feed are successful in the hospital and for a number of days or weeks afterward (with the possible exception of the first day or two at home). Then too many of them feel that they are failing and give up. They say, "I didn't have as much milk," or "My milk didn't seem to agree with the baby," or "As he grew bigger my milk was no longer sufficient."

Why is it that throughout most of the world a mother's milk takes care of the baby for many months and that it's only in bottle-feeding countries like ours that the breast-milk supply seems to fail so early in a majority of cases? I don't believe that American mothers are that nervous. They are certainly as healthy as any. I think there is one main reason. The mother here who is trying to breast-feed, instead of feeling that she is doing the most natural thing in the world and assuming that she'll succeed like everyone else, feels that she's attempting to do the unusual, the difficult. Unless she has tremendous self-confidence, she keeps wondering whether she won't fail. In a sense, she's looking for signs of failure. If her baby cries one day a bit more than usual, her first thought is that her milk has decreased. If he develops indigestion or colic, or a rash, she is quick to suspect her milk. Her anxiety makes her feel sure that the bottle is the answer. And the trouble is that the bottle is always available. Probably she was given formula directions when she left the hospital ("just in case"), or she can call the doctor or the public-health nurse and get directions. Babies on the breast who begin to receive ample amounts of formula several times a day practically always nurse less eagerly at breast. And milk left in the breast is Nature's method of signaling to the glands, "Make less, make less."

In other words, the combination of a mother lacking confidence in her ability to breast-feed and the availability of bottles of formula is the most efficient method of discouraging breast feeding.

To put it positively: the way to make breast feeding a success is to go on breast feeding and keep away from formula (except possibly for one relief bottle a day after the breast supply is well established). See Sections 123, 124.

Under normal conditions the amount of milk supplied by the breasts is not a stationary quantity. The breasts are ready at any time to decrease or increase gradually the amount, depending on whether the baby wants less or more. As a baby grows and his appetite increases, he empties the breasts more completely and sometimes more frequently. This is the stimulation that encourages a larger supply.

122. Hunger is not the commonest reason for crying. The most common reason for a mother to start worrying is that her baby begins to fret right after feedings, or between feedings. Her first thought is that her milk supply is failing. But this assumption is not correct. The fact is that a majority of babies—especially first babies—get into fretful spells by the time they are a couple of weeks old, most often in the afternoon or evening. Bottle-fed babies fuss as much as breast-fed babies. Babies who are getting all the milk they can possibly hold have crying spells just the same as babies who are receiving less. These fretful spells are discussed in Section 275, on colic, and Section 273, on general fretfulness. If a mother realizes clearly that most of the fussing in the early weeks is not caused by hunger, she won't be so quick to lose confidence in her breast-milk supply.

Though it is much less likely, it is, of course, possible that a baby is beginning to fret because he's hungry. However, hunger is much more apt to wake a baby a little earlier for the next feeding than to bother him in the first hour or two after the last feeding. If he **is** hungry it may be because his appetite has taken a sudden spurt or it may possibly mean that his mother's milk has decreased slightly because of fatigue or tension. In either case the answer is the same: take it for granted that he'll wake and want to nurse more frequently and more vigorously for a day or for a few days until the breasts have adjusted to the demand. Then he will probably go back to his previous schedule.

In case the fussing was **not** due to hunger at all, the extra nursing has done no harm.

The treatment of fretfulness seems clear to me. Any thought of giving a bottle of formula should be postponed for at least a week or two. The baby should be allowed to nurse as often as every 2 hours, for 20 to 40 minutes. If he makes a reasonable weight gain in that week or two, consideration of formula should again be put off, for at least 2 more weeks. The baby can be comforted during his fretful periods with a pacifier or with a bottle of water or possibly sugar water (Sections 192 and 193). The mother may occasionally want to nurse him even more frequently than every 2 hours. It certainly won't do the baby any harm. I'm only thinking of the mother: she can't help becoming frantic if she's nursing all day long, and it won't do that much good. Emptying the breasts 10 times a day will give them about as much stimulation as they can use. It is also necessary for the mother to have some rest and relaxation.

123. A relief bottle is all right. Does all this mean that a mother who wants to continue breast feeding must never give a bottle under any circumstances? No, it isn't that crucial. Most of the mothers who want to give a relief bottle regularly once a day find that they can do so without discouraging the breast-milk supply, provided the supply has been well established for a few weeks and provided it's only one bottle a day.

And certainly a mother who has not been giving a bottle regularly can give one occasionally. Perhaps she must be away for a feeding. Or perhaps she has become extremely tired or upset and the baby has acted entirely dissatisfied with one feeding. One bottle doesn't stop breast feeding. What I have been advising against is regularly giving a complementary bottle (a bottle given **in addition** to a breast feeding) 2 or 3 times a day, if you hope to continue with breast feeding.

124. A relief bottle. The relief bottle can be given every day if desired, at the 10 A.M., 2 P.M., or 6 P.M. feeding. (When the baby is off the 2 A.M. feeding, the mother will usually be too uncomfortable to omit either the 10 P.M. or the 6 A.M. nursing, since this would leave the breasts full for 12 hours. Also, such a long interval might discourage the breast-milk supply.)

If a mother plans to wean her baby from breast to bottle sometime between 2 and 7 months, it's a good idea to offer a relief bottle at least twice a week, even though she could nurse just as well. The reason is that some babies become so set in their ways during this age period that they will refuse to take a bottle of milk if they have not been used to it, and this may make quite a struggle. A baby rarely gets this opinionated before the age of 2 months. And after 7 months he will probably be weaned directly to the cup.

It is sometimes recommended that **all** breast-fed babies get a bottle once or twice a week, even though the mother is planning to nurse her infant until he is weaned to the cup. This is on the theory that the mother might have to stop nursing for some unexpected reason. You can decide for yourself, balancing the inconvenience of making the bottle against risking the baby's putting up a struggle if weaned suddenly.

Your doctor will give you a formula for a single bottle. If you cannot consult a doctor you can try the following: 4 ounces of pasteurized whole milk (shake the bottle, if you do not use homogenized milk), 2 ounces of water (as in all formula-making, you will have to add an extra ounce or two of water to the original mixture to allow for evaporation), 2 level teaspoonfuls of granulated sugar. Mix, bring to a boil, simmer for 3 minutes, strain into a sterilized bottle. See Sections 171 to 175.

You should end up with 6 ounces of formula. Let the baby take as much of this as he wants. A small baby won't want it all. It will be about enough for the average 10-pounder. If it's insufficient for a big baby, make it 6 ounces of milk, 2 teaspoonfuls of sugar, no water (except what you add to allow for evaporation).

For most families, it is more convenient to make a formula for a single bottle from pasteurized milk than from evaporated milk, because only a very small amount of the can of milk is used. However, if you don't have pasteurized milk, or if you can use up the rest of the evaporated milk for other purposes, you may prefer to use evaporated milk for the relief bottle. You can buy evaporated milk in small, 6-ounce cans. To make a 6-ounce formula, use 2 ounces of evaporated milk, 4 ounces of water, 1 or 2 more ounces of water for evaporation, 2 level teaspoonfuls of granulated sugar. Bring to a boil, simmer 3 minutes. A stronger formula would be 3 ounces of evaporated milk, 3 ounces of water, 2 teaspoonfuls of sugar.

125. Breast and bottle both. If a mother who can't produce enough milk to completely satisfy the baby wants to go on with a combination of breast and bottle, there is no reason why she shouldn't. However, in many cases of mixed feedings, the breast-milk supply gradually decreases. Also, the baby may come to prefer the bottle and reject the breast altogether.

Most women don't want to go on with both, because it means all the trouble of formula-making **and** being tied down by the nursing schedule. The most sensible thing to do when the mother is producing a reasonable amount of milk (say half or more of what the baby needs) is to first make a real effort to dispense with the formula altogether (Section 118). If this does not increase the breast-milk supply sufficiently, then she can wean the baby completely to the bottle, knowing that she has tried as hard as she could.

126. How to supplement the breast with the bottle (if you cannot consult a doctor). Let's say that you have tried to get along on breast feeding alone, but that it is not providing sufficient milk. You have to give some formula to satisfy the baby, but you want to do it in the way that is least likely to decrease the breast-milk supply. I will discuss the subject in different paragraphs, depending on how much extra the baby needs, and use the word **complemental** to mean a bottle that is given right after (in addition to) a breast feeding, and **supplemental** to mean a bottle that is given **instead** of a breast feeding. In a general way, it's more convenient to omit certain breast feedings altogether and give supplemental bottles instead. On the other hand, there's slightly more chance of keeping up the breast-milk supply if you continue to give the breast at every feeding, with a complemental bottle in addition at certain feedings when the baby doesn't get enough at breast.

Suppose the breasts are supplying enough at all but one feeding. Six P.M. is apt to be the scantiest. 2 P.M. the next. You could try giving a complemental bottle in addition to the 6 P.M. nursing. Or you could give a supplemental bottle instead of the 2 P.M. nursing; then there might be enough breast milk stored up at 6 P.M.

Suppose the breasts are supplying less than enough at two or more feedings. You could give complemental bottles after the breast feedings at 10 A.M., 2 P.M., and 6 P.M. The 6 A.M. breast feeding is apt to be the largest of the day and may supply all that the baby needs at that time. The 10 P.M. breast feeding is also apt to be fairly large. Another method, if the breasts are supplying less than enough at several feedings, would be to breast-feed alone at 6 A.M., 2 P.M., 10 P.M., and give supplemental bottles alone at 10 A.M. and 6 P.M. (also at 2 A.M. if the baby still needs to be fed then).

If the breast-milk supply is insufficient at all feedings, you will need a bottle at all feedings, whether you give the breast first or not.

How much formula do you put in each bottle, whether it is a complemental or a supplemental bottle? The answer is, As much as the baby seems to need. If your baby weighs 9 pounds or more, he may want 6 ounces in his supplemental bottle; if he is smaller, he may want less. If it's a complemental bottle after a breast feeding, he may want 2 to 3 ounces. If so, offer 3 ounces and let him take what he wants.

If your doctor has not given you a formula and you cannot reach him, you can try the formulas in this book. In Section 124 there are directions for making a formula for a 6-ounce relief bottle. You could use this for making one 6-ounce supplemental bottle, or for two 3-ounce complemental ones. If you need 12 ounces altogether, for two 6-ounce bottles or for three 4-ounce bottles, then double the quantities listed. If you need only 3 ounces altogether, use half the quantities listed. Don't worry too much about coming out even. If, for instance, you need one 4-ounce bottle a day, make a 6-ounce bottle and throw out what the baby doesn't want.

You can go on multiplying the 6-ounce relief-bottle formula as you need more, or you can turn to Section 164.

SPECIAL PROBLEMS OF BREAST FEEDING

127. The fiddler, the fusser, the sleeper, and the waker. There are several patterns of behavior in the early weeks of nursing that complicate the mother's job and nearly drive her mad. The first is that of the baby who never seems to nurse very vigorously and falls asleep 5 minutes or so after starting. You don't know whether he has taken a reasonable amount or not. (A baby usually gets a major part of what's in the breast in 5 minutes of steady nursing.) It wouldn't be so bad if he'd sleep for 2 or 3 hours, but he may wake and cry again in a few minutes after he's put back to bed. We don't really know what causes this ineffi- cient nursing **or** the prompt waking. One possibility is that the baby's nervous system and digestive system are not yet working well enough together. Perhaps the comfort of his mother's arms and the breast in his mouth is enough to put him back to sleep. When he's a little older and knows what it's all about, his hunger will keep him awake until he's well satisfied. In the bottle-fed baby, a contributory cause of falling asleep may be nipple holes that are too small. In the breast-fed baby, it may be that although the mother has plenty of milk, the baby cannot get it well enough.

It's probable that a mother's feelings control the ease with which the milk flows. Many mothers after a few weeks of nursing notice that as soon as they hear the baby cry with hunger, the milk starts to leak from the breasts. And feelings of anxiety or other tension probably hold the milk in. (Farmers know that cows can't "let down" the milk if they are tense.)

One baby who finds that he's getting little result from nursing goes back to sleep. Then when he's put back into the harder, cooler bed, his hunger wakes him up again. Another baby, who's hungrier or more wide- awake or more assertive, reacts with irritation when he finds he can't get enough milk. He jerks his head away from the breast and yells, tries again, gets mad again.

The fact that the baby doesn't nurse well only increases the mother's uneasiness, so a vicious cycle sets in. If a mother understands this mechanism, she can use all her ingenuity in finding her own best way to relax before and during nursing. It's different with each individual. Mu- sic, a magazine, a glass of beer, a cigarette, television—whatever works best is what she should adopt.

If the baby gets sleepy or restless after a few minutes at one breast, you can try shifting right away to the other breast, to see if the easier flow of milk will help. Of course, you'd like him to work for at least 15 minutes on one breast to be sure that it is well stimulated, but if he won't, he won't.

If the baby is one of those "resters" who doze, off and on, but suck well in between, let him continue. But if he doesn't resume nursing, it works better not to prolong the nursing or to keep trying to wake him up again. In the long run you only take away his enthusiasm and make him an indifferent eater.

What do you do if he wakes as soon as you put him to bed or a little later? I think it's better to assume first that if he has nursed for 5 min- utes he's had enough to keep him satisfied for a couple of hours, and try not to feed him again right away. Let him fuss for a while if you can stand it. Give him a pacifier if you and your doctor approve. See if a hot-water bottle will make him feel cozier (see Section 276).

The purpose is to teach him that feedings come every few hours and that it's his eagerness that brings the satisfaction. To keep feeding him off and on for an hour and a half tends to teach him that feedings are always chasing him and that sometimes the only way to escape them is to go to sleep. However, the chances are that the baby will outgrow this inconvenient pattern in a few weeks, no matter how you handle it. So if he wakes as soon as he's in bed and can't be comforted and gets crying frantically, you'd better feed him again, anyway, and never mind the theory. You can at least give him a second chance. But don't go on to a third and a fourth feeding if you can help it. Make him wait an hour or two, anyway.

128. Retracted nipples. If a mother's nipples are flat or retracted (drawn back into the breast by the supporting tissue), it may further complicate the business of getting a baby started at the breast, especially if he is the excitable type. If he searches around and can't find the nipple, he may cry angrily and pull his head back. There are several tactful things you can try. If possible, put him to breast when he first wakes up, before he gets too cross. If he starts crying at the first attempt, stop right away and comfort him before trying again. Take your time. It sometimes makes a nipple stand out better to massage it lightly with the fingers first. Or the baby can, for a couple of days, nurse for a minute or two through a nipple shield (Section 140), to draw the nipple out, before taking the mother's nipple directly.

Actually, the nipple is not so important in nursing (as explained in Section 103) as it is in guiding the baby to draw the entire areola into his mouth. However, the supporting tissues that retract the nipple also make it more difficult for the baby to draw the areola forward and shape it to his mouth. Probably the most valuable procedure is for the mother (or nurse) to squeeze some of the milk from the sinuses by manual expression (see Sections 137, 138) so that the areolar region will be softer and more compressible. Then press the areola into a flatter shape, between thumb and finger, when putting it into the baby's mouth.

129. Pains during nursing. You may be bothered the first week or so by cramps in your lower abdomen as soon as the baby starts nursing. This is the normal reflex action by which nursing causes the uterus to contract. It is intended to help the uterus get back to its nonpregnant size. These cramps disappear after a while.

Twinges of pain in the nipple that last a few seconds after the baby begins to nurse, for the first few days or weeks, are very common, mean nothing, and will soon go away.

130. Sore or cracked nipples. Pain that persists throughout the nursing may point to a cracked nipple, and a careful search should be made. (A very few mothers are unusually sensitive and continue to feel pain even though the nipples remain healthy.) If a nipple is cracked (often because a baby has chewed on it instead of taking the whole areola into his mouth), it is usually recommended that nursing be stopped on that breast for 24 to 48 hours (or at least cut down to perhaps 3 minutes every 8 hours). The physician may prescribe an ointment for the sore nipple. Another method is to leave the nipple dry, protected from any chafing, but not cut off from some circulation of air. Leave it exposed for 15 minutes after nursing. Remove the waterproof lining from the brassiere. One mother found successful a small tea strainer (the kind that can be detached from the handle) over the nipple, inside an ample brassiere.

To provide continued stimulation of the breast or to relieve fullness, milk can be expressed manually, 2 or 3 times in the 24 hours. The baby nurses at the other breast at each feeding.

If the nipple is much improved after 12 to 48 hours of rest, the baby may be allowed to nurse at it very briefly (perhaps 3 minutes), provided this is not painful. If all goes well, he continues to nurse a limited amount at that breast—for example, not more than 5 minutes each time the first day, 10 minutes the second, 15 minutes the third. If the crack and pain return, the rest treatment is repeated.

Another method of treating cracked nipples is to let the baby continue nursing but through a nipple shield (Section 140). This is apt to be less successful, because it does not give the mother's nipple a complete rest and because it usually produces less milk than a mother can get by manual expression.

131. Distended breasts; areolar engorgement. There are three different ways in which the breasts may become over-distended or engorged. The commonest and simplest is caused by overfilling of the sinuses, the storage spaces located behind the areola. This is not uncomfortable for the mother, but it may make the areolar region so firm and flat that the baby cannot take it into his mouth in order to compress it with his gums. The only thing he can get hold of is the nipple, and he is apt to chew on it and perhaps make it sore. It is important, therefore, for the mother or nurse to express sufficient milk from the sinuses so that the areolar region will become soft enough and compressible enough for the baby to take it into his mouth (Sections 137, 138).

It is not necessary to express much milk to soften the areolar region. Two to 5 minutes on each breast should be sufficient. Then the mother can compress the areolar region from above and below as she puts the breast into the baby's mouth, to help him get started. This type of engorgement is most likely to occur in the latter half of the first week, to last 2 or 3 days, and not to return, as long as nursing continues normally.

132. Peripheral engorgement. Another type of engorgement involves not just the areolar region but the whole breast. The entire breast becomes firm and uncomfortable. Most cases are mild, but in the infrequent case that becomes severe, the breast is enlarged, surprisingly hard, and very painful.

The usual mild case can be relieved promptly by having the baby nurse. It may be necessary to soften the areolar region first by manual expression if it is too firm for the baby to get into his mouth.

The severe case may require several different kinds of treatment. If the baby cannot consume enough milk to relieve the distension, the entire breast needs to be massaged, starting at the outer edges and working toward the areola. Cocoa butter or cold cream should be used during the massage to avoid irritating the skin, but the ointment should be kept off the areola, because it makes it too slippery for areolar expression, which comes next. Massage of the entire breast is tiring to the mother and should be carried on only long enough to partially relieve the engorgement. It may be performed once or several times a day. The difficulty usually lasts only 2 or 3 days. The application of cloths wet with comfortably hot water seems to help prepare the breasts for massage. If massage and manual expression cannot be used successfully because there is no one available to do it or to teach the mother how, a breast pump can be tried (Section 139). Between nursings or treatments, a firm support should be given to the breasts from all sides by a large firm brassiere or by a binder that gives support from the shoulders. The binder should be used not to flatten the breasts against the chest but to support them firmly from below and both sides. An ice bag or hot-water bottle can be applied for short periods. There are various medications that the physician may prescribe. This total engorgement practically always occurs, if at all, in the latter half of the first week. It is rare after that.

133. Caked breast and breast abscess. A third type of engorgement is similar to total engorgement in that it is outside the areolar region and is painful. But it is confined to only one segment of the breast. This type is sometimes called caked breast. It is more likely to occur after the hospital period. Treatment is similar to that of total engorgement: hot applications followed by massage of the engorged area, support by an efficient brassiere or a binder, ice bag or hot-water bottle between treatments, continuation of nursing.

If a sore spot develops inside the breast, this may be an infection, or breast abscess. The skin may become red over it. You should take your temperature and get in touch with your doctor. However, with modern methods of treating infections, it may not be necessary to keep the baby from nursing at that breast, even temporarily.

134. When the mother is ill. In the ordinary illnesses during which the mother stays at home, it is customary to allow the baby to continue to nurse as usual. To be sure, there is a chance of the baby's catching the ailment, but this would be true even if he weren't being nursed. Besides, most infections are contagious before any symptoms are noticed. Babies on the average have milder colds than older members of the family.

135. Biting the nipple (when the baby gets teeth). You can't blame the baby for trying a few bites when his gums are tingling during teething or when a couple of teeth have come in. He doesn't realize it hurts. But it's not only painful; it may make the nipples so sore that nursing has to be stopped.

Most babies can be taught quickly not to bite. Instantly slip your finger between his gums and say "No" very firmly. This surprises him and usually inhibits him. If he does it again, put your finger in again, say "No" and end the feeding. It's usually late in the feeding, anyway, when a baby starts to bite.

MANUAL EXPRESSION AND BREAST PUMPS

136. The purpose. Manual expression or breast pumps are used to obtain milk for the baby when he cannot or will not nurse at the breast, although the mother has plenty of milk. A small, premature baby may be too weak to nurse or to be taken out of the incubator. He can be fed breast milk from a bottle or medicine dropper. When an ill mother is away in a hospital, or when it is considered unwise, in the home, to expose the baby to her directly, her milk can be collected and given to the baby from a bottle (or discarded) until she can nurse him again.

When it is desired to obtain plenty of milk or to keep the breasts functioning, they are emptied at regular intervals. When the breasts are partially emptied to spare the mother pain during weaning, it is done only as often as necessary and only long enough to relieve the pressure.

The best way to learn manual expression is from an experienced nurse while you are in the hospital. It's a good idea to get some instruction even though you don't anticipate using it. Or a public-health nurse or a visiting nurse can teach you at home. A mother can learn by herself, but this takes a little longer. In any case, it seems like an awkward business at first, and several practice sessions will be necessary before you become very efficient. Don't be discouraged.

The milk produced in the glandular tissue throughout the breast flows through tiny tubes toward the center of the breast and is stored in 15 to 20 sinuses, or sacs, which are located behind the areola, the dark-colored skin around the nipple. In manual expression, the milk is squeezed out of the sinuses, each of which has a small tube leading through the nipple to the outside.

If you are going to express only a small amount of milk—for instance, to relieve engorgement in the areolar area—you can use any handy cup to catch it. If you are going to express as much as you can and will be giving it to the baby right afterward, you should wash the cup with soap. rinse it, and dry it with a clean towel. After expressing the milk, you pour it into a nursing bottle and cap with a nipple, both of which should have been washed with soap and rinsed since the last use. If you are going to save the milk for a number of hours—for instance, if you are delivering it once a day to the hospital for a premature baby—it should be kept as sterile as possible. Either you can express the milk into a sterilized cup and then transfer it to a sterilized bottle with cap and nipple (sterilized by boiling for 5 minutes), or you can use a washed cup, bottle, cap, and nipple, and sterilize after the milk is in the bottle (see terminal sterilization, Sections 168–170).

137. The finger-and-thumb method. In the commoner method of manual expression, the sinuses are repeatedly squeezed between thumb and finger. First, of course, you wash your hands with soap. To apply the pressure where the sinuses lie, deep behind the areola, it is necessary to place the tips of thumb and finger on opposite sides of the areola (just at the edge where the dark skin meets the normally colored skin). Then press thumb and finger in deeply until they meet the ribs. In this position, squeeze them rhythmically together. The right hand is usually used to express the left breast, and in this instance the left hand holds the cup that catches the milk.

The main thing is to press in deeply enough and at the edge of the areola. The nipple itself is not squeezed or fingered. You may be able to get more milk with each squeeze if you not only press thumb and finger toward each other but pull slightly outward with them (toward the nipple) at the same time, to complete the milking motion.

After a bit, the thumb and finger can be shifted, part way "around the clock" to be sure that all the sinuses are being pressed. If the finger

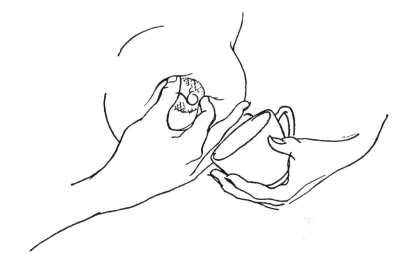

and thumb become tired—and they will at first—you can shift back and forth from side to side.

138. The thumb-and-cup method. Another method, less commonly used but very efficient when learned, is to press the sinuses between the thumb and the inside edge of a teacup that has a flared edge (it's too hard to get the areola and the thumb down inside a cup with straight sides). If you will be saving the milk for hours, the cup should be sterilized.

First, wash your hands with soap and water. Tuck the lower edge of the cup **deep** into the left breast, at the lower edge of the areola, and tip the cup up, part way, holding it with the left hand. Place the thumb of the right hand on the **upper** edge of the areola. Now the areola is being

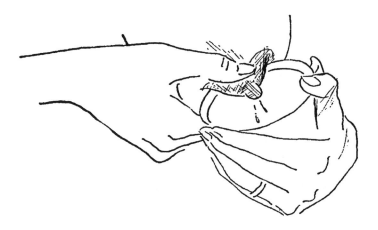

pressed between the right thumb and the rim of the cup. Press the right thumb firmly inward (toward the rim) and then downward (toward the nipple). This squeezes the milk from the sacs into the tubes running through the nipple. When you press toward the nipple, don't slide your thumb across the dark skin; the skin moves with the thumb. It is not necessary to squeeze or even touch the nipple.

With a little practice, you will be able to press the milk out in a fine spray. The first few days your thumb may be tired and lame, but this won't last. If you are emptying a full breast, it may take 20 minutes—more if you are just learning. If you are attempting to empty the breasts completely after the baby has finished nursing, it will take only a few minutes. When the breast is full, the milk comes in a spray. When it is partly empty, it comes in drops. Stop when no more milk comes. Naturally, if you wait 10 minutes the breast will have made more milk, but you don't have to empty it again.

139. Breast pumps. There are three kinds of breast pumps. The simplest, least expensive, and easiest to find is of glass, with a rubber bulb to apply the suction. More efficient but harder to find is a water-type breast pump. One part of the pump attaches to an ordinary water faucet. As the faucet is repeatedly turned on and off, it rhythmically creates suction at the breast. Then there are electric breast pumps, which can be rented from some hospitals and surgical-supply stores.

140. A nipple shield consists of a rubber nipple attached to a glass cone that fits over the front of the breast. As the baby sucks on the rubber nipple, a vacuum is created in the cone and this draws the areola into the cone and draws out some of the milk. A nipple shield is used temporarily when the mother's nipples are sore or retracted. It is not very efficient, because the milk is not squeezed out of the sinuses. A baby has to be able to suck vigorously to get much milk. (Old-fashioned lead nipple shields should not be used, because they may cause lead poisoning.)

WEANING FROM THE BREAST

Weaning is important not only for the baby but for the mother, and not only physically but emotionally. A mother who has set great store by nursing may feel mildly let down and depressed after she stops—as if she has lost some of her closeness to the baby or as if she has become a less worthwhile person. This is an additional reason for making weaning a gradual process whenever possible.

141. Weaning when there is little breast milk. Weaning from the breast is quite easy when the mother is producing only a **small** amount of milk. It's usually not necessary for her to bind her breasts or limit her own fluids. She can just stop putting the baby to breast and wait. If the breasts get so full that they are uncomfortable, she can nurse him for 15 or 30 seconds. This will relieve the pressure without really stimulating the breast. If the breasts should become uncomfortable again, she can repeat this. If she is producing a **moderate** amount of milk, she should plan to wean more gradually. It still isn't necessary to bind the breasts or to limit fluids. Try omitting every other breast feeding. If, in a day or two, the breasts have not become uncomfortably full, stop all regular nursing, but put the baby to breast for a short period if the breasts then become uncomfortable.

If you have no doctor to advise you, use the formula in Section 164.

142. Sudden weaning from the breast (if you cannot consult a doctor). You may have to suddenly wean the baby from the breast if, for instance, you become seriously ill or you have to go out of town for an emergency. (It is not usually necessary to wean the baby because of mild or moderately severe illness in the mother. Your doctor is the one to decide this.) One method is to limit the fluids that the mother drinks and to apply a tight binder and ice bags to her breasts. This is a pretty uncomfortable business. A better way is to relieve the breasts whenever they become uncomfortably full, either with a breast pump or by manual expression. If you consult a doctor, he may recommend several days of injections with a special preparation that decreases milk production.

If you have no doctor to advise you, use the formula in Section 164.

143. Gradual weaning from breast to cup in the last part of the first year. If a mother is producing plenty of milk, how long should she plan to nurse? Best of all, most natural of all, is to nurse until the baby is ready for weaning to the cup. As is pointed out in Section 225, one baby is ready for weaning earlier than another. Most breast-fed babies are ready somewhere between the ages of 7 and 10 months. (This is in contrast to bottle babies, many of whom are unwilling to give up the bottle until they are well over a year old.)

It's a good idea to begin offering a sip of milk from the cup from the age of 5 months, so that the baby gets used to it before he is too opinionated. By 6 months encourage him to hold the cup himself (see Sections 222–224). Then sometime in the second half of the first year, most commonly between 7 and 10 months, you notice he is beginning to be less eager for the breast. He nurses for shorter periods. If he is also drinking well from the cup, I would assume he is ready for gradual weaning. Now offer him the cup at all his meals and increase the amount as he shows his willingness to take more, but continue to breast-feed him at the end of the meal. Next, leave out one of his daily breast feedings, the one that he seems the least interested in, giving him only the cup. This is usually at breakfast or lunch. In a week, omit another breast feeding if he seems willing, and in another week, the last one. Don't rush him. His willingness to be weaned may not progress steadily. If he gets into a period when he is miserable from teething or illness, he may want to retreat a little. This is natural enough, and there is no danger in accommodating him. When you stop to think for a minute what a tremendous joy nursing has been to him from the day he was born, you don't wonder that he wants to go back to more nursing when life looks dark. It's better to avoid making other important changes in a baby's life (for instance, moving to another house or starting toilet training) during the period when he is being weaned.

When weaning is carried out this gradually, there is usually no problem about the mother's breasts. If, however, they become uncomfortably full at any time, the mother only needs to allow the baby to nurse for 15 to 30 seconds to relieve the pressure. Don't let him nurse for 5 minutes— that will encourage the breasts too much.

Sometimes a mother will be afraid to give up nursing altogether, because the baby is not taking as much milk from the cup as he used to take from the breast. This may postpone the weaning indefinitely. I would stop the nursing if the baby is taking an average of 4 ounces from the cup at each meal, or a total of 12 to 16 ounces a day. After the nursing is stopped, he will probably increase the amount from the cup up to a total of 16 ounces or more. This is usually enough, with all the other things he is eating.

I think it is preferable to have a baby weaned from the breast by a year if he seems ready for it. A child seldom demands the breast after that, and it's apt to be continued just to get him to sleep or for some other reason. When breast feeding is continued beyond the age that the child really needs it, it may become a habit that makes him unnaturally dependent on his mother.

Some other points about weaning are taken up in Sections 222 to 228.

144. Gradual weaning from breast to bottle in the first 6 months. There are lots of mothers who either aren't able or don't want to nurse a baby until he is ready to be weaned to the cup, toward the end of his first year. In one case the milk supply becomes insufficient. The baby cries from hunger and fails to gain sufficient weight. A hungry baby like this seldom puts up any fuss over weaning to the bottle. How fast the weaning to the bottle goes will depend on how much the mother is producing.

If you find that your breast-milk supply is failing rapidly and the baby is quite hungry, and if you have no doctor to consult, make up a complete formula from Section 164 or 165. Give him a bottle at each feeding, after the breast, letting him take as much or as little of it as he wants. Omit the breast feeding at 6 P.M. Two days later omit the 10 A.M. breast feeding also. Discontinue the remaining breast feedings, one every 2 or 3 days, in the following order: 2 P.M., 10 P.M., 6 A.M. (If the mother's milk is decreasing only gradually and the baby is only slightly dissatisfied, it will work better to introduce the bottles one feeding at a time, as in the third paragraph below.)

But suppose there is no problem of the milk supply's giving out. Let's say a mother wants to nurse her baby for a few months to give him a good start, but not for most of the year. How long is it important to nurse? There's no hard-and-fast answer to this, of course. The physical advantages of breast milk, its purity, its easy digestibility, are most valuable to the baby at first. But there is no age at which they suddenly become of no benefit. The emotional advantages of breast feeding will not cease at any definite period, either. One sensible time to wean to the bottle is at about 3 months. By this age, the baby's digestive system will have settled down. He will be about over any tendency to colic. He will be pretty husky and still gaining rapidly. But if a mother would like to go on nursing until her baby is 4, 5, or 6 months old, or stop at 2 months, those are satisfactory times to wean, too. It is a little safer not to wean in very hot weather.

If you plan to wean to the bottle at some age beyond 2 months, it is wiser to keep the baby accustomed to the bottle from the age of 2 months on, by giving him one regularly 2 or 3 times a week, every day if you prefer.

If the breasts have been producing a good amount of milk, the weaning should preferably be gradual from the beginning. First, omit one breast feeding a day, say at 6 P.M., and give a bottle instead. Let the baby take as much or as little of this as he wants. Wait 2 or 3 days until the breasts become adjusted to the change, then omit the 10 A.M. breast feeding, too, and substitute the second daily bottle. Again wait 2 or 3 days, and then omit the 2 P.M. breast feeding. Now the baby is getting the breast only at 6 A.M. and 10 P.M. and a bottle at each of the other three feedings. You will probably need to wait 3 or even 4 days each time before omitting these last two nursings. Any time the breasts become uncomfortable, even though it isn't time for a scheduled nursing, let the baby nurse for a few seconds, or use manual expression or a breast pump for a few minutes, just to relieve the pressure. Then it should not be necessary to use a binder or to limit your fluids.

145. If the baby won't take the bottle. A baby of 2 months or more who has not regularly had a bottle may balk completely. Try for a week offering him a bottle once or twice a day, before the breast or solid food. Don't force it; don't get him angry. Take it away if he refuses, and give him the rest of his meal, including the breast. In a few days' time, he may change his mind.

If he's still adamant, omit the 2 P.M. breast feeding altogether and see if this makes him thirsty enough so that he will try the bottle at 6 P.M. If he still holds out, you will probably have to give him the breast anyway at the 6 P.M. feeding, because it will be uncomfortably full. But continue to omit the 2 P.M. nursing for several days. It may work on a subsequent day, though it didn't the first.

The next step is to try omitting every other breast feeding throughout the 24 hours (nurse at 6 A.M., 2 P.M., 10 P.M.) and hold down on the solid foods so that he's pretty hungry—or omit solids altogether.

The only alternative left is to stop breast feeding entirely and starve him into capitulation. I put this last, because it is drastic for both baby and mother.

The mother can use a breast pump or manual expression (Sections 137–139) just enough to relieve the pressure and discomfort.

Bottle Feeding

VARIOUS MILKS

146. What is a formula? There is nothing mysterious about a formula. It is a mixture of cow's milk, water, and sugar. (Sometimes the doctor omits sugar.) The water and sugar are put in to make the mixture more like mother's milk in composition. The cow's milk that you use may be evaporated milk or pasteurized whole milk, or powdered milk. Each has its special advantages. A variety of sugars are used. The commonest are granulated sugar, corn syrup, brown sugar, and mixtures of dextrins and maltose.

The reason you have to sterilize carefully the ingredients and the bottles is that germs thrive on milk, just the way babies do. If a few bacteria get into the formula when you make it on Tuesday, they may have multiplied a lot by the time the baby drinks the last of it on Wednesday, especially if the formula has not been well refrigerated. Boiling the formula also makes it more digestible.

Your doctor will prescribe the best kind of milk for your baby, taking into account his particular needs and what is available. The commonest milks used in formula-making are listed for general information.

147. Evaporated milk. Evaporated milk is canned milk from which a little more than half the water has been removed. (It should not be confused with **condensed** milk, which is heavily sweetened with sugar and is not suitable for infants.) The advantages of evaporated milk are several. It is thoroughly sterilized in the process of canning, so it is free of germs when you open it. It is, in most localities, cheaper than fresh milk. It can be kept indefinitely in the unopened can without refrigeration. It's the same wherever you buy it, so a baby who travels doesn't have to adjust to different kinds of milk. It is a little easier to digest than fresh milk and less apt to cause allergies, like eczema.

When you have listed all these advantages, you wonder why anyone uses fresh milk. The main reasons are custom and taste. The taste of evaporated milk doesn't appeal to some older children and adults who have become accustomed to fresh milk. But babies love it, and they rarely object to changing back and forth. There's no reason why a baby shouldn't go on drinking evaporated milk for years. See Section 221.

Since evaporated milk is about twice the strength of fresh milk, you always dilute it with at least an equal amount of water. In our country, vitamin D is added to evaporated milk.

There are many brands of evaporated milk. All are of about the same composition. You do not have to worry about switching from one brand to another.

148. Modified evaporated and powdered milks. A number of evaporated and powdered milks, with special brand names, have already been modified to make them closer to breast milk in composition, and many doctors prescribe them routinely. In all of them more sugar has been added (so that the mother does not have to do this herself), and in some of them the protein has been decreased. These milks should be used on a doctor's recommendation and diluted according to directions.

149. Pasteurized milk. If you are going to make your baby's formula from fresh rather than evaporated milk, it is very desirable that it be pasteurized. In pasteurization, the milk is heated, before being bottled in the dairy, to kill the bacteria dangerous to human beings.

150. Homogenized milk is pasteurized milk in which the fat droplets have been broken up into much smaller particles, making the fat easier to digest. The cream does not rise to the top but stays mixed throughout the milk. Homogenized milk has some advantages for a baby who digests milk poorly. It causes less scum than ordinary milk and will be helpful if you are having trouble with clogged nipples.

151. Vitamin D (pasteurized) milk is available in some localities.

152. Raw milk is unpasteurized. It is milk just as it comes from the cow. It should be boiled for 5 minutes, not only for babies but for children of all ages. This is to be sure that it does not contain bacteria that cause diarrhea, sore throat, tuberculosis, or other infections. Raw milk from Jersey and Guernsey cows is apt to be richer in cream than ordinary commercial milk, and so may upset a baby's digestion. If you move to the country and get this rich milk, you should pour off a little of the cream, so that what's left looks about like commercial milk.

153. Whole milk is an expression used in formula-making. It means that the normal amount of cream is mixed throughout the milk. To obtain whole milk, you shake up the bottle of pasteurized milk, if it is not homogenized, to mix the cream with the rest of the milk. You do this before using any for the formula. If you leave the cream on top and use only the milk in the upper part of the bottle, the formula will be too rich in butter fat. On the other hand, if you are using a bottle of milk from which the top cream has already been used, the formula will be too thin. You don't have to shake homogenized milk, because the cream does not separate.

154. Half-skimmed milk, in which about half the cream has been removed, is preferred by some doctors for feeding **premature babies** until they weigh about 5 pounds, because it is more easily digested than milk with all the cream still in it. (Skimmed milk with **all** the cream removed is too weak for feeding prematures.)

You may be able to buy half-skimmed powdered milk in cans at the grocery or drugstore. Most brands are converted back to liquid half-skimmed milk by mixing in water in the ratio of 2 ounces of water to 1 level tablespoonful of powdered milk (consult the label). Directions for liquefying are in Section 156.

Some commercial dairies sell pasteurized half-skimmed milk in bottles. Or you can buy pasteurized whole milk and remove half the cream with a skimming spoon (or a round measuring spoon, the bowl of which is bent at right angles to the handle).

155. Skimmed milk (for diarrhea). Skimmed milk, or skimmed milk diluted to half strength, if often prescribed for diarrhea, because milk is easier to digest when there is no cream in it.

You can probably buy powdered skimmed milk in cans at the grocery or drugstore. Most brands are converted back to liquid skimmed milk by mixing in water in the ratio of 2 ounces of water to 1 level tablespoonful of powder (consult the label), as in Section 156. Some dairies sell skimmed pasteurized milk.

When you are making **diluted** skimmed milk for diarrhea, you use only half that amount of powder: 1 level tablespoonful of powder to 4 ounces of water.

156. Powdered milk. Powdered whole milk is useful if you are traveling with your baby, or if you are going to live in an uncivilized spot where you can't get evaporated or safe fresh milk. You can carry a large supply with you, and it won't weigh too much. It is more expensive than fresh or evaporated milk. You turn it back into liquid **whole** milk by mixing in the proportion of 1 level tablespoonful of powdered milk to 2 ounces of water. If your baby is taking a formula of 10 ounces of evaporated milk, 20 ounces of water, and 2 tablespoonfuls of granulated sugar, you use 10 tablespoonfuls of powdered milk. You mix this with 30 ounces of water and 2 tablespoonfuls of sugar.

You boil the required amount of water, and dissolve the sugar in it. When this has cooled at least to body heat, place the powder on top and beat it in with a sterilized fork or egg beater.

Powdered milk should be kept in the refrigerator after the can has been opened.

We have been talking about powdered **whole** milk. There are other varieties of powdered milk in which the proportions of the different elements have been changed. The latter should be used only under a physician's supervision.

157. Lactic-acid milk. Lactic-acid milk is a sour milk. It can be made in two ways. In a commercial dairy or in a formula room in a hospital, they put lactic-acid bacilli into pasteurized milk. The bacilli produce the lactic acid, which sours the milk.

The other way is to add the chemical **lactic acid** to pasteurized or evaporated milk. This can be done in the home.

Lactic-acid milk is more easily digested by some babies than ordinary sweet milk. Doctors often prescribe it for those who have painful indigestion, or who vomit a lot, or who have a tendency to diarrhea. Some doctors prefer to use it routinely for all babies. It discourages the growth of harmful bacteria, so it is safer than sweet milk when refrigeration is poor. The amounts of milk, water, and sugar are the same as in an ordinary formula.

Lactic-acid milk is a little tricky to make in the home. The three important things are to have the milk and water well chilled, to acidify the milk very gradually, and not to get the milk too hot after it is acidified.

You boil your milk in one saucepan, cool it, then chill it in the refrigerator. In a separate saucepan, boil your water and sugar, then cool and chill it. Now add 1 teaspoonful of "U.S.P. Lactic Acid" to the water and sugar. (This is the usual amount for a total formula of 24 to 30 ounces. For a smaller formula, use proportionately less.) Now add the acidified water to the milk very slowly, stirring constantly. If someone can help you, have her pour the acidified water into the milk while you stir continuously with an egg beater. You are trying to avoid getting too much acid in any one part of the milk, because that makes a large, tough curd, which won't go through the nipple. That's why you add the acid to the water first, so that it will be diluted before it touches the milk. If you have a formula calling for just milk and sugar, no water, I would add the lactic acid to 1 or 2 ounces of water anyway, before adding it to the milk.

When you come to warm the bottle for the baby, don't heat it too rapidly or too hot. Heat it in a pan of warm water. If you prepare lactic-acid milk carefully, the curds will be fine enough to go through the ordinary-sized nipple holes. If necessary, enlarge the nipple holes.

You can buy prepared whole lactic-acid milk in some large cities. It is usually quite expensive. You can also buy it in powdered form, through your druggist. In using it in a formula, you add water and sugar, the same way as in a sweet-milk formula.

158. Artificial milks, for babies and children who are allergic to real milk, are made from a mixture of foods, such as soybean flour and sugar. They require larger nipple holes.

VARIOUS SUGARS

The doctor will prescribe the sugar that he thinks best for your baby (or none at all). The usual sugars are listed here.

159. Ordinary granulated sugar (cane sugar) is commonly used in formula-making, because it is cheap, available, and usually satisfactory. Being highly refined, it has nothing in it to counteract constipation, if a baby has that tendency. The largest amount usually added to a 24-hour formula is 2 or 3 tablespoonfuls.

160. Brown sugar is unrefined cane sugar. It is useful when the baby's stools are too dry and firm. A tablespoonful has the same food value as a tablespoonful of granulated sugar.

161. Corn syrup is also commonly used in formulas. It contains a mixture of sugar and dextrins. A dextrin is halfway between a sugar and a starch. In the intestine, it is only slowly converted into sugar, so that at any one time there is less sugar in the intestine to make gas. That's why a dextrin mixture is thought to be better for a baby who is forming lots of gas or has a tendency to looseness. However, it can be used for babies with good digestions, too. It is inexpensive. You use the same number of tablespoonfuls of it as you would of granulated sugar. The maximum for a 24-hour formula is usually 2 or 3 tablespoonfuls. The light syrup is ordinarily used, unless there is a tendency to constipation. The dark syrup, being less refined, is slightly more laxative.

162. Dextrin and maltose preparations are much like corn syrup, except that they are in powder form and are more expensive. A tablespoonful contains only half as much nourishment (calories) as granulated sugar. Therefore, if you are changing, you use 2 tablespoonfuls of a dextrin and maltose preparation in place of 1 tablespoonful of granulated sugar. The maximum for a 24-hour formula is usually 4 to 6 tablespoonfuls.

163. Lactose is the sugar that naturally occurs in human and cow's milk. It is satisfactory for formulas, but expensive. It takes 1½ tablespoonfuls of it to equal 1 tablespoonful of granulated sugar.

FORMULAS FOR EMERGENCY USE

In the next pages are a couple of formulas for parents who are completely unable to consult a doctor about a baby's feeding. If you bring your baby to a private doctor, clinic, baby-health station, or have the help of a visiting or public-health nurse, you will be given formulas based on your baby's age, weight, rate of gain, and digestion. That is the only sound way to decide on the right formula. If you are completely out of reach and if your baby is healthy and normal, you can probably make out with the formulas in this book and a little common sense.

164. A moderately dilute formula suitable for a newborn baby or for a baby with a small appetite:

evaporated milk	10 ounces
water	20 ounces
corn syrup	2 level tablespoonfuls

This will make 30 ounces of formula, which will probably be more than the average baby will need in 24 hours until he weighs 9 or 10 pounds.

How many ounces in how many bottles? A 6-pounder may want about 3 ounces roughly every 3 hours during the day (6 A.M., 9 A.M., 12 noon, 3 P.M., 6 P.M.) and about every 4 hours at night (10 P.M., 2 A.M.), a total of about 21 ounces in the 24 hours.

A 7- or 8-pounder may want about 4 ounces on an average of every 4 hours day and night (6 A.M., 10 A.M., 2 P.M., 6 P.M., 10 P.M., 2 A.M.) for the first week or so, a total of about 24 ounces. But usually, by the time he is a few weeks old, he is willing, if waked and fed at 10 or 11 P.M., to sleep through the 2 A.M. feeding. Then you can put larger amounts in fewer bottles.

You can divide your total formula any way that is most convenient, depending on how many bottles your baby wants in the 24 hours and how many ounces he usually wants at each feeding.

In the early weeks, for instance, if you are making a total of 30 ounces of formula for a 7- or 8-pound baby, you can put 3¾ ounces in each of 8 bottles. If he is unusually regular and needs only 6 bottles in 24 hours, you can use the extra bottles for the first two feedings of the next 24-hour period and then make up the next formula later in the day. Or you can discard the extra bottles (or use the formula for cooking) and make up the new formula at always the same time of day.

But most babies wake somewhat irregularly at first. If your doctor has recommended a flexible schedule (feeding the baby—at least during the day—whenever he seems really hungry, regardless of the clock), the two extra bottles may well be called for by a baby who wakes more frequently than six times in the 24 hours. It is unlikely, though, that a 7- or 8-pounder will want more than 20 to 24 ounces in the 24 hours, so you can expect several bottles to be only partly finished.

If in the early weeks your baby wakes and is hungry for more feedings than you have bottles for, you can make the next formula early. If this works you back to an inconvenient hour for formula preparation, you can make formula twice in one day to catch up.

As your baby gets older and grows bigger, you can expect him to cut down gradually on the number of feedings each day, to increase the amount he wants in an average feeding, and to increase his total amount for the day. As you watch his changing pattern, you will be able to decide when to increase the amount in each bottle and cut down on the number of bottles. Thirty ounces of total formula make about 3¾ ounces in 8 bottles, 4¼ ounces in 7 bottles, 5 ounces in 6 bottles, 6 ounces in 5 bottles.

165. A full-strength formula for a baby who has become dissatisfied with the more dilute formula (probably when he weighs about 10 pounds):

evaporated milk . . . . 13 ounces (1 can)
water (to make a total of one
  quart) . . . . 19 ounces
corn syrup . . . . 3 tablespoonfuls.

This will make about 5¼ ounces in 6 bottles, 6½ ounces in 5 bottles, 8 ounces in 4 bottles.

166. Weakening the formula temporarily. (Directions for those who cannot consult a doctor. If you can reach a doctor, he is the one to advise you about **any** changes.) The formula may be weakened temporarily, for example, if a baby is having a spell of indigestion or mild diarrhea or if a newborn baby has a poor appetite and is finishing only about half of each bottle.

If the bottles have already been prepared with the usual formula, pour off half the quantity, add an equal amount of boiled water. Make one or two extra bottles with the formula you are pouring off. If you are just making the formula, do it the usual way but put only half the usual amount into each bottle and then add an equal amount of boiled water. Make one or two extra bottles with the remaining formula, weakened the same way.

This method of weakening a formula may sound wasteful, but it's safer than getting all mixed up in more complicated arithmetic. Besides, it's convenient to have an extra bottle or two of formula. A baby whose formula has been weakened may suddenly get very hungry.

PREPARING A FORMULA

There are various ways of preparing a formula. Which one you use depends on what the doctor or nurse who teaches you recommends, how much special equipment you have, what you find easiest.

There are in general two different methods. The first is called **terminal sterilization,** because the sterilizing of the formula and of the bottles takes place at the end of the preparation, after the formula is all in the nursing bottles. This method is the simplest and the safest. The only trouble is that there is apt to be more scum to clog the nipple holes, because there is no chance to strain the formula after it has been boiled.

The second method is sometimes called the **aseptic** method because the formula, the bottles, and the other equipment get sterilized separately. Then you have to use aseptic care (just as doctors and nurses do in an operation) in straining the formula into the nursing bottles and capping them so as not to introduce germs.

The reason for all this sterilizing is that germs grow readily in milk, and germs added at the time the formula is prepared may multiply a lot by the time the baby drinks it if it is not well refrigerated.

167. Care of bottles and nipples after use. After the baby has finished with a bottle, rinse it, squirt a little water through the nipple to remove

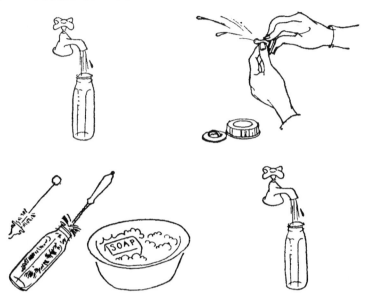

scum, wash the bottle, nipple, and bottle cap briefly but vigorously with hot water, soap, and a bottle or jar brush. Rinse and set to drain.

It is easier to get the equipment clean if you wash it right after use. But if you prefer, you can wash all the bottles, nipples, and caps together before making formula.

If you have trouble with clogged nipples, clean each nipple hole daily by rotating a toothpick in it. (See also Section 182.)

PREPARING FORMULA—TERMINAL METHOD

In this method you do not sterilize anything until the formula is in the nursing bottles, and then you sterilize everything together.

168. Equipment (see Sections 48–53 for description of equipment).

1. **8-ounce nursing bottles.** As many as the baby will need for taking the total amount of formula, probably 6 to 8 bottles for 24 hours in the beginning. You may want an extra bottle for water if the baby takes it.
2. An equal number of **nipples, bottle caps,** and **disks.**
3. A **quart measure** of glass or enamelware or some substitute (Section 52).
4. A **tablespoon** for stirring.
5. A set of **measuring spoons,** and if you are using a dry sugar, a knife to level the sugar in the spoon.

6. **A can opener,** for evaporated milk. (A beer-can opener is easiest.)

7. **A sterilizing pail** with **lid** and **bottle rack.**

169. Mixing the formula. Let's, for an example, assume that the formula will be:

evaporated milk . . . . 10 ounces
water . . . . .20 ounces
corn syrup . . . . 2 tablespoonfuls

with which you expect to make 7 bottles of about 4¼ ounces each.

Run faucet water (hot or cold) into the quart measure up to the 20-ounce mark.

Put the 2 level tablespoonfuls of corn syrup into the water and stir until dissolved (syrup or sugar dissolves faster in warm water).

Briefly wash the top of a 13-ounce can of evaporated milk with soap; rinse; then make two openings with the can opener on opposite sides of the top, one to let the milk out, the other to let air in.

Pour 10 ounces of the evaporated milk into the quart measure, bringing the total to 30 ounces.

Stir with the tablespoon and pour about 4¼ ounces into each of 7 bottles.

170. Sterilizing the formula. Now cap the bottles. If you are using the kind of nipple that is held in place by a plastic cap, you insert the nipple

upside down in the cap, cover with a disk, then screw the cap on. Leave the caps only partly screwed on so that there will be a space for hot air to escape as the bottles heat up, and to re-enter as the bottles cool again.

If you are using the kind of nipple that is stretched over the neck of the bottle, you do not put it on the bottle until feeding time. Meanwhile you cap the bottle with a glass or aluminum cap.

Place the bottles in the wire rack in the sterilizing pail, put an inch or two of hot water in the bottom, put the pail on the stove, and heat. The water should boil for a full 25 minutes.

It has been discovered recently that there will be the least scum to clog the nipple holes if the formula is allowed to **cool slowly without being shaken** at all. So leave the sterilizing pail (with its cover on) right on the stove (with the heat off).

When the bottles are lukewarm or cool, screw the caps down and place the bottles in the refrigerator.

If you are using nipples that stretch over the neck of the bottle, boil them for 3 minutes in a small saucepan with cover, drain, leave the cover off until they are dry, then re-cover, and leave in the saucepan until used.

PREPARING FORMULA—ASEPTIC METHOD

In the aseptic method, you sterilize the bottles, nipples, and other equipment by boiling, and you sterilize the formula in a quart measure or saucepan. Then you pour the sterilized formula into the sterilized bottles and cap them.

This method takes more time and care than terminal sterilization, but there is less trouble with clogging of the nipple holes, because the formula is strained as it is poured into the bottles.

171. Equipment (see Sections 48–53 for description).

1. **Eight-ounce nursing bottles,** probably 6 to 8 at first. If the baby takes water, you may want an extra bottle for it.
2. **Nipples.** Same number.
3. **Bottle caps.**
4. **Funnel** and **strainer.**
5. **Can opener** for evaporated milk.
6. **Quart measure** of enamelware, or something else to measure and boil formula in (Section 52).

7. Set of **measuring spoons.**

8. A long **tablespoon** for stirring (with a handle that doesn't get too hot).

9. A **sterilizing pail** with **cover** and a **wire rack.**

172. Sterilizing the bottles and equipment. The nipples and bottle caps (and disks) can be more conveniently boiled in a separate saucepan, with cover for draining. In order to preserve the nipples, boil for only 3 minutes, drain, and let cool with cover off.

nipples, caps, disks in saucepan

Wash your hands with soap.

Place bottles upside down in wire rack in sterilizing pail, which contains about an inch of hot water. Also put the funnel and strainer into the pail. Boil vigorously for 5 minutes. While it is cooling (with cover off), you can be mixing and boiling the formula.

173. Making the formula. Into the quart measure, run the amount of water (hot or cold) called for in your formula, plus 2 extra ounces for evaporation. Add the amount of sugar or syrup called for. The sugar in the tablespoon should be scraped level with a knife. Stir the sugar or syrup till dissolved.

Now add the number of ounces of milk required for the formula. If the formula calls for 10 ounces evaporated milk, 20 ounces water, you will first run in the water, up to the 22-ounce mark (20 ounces for the formula, 2 ounces for evaporation). Adding 10 ounces of evaporated milk will bring the level up to 32 ounces before boiling.

(A can of **evaporated milk** should be washed briefly on top with soap, opened with two holes, one for the milk to come out, the other for air to go in.)

(Homogenized milk needs only to be opened and poured.)

(Pasteurized milk that is not homogenized should be turned upside down for a minute and shaken before opening, to mix the cream.)

Place the filled quart measure over flame, bring to a boil, and simmer for 5 minutes, stirring constantly to keep it from boiling over and from burning on the bottom. (The quart measure or saucepan and the stirring spoon don't have to be sterilized ahead of time. They will be sterilized while the formula is simmering.)

174. Bottling the formula. When the sterilizer containing the bottles is cool enough to handle, move it to the table. Remove the funnel and strainer and place them in the upside-down pail cover, which is sterile inside.

Avoid touching the openings of the bottles, the inside of the funnel, the mesh of the strainer.

Lift out the rack of bottles and set them right side up on the table.

Pour the required amount into each bottle, using the funnel and strainer.

Put on nipples and bottle caps (nipples upside down in the bottles and covered with disks if you are using screw-on caps), being careful to handle nipples only by the rims.

When cool, place in refrigerator.

175. You can bake the bottles. Instead of boiling the bottles and funnel and strainer, you can, if you prefer, bake them in the oven for 15 minutes at about 250°. Don't try to bake the nipples and bottle caps.

FORMULA REFRIGERATION

176. Insufficient space in refrigerator. If you don't have enough room in the refrigerator for all the bottles, you can pour the boiled formula, through a strainer, into a sterilized quart bottle (there probably isn't room for it in your sterilizer, but you can boil it separately in a pan). Cover the top with waxed paper held on with a rubber band, and keep this bottle in the refrigerator. Your sterilized nursing bottles can be set aside on a shelf. At each feeding you fill one from the quart bottle.

177. Saving the unused evaporated milk. When you use less than a full can of evaporated milk, you can save what is left for the next day. Leave it in the can and cover the top with a fresh piece of waxed paper held with a rubber band to keep bacteria, molds, and dust particles from drifting in. Keep the covered can in the refrigerator, and use it all up the next day.

178. If you cannot keep the formula cold. If you ever get into a situation where you can't keep the baby's bottles cold until feeding time—for instance, if your refrigerator stops working—you will be pretty safe if you heat each bottle to the boiling point before giving it. Put the bottle in hot water, bring to a boil, boil 10 minutes, then cool it down to body temperature before giving it.

GIVING THE BOTTLE

179. The first few days. Usually the first bottle is offered about 12 hours after the baby is born, though it can be started earlier if he seems hungry. The baby is apt to want little the first few feedings. Even if he takes only half an ounce, don't try to get more into him. It's often 3 or 4 days before he wants the amounts you expect him to need, and it may take a week or more. Don't worry; it may be better for his digestion to start gradually. He'll find out what he needs when he comes more to life in a few days.

180. Warming and giving the bottle. Shake the bottle when you remove it from the refrigerator, to mix the cream. You can warm the bottle in a saucepan or pitcher of hot water, or in a washbasin. It is more convenient, if there's no hot water near the baby's room, to use an electric or a chemical bottle warmer. Most babies like the formula at just about body heat. The best way to test this is to shake a few drops onto the inside of your wrist. If it feels hot, it is too hot. Sit in a comfortable chair and hold the baby cradled in your arm, just as in breast feeding. Some mothers find a rocking chair is perfect.

Keep the bottle tilted up, so that the nipple is always full. Most babies want to work steadily until they have taken all the formula they need. There are some, though, who swallow a lot of air during nursing, and if the air bubble in the stomach gets too big, they feel uncomfortably full and stop nursing in the middle of the bottle. If this happens, bring up the bubble (see Section 90) and go on with the feeding. A few babies need to be bubbled 2 or even 3 times in the course of a bottle—others not at all. You will soon find out which type your baby is.

As soon as your baby stops nursing and seems satisfied, let that be the end of the feeding. He knows better than anyone else how much he needs.

181. Can you prop the bottle? It's good for the mother to hold her baby in her arms during bottle feedings. This is the position that Nature intends. The baby and mother are as close as can be, and they can watch each other's face. Feeding is a baby's greatest joy, by far, and it's good for him to link this with his mother's presence and his mother's face.

On the other hand, some busy mothers, with other children and a husband to take care of, feel compelled to prop the bottle at certain feedings. Most mothers of twins find it essential to prop the bottle for one or both babies at each feeding. These mothers point out that there are a number of chances every day for a mother to talk to her baby and cuddle him and that these other times may be calmer and happier than certain hectic feeding times. I agree that there are a hundred different ways to show a baby that you love him and that no single one of them is essential in itself. I agree that it does no harm for a loving but busy mother to prop some of the bottles if she can make it up to the baby in other ways. I'd still advise a mother who's not too busy not to prop.

Most mothers prop with a folded diaper, but there are bottle holders that are more efficient.

Many babies by the time they are 7 or 8 months old feel so grown-up that they don't want to take the bottle cuddled in their mother's arms. They want to sit up straight and hold the bottle themselves. Of course, here's no point insisting on a baby's being in your lap when he'd prefer something else. (See Section 188.)

182. Making the nipple holes right. If the nipple holes are too small, the baby will get too little. He'll start fussing, or he'll become tired long before he's finished and go to sleep. If they are too large, he may choke or get indigestion; in the long run, he may get too little sucking satisfaction and suck his thumb more. For most babies, the right speed is when the bottle takes about 20 minutes of straight sucking time. The holes are generally right for a young baby if, when you turn the bottle upside down, the milk comes out in a fine spray for a second or two and then changes to drops. If it keeps coming in a spray, it is probably too fast. If it comes in slow drops from the beginning, it is probably too slow.

Many new nipples are too slow for a young baby but are right for an older, stronger one. If they are too slow for your baby, enlarge them carefully as follows: Stick the dull end of a fine (No. 10) needle into a cork. Then, holding the cork, heat the needle point in a flame until it's red-hot. Stick it a short distance into the top of the nipple. You don't have to poke it into the old hole. Don't use too large a needle or poke it in too far, until you can test your results. If you make the holes too large, you'll have to throw the nipple away. You can make 1, 2, or 3 enlarged holes. If you have no cork, you can wrap a piece of cloth around the dull end of the needle or hold it in pliers.

If you have trouble with clogged nipple holes, especially in terminal sterilization, you can buy small wire strainers that fit inside the base of each nipple. Insert a strainer in each nipple before putting the nipple in bottle and then sterilize. Or you may find it adequate to clean each nipple hole daily by rotating a toothpick in it.

Another way to prevent clogging is to buy nipples that, instead of having small holes, are "cross cut." This means that a small cross has been cut in the tip of the nipple. The milk does not pour out, as you might expect, because the edges of the cut stay together until the baby sucks. You can make small cross cuts in your regular nipples with a razor blade. First pinch the nipple tip to make a narrow ridge, then cut through it. Then pinch again (at a right angle to the first pinch) and make another cut.

183. Don't urge the baby to take more than he wants. The main trouble with bottle feeding, to my mind, is that the mother can see how much formula is left. Some babies always want the same quantity at every feeding of the day. But there are others whose appetites are much more variable. You mustn't get the idea that your baby has to have a certain amount at each feeding. It may help you acquire a more relaxed feeling about this to realize that a breast-fed baby may get as much as 10 ounces at the 6 A.M. nursing and as little as 4 ounces at the 6 P.M. feeding and be perfectly happy with each. If you can trust a breast-fed baby to take what he needs, you can trust a bottle-fed baby, too.

It is necessary to make this point because quite a number of children become feeding problems. They lose the natural appetite that they were born with and balk at all or many of their foods. These problems develop, in nine out of ten cases, because the mother has been trying, sometimes since infancy, to get her child to eat more than he wants. When you succeed in getting a baby or child to take a few more mouthfuls than he is eager for, it looks to you as if you have gained something. But this isn't so. He will only cut down at his next feedings. He knows the amounts and he even knows the different kinds of foods that his body is calling for. Urging your child isn't necessary, doesn't get you anywhere. It is harmful because it begins, after a while, to take away his appetite, and makes him want to eat **less** than his system really needs.

In the long run, urging does more than destroy appetite and make a thin child. It robs him of some of his positive feeling for life. A baby is meant to spend his first year getting hungry, demanding food, enjoying it, reaching satisfaction—a lusty success story, repeated at least 3 times a day, week after week. It builds into him self-confidence, outgoingness, trust in his mother. But if mealtime becomes a struggle, if feeding becomes something that is done **to** him, he goes on the defensive and builds up a balky, suspicious attitude toward life and toward people.

I don't mean that you have to snatch the bottle away for good the first time your baby pauses. Some babies like to rest a bit several times during a feeding. But if he seems indifferent when you put the nipple back in his mouth (and it's not due to a bubble), then he's satisfied, and you should be, too. You may say, "If I wait 10 minutes, he'll sometimes take a little bit more." Better not.

184. The baby who wakes in a few minutes. What about the baby who goes to sleep after he's taken 4 of his 5 ounces and then wakes up and cries a few minutes later? This is more apt to be due to an air bubble or colic or periodic irritable crying than to hunger. A baby won't notice a difference of an ounce, especially if he's gone to sleep. In fact, a baby will often sleep just as well when he's taken only half his usual amount, though he may wake a **little** early.

It's perfectly all right to occasionally give your baby the rest of the formula a little later, if you feel sure that he's hungry for it. But I think it's better to assume first that he is not really hungry and give him a good chance to go back to sleep—with or without a pacifier. In other words, try to postpone the next feeding for 2 or 3 hours.

185. The young baby who only half finishes. A mother may bring a baby home from the hospital and find that he stops taking his bottle and falls asleep when it's still half full. Yet they said in the hospital that he was taking it all. The mother keeps trying to rouse him, to wedge another quarter of an ounce in, but it's slow, hard, frustrating work. What's the trouble? He may be a baby who hasn't quite "come to" yet. (An occasional baby stays sluggish like that for the first 2 or 3 weeks and then comes to life with a bang.)

The constructive thing to do is to let the baby stop when he wants to, even if he's taken only an ounce or two. Won't he get hungry then, long before it's time for the next feeding? He may, or he may not. If he does, feed him. "But," you say, "I'd be feeding him all day and night." It probably won't be that bad. The point is that if you let a baby stop when he feels like it and let him come to feel his own hunger, he will gradually become more eager for his feedings and take larger amounts. Then he will be able to sleep for longer periods. You can help him to learn to wait longer and be hungrier by trying to stretch out the interval to 2, 2½, then 3 hours. Don't pick him up just as soon as he starts fussing but wait a while. He may go back to sleep. If he gets crying hard, you'll probably have to feed him.

If you keep urging him to finish, there's a chance that he'll go right on being indifferent.

If his appetite doesn't begin to improve in a few days and he's still taking all together only about half of his formula, and if you have no doctor to advise you, you can dilute his formula in half for a day or two (Section 166). When he's dissatisfied with that, go back to his full-strength formula.

186. The baby who fusses soon after starting a bottle or who promptly goes to sleep may be frustrated by a nipple hole that is clogged or too small. See if the milk comes in a fine spray when the bottle is first inverted. Try enlarging the nipple hole a little anyway, as an experiment (Section 182).

The older baby who refuses to nurse is discussed in Section 89.

187. How long after a bottle has been taken out of the refrigerator can you still use it? During the time when a bottle is at drinking temperature or room temperature or pleasant outdoor temperature, any bacteria that may have gotten into the formula will be able to multiply rapidly. That is why it is unwise to give a baby a bottle that has been sitting around the house or carriage or car for several hours, whether it's a full bottle or one that has been partly consumed.

If you will need to feed the baby a couple of hours after leaving home, put the bottle, as soon as you take it out of the refrigerator, into an insulated bag designed to keep things cold or wrap it in 10 layers of newspaper (which is a pretty good insulator).

If you have a young baby who sometimes goes to sleep after half a bottle and then wakes in a couple of hours for the rest, you can promptly put his half-finished bottle back into the refrigerator. I wouldn't use such a bottle more than twice.

188. Avoiding a bedtime bottle through the second year. Some parents are bothered if a baby wants a bottle far into the second year; others don't mind at all. If you care a lot, one precaution you can take is not to get your baby used to taking his own bottle in bed. Between 7 and 10 months, many babies come to feel so grown-up that they don't want to be cradled in their mother's arms at nursing time; they want to sit up. And they also want to take the bottle away from the mother and hold it themselves. A practical mother, seeing she's not much use, is apt to put such a baby in his crib, where he drinks his bottle and puts himself to sleep all in one operation. This pattern is a handy one for putting babies to sleep, but in the long run it makes it impossible for some of them to go to sleep without a bottle. When the mother tries to withhold the bedtime bottle at 15 or 18 or 21 months, such a baby will cry frantically and be unable to fall asleep for a long time. I'm not saying that this dependence on the bottle in bed always develops. And I'm not saying that if you avoid the bottle in bed, your baby will surely be willing to be weaned early—but it should help somewhat. Let him hold his own bottle, on your lap or in his chair, and then put him to bed afterward.

If you prefer the bottle in bed as a sort of sedative and won't mind continuing to give it through a good part of the second year, then there's no harm.

Adding Vitamins and Water

VITAMINS IN INFANCY

189. Babies definitely need extra vitamin D and vitamin C. (They are discussed in Sections 421–422.) There are only small amounts of these in milk as it comes from the cow and in solid foods that are given early. However, in the United States vitamin D is added to all brands of evaporated milk and to pasteurized milk that is labeled "vitamin D milk."

Breast milk may contain sufficient vitamin C if the mother's diet is rich in citrus fruits and certain vegetables (Section 421), but breast milk doesn't contain enough vitamin D.

Previously vitamin D was most often given in the form of fish-liver oil, and vitamin C in the form of orange juice. But fish-liver oil is strong-smelling, stains the clothes, and is irritating to the lungs if choked on; orange juice is often spit up and sometimes causes rashes in the first few months. So nowadays many doctors prescribe a concentrated commercial preparation that contains vitamins D, C, and A. The dropper that comes with the bottle has lines showing 0.3 cc. and 0.6 cc. (three tenths and six tenths of a cubic centimeter). The fluid is drawn up in the dropper to the line that the doctor prescribes and then squirted directly into the baby's mouth at the beginning of one of the feedings of the day.

If you have no doctor to advise you, give 0.6 cc. (in most preparations this contains 1,000 units of D, 5,000 units of A, and 50 milligrams of C) winter and summer. Start at 1 month or earlier.

190. "Multivitamins" not usually essential. Doctors sometimes advise a "multivitamin" or "polyvitamin" preparation that contains a number of B vitamins, in addition to the A, C, and D, to be doubly sure that all the B-vitamin requirements are covered. However, milk, cereals, and the other foods that babies and children eat usually provide sufficient B vitamins. The dosage of many multivitamin preparations is also 0.6 cc., which is squirted directly into the mouth before one feeding of the day. The main reason for not using one of these products routinely for children, aside from the fact that the added B vitamins are not necessary, is that they are more expensive.

191. Orange juice. When your baby is a few months old, the doctor will probably suggest adding orange juice to his diet. It can be fresh, frozen, or canned. Orange juice is usually mixed with an equal amount of boiled water so that it won't taste too strong. One way is to start with 1 teaspoonful of orange juice and 1 teaspoonful of water. The next day give 2 teaspoonfuls of orange juice and 2 teaspoonfuls of water. The third day, 3 teaspoonfuls of each. And so on, up to an **ounce of each.** Then gradually decrease the water and increase the orange juice, until you are giving **2 ounces of straight orange juice.** You strain the orange juice, so that the pulp won't clog the nipples. The baby usually takes it from the bottle until he's 5 or 6 months old; after that, from a cup or glass. Orange juice is often given before the baby's bath, because this is a time when he is always awake for about an hour before his next feeding. You can give it at room temperature or slightly warmed. Don't get it hot. Heat destroys vitamin C.

Most babies love orange juice and digest it easily. Some young babies always vomit it. An occasional baby seems to be made uncomfortable by it or gets a rash from it. Very few babies dislike it at first, but some turn against it later. If for any of these reasons your baby can't take orange juice, you can postpone it for a month or two or you can try tomato juice (4 ounces a day). Unfortunately, if a baby is upset by orange juice or dislikes it, he usually is upset by or dislikes tomato juice, too. If he doesn't take orange juice or tomato juice, he should continue with drops that contain vitamin C.

DRINKING WATER FOR A BABY

192. Some want water; others don't. It is often recommended that a baby be offered a few ounces of water between meals, once or twice a day. It is not absolutely necessary, because the amount of fluid in the formula is probably calculated to satisfy the baby's ordinary needs. It is more important to offer water during excessively hot weather or when the baby has a fever. Babies who ordinarily refuse water often take it at these times.

As a matter of fact, a lot of babies don't want any water from the time they are a week or two old until they are about a year. During this age they fairly worship anything with nourishment in it, but they feel insulted by plain water. If your baby likes it, by all means give it to him once or several times a day when he is awake between meals (not just before the next meal). You can give him as much as he wants. He probably won't want more than 2 ounces. But don't urge him to take water if he doesn't want it. There's no point in getting him mad. He knows what he needs.

If your baby takes water, boil for 3 minutes a sufficient quantity for the day; keep it in a sterilized bottle. When you need some, pour it into another bottle, which you then warm like a bottle of milk.

Boil the water that your baby drinks through the first year anyway, and through the second year also if you aren't sure that the water from your faucet or well is absolutely pure.

If you are using well water, it is important to have it tested for bacteria and for nitrates before the baby arrives. (Nitrate salts in well water cause blueness of the lips and skin of babies.) Write your state health department.

193. Sugar water. If your baby won't take his water plain, you can try him on sugar water. You may particularly want him to take water if you are trying to get him off a night feeding or if he is taking little milk because of an illness or if the weather is very hot.

Add 1 level tablespoonful of granulated sugar or corn syrup to a pint of water before boiling it for 3 minutes.

194. You don't have to boil everything. You sterilize the formula and nursing equipment because germs multiply in milk. You boil drinking water because there is a chance that harmful germs will get into the reservoir or well, or into your pipes through faulty plumbing. Sometimes mothers get so scared by the care that they take in preparing the formula and drinking water that they think they have to sterilize everything that goes into the baby's mouth. You don't have to be so fussy with all the other things that your baby will eat and drink. You don't have to boil dishes and cups and feeding spoons, because germs don't get a chance to grow on clean, dry utensils. It's sensible to wash the outside of the baby's orange, since it may have been recently handled by someone with a cold. There's no need to sterilize the knife you cut it with. Germs won't multiply in orange juice that a baby is going to drink 10 minutes after it is squeezed.

You can wash with soap the teething rings, pacifiers, and toys that a baby puts in his mouth, when you first buy them. But there is no need to keep on washing them afterward, unless they fall on the floor, because the only germs on them will be the baby's own germs that he's used to.

Changes in Diet and Schedule

The doctor who is taking care of your baby and knows his digestion is, of course, the one to advise you about these changes. The specific directions in this chapter are for parents who are unable to consult a doctor regularly.

ADDING SOLID FOODS

195. There's no set age when it's important to start solid food. Fifty years ago it was begun when a baby was a year old. As the years have passed, doctors have experimented with giving it earlier and earlier, and found that babies took it and prospered. There are two definite advantages in starting in the first half year. Babies take to the idea more easily than when they are older and more opinionated. And a variety of solid foods adds to the diet substances that are scanty in milk, particularly iron.

Nowadays doctors customarily recommend the first solid food sometime between 1 and 4 months. There is no great advantage in extreme earliness. A baby usually gets all the calories he needs from milk for the first 2 or 3 months. His immature digestive system doesn't make much use of starch at first; much of it comes out in the bowel movement.

When there is a family history of allergy, the doctor may wait longer to introduce other foods than milk, because the older a baby is when he receives a new food the less apt he is to develop an allergy to it.

The baby's hunger and digestive system may both influence the age at which the doctor suggests starting solids. A baby of 6 weeks who is not getting quite enough breast milk to satisfy him might well be started early on his solid food to avoid a supplementary formula. On the other hand, if a baby has been on the edge of looseness all the time he was on formula alone, the doctor may prefer to wait longer than usual before introducing solids, for fear of upsetting the digestion further. A big factor in giving solids earlier has been the eagerness of mothers who don't want their baby to be one day later than the baby up the street. They put strong pressure on doctors.

196. Solids before or after the milk? Most babies who are not used to solids expect their milk and want their milk first when it's feeding time. They become indignant if offered a spoonful of something solid instead. So start with the formula or the breast feeding. A month or two later, when a baby has learned that solid foods can ward off starvation just as well as milk, you can experiment with moving his solids up to the middle or the beginning of the meal. Eventually almost all babies are happy to take all their solid food first and then top it off with the beverage, the way so many adults do. Shortcuts are mentioned in Section 762.

197. What kind of spoon? A teaspoon is pretty wide for a baby's mouth, and most spoons have a bowl so deep that the baby can't scoop all the contents out. A small coffee spoon (*demi-tasse* spoon) is better, preferably one with a shallow bowl. Some mothers like to use a flat butter-spreader or wooden tongue blades—the kind that doctors use—which can be bought in bulk at the drugstore.

198. Cereal. The exact order in which solids are introduced is not important. Cereal is commonly given first. The only disadvantage is that its taste doesn't have great appeal for many babies. Different babies prefer different ones. There is some advantage in getting a baby used to variety.

199. Give him time to learn to like it. A doctor usually recommends starting with a teaspoonful or less and working up gradually to 2 or 3 tablespoonfuls if the baby wants it. This gradualness is to make sure the baby learns to like it and won't be upset. Just give him a taste for several days, until he shows signs of enjoying it. There's no rush.

A baby taking his first teaspoonful of solid food is quite funny and a little pathetic. He looks puzzled and disgusted. He wrinkles up his nose and forehead. You can't blame him. After all, the taste is new, the consistency is new, the spoon may be new. When he sucks on a nipple, the milk gets to the right place automatically. He's had no training in catching hold of a lump of food with the front of his tongue and moving it back into his throat. He just clacks his tongue against the roof of his mouth, and most of the cereal gets squeezed back out onto his chin. You will have to shave it off his chin and scoop it back into his mouth. Again a lot will be oozed out frontward, but don't be discouraged—some goes down inside, too. Be patient until he is more experienced.

It doesn't matter much at which meals you start the solids. Just don't give it at the feeding when he's least hungry. Cereal is usually given at the 10 A.M. and 6 P.M. feedings.

It's a good idea, if you are starting with cereal, to mix it (with formula or milk) thinner than the directions on the box say. Then it will seem more familiar to the baby and be easier for him to swallow. Also, babies and small children dislike food with a sticky consistency. If your baby is on a formula, you will use some of that to mix with the cereal. Some babies, however, miss any formula that is taken out of the bottle. In that case, or if the baby is on the breast, use pasteurized milk to make the cereal. You do not need to boil it, if your doctor agrees it is safe enough. If you have no fresh milk, use equal parts of evaporated milk and water to mix with the cereal. Of course, you can use plain boiled water, but this is less likely to appeal to the baby.

200. Which cereals? Most mothers give the precooked cereals made especially for babies, of which there is a wide variety. They are ready for eating as soon as mixed, which is a great convenience.

Sometimes, if the baby belongs to an allergic family, the doctor may prefer to start cereals at a later age than usual. Then he may start with rice, oats, corn, or barley, omitting wheat for several more months, because wheat causes allergy more often than other cereals. Also, he may delay the mixed cereals until the baby has shown he can take each of the separate kinds without trouble.

If you prefer to give the baby the same cooked cereals as the other members of the family, you can start with a white (refined) wheat cereal. This has small grains and a little roughage. By the time he is 5 or 6 months old, you can branch out into whole wheat, oatmeal, hominy, rice. A few babies get loose bowel movements from the roughage of whole wheat and oatmeal until they are older. Wheat, oat and barley cereals are the most valuable in terms of vitamins and proteins. Add salt to taste.

201. The baby who balks at cereal. You will know within a day or two after starting how your baby is going to take to cereal. Some babies seem to decide, "It's queer, but it's nourishment, so I'll eat it." As the days go by they grow more and more enthusiastic. They open their mouths for it like birds in the nest.

But there are other babies who decide on the second day of cereal that they don't like it at all. And on the third day they dislike it more than on the second. If your baby feels this way, be careful. Take it easy. If you try to push the cereal into him against his will, he will get more and more rebellious. You will get exasperated, too. In a week or two he may become so suspicious that he balks at the bottle, too. Offer the cereal just once a day. Give him only enough to cover the tip of the teaspoon until he is used to it. Add a pinch of sugar to see if he likes it better sweet. If in 2 or 3 days he is getting more set against it in spite of all these precautions, then stop altogether for a couple of weeks. If he still balks when you try again, report it to your doctor.

I think it's a great mistake to get into an argument with a baby about his first solid food. Sometimes a long-lasting feeding problem starts in this way. Even if it doesn't last, it's bad for mother and baby to go through an unnecessary fight.

If you have no doctor to advise you, I suggest that you start with fruit instead of cereal. Babies are puzzled by fruit, too, the first time they have it. But within a day or two practically all of them decide they love it. By the end of 2 weeks they are ready to assume that anything that comes on a spoon is wonderful. They you can add cereal, too.

202. Starting fruit. Fruit is often the second solid added to a baby's diet, a few weeks after he has become used to cereal. Some doctors prefer it as the first solid food because babies usually take to it so enthusiastically.

For the first 6 or 8 months of a baby's life, his fruit is stewed, except for raw ripe banana. Apples, peaches, pears, apricots, prunes, and pineapple are the usual fruits. You can buy the small jars of strained fruits for babies. You can use fresh or frozen fruit that you have stewed for the rest of the family, but strain or sieve it for the baby and add enough sugar to keep it from tasting sour. Or you can use canned fruit that you serve to other members of the family. Much canned fruit for adults is undesirably sweet, so pour off the excess syrup before straining it for the baby.

Fruit can be given at any one of the baby's feedings, even twice a day, depending on his appetite and digestion. The most popular time is 2 P.M. or 6 P.M.

Increase each fruit gradually as the baby learns to like it. Most babies are satisfied with half a baby jar. You can give the other half next day. Fruit can be kept 3 days if it is well refrigerated.

Banana should be **very** ripe. It should have black spots on the skin and be tan-colored inside. Mash it fine with a fork. Add a little formula or milk if it seems too thick for your baby.

Fruit has the general reputation of being laxative. But most individuals, including infants, don't show any definite looseness or cramps from any of the fruits mentioned above, except for prunes or prune juice. Prunes are mildly laxative for almost all babies, and this makes them a doubly valuable food for those who have a chronic tendency to constipation. For the baby who needs it and likes it that regularly, puréed prunes or prune juice can be given at one feeding and some other fruit at another feeding each day.

If your baby's bowels become loose too easily, you will probably omit prunes altogether and give other fruits only once a day.

In the second half of the first year, you can begin adding or substituting other raw fruits besides bananas: scraped apple, pear, avocado. (Berries and seedless grapes are usually postponed till the baby is 2 years of age.)

203. Vegetables. Strained boiled vegetables are commonly added to a baby's diet 2 to 4 weeks after he has gotten used to cereal or fruit or both.

The ones usually offered are string beans, peas, spinach, tomatoes, squash, carrots, beets, sweet potatoes, celery.

There are other vegetables—such as broccoli, cauliflower, cabbage, turnips, onions—which, as usually cooked, are so strong-tasting that most babies don't like them and most parents don't bother to try them. However, if your family likes some of them (and they can be made much less strong by boiling in two changes of water), there is no harm in straining some and offering it to your baby, too. Corn is not given because of the large husks on the kernels.

You can serve your baby fresh or frozen vegetables, boiled and strained, or the ones in cans already puréed for babies, or the ordinary canned vegetables that you serve the rest of the family, but strained.

Babies are more likely to be choosy about vegetables than about cereals or fruits. You will probably find that there are one or two vegetables that your baby doesn't like. Don't urge them, but try them again every month or so. There's no point fussing over a few foods when we have so many to choose from. Some babies are much more enthusiastic about vegetables if a little salt is added for flavoring, and there is no harm in this.

It's common for undigested vegetable to appear in the bowel movements when the baby is first taking it. This is not a bad sign so long as there is no looseness or mucus, but increase slowly until his digestion learns to handle it. If a vegetable causes looseness or much mucus, omit it for the time being and try a very small amount in another month.

Beets may show up red in the bowel movements or color the urine, which is nothing to worry about if you can remember that it is caused by beets and not blood.

Spinach causes chapping of the lips and around the anus in some babies. If it does, omit it for several months and try again.

Lunchtime—2 P.M. for a baby still on a roughly 4-hour schedule, noon for an older baby on 3 meals a day—is the conventional time for vegetables.

Work up to several tablespoonfuls as desired or half a baby jar. The rest of the jar, if refrigerated, can be given the next day. If you have no refrigerator, don't keep vegetables. Cooked vegetables spoil fairly rapidly.

204. Eggs. Egg yolk is important because it contains valuable iron. Babies begin to need more iron for their red blood cells around the middle of the first year, because with their rapid growth, they begin to outgrow the limited amount that was in their bodies at birth. (Milk contains practically no iron, and many other foods provide very little. However, a majority of the cereals prepared for babies contain good amounts of iron.)

Egg should be started with a little caution, because it is one of the foods that is most apt to cause allergy, especially in allergic families. The commonest form of allergy in babies is eczema, in which the skin, particularly around the face and ears, first becomes rough, red, scaly, and then may go on to oozing and crusting. It itches.

In order to lessen the chance of egg allergy, several precautions can be taken. The yolk only can be used until the baby is nearer to a year of age, since the iron is in the yolk and it's the white that usually causes the allergy. The yolk can be served hard-boiled, because thorough cooking of any food lessens the likelihood of its causing trouble. You can start by offering less than a quarter of a teaspoonful and increase gradually.

So you hard-boil an egg for 20 minutes, take off the white, and crumble the yolk. Some babies dislike the taste of plain hard-cooked egg yolk. You can try adding salt to give it some flavor, or mix it with the baby's cereal or vegetable. If this makes him balk at the cereal or vegetable, don't persist.

Egg yolk is most commonly started between 4 and 6 months of age, but some doctors prefer to wait until 7 or 8 months, especially in an allergic family.

If you have no doctor to advise you, start egg yolk at 4 months unless there is allergy in the family. Better wait till 9 months to offer soft-cooked or scrambled eggs, which contain the white, and then start very gradually, as if it were a new food.

Egg can be given at breakfast, lunch, or supper. When you add meat to the diet, serve the egg at breakfast or at supper.

205. Meats. Nutrition studies have shown that babies profit by meats during the first year, so many doctors recommend them as early as 2 to 6 months of age. Meats for babies are finely ground or "strained" or "scraped," so they can be swallowed easily before the baby has any teeth.

You can give your baby jars or cans of strained meats, such as beef, beef heart, liver, lamb, chicken, veal, pork; or you can prepare the meat yourself. The simplest way to cook beef or lamb chop for a baby is to scrape it, while still raw, with a dull knife or tablespoon. Put this soft pulp in a custard cup and set it in a pan of slowly boiling water. Cook until the color changes. If desired, milk or water can be added, before cooking, to make the meat more moist. Another method is to briefly broil a piece of beef (top round, for instance) or lamb chop, to sterilize the surface, and then, grasping it firmly, scrape it with a tablespoon. This scrapes out the soft red meat and leaves the tough white fibers behind. A piece of liver can be plunged into boiling water, cooked until the color changes, and then pressed through a sieve. Pork should be well cooked. Salt to taste.

After your baby has become used to strained or scraped meat, you can give him beef that you have briefly broiled and put through a fine grinder. It is preferable not to give meat ground by the butcher, because the meat surfaces that have been handled and those that have come in contact with the grinder are mixed through the rest of the meat. Also, it may contain a lot of fat and tough fiber.

By the time the baby is used to ground beef, he can also have ground or fine-minced chicken, lamb, liver, bacon, veal, and pork. Pork should always be cooked through.

206. Meat soups. There are a variety of meat soups in jars for babies. They usually consist of small amounts of a meat and a vegetable with a larger amount of a cereal such as rice or barley. In adding them to a meal with other foods, it is sensible to consider them as primarily a starch. Don't count on them regularly as a source of meat.

When there is a tendency to allergy, such mixtures may be confusing unless the baby has already taken each of the foods included in the mixture without reaction.

Meat soups are appropriate for occasional use any time after the baby has begun to have plain meats.

207. The meals at six months (if you cannot consult a doctor). By the time your baby is 6 months old, he will probably be eating cereal, egg yolk, and a variety of fruits, vegetables, and meats. A common arrangement for a moderately hungry baby is cereal and egg yolk for breakfast, vegetable and meat for lunch, cereal and fruit for supper. But there are no hard and fast rules. It all depends on your convenience and your baby's appetite. For instance, if he's not a very hungry baby, you could give fruit and egg at breakfast, vegetable and meat at lunch, cereal alone at supper. If he tends to be constipated, you can give him prunes every night along with his cereal, and another fruit at his breakfast or lunch.

208. Simple puddings if convenient. Puddings aren't so important for most babies as other foods. They don't add any new element to the diet; they take time to prepare. Fruit makes, in some respects, a more valuable dessert. However, if you are making puddings for your family anyway, you can begin giving them to the baby for lunch or supper any time after 6 months.

Puddings may be important in special cases. If when your baby is about a year old, he loses most of his desire for milk as a drink, you can get several ounces into him each day in pudding form. Puddings may also be helpful for the rare baby who is "fed up" with each food after a few spoonfuls. He may like pudding as an extra dessert, in addition to fruit. Puddings are also helpful when a baby turns against cereal for supper. Then supper can be fruit and pudding, or vegetable and pudding.

The more valuable and common puddings are those made mainly of milk (junket), milk and egg (boiled and baked custard), milk and starch (tapioca, rice, cornstarch). The gelatin in gelatin desserts is relatively unimportant, but there is value in the fruit that is added to it.

Some puddings come in jars for babies. Many of the packaged cornstarch puddings that come in various flavors and are meant for family use are sweetened excessively, and it is better to avoid these.

So if your child likes fruit for dessert and digests it well, is drinking plenty of milk and is well nourished, there is no reason for you to prepare puddings regularly unless you want to. Even if you do serve puddings, it is desirable that half the baby's desserts be raw or stewed fruit.

209. Adding potato if your baby likes it and needs it. Other starch. Potatoes are good as a source of starch at lunch for a child who is hungry or in place of cereal at supper. They also contain appreciable amounts of iron, other salts, and vitamin C, so that they have food values aside from the starch.

Potato, baked or boiled, can be introduced into the diet any time in the last half of the first year. A logical time is when the baby goes onto a 3-meals-a-day schedule. When his lunch is 5 hours away from his supper, the starch, which a potato is mostly made of, supplies lots of energy (calories) to last through the afternoon.

A word of caution about potato. Babies are more apt to gag and rebel against it than any other food. I don't know whether this is because it is grainy or because it is sticky. So mash it very smooth at first, make it thin by mixing with plenty of milk, and offer it in very small amounts until he gets used to it. Flavor it with salt. Don't urge it on him if he continues to gag; forget about it, at least for a month, and then try again.

If your baby is pretty fat and seems content with a lunch of green vegetable, meat, milk, and perhaps fruit, leave out potato. It doesn't add anything new to his diet.

You can occasionally substitute macaroni, spaghetti, noodles, or rice for potato. Strain or mash them fine at first.

210. Adding fish. By 10 or 12 months, you can also add the white, nonoily fish, such as flounder, haddock, and halibut, if the child likes them. You can poach them in pieces in slowly boiling water. Or you can place small pieces in a custard cup, cover with milk, and then place the cup in a pan of boiling water until the fish is cooked through. Or you can serve the baby the fish you have boiled, baked, or broiled for the rest of the family. In any case, crumble the flakes in your fingers to be sure there are no bones.

Substitute fish for meat at lunchtime. Some babies love it, and then it's a great help. But a lot of babies turn thumbs down. Don't try to force it.

The oily fish, like mackerel, are liable to be harder to digest and less appealing.

211. Finger foods. By the time a baby is 6 or 7 months old, he wants to and can pick foods up in his hand and suck and munch on them. This is good training for him as preparation for spoon-feeding himself at about a year. If a baby is never allowed to feed himself with his fingers, he's less likely to have the ambition to try the spoon.

The traditional first finger food is a crust of stale bread or toast or zwieback at 6 or 7 months. The baby sucks at it and chews at it with his bare gums (they may be tingling with teething, and in that case he'll enjoy the biting). As it softens gradually with his saliva, some of it rubs or dissolves off into his mouth, enough to make him feel he's getting somewhere. Most of it goes on his hands, face, hair, and the furniture.

By 9 months you are mashing his food instead of straining it, and you can leave unmashed some of the pieces of string beans and carrots. He will want to pick up these pieces, along with particles of meat, and put them in his mouth. He can also chew on a slice of raw apple or pear.

The average baby gets his first tooth at about 7 months, and at a year may have 4 to 6 sharp biting teeth. But he probably won't get his first molars for grinding until sometime around a year and a quarter. Therefore you can't expect him to do much efficient grinding of food till then.

212. Lumpy foods by a year. Somewhere between 9 and 12 months, you want to get your baby used to lumpy or chopped foods. If he goes much beyond a year eating nothing but puréed things, it gets harder and harder to make the change. People have the idea that a baby can't handle lumps until he gets a fair set of teeth. This isn't true. He can mush up lumps of cooked vegetables or fruit and pieces of zwieback with his gums and tongue.

Some babies seem to be born more squeamish about lumps than others. But most babies and older children who gag easily on particles of food have become that way either because the mother tried to make the change to chopped foods too abruptly or too late, or because she had been forcing food when the child didn't want it.

There are two important points in shifting to chopped foods. Make the change a gradual one. When you first serve chopped vegetables, mash them up pretty fine with a fork. Don't put too much in the baby's mouth at a time. When he's used to this consistency, gradually mash less and less. The other way a baby gets used to lumps is by being allowed to pick up a cube of cooked carrot, for instance, in his fingers and put it in his mouth himself. What he can't stand is to have a whole spoonful of lumps dumped into his mouth when he's not used to it.

So start the change at 9 months. You can serve the baby the boiled vegetables and stewed fruits that you cook for the rest of the family or you can buy the chopped (junior) foods in jars prepared for babies.

You don't have to make all his foods lumpy. It is necessary only that he get used to eating some lumps each day.

Meats should generally continue to be served ground or minced fine. Most small children dislike chunks of meat that don't chew up easily. They often chew on such a piece for a long time without getting anywhere. They don't dare try to swallow a too big piece, as adults do when they are desperate. This may lead to gagging or at least to a loss of appetite for this particular kind of meat.

Gagging is also discussed in Section 595.

213. Diet by the end of the first year. In case you are mixed up by all the things that have been added to the diet, here is a rough list of what babies are apt to be eating by the end of the year:

Breakfast: cereal (preferably brown), egg (whole, soft), toast, milk
Lunch: vegetable (green or yellow, in lumps), potato (or macaroni, etc.), meat or fish, fruit, milk
Supper: cereal, fruit, milk

Fruit juice (including orange juice) is given daily between meals or at breakfast. Zwieback, toast, bread (preferably whole-grain), can be given at meals or between, with a little butter or margarine. A simple pudding can be substituted for one of the fruit desserts. The fruit is stewed except for banana, scraped apple, pear, avocado.

In other words, a pretty grown-up diet.

CHANGES IN SCHEDULE AND BOTTLE

214. When to omit the 10 P.M. feeding. When you give up the 10 or 11 P.M. feeding should depend most on when the baby is ready. There are two things to consider.

The first is whether he is ready to sleep through the night. You can't be sure that he's ready just because he always has to be waked up at 10 or 11. If you don't wake him, he may wake himself around midnight. Better wait until you have had to wake him for several weeks. Then see if he sleeps through. If he wakes hungry later in the night, feed him and go back to the evening feeding for a few more weeks.

Of course, if a baby is very small or gaining slowly or having trouble with his digestion, it may be better to keep the evening feeding going a while longer, even if he is willing to sleep through without it.

Another point is whether he is sucking his thumb a lot. If he is, it may mean that he is not getting as much sucking as he'd like from breast or bottle. If you cut out a feeding at this time, you reduce his sucking time further still. However, if he continues to be a thumb-sucker in spite of all your efforts, you don't have to go on **forever** giving him the evening feeding. For one thing, as he gets older he may refuse to wake up, no matter how hard you try, or fall asleep again as soon as he has taken a couple of ounces. I'd stop the feeding by this time anyway, whether he is sucking his thumb or not.

In a general way, then, let your baby give up his 10 P.M. feeding when he shows that he can sleep through without it and get enough sucking satisfaction without it. This will probably be between the ages of 3 and 6 months. Wait till 5 or 6 months if he is sucking his thumb much and is willing to take the evening feeding.

Most babies get themselves off the evening feeding as soon as they can. But an occasional one will continue it indefinitely, especially if the mother rushes in as soon as he first murmurs. If your baby is still waking for this feeding at 7 or 8 months, I'd try to get him over the habit. At this age he certainly doesn't need nourishment at night if he is eating well in the daytime and gaining satisfactorily. Let him fuss for 20 or 30 minutes (without going to him at all) and see if he won't go back to sleep.

When you omit the evening bottle, distribute the formula into the other 4 bottles. This probably makes about 7½ ounces in each bottle. But if he wants only his usual 5 or 6 ounces, let it go at that without any urging. Twenty-four ounces a day is plenty if he's satisfied.

215. If your baby loses his appetite between three and nine months. A baby may take solids eagerly for the first couple of months and then rather suddenly lose a lot of his appetite. One reason may be that at this age period he is meant to slow down in his weight-gaining. In his first 3 months he has probably gained close to 2 pounds a month. By 6 months he is apt to be down to a pound a month. Otherwise he would become too fat. Also, he may be bothered by teething. One baby wants to leave out a lot of his solid food; another turns against his milk.

If your baby loses a lot of his appetite, **don't** urge him. There are two things you can do. The first is to gradually remove the sugar from his formula (Section 216). The sugar was there in the early months principally to give him enough calories while he was on a diluted formula. He doesn't really need these sugar calories when he is eating a good helping of solid food 3 times a day. In fact, the very sweetness of the formula may be killing his appetite for unsweetened foods.

The other thing you can do is to go from the approximately 4-hour schedule during the daytime (6 A.M., 10 A.M., 2 P.M., 6 P.M.) to a 3-

meals-a-day schedule (approximately 7 A.M., 12 noon, 5 P.M.), whether or not he is still on an evening feeding (Section 217).

If a baby's appetite still doesn't revive with these two measures, it's important to get him to the doctor, to be sure that he's otherwise healthy.

216. When to remove the sugar from the formula. You want to remove the sugar from the formula gradually, when your baby is somewhere between 4 and 9 months of age. The time depends on his appetite. If he goes through a phase of poor appetite at the age of 4, 5, or 6 months, that is a good time to take out the sugar. If, on the other hand, he is the kind of baby who never seems to get enough to eat and is always hungry ahead of mealtime, then leave the sugar in until he is 7 or 8 months old.

Remove the sugar gradually, so that he doesn't notice any sudden change in taste. You can remove about a quarter of a tablespoonful a day from the formula until there is none left.

217. When to put the baby on three meals a day. This depends on when your baby is ready for it. It may be anywhere between the ages of 4 and 10 months. A 3-meal schedule means about 5 hours between meals. If your baby is starved at the end of 4 hours and crying with hunger, he isn't ready for a 3-meal schedule, no matter how old he is. If he has to have his first feeding by 6 A.M., there's usually not much use talking about 3 meals a day.

On the other hand, your baby may show clearly at a certain stage that he is ready for 3 meals. A mother will say, "He only eats well at every other meal. If he finishes his 6 A.M. bottle, he'll eat poorly at 10, well at 2, and poorly at 6 P.M." Babies who are acting like this need to be changed to a 3-meals-a-day schedule so that they will be hungry at mealtime. Otherwise they are apt to become feeding problems.

If a baby is thumb-sucking a lot and is still ready to eat every 4 hours, this is a reason for leaving in the fourth feeding for a while longer.

Once in a while there is a baby who is no longer ready to eat every 4 hours during the daytime, but who still wakes up like clockwork for his 10 P.M. bottle. There's no problem here. You try to adjust to the baby's needs, as usual, putting him on 3 meals during the day and continuing to give the 10 P.M. feeding until he is ready to sleep through.

There's another problem that turns up occasionally. A baby seems to have outgrown the 4-hour schedule. He's not hungry for some of his meals. And yet he's still waking around 6 A.M. yelling with hunger. How do you put him on 3 meals a day and still feed him at 6 A.M.? The easiest way is to give him his milk from breast or bottle as soon as he demands it in the morning, and give him his cereal, or his cereal and fruit, a little later, as soon as it is convenient (for instance, between 7 and 8). His next meal will be lunch, around noon. Of course, the baby who is hungry early is no problem if the whole family breakfasts around 6 A.M. Some babies who wake early are quite satisfied with a bottle of orange juice for the time being. Then they can have their milk along with the rest of their breakfast, later.

Another factor is the mother's convenience. Suppose she has her hands full preparing meals for her older children, and her baby is **able** to go more than 4 hours between meals, even though he is still willing to eat that often. This mother naturally wants to get the baby onto the same 3 meals as the older children now, and there is no reason why she shouldn't, especially if he isn't thumb-sucking much. There are other mothers, especially with the first baby, who find the 4-hour schedule fits their own convenience better than 3 meals a day. There is no reason why these babies shouldn't stay on the 4-hour schedule longer than average as long as they remain hungry for their meals that often. In other words, there is no rule about making such a change in a baby's routine. It's just a matter of reasonableness and common sense. You see what the baby is ready for and fit it in with your convenience.

The hours at which a baby is fed when he goes onto 3 meals a day depend largely on the family's habit, somewhat on the baby's hunger. Breakfast is usually between 7 and 8, but can be later if he's willing. He gets cereal and fruit (one **or** the other if he has a small appetite), his milk, and probably his egg. In the middle of the morning, he probably needs something to help him last through until lunch. Orange juice, about 2 ounces, is best. If he doesn't drink orange juice, you could give him pineapple juice, prune juice, or tomato juice. If he gets **very** hungry before meals, add a piece of zwieback or dry bread crust or plain cracker.

Lunch comes in the neighborhood of 12 o'clock. Some babies must have it by 11:30. It probably consists of a green or yellow vegetable, meat, potato, and milk. Potato is usually added at the time a baby goes on 3 meals a day, to give him enough extra energy to last through the afternoon. You don't bother with it if your baby has a small appetite or is getting fat. Fruit or pudding may be given at lunch, if this is the most convenient time of day or if your baby is hard to fill up. A baby should get fruit once or twice a day, but there is no harm in 3 times a day if it agrees with his digestion.

In the middle of the afternoon, if he needs a snack, another 2 ounces of orange juice or another fruit juice. Occasionally a mother says that it suits her baby best, for the first month or two after he gets on a regular breakfast-lunch-supper schedule, to give him an extra breast or bottle feeding at about 3 P.M. Of course, this still means 4 milk feedings a day, though such a baby may want only half a bottle at 3 P.M. and 6 P.M. This extra bottle or half bottle in the middle of the afternoon is called for only if the mother wants his supper to be late, around 6, and if the baby has a very large appetite. Ordinarily, milk is not given between meals, because it stays in the stomach for 3 or 4 hours and takes away the appetite for the next meal.

Supper is usually given sometime between 5 and 6 P.M. when a baby goes on 3 meals a day. Most babies can't last beyond 5 if lunch is at 12, and some need to be fed even earlier. Supper is usually cereal, fruit, and milk.

When a baby is taking milk only 3 times a day, he is probably getting a smaller total for the day than formerly, because he probably does not want more than his usual 6 to 8 ounces a meal. Don't worry about this. Don't try to tuck a few extra ounces into him at odd hours to keep up to the old 30-ounce total. Most babies are quite safe if they are taking as much as 24 ounces a day. On the other hand, if your baby is the unusual one who wants as much as 10 ounces a meal, give it to him.

218. When can you stop sterilizing the formula and bottles (if you cannot consult a doctor)? The answer to this question depends on so many different things that you ought to take it up with your doctor even if you can consult him only on rare occasions. But for those who can't, I'll mention some of the factors.

There are four reasons why you have to sterilize the formula in bottles when you are making a formula that contains water and that will last for a day. (1) There may be dangerous germs in the water (especially if the supply is unreliable). (2) Germs may be introduced in preparing the formula. (3) Germs multiply rapidly in milk over a period of hours, especially if it is not well refrigerated. (4) Babies develop intestinal infections easily. (This susceptibility is not outgrown until the second year, and then only gradually.)

So, as long as you are making a 24-hour formula that contains water, you have to sterilize the formula and bottles.

219. The answer in the case of straight pasteurized milk. If a baby of 9 months, for instance, has graduated to straight pasteurized milk in the bottle (or cup), the doctor **may** say it is safe to stop sterilizing milk and bottles **if** the mother fills each clean bottle **just before giving it.** The few germs left in such a bottle have no chance to multiply in the few minutes it takes the baby to drink it. The pasteurized milk should have no dangerous germs in it, and no water has been added. However, a doctor may be slower to advise giving unboiled pasteurized milk if a baby is particularly susceptible to diarrhea, if the weather is hot, or if there isn't a good refrigerator in which to keep the quart container from the dairy. Raw (unpasteurized) milk should be boiled throughout childhood.

220. The answer in the case of evaporated milk. The situation is different for a baby on an evaporated-milk mixture. The milk is sterile as it comes from the freshly opened can. If the opened can is kept in the refrigerator, it is safe for 24 hours anyway. It is the water that is the more doubtful factor. Some tap water and well water is not safe enough for the doctor to recommend using it unboiled until the baby is a year or more old; and there is always at least a slight risk of contamination of **any** water supply under special circumstances. So the water should be sterilized before or after being mixed with evaporated milk until the doctor says it is safe to stop. However, this is no problem. A day's supply of water can be boiled in 5 minutes and kept in its container for use throughout the day. Then at each feeding the mother can combine equal parts of evaporated milk and boiled water to give to the baby, either by cup or by bottle. As explained in the previous paragraph, the cup or bottle needs only to be washed clean with soap and water, because the milk will be in it only a few minutes. (Of course, you may feel that it's just as easy to continue to boil all together the formula and bottles needed for 24 hours.)

221. When do you change from evaporated to pasteurized milk? The really sensible answer would be "Never." Evaporated milk is sterile, cheaper, easier to store, easier to digest, less likely to cause allergy. It's only slightly less convenient to serve. When the baby is off formula, you merely mix equal parts of evaporated milk and boiled water in the cup or bottle just before feeding. When your doctor says you no longer need to boil the baby's water, you can mix equal parts of evaporated milk and tap water in the cup or bottle.

With all the advantages of evaporated milk, why are most babies changed to pasteurized milk? It's rarely at the insistence of the doctor. It's usually the strong wish of the mother. I think there are two reasons for this. Proud mothers delight in seeing their babies make advances, and for some reason the change from evaporated to pasteurized milk seems as important to them as learning to walk or becoming toilet-trained or entering school. Also, some mothers who don't like the taste of evaporated milk seem to assume that the baby will turn against it, too, just as soon as he is old enough to have any discrimination. They are sure this moment has come the first time he takes less than his usual amount of formula. I don't think there is any evidence that babies prefer pasteurized milk, but I've rarely been able to convince a mother of this. Anyway, there's no medical reason why a baby needs to change, so keep him on evaporated milk as long as you are willing to.

Weaning from Bottle to Cup

READINESS FOR WEANING

222. Starting sips of milk from the cup at five months. It's a good idea to begin offering your baby a sip of milk from the cup each day by the time he's 5 months old. You aren't going to try to wean him to the cup right away. You only want to accustom him, at an age when he's not too opinionated, to the idea that milk comes in cups, too. If you wait till he's 9 or 10 months old to start, he is likely to bat the cup away indignantly, or at least pretend that he doesn't know what it is for.

Pour half an ounce of the formula into a small cup or glass once a day. He won't want more than one sip at a time, and won't get much at first, but he'll probably think it is fun. If he is a breast-fed baby, pour half an ounce of pasteurized milk (from a well-shaken up bottle) into a cup. It isn't usually necessary to boil this if it is pasteurized, but your doctor is the one to advise you on this point.

223. Orange juice doesn't count toward weaning. You may already have begun to give your baby orange juice from a cup or glass. If not, you can start that now, too. But the thing to remember is that a baby who is getting used to orange juice from a cup isn't getting used to the idea that milk can also come that way.

224. Helping a baby to like the cup. When he's 6 months old and wants to grab everything and put it in his mouth, give him a small, narrow, empty glass or cup that he can hold easily by himself and pretend to drink from. When he does it fairly well, put a few drops of milk in the cup. Increase the amount as he gains in skill. If he takes to the idea of drinking by himself between 6 and 8 months, he is much less likely to turn against the cup at 9 or 10 months. If he stops drinking for a few days, resist the temptation to pick up the cup and offer it to him, as this might only make him more balky. Remember in the early months of cup drinking that he'll probably want only one swallow at a time. Many babies don't learn to take several gulps in succession until they are 1 to 1½ years old.

The child between 1 and 2 who is suspicious of the old cup he has always been offered may be delighted with a new cup or glass of a different shape or color. Changing to cold milk sometimes changes his mind. If the doctor thinks it's advisable, a little flavoring or coloring in the milk may help. Some mothers have found that adding a little cereal to the cup of milk makes it different enough to be acceptable for drinking. The cereal can gradually be removed a few weeks later.

225. Some are ready for weaning early, others not. The baby who has been satisfied with a moderate amount of sucking at breast or bottle may show his readiness to be weaned to the cup as early as 7 or 8 months of age. His mother says, "He's getting bored with the bottle. He often leaves a lot and stops to play with the nipple with his fingers. [On the breast he may be nursing for shorter and shorter periods.] When I offer him milk from the glass, he takes it eagerly." The baby who acts this way is showing, I think, that he's ready for gradual weaning.

At the opposite extreme is the baby with a great love of sucking. (He's more apt to be a thumb-sucker.) At 9 or 10 months his mother says of him, "Oh, Doctor, how he loves his bottle! He watches it all the time he's taking his solid food. When it's time, he snatches it eagerly. He strokes the bottle lovingly and murmurs to it all the time he's taking it. He always finishes it to the last drop. He's very suspicious of milk in the cup. Sometimes he won't touch it at all; other times he takes a sip or two and then pushes it away impatiently."

WEAN HIM GRADUALLY

226. Take it easy and follow his lead. Let's say you have been giving your baby a sip of milk a day from the cup from the age of 5 months. When he's 8 or 9 months old, you ask yourself, "How's he doing?" If he's becoming a little bored with his bottle and likes milk from the cup, gradually increase the amount in the cup. Give him the cup at every meal. This leaves less and less in the bottle. Then leave out the bottle that he takes least interest in, probably the lunch or breakfast one. In a couple of weeks, give up the second bottle if he's progressing, and then the third. Most babies love their supper bottle most and are slowest to give it up. Others feel that way about the breakfast bottle.

Willingness to be weaned doesn't always increase steadily. Misery from teething or a cold often makes a baby want more of the bottle for the time being. Follow his needs. The trend that made him start to give up the bottle before will set in again when he feels better.

227. The reluctant weaner. But suppose yours is another kind of baby. He's had a sip of milk daily, from 5 months. At 9 months, instead of being willing to take more, he's turning against it. Sometimes he's willing to take one sip from the cup and then pushes it away impatiently. A cagey baby pretends he doesn't know what it's for. If his mother holds the cup, he lets the milk run out at the sides of his mouth, smiling innocently. Or he may refuse to let the cup near his lips. The baby who is against the cup at 9 or 10 months is apt to be devoted to his bottle. He's nowhere near ready to give it up yet. Let him go on with it. Put an ounce of milk in a small glass that he can handle and just set it on his tray every day or so, hoping that he'll drink it. If one sip is all he takes, don't even try to give him two. Act as if it doesn't make any difference to you.

He may relent a little at 12 months, but it is more likely that he'll remain suspicious till 15 months or even later. If you take it seriously, you'll get exasperated, which won't get you or the baby anywhere. Try to relax; forget when the neighbor's baby was weaned. Think how you'd feel if a big bossy giant who had you in his power and who didn't understand your language kept trying to take your coffee away and make you drink warm water out of a pitcher. If you get into a real struggle, he will probably cling to his bottle much longer than he would have otherwise, and possibly refuse milk in a glass for months or even years. Sometimes a battle over weaning starts a feeding problem, and this may bring other behavior problems in its wake.

When a suspicious baby does start to take a little milk from the cup, you must still be patient, because it will probably take several more months before he is ready to give up the bottle altogether. This applies particularly to the supper or bedtime bottle. That's the time of day when most babies and children want their old-fashioned comforts. Many late weaners insist on a bedtime bottle till about 2 years of age, and I don't think there is any harm in this.

228. Sometimes it's the mother who delays weaning. So far, I have been cautioning you against forced weaning, against taking away the bottle that the baby is still eager to have, against pushing at him a cup that only makes him angry. Now I had better turn around and say that sometimes a baby is kept on the bottle longer than he needs to be because his mother worries about the fact that he isn't taking as much from the cup as he used to take from the bottle. Let's say that at 9 months he's drinking about 6 ounces from the cup at breakfast, 6 ounces at lunch, and about 4 ounces at supper, and that he's not especially eager for the bottle but if his mother gives it to him at the end of the meal he is willing to take a few ounces more that way. I think that a baby over 8 months who is taking as much as 16 ounces a day from the cup, and not acting as if he misses the bottle, might better be off the bottle altogether. If he is kept on it now, he may become **less** willing to give it up at that suspicious age between 10 and 15 months.

Another problem may develop for the mother who uses the bottle as a pacifier during the second year. Whenever her child has a crying spell in the daytime or wakes at night, she kind-heartedly makes another bottle for him. The child may get as many as 8 bottles in the 24 hours—a total of 2 quarts of milk. This naturally takes away most of his appetite for meals, and he is then likely to develop a severe anemia. (There's practically no iron in milk.)

It's important from a nutritional point of view that a child not take more than a quart of milk a day. And from the point of view of emotional development, he should feel that he is being encouraged by his mother to grow out of babyhood. One of the most important ways she achieves this is by helping him to give up his bottles, one by one, as soon as he feels able to do so.

Daily Care

THE BATH

229. Before any feeding. It's usually most convenient in the early months to give the bath before the 10 A.M. feeding, but before any feeding is all right (not after a feeding, because you want him to go to sleep then). The father may even enjoy bathing him before the 6 P.M. or 10 P.M. feeding. By the time your baby is on 3 meals a day, you may want to change to before lunch or before supper. As the child gets older still and stays up for a while after supper, it may work out better to give the bath after supper, especially if he needs his supper early. If you give him his orange juice before the bath, it keeps him from getting too hungry. Bathe him in a reasonably warm room—the kitchen, if necessary.

230. A sponge bath if you prefer. Though it's the custom to give a complete tub or sponge bath every day, it certainly isn't necessary more than once or twice a week in cool weather, so long as the baby is kept clean in the diaper area and around the mouth. On the days when you don't give him a full bath, give a sponge bath in the diaper area. The tub bath is apt to be frightening at first to the inexperienced mother—the baby seems so helpless, limp, and slippery, especially after he has been soaped. A baby may feel uneasy in the tub at first, because he can't be well supported there. You can give him a sponge bath for a few weeks until you and he feel more secure, or even for months—until he can sit up—if you prefer. It is often advised that a tub bath not be given until the navel is healed.

You can give a sponge bath on a table or in your lap. You'll want a piece of waterproof material under the baby. If you are using a hard surface like a table, there should be some padding over it (large pillow or folded blanket or quilt) so that the baby won't roll too easily. (Rolling frightens young babies.) Wash the face and scalp with a washcloth and clear warm water. (The scalp can be soaped once or twice a week.) Lightly soap the rest of the body with the washcloth or your hand. Then wipe the soap off by going over him at least twice with the rinsed washcloth, paying attention to creases.

231. The tub bath. Before starting the bath, be sure you have everything you need close at hand. If you forget the towel, you'll have to go after it holding a dripping baby in your arms.

Take off your wrist watch.

An apron keeps your clothes drier.

Have at hand:

> soap (any mild toilet soap)
> washcloth
> towel
> absorbent cotton for nose and ears if necessary
> oil or powder if you use either
> shirt, diaper, pins, nightie

The bath can be given in a washbowl, dishpan, kitchen sink, or enamelware tub. The regular bathtub is hard on a mother's back and legs. Some mothers prefer a baby's fabric tub on high legs if there is room for it. For your own comfort, you can put a dishpan or enamelware tub on a table at which you sit or on something higher like a dresser, at which you stand. You can sit on a stool at the kitchen sink. The water should be about body temperature (90–100°). A bath thermometer is a comfort to the inexperienced mother but is not necessary. Test the temperature with your elbow or wrist. It should feel comfortably warm. Use only a small amount of water at first until you get the knack of holding the baby securely. A metal tub is less slippery if you line it with a diaper each time. Hold the baby so that his head is supported on your wrist, and the fingers of that hand hold him securely in the armpit. Wash his face first, with a soft washcloth, without soap, then his scalp. His scalp needs to be soaped only once or twice a week. Wipe the soapsuds off his scalp with a damp washcloth, going over it twice. If the washcloth is too wet, the soapy water may get into his eyes and sting. (There are shampoos that do not sting the eyes.) Then soap the rest of the body, arms, and legs, using the washcloth or your hand. (It's easier to soap your hand than a washcloth when your other hand is occupied.)

Your hand under his arm, your wrist supporting his head.

If you feel nervous at first for fear you'll drop the baby in the water, you can soap him while he is on your lap or on a table. Then rinse him off in the tub, holding him securely with both hands.

Use a soft bath towel for drying him, and blot rather than rub. If you begin giving the tub bath before the navel is completely healed, dry it thoroughly after the bath with sterile cotton. Most babies, after a few weeks' experience, have a wonderful time in the bath, so don't rush it. Enjoy it with him.

232. Ears, eyes, nose, mouth, nails. You need to wash only the outer ear and the entrance to the canal, not inside. Wax is formed in the canal to protect and clean it. Tiny, invisible hairs keep slowly moving the wax, and any dirt that it has collected, toward the outside.

The eyes are bathed constantly by the steady flow of the tears (not just when the baby is crying). This is why it is unnecessary to put any drops in the eyes while they are healthy.

The mouth ordinarily needs no extra care.

The nails can be easily cut while the baby sleeps. Clippers may be easier than nail scissors.

The nose has a beautiful system for keeping itself clear. Tiny, invisible hairs in the cells lining the nose keep moving the mucus and dust down toward the front of the nose, where it collects on the large hairs near the opening. This tickles the nose and makes the baby sneeze or rub the collection out. When you are drying the baby after the bath, you can first moisten and then gently wipe out the ball of dried mucus with the corner of the washcloth, or with a piece of absorbent cotton that has been twisted into a point and then wet, or, if necessary, with cotton carefully wrapped around the end of a toothpick or match stick so that the wood does not protrude. Don't fuss at this too long if it makes him angry.

233. Dried mucus obstructing the nose. Sometimes, especially when the house is heated, enough dried mucus collects in the nose of a small infant to partially obstruct his breathing. Then each time he breathes in, the lower edges of his chest are pulled inward, or "retracted." An older child or adult would breathe through his mouth, but most babies can't leave their mouths open. If your baby's nose becomes obstructed at any time of day, you can first moisten and then remove the mucus as in the previous paragraph.

234. Oil or powder? It's fun to apply oil or powder to a baby after his bath, and the baby likes it, too, but neither is really necessary in most cases. (If it were, Nature would provide it.) Powder is helpful if the baby's skin chafes easily. It should be dusted on your hand first—away from the baby, so that he won't breathe a cloud of powder—and then rubbed gently on his skin. It should be applied thinly, so that it won't form lumps. Any baby powder or plain talcum is satisfactory. (Don't use zinc stearate powder; it's irritating to the lungs.) When a baby has a dry skin, you can use mineral oil (liquid petrolatum) or any of the commercial baby skin oils (these are medicated, scented mineral oil).

THE NAVEL

235. The healing of the navel. When the baby is still in the mother's womb, he is nourished through the blood vessels of the umbilical cord. Just after birth, the doctor ties it and cuts it off close to the baby's body. The stump that's left withers and eventually drops off, usually in about a week, though it may take longer. When the cord falls off, it may leave a raw spot, which takes a number of days, occasionally a number of weeks, to heal over. If healing is slow, the raw spot may become lumpy with what's called granulation tissue, but this is of no importance. The raw spot should merely be kept clean and dry, so that harmful germs will not infect it. If it is kept dry, a scab covers it until it is healed. Nowadays most doctors recommend that no dressing be put over the navel while it heals. In this way it is likely to stay driest. It is sometimes recommended that the baby not be given a tub bath until the navel is completely healed, but this rule is not essential if the navel is wiped dry with sterile cotton. It is wise to keep the diaper below the level of the unhealed navel, so that it doesn't keep it wet.

If the unhealed navel becomes moist and discharges, it should be protected more carefully from constant wetting by the diaper, and cleaned each day with alcohol. The doctor may recommend touching it with an antiseptic powder or powdered alum to hasten drying and healing.

If the navel and the surrounding skin become red, infection is present and you should get in touch with your doctor right away. Until you can reach him, you should apply continuous wet dressings (Section 711).

If the scab on the unhealed navel gets pulled by the clothing, there may be a drop or two of blood. This amount is of no importance.

236. Umbilical hernia. After the skin of the navel heals over, there is usually still an opening in the deeper, muscular layer of the abdomen where the umbilical vessels passed through. When the baby cries, a small part of the intestine is pushed through this hole (umbilical ring) and it makes the navel puff out somewhat. This is called an umbilical hernia. When the ring is small, the protrusion of the hernia is never much larger than a pea and the ring is likely to close over in a few weeks or months. When the ring is large, it may take months or even years to close and the protrusion may be larger than a cherry.

It used to be thought that the closing of the umbilical ring could be hastened by putting a tight strap of adhesive across the navel to keep it from protruding. It is now believed that strapping makes no difference. It is much easier not to bother with the adhesive, which always became soiled, soon loosened, and left raw places in the skin.

You don't have to worry about the protrusion of the hernia. It rarely causes any trouble, as other hernias sometimes do (Section 695). There is no need to try to keep the baby from crying.

In the well-padded, older child or adult, the fat over the abdomen is thick enough to make the navel appear to be at the bottom of a hole. This is rarely the case in the first 2 or 3 years of life. The folds of skin of the navel (looking something like a rosebud) stand right out on the full abdomen. This prominence of the skin folds of the navel should not be confused with a hernia. A hernia can be felt underneath the skin folds, like a small, soft balloon. A hernia makes the navel stick out farther than it would otherwise.

THE PENIS

237. Circumcision and other ways to care for the penis. Should a baby boy be circumcised? If not, what care should be given the penis (the genital)? There's no single answer.

Circumcision is the cutting off of the sleeve of skin (called the foreskin) that normally covers the head of the penis. The advantages of circumcision are cleanliness and practicality. A cheeselike material called smegma is secreted by the skin of the head of the penis. When the foreskin remains, the smegma collects. Sometimes ordinary germs get into this smegma-filled space and cause an irritation or mild infection. If the foreskin has been removed, the smegma does not collect and there is no place for infection to occur. If circumcision is performed in early infancy, there will be no risk of psychological harm from having to do it later. I think circumcision is a good idea, especially if most of the boys in the neighborhood are circumcised—then a boy feels "regular." However, it is not absolutely necessary. It is usually done before the baby leaves the hospital.

If your baby has been circumcised, the wound will not heal for a number of days. To protect the wound and to keep the scab from sticking to the diaper, put petrolatum (petroleum jelly) or boric acid ointment on a single layer of gauze about the size of a large postage stamp and wrap this around the end of the penis. The ointment will hold the gauze in place. If the wound gets rubbed by the diaper, a few drops of blood or a pink stain appears on the diaper. This is of no importance.

Another method of keeping the penis clean is to pull back (retract) the foreskin each day in the bath and briefly wash the head of the penis. This is painful to the baby at first because of the smallness of the opening in the foreskin in infants, and is difficult for mothers to do efficiently. I think it is an unsatisfactory method, psychologically and physically.

The third method of care is to leave the foreskin alone. This is the simplest way and the one used throughout a great part of the world. Its disadvantages are the slight risk of an infection under the foreskin, and the possibility, on this account, of having to consider circumcision at a later age when the child is very likely to be made nervous by the operation.

238. Why circumcision is harmful after infancy. The question of circumcision is often raised later in childhood, either because there has been an irritating infection beneath the foreskin or because the child is masturbating. In the days before the importance of the child's emotions was recognized, it seemed logical to circumcise for either of these reasons. The parents or the doctor might say, "Maybe he's masturbating because there is discomfort from a little infection." The trouble is that this theory often puts the cart before the horse. We know now that a boy, especially between 3 and 6, often becomes nervous about his penis for fear some injury might happen to it (explained in Section 515). This worry may *cause* him to handle himself and produce a little irritation. If this should be the real sequence of events, you can see that an operation on the penis would be a bad thing for his fears.

The danger of psychological harm from circumcision is greatest between 1 and 6 years, but there is some risk up through adolescence. I think it's wise to avoid the operation after the baby is a few months old, especially as a treatment for masturbation. The possibility of psychological harm from a later circumcision is a very good reason for performing the operation right after birth.

239. Erections. It is common for boy babies to have erections of the penis, especially when the bladder is full or during urination. This has no importance.

THE FONTANEL

240. The soft spot on the top of a baby's head is where the four pieces of bone that make up the top of the skull have not yet grown together. The size of the fontanel at birth is different in different babies. A large one is nothing to worry about, and it's bound to be slower to close than a small one. Some fontanels close as early as 9 months and slow ones not till 2 years. The average is at 12 to 18 months.

If the light is right, you can see that the fontanel pulsates with the beat of the heart.

Mothers worry unnecessarily about the danger of touching the soft spot. Actually, it is covered by a membrane as tough as canvas, and there is very little risk of hurting a baby there.

CLOTHING, FRESH AIR, AND SUNSHINE

241. Coverings and room temperature. The hardest question for a doctor to answer, in a book or in his office, is how much covering to put on a baby. All he can give are some rough guides. A baby under 5 pounds hasn't a very good system for keeping his body at the right temperature and has to be in an incubator. Between 5 and 8 pounds, he doesn't usually need to be heated from the outside. He can take care of himself in a comfortable room, say 68 to 72°, with 1 or 2 light wool blankets and his cotton sleeping clothes.

By the time he weighs 8 pounds, his heat regulator is working well and he is getting a layer of fat that helps him stay warm. Now his room for sleeping can and probably should be allowed to go down to 60° in cool or cold weather.

It isn't necessary to try to get a baby's sleeping room below 60° (which is mildly cold). At 60° he probably needs a sweater to keep his shoulders warm, and 2 or 3 layers of light wool blanketing.

A room temperature of 68 to 72° for eating and playing is right for babies weighing over 5 pounds, just as it is for older children and adults. In such a room he needs to be wrapped in a thin blanket, and perhaps wear a thin sweater, at least while he is small.

Babies and children who are reasonably plump need less covering than an adult. More babies are overdressed than underdressed. This isn't good for them. If a person is always too warmly dressed, his body loses its ability to adjust to changes. He is **more** likely to become chilled. So, in general, put on too little rather than too much and then watch the baby. Don't try to put on enough to keep his hands warm, because most babies' hands stay cool when they are comfortably dressed. Feel his legs or arms or neck. Best guide of all is the color of his face. If he is getting cold, he loses the color from his cheeks, and he may begin to fuss, too.

When putting on sweaters and shirts with small openings, remember that a baby's head is more egg-shaped than ball-shaped. Gather the sweater into a loop, slip it first over the back of the baby's head, then forward, stretching it forward as you bring it down past the forehead and nose. When taking it off, pull the baby's arms out of the sleeves first. Gather the sweater into a loop as it lies around his neck. Raise the front part of the loop up past his nose and forehead (while the back of the loop is still at the back of his neck), then slip it off toward the back of his head.

242. Practical coverings. It is better to use all-wool (or synthetic) blankets. They give the most warmth with the least weight. Best of all are the knitted ones (shawls). They wrap more easily when the baby is up, and because they are thinner, you can adjust the amount of covering to the temperature more exactly than with thick blankets. Avoid coverings that are heavy, such as solid-feeling quilts.

All blankets, quilts, sheets, should be large enough to tuck securely under the mattress, so that they will not work loose. Waterproof sheets and pads should either be large enough to tuck in securely or should be pinned or tied down at all corners so that they will not come loose. The mattress should be firm and flat enough so that the baby will not be lying in a depression. A carriage mattress should fit well, so that there is no space around the edge in which he might get wedged. Use no pillow in crib or carriage.

A cap in which to sleep should be of knitted wool, so that if it slips over the baby's face he can breathe through it. Fancier caps are all right when the mother is with the baby.

There are different kinds of sleeping bags for the purpose of keeping a small child down in bed and under the covers. Most of them tie to the sides of the bed, and some of them close tight at the neck with a zipper. They are very convenient, but I would not recommend them, for two reasons. There is a slight danger of a baby's strangling himself in any arrangement that holds him around the neck and is at the same time tied to the bed. And some psychologists have wondered if it might cramp a child's spirit and his sense of bodily freedom to spend so much of his early formative period tied down, helpless, and immobile. It seems better to me to give the baby the benefit of the doubt.

However, you can use a sleeping suit made out of thick blanketing. Those made of synthetic material can be washed frequently without shrinking. Another suggestion is a snow suit that an older child has outgrown. Or you can use a bag that reaches up to the baby's armpits and is pinned snugly around him. A sweater or two will keep his shoulders warm. When he gets to the standing age, he can stand up and still be well covered. You can buy such a blanket bag or make one from an old blanket. Leave the lengthwise seam open in its upper third. Then you can overlap the two flaps snugly across his back and pin them in two places close to his shoulder blades, where he can't get at them. In very cold weather, use two bags.

243. Fresh air. Changes of air temperature are beneficial in toning up the body's system for adapting to cold or heat. A bank clerk is much more likely to become chilled staying outdoors in winter than a lumberjack who is used to such weather. Cool or cold air improves appetite, puts color in the cheeks, and gives more pep to humans of all ages. A baby living continuously in a warm room usually has a pasty complexion and may have a sluggish appetite.

In cold weather the air contains much less moisture. When this air is heated in a house it becomes relatively drier still, especially when the temperature rises above 72°. Dry, hot air dries and hardens the mucus in the nose and parches the air passages generally. This makes the baby uncomfortable and probably lowers his ability to resist infections.

It's good for a baby (like anyone else) to get outdoors for 2 or 3 hours a day, particularly during the season when the house is heated.

When he is sleeping indoors during cold weather, his window should be open wide enough (and the radiator turned off) so that the temperature falls to about 60°.

When he is awake and with the family, the room temperature should be kept between 68 and 72°.

Most people accustomed to heated houses let the temperature gradually get hotter all winter, without noticing it, and come to demand excessive heat. One way to counteract this in a private house is with a thermostat, which turns the furnace down when the desired temperature (70°) is reached. In an apartment or private house without a thermostat, the mother should hang a house thermometer in a prominent place and glance at it several times a day until she becomes so attuned to a range of 68 to 70° that she notices a higher temperature without looking.

The problem of providing cool enough air for a baby is further complicated by the inexperienced mother's natural anxiety and protectiveness. She tends to keep her baby in a too hot room and too well covered, besides. Under these conditions some babies even develop heat rash in winter.

244. Getting the baby out of doors. Let's say, to start the discussion, that it would be good for every baby weighing 10 pounds or more to be outdoors, when it isn't raining, for 2 or 3 hours a day, as long as the temperature is above freezing and the wind isn't bitterly cold. An 8-pounder can certainly go out when it's 60° or above. The temperature of the air is not the only factor. Moist, cold air is more chilling than dry air of the same temperature, and wind is the greatest chiller. Even when the temperature is below freezing, a 12-pound baby can be comfortable in a sunny, sheltered spot for an hour or two.

In winter the best time to have the baby out is in the middle of the day (between the 10 A.M. and 2 P.M. feedings in the early months). If you live in the country or have your own yard, you can put him out for even longer than 3 hours in reasonable weather. Let the sun fall on his face for a short time if this does not make him uncomfortable (see Section 245 on sun bathing).

As he grows older, is awake for longer periods, and appreciates company more, I wouldn't keep him out **all by himself** for more than an hour when he is awake. By the second half of the first year, a child is entitled to have people nearby most of the time he's awake, even though he's amusing himself. It's fine for him to be out for 2 or 3 hours with his mother or when he's asleep.

If you live in a city and have no yard to park the baby in, you can push him in a carriage. Long woolen underwear, slacks, woolen stockings, and galoshes make your life a lot more pleasant during this period. If you enjoy being out and can afford the time, the more the better.

In summer, if your house gets stifling hot and you can find a fairly cool place outdoors, the longer the baby stays out when asleep the better. If your house stays cool, I would still try to have the baby out for a couple of hours a day, but in the first part of the morning and the end of the afternoon.

When your baby first goes on 3 meals a day, you may need to shift the hours outdoors somewhat to suit your and his convenience. But the general principle of trying to get him out for 2 or 3 hours a day remains the same. As he gets nearer to a year old, he becomes more interested in his surroundings. He may refuse to go to sleep after lunch if he is being pushed around in his carriage. Then you may have to let him have his nap in his crib after lunch. That leaves very little of the afternoon for an outing, especially in winter. You might keep him out for 1 to 2 hours in the morning and an hour in the afternoon. What part of the morning you take him out also depends on when he takes his morning nap. Some babies in the last part of the first year fall asleep right after breakfast, others not until the end of the morning. If your baby won't sleep while he is outdoors, you have to fit in the outings when he is awake.

245. Sunshine and sun baths. Direct sunshine contains ultraviolet rays, which create vitamin D right in the skin. On general principles it's sensible for babies and children to be in the sun for part of the time. There are three cautions. Exposure to sunshine should be increased very gradually to avoid burns, especially where the sun is hot and the air is clear. Secondly, excessive exposure is probably unwise even when the skin has been gradually tanned. The reason the skin becomes tanned is to protect the body from the effects of too much sun. In other words, the body can't use more than a moderate amount. Excessive amounts may be harmful to the skin. Thirdly, a severe sunburn is just as dangerous as a heat burn. When you put a baby out to sleep in a carriage, you must take into account how much sunshine he will get on his skin, especially if you are putting him in a new spot in a season when the sun is bright.

In summer you can begin exposing the baby's body to the sun as soon as the weather is warm enough and as soon as he weighs about 10 pounds. This means that he is plump enough so that he won't get chilled when he is partly undressed outdoors. In cooler weather you may be able to expose his legs alone. You have to wait longer to expose his face, until his eyes are no longer bothered by the bright light. This varies in different babies. When you do expose his face, turn him so that the top of his head is toward the sun. Then his eyebrows will shield his eyes.

In winter you can, if you wish, give him sun baths at an open window if the room is warm enough and the wind does not blow on him.

Begin with 2 minutes and increase the exposure gradually—adding 2 minutes each day is fast enough. Divide the time between back and stomach. I wouldn't suggest going beyond 30 or 40 minutes of full exposure, especially in summer. In warm weather it is important that the baby not get overheated during his sun bath. Put him on a pad on the floor or on the ground where the air will cool him, not down inside a bassinet or carriage. If he becomes flushed, he's too hot.

When the sunshine is intense, as at the beach, a baby should be in the shade all the time the first day or two, and even then he may get enough reflected glare to give his tender skin a burn. A baby old enough to sit up and crawl around needs a hat at the beach or any equally sunny place. Remember that the redness of sunburn doesn't show up until several hours after the damage is done.

SLEEP

246. How much should a baby sleep? Mothers often ask this question. Of course, the baby is the only one who can answer it. One baby seems to need a lot, and another surprisingly little. As long as a baby is satisfied with his feedings, comfortable, gets plenty of fresh air, and sleeps in a cool place, you can leave it to him to take the amount of sleep he needs.

Most babies in the early months sleep from feeding to feeding if they are getting enough to eat and not having indigestion. There are a few babies, though, who are unusually wakeful right from the beginning, and not because anything is wrong. If you have this kind of baby, there's nothing you need to do about it.

As your baby gets older, he gradually sleeps less and less. You're apt to notice it first in the late afternoon. In time he becomes wakeful at other periods during the day. Each baby develops his own pattern of wakefulness and tends to be awake at the same time every day. Toward the end of his first year, he probably is down to 2 naps a day; and between 1 and 1½ years, he probably gives up one of these. It is only during infancy that you can leave the amount of sleep entirely up to the baby. A child by the age of 2 is a much more complicated being. Excitement, worries, fear of bad dreams, competition with a brother, may keep him from getting the sleep he needs.

247. Going to bed. It is preferable to get your baby used to the idea that he always goes to bed and to sleep right after a meal. (An occasional baby won't fall easily into this pattern but insists on being sociable after his meals. I'd try to change his mind.) It is good, too, for him to get used to falling asleep in his own bed, without company, at least by the time any 3-month colic is over.

Most babies can get accustomed to either a silent home or an average noisy one. So there is no point tiptoeing and whispering around the house at first—you'd only be training the baby to be easily wakened by unexpected sounds. The infant and child who, awake or asleep, is used to ordinary household noises and human voices usually sleeps right through a visit of talking, laughing friends, a radio or TV tuned to a reasonable level, even somebody's coming into his room.

248. On back or stomach? A majority of babies seem, from the beginning, to be a little more comfortable going to sleep on their stomach. This is particularly true of the baby who develops colic: the pressure on the abdomen seems to partly relieve the gas pains.

Others either don't care at first or prefer sleeping on their back. There are two disadvantages to a baby's sleeping on his back. If he vomits, he's more likely to choke on the vomitus. Also, he tends to keep his head turned toward the same side—usually toward the center of the room. This may flatten that side of his head. It won't hurt his brain, and the head will gradually straighten out, but it may take a couple of years. If you start early, you may be able to get him used to turning his head to both sides by putting his head where his feet were the time before, each time you put him to bed. Then if there is one part of the room he likes to look at, he will turn his head in each direction half the time. Within a few weeks a baby usually develops such a strong preference for his usual position, stomach or back, that it's quite a struggle to change him.

I think it is preferable to accustom a baby to sleeping on his stomach from the start if he is willing. He may change later when he learns to turn over.

249. See if you can train the baby to sleep later or be happy in his bed in the morning. In the middle part of the first year, most babies become willing to sleep a little later than that uncivilized 5 or 6 A.M. waking hour that they all love at first. However, most parents develop such a habit of listening for the baby in their sleep and jumping out of bed at the first murmur that they never give him a chance to go back to sleep if he's willing, or to become accustomed to amusing himself for a while. As a result, they may find themselves still getting up before 7 A.M. when the child is 2 or 3 years old. And a child who has been used to early company for so long will demand it.

So if you like to sleep till 7 or 8, use your alarm clock again instead of the baby. Set the alarm 5 minutes later than he usually wakes, and every few days move it 5 minutes later still. If he wakes before the alarm, he may go back to sleep without your hearing him or he may learn to stay awake contentedly for a longer and longer period. If he fusses, wait a while to see if he quiets down. Of course, if he works himself up to indignant crying and it persists, you've got to get up. But try again in another month.

250. Out of the parents' room by six months if possible. A child can sleep in a room by himself from the time he is born, if convenient, as long as the parents are near enough to hear him when he cries. If he starts with his parents, 6 months is a good age to move him. He has the strength to take care of himself pretty well, and he doesn't yet have set ideas about where he wants to be. It is preferable that he not sleep in his parents' room after he is about 9 months old. Otherwise there is a chance that he may become dependent on this arrangement and be afraid and unwilling to sleep anywhere else. The older he is, the harder it may be to move him.

Another trouble is that the young child may be upset by the parents' intercourse, which he misunderstands and which frightens him. Parents are apt to think there is no danger if they first make sure the child is asleep. But children's psychiatrists have found cases in which the child awakened and was much disturbed without the parents' ever being aware of it. However, the risk of a child's becoming dependent or upset if he continues to sleep in the parents' room is not so great that the parents should worry when no other sleeping arrangement is possible. Perhaps there is room for a screen between the beds.

Whether a child should sleep in a room by himself or with another youngster is largely a practical matter. If it's possible, it's fine for each child to have a room of his own, especially as he grows older, where he can keep his own possessions under control and have privacy when he wants it. The main disadvantage of two young children in the same room is that they are apt to wake each other up at the wrong times.

251. Better not let the child in your bed. Sometimes when a small child is going through a period of waking up frightened at night—perhaps coming repeatedly into the parents' room, perhaps crying persistently— the parents take him into bed with them so that they can all get some sleep. This seems like the most practical thing to do at the time, but it usually turns out to be a mistake. Even if the child's anxiety improves during the following weeks, he is apt to cling to the security of his parents' bed, and there is the devil to pay getting him out again. So, **always** bring him promptly and firmly back to his own bed. I think it's a sensible rule not to take a child into the parents' bed for any reason (even as a treat when the father is away on a business trip).

PLAY PERIODS

252. Being companionable with your baby. Be quietly friendly with your baby whenever you are with him. He's getting a sense of how much you mean to each other all the time you're feeding him, bubbling him, bathing him, dressing him, changing his diapers, holding him, or just sitting in the room with him. When you hug him or make noises at him, when you show him that you think he's the most wonderful baby in the world, it makes his spirit grow, just the way milk makes his bones grow. That must be why we grownups instinctively talk baby talk and waggle our heads when we greet a baby, even grownups who are otherwise dignified or unsociable.

One trouble with being an inexperienced parent is that part of the time you take the job so seriously that you forget to enjoy it. Then you and the baby are both missing something.

Naturally I don't mean that you should be talking a blue streak at him all the time he's awake, or constantly joggling him or tickling him. That would tire him out, and in the long run would make him tense and spoiled. You can be quiet nine tenths of the time you are with him. It's the gentle, easygoing kind of companionship that's good for him and good for you. It's the comfortable feeling that goes into your arms when you hold him, the fond, peaceful expression on your face when you look at him, and the gentle tone in your voice.

253. Companionship without spoiling. Though it's good for a baby during his play periods to be somewhere near his mother (and brothers and sisters, if any) so that he can see her, make noises at her, hear her speak to him, have her show him a way to play with something occasionally, it isn't necessary or sensible for him to be in her lap or arms or to have her amusing him much of the time. He can be enjoying her company, profiting from it, and still be learning how to occupy himself. If a new mother is so delighted with her baby that she is holding him or making games for him a good part of his wakeful period, he may become quite dependent on these attentions and demand more and more of them. See Sections 280, 281.

254. Things to watch and things to play with. Young babies begin waking earlier and earlier, especially at the end of the afternoon. At such times they want something to do and they want **some** companionship. At 2, 3, and 4 months, they enjoy looking at bright-colored things and things that move. Outdoors, they are delighted to watch leaves and shadows. Indoors, they study their hands, pictures on the wall. There are bright-colored plastic shapes on strings that you can suspend between the top rails of the crib. Place them just within arm's reach—not right on top of a baby's nose—for the time when he begins reaching. You can make mobiles yourself—cardboard shapes covered with colored paper that hang from the ceiling or from a lighting fixture and rotate in slight drafts (they aren't strong enough for playing with or healthful for chewing)—or you can hang suitable household objects within reach—spoons, plastic cups, for instance. Remember that eventually everything goes into the mouth. As a baby gets toward the middle of his first year, his greatest joy is handling and mouthing objects: collections of plastic objects linked together (made for this age), rattles, teething rings, animals and dolls of cloth, household objects that are safe in the mouth. Don't let a baby or small child have objects or furniture that has been repainted with outdoor paint that contains lead, or thin celluloid toys that can be chewed into small, sharp pieces, or small glass beads and other small objects that can be choked on. Take the metal whistles out of rubber animals.

Each afternoon when the baby becomes bored with his crib, put him in the play pen near where you are working or sitting. If you are going to use a pen, the baby should become accustomed to it at 3 or 4 months, before he has learned to sit and crawl and before he has had the freedom of the floor. Otherwise he considers it a prison from the start. By the time he can sit and crawl, he has fun going after things that are a few feet away, handling larger objects like cooking spoons, saucepans, strainers. When he becomes bored with the play pen, he can sit in a bouncing chair or a chair-table arrangement. It's good for him to end up with some free creeping.

255. When to get a play pen. You don't have to have a play pen. Some psychologists and physicians disapprove, feeling that it prevents the creeping baby from exploring and gaining independence. I understand this theoretical objection, though I don't believe there is any proof one way or the other. I have usually suggested a play pen on purely practical grounds as a great help, especially for the busy mother. Set up in the living room or the kitchen, where the mother is working, it gives the baby the company that he can't have in his own room and a chance to see everything that is going on. Later he has fun by the hour putting toys out onto the floor and getting them back again. When he is old enough to stand up, the pen gives him slats and railings to hold onto and a firm foundation under his feet. In good weather he can sit safely in his play pen on the porch and watch the world go by.

256. A bouncing chair is useful, too, after a baby has learned to sit with a straight back and before he has learned to walk. In some of these, the base that rests on the floor does not reach far enough forward, so that when the baby gets bouncing hard, he can tip the chair over forward. A father can remedy this by attaching longer wooden runners to the base. Another remedy is to limit the up-bounce by strapping the rear of the springs to the base so that the seat can't rise so high.

I wouldn't keep a child in a seat all his waking hours. He needs chances to creep and to learn to stand.

THE BOWEL MOVEMENTS

257. Meconium. For the first day or so after birth, the baby's movements are composed of material called meconium, which is greenish-black in color and of a smooth, sticky consistency. Then they change to brown and to yellow. If a baby hasn't had a movement by the end of his second day, the doctor should be notified.

258. The breast-fed baby may have many or few movements. A breast-fed baby usually has several movements a day in the early weeks. Some have a movement after every nursing. They are usually of a light-yellow color. They may be pasty or they may have the consistency of thick cream soup. They are practically never too hard. Many breast-fed babies change from frequent to infrequent movements by the time they are 1, 2, or 3 months old. Some then have 1 movement a day, others a movement only every other day or even further apart. This is apt to alarm a mother who has been brought up to believe that everyone must have a movement every day. But there is nothing to worry about so long as the baby is comfortable. The breast-fed baby's movement stays just as soft, even when it is passed every 2 or 3 days.

Some of these breast-fed babies who have infrequent movements begin to push and strain a lot when 2 or 3 days have gone by. Yet the movement is like creamed soup when it does come out. The only explanation I can make for this is that the movement is so liquid that it doesn't put the right kind of pressure on the inside of the anus, where the movement comes out. Consult the doctor about this. Adding a little solid food to the diet usually helps, even though the baby doesn't otherwise need solid food yet. Two to 4 teaspoonfuls of puréed prunes daily (stewed or canned) generally works well. There is no call for cathartics in this kind of difficulty. I think it is better not to use suppositories or enemas regularly, for fear the baby will come to depend on them. Try to solve the problem with prunes or other solid food.

259. The bottle-fed baby's movements. The baby fed cow's milk usually has between 1 and 4 movements a day at first, though an occasional baby has as many as 6. As he grows older, the number tends to decrease to 1 or 2 a day. The number is unimportant if the consistency of the movement is good and if the baby is doing well.

Cow's-milk movements are most often pasty and of a pale-yellow or tan color. However, some young babies always have stools that are more like soft scrambled eggs (curdy lumps with looser material in between). This is not important if the baby is comfortable and gaining well.

The commonest disturbance of the bowel movements in the baby on cow's milk is a tendency to hardness. This is discussed in the section on **constipation** (Section 292).

A very few bottle-fed babies have a tendency to loose, green, curdy movements in the early months. This is usually worse as more sugar is added to the formula. A severe case needs a lot of supervision by the doctor. If you are completely out of reach of a doctor, you can omit the sugar from the formula altogether. However, if a baby's movements are always just a little loose, it can be ignored, provided he is comfortable, gaining well, and the doctor finds nothing wrong.

260. Changes in the movements. You can see that it doesn't matter if one baby's movements are always a little different from another baby's, as long as he's doing well. It's more apt to mean something, and should be discussed with the doctor, when his movements undergo a real change. If they were previously pasty and then turn lumpy, slightly looser, slightly more frequent, it may be a spell of indigestion or a mild intestinal infection. If they become definitely loose, frequent, greenish, and the smell changes, it is almost certainly due to an intestinal infection (diarrhea), whether mild or severe. When a bowel movement is delayed and then comes unusually firm, it sometimes means the beginning of a cold, sore throat, or other disease, but not necessarily. (The infection makes the intestine more sluggish, just as it's apt to diminish the appetite.) Generally speaking, changes in the number and color of the movements are less important than changes in the consistency and smell.

Mucus in the bowel movements is common when a baby has diarrhea, and it is just another sign that the intestines are irritated. Similarly, it may occur in indigestion. It can also come from higher up, from the throat and bronchial tubes of a baby with a cold, or of a healthy newborn baby. Some babies form a great deal of mucus in the early weeks.

When a **new vegetable** is added to the diet (less frequently in the case of other foods), part of it may come through looking just the same as it went in. If it also causes signs of irritation, such as looseness and mucus, give much less the next time. If there is no irritation, you can keep on with the same amount or increase slowly until he learns to digest it better. Beets can turn the whole movement red.

A bowel movement exposed to the air may turn brown or it may turn green. This is of no importance.

Small streaks of blood on the outside of a bowel movement usually come from a crack, or "fissure," in the anus, caused by hard bowel movements. The bleeding is not serious in itself, but the doctor should be notified so that the constipation can be treated promptly. This is important for psychological as well as physical reasons (see Section 382).

Larger amounts of blood in the movement are rare and may come from malformations of the intestines, from severe diarrhea, or from intussusception (Section 690). The doctor should be called or the child taken to a hospital immediately.

Diarrhea is discussed in Sections 298–300.

DIAPERS

261. Diapering. How to fold a diaper depends on the size of the baby and of the diaper. The only important things in putting it on are to have the most cloth where there is the most urine, and not to have so much diaper bunched between the legs that they are kept widely separated. With a full-sized newborn baby and the usual large diapers, you can fold as in the pictures. First fold lengthwise so that there are 3 thicknesses. Then fold about one third of the end over. As a result, half of the folded diaper has 6 layers, the other half 3 layers. A boy needs the double thickness in front; a girl needs the thickness in front if she lies on her abdomen, in back if she lies on her back. When you put in the pin, slip two fingers of the other hand between the baby and the diaper to prevent sticking him.

Most mothers change the diapers when they pick the baby up for his feeding and again before they put him back to bed. Mothers who are

One way to fold a diaper.

very busy, though, have found they can save time and laundry by changing only once at each feeding, either before or after. Most babies are not bothered by being wet. But a few are extra sensitive and have to be changed more often. If a child has sufficient covers over him, his wet diaper does not feel cold. It is when wet clothing is exposed to the air that evaporation makes it cold.

If a baby drenches himself and his bed, it may be worth while using 2 diapers at a time. The second one may be too bulky if put on the same way as the first. You can pin it around his waist like an apron.

Disposable diapers are handy for traveling. Some mothers find them convenient for every day if the added expense is not important. The full-sized ones are rather bulky. The small ones that fit into a waterproof cover do not absorb as much urine as a cloth diaper and do not retain a bowel movement as well.

In cleaning the baby after a bowel movement, you can use oil (baby oil or liquid petrolatum) on a piece of absorbent cotton, or plain water on cotton or a washcloth. If necessary, you can use soap and water on cotton or a washcloth (the soap should be wiped off). It isn't necessary to wash the baby when changing a wet diaper.

262. Washing the diapers. You want a covered pail partially filled with water to put used diapers in as soon as removed. If it contains soap or detergent, this helps in removing stains. Be sure the soap is well dissolved, to prevent lumps of soap from remaining in the diapers later. When you remove a soiled diaper, scrape the movement off into the toilet with a knife, or rinse it by holding it in the toilet while you flush it (hold tight).

You wash the diapers with mild soap or mild detergent in washing machine or washtub (dissolve the soap well first), and rinse 2 or 3 or 4 times. The number of rinsings depends on how soon the water gets clear and on how delicate the baby's skin is. If your baby's skin isn't sensitive, 2 rinsings may be enough.

If your baby has a tendency to diaper rash, you may need to take additional precautions—at least at the times the rash appears, and perhaps regularly. Bacteria that sometimes collect in diapers manufacture ammonia from the urine. This ammonia is the main cause of diaper rash. These bacteria are not completely removed by washing. They must be destroyed if there is much diaper rash, either by boiling the diapers or by adding a special antiseptic to the last rinsing water. Ask your doctor for the name of a diaper antiseptic that is safe and convenient. Some clothes washers and dryers effectively kill these bacteria (depending on the heat).

Sunshine is a potent destroyer of many bacteria. There is probably less chance of diaper rash if you hang the diapers (and also the other things that are wet by the urine: nighties, shirts, sheets, pads, waterproof sheeting, waterproof pants) in the sun to dry. See Section 302 on diaper rash.

263. Diaper liners. There are diaper liners, made of paper, to put in the diaper at the times of day when bowel movements are expected, to keep the diaper from becoming soiled.

There are liners, made of treated cloth that dries rapidly, that are meant to keep the baby's skin from staying too wet.

264. Waterproof pants or "soakers" (the latter are knitted wool pants), over the diapers, are a special help when you are going places with the baby. You may want to use the soakers at home, too, if washing them is not a burden. Whether you use waterproof pants at home depends on how well the baby's skin stands up. When a baby has no waterproof pants on, a lot of the urine in the diaper is absorbed into the surrounding clothing or evaporated. With waterproof pants the diapers stay much wetter and warmer, and bacteria accumulate in them. This favors the formation of ammonia and diaper rash. As long as your baby's skin is clear in the diaper region, you can use pants as much as is convenient. When there is diaper rash, leave them off. It probably helps to wash the pants with soap and water each day and hang them in the sun to kill the germs that make ammonia.

Problems of Infancy

CRYING IN THE EARLY WEEKS

265. What does it mean? This is usually an important question with a first baby. As he grows older, crying is much less of a problem because you worry less, you know what to expect from him at different times of the day, you are able to distinguish between different cries, and he has fewer causes for crying.

Several questions pop into your mind: Is he hungry? Is he wet? Is he sick? Does he have indigestion? Is a pin sticking into him? Is he becoming spoiled? Parents are not apt to think of fatigue, but it's one of the commonest causes. It is fairly easy to answer these questions, one by one.

But there is a lot of fretting and crying that can't be explained by any of these reasons. In fact, by the time they are a couple of weeks old, a majority of babies—especially first babies—get into fretful periods that we can give names to but can't explain exactly. When the crying is regularly limited to one period in the evening or afternoon, we can call it **colic** (if there is pain, distension, and gas) or **periodic irritable crying** (if there is no distension). If the baby is fussing off and on, any old time of the day or night, we can sigh and say that he is just a **fretful baby** at this stage. If he's unusually tense and jumpy, we use the term **hypertonic baby.** But we don't know the meaning of these patterns of behavior. We only know that they commonly occur and that they gradually peter out—usually by 3 months of age. Maybe they are different variations of one condition. In a vague way we can sense that the age period between birth and about 3 months is one of adjustment of the baby's immature nervous system and immature digestive system to life in the outside world and that a smooth adjustment is harder for some babies to achieve. Anyway, the important thing to remember is that these most common types of crying in the early weeks are temporary and are not a sign of anything serious.

266. Hunger? Whether you're feeding your baby on a fairly regular schedule or according to his desire, you soon get an idea of what his pattern is like—at what times of day he wants more to eat, at what times he's apt to wake early. This should help you to decide whether unusual crying is due to hunger. If a baby took less than half his usual amount at his last feeding, it **may** be the reason why he's awake and crying in a couple of hours instead of in 3 or 4 hours. But not necessarily. A baby who has taken much less than his usual amount may, just as often, sleep contentedly for the full 4-hour period.

If a baby took an average amount at his last feeding and wakes crying before 2 hours, it is even less likely that he is hungry. (If he wakes within an hour, especially in the evening or afternoon, it's most apt to be colic.) If it's 2½ or 3 hours after the last feeding, then consider hunger first.

Could it be that he has outgrown his formula or the breast-milk supply, or that the breast supply is decreasing? A baby doesn't outgrow his formula all of a sudden, from one day to the next. He will have been finishing every bottle for several days and looking around for more. He begins to wake and cry a **little** earlier than usual, not a lot. In most cases, it's only after he has been waking early from hunger for a number of days that he begins crying **after** a feeding.

Normally the breast-milk supply increases as the baby demands it. The more complete and more frequent emptying of the breast stimulates it to greater production. Of course, it is possible for a mother to have less breast milk occasionally if she is fatigued or worried.

I'd sum it up with the following rule of thumb: If a baby has been crying hard for 15 minutes or more and if it's more than 2 hours after the last feeding—or even if it's less than 2 hours after a **very small** feeding—give him another feeding. If this satisfies him and puts him to sleep, it's the right answer. If it's less than 2 hours after a **full** feeding, it's unlikely that he's hungry. Let him fuss or cry for 15 or 20 minutes more, if you can stand it, or give him a pacifier, and see if he won't go back to sleep. If he's crying harder than ever, there's no harm trying a feeding.

(Don't start giving a bottle the first time you suspect the breast milk is insufficient; give the breast.)

267. Is he sick? Babies catch colds and they catch intestinal infections during their early months, but these show themselves in running noses, coughs, or loose bowel movements. Other infections are pretty rare. If your baby is not only crying but **looks different** in general appearance and color, take his temperature and report to the doctor.

268. Is he crying because he's wet or has had a bowel movement? A very few young babies seem uncomfortable when wet or soiled. Most don't mind at all. You can change him, anyway.

269. Is it a safety pin? This doesn't happen once in a hundred years, but you can look to be sure.

270. Is it indigestion? You can try bubbling him again even though you got a bubble up before. Indigestion with spitting and loose, curdy, green stools is discussed in Section 290, colic in Section 275.

271. Is he spoiled? Though older babies can be spoiled (Section 279), I think you can assume that in the first month your baby is not crying because he's spoiled.

272. Fatigue? When a young baby has been awake an unusually long while or when he has been stimulated more than usual by being with strangers or by being in a strange place or even by being played with by his parents, he may react by becoming tense and irritable. Instead of being easier for him to fall asleep, it may be harder. If the parents or strangers then try to comfort him with more play, more talk, more jouncing, it may make matters worse.

Some young babies seem to be made in such a way that they can **never** drift peacefully into sleep. Their fatigue at the end of every period of being awake produces a tension that is a sort of hump they must get over before falling asleep. They have to cry. Some of them cry frantically and loudly. Then gradually or suddenly the crying stops and they are asleep.

So if your baby is crying at the end of a wakeful period and after he has been fed, try assuming first that he's just tired and put him to bed. Let him cry for 15 to 30 minutes if he has to. Some babies fall asleep faster if left in the crib, and this is the method to strive for in the long run. Another baby who has become overfatigued relaxes sooner if kept in gentle motion—by being pushed back and forth in a bassinet that has wheels or by being rocked in the carriage or by being held in the arms and walked quietly, preferably in a darkened room. I would try walking a baby occasionally during an unusually tense spell (or rocking him in a rocking chair), but I wouldn't go on week after week putting him to sleep this way. He might become more and more dependent on it and demand more of it. You'd surely resent it sooner or later.

273. Fretful babies. Most babies have at least a few fretful spells during the early weeks, especially first babies. A few babies are excessively fretful—on certain days or a good part of the time. These fretful periods may alternate with unusually long stretches during which they sleep like a log and are almost impossible to wake. We don't really know what the cause is, whether it is indigestion because of an immature digestive system or whether it is the irritability and instability of a nervous system that hasn't settled down yet. This tendency doesn't mean anything serious and it passes with time, but it's hard on the parents while it lasts.

There are various things you can try: Try a pacifier between feedings if the doctor approves. Try swaddling the baby snugly in a receiving blanket. Some mothers and experienced nurses insist that a fretful or tense baby is much happier if he sleeps in a small space—a small bassinet, a car bed, even a cardboard carton fitted with a folded pad or blanket for a mattress and lined with a blanket. If you have a carriage or can borrow a cradle, you can see whether motion soothes him. A car ride works like magic with many fretful babies, but the trouble may return as soon as you get home, or even at every red light. A hot-water bottle may comfort him (see Section 276). You can also try music. Read Section 277 on getting some relief yourself. Doctors often prescribe a sedative.

274. A hypertonic baby is one who is unusually tense and restless during the early weeks. His body doesn't relax well. He startles excessively at slight noise or on any quick change of position. If, for instance, he is laid on his back on a firm surface and rolls to one side, or if he is held too loosely in the arms, or if the person carrying him moves him too suddenly, he may almost jump out of his skin. He may hate a tub bath for a couple of months. A hypertonic baby may also have colic or periodic irritable crying.

Hypertonic babies usually do best on a quiet regime: quiet room, few visitors, low voices, slow movements in handling him, a firm hold in carrying him, a big pillow (with a waterproof cover) to lie on while being changed and sponge bathed so that he won't roll, swaddling in a receiving blanket most of the time, lying on his stomach in bed, a small confining bassinet (see Sections 273 and 277). Doctors frequently prescribe a sedative.

275. Three-month colic and "periodic irritable crying." In this section I am describing two somewhat similar conditions that may be related to each other. The first is colic (sharp pains in the intestine). The baby's abdomen becomes distended with gas, he pulls up or stiffens his legs, screams piercingly, and may pass gas by rectum. The second condition I call "periodic irritable crying." The baby, even though he has had plenty to eat, cries miserably for several hours at one regular time of day without definite signs of pain or gas. He may be pacified as long as you hold him and carry him about. One baby has colic, another has irritable crying, a third seems to have a mixture. The two conditions may be related to each other, because both commonly start around 2 to 4 weeks of age and are usually over by the time the baby is about 3 months old. Both conditions cause trouble most often between 6 and 10 P.M.

The commonest story is this: The baby was said to be well behaved and quiet in the hospital, but a few days after going home he suddenly has a crying spell that lasts for 3 or 4 hours straight. His mother changes him, turns him over, gives him a drink of water, but nothing works for long. After a couple of hours, she wonders if he is hungry ahead of time, because he seems to be trying to get everything into his mouth. She warms up a bottle and he takes it eagerly at first, but before it's finished he lets go and cries again. The screaming often continues for the full 4-hour interval between feedings. After he has finished his next regular bottle, he may be miraculously relieved.

Lots of babies have just a few attacks scattered through the early months. At the other extreme is the infant who has trouble every night until he's 3 months old (that's why the severer cases have always been called three-month colic).

One baby is very regular about his colic or irritable crying. He sleeps like an angel after every feeding but one, and always screams from 6 P.M. to 10 P.M. or from 2 P.M. to 6 P.M. Another baby spreads his unhappiness through a longer period, and the mother says, "He sleeps like a lamb all night, but cries off and on for half the day." This is not so bad as the baby who sleeps all day and cries half the night. Another starts out being restless in the daytime and then gradually shifts to night, or vice versa. The crying of colic most often begins after a feeding, sometimes right after, sometimes half an hour or so later. In this way it is different from the crying of the hungry baby, which usually occurs **before** the feeding.

A mother is distressed to have her baby so unhappy and thinks that something is terribly wrong. She wonders how long he can keep this up and not become exhausted. She wonders how long **she** can stand it. The strange thing is that the colicky or crying baby usually prospers from the physical point of view. In spite of hours of crying, he continues to gain weight, not just average-well but better than average. He is a hungry baby. He gulps down his whole feeding and always seems to be demanding an increased amount.

When a baby turns colicky, the mother's first thought is apt to be that his feeding is wrong. If he is on the breast, she thinks her milk is to blame. If he is on a formula, she wonders if it needs some fundamental change—perhaps from evaporated milk to fresh milk or perhaps from granulated sugar to a fancier sugar, like the baby next door. Changing the formula may bring about improvement in some cases, but not in most. It is plain to see that the quality of the feeding is not the main cause of colic. Otherwise why should the baby be able to digest it perfectly 4 out of 5 feedings a day, and get into trouble only in the evening? Colic occurs with breast milk, with cow's milk, and with all kinds of formulas. Once in a while, orange juice is suspected of being the cause.

We don't know the basic cause of most colic or irritable crying. One guess is that both conditions are due to a periodic tension in the baby's immature nervous system. Some of these babies are hypertonic all the time (Section 274). The fact that the trouble is commonest in the evening or late afternoon suggests that fatigue plays a part. Many babies up to the age of 3 months are on edge just before falling asleep. Instead of being able to slip peacefully off, they must let out at least a few piercing cries.

276. The treatment of colic. The most important thing is for the mother and father to recognize that the condition is fairly common, that it doesn't seem to do the baby any permanent harm, that, on the contrary, it occurs most often in babies that are developing and growing well, and that it will probably be gone by the time the baby is 3 months old, if not before, leaving him none the worse for wear. If the parent can accept the condition in a fairly calm and resigned way, the battle is half won.

Some colicky babies (the hypertonic ones) seem to be definitely better when they lead quiet, calm lives—sleeping in a quiet room, being handled slowly and gently, being talked to softly, not seeing any visitors (at least closely), not being tickled or rough-housed in any way, avoiding noisy places outdoors, and perhaps, in an extreme case in a city, not going outdoors at all till the colic improves. The colicky baby, like others, must have company and cuddling and be smiled at, but it can be done gently. It is important to get his bubble up after feedings. The mother should keep closely in touch with the doctor. He may prescribe a sedative or other relaxing drugs. A sedative properly prescribed is not harmful or habit forming, even if used for months.

But suppose it is not possible to get in touch immediately with the doctor. What home remedies are useful?

In many cases, a **pacifier** is by far the most effective remedy, but pacifiers are disapproved of by some parents and some doctors (Section 329).

The colicky baby is usually more comfortable on his stomach. He may get more relief still by being laid across his mother's knees or a hot-water bottle, and rubbed on his back.

Hot-water bottle. You should be able to rest the inside of your wrist against the hot-water bottle without discomfort. Then, as an extra precaution, wrap it in a diaper or towel before laying the baby against it or half on it.

When the colic is agonizing, a warm enema may give dramatic relief. (See "Enemas," Section 610.) This is not a remedy that should be given regularly; use it only on especially severe occasions.

Should you pick a baby up, or rock him gently, or carry him around while he has colic? Even if it makes him stop crying, won't it spoil him? We aren't as scared nowadays of the danger of spoiling a baby as we used to be. If a baby is comforted when he is miserable, he usually doesn't go on demanding that comfort when he isn't miserable. If a baby is screaming with colic or irritability, and picking him up or rocking him seems to help him, then do it. If, however, holding him makes him feel no better, it's just as well not to get him used to being held so much (Section 278).

Babies who are unusually miserable or unusually tense need especially to be under close medical supervision. Most of them improve steadily as they grow older, but the first 2 or 3 months may be rough on them and on their parents.

277. It's hard on the parents of a fretful, hypertonic, colicky, or irritable baby. If your baby is colicky or irritable, he may be soothed when you first pick him up. But after a few minutes he's apt to be screaming harder than ever. He thrashes with his arms and kicks with his legs. He not only refuses to be comforted—he acts as if he were angry at you for trying. These reactions are painful for you. You feel sorry for him, at least in the beginning. You feel increasingly inadequate, because you're not able to do anything to relieve him. Then as the minutes go by and he acts angrier and angrier, you feel that he is spurning you as a parent and you can't help feeling mad at him underneath. But getting angry at a tiny baby makes you ashamed of yourself, and you try hard to suppress the feeling. This makes you more tense than ever.

Every parent gets angry at such times, and there's no need to feel guilty. If you can admit the feeling and laugh about it with your husband, you will be able to stand it more comfortably. The other thing to remember is that the baby is not mad at you. He doesn't know yet that you are a person or that he is a person. He's just a bundle of organs and nerves during his first month. Some kind of pain is spreading through his system, and it automatically sets all his limbs to thrashing, just as a tap on his knee automatically makes his leg kick.

If you have the bad luck to have a baby who cries a great deal from colic or irritability or fretfulness, despite your own and your doctor's efforts, you have to think of yourself, too. You may be the kind of mother who isn't bothered too much after you have found out that there is nothing seriously wrong with him and after you have done all that you can to make him happy. That's fine, if you are made that way. But many mothers get worn out and frantic listening to a baby cry, especially when it's the first. You should make a great effort to get away from home and baby for a few hours at least twice a week—oftener if you can arrange it. Hire someone, or ask a friend or neighbor to come in and relieve you. If you're like most people, you hesitate to do this. "Why should I inflict the baby on somebody else? Besides, I'd be nervous being away from him for so long." But you shouldn't think of a vacation like this as just a treat for you. It's very important for you, for the baby, and for your husband that you do not get exhausted and depressed. If you can't get anyone to come in, let your husband stay home one or two evenings a week while you go out to visit or see a movie, and encourage him to take one or two nights off a week. The baby doesn't need two worried parents at a time to listen to him. Try also to get friends to come in and visit you. Remember that everything that helps you keep a sense of balance, everything that keeps you from getting too preoccupied with the baby, helps the baby and the rest of the family in the long run.

SPOILING

278. Can you spoil a baby? This question comes up naturally in the first few weeks at home if a baby is fussing a lot between feedings instead of sleeping peacefully. You pick him up and walk him around and he stops crying, at least for the time being. Lay him down, and he starts all over again. I don't think you need to worry much about spoiling in the first month or even the first 2 months. The chances are great that such a young baby is feeling miserable inside. If he stops fussing when picked up, it's probably because the motion and distraction, and perhaps the warm pressure on his abdomen from being held, make him forget his pains or tensions at least temporarily. Even if you decide later that he has been somewhat spoiled from an early age, you can usually undo the harm in a few days, in the first 4 or 5 months.

279. You can be a little more suspicious by three months. By the time babies are about 3 months old, the commonest causes of physical misery—colic, irritable crying, fretfulness—are over in a great majority of cases. (A very few babies go on having severe colic until 4 or 5 months old.) You notice that the baby who was previously colicky no longer wakes suddenly with cramps and distension. The baby who suffered from irritable crying or fretfulness no longer has distinctly miserable spells that contrast with comfortable periods. Naturally, some of these babies who have been held and walked a great deal for 3 months straight are mildly spoiled. They want their walking and their company, anyway. Now it's sensible to become a little less tender-hearted. I don't mean that you should turn severe all of a sudden. But when it's bedtime you can tell your baby cheerfully but firmly that he has to sleep and that you have to go, even if he yells for a few minutes. (The more severe form of this problem is discussed in Section 284.)

There are other types of spoiling that a mother can gradually slip into as a baby comes to the middle and last parts of the first year.

280. A parent who's too eager to amuse. A mild kind of spoiling occurs when a mother (or father or grandmother) is so delighted with her baby that she is regularly playing with him most of the time he's awake—carrying him around or dancing with him or jouncing him on her knees or playing pat-a-cake or making him laugh. (Everyone does these a little.) Gradually he forgets how to amuse himself. He feels bored, deserted, and miserable when left alone and cries for attention. What started out as fun for the mother becomes an endless chore.

281. Parents who submit too easily. If a mother is too ready to pick a baby up and carry him around whenever he fusses, she may find after a couple of months that he is fretting and holding out his arms to be carried almost all the time he is awake. If she continues to give in, he realizes after a while that he has his poor tired mother under his thumb and he becomes increasingly disagreeable and tyrannical in demanding this service. The mother can't help resenting such an unreasonable attitude and gets to dislike him heartily. But these emotions are apt to make her feel guilty, and besides, she doesn't know how to get out of the jam.

282. Some causes of spoiling. Why does a parent get involved in these ordinary types of spoiling? In the first place, it usually happens with the first baby and all of us come near it with our first. For most people a first baby is the most fascinating plaything in the world. If a man can be obsessed for a while with a new car and a woman with a fur coat, it's easy to see why a baby is all-absorbing for months. But delight is not the only factor. Parents are apt to project all the hopes and fears they've had about themselves onto their first-born. There's the anxiety, too, the unfamiliar sense of being entirely responsible for the safety and happiness of a helpless human being. His crying makes a powerful demand on you to do something. With your second baby you have more assurance and a sense of proportion; you know that a child has to be denied some things for his own good, and you don't feel guilty about being hard-hearted when you know for sure it's right.

But some parents are more easily drawn into spoiling than others—for instance, parents who have had to wait a long time for a baby and suspect that they may not be able to have another; parents with too little confidence in their own worthiness who become willing slaves to a child and expect him to be all the things they felt they never could be; parents who have adopted a baby and feel that they have to do a super-human job to justify themselves; parents who have studied child psychology in college or nursing or medicine or worked professionally in the field and feel doubly obligated to prove their capability (actually, it's a tougher job when you know the theory); parents who are ashamed when they've felt cross at the baby and try to even things up by giving him anything he wants; parents who feel too angry or guilty when they hear a baby crying and find the tension unbearable. See also Section 497 on overprotection.

Whatever the underlying factor, all these parents are a little too willing to sacrifice their own comforts and their own rights, too anxious to give the baby anything he asks for. This might not be too bad if a baby knew what was sensible to ask for. But he doesn't know what's good for him. It's his nature to expect firm guidance from his parents. This comforts him. When they are hesitant it makes him uneasy. If they always anxiously pick him up whenever he fusses—as if it would be terrible to leave him there—he, too, gets the feeling that this would be terrible. And the more they submit to his orders, the more demanding he becomes. (A human being of any age finds himself imposing on a person who is too submissive.)

283. How do you unspoil? The earlier you detect the problem, the easier it is to cure. But it takes a lot of will power and a little hardening of the heart. To get yourself in the right mood you have to remember that, in the long run, unreasonable demandingness and excessive dependence are worse for the baby than for you. They get him out of kilter with himself and with the world. So you are reforming him for his own good.

Make out a schedule for yourself, on paper if necessary, that requires you to be busy with housework or anything else for most of the time the baby is awake. Go at it with a great bustle—to impress the baby and to impress yourself. When he frets and raises his arms, explain to him in a friendly but very firm tone that this job and that job **must** get done this afternoon. Though he doesn't understand the words, he does understand the tone of voice. Stick to your busy work. The first hour of the first day is the hardest. One baby accepts the change better if his mother stays out of sight a good part of the time at first and talks little. This helps him to become absorbed in something else. Another adjusts more quickly if he can at least see his mother and hear her talking to him, even if she won't pick him up. When you bring him a plaything or show him how to use it, or when you decide it's time to play with him a bit at the end of the afternoon, sit down beside him on the floor. Let him climb into your arms if he wants, but don't get back into the habit of walking him around. If you're on the floor with him, he can crawl away when he eventually realizes you won't walk. If you pick him up and walk him, he'll surely object noisily just as soon as you start to put him down again. If he keeps on fretting indefinitely when you sit with him on the floor, remember another job and get busy again.

284. Chronic resistance to sleep in infancy—Going-to-bed type: This is a difficulty that develops insidiously. In most cases it grows out of a case of colic or irritable crying. It can be thought of as a form of spoiling. A baby has been miserable with colic most evenings for his first 2 or 3 months. His mother has found that he is more comfortable when she carries him around. This makes her feel better, too. But by the time he is about 3 or 4 months old, it gradually dawns on her that he doesn't seem to be in so much pain or misery any more—his cry is now angry and demanding. He wants his walking because he's used to it and thinks he's entitled to it. He almost glares at his mother when she sits down for a well-needed rest as if to say, "Woman, get going!"

A baby who becomes engaged in a nightly struggle to keep his mother walking has to really train himself to stay awake, and he succeeds step by step as the months go by—first to 9 P.M., then to 10, 11, even midnight. His mother says that his lids often close and his head droops while she's carrying him, but that as soon as she starts to lay him down he wakes with an indignant yell.

Such a sleep problem is exhausting to baby and parents. The baby is apt to become more irritable in the daytime, too, and may eat less well. The parents can't help getting more and more irritated and resentful. A baby shouldn't be able to put adults through a performance like this every night. They know it but don't know what to do about it. Even a baby senses, I think, that he shouldn't be able to get away with such tyranny.

The habit is usually easy to break once the parents realize that it is as bad for the baby as it is for them. The cure is simple: put the baby to bed at a reasonable hour, say good night affectionately but firmly, walk out of the room, and don't go back. Most babies who have developed this pattern cry furiously for 20 or 30 minutes the first night, and then when they see that nothing happens, they suddenly fall asleep! The second night the crying is apt to last only 10 minutes. The third night there usually isn't any at all.

It's hard on the kind-hearted parents while the crying lasts. They imagine the worst: that his head is caught in the slats of the crib, or that he has vomited and is lying in a mess, that he is at least in a panic about being deserted. From the rapidity with which these sleep problems can be cured in the first year, and from the way the babies immediately become much happier as soon as this is accomplished, I'm convinced that they are only crying from anger at this age. It's important not to tiptoe in to be sure the baby is safe or to reassure him that you are near by. This only enrages him and keeps him crying much longer. See Section 497 on overprotection.

If the several nights of crying will wake other children or anger the neighbors, you can muffle the sound by putting a rug or blanket on the floor and a blanket over the window. Soft surfaces of this kind absorb a surprising amount of the sound.

It's sometimes worth while to explain the program to touchy neighbors in order to reassure them that it will take only a few nights and to ask their indulgence.

285. Waking-in-the-night type: In this form the baby goes to bed and right to sleep like an angel but develops a habit of regularly waking in the middle of the night. Sometimes it starts from a bad cold or ear infection that wakes him with real discomfort. This makes his parents quick to run to him again on subsequent nights when they hear a whimper, even though the cold is subsiding. Sometimes the wakefulness seems to start during a painful stage of teething. I imagine that all babies, like older people, half-wake a number of times every night to shift position. When a baby has been picked up and treated to company for a number of nights, I think he learns to rouse himself from half awake to wide awake to have more of the fun.

If the parents don't know how to put a stop to it, a baby may learn to wake not once but several times, to stay awake longer and longer each time, to demand not just company but walking, and to resist being put back to bed by furious crying. I've heard of cases in which it amounted eventually to 3 or 4 hours of walking each night. This is even more exhausting and irritating to baby and parents than a going-to-bed problem. See Section 497 on overprotection.

Most cases can be cured easily. The baby has to learn that there is nothing to be gained by waking and crying. This can usually be accomplished in 2 or 3 nights by letting him cry and not going to him at all. It is apt to be 20–30 minutes the first night (it may seem much longer), 10 minutes the second night, none the third.

One additional requirement is necessary, in my experience. The baby must not see the parents when he wakes up. If he sees them, even though they pretend to be asleep, this angers him and stimulates him to keep up the crying indefinitely. It is essential to put his bed in a different room from theirs, at least for a few nights, until the habit is broken, no matter how inconvenient this may be. If this is absolutely impossible, a screen or curtain can be rigged to prevent his seeing them. Read the other suggestions in the previous section.

286. The spoiled baby who vomits. Some babies (and young children) vomit easily when enraged. The mother is apt to be upset and shows it by her anxious looks, by rushing to clean up, by being more sympathetic afterward, by being quicker to come to the baby the next time he screams. This lesson is not lost on the child, and he is likely to vomit more deliberately the next time he's in a temper. And he also comes to be frightened by the vomiting he induces, because his mother is frightened by it. I think it is essential that a mother harden her heart to the vomiting if her baby is using it to bully her. If she is trying to get him over a refusal to go to bed, she should stick to her program and not go in. She can clean him up later after he has gone to sleep.

COMMON KINDS OF INDIGESTION

Consult the doctor promptly about any change in your baby's digestion. Don't try to diagnose it yourself—there is too much chance of error. There are many other causes of vomiting, cramps, and loose movements besides those mentioned here. This discussion is primarily to help parents to adjust to a few common types of mild chronic indigestion of early infancy, after the doctor has made the diagnosis.

287. Hiccups. Most babies hiccup pretty regularly after meals in the early months. It doesn't seem to mean anything, and there is nothing that you need to do, aside from making sure he has no bubble. If a drink of warm water stops him, there's no harm in giving it.

288. Spitting and vomiting are common. Spitting and vomiting are really the same thing. The word **spitting** is popularly used when only small amounts of milk are brought up. Most babies do considerable spitting during the early months, and this usually means nothing. Some spit several times after every feeding. Others do it only occasionally. (Milk stains can be more easily removed from sheets, diapers, and clothing if they are first soaked in cold water.)

It alarms a new mother when her baby first vomits a large amount of milk. But this is not serious in itself if the baby seems otherwise healthy. There are a few babies who vomit a large amount as often as once a day, especially the hypertonic babies (Section 274) and especially in the early weeks. Naturally, if your baby spits or vomits regularly even though he is continuing to gain, you should discuss it with the doctor—particularly if there are other signs of indigestion. It is worth while taking extra care to bring up the bubble. In most cases, the spitting goes right on, no matter how you change the formula or decrease the quantity.

The question occurs to you, If a baby has vomited what seems like his whole feeding, should he be fed again right away? If he seems happy enough, don't feed him, at least until he acts very hungry. His stomach may be a little upset, and it is better to give it a chance to quiet down. Remember that the amount vomited usually looks larger than it actually is. There are babies who you would swear are vomiting most of every feeding but who still go on gaining satisfactorily.

Whether or not the spit-up milk is sour and curdled is not important. The first step in digestion in the stomach is the secretion of acid. Any food that has been in the stomach for a while is acidified. The effect of acid on milk is to curdle it.

All that I have been saying about how common it is for babies to spit and to vomit occasionally doesn't mean that you never have to take vomiting seriously. A baby who begins vomiting all his feedings right after birth must be watched carefully by the doctor. Usually it's due to mucus in the stomach and clears up in a few days, but once in a great while it's more serious, especially if there is green bile in it, and requires prompt medical or surgical treatment.

289. Projectile vomiting in pyloric stenosis. Another uncommon form of vomiting is most apt to begin when the baby is several weeks old. It is called pyloric stenosis. In this condition, the valve leading from the far end of the stomach into the intestines will not open up satisfactorily to let the food through. It is more common in boy babies. The food is vomited out with great force (projectilely), so that it lands at a distance from the baby's mouth. The vomiting may occur during or shortly after the feeding. It doesn't mean that your baby has this condition if he has projectile vomiting once in a while. But if he has projectile vomiting as often as twice a day, he **must** be under careful medical observation. If other methods of treatment fail and if he continues to vomit most of his feedings and fails to gain, he may have to be cured by operation.

If your baby has not been a vomiter and then suddenly vomits a large amount for the first time, it's a good idea to take his temperature to make sure that he is not sick. Many different infections start with vomiting in a baby. If he has no fever and looks entirely normal, don't worry. If he seems sick in any other way or vomits again, call the doctor.

Vomiting that comes on suddenly later in infancy, especially if there is pain or if there is green bile in the vomitus, may mean obstruction of the intestines, as in intussusception (Section 690) or strangulated hernia (Section 695). It requires immediate attention.

In most babies the tendency to spitting is greatest in the early weeks and months, and decreases as they get older. Most have stopped it altogether by the time they can sit up. An occasional one goes on until he is walking. Once in a while a baby only starts his spitting when he is several months old. Sometimes teething seems to make it worse for a while. Spitting is messy and inconvenient but not important if he's gaining well and is happy.

290. Mild indigestion and gas. In three-month colic the baby has regular spells of misery that seem to have more to do with the time of day than with what he is having to eat. But another baby may develop a spell of indigestion that's more continuous. Common symptoms are discomfort and fretting, passing gas by rectum, increased spitting and vomiting, bowel movements that are partly loose, partly curdy, and perhaps greenish. These cases are more likely to be improved by changes in the formula than are cases of three-month colic. If you have a doctor or can reach one, you should, of course, consult him about the baby's indigestion even if the baby is gaining. It is absolutely necessary to consult a doctor if a baby is having trouble and not gaining weight.

If you are completely out of reach of a doctor and indigestion is persisting, you can try omitting all sugar from the formula. The baby may need a larger total amount of the sugarless formula to make up for the sugar calories. If he is on a weak beginning formula, you may need to increase the evaporated milk to the full can (13 ounces of evaporated milk, 19 ounces of water). If the indigestion is not improved, you can acidify the formula (Section 157). If these changes are successful, keep them up for a couple of months or until you can consult a doctor.

CONSTIPATION

291. What's constipation and what isn't? One baby always has his bowel movement at the same time of day, another at a different time each day. One is just as healthy as the other. There is no advantage to be gained by trying to make the irregular baby regular. In the first place, it can't usually be done. In the second place, there's a danger, in the long run, of upsetting the baby emotionally if you keep trying to get a movement out of him when he isn't ready.

It isn't constipation when a breast-fed baby has a movement only every other day, because the movement is still very soft, and there is no reason why a baby needs to have a movement every day. Perhaps you could call it a kind of constipation when he strains unsuccessfully to get this liquid movement out, but it's not the ordinary kind.

292. Hard movements with the bottle-fed baby. One type of constipation is when the movements of a baby on cow's milk become hard and formed. They may be uncomfortable for him to pass. Consult your doctor about this. If you cannot reach a doctor, there are two remedies you can try. The simplest is to change the sugar in the formula to one that is more laxative. If you have been using light corn syrup, change to the dark. If this is not sufficient or if the baby has been on granulated sugar, use brown sugar. (You use the same amount as you were using of granulated sugar or corn syrup.) This kind of constipation is also helped by adding prune juice or puréed prunes to the baby's diet. You can start with 2 teaspoonfuls of the prunes (stewed or canned) or of the juice (homemade, from stewed prunes, or canned prune juice) at the 6 P.M. feeding. If this isn't enough, increase to 4 teaspoonfuls of prunes or juice, or even more. Some babies get cramps from prunes or prune juice, but most take it all right.

293. Chronic constipation is less common in the older baby or child, especially if he is taking a varied diet including whole-grain cereals, vegetables, and fruits. If your child becomes constipated, take it up with the doctor—don't try to treat it yourself, because you aren't sure what it is due to. It's very important, whatever treatment you use, that you do not get the child concerned about his bowel function. Don't get into serious conversations about it with him, or connect it with germs or his health or how he feels. Don't encourage him to keep track of his movements, or seem to pay too much attention to them yourself. Avoid enemas. Do what the doctor recommends as matter-of-factly, cheerfully, and briefly as possible, whether it's diet, medication, or exercise, without going into the whys and wherefores with the child; otherwise you may turn him into a hypochondriac.

But suppose you are unable to consult a doctor, and your child, otherwise healthy, gradually gets into a spell of constipation. (Naturally, if he has any symptoms of illness, you get him to the doctor or hospital somehow.) Give him more fruit or vegetables, if he likes either, 2 or 3 times a day. If he likes prunes or figs, serve them every day. Fruit and vegetable juices help, too. See that he has plenty of exercise. If he is 4 or 5 or older, and in spite of your efforts with diet, continues to have rather constipated and irregular movements that don't hurt him, relax until you can get a doctor's help.

Mineral oil is not considered safe for a baby. If he chokes on it, some may get breathed into the lungs and possibly cause a chronic kind of pneumonia.

294. Painfully hard movements in the early years should be treated promptly. If you have a child of 1, 2, or 3 years whose movements are hurting him, it's urgent to relieve him. Otherwise he may become worried because of the pain. It's a psychological emergency (Sections 295 and 382). If you cannot reach a doctor and are compelled to treat the condition yourself, a reasonably safe thing to use is a commercial preparation made of acidophilus bacilli, mineral oil, and chocolate flavoring; a teaspoonful of this each evening is usually sufficient to prevent hard movements. This is not a cathartic and does not soften up an already hard movement. You give a teaspoonful every night after supper for at least a month or until you can get advice from your doctor. If the movements are then good, cut down gradually, to ¾ teaspoonful for 3 nights, ½ teaspoonful, and so on. If the constipation starts to return, give the full dose for another month.

295. Psychological constipation. There are two varieties of constipation that are largely psychological in origin and that start most frequently between the ages of 1 and 2. If a child at this age has one or two painfully hard movements, he may tend to hold back for weeks or even months afterward for fear of being hurt again. If he holds the movement in for a day or two, it's apt to be hard again, and this keeps the problem going. It's discussed in Section 382. Occasionally when a mother goes at toilet training in too determined a manner, the small child, being in an independent stage in his development, automatically resists and holds the movement back, which leads to constipation. This is discussed in Section 381.

296. Temporary constipation is common during illness, especially if there is fever. In former days parents and doctors often felt it was the most important symptom to treat and that the child couldn't begin to recover until he was "cleaned out." Some people even believed that the constipation was the main cause of the illness. It's more sensible to realize that any disease that can make a person feel sick all over is apt to affect his entire stomach and intestinal system, slowing down his bowels, taking away his appetite, perhaps causing him to vomit. These symptoms may appear several hours before any others. The doctor may prescribe a cathartic on general principles, but if he is delayed in coming, the parent needn't feel that valuable time is being lost.

If you **have** to treat a sick child without a doctor, don't worry too much about his bowels. It's better to do too little than too much. If he isn't eating anything, there isn't much for his bowels to move. If you are sure that he has only a cold or a contagious disease and he hasn't moved for 3 days, you can give him an enema (Section 610).

297. Spastic constipation. In this kind of constipation, the movement comes out as a collection of small hard balls. It occurs on a cow's-milk formula or on a regular solid-food diet. The sections of the large intestine go into spasms and hold small pieces of the bowel movement until they become dried into little balls. Nobody knows why the intestines of some people have this tendency. It may be due to nervous tension in some cases. It is often hard to cure. Sometimes it is helped by changes in the formula or diet, but frequently not. A child may outgrow spastic constipation at any age. If there is a delay in consulting a doctor, you can try the suggestions in Section 294.

DIARRHEA

298. Diarrhea in babies. A baby's intestines are sensitive the first year or two. They may be upset not only by the germs that cause diarrhea in older individuals but by one or another vegetable, by cold germs, and by other germs that don't affect older children and grownups at all. This is why we try to protect babies from infections in others, sterilize their milk so carefully, make formula changes gradually, add new foods slowly.

If a baby's movements have been good but suddenly turn loose, you should assume that he has an intestinal infection. There are usually other changes, too. The stools are likely to be more numerous. The color often changes, most commonly to greenish. The odor is usually different.

Most diarrheas are mild and can be cured easily if they are treated early. A diarrhea should be considered **severe** if **any** of the following symptoms are present: watery stools; pus or blood in the stools; vomiting; fever of 101° or more; the baby looks prostrated or has sunken eyes with gray circles under them.

Even for a mild diarrhea you ought to get in touch with the doctor promptly, because the sooner treatment is started the lighter the disease will be and the quicker over. If the baby has any of the symptoms that point to a severe diarrhea, it is vitally important to get the doctor or to take the baby to a hospital, even if this involves a long trip.

Two rare types of chronic diarrhea are discussed in Sections 692 and 693.

299. Emergency treatment of mild diarrhea, until you can consult a doctor. It will often be several hours before you can get advice from the doctor, and in the rare case of a baby who is hundreds of miles from nowhere, it may not be possible to reach one at all. So the following emergency suggestions are given. But they should not encourage any mother to treat diarrhea herself if she can possibly consult a doctor.

If the baby is on the breast alone, let him continue to nurse. If he wants less than usual, so much the better. If he is taking solids, too, omit them until you can talk to the doctor or the diarrhea is cured. Most diarrheas do well with breast milk.

If your baby is on formula alone and develops a mild diarrhea, dilute each bottle in half until you can speak to the doctor (Section 166). Even better than half-strength formula is diluted skimmed milk if you can get it. See Section 155. Let the baby take as little of each bottle as satisfies him. But if on this weak formula he gets hungry more often, feed him more frequently. If you **have** to continue to treat him yourself, try to keep him on half-strength formula or diluted skimmed milk until his movements have been normal or nearly normal for a whole day and until he is hungry for more. If he isn't hungry enough to demand a stronger formula, it's probably a sign that he's still ill and that it's safer not to increase yet. If a mild diarrhea isn't much improved in 2 or 3 days, you should consider it more serious and make a greater effort to reach the doctor.

If a baby on both formula and solid foods develops a mild diarrhea, omit all solids until you consult the doctor or until the diarrhea is over. If the baby is not hungry for his formula or if he is not improved in a day, dilute the formula as directed in Section 166, or give diluted skimmed milk (Section 155). When he is well, get the formula back to normal first before resuming the solids. In putting the solids back, go slowly. Add only one more type of food each day. Give one third the usual amount the first day, two thirds the second day, the full amount the third day. Resume his usual foods in something like the following order: (1) gelatin or junket, (2) applesauce and orange juice, (3) meat and egg, (4) white cereal, (5) vegetables, (6) potato or other starch, (7) other fruits. For example, the first day you might give a third of his usual serving of junket; the second day two thirds of his usual amount of junket and a third of his usual serving of applesauce. Naturally, you don't add any foods at this time that he was not taking before.

300. Emergency treatment of severe diarrhea, until you can reach a doctor. If a baby develops any of the symptoms pointing to a severe diarrhea (watery stools, pus or blood in the stools, vomiting, fever of 101° or more, prostration or sunken eyes), give only a special formula made without milk as follows:

water .... 1 quart
his usual sugar .... 1 level tablespoonful
salt .... ¾ level teaspoonful

Give 1 to 4 ounces every 2 or 3 hours if he is awake and wants it, until you can talk to the doctor. If you are compelled to go on treating the illness yourself, keep him on this special formula alone for 24 to 72 hours, depending on how soon the bowel movements improve in appearance. Then proceed **very** gradually. I will list the possible stages in increasing the diet. If he recovers fairly rapidly, advance one stage each day. If he's improving slowly, take two days for each step.

Stage 1: Give him diluted skimmed milk. This is skimmed milk diluted with an equal amount of water (Section 155). If this is not available, make a formula using half his usual amount of his usual milk, no sugar, and enough water to make the usual total volume. Put only about two thirds of the usual amount into each bottle; use the rest to make a couple of extra bottles in case he has to be fed every 3 hours. Let him take just as little at each feeding as satisfies him; better too little than too much.

Stage 2: Use diluted skimmed milk with 1 tablespoonful of his usual sugar. If this is not available, use half the usual amount of his usual milk, enough water to make up the usual total, 1 tablespoonful of sugar.

Stage 3: Use full-strength skimmed milk and 2 tablespoonfuls of sugar. If not available, use half the amount of his usual milk, enough water to make up the usual total, 2 tablespoonfuls of sugar.

Stage 4 (if the bowel movements are normal): His usual formula.

Stage 5 and after: Add solids gradually, as in the last section.

If the movements become somewhat looser, drop back two stages. If the diarrhea becomes severe again, go all the way back to the special formula without milk and make a greater effort to get to a doctor.

When a diarrhea is improving, the first movement of the day is apt to look better, and a later one not so good. This in itself should not make you discouraged, but it shows that it is safer to see what the afternoon movements are like before strengthening the formula or adding to the diet. A sympathetic parent who is told to cut a baby's formula or diet way down during diarrhea is apt to cry out, "But he'll be hungry." Maybe he will be, maybe not. But it's kinder to make him a little unhappy for a day or two than to let his diarrhea get worse, for in the latter case you would have to starve him for longer in the end.

By the time a child is 2 or more, there is much less chance of severe or prolonged diarrhea. Until the doctor can be reached, the best treatment is bed rest and such fluids and soft solids as water, skimmed milk, gelatin, junket.

RASHES

Consult the doctor about all rashes. It's easy to be mistaken.

301. Bluish mottling. Babies who have pale skins often show a bluish mottling of the skin of the body when undressed.

302. Diaper rash. Most babies have sensitive skins in the early months. The diaper region is particularly apt to suffer. You may bring your baby home from the hospital with a sore behind. This doesn't mean that the hospital has been neglectful, but only that his skin needs extra care. The commonest forms of diaper rash are collections of small red pimples and patches of rough, red skin. Some of the pimples may become mildly infected and develop whiteheads (pustules) on them. If the rash is bad, raw spots may appear.

Diaper rash is mostly caused by ammonia. This is often mistakenly blamed on something in the baby's diet. But the ammonia is not passed in the urine. It is formed in the diaper and wet bedclothes by bacteria working on the urine. In the case of diaper rash, you boil the diapers, or dry them in the sun, or use a special antiseptic in them to discourage the bacteria that make ammonia.

Almost all babies develop a few spots of diaper rash from time to time. If it is slight and goes away as fast as it came, no special treatment is necessary. It is wise to discontinue the use of waterproof pants while there is any rash. Keep the rash covered with a protective ointment. Zinc ointment or Lassar's paste stays in place for a long while. Mineral oil, baby oil, and petroleum jelly get wiped off or absorbed too fast to give long-lasting protection.

If a diaper rash persists for days or gets worse, the most important step is either to boil the diapers or to use the diaper antiseptic your doctor recommends in rinsing them. **When a rash is bad, it is also important to boil or use antiseptic in rinsing the nighties, shirts, sheets, pads, waterproof sheeting—everything that gets wet with urine.** (Some waterproof sheeting can't be boiled but can be scrubbed with soap and soaked in diaper disinfectant.)

When a rash is bad, and especially if there are a lot of pustules (whiteheads), it usually works better not to use an ointment but to expose the whole diaper area to the air for several hours a day, keeping the baby in a warm room. You can cover his chest and his legs with two separate light blankets. Fold his diaper underneath him to catch some of the urine. Exposing a bad diaper rash to the air is the surest method of curing it, whether there are pustules or not.

If your baby has a tendency to develop bad diaper rash easily and frequently, you can experiment to see which precautions, used regularly, work best and with least effort: drying the diapers in the sun, or using a special diaper antiseptic in the last rinse, or boiling the diapers, or using ointment. Used regularly, one or the other of these or a combination may do the trick. If it seems necessary, you can change diapers not only before and after feedings but also midway between feedings.

Diapers from a diaper service are usually sterilized, so there is no point in boiling them again. Some diaper services also use a special antiseptic in the last rinse to discourage any growth of bacteria after the diaper has been wet by the baby.

Irritating bowel movements during an attack of diarrhea sometimes cause a very sore rash around the anus. The treatment is to try to change the diaper just as soon as it is soiled, clean the area with oil, and apply a thick covering of zinc ointment. If this does not work, the diaper should be left off and the diaper area exposed to the air.

303. Mild face rashes. There are several mild face rashes that babies have in the first few months that aren't definite enough to have names but are very common. First of all, there are minute shiny white pimples without any redness around them. They look like tiny pearls in the skin. They will surely go away as the baby gets older. Then there are collections of a few small red spots or smooth pimples on the cheeks. These may last a long time and get a mother quite upset. At times they fade and then get red again. Different ointments don't seem to do much good, but these spots always go away eventually. Less common is a rough, red patch on the cheeks that comes and goes.

Babies in the early weeks often have white blisters in the middle part of their lips from sucking. Sometimes the blisters peel. These clear up in time and need no treatment.

304. Prickly heat. Prickly heat is very common in the shoulder and neck region of babies when hot weather first begins. It is made up of clusters of minute pink pimples surrounded by blotches of pink skin. Tiny blisters form on some of the pimples, and when they dry up they give the rash a slightly tan look. Prickly heat usually starts around the neck. If it is bad, it can spread down onto the chest and back and up around the ears and face. It seldom bothers a baby. You can pat the rash several times a day with a bicarbonate of soda solution (1 teaspoonful of bicarbonate of soda to 1 cup of clean water) on absorbent cotton. Another treatment is dusting with cornstarch powder. It is more important to try to keep the baby cool. Don't be afraid to take off his clothes in very hot weather.

305. Cradle cap. Cradle cap is a mild disorder of the skin of the scalp. It is quite common in the early months. It appears as scaly patches that look dirty. The best treatment is to keep water and soap off the scalp altogether. Instead, clean the scalp with mineral oil or baby oil on a piece of absorbent cotton. Oiling the spots twice a day softens the crusts, which can then usually be combed off with a very fine-toothed comb. If this method is not successful, consult your doctor. Cradle cap rarely persists beyond the early months.

Eczema is discussed in Section 652.

Impetigo and other common rashes are discussed in Section 658.

MOUTH AND EYE TROUBLES

306. Thrush. Thrush is a mild fungus infection of the mouth. It looks as if patches of milk scum were stuck to the cheeks and tongue and roof of the mouth. But, unlike scum, it does not wipe off easily. If you do rub it off, the underlying skin bleeds slightly and looks inflamed. Thrush usually makes a baby's mouth sore. He shows the discomfort when he is trying to nurse. A baby's mouth is more apt to become infected with thrush if the nipples are handled carelessly. But it also occurs in babies who are taken care of to perfection. If you suspect it, consult the doctor promptly for diagnosis and treatment. If there is a delay in getting medical advice, it is helpful to have the baby drink half an ounce of boiled water, or suck it from a piece of sterile absorbent cotton, after his milk. This washes the milk out of his mouth and gives the thrush fungus less to live on.

Don't be fooled by the color of the inner sides of the gums where the upper molar teeth are going to be. The skin color here is normally very pale, and is sometimes mistaken for thrush by mothers who are on the lookout for it.

Cysts on the gums. Some babies have one or two little pearly-white cysts on the sharp edge of their gums. They may make you think of teeth, but they are too round and they don't make a click on a spoon. They have no importance and eventually disappear.

307. Discharge and tearing of the eye. Many babies develop a mild inflammation in the eyes a few days after birth. This is caused by the medication that is always used right after birth, to avoid infection.

If at any later time the baby has an inflammation that makes the whites of his eyes look bloodshot or even pink, it is probably an infection, and the doctor should be called promptly.

There is another kind of very mild but chronic infection of the eyelids that develops off and on in the early months in quite a number of babies, most commonly in only one eye. The eye waters and tears excessively, particularly in windy weather. White matter collects in the corner of the eye and along the edges of the lids. This discharge may keep the lids stuck together when the baby first wakes up. The condition is caused by obstructed tear ducts. The tear ducts lead from small openings on the edges of the eyelids, first toward the nose, then down the side of the eye socket and into the nose cavity. When this duct is partly plugged, the tears are not drained off as fast as they form. They well up in the eye and run down the cheek. The lids keep getting mildly infected, just because the eye is not being cleansed sufficiently by the tears. The doctor should, of course, see the eyes and make the diagnosis.

The first thing to realize about this condition is that it is fairly common, not serious, and does not injure the eye. It may last for many months. The tendency is outgrown in most cases even if nothing is done. If by a year it is still bothersome, an eye doctor can clear the duct with a simple procedure. When the lids are stuck together, you can soften the crust by laying over the lids a piece of sterile cotton wet with a sterile solution of boric acid, which you can get in the drugstore. The doctor sometimes advises massage of the duct, but don't do this without his directions. A plugged tear duct does not cause inflammation of the white of the eye. If the eye is bloodshot, something else is wrong and you should call the doctor.

308. Crossed eyes. It is common for a baby's eyes to turn in or out too much **at moments** in the early months. In most cases they become steady and straight as he grows older. If, however, the eyes turn in or out **all the time** or **much of the time,** even in the earliest months, or if they are not steady by 3 months, an eye doctor should be consulted. Many times a mother thinks her baby's eyes are crossed when they are really straight. This is because the skin area between the eyes (over the root of the nose) is relatively wider in a baby than in an older person.

Mothers often ask whether it is safe to hang toys over a baby's crib, since he sometimes is cross-eyed looking at them. Don't hang a toy right on top of a baby's nose, but it's perfectly all right to hang it at arm's reach. You have to remember that when a baby is looking at something in his hands, he has to turn his eyes in more than an older person does because his arms are so short. He is only converging his eyes normally, the way we all do to a lesser extent. His eyes won't get stuck that way.

It's not uncommon in a newborn baby for the lid of one eye to droop a little lower than the other or for one eye to look smaller. In most cases, these differences become less and less noticeable as the baby grows older.

SWOLLEN BREASTS

309. When the baby has swollen breasts. Many babies, both boys and girls, have swollen breasts for some time after birth. In some cases a little milk runs out. This is caused by the glandular changes in the mother just before the baby is born. Nothing needs to be done for swollen breasts in the baby; the swelling will surely disappear in time. The breasts should **not** be massaged or squeezed, since this is likely to irritate and infect them.

BREATHING TROUBLES

310. Sneezing. Babies sneeze easily. Sneezing doesn't usually mean a cold unless the nose begins to run, too. It is most often caused by dust and dried mucus that has collected in a ball in the front of the nose and tickles. If the breathing is obstructed, see Section 233.

311. Faint breathing. New parents usually worry a little about a new baby's breathing because it is often irregular and at times so shallow that they can't hear it or see it. They may worry, too, the first time they hear their baby snoring faintly in his sleep. Both conditions are normal.

312. Chronic noisy breathing occurs in a certain number of young babies. In one form the baby makes a snoring noise in the back of his nose. It's just like a grownup's snoring, except that the baby does it while he is awake. It seems to be caused by the fact that he hasn't yet learned to control his soft palate. He'll outgrow it.

The commoner type of chronic noisy breathing is caused in the larynx (voice box). The epiglottis, a fleshy structure just above the vocal cords, is so soft and floppy in some babies that it is sucked down and made to vibrate. This causes a loud rattling, snoring noise during breathing in, which doctors call stridor. It sounds as if the baby were choking, but he can breathe that way indefinitely. In most cases the stridor occurs only when the baby is breathing hard. It usually goes away when he is quiet or asleep. It may be better when he lies on his abdomen. It should be discussed with the doctor, but no treatment is necessary or does any good. Stridor goes away as the baby grows older.

Noisy breathing that comes on acutely, particularly in an older infant or child, has an entirely different significance from the chronic variety. It may be due to croup, asthma, or other infection, and requires **prompt** medical attention.

Every baby with noisy breathing, chronic or acute, should be examined by a doctor.

Obstruction in the nose from dry mucus is discussed in Section 233; obstruction from moist mucus during a cold, in Section 628.

313. Breath-holding spells. Some babies get so furiously angry when they cry, and hold their breath so long, that they turn blue. When this first happens, it scares the wits out of the parents. It seldom means anything except that the baby has that kind of temperament. (It's often a baby who's unusually happy at other times.) The doctor should be told about it so that at the next visit he can make sure that everything is all right physically; otherwise nothing needs to be done. It's not a reason for keeping the baby from ever crying. If you pick him up every time he cries, he's likely to get spoiled.

314. The thymus gland. You hear people talking about the thymus gland with great awe. You'd think it was a very dangerous gland indeed. It is sometimes blamed on those very rare occasions when a baby dies for no apparent reason. Most of this bad reputation is not deserved at all. Every baby has a thymus gland in the upper part of his chest. A normal thymus may be large enough so that it presses slightly on the windpipe, but this almost never causes any symptoms or trouble. It is no longer considered necessary or wise to give X-ray treatment for the thymus gland.

The old idea that enlarged thymus could cause sudden death came about because of a misunderstanding about what size the gland is meant to be. Now that we know more about it, we realize that those glands that were found in cases of sudden death, and that were thought to be enlarged, were really normal-sized glands. Those rare cases of sudden death are usually found, on very careful examination, to have been caused by sudden severe infection.

So don't worry about the thymus. There's no good reason why a healthy newborn baby needs an X-ray picture to show how big his thymus is.

COMMON NERVOUS SYMPTOMS

315. Babies who startle easily. Newborn babies are startled by loud noises and by sudden changes in position. Some are much more sensitive than others. When you put a baby on a flat, hard surface and he jerks his arms and legs, it's likely to rock his body a little. This unexpected motion is enough to make a sensitive baby nearly jump out of his skin and cry with fright. He may hate his bath because he is held so loosely. He needs to be washed in his mother's lap and then rinsed in the tub, while held securely in both her hands. He should be held firmly and moved slowly at all times. He will gradually get over this uneasiness as he grows older. (See Section 274 on the hypertonic baby.)

316. The trembles. Some babies have trembly moments in the early months. The chin may quiver, or the arms and legs may tremble, especially when the baby is excited or when he is cool just after being undressed. This trembling is nothing to be disturbed about. It is just one of the signs that the baby's nervous system is still young. The tendency passes away in time.

317. Twitching. Some babies twitch occasionally in their sleep, and once in a while there is one who twitches frequently. This, too, usually disappears as the baby grows older. Mention it to the doctor so that he can check.

318. Head-rolling, head-banging, jouncing. It's disturbing to a mother to have her baby take up the habit of banging his head. It seems so senseless and painful that it makes her doubt whether he's really bright, after all. She wonders if the repeated blows can injure his brain. Even if she doesn't have these worries, she finds it nerve-racking to sit in the next room and listen to the steady thud, thud, thud.

As one baby bangs his head against the bed, another rolls it from side to side. Still another gets up on his hands and knees and rhythmically jounces down against his heels. This moves the crib across the room until it bangs against the wall.

What is the meaning of these rhythmic movements? I don't think we know for sure, but here are some suggestions. In the first place, these motions usually appear in the second half of the first year, in the age period when babies naturally begin to get a sense of rhythm and try to sway in time to music. But this is at best only a partial explanation. Jouncing and head-banging occur mostly when a baby is going to sleep or is partly awakened. We know that many babies when they are tired do not go directly and peacefully to sleep, but must go through a slightly tense period first. There are the 2- and 3-month-old infants who always scream for a few minutes before dropping off. Perhaps those older babies who suck their thumbs to go to sleep, and the others who bang their heads or jounce, are also trying to soothe away a tense feeling.

I think that the first baby is more likely to bang his head or jounce than his younger brothers and sisters, and the solemn, high-strung one more often than the jolly, easygoing one. Some doctors have the impression that these rhythmic movements are commoner in babies who don't get quite enough cuddling. Maybe these notions have some connection with each other. It's natural for parents with their first baby to be more serious. They forget at times to relax, to be natural and comfortable, to show physical affection for the baby. As a result, he may be less cuddly, less sociable, less easygoing.

This idea may give a useful clue to some parents of jouncing, head-rolling, or head-banging babies, but I certainly don't want to give you the impression that it applies to all the babies who do these things, or that it's a proved theory for even a few. These habits do not mean that a baby is lacking in intelligence. They do not injure his brain.

If a baby bangs his head, you can pad his crib to keep him from bruising himself. One father solved his baby's head-banging by sawing the headboard out of the crib and tacking a piece of canvas in its place. For the jouncing baby who rattles the whole house, you can put the crib on a carpet and tack the carpet to the floor, or tie some kind of homemade pads, preferably of rubber, onto the feet of the crib. Or you can put the crib against the wall, where it's going to end up anyway, and place a big wad of padding between the crib and the wall.

In any case, I would not scold the baby or try to restrain him physically. Either of these measures would only make him more tense.

THUMB-SUCKING

319. Thumb-sucking is a subject about which there is yet no final agreement. I'll give you an idea of what is known and my suggestions of what to do about it. It used to be thought of as just a bad habit. That's why, when a baby first started, the mother would try to prevent it before it became a "habit." But we now know that it isn't this kind of habit, at least in the beginning. The main reason that a young baby sucks his thumb seems to be that he hasn't had enough sucking at the breast or bottle to satisfy his sucking need. Dr. David Levy pointed out that babies who are fed every 3 hours don't suck their thumbs as much as babies fed every 4 hours, and that babies who have cut down on nursing time from 20 minutes to 10 minutes (because the nipples have become old and soft) are more likely to suck their thumbs than babies who still have to work for 20 minutes. Dr. Levy fed a litter of puppies with a medicine dropper so that they had no chance to suck during their feedings. They acted just the same as babies who don't get enough chance to suck at feeding time. They sucked their own and each other's paws and skin so hard that the fur came off.

If your baby begins to try to suck his thumb or finger or hand, I think it's preferable not to stop him directly but to try to give him more opportunity to suck at the breast or the bottle or the pacifier (Section

329). There are two things to consider: the number of feedings, and how long each feeding takes.

320. The time to pay attention to thumb-sucking. The time to pay attention to thumb-sucking is when the baby first tries to do it, not when he finally succeeds. I make this point because there are lots of babies who, for the first few months of their lives, haven't much control over their arms. You see such a baby struggling to get his hands up, and searching around with his mouth. If by good luck he gets his fist to his mouth, he sucks it vigorously as long as it happens to stay there. This baby, just as much as the real thumb-sucker, is showing a need to suck longer at the breast or bottle.

The very young baby needs help most, because the sucking need is strongest in the first 3 or 4 months. From then on it tapers off gradually. One baby seems to have had enough sucking as early as 7 months, another not till he is over a year.

All babies aren't born with the same amount of instinct to suck. One baby never nurses more than 15 minutes at a time and yet never once has put his thumb in his mouth, and another whose bottles have always taken 20 minutes or more thumb-sucks excessively. A few begin to thumb-suck in the delivery room, and they keep at it. I suspect that a strong sucking instinct runs in some families.

You don't need to be concerned when a baby sucks his thumb for only a few minutes just before his feeding time. He is probably doing this only because he's hungry. It's when a baby tries to get his thumb just as soon as his feeding is over, or when he sucks a lot between feedings, that you have to think of ways to satisfy his sucking craving. Most babies who thumb-suck start before they are 3 months old.

I might add here that the thumb-, finger-, and hand-chewing that almost every baby does from the time he begins to teethe (commonly around 3 or 4 months) should not be confused with thumb-sucking. Naturally, the baby who is a thumb-sucker is sucking at one minute, chewing at another, during his teething periods.

321. Thumb-sucking in breast-fed babies. I have the impression that a breast-fed baby is less apt to be a thumb-sucker. This is probably because the mother is inclined to let him go on nursing as long as he wants to. She doesn't know whether her breast is empty, so she leaves it up to the baby. When a baby finishes a bottle, it's done. He stops because he doesn't like to suck air or because his mother takes away the bottle. The first question, then, about a breast-fed baby who is trying to suck his thumb is, Would he nurse longer if allowed to? If so, let him nurse for 30 or even 40 minutes at times if this is convenient for you. A baby gets most of the milk from a breast in 5 or 6 minutes; the rest of the time he's satisfying his craving to suck, lured on by a small trickle of milk. In other words, if he nurses for 35 minutes, he gets only slightly more milk than if he had nursed for 20. A breast-fed baby, allowed to nurse as long as he wants, may vary surprisingly. He is satisfied with 10 minutes at one feeding and wants as much as 40 minutes at another. This is an example of how breast feeding is adaptable to a baby's individual needs.

If a baby being nursed on one breast each feeding doesn't want to nurse any longer, there's nothing that you can do to make him. The baby who is getting **both** breasts at each feeding and begins to suck his thumb presents a different problem. Suppose he is usually taken off the first breast after 10 minutes and put on the second. He may get so much milk on the second breast that he's uncomfortably full after 5 minutes. So he stops nursing, even though he may not have satisfied his sucking instinct yet, and begins to suck his thumb. There are two methods you can try to make him nurse longer. See if he can be satisfied with one breast at each feeding, nursing as long as he will. If his hunger can't be satisfied that way, then at least let him nurse longer at the first breast. Instead of taking him off in 10 minutes, let him stay on for 20, if he will. Then put him to the second breast for as long as he wants.

322. Thumb-sucking in the bottle baby. With the average bottle-fed baby, thumb-sucking is most likely to begin at about the time he learns to finish his bottle in 10 minutes instead of in 20. This happens because the baby gets stronger as he gets older, but the rubber nipples get weaker. Whatever length of time he is taking to finish the bottles, the first thing to do is to get new nipples, leave the holes as they are, and see if that lengthens the bottle time. Of course, if the nipple holes are **too** small, some babies stop trying altogether. Try to keep the nipple holes small enough so that a bottle takes 20 minutes anyway, at least during the first 6 months. In this discussion, I am talking about the actual number of minutes that the baby is sucking. Naturally, it wouldn't help to lengthen the feeding time by pausing in the middle of the feeding.

If you have a strong baby, he may be able to empty a bottle in 10 or 12 minutes, even with brand-new nipples with holes that haven't been enlarged. If this is so, buy "blind" nipples. These are made without any holes. You have to burn the holes yourself with a red-hot needle (see Section 182). Start with a fine needle and burn briefly until you see how fast the milk or formula flows.

Bottles with plastic screw-on caps have nipples with a special opening near the edge for air intake. You can slow down this kind of bottle by screwing the cap on tighter. This partly blocks the air intake, keeps more of a vacuum in the bottle.

323. With a thumb-sucker, it's better to go slow in omitting feedings. It's not just the length of each feeding, but also the number or frequency of feedings in the 24 hours that determines whether a baby satisfies his sucking instinct. So if a baby is still thumb-sucking even though you have made each breast or bottle feeding last as long as possible, it is sensible to go slow in dropping other feedings. For example, if a 3-month-old baby seems willing to sleep through the 10 P.M. feeding but is doing a good deal of thumb-sucking, I would suggest waiting a while longer before dropping it—perhaps a couple of months, provided he is still willing to drink it when he's waked. The same thing applies to the change from 4 feedings a day to 3 meals.

324. The effect on the teeth. You may be worried about the effect of thumb-sucking on the baby's jaws and teeth. It is true that thumb-sucking often pushes the upper front baby teeth forward and the lower teeth back. How much the teeth are displaced depends on how much the child sucks his thumb and, even more, on what position he holds his thumb in. But dentists point out that this tilting of the baby teeth has no effect on the permanent teeth that begin coming in at about 6 years of age. In other words, if the thumb-sucking is given up by 6 years of age—as it is in a great majority of cases—there is very little chance of its hurting the permanent teeth.

But whether thumb-sucking displaces the teeth or not, you naturally prefer to have your child give it up as soon as possible. The suggestions I have been making are the ones that I think will end thumb-sucking soonest.

325. Why not use restraints? Why not tie a baby's arms down or put aluminum mittens over his hands to keep him from thumb-sucking? This would frustrate him a great deal, which theoretically is not a good idea. Furthermore, it usually doesn't cure the baby who is thumb-sucking a lot. We have all heard of despairing mothers who use elbow splints or metal mitts or bad-tasting paint not just for days but for months. And the day they take off the restraint, the thumb pops back in the mouth. To be sure, there are some mothers who say they have had good results from using such restraints. But in most of these cases, the thumb-sucking was very mild. Many babies do a little thumb-sucking off and on. They get over it quickly, whether you do anything or not. I think, myself, that restraints only make the confirmed thumb-sucker do it more in the long run.

326. Thumb-sucking in the older baby and child. Up to now we have been talking about how thumb-sucking begins in the early months. But by the time a baby is getting near the age of a year, his thumb-sucking seems to be turning into something different. It is a sort of comfort that he needs at special times. He sucks when he is tired or bored or frustrated, or to put himself to sleep. When he can't make a go of things at the more grown-up level, he retreats to early infancy when sucking was his chief joy.

Even though thumb-sucking satisfies a different need after the age of a year, it's the baby who first sucked his thumb to satisfy his sucking need who goes on doing it now. It's very rare for a child beyond the age of 1 to begin to thumb-suck for the first time.

There is no point worrying about lengthening the sucking time of the 1-, 2-, or 3-year-old. Is there anything that the parents need to do? I don't think so, if the child is generally outgoing, happy, and busy, and sucks only at bedtime and occasionally during the day. On the other hand, if he is sucking a great deal of the time instead of playing, his parents should only ask themselves whether there is anything they ought to do so that he won't **need** to comfort himself so much. A child may be bored from not seeing enough of other children and from not having enough things to play with. Or perhaps he's having to sit in his carriage for hours. A child of 1½ may be at loggerheads with his mother all day if she is always stopping him from doing all the things that fascinate him instead of diverting him to playthings that are permissible. Another child has children with whom he can play and freedom to do things at home, but he's too timid to throw himself into these activities. He thumb-sucks while he watches. I do not mean to suggest that every child who sucks his thumb is a problem. Even the happiest and best-adjusted of children have their off moments, and many small children who are sucking their thumbs regularly don't seem to need any change in their handling; in fact, they are unusually happy. I give the examples only to make it clear that if **anything** needs to be done for excessive thumb-sucking, it is to make the child's life more satisfying.

What has been said above probably applies equally to the child who must be sucking a corner of his blanket or chewing the collar of his coat when he's sleepy or bored or feels left out.

Elbow splints, mitts, and bad-tasting stuff on the thumb only make the child miserable and don't stop the habit any more often in older children than they do in small babies. I think that they tend to prolong the habit. The same applies to scolding a child or pulling his thumb out of his mouth. I remember the story of Anne, who finally stopped sucking her thumb of her own accord at 3. Six months later her Uncle George, who had been the member of the family who used to nag her about it, came back to the house to live. Anne's thumb-sucking began again the minute he entered the house. You often hear the recommendation that you give the child a toy when you see him thumb-sucking. It certainly is sound to have enough interesting things around for him to play with, so that he won't be bored. But if every time his thumb goes in his mouth, you jump toward him and poke an old toy into his hands, he'll soon catch on. What about bribing? If your child is one of the rare ones who is still sucking his thumb at the age of 5, and you are beginning to worry about what it will do to his permanent teeth when they come in, you will have a fair chance of succeeding if the bribe is a good one. A girl of 4 or 5 who wants to get over her thumb-sucking may be helped by having her fingernails painted like a lady's. But practically no child of 2 or 3 has the will power to deny an instinct for the sake of reward. You're apt to make a fuss and get nowhere.

So if your child is thumb-sucking, see to it that his life is good. In the long run it will help him if you remind him that someday he will be grown-up enough to stop. This friendly encouragement makes him want to stop as soon as he is able. But don't nag him. Most important of all, try to stop thinking about it. If you keep on worrying, even though you resolve to say nothing, the child will feel it and react against it. Remember that thumb-sucking goes away all by itself in time. In the overwhelming majority of cases, it is over before the second teeth appear. It doesn't go away steadily, though. It decreases rapidly for a while, and then comes back part way during an illness or when the child has a difficult adjustment to make. Eventually it goes for good. It rarely stops before 3 years. It usually peters out between 3 and 6.

327. Stroking movements and comforters with thumb-sucking. Most of the babies who go on thumb-sucking until they are 1 or more years old do some kind of stroking at the same time. One rubs or plucks a piece of blanket, or diaper, or silk, or a woolly toy. Another strokes his ear lobe or twists a lock of hair. Still another wants to hold a piece of cloth right up close to his face and perhaps stroke his nose or lip with a free finger. These motions remind you of how the younger baby used to be gently feeling his mother's skin or clothing when he was suckling at the breast or bottle. And when he presses something against his face, it looks as though he were remembering how he felt at the breast. These habits usually go away when the thumb-sucking goes.

When a child becomes deeply attached to an old piece of cloth or a worn-out soft toy, which he must fondle during thumb-sucking, this is apt to be distressing to a mother who cares about appearance. She may be able to sneak it away for a few hours to get it washed and dried, but there is not much more she can do. Sometimes a child permits a substitution of a new object exactly like the old one, but not usually. Considering the enormous amount of comfort and security a child gets from such a cuddly object, I think it's wrong to try to force him to part with it. He wants to give it up as soon as he is able, sensing that it is babyish. He outgrows it gradually—in spurts and starts, with relapses in between.

328. Ruminating. Sometimes a baby or young child gets in the habit of sucking and chewing on his tongue until his last meal comes up (somewhat the way a cow's does), a practice known as ruminating. It's a rare condition. Some cases begin when a thumb-sucking baby has his arms restrained. He turns to sucking his tongue instead. I would certainly advise letting such a baby have his thumb back immediately, before the ruminating becomes a habit. Be sure, also, that he has enough companionship, play, and affection. It is said that the meals stay down better when they consist entirely of solids. That means cooking the milk into his cereals, puddings.

THE PACIFIER

329. A pacifier is helpful for colic and to prevent thumb-sucking. A pacifier is a "blind" nipple (without a hole in it), attached to a plastic disk that rests against the baby's lips. He can suck vigorously on the nipple, and the disk keeps it from being pulled entirely into his mouth.

In former times pacifiers were used freely for colic and fretfulness. But in the first half of the twentieth century, when so much emphasis was put on cleanliness and proper habits, they came to be frowned on as unhygienic and disgusting. In the past few years they have returned to favor with some parents and some doctors for use in treating colic or preventing thumb-sucking. Other doctors and parents still disapprove quite strongly.

It has been observed by parents and doctors that very few babies who have used pacifiers in their early months ever turn to thumb-sucking. On the other hand, a fair proportion of the pacifier babies continue to want the pacifier until they are 1 to 2 years old and a few until 3 years old. Some parents feel this is as unattractive as thumb-sucking, or even worse. This is a matter of personal opinion. However, pacifier sucking has some distinct advantages over thumb-sucking. A great majority of the babies who were regularly sucking their thumbs or fingers at 3 months of age are still doing so at 1 and 2 and 3 years. It's between 3 and 6 years of age that most of them gradually stop. A few go on past 6. In contrast, about half the babies who were on pacifiers in the early months give them up between 3 and 6 months of age, and most of the rest give them up by 1 or 2 years. This is a big difference.

Another advantage is that pacifier sucking is much less likely to push the teeth out of position than thumb-sucking.

I have a theory about why a baby or child is able to give up the pacifier earlier than the thumb. The greatest sucking need is in the first 3 or 4 months of life. Yet most babies can't get their thumbs into their mouth or keep them there until they are about 3 months old. So perhaps the longing for more sucking has added up to a greater total in the would-be thumb-sucker by the time he can finally manage to do it. He has a lot of missed sucking to make up. The baby whose mother gives him the pacifier freely after meals, from his earliest weeks, can suck as long as he wants and gets his craving well satisfied during those early months when it's greatest.

But if you are disgusted by the appearance of a pacifier in a baby's or child's mouth, you'd better not use one; it wouldn't be good for you or for your feelings for the child. If you feel that your baby needs a pacifier and are worried only about what the neighbors or relatives will say, tell the neighbors that this is a very modern practice (or tell them that this is your baby).

330. How to use a pacifier. If you are using a pacifier mainly for colic, you naturally use it most during the hours when the baby is suffering from the discomfort. In a great majority, the colic is over by 3 months of age.

How would you use the pacifier to prevent thumb-sucking? In the first place, many babies—perhaps 50%—never try to thumb-suck at all or do it only casually and for brief periods. In these, there is nothing to prevent and no need to get involved with the pacifier (unless there is colic). On the other hand, you have to decide, not on the basis of what a baby is actually accomplishing, but from what he is **trying** to do. If he tries after meals to get his thumb in his mouth and sucks eagerly when he succeeds, then there is good reason to consider the pacifier.

What age to start? If a baby becomes used to his thumb over a period of weeks or months, the chances are that he will refuse the pacifier. He has learned to enjoy not only the sensations in his mouth but the sensations in his thumb. So if you are going to use a pacifier, start it in the first few weeks of life.

What times of day? The logical time to offer the pacifier is whenever the baby is searching around with his mouth and trying to suck on thumb, fingers, wrist, clothing, or anything else he can reach. In the early months, a baby is seldom awake except before and after feedings, so these are the usual times. But if he's awake between feedings, I'd give it to him then, too. The idea is to give it to him not as little as possible, but as much as he can use it in the first 3 months, so that he will be satisfied and give it up as soon as he can.

I think it is preferable to remove the pacifier when the baby begins to be drowsy, if he doesn't object too strongly, or just as soon as he is asleep. There are two reasons. A baby who is accustomed to having a pacifier in his mouth when asleep may, if it falls out, wake and cry unhappily until it is replaced. This can happen a dozen times a night—especially when a baby who has previously slept on his back learns to turn over on his abdomen—and it can be an awful nuisance. The other reason for not letting a baby form the habit of falling asleep with a pacifier (or bottle) in his mouth is that after a few months he may become utterly unable to fall asleep without it, no matter how tired he is. This problem can postpone the giving up of pacifier or bottle for many months.

331. Giving up the pacifier. When does the baby give up the pacifier? Many mothers who have tried pacifiers report that between 3 and 6 months of age their baby has shown a decreasing desire to suck the pacifier. Some of these infants have even come to the point of spitting out the pacifier and refusing to take it again. When the baby's interest has lessened a great deal, mothers report no difficulty or unhappiness when they remove the pacifier for good. I'd advise parents who see lack of interest at 3 or 4 or 5 months to take advantage of it and get rid of the pacifier if the baby is willing. I don't mean that I'd try to dispose of it the first day a baby cuts down his use of it. He couldn't outgrow his need that fast. But I'd follow his lead closely and begin omitting it gradually, first at one and then at another time of day when he sucks it least. If I found that I was going too fast for him or that he had off days when he was looking for it anxiously, I wouldn't be afraid to give in to him for a day or so. On the other hand, I wouldn't be so hesitant that I failed to take full advantage of his readiness.

Though the majority of babies seem willing to give up the pacifier in the 3-, 4-, 5-month-old stage, there are some who are unready until the last half of the first year, others who are not ready until some time in the second year, and a very few who cling to it beyond the age of 2. If your baby is clinging to the pacifier, should you insist that he give it up? I think it is unwise to take it away forcibly, to refuse to give it to him, or to pretend that it is lost when he's begging for it. I wouldn't nag and tease him about it. In other words, it's fine to help him outgrow it, a mistake to make him miserable by taking it away.

332. Precautions with the pacifier. If, when he's older, it's going to embarrass you to take him out in public with a pacifier, you may be able to accustom him from the start to going without it when away from home.

If your baby has already become dependent on a pacifier through the night but keeps losing it in his sleep, you can probably help him over this hump by putting 2 or 3 in his crib so that he is more likely to find one by himself.

In any case, have several pacifiers in the house so that the baby and you won't be frantic if one gets lost or broken.

There is another precaution that you ought to take. When a baby has a few teeth, he can pull the nipple of an old, tired pacifier off the disk or chew pieces out of the nipple. These pieces may cause serious choking if swallowed the wrong way. So buy new pacifiers when the old ones become at all weak or crumbly.

Some pacifiers are too long in the nipple for a newborn baby. They hit against the back of his throat and gag him. If so, try to find shorter ones.

Inoculations

333. Keep a record with you. It's a good idea to keep a record (signed by your doctor) of all your children's inoculations (and sensitivity to drugs, if any) in your home, and to carry it with you when the family goes on trips. It's also valuable if you move or if you change doctors. To be sure, you can always write or phone the doctor who gave the inoculations, but this is often impossible to do in a hurry during an emergency. The commonest emergency is when a child away from home receives a wound that calls for extra protection against tetanus (lockjaw). Then it is very important for the attending doctor to know for certain whether the child has received tetanus inoculations.

334. Diphtheria, pertussis (whooping cough), tetanus inoculations (D.P.T. shots). Inoculations against these three diseases are usually given together in a combined form (three materials in one shot). They should be started very early, preferably at 1 month of age. Three shots are given (each shot containing diphtheria, pertussis, and tetanus material), most commonly 1 month apart. However, if the interval between inoculations is longer than a month the effect is just as good.

The protection from the three shots is usually very high, but after a few months it begins to taper off. So a booster shot is given a year later (at 12 to 18 months of age) to bring the protection back to a high level, and again at about 4 years of age.

These combined inoculations often cause a reaction (on account of the whooping-cough material), consisting of fever, crankiness, loss of appetite, soreness around the injection, which usually starts 3 or 4 hours after the shot. The doctor can prescribe medication to relieve the symptoms. The baby should feel better the next day. If he has a fever after that, it should not be blamed on the inoculation; it is due to some new infection. These shots do not cause cough or cold symptoms.

Doctors usually don't give these inoculations when a baby has a fresh cold or other infection. They are not usually given to children over a year of age during a poliomyelitis epidemic for fear of temporarily lowering resistance to that disease. There is little risk under a year.

It is common for a firm lump, or "knot," to remain in the buttock or arm where the child has received a shot. It remains for several months and is nothing to worry about.

Now we should discuss the three materials that go into these combined inoculations.

335. Pertussis (whooping-cough) vaccine is one of the materials that go into D.P.T. inoculations. It is made from killed whooping-cough germs. It may not give complete protection from whooping cough, but if an inoculated child does catch the disease it is apt to be mild. Whooping cough is a dangerous disease for babies, and this is one reason the inoculations are started so early in infancy.

It takes two or three shots and some time before the vaccine stimulates the body to build a high resistance. So no immediate help can be expected from a first inoculation given after a child has already been exposed to the disease.

336. Diphtheria toxoid is another of the materials that goes into D.P.T. shots. The poisonous substance from diphtheria germs, called diphtheria toxin (which is what does the damage when a person has the disease), is treated chemically so that it is changed to a nonpoisonous substance—a toxoid. Diphtheria toxoid, when injected, can stimulate the body to build protection against diphtheria toxin. It is recommended that a child have three shots in early infancy and boosters at 1 year of age and every 3 years thereafter. In this way, he is almost certainly protected against diphtheria.

337. Tetanus toxoid is the third material that goes into D.P.T. shots. It is made from the poisonous substance (tetanus toxin) in tetanus germs, and when several shots are injected, they stimulate the body to **slowly** build its own, long-lasting protection against tetanus. It must be differentiated from tetanus antitoxin, which is a horse serum that gives prompt but only temporary protection.

Tetanus, or lockjaw, is a serious infection that sometimes gets into a wound. The germs occur most commonly in soil and other places where horse manure and cow manure have been. The germs can still be found fairly regularly in city streets. A wound is more liable to be infected with tetanus if it is deep. A deep puncture from a nail in a barnyard is therefore the riskiest kind. Lots of people think that the rust on a nail brings the danger of tetanus. This is not true. The important thing is where the nail has been.

Nowadays if a child who has already built his own protection as a result of tetanus **toxoid** injections receives a dangerous wound, the doctor merely gives another toxoid booster to be sure the protection is high. But if the doctor has no proof that toxoid inoculations have been given, he has to give horse serum (Section 338) in order to play safe. That is why you should carry a record of a child's inoculations with you when you are away from your own doctor.

The protection a child builds up from tetanus toxoid develops slowly and reaches a safe height only after the second shot. Therefore, there is no use **starting** this method at the time he gets a dangerous wound. He needs a shot of horse serum to give him immediate protection.

A booster shot is given a year after the original injections and then repeated every 3 years. In addition, if the child gets a dangerous wound at any time, he should have another toxoid injection. This immediately boosts his protection to a good, high level.

338. Tetanus antitoxin (horse serum). Long before we had tetanus toxoid for long-lasting protection, we had tetanus antitoxin horse serum. A horse is inoculated with tetanus germs until his blood serum contains a lot of protection against this disease. Some of this serum is injected into a person who has had a dangerous wound. The person in this way borrows some of the horse's protection, but it lasts only a few weeks. The trouble with a horse-serum injection is that it is apt to produce serum sickness (hives and fever) a couple of weeks later. It may also make a person highly sensitive to horse serum. If this happens, a second injection might make him very sick indeed, unless given with extreme care.

If an injured child or adult has not already built his own protection from toxoid inoculations, or if proof of these is lacking, it is often hard to decide whether horse serum is necessary—for instance, when a wound is not very deep and when there is a question whether any tetanus germs could have gotten in. It's a matter that has to be decided each time between the parents and the doctor. Serum isn't usually given for cuts and scratches that a child receives indoors.

339. Vaccination against smallpox. This is a must for all babies. It's best done sometime before your baby is a year old, when it's less apt to make him sick. Smallpox is a serious disease, and vaccination is a sure preventive. The vaccine contains the virus or germ of **cowpox,** and when the vaccination "takes," the baby is having a light case of cowpox. The wonderful thing about cowpox is that, though it is a very mild disease, it protects a person from getting the severe disease smallpox.

Once in a while there's a baby who shouldn't be vaccinated during his first year. If he has eczema or any other skin disease, vaccination should be postponed until his rash has cleared up (unless there are cases of smallpox in the community). Babies with eczema or other rashes sometimes get severe reactions from vaccination. Vaccination should also be postponed if a baby has been frail or sickly. It's wise not to vaccinate during a very hot spell, or when other members of the family have fresh colds, or when the baby has a cold or any other upset. It should also be postponed if there is in the family another child with eczema who has never been vaccinated. He might become accidentally inoculated from the vaccination. To be absolutely safe, a child should be revaccinated every 5 years. When cases of smallpox appear in a neighborhood, everybody should be immediately revaccinated.

The doctor puts a drop of the vaccine material on the baby's skin, and then pricks or scratches the skin through the drop. Nothing happens right away. In about 3 days a little red pimple appears, which soon gets a whitish blister on it. It gradually enlarges and is surrounded by a reddened area. It's at its worst on about the eighth or ninth day. In a mild vaccination the whole thing may be no larger than a nickel. In a moderate reaction the redness and swelling may cover an area larger than a silver dollar. When the vaccination is mild, a baby may show no ill effects at all. If it is moderate, he feels sick and cranky, loses his appetite, and runs a fever. Don't have your baby vaccinated when you are going to be traveling or unusually busy a week later.

After the height of the reaction, the vaccination dries up and turns into a tough, brown scab, which takes several weeks to fall off.

The air should not be shut out from a vaccination. A celluloid shield should never be used. It is best of all to leave the vaccination uncovered, except by the clothing, as long as the baby does not scratch at it. If it is on his upper arm and he is scratching it, you can pin a square sterile gauze dressing on the inside of his nightie or shirt, so that it lies over the vaccination. If a girl is vaccinated on the thigh (to avoid the arm scar) and there is no clothing to protect it from scratching, you can place a square sterile gauze dressing over the vaccination and attach it with two narrow strips of adhesive plaster running up and down the thigh. Don't run adhesive plaster around the leg or arm. It may cut off the circulation.

You don't need to do anything about the vaccination for the first 3 or 4 days. After the blister or white top appears, the baby is usually kept out of the tub bath, because it's better to keep the top from being softened and broken, if possible. Give him a sponge bath from the time the blister appears until the scab falls off.

Even though severe reactions to vaccinations are uncommon and rarely lead to complications, you should keep in touch with your doctor if your baby's arm is widely inflamed, or the fever is high, or the reaction lasts after the tenth day.

If a vaccination doesn't take, it doesn't mean that the person is immune. It shows only that the vaccine material was weak or that it didn't get through the skin. He should be vaccinated again and again, if necessary, until there is a take.

When a person who had a successful vaccination years before is vaccinated again, he should show some reaction on his skin. If most of his former protection has worn off, his new vaccination develops much like the previous one. If he still has most of his old protection, a small pimple forms, lasts a few days, and goes away without ever coming to a head. If nothing shows at all, it means that the vaccine material was weak or did not get through the skin. The vaccination should then be repeated.

340. Poliomyelitis vaccine. The Salk vaccine for protection against poliomyelitis (infantile paralysis) is now available and should be given to all children. It decreases greatly the chances of a child's having a paralytic case of the disease. Your doctor will advise you at what age to start and the best interval between inoculations.

The world had to wait a long time for this vaccine. Any vaccine has to be made from the germs of the disease. Polio is caused by a virus, and the virus, like the other viruses that cause human diseases, was extremely difficult to grow outside the human body. Three scientists, Drs. John Enders, Frederick Robbins, and Thomas Weller, finally discovered how to grow it in tissue cells from monkeys. With this step solved,

Dr. Jonas Salk was able to tackle the complex job of developing an effective and safe vaccine. (See Section 671.)

Your Baby's Development

WATCHING HIM GROW

341. He's repeating the whole history of the human race. There's nothing in the world more fascinating than watching a child grow and develop. At first you think of it as just a matter of growing bigger. Then, as he begins to do things, you may think of it as "learning tricks." But it's really more complicated and full of meaning than that. Each child as he develops is retracing the whole history of mankind, physically and spiritually, step by step. A baby starts off in the womb as a single tiny cell, just the way the first living thing appeared in the ocean. Weeks later, as he lies in the amniotic fluid in the womb, he has gills like a fish. Toward the end of his first year of life, when he learns to clamber to his feet, he's celebrating that period millions of years ago when man's ancestors got up off all fours. It's just at that time that the baby is learning to use his fingers with skill and delicacy. Our ancestors stood up because they had found more useful things to do with their hands than walking on them. The child in the years after 6 gives up part of his dependence on his parents. He makes it his business to find out how to fit into the world outside his family. He takes seriously the rules of the game. He is probably reliving that stage of human history when our wild ancestors found it was better not to roam the forest in independent family groups but to form larger communities. Then they had to learn self-control, how to cooperate with each other according to rules and laws, instead of depending on the old man of the family to boss them around.

To appreciate your child's development up to 5, you ought to read *Infant and Child in the Culture of Today,* by Arnold Gesell and Frances L. Ilg.[1] They have studied hundreds of babies and children and can tell you not just what a child will probably do at different age periods but something about what it means. Understanding what your child is up to is the first step in learning how to get along with him. As you watch your own baby grow, remember the advice in Section 69 of this book.

[1] New York: Harper & Brothers, 1943, $4.50.

342. Slow developers. You watch your child grow with a mixture of strong feelings. When he is coming along speedily, you are proud of him and proud of yourself for having produced him. As he shows his delight in his new accomplishments and in discovering the amazing world around him, you live over again the pleasantest parts of your own childhood. But always you find that you are quick to worry if there are any signs that he is failing to keep up with his own progress or to keep up with other children you know about. You feel not only anxious but vaguely guilty. That's the way all good parents are made. Anything the slightest bit out of line makes them wonder whether they are caring for their child properly, whether they have given him a worthy inheritance, whether something they were made to feel guilty about in their own past is affecting him. The Bible speaks ominously of the sins of the father being visited on the children, and many of us parents were warned in similar words in our own upbringing.

Rarely does slow development have anything to do with inadequate care or inherited defects or the sins of the parents (real or imaginary).

Every child's development is different from every other child's and is a complex mixture of patterns, as was explained in Section 69. These are determined mainly by his inheritance—normal inheritance, not faulty inheritance. Slow or fast walking, teething, talking, early or late puberty development, tallness or shortness, tend to run in families. But all these characteristics vary in the same family, because each family's inheritance is a great mixture.

Motor development covers such skills as holding the head erect, sitting, creeping, standing, walking. We have average figures for each of these, but the variations are great among babies who are entirely healthy and normal.

There are a few rare diseases that interfere with motor development, but these can usually be diagnosed by a doctor.

The overwhelming majority of cases of slow motor development—more than 9 out of 10—are simply a matter of normal variation.

Development of intelligence. It's particularly important for parents of a child who is slow in his motor development to know that there is very little connection between this and his intelligence. More than 9 out of 10 of the babies who are distinctly slow in motor development turn out to have normal intelligence. Incidentally, the developmental tests that are sometimes given in infancy (particularly in cases for adoption) are mainly tests of motor ability and social responsiveness. They reveal whether a baby has had a disease or injury to his brain and whether he has suffered emotionally from neglect. But aside from these conditions, they do not tell in the first year anything about what his intelligence will be in the future. Intelligence, which has to do with such abilities as reasoning and memory, cannot begin to be tested reliably until about 2 years of age.

Intelligence, in contrast to motor development, has a lot more to do with environment than with inheritance. Babies born to mothers with low intelligence but adopted into average or bright families, tend to develop an intelligence like that of their adopted parents.

Social and emotional development may depend somewhat on the temperament that a baby is born with—whether he is quiet or active, for instance—but most of all they depend on what experiences he has. There is no evidence that specific disturbances like alcoholism, untruthfulness, meanness, and delinquency are inherited.

A baby who is slow in his development certainly needs to be checked regularly by his doctor to be sure that there is no disease or condition that needs correcting. This is especially true if he is not only slow in motor development but also unresponsive to the people and things around him. Then he should have at least one consultation with a pediatrician, an eye specialist, and a hearing specialist.

343. He's wrapped up in himself the first two or three months. In the period up to 2 or 3 months, a baby hasn't much contact with the outside world. Most of the time he seems to be listening to what his insides tell him. When they tell him that all is well, he is very peaceful. When they tell him about hunger, or indigestion, or tiredness, he feels wholeheartedly wretched because there's nothing to distract him. It's an irritable period for some babies. One has colic, another has spells of irritable crying, a third always screams for a few minutes just before falling asleep.

As a baby gets beyond the 3-month period, he takes a lot more notice of the world around him. He turns his head in all directions, all by himself, and seems pleased with what he sees.

344. He starts by using his head. It's a gradual process by which a baby learns to control his body. It starts with the head and gradually works down to the hands, trunk, and legs. Just as soon as he's born, he knows how to suck. And if something touches his cheek—the nipple or your finger, for example—he tries to reach it with his mouth. He's ready to do his part in nursing. If you try to hold his head still, he becomes angry right away and twists to get it free. Probably he has this instinct to keep from being smothered.

Mothers ask, "When does he begin to see?" This is a gradual process, like everything else. As soon as he's born, he can tell light from dark. A bright light bothers him and makes him shut his eyes. In the early weeks he begins to fix his gaze on objects that are near. By the time he's 1 or 2 months old, he recognizes a human face and responds to it. By 3 months he looks around in all directions. In the early months he can't coordinate his two eyes very efficiently and often looks cross-eyed. Also, the surface of his eyes isn't sensitive, and a piece of fuzz there may not bother him at all.

A newborn baby seems to be deaf the first day or two because of fluid in his inner ear. But soon he is apt to have a sharp sense of hearing and may startle all over when he hears a loud noise. A few babies remain deaf for a number of weeks, apparently because the fluid in the ear is slow to absorb.

345. He smiles early, because he's a social being. Somewhere between 1 and 2 months of age, your baby smiles at you one day when you are talking and smiling to him. It's an exciting moment for you. But think what it means about his development. He knows little at this age; he can't use his hands or even turn his head from side to side. And yet he already knows that he's a sociable being, that it's nice to have loving people around, that he feels like responding to them. And if he's handled with plenty of affection and sensible firmness, he'll go on being friendly and reasonable just because it is his nature.

346. Using his hands. As soon as they are born, a very few babies can put their thumbs in their mouth any time they want to. But most can't get even their hands to their mouths with any regularity until they are 2 or 3 months old. And because their fists are still clenched tight, it usually takes them longer still to get hold of a thumb separately.

But the main business of hands is to grab and handle things. A baby seems to know ahead of time what he's going to be learning next. Weeks before he can actually grab an object, he looks as if he wanted to and were trying. At this stage, if you put a rattle into his hand, he holds onto it and waves it. Around the middle of the first year, he learns how to reach something that's brought within arm's reach. Gradually he handles things more expertly. In the last quarter of his first year, he loves to pick up tiny objects, like a speck of dust, carefully and deliberately.

347. Right- and left-handedness. The subject of handedness in children is a somewhat confusing one. Some babies stay ambidextrous for the first year or so and then gradually become right- or left-handed. Others show an early preference for the right or left hand that seems permanent. Others use one hand predominantly for several months and then shift to the other.

Formerly most scientists who were interested in handedness believed it was an inborn trait that would sooner or later become evident in each individual. And since many speech and reading specialists believed that changing a left-handed child to right-handed sometimes caused stuttering or reading difficulties, it seemed best not to try to influence any baby or small child, for fear of confusing a possible left-hander. More recently, Dr. Abram Blau wrote a book, The Master Hand, giving evidence in support of his belief that right- or left-handedness is not inborn but acquired as a habit. He recommends that parents tactfully help the baby and small child to favor the right hand from the beginning. He believes that the child who prefers his left hand despite his mother's efforts is most likely doing so because of contrariness ("negativism").

Faced with two opposite theories, what is a parent to do? I think there is a fairly safe compromise course. If a baby seems ambidextrous, as he is likely to be when he first begins to hold things in the middle of the first year, or right-handed, then assume he is right-handed and favor his right hand as you hand him toys and finger foods and, later, a spoon. But if from the very beginning he has a definite preference for the left or if later he begins to insist on using his left, I wouldn't argue or fight with him but leave him to his preference. Even if his left-handedness **is** an expression of contrariness, it would only make matters worse to get him more antagonistic and obstinate.

The cue then is to guide him tactfully if he is willing to be guided but not to fight him.

348. How a baby feels about strangers. You can get an idea of how a baby goes from phase to phase in his development by watching his reaction to strangers at different ages. This is how it goes in a doctor's office. A 2-month-old baby doesn't pay much attention to the doctor. As he lies on the examining table, he keeps looking over his shoulder at his mother. The 3-month-old is the doctor's delight. He breaks into a body-wiggling smile just as often as the doctor is willing to smile and make noises at him. By about 5 months, a baby is apt to have changed his mind. When a stranger approaches, he stops his kicking and cooing. His body freezes, and he eyes him intently, suspiciously, maybe for 10 or 20 seconds. Then his stomach begins to rise and fall rapidly. Finally his chin puckers, and he begins to shriek. He may get so worked up that he cries long after the examination is over. This is a sensitive period, when a baby may take alarm at anything unfamiliar, such as a visitor's hat or even his father's face. Probably the main cause of this behavior is that he is now smart enough to distinguish between friend and stranger. If your baby is sensitive about new people, new places, in the middle of his first year, I'd protect him from too much fright by making strangers keep at a little distance until he gets used to them, especially in new places. He'll remember his father in a while.

Some babies treat strangers in a fairly casual way toward the end of the first year. They are now more interested in objects and in things to do than in new faces. But everything changes at about a year. I think 13 months is the most suspicious age of all. The usual baby at this age scrambles to his feet when the doctor approaches and tries to climb off the table and onto his mother. He cries furiously, buries his face in his mother's neck, ostrich-fashion. Every once in a while he stops just long enough to peer over his shoulder at the doctor, with looks like daggers. He usually stops crying and struggling soon after the examination is over. A few minutes later he may be happily exploring the office and even making friends with the villain himself. There is more about handling the sensitiveness of the 1-year-old in Section 400.

349. Rolling over and sitting up. The age when babies roll over, sit up, creep, stand up, or walk is more variable than the age when they get control of their head or arms. A lot depends on temperament and weight. A wiry, energetic baby is in a great rush to get moving. A plump, placid one is willing to wait until later.

A baby, by the age he first tries to roll over, shouldn't be left unguarded on a table for as long as it takes the mother to turn her back. unless he is secured with a strap (such as comes with fabric bathtubs). By the time he can actually roll over, it is not safe to leave him even in the middle of an adult's bed. It is amazing how fast such a baby can reach the edge.

Most babies learn to sit steadily (after being helped up) between 7 and 9 months. Some normal, intelligent ones wait till as late as a year. But before a baby has the coordination to succeed, he wants to try. When you take hold of his hands, he attempts to pull himself up. This eagerness always raises the question in the mother's mind, How young can I prop him up in the carriage or high chair? Doctors feel that in general it's better not to prop a baby straight up until he can sit steadily himself for many minutes. This doesn't mean that you can't pull him up to a sitting position for fun, or sit him in your lap, or prop him on a slanted pillow in the carriage, just as long as his neck and back are straight. It's the curled-over position that's not so good for long periods.

This brings up the question of a **high chair.** It is of greatest advantage when the baby is eating his meals with the rest of the family. On the other hand, falling out of a high chair is a common accident. If a baby is going to be eating most of his meals by himself, I think it is preferable to buy him a low chair-table arrangement. If you are going to use a high chair, get one with a broad base (so that it doesn't tip over easily) and a strap to buckle the baby in. Don't leave a baby for long periods in a high or low chair after he has learned to creep or stand. He needs more freedom.

350. A toy or food while being changed. One of the things a baby never learns is that he ought to lie still while his mother changes or dresses him. It goes completely against his nature. From around half a year, when he learns to roll over, until his mother dresses him standing up at about a year, he struggles or cries indignantly against lying down, as if he has never heard of such an outrage.

There are a few things that help a little. One baby can be distracted by a mother who makes funny noises, another by a small bit of zwieback or cracker. You can have a special fascinating toy, like a music box, that you hand him at dressing time only. Distract him just before you lay him down, not after he starts yelling.

351. Creeping. Creeping can begin any time between 6 months and a year. Some babies never creep at all; they just sit around until they learn to stand up. There are a dozen different ways of creeping, and a baby may change his style as he becomes more expert. One first learns to creep backward, another somewhat sideways. One wants to do it on hands and toes with legs straight, another on hands and knees, another still on one knee and one foot. The baby who learns to be a speedy creeper may be late in walking, and the one who is a clumsy creeper, or who never learns to creep at all, has a good reason for learning to walk early.

352. Standing. Standing usually comes in the last quarter of the first year, but a very ambitious, wiry baby may do it as early as 7 months. Occasionally you see one who doesn't stand until after a year who seems to be bright and healthy in all other respects. Some of these are plump, easygoing babies. Others just seem to be slow getting strength in their legs. I wouldn't worry about such a child so long as the doctor finds that he is healthy and so long as he seems bright and responsive in other ways.

Quite a number of babies get themselves into a jam when they first learn to stand up but don't yet know how to sit down again. The poor things stand for hours until they are frantic with exhaustion. A mother takes pity on such a child, unhitches him from the railing of his play pen, and sits him down. But instantly he forgets all about his fatigue and pulls himself to his feet again. This time he is crying within a few minutes. The best that a mother can do is to give him especially interesting things to play with while he's sitting, wheel him in the carriage longer than usual, and comfort herself that he'll probably learn how to sit down within a week. One day he tries it. Very carefully he lets his behind down as far as his arms reach and, after a long hesitation, lets go. He finds that it wasn't such a long drop and that his seat is well padded.

As the weeks go by, he learns to move around hanging on, first with two hands, then with one. Eventually he has enough balance to let go altogether for a few seconds when he is absorbed and doesn't realize what a daring thing he's doing. He is getting ready for walking.

Parents sometimes ask whether "walkers" are advisable. These are various contraptions in which a baby who hasn't yet learned to walk can sit and push himself around the floor. The purpose is to give him something interesting to do, keep him happy and out of trouble. Occasionally a doctor advises against a walker for a child who has a tendency to toe in or toe out too much, because the walker may encourage either condition. Take this question up with the baby's doctor. In any case, I would keep a child in a walker only part of his waking hours and allow him plenty of chance to creep and explore.

353. Walking. Lots of factors determine the age when a baby walks alone: ambitiousness, heaviness, how well he can get places by creeping, illnesses, bad experiences. A baby just beginning to walk when an illness lays him up for 2 weeks may not try again for a month or more. Or one who is just learning and has a fall may refuse to let go with his hands again for many weeks.

Most babies learn to walk between 12 and 15 months. A few muscular, ambitious ones start as early as 9 months. A fair number of bright children, without rickets or any other physical disease, do not begin until 18 months or even later.

When a baby begins to walk, it raises a lot of minor problems, like shoes and discipline, but these are taken up in later sections.

You don't have to do anything to teach your child to walk. When his muscles, his nerves, and his spirit are ready, you won't be able to stop him. I remember a mother who got herself into a jam by walking her baby around a great deal before he was able to do it by himself. He was so delighted with this suspended walking that he demanded it all day long. Her back was almost broken.

A mother of a baby who walks early may wonder whether it won't be bad for his legs. As far as we know, a child's physique is able to stand whatever he's ready to do by himself. Babies sometimes become bowlegged or knock-kneed in the early months of walking, but this happens with late walkers as well as with early walkers.

354. Feet and legs. All babies have feet that look flat the first couple of years, partly because they haven't built their arches yet, partly because their feet are so plump. As they learn to stand and walk, they exercise the muscles that help create the arch of the foot. (See next section.)

How straight the legs, ankles, and feet grow depends on several factors, including the pattern of development a baby is born with and whether he has rickets (soft bones due to insufficient vitamin D). Some babies seem to have a tendency to knock-knees and ankles that sag inward even though there is never any rickets. The heavy child is more apt to develop these conditions. Other babies seem to be born with a tendency to bowlegs and toeing in, quite apart from rickets. I think this is especially true of the very active, athletic ones. If a baby has a tendency to knock-knees, and also has soft bones due to rickets, you can see why his knock-knees will develop more rapidly and more severely. The same applies to bowlegs. Another factor may be the position a baby keeps his feet and legs in. For instance, you occasionally see a foot that becomes turned in at the ankle because the baby always sits with his foot tucked under him in that position. It is sometimes suspected that a baby has been made to toe in by always lying on his stomach with his feet pointed toward each other, or by pushing himself in a walker with the outside edges of his feet.

All babies toe out to some degree when they start to walk, and then gradually bring the front part of the feet in as they progress. One starts with his feet sticking right out to the side, like Charlie Chaplin, and ends up toeing out only moderately. The average baby starts toeing out moderately and ends up with his feet almost parallel. The baby who starts out with feet almost parallel is more apt to end up toeing in. Toeing in and bowlegs often go together.

The doctor at the regular examinations watches the baby's ankles and legs from the time he begins to stand up. This is one reason why regular visits are important during the second year. If weak ankles, knock-knees, bowlegs, or toeing in develop, he may recommend corrective shoes. If there is any suspicion of rickets, he may have an X-ray picture taken.

355. Shoes: when and what kind? In most cases there's no need to put anything on a baby's feet until he's walking outdoors. Normally his feet stay cool just the way his hands do, and this doesn't bother him. In other words, there's no necessity for knitted booties or soft shoes in the first year unless the house or the floor is unusually cold.

After a baby is standing and walking, there's a real value in leaving him barefoot most of the time when conditions are suitable. A baby's arches are relatively flat at first. He gradually builds his arches up and strengthens his ankles by using them vigorously in standing and walking. (I suppose the reason that the soles of the feet are ticklish and sensitive under the arch is to remind us to keep that part arched up off the ground.) Walking on an uneven or rough surface also fosters the use of the foot and leg muscles. When you always provide a baby with a flat floor to walk on and always enclose his feet in shoes (with their smooth insides), especially if the soles are stiff, you encourage him to relax his foot muscles and to walk flat-footed.

Of course, a child who is walking needs shoes when he goes outdoors in cold weather and when he walks on pavements and other surfaces that are hazardous. But it's good for a child to continue to go barefoot indoors till the age of 2 or 3, and outdoors, too, in warm weather at the beach, in the sand box, and in other safe places.

Doctors most commonly recommend semisoft soles at first, so that the child's feet have a better chance to move. The important thing is to have the shoes big enough so that the toes aren't cramped, but not so big that they almost slip off. Socks should always be large enough, too.

Small children outgrow their shoes at a discouragingly fast rate, sometimes in 2 months, and a mother should form the habit of feeling the shoes every few weeks to make sure they are still large enough. There must be more than **just** enough space for the toes, because as the child walks, his toes are squeezed up into the front of the shoe with each step. There should be enough empty space in the toe of the shoe, as the child stands, so that you can get about half your thumb nail onto the tip of the shoe before running into the child's toe. You can't judge while he is sitting down; the feet don't fill as much of the shoe unless he's standing up. Naturally, the shoes should be comfortably wide, too.

If the doctor is prescribing wedges in the shoes to correct such things as weak ankles, toeing in, bowlegs, knock-knees, he may specify firm shoes. Corrective shoes don't do so much good if they are limp, and they usually need to be high.

But if your baby's feet and legs are strong, you can get medium-soft shoes, even inexpensive ones if they fit well and are large enough. Sneakers are considered satisfactory by many doctors as long as they don't cause sweating. The feet are pudgy the first couple of years, and as a result low shoes sometimes do not stay on so well as high shoes.

356. Talking. Most babies begin to use a few sounds that mean something when they are in the neighborhood of a year old. But there are perfectly normal children who wait months longer. It seems to be largely a matter of temperament or personality. Your friendly, outgoing baby just naturally wants to talk young. The quiet, observer type seems to want to spend a long time solemnly watching the world go by before he feels like saying anything about it.

The atmosphere around a baby and the way he is handled are impor-tant, too. If a mother, under nervous tension, is always silent when she does things for her child, he feels the lack of communication and re-mains in his own shell. At the other extreme, if the adults in a family are going at a baby too hard, talking at him and bossing him continually, he may feel uncomfortable and unresponsive whenever people are around. He's not at an age when he can talk back or go out for a walk to get away from it all. People young and old feel like talking when they are around easygoing, sympathetic friends. The only difference with a baby is that he has to have more desire in order to learn the words in the first place.

It's sometimes said that a certain child hasn't learned to talk because the whole family waits on him hand and foot, gives him everything be-fore he's had time to realize that he wants it. This kind of service might slow a baby down a little in learning new words, but I don't think it would make him silent unless the family were also keeping after him too much and squelching his outgoingness.

Once in a while you suspect that a baby is slow to pick up words because his mother talks to him in long sentences and he never has a chance to grab hold of a single word at a time to learn. This isn't common, because it comes instinctively to most people to use single words at first with a baby, or to stress the important word in a phrase.

Does slow talking point to slow mental development? This is apt to be the first awful thought that occurs to parents. It is true that some children who are mentally slow are late talkers, but plenty of them use words at the regular age. Naturally, the child who is **severely** retarded, who can't sit up, for instance, until he's 2, will be really delayed in his talking also. But the fact is that a great majority of late talkers, even those who don't talk much until 3, have normal intelligence, and some of them are unusually bright.

I think you can guess what to do if your child is a late talker. Don't fret about it and don't jump to the conclusion that he's stupid. Show him comfortable affection, and try not to boss him too much. Give him chances, if possible, to be around other children where he can make his own way. Talk to him with simple words in a friendly manner. Encourage him to ask for things by name, but try to avoid angry demands that he speak.

All babies start out mispronouncing most of the words that they use, and gradually improve. But one continues to have trouble with one sound and another with another. Some of these mispronunciations are apparently due to real clumsiness of the tongue or other part of the speech apparatus. After all, some grownups still lisp, no matter how hard they try. Other mispronunciations seem to be due to quirks in the child's feelings. He clings to the mispronunciation of one word long after he's learned to make the same sound correctly in another word. Minor delays like this are not important if the child is generally well adjusted and outgoing, and is growing up in other respects. It's all right to correct a child occasionally in a friendly way. It's a mistake to be too serious or argumentative about it.

What about the child who has such clumsy speech at 3 or 4 or 5 or older that other children can't understand him and make fun of him? In the first place, he needs to have his hearing checked by a specialist. He might go to a speech expert if there is one who knows how to get along with a small child easily and can make the lessons appeal to him. But whether or not an expert is available, such a child needs regular association with other children as close to his own age as possible, preferably in a good nursery school, until he's ready for the grades. A good teacher can protect the child with a defect from the scorn of the other children in tactful ways, and can often coach him in talking more easily than the parent because she isn't so worried about it. Some grade schools have trained speech teachers.

Deliberate baby talk comes up most often in the child who is jealous of a younger member of the family, who he feels is getting too much admiration and affection (see Section 484). There is another kind of affected baby talk in the child who has no rivals to worry about. I am thinking, for instance, of the little girl with corkscrew curls and fancy clothes who is the only child of a doting family. They are so pleased with her as a plaything that they forget she has to grow up. They keep talking baby talk to her long after it is natural, and show her that they love her best when she acts babyish and "cute." You can't blame her for playing up to them. But she will have a tough time when she gets around children her own age, because they won't think she's cute; they'll think she's awful.

TEETHING

357. Age of teething means little. Teething is quite different in different babies. One chews things, frets, and drools for 3 or 4 months before each tooth comes through, and makes life miserable for the whole family. In another case, a mother discovers a tooth one fine morning without ever having suspected that her baby was teething.

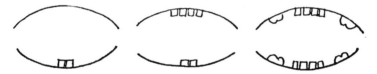

One baby gets his first tooth at 3 months, another not till a year. Yet both are healthy, normal infants. It is true that certain diseases once in a while influence the age of teething. But this is rare. In a baby who is reasonably healthy, the age of teething is simply a matter of the pattern of development he was born with. In one family most of the children teethe early, in another late. You can't decide your baby is extra bright because he teethes early, that he's generally backward because he teethes late.

358. How the average baby's teeth come through. The average baby gets his first tooth around 7 months, but he has been drooling, biting, and having periods of fretfulness from the age of 3 or 4 months. Since a baby gets 20 teeth in his first 2½ years, it is easy to see why he is teething most of that whole period. This also explains why it's so easy to blame every ailment on teething.

In the olden days it was the custom to blame teeth for colds, diarrheas, fevers. Of course, these diseases are caused by germs and not by teething. However, in some babies it looks as though teething lowers resistance, making it **easier** for an infection to start at that time. But if your baby becomes sick while he's teething, or has a fever as high as 101°, he needs a doctor to diagnose and treat the disease just as much as if he had gotten sick when he wasn't teething.

Usually the first 2 teeth are the lower central incisors. (**Incisor** is the name given to the 8 front teeth, which have sharp cutting edges.) After a few months come the 4 upper incisors. The average baby has these 6 teeth, 4 above and 2 below, when he is a year old. After this there's usually a pause of several months. Then 6 more teeth are apt to come in, without much pause in between—the 2 remaining lower incisors, and all 4 first molars. The molars don't come in next to the incisor teeth but farther back, leaving a space for the canine teeth.

After the first molar teeth, there is a pause of several months before the canines (the pointed "dog teeth") come through in the spaces between the incisors and the molars. The commonest time is in the sec-

ond half of the second year. The last 4 teeth in the baby set are the second molars. They come in right behind the first molars, usually in the first half of the third year.

359. Wakefulness with teething. The first 4 molar teeth, which in the average baby come through between a year and a year and a half, are more likely to cause a baby trouble than the others. He may be cranky and lose his appetite for days at a time. He may wake crying a number of times each night. This can be quite a problem if he doesn't fall asleep again quickly. A small bottle or cup of milk may seem to be the easiest way to pacify him. Is this risky? In most cases, the baby stops waking when the teeth are through. But an occasional baby develops a persistent habit of waking, especially if he is picked up for the bottle and given a sociable time (Section 285). Therefore, I think it's preferable not to get into the habit of giving a night feeding at this age or of picking the baby up, if he quiets down in a few minutes by himself. If you do have to give a bottle, give it in the crib, and stop it firmly when the teeth are through.

The coming of the first teeth, in the middle of the first year, may cause waking, too.

Refusal to take bottle or breast during teething is discussed in Section 89.

360. Let him chew. Sometimes a mother thinks it's her duty to keep her baby from putting things in his mouth and chewing. This notion will surely drive her and the baby frantic in time. Most babies **must** put things in their mouths, off and on, at least from 6 months to 15 months. The best that a mother can do is to provide chewable objects that are dull enough so that if the baby falls with them in his mouth they won't do too much damage. Rubber teething rings of various shapes are good, but any piece of rubber that the baby can hold easily will do. You have to be careful about toys made from thin celluloid. Babies sometimes break off and swallow small bits or choke on them. You also have to be careful that the baby doesn't gnaw the paint off furniture and other objects if there is any danger that the paint is made with lead. Nowadays practically all babies' furniture and painted toys are painted with leadless paint. You have to think about objects that have been repainted at home or that were never expected to be chewed by babies. Some babies prefer a certain kind of cloth for chewing on. Let him have what he seems to want as long as it's not dangerous. You don't have to fret about the germs on a teething ring or a favorite piece of cloth. They are his own germs, anyway. Of course, it's a good idea to wash the teething ring with soap after it has fallen on the floor or after the dog has gotten it. If the baby chews on a piece of cloth, you can boil it occasionally. Some babies love to have their gums firmly rubbed at times. Don't use any medicine without the doctor's recommendation.

361. What makes good teeth. The first thing to realize is that the crowns of all the baby teeth (the parts that will show) are formed in his gums before he is born. In other words, they are made from what the mother eats during her pregnancy. Research shows that among the food elements necessary to make strong teeth, the following are particularly important: calcium and phosphorus (milk and cheese), vitamin D (vitamin drops and sunshine), vitamin C (vitamin drops, oranges, other citrus fruits, raw tomatoes, cabbage). Other factors are probably necessary, too, including vitamin A and some of the B vitamins.

The baby's permanent teeth, the first of which won't appear until he is about 6 years old, already **are being formed within a few months**

after his birth. A baby at this age is, of course, getting plenty of calcium and phosphorus from his milk diet. He should get C and D vitamins by the time he is a month old. (These are usually added in the form of concentrated drops.)

362. Fluoride in the water makes stronger teeth. One element known to be valuable in the **formation** of a child's teeth is fluoride—a minute amount in the diet of the mother while she is pregnant, and in the diet of the baby and small child while his permanent teeth are being formed. There is much less tooth decay in those parts of the country where fluoride occurs naturally in the water. It is now added, in minute, safe amounts, to the water of many progressive communities as a public-health measure. If there is no fluoride in the water, the dentist can give a child part of the benefit by painting fluoride on his teeth. Whenever it is proposed that fluoride be added to a city's water supply, it makes some citizens anxious. They discover literature that claims fluoridation is harmful, and they may invite speakers from other cities, who are known as opponents of fluoridation, to testify against it. Since some of the statements are very alarming, they raise questions in the minds of all citizens. It is well to remember that intensive and extensive studies were made by responsible scientists before artificial fluoridation was ever proposed and that all the possible dangers and objections were carefully checked. Then committees of experts of the American Public Health Association, the American Dental Association, the American Medical Association, and the United States Public Health Service reviewed the evidence before publicly recommending fluoridation.

It gives you a better perspective to realize that similar alarm was raised about vaccination, diphtheria inoculation, and chlorination of water before these procedures became generally accepted.

363. Decay is favored by frequent contact with sugars and starches. Dental scientists haven't yet been able to find all the answers to decay (caries) of the teeth. The diet of the pregnant mother and of the baby are important in the formation of the teeth. Heredity probably plays a part.

But some teeth that look strong decay later. Dentists believe that the principal cause of tooth decay is lactic acid. This lactic acid is manufactured by bacteria that live on sugars and starches that are in contact with the teeth. The more hours of the day there are starches and sugars on the teeth, the greater the number of bacteria there are and the more lactic acid is produced to dissolve holes in the teeth. That is why frequent between-meal sucking of lollipops, eating of sticky candy and dried fruit, drinking of sodas, and nibbling of cookies and crackers (which so often stick to the teeth) are particularly liable to cause decay.

Of course, most fruits contain some sugar, and even vegetables contain a little. But the sugar is dilute and as a result is washed away sooner. And the rough fibers of fruit have a brushing action on the teeth. All of us eat starches to a greater or lesser extent, but we usually take them only at meals and many of them—especially those containing roughage, such as whole grains and potatoes—don't stick long to the teeth. It's the frequent between-meal eating of sugars and starches, which stick, that is particularly hard on the teeth.

364. Care of the teeth. It is sometimes recommended that a baby's teeth be brushed when he has his first set of molars. For most babies this would be in the first half of the second year. I think, myself, that there is something to be said for waiting until the child is nearly 2. At this age he has a passion to copy everything he sees done around him. If his mother and father brush their teeth, he one day grabs one of their brushes and insists on trying it himself. This is a good time to buy him a brush and let him go to it. Naturally, he won't be very efficient at first,

Children want to do grown-up things.

but you can help him tactfully. Perhaps I am making too much of a point of this, but it's a good example of a basic truth. Three quarters of the things that we think we must impose on children as unpleasant duties are things that they enjoy learning to do themselves at a certain stage of their development, if we only give them a chance.

The main purpose of brushing the teeth is to remove the lumps of food from around the teeth. **The logical time is after meals, three times a day.** (Hang toothbrushes in the kitchen as well as in the bathroom.) Most important is after supper, so that the teeth are clean for the long night period when the mouth is quiet and the saliva is flowing slowly. There is no proof that the green film that forms on some children's teeth is harmful.

365. Dental examination twice a year from the age of three. It's wise to begin taking a child to the dentist every 6 months, beginning when he is 3 years old. He is coming into the period when tooth decay may start. The time to fill cavities is when they are small. This saves the teeth, and it hurts the child less. Even if your child doesn't have a cavity at the 3- or 3½-year-old visit to the dentist, it is worth the expense for two reasons. It's insurance that the teeth are healthy. It gets the child used to going to the dentist without fear. This confidence makes a big difference when he has to have his first filling.

Parents sometimes think that they don't have to worry about decay of the baby teeth because they are all going to be lost anyway. This is wrong. A decayed tooth may cause the child pain, and it sometimes leads to infection of the jaw. And if a baby tooth is so decayed or causes so much pain that it has to be pulled, it leaves a space in the jaw that allows near-by teeth to grow out of position. Then there isn't enough room for the permanent tooth when it's ready to come through. Remember that the last baby teeth are not lost until the child is 12 years old. So they need just as careful care as the permanent ones.

366. The permanent teeth. The permanent teeth begin to appear when the child is about 6 years old. The 6-year-old molars come through farther back than the baby molars. The first baby teeth to be lost are the lower central incisors. The permanent incisors, pushing up underneath, destroy the roots of the baby teeth, which get loose and then fall out. The baby teeth are lost in about the same order they come in: the incisors, the molars, the canines. The permanent teeth that take the place of the baby molars are called bicuspids. The substitution of the new teeth is completed somewhere around 12 to 14 years of age. Meanwhile, the 12-year-old molars have come through behind the 6-year molars. The "18-year molars," or "wisdom teeth," come considerably later (sometimes never).

When teeth come through crooked or out of place, there is some tendency for them to straighten out later, how much one cannot tell ahead of time. Your regular dentist, who should be seeing your child's teeth every 6 months, can advise you whether he needs special treatment for this.

Toilet Training

BOWEL TRAINING

367. Readiness for toileting depends on age and the individual child. From what some people say, you might get the impression that the only way a baby becomes trained is by the parent's strenuous efforts. It's a lot easier than that. Generally speaking, babies gradually gain control of their bowels and bladders as they grow. The most that a mother needs to do is to watch her child—to see what stage of readiness he is in—and give him some positive encouragement.

The first thing to realize is that there are real differences, at different ages and between different babies, in how the bowels and bladder function and in the child's attitude.

368. Regular and irregular babies. During the first year, most babies don't seem to pay much attention to these functions. When the lower intestine is full, the movement is apt to be passed with such brief pushing that the mother hardly notices it.

One baby quite regularly has his first or only movement of the day within a few minutes after breakfast. This is because a full stomach tends to stimulate the entire intestinal tract to activity, especially after the long night's rest. It's fairly easy to catch the movements of a baby who is naturally regular, but he isn't really trained during the first year because he's hardly aware of what it's all about. It's his mother who is trained. He is only becoming accustomed to the potty or toilet seat.

Another baby has one or several movements at any old time of day. While he is as irregular as this, it is useless to start toileting him during his first year. You'd have to put him on the seat so often and for so long that you'd be apt to make him angry and resistant.

369. The second year. The desire to please the mother. During the second year, several important changes of attitude take place in children that have a great influence on training. A child at this stage becomes gradually more aware of his fondness for his mother and enjoys pleasing her. If she shows him in a friendly way that she would like him to use the seat and acts proud of him when he succeeds, this gives him a strong motive to become trained. However, there are other factors that work in the opposite direction.

370. Second-year possessiveness and balkiness. Early in the second year, a child becomes more aware of his bowel movements. He can hold back or push more deliberately. If he sees his movements—either in the potty or toilet if he is having them there, or on the floor if they come occasionally when he has no diaper on—he acquires a personal and possessive feeling about them. He realizes that they are his very own—he made them. He feels kind of proud of them. If his mother is sympathetic, he may go into the next room to fetch her, so that she can admire, too. He has not learned any disgust, in the early part of the second year, and he may play with them if he has the chance or put some in his mouth, as he does everything else.

But many a baby who has been willingly using the seat for several months suddenly changes his pattern at some time between 12 and 18 months. He sits down obediently but never has a movement so long as he stays there. Right after getting up, he moves his bowels in the corner or in his pants. A mother says, "He seems to have forgotten what it is all about." I don't believe a child forgets that easily. I think that his possessive feeling about his movements has become stronger than ever and that he's simply unwilling to give them up so readily to the potty or toilet or to his mother. Besides, he wants to do everything by himself, in his own way, at this age, and that goes for moving his bowels, too. So he just holds the movement in—at least until he can get away from the seat, which symbolizes giving it up and giving in.

If his mother becomes more insistent, it increases his conviction that he must hold onto his possession more obstinately. If she becomes cross and tries to get his movement out with an enema or a suppository or if he is worried by seeing it flushed away in the toilet, he may hold back **anxiously** the next time, as if he were trying to save a part of his body.

All babies who have been previously accustomed to the seat don't go through this rebellion in the second year. It's more often the ones who have been assertive all along—boys particularly. A lot depends, too, on whether the mother has been encouraging or a bit too bossy in her efforts.

371. Signaling in the second half of the second year. In the second half of the second year (from 18 to 24 months) a good proportion of children begin to give their mothers some definite signal of an approaching movement (or urination)—the family word for it or a meaningful grunt. In a few children this occurs even before 18 months, in others not till after 2 years.

There are several factors that may prompt a child to begin to signal, and they vary in different individuals. If a mother has been catching her child's movements regularly, he gradually takes on some of her concern. If she is tactfully encouraging him to notify her, his desire to cooperate sharpens his awareness. But there are also children who begin signaling whose mothers have never toileted them or asked for a signal. Some of them, toward the end of the second year, begin to feel uncomfortable when soiled and wet or they begin to be disgusted by the sight and smell of the movement. If a mother has been suggesting that accidents are uncomfortable or unpleasant, it is easy to see why the child is likely to pick this up. But there are other cases in which the mother hasn't expressed such attitudes, so far as she knows, and yet the child acquires them just the same. This makes us think that discomfort and disgust at being soiled come naturally to children at a certain stage of development, more in one case, less in another.

372. Self-training by imitation around two years. One other factor that occasionally plays a large role in training is the intense imitativeness of the last part of the second year. A child whose mother has never put him on the seat may suddenly become interested in the fact that his brother or sister or friend uses it, and insist on doing the same thing. When a child gets this idea, he's apt to go at it with great enthusiasm and to train himself for both bowel movements and urine in a couple of days. In fact, it may be a nuisance for a few days: he's so proud of his new accomplishment that he wants to try every ten minutes.

373. The final stage—doing it all by himself. When a child has reached the stage of being quite reliable about signaling to his mother, he still expects her to get him to the seat and take his clothes down. He won't really have reached the last stage of training until he does these jobs by himself, usually between 2 and 2½ years. A lot depends on whether his mother is encouraging him to take over and on how easily he can get his clothes down. Even so, there are apt to be occasional accidents— when playing outdoors, when away from home, or when there is diarrhea—until he is about 3 years old.

374. Parents' feelings about toilet training are just as important and just as variable as children's. At one end of the scale are the parents who are naturally very casual about training. They'd just as soon postpone it as not. They're not upset by having to change soiled diapers until the age of 2 or by occasional accidents after 2 years. At the other end of the scale are the conscientious parents who feel strongly that it's important for a child's development and character to get him clean and dry as early as is safe. Bowel movements that have to be cleaned up are distinctly unpleasant to them, and they can't help being irritated by the child who continues to soil after 1 or 1½ years. All of us parents fall somewhere on this scale. These differences in attitude can often be traced back to our own childhood, to how much emphasis was put on our own training. Most of us are inclined to bring up our children about the same way we were brought up, and this is as it should be. If we don't bring them up according to our beliefs, we will be dissatisfied with them.

375. Difficulties when parents are too afraid to lend a hand. The subject of toilet training has been made more complex for parents by the studies of psychiatrists, psychologists, and pediatricians.

Psychiatrists in their work with nervous adults and children came to the conclusion that excessively early and severe training, which used to be popular, would sometimes make a child into a very balky person or one who was too fussy about cleanliness and neatness. Pediatricians taking care of babies and young children noticed the same thing; they also heard an occasional mother report that she had gone through a long and unsuccessful training struggle with her first child, felt too discouraged to even get started with her second, and then was amazed to have him suddenly train himself at about the age of 2 by signaling or imitation. This gave some pediatricians (including me) the hope that if they could persuade parents to give up trying so hard, children might be willing to do almost all the work. But when we doctors recommended this method, we found that waiting for the child to take the initiative didn't work for some parents at all—particularly those parents who believed in early training and were delaying it only because the doctor advised it, and those parents who became so worried about overtraining that they hesitated to give the child any positive encouragement at all.

376. Programs for training. I don't think there is any one right time or way to toilet-train. What works for one parent may not for another, and certainly what works for one child may not be right for another. There are occasional problems with every approach. What's important is to know how you feel, to know how different children may react, to watch for your child's readiness, and then to use encouragement rather than disapproval.

It used to be the style to try to catch the baby's movements in the potty in the first few months of life. It doesn't really accomplish much, because many months pass before the baby realizes what the purpose is or has a chance to cooperate voluntarily. The main disadvantage of such very early efforts, I think, is that they encourage the mother to overemphasize the importance of training, to become too insistent about it, and to forget that the chief aim should be to secure the child's cooperation. It seems to me sensible to give the baby the benefit of the doubt and not fuss at him until he is old enough to understand a little better what it's all about and can at least sit up by himself.

377. The method of accustoming the baby to the seat in the latter part of the first year. If a baby always has his movement at the same time of day, some parents start putting him on the seat at some time between 7 and 12 months. This seems to me a reasonable method for those parents who want to get training started as early as possible. The baby is able to sit up steadily and comfortably by this time and has some degree of voluntary control over the lower part of his body. If he always has his movement within ten minutes after breakfast, the job is soon accomplished without fuss and there is little chance of his becoming impatient from having to sit too long. Of course, this is only the very first stage of training, because a baby under the age of a year is still not much aware of what he is doing and he is certainly taking no responsibility. He is merely becoming accustomed to sitting there and to having these sensations there. You might say it is preparation for training. If he is a baby who has a second movement later in the day, it is not likely to come at such a regular time and therefore it is better not to try to catch it.

If a baby's first movement of the day is quite irregular, I think it's much wiser not to try to catch it at this age. You would have to put him on the seat so often and keep him there so long that you'd be too apt to make him impatient and rebellious. (Children around the age of a year are naturally very restless.)

378. The method of accustoming the child in the first part of the second year. Quite a few parents start toileting in the first part of the second year. The child seems more grown-up; he's beginning to notice the parts of his body, and to notice his urination and his bowel movement, if he has the opportunity. If his movement comes at a regular time of day, he can be put on the seat for five or ten minutes. When he has a movement there, it makes some impression on him, and his mother can increase his satisfaction with her compliments. He is apt, as the weeks go by, to take more pride in his accomplishment. This is coming closer to real training, because he's getting the idea that he's doing a job and that this is where the movement belongs.

This approach to training, early in the second year, is successful in a majority of cases, particularly if the child is an agreeable type. The most common problem is that the child may soon develop such a sense of independence and of possessiveness of his movement that he may then refuse to cooperate for a number of weeks or months. It's wise to keep in mind the child's sensitivity about his rights and dignity at this age, especially if he's the assertive type, to be tactful and friendly and encouraging about the toilet, rather than bossy. The treatment of resistance is discussed in Section 381.

379. The method of waiting until later in the second year and encouraging the child to give a signal. Many parents prefer not to take so much initiative in accustoming the child to the seat but to wait until he shows more interest, in the middle part or the latter half of the second year. This is the age that seems most natural to me.

Some children become so aware at this age of the sensation of a coming movement (or a full bladder) that they give a signal without any coaching.

Children who don't signal but whose movements come right after breakfast can, for a number of days, be placed briefly on the seat, at about 1½ years of age. When the movement comes each day, the mother can show her pleasure and suggest that the child tell her tomorrow when he's ready. The point is that he's likely to pick up the idea from her more quickly at this age.

If the child begins to show discomfort or disgust about the movement in diaper or pants, the mother can explain, as she cleans up, that he will be more comfortable and more like grownups if he will tell her beforehand next time so that she can put him on the seat.

In the case of the child who is still irregular and showing no signs of interest or discomfort or disgust by the second half of the second year, the mother can leave him in training pants or no pants at all for part of the day (while he is in a room with no carpet) so that when the movement comes he will realize what is happening. Then she can encourage him to tell her next time.

The mother's suggestions, to encourage the child to give her a signal, should be started gradually and gently (don't go at him hammer and tongs), and usually have to be repeated for several weeks before the child gets the hang of it. He may first begin to notify her after the accident has occurred. This is really a sign of progress, even though it doesn't seem so to the parent. He should be praised for telling and encouraged to tell again tomorrow—so that they can make the movement go in the potty or toilet and so that they won't have to clean it up.

The main cue for the mother is to remain friendly, encouraging, and optimistic about tomorrow. She can talk about how she, Daddy, brothers, sisters, friends, use the toilet, how the child is growing bigger every day, how nice it feels to be clean and dry. I don't mean a whole sermon every day, just a reminder.

All this takes a lot of patience. Some days the mother will be irritated and angry that no progress is apparent. If you see you are making no progress, drop the effort for a few days or weeks. It's better not to get yourself frustrated. It's better not to scold or shame or punish. If encouragement doesn't work. stronger methods will only set you back further.

380. The regular toilet or a child's seat on the floor? Many babies become accustomed from the start to a baby's toilet seat attached to the regular toilet seat. If such an arrangement is used, it's preferable to have a footrest attached to the baby's seat so that he can feel more steady. It's also a sensible precaution during the second year for the mother to wait until the child has gone away from the bathroom before flushing the toilet. Most 1-to-2-year-olds are fascinated with the flushing at first and want to do it themselves. But a small proportion of them later become frightened by the violent way the water flushes the movement away and then are afraid to sit on the seat. One child probably fears that he might fall in and disappear likewise. Another is apparently worried to see this object. which he considers part of himself, snatched away.

I myself think it's preferable to use a child's seat over a potty, close to the floor, up to the age of 2 or 2½ years. A child feels more friendly toward a small piece of furniture that is his own and that he can sit down on by himself. His feet can stay on the floor, and there is no height to make him feel insecure. Until past the age of 2, I'd empty the potty and flush the toilet after he has gone away.

A child's seat designed to fit on an adult toilet can be adapted for use over a potty by attaching two upright boards to the underside.

Incidentally, I think it's a good idea to give the small seat to the child just to play with for several days. You can explain what it is for but not try to persuade him to use it properly at first. Let him sit on it when the spirit moves him, let him lug it around. let him become friendly with it.

When he is fond and proud of it as his very own, he may begin to try to have a movement there. If not, you can suggest it.

381. Resistance to bowel training. The mildest form of resistance to training was mentioned in Section 370: the child no longer moves his bowels on the seat as he used to but waits until just after getting up.

If the resistance persists for many weeks and increases, the child may hold back his movement not only while he is on the seat but for the rest of the day, too, if he can manage it. This is a psychological type of constipation. It is rarely unhealthy from a physical point of view, but it is a sign of how concerned the child feels.

Sometimes these forms of resistance can be eased if the mother stays with him while he is on the seat, agreeably keeping him company and perhaps giving him occasional encouragement. In other words, humor him into being compliant. If this doesn't work in ten minutes, it usually is better not to prolong the issue but to let him up. If he later soils the floor or his clothes, a mother can't help feeling cross. But if she can remind herself that this seems to him to be his best way of showing how grown-up and independent he feels, she may be able to take it with more humor. Her best approach is to encourage him that tomorrow perhaps he'll be a big boy and do it in the potty. She shouldn't be surprised, though, if the resistance lasts for a number of weeks. Of course, it isn't worth while making the same speech every day. Better try to ignore the whole business for a spell and then try again someday when he seems to feel more grown-up and cooperative.

Since the small child at this stage is unwilling to give up his movement because he considers it a rather precious possession, it may help to remind him that it's all right to let this one go because he will be able to make another one tomorrow and tomorrow and tomorrow.

If the resistance becomes more marked, the child may object to sitting down on the toilet seat at all or even to going into the bathroom. If the objection is mild, his mother may be able to humor him along with friendly talk and distraction. If his objection is strong, it shows that he is really frightened about moving his bowels, and then it's a mistake to try to force the issue. Better to drop the matter for a while, remind him every couple of weeks in a friendly, encouraging tone that someday he'll use the seat again like others, and watch for a day when he feels more ready. On the other hand, if his mother becomes too timid to **ever** speak of the subject, this can strengthen his opinion that what she wants him to do is unfair or dangerous. Her occasional confident reminder in a pleasant tone helps him to get back to his previous attitude that toileting is a routine part of growing up, even something to be proud of.

In some cases, the child can be encouraged to take a new view of training by being offered new clothes as a reward: some fancy panties for the girls instead of the plain white training pants, some costume that appeals to the boy. Seeing other young friends proudly use the toilet or small seat inspires some children.

382. Fear of painfully hard movements. Sometimes a child gradually or suddenly gets into a spell of unusually hard movements that are painful to pass. Not all hard movements are painful. The collections of small hard pellets—the result of what is sometimes called spastic constipation —are rarely painful. It's usually the hard movement in one large piece, with a wide diameter, that is to blame. As it is passed, it may tear a tiny slit, or "fissure," in the edge of the stretched anus. When a fissure has occurred, it is likely to be stretched open again each time another movement is passed. This is quite painful, and the fissure may thus be kept from healing for many weeks. You can easily see how a child who has once been hurt may dread a repetition and fight against toileting again. It may become a vicious circle, because if the child succeeds in holding back his movement for several days, it is more likely to be hard.

It's important to notify the doctor promptly if a child begins to have hard movements, particularly in this sensitive second year, so that he can consider a change in the diet or a medication to keep them soft. Adding prunes or prune juice to the diet every day, if the child likes them, usually works. More whole-grain wheat and oats in cereal, bread, and crackers may help some. If you have such an emergency and cannot reach a doctor soon, you can get from the druggist one of the commercial preparations that contain acidophilus bacilli in mineral oil (Section 294).

It helps to keep reassuring the child for a while that you know he is worried for fear another movement will hurt the way the previous one did but that he doesn't need to worry any more because the movements are now kept soft by the medicine.

If a child remains frightened and resistant or if he seems to continue to have pain, the doctor should examine him for the possibility that a fissure has been created and is not healing. It is sometimes necessary to stretch the fissured anus while the child is under anesthesia.

383. Things to avoid during intense resistance to toilet training. Though a mother can't help being frustrated and irritated when her child continues to balk against training, it's good for her to know that there are things that only make the problem worse. Insisting that he sit on the toilet more and more often and for longer and longer periods, despite his absolute refusal to do anything there, only increases his obstinacy.

Parental angriness, if it doesn't succeed right away in small doses, only makes him feel guilty; it doesn't make him good. Excessive shaming about his messes, trying to develop in him an intense sense of disgust, usually doesn't make his training go any faster. But after he finally gives in, it may make him an overly fussy person—the kind who's afraid to enjoy himself or try anything new, the kind who is unhappy unless everything is just so.

The very occasional enema or suppository the doctor may prescribe is not harmful in a child who has no training problem. But during a training struggle, when a child has been hanging onto his movement for dear life, if his mother in desperation resorts to an enema or suppository to get it out, he is apt to fight in rage and terror, as if he thought she was going to remove a very part of his body. In a training problem, it's much safer psychologically to use a cathartic by mouth if the doctor thinks it is necessary.

URINE TRAINING

384. Readiness for urine training. In one sense, bladder training is more difficult or at least slower than bowel training—it's easier for a person of any age to control a movement than to control urine. Whereas most children have complete control of their bowels by about 2 years (if they have a mind to), plenty of 2½-year-olds are still wetting fairly often either in the daytime or at night. On the other hand, children rarely make an issue of daytime urination. When they are physically able to control the bladder, they are usually quite agreeable to doing so. That is to say, they don't refuse to go to the toilet or to release the urine when they get there. It seems as though urine doesn't matter to them as a possession, the way the bowel movement often does.

385. The bladder begins to retain more urine sometime between 12 and 18 months. In most babies, the bladder empties itself automatically quite often during the first year and the first few months of the second year. Then it begins to retain urine for longer periods. Often it's around the age of 15 or 16 months that a mother first notices—with surprise and pleasure—that her child is dry for as long as 2 hours, usually during the nap. This isn't due to any training efforts. It's simply the maturing of the baby's bladder. This is shown clearly in the story of the occasional baby who becomes dry at night by the age of 12 months—before the mother has ever sat him on the seat for either bowels or urine. On the average, boys are slower than girls in urine training, day or night. A few children have bladders that are still emptying frequently, every half hour to an hour, at 2 years of age.

Though many a child's bladder retains urine for 2 hours by the time he is 1¼ or 1½ years old, this does not mean, of course, that he is trained. If a mother keeps it in mind and goes at it tactfully, she may be able to catch his urine several times a day. But it's very unusual for a child of this age to keep it in mind or to make any signal. He doesn't seem to be enough aware of it.

386. Notifying between 18 and 24 months. Sometime in the latter part of the second year, many children do become enough aware of a full bladder to say a word or to make some special signal to the mother. Signaling is commoner at this age in those children whose mothers have been catching them fairly regularly; this has focused the child's attention. As a matter of fact, for the first few weeks the child often notifies his mother **after** he has wet. This seems pointless to some mothers and others even suspect their child is teasing them, but they shouldn't be so pessimistic. It's simply that at first the feeling of being wet is more noticeable to the child than the feeling of a full bladder. His intentions are good, he's doing his best for the time being, and soon he'll be calling in time if he sees that his efforts are appreciated.

But even after a child has begun notifying, he's not solidly trained yet. He's too busy at times to notice his full bladder, so there continue to be frequent accidents except when his mother keeps the time in mind. And he still has to progress to the final stage—when he notices in time and has skill enough and sense of responsibility enough to take himself to the toilet, manage his clothes, and carry out the whole job. Studies of average children show that most of them are still having frequent accidents at 2½ years and plenty aren't able to take over full responsibility until they are about 3.

387. Catching in the first half of the second year. There are two general approaches to bladder training. The mother who prefers to get at it as early as is sensible (the mother who also starts to catch regular bowel movements in the last part of the first year or the first part of the second) can start gradually to catch the urine any time when the bladder shows that it is retaining urine for a couple of hours. If you wait until you find your child dry after two hours, you can be reasonably sure of three things:

1) The bladder is grown-up enough to cooperate. You won't be trying to train something that is nowhere near ready for training.

2) Your child's bladder will be full after 2 hours. That means that he is ready to urinate pretty soon. You won't have to keep him on the seat for long.

3) If you wait to put him on until he's been dry for 2 hours, you won't be going at his training too suddenly, because you will find him dry only every few days at first. Gradually, as the weeks pass, you'll find him dry more regularly.

This is a practical time to change to training pants.

In a majority of children, dryness first shows up at the end of the nap. A few are first found dry at another time of day. In a few, it is first discovered on waking in the morning.

388. Waiting for notification. Parents who prefer to go slow on training (who wait on bowel training for signals or imitation in the last half of the second year) are naturally waiting on bladder training, too. The child who has learned somewhere between 18 and 24 months to make a sign that a bowel movement is coming, usually, a month or so later, becomes aware enough of a full bladder to tell his mother about that, too, if she encourages him a little by using the word and by suggesting that he can tell her about this also.

If a mother is waiting for her child to do most of the training himself (through his own desire to use the toilet just like others in the family), he will, toward the end of the second year, probably achieve most of his bowel and urine training at the same time. As I said in the discussion of bowel training, this can be a nuisance for a few days, because at times he'll want to go to the toilet every ten minutes in hopes he can perform again.

I want to add again that the parent who prefers to wait for the child to start the training, with signal or imitation, shouldn't get the idea that any suggestion on her part is wrong and will spoil the method. Most children are quite ready and willing in the last part of the second year to begin to try to cooperate with a mother's wishes if she expresses them in an agreeable and encouraging manner and if she takes into account her child's readiness. To put it the other way around, it's unnecessary and sometimes confusing to a child if the mother is so afraid of interfering that she tries to keep it a secret that she wishes him to become trained.

389. Inability to urinate away from home. It sometimes happens that a child around 2 has become so well trained to his own potty chair or toilet seat that he can't perform anywhere else. You can't urge him or scold him into it. He will probably wet his pants eventually, for which he shouldn't be scolded. If he is painfully full, can't let go, and you can't get home, put him in a hot bath for half an hour. This will probably work. Keep this possibility in mind when you take him traveling, and bring along his own seat if necessary. It's better to get a child used early to urinating in different places, including outdoors.

390. Standing up to urinate comes later. Parents are sometimes worried because a 2-year-old boy won't make the change to urinating standing up. It isn't necessary to make an issue of this. He'll get the idea sooner or later, when he has a chance to see other boys occasionally or his father once or twice. (See Section 532 on parental nudity.)

391. Staying dry at night. Many inexperienced and experienced parents assume that the only reason a child learns to stay dry through the night is because the parent picks him up late in the evening. They ask, "Now that he is reasonably dry in the daytime, when should I begin to pick him up at night?" This is a mistaken idea, and it makes night dryness sound like too much of a job. It's closer to the facts to say that a child just naturally becomes dry at night when his bladder becomes mature enough, provided he isn't nervous or rebellious (Section 679). This is shown clearly by the fact that one baby in a hundred regularly stays dry at night from the age of 12 months, although the mother has made no training effort at all and although the child wets throughout the day. And quite a few children, late in the second year or early in the third, become dry at night before they have much control in the daytime. The reason the bladder can retain urine for longer periods during sleep than in the daytime is that the kidneys automatically produce less urine when a person is quiet and asleep and make the urine more concentrated.

Most children become dry at night between 2 and 3 years of age, a smaller number between 1 and 2, a few not till after 3. Boys tend to be later than girls, high-strung children later than relaxed ones. Sometimes slowness in becoming dry seems to be a family trait.

I don't think it is necessary for parents to do anything special about night training. The natural maturing of the bladder plus the idea that the child gets in the daytime—that urine belongs in the toilet—takes care of most cases. Of course, it helps a little if the parents share in the child's pride when he begins to have dry nights.

Some parents prefer to take a more active part and begin picking the child up at 10 P.M. just as soon as he has become responsible in the daytime. It may be possible to hasten night dryness a bit in this way, since a bladder that is emptied in the evening is not so full in the early morning. Some children wake easily in the evening and perform readily. Others are hard to wake or have trouble performing or become very upset. I think that if the parents run into any trouble, they should call it off.

The One-Year-Old

WHAT MAKES HIM TICK

392. Feeling his oats. One year old is an exciting age. Your baby is changing in lots of ways—in his eating, in how he gets around, in what he wants to do, and in how he feels about himself and other people. When he was little and helpless, you could put him where you wanted him, give him the playthings you thought suitable, feed him the foods you knew were best. Most of the time he was willing to let you be the boss, and took it all in good spirit. It's more complicated now that he is around a year old. He seems to realize that he's not meant to be a baby doll the rest of his life, that he's a human being with ideas and a will of his own.

When you suggest something that doesn't appeal to him, he feels he **must** assert himself. His nature tells him to. He just says No in words or actions, even about things that he likes to do. The psychologists call it "negativism"; mothers call it "that terrible No stage." But stop and think what would happen to him if he never felt like saying No. He'd become a robot, a mechanical man. You wouldn't be able to resist the temptation to boss him all the time, and he'd stop learning and developing. When he was old enough to go out into the world, to school and later to work, everybody else would take advantage of him, too. He'd never be good for anything.

393. The passion to explore. He's a demon explorer. He pokes into every nook and cranny, fingers the carving in the furniture, shakes a table or anything else that isn't nailed down, wants to take every single book out of the bookcase, climbs onto anything he can reach, fits little things into big things and then tries to fit big things into little things. A tired out mother calls this "getting into everything," and her tone of voice says that he's a nuisance. She probably doesn't realize what a vital period this is for him. A baby **has** to find out about the size and shape and movableness of everything in his world and test out his own skill before he can advance to the next stage, just the way he'll have to go through the grades before he can go to high school. That he "gets into everything" is a sign that he's bright in mind and spirit.

Incidentally, you've probably realized by now that he is never quiet while he's awake. It isn't nervousness—it's eagerness. He's made that way so that he will surely keep learning and practicing all day long.

AVOIDING ACCIDENTS AND FEARS

394. One year is a dangerous age. Parents cannot prevent all accidents. If they were careful enough or worrisome enough to try, they would only make a child timid and dependent.

On the other hand, a great majority of serious accidents can be easily prevented if you know where the common dangers lie and are sensible in avoiding them. Here is a list:

Low chair-table combinations are safer than **high chairs.** If you use a high chair, it should have a broad base so that it won't tip, a harness to hold a climbing baby, a latch to keep him from raising the tray. A **baby carriage** should have a harness for a baby who has reached the climbing age. There should be gates at the top and sometimes at the bottom of **stairs,** including porch stairs, until the child can go up and down steadily. Upstairs **windows** should have guards, or be opened only at the top.

It is not wise to let a baby be crawling or a small child be walking around the **kitchen** during the cooking or serving of meals. There is danger from spattering grease, from the mother's tripping and spilling something hot, from the child's pulling a pot off the stove. This is the best time for the play pen or a pen made by laying chairs on their sides, or for his chair. His chair or pen should be well away from the stove. A baby can reach a surprising distance when he tries. Get in the habit of turning **pot handles** away from the front of the stove. When serving the meal, put a coffee pot or other **hot container** in the middle of the table. Take the same precautions with oil lamps. Avoid tablecloths that hang over the edge and so can be pulled off.

A baby or small child who still puts things in his mouth should not have **small objects** like buttons, beans, peas, or beads to play with, or nuts or popcorn to eat, because they are easily breathed into the windpipe and cause choking. Take away a pencil or other **sharp object** if a small child keeps it in his mouth when he plays or runs.

As a matter of habit, always feel the temperature of a **bath** just before you put a child in, even if you remember doing it earlier. Hot faucets sometimes cause burns. Don't touch, or let a child touch, electrical equipment while in a bath or while holding onto a faucet. Don't leave pails of hot water on the floor.

Electric cords should be in first-class condition. Train the baby early not to pull or chew them (Section 404). Cover unused **wall sockets** with adhesive tape or put solid furniture in front of them so that pins can't be poked into them. Put bulbs into empty **lamp sockets** if they are within reach.

Keep **matches** in containers in high places that are impossible for even a determined 3- or 4-year-old to reach.

Wells, pools, cisterns, should be well protected.

Put **broken glass, opened cans,** into a covered, hard-to-open receptacle. Use a can with a slot in the top for used **razor blades.**

Don't let a baby go close to strange dogs at an age when he is likely to startle or hurt them.

395. Now's the time to put poisons out of reach. A fifth of all accidental poisonings occur in the second year of life. Children in this exploring and tasting age will, when the spirit moves them, eat almost anything, no matter how it tastes. They especially love pills, good-tasting medicines, cigarettes, and matches. You will be surprised to read the list of the substances that most frequently cause dangerous poisoning in children:

Aspirin and other drugs
Insect and rat poisons
Kerosene, gasoline, benzene, and cleaning fluids
Lead in paint that a child has chewed off something.
    (Most indoor paint and toy paint contains no lead. The danger
    is from outdoor paint on window sills, porches, etc., and from
    outdoor paint that has been used at home to repaint toys, cribs,
    and other furniture.)
Liquid furniture and auto polish.
Lye and other alkalis used for cleaning
Oil of wintergreen
Plant sprays
Stove cleaners

Now is the time to inspect your home with an eagle eye—or, rather, a baby's eye. Put all **medicines** surely out of reach. Find very safe places for **cleaning fluids and powders, shoe polish, ink, cigarettes, tobacco, plant sprays.** Keep dangerous substances in different cupboards or on shelves far away from relatively harmless medicines and substances used in cooking so you won't grab the wrong one in a hurry. Never give a child a bottle or package of medicine or other poisonous substance to play with, no matter how tightly stoppered. Put bold labels on all medicines so you won't use the wrong one. Stop using rat **poisons** and insect pastes and powders. Get rid of them. Be careful in disposing of bottles and cans that have contained poisons.

396. Protect him from frightening sounds and sights. A baby at a year may become fascinated with one thing for several weeks on end—for instance, the telephone, or planes overhead, or electric lights. Let him touch and become familiar with objects that are not dangerous or disturbing. However, in some cases the child is half frightened of the object. Then it's wiser for the parents not to play up to his interest, or if it's something dangerous, not to dwell on the danger. Better to distract him with something else than to increase his awe.

At this age a baby may be frightened by strange objects that move suddenly or make a loud noise, such as folded pictures that pop up from a book, the opening of an umbrella, a vacuum cleaner, a siren, a barking, jumping dog, a train, even a vase of rustling branches.

Try not to have these startling things too close to a 1-year-old until he gets used to them. If the vacuum cleaner bothers him, don't use it for a few months, at least while he is indoors. Then try it the first time when he is some distance away.

397. Fear of the bath. Between 1 and 2 years, a child may become frightened of the bath, because of slipping under water, or getting soap in his eyes, or even seeing and hearing the water go down the drain. To avoid soap in the eyes, soap with a washcloth that is not too wet and rinse several times with a damp but not dripping washcloth. There are also special shampoos for children that don't sting the eyes. If he becomes afraid to get into the bathtub, don't force him at all. You can try a dishpan, but if he's afraid of that, give him a sponge bath for several months, until he gets back his courage. Then start with an inch of water and remove him before you pull the stopper.

If your baby, toward the end of the first year, begins to fight having the food washed off his face and hands with a cloth after meals, set a pan of water on the tray in front of him and let him dabble his hands while you wash his face with your wet hand.

Fear of strangers is discussed in Sections 348 and 400, fear of the flushing toilet in Section 380.

INDEPENDENCE AND OUTGOINGNESS

398. He gets more dependent and more independent at the same time. This sounds contradictory. A mother complains of a year-old baby, "He's getting to cry every time I go out of the room." This doesn't mean that he is developing a bad habit, but that he's growing up and realizing how much he depends on his mother. It's inconvenient, but it's a good sign.

But at the very age when he is becoming more dependent, he is also developing the urge to be on his own, discover new places, make up to unfamiliar people.

Watch a baby at the creeping stage when his mother is washing the dishes. He plays contentedly with some pots and pans for a while. Then he gets a little bored and decides to explore in the dining room. He creeps around under the furniture there, picking up little pieces of dust and tasting them, carefully climbing to his feet to reach the handle of a drawer. After a while he seems to feel the need of company again, for he suddenly scrambles back into the kitchen. At one time you see his urge for independence getting the upper hand, at another the need for security. He satisfies each in turn. As the months go by he becomes more bold and daring in his experiments and explorations. He still needs his mother, but not so often. He is building his own independence, but part of the courage comes from knowing he can get security when he feels he needs it.

I am making the point that independence comes from security as well as from freedom, because a few people get it twisted around backward. They try to "train" independence into a child by keeping him in a room by himself for long periods even though he is crying for company. I think that when the issue is being forced this hard a child is not learning anything very good.

So the baby at around a year is at a fork in the road. If he's given a chance, he gradually becomes more independent: more sociable with outsiders (grownups and children), more self-reliant, more outgoing. If he's confined a great deal, kept away from others, used to having only his mother hovering over him (see Section 497), he is apt to become tied to her apron strings, more timid with strangers, wrapped up in himself. How is independence encouraged?

Let him out of the carriage when he can walk. When a baby has learned to walk, it's time to let him out of his carriage on his daily outings. Never mind if he gets dirty; he should. Try to go to a place where you don't have to be after him every minute and where he can get used to other children. If he picks up cigarette butts, you have to jump, take them away, and show him something else that's fun. You can't let him eat handfuls of sand or earth because it irritates his intestines and may give him worms. If he puts everything in his mouth, try giving him a hard cracker or some clean object he likes to chew on, to keep his mouth busy. Keeping an able-bodied walking baby tucked in his carriage may keep him out of trouble, but it cramps his style and hinders his development. Some parents find a harness is very practical for shopping and walks at this age. It shouldn't be used for hitching him in one place for long.

399. Let him out of the play pen when he insists. One child is willing to stay in the play pen, at least for short periods, as late as a year and a half. Another thinks it's a prison by the time he's 9 months. Most like it well enough until they learn to walk, around the age of a year and a quarter. I'd say let your baby out of the pen when he feels unhappy there. I don't mean at the first whimper, for if you give him something new to play with, he may be happy there for another hour. Outgrowing the pen is a gradual process. At first he gets sick of it only after a long spell. Gradually he gets impatient earlier. It may be months before he objects to being put in at all. In any case, let him out each time he's sure he's had enough.

400. Get him used to outsiders. At this age a baby's nature tells him to be leery and suspicious of strangers till he has had a chance to look them over. But then he wants to get closer and eventually make friends, in a 1-year-old fashion, of course. He may just stand close and gaze, or

Let him out when he's had enough.

solemnly hand something to the newcomer and then take it back, or bring everything movable in the room and pile it in the person's lap.

Many adults don't have the sense to let a small child alone while he sizes them up. They rush up to him, full of talk, and he has to retreat to his mother for protection. Then it takes longer for him to work up his courage to be friendly. I think it helps for a mother to remind a visitor in the beginning, "It makes him bashful when you pay attention to him right away. If we talk for a while, he'll try to make friends sooner."

When your baby is old enough to walk, give him plenty of chances to get used to strangers and make up to them. Take him to the grocery store a couple of times a week. If possible, take him every day where other small children play. He isn't able to play **with** them yet, but at times he wants to watch. If he is used to playing near them now, he will be ready for cooperative play when the time comes, between 2 and 3. If he's never been around other children by 3, it will take him months just to get used to them.

HOW TO HANDLE HIM

401. He's very distractible, and that's a big help. The year-old baby is so eager to find out about the whole world that he isn't particular where he begins or where he stops. Even if he's all absorbed in a ring of keys, you can make him drop it by giving him an egg beater. His distractibility is one of the handles by which his wise parent guides him.

402. Arranging the house for a wandering baby. When you tell a mother that her baby has outgrown the play pen or the crib and that she ought to let him on the floor, she is apt to look unhappy and say, "But I'm afraid he'd hurt himself. At least he'd wreck the house." Sooner or later he must be let out to roam around, if not at 10 months, at least by 15 months, when he's walking. And he's not going to be any more reasonable or easier to control then. At whatever age you give him the freedom of the house, you have to make adjustments, so it's better to do it when he is ready.

How do you keep a year-old baby from hurting himself or the household furnishings, anyway? First of all, you can arrange the rooms where he'll be so that he's allowed to play with three quarters of the things he can reach. Then only a quarter have to be forbidden. Whereas, if you try to forbid him to touch three quarters of the things, you will drive him and yourself mad. If there are plenty of things he can do, he's not going to bother so much about the things he can't do. Practically speaking, this means taking breakable ash trays and vases and ornaments off low tables and shelves and putting them out of reach. It means taking the valuable books off the lower shelves of the bookcases and putting the old magazines there instead. Jam the good books in tight so that he can't pull them out. In the kitchen, put the pots and pans on the shelves near the floor and put the china and packages of food out of reach. One mother filled a lower bureau drawer with old clothes, toys, and other interesting objects and let the baby explore it, empty it, fill it, to his heart's content.

403. How do you make him leave certain things alone? This is the main problem between 1 and 2 years. There are always a few things that you have to teach him to let alone. There have to be lamps on tables. He mustn't pull them off by their cords or push tables over. He mustn't touch the hot stove, or turn on the gas, or crawl out a window.

404. "No" isn't enough at first. You can't stop him by just saying No, at least not in the beginning. Even later, it depends on your tone of voice and how often you say it and whether you really mean it. It's not a method to rely on heavily until he has learned from experience what it means—and that you mean it. Don't say "No" in a challenging voice

Better to remove and distract him than to just say, "No, no!"

from across the room. This gives him a choice. He says to himself, "Shall I be a mouse and do as she says, or shall I be a man and grab the lamp cord?" Remember that his nature is egging him on to try things and to balk at directions. The chances are he'll keep on approaching the lamp cord with an eye on you to see how angry you get. It's much wiser, the first few times he goes for the lamp, to go over promptly and whisk him to another part of the room. You can say "No" at the same time to begin teaching him what it means. Quickly give him a magazine, an empty cigarette box, anything that is safe and interesting. There's no use tossing him a rattle that he was bored with months ago.

Suppose he goes back to the lamp a few minutes later? Remove him and distract him again, promptly, definitely, cheerfully. Say, "No, no," at the same time that you remove him, adding it to your action for good measure. Sit down with him for a minute to show him what he can do with the new plaything. If necessary, put the lamp out of reach this time, or even take him out of the room. You are tactfully but firmly showing him that you are absolutely sure in your own mind that the lamp is not the thing to play with. You are keeping away from choices, arguments, cross looks, scoldings—which may not do the job and which are likely to get his back up.

You might say, "But he won't learn unless I teach him it's naughty." Oh yes, he will. In fact, he can accept the lesson more easily if it's done in this matter-of-fact way. When you disapprovingly waggle a finger from across the room at a baby who hasn't yet learned that **no** really means **no,** your crossness rubs him the wrong way. It makes him want to take a chance on disobeying. And it's no better if you grab him, hold him face to face, and give him a talking-to. You're not giving him a chance to give in gracefully or forget. His only choice is to surrender meekly or to defy you.

I think of a Mrs. T. who complained bitterly that her 16-month-old daughter was "naughty." Just then Suzy toddled into the room, a nice girl with a normal amount of spunk. Instantly Mrs. T. looked disapproving and said, **"Now remember,** don't go near the radio." Suzy hadn't been thinking of the radio at all, but now she had to. She turned and moved slowly toward it. Mrs. T. gets panicky just as soon as each of her children in turn shows signs of developing into an independent person. She dreads that she won't be able to control them. In her uneasiness, she makes an issue when there doesn't need to be any. It's like the person learning to ride a bicycle who sees a rock in the road ahead. He is so nervous about it that he keeps steering right for it.

Take the example next of a baby who is getting close to a hot stove.

A mother doesn't sit still and say, "No-o-o," in a disapproving voice. She jumps and gets him out of the way. This is the method that comes naturally if she is really trying to keep him from doing something, and not just engaging in a battle of wills.

405. Take lots of time or be masterful. A mother of a 1¾-year-old boy takes him with her every day to the grocery store. But she complains that instead of walking right along, he wanders up the walk and climbs the front steps of every house they pass on the way. The more she calls to him, the more he lingers. When she scolds him, he runs in the opposite direction. She is afraid he is turning into a behavior problem. This baby isn't a behavior problem, though he may be made into one. He's not at an age when he can keep the grocery store in mind. His nature says to him, "Look at that walk to explore! Look at those stairs!" Every time his mother calls to him, it reminds him of his new-felt urge to assert himself. What can the mother do? If she has to get to the store promptly, she can take him in his carriage. But if she's going to use this time for his outing, she should allow four times as long as if she were going alone, and let him make his side trips. If she keeps moving slowly, he'll want to catch up to her every once in a while.

Here's another tight spot. It's time to go in for lunch, but your small child is digging happily in the dirt. If you say, "Now it's time to go in," in a tone of voice that means, "Now you can't have any more fun," you get resistance. But if you say cheerfully, "Let's go climb the stairs," it may give him a desire to go. But suppose he's tired and cranky that day, and nothing that's indoors makes any appeal. He just gets balky right away, disagreeably balky. I'd pick him up casually and carry him indoors, even if he's squealing and kicking like a little pig. You do this in a self-confident way, as if you were saying to him, "I know, you're tired and cross. But when we have to go in, we have to." Don't scold him; it won't make him see the error of his ways. Don't argue with him, because that won't change his mind; you only get yourself frustrated. A small child who is feeling miserable and making a scene is comforted underneath by sensing that his mother knows what to do without getting angry.

406. Dropping and throwing things. Around the age of 1 year, a baby learns to drop things on purpose. He solemnly leans over the side of his high chair, and drops food on the floor, or tosses his toys, one after the other, out of his crib. Then he cries because he hasn't got them. An irritated mother is apt to think he's deliberately making a monkey out of her. But he isn't thinking of her; he is fascinated by a new skill. He wants to do it all day long, the way a boy wants to ride his new two-wheeler.

Dropping is a new skill.

If you pick up the object, he realizes it's a game that two can play and is more delighted. It's better not to get in the habit of picking up his dropped toys right away. Put him on the floor or ground when he gets in this mood. You can tie his favorite bed toys to the slats of his crib on strings a foot long. (A baby may become dangerously entangled in a long string.) Tie others to his carriage. You don't want him throwing food out of the high chair in any case, but he won't start until his appetite is pretty well satisfied. Take the food away promptly and firmly when the dropping begins, and put him down to play. Trying to scold a baby out of dropping things leads to nothing but frustration for the mother.

NAP HOURS ARE CHANGING

407. Naptimes are shifting in most babies around the age of a year. One who was taking a nap at about 9 A.M. may refuse it altogether or show that he wants it later and later in the morning. If he takes it late, he is unready for his next nap until the middle of the afternoon, and this probably throws off his bedtime after supper. Or he may refuse the afternoon nap altogether. A baby may vary a lot from day to day at this period, and even go back to a 9 A.M. nap that he has refused for 2 weeks, so don't come to final conclusions too soon. You have to put up with these inconveniences as best you can, realizing that they are temporary. With some babies who are not ready to sleep in the first part of the morning, you can remove the need for the before-lunch nap by putting them in their beds anyway, around 9 in the morning, if they are willing to lie or sit quietly for a while. Of course, another kind of baby only gets in a rage if put to bed when not sleepy, and nothing is accomplished.

If a baby becomes sleepy **just** before noon, it's the mother's cue to move lunch up to 11:30 or even 11 for a few days. Then the long nap comes after lunch. But for a while after a baby has cut down to one nap a day, whether morning or afternoon, he may get frantically tired before suppertime. As a doctor friend of mine put it, "There's a stage in a baby's life when two naps are too many and one is not enough." You can help your baby through this period by giving him his supper and putting him to bed for the night a little earlier for the time being.

Don't get the idea from this section that all babies give up their morning nap in the same way or at the same age. One is through with it at 9 months; another craves it and benefits by it as late as 2 years.

HE'S APT TO CHANGE HIS EATING HABITS

408. He gets more choosy for several reasons. Somewhere around a year a baby is apt to change his feeling about his food. He becomes more choosy and less hungry. This is not surprising. If he kept on eating and gaining the way he did when he was a little baby, he'd turn into a mountain. Now he seems to feel that he has time to look the meal over and ask himself, "What looks good today and what doesn't?" What a contrast to his behavior at 8 months! In those days he felt he was starved to death when mealtime came around. He'd whimper pathetically while his mother tied his bib and lean forward for every bite. It wouldn't matter much what she was serving him. He was too hungry to care.

There are other reasons, aside from not being so hungry, that make him choosy. He's beginning to realize that he's a separate person with ideas of his own, so he becomes definite in his dislike of a food that he was doubtful about before. His memory is getting better, too. He probably realizes, "The meals here are served up pretty regularly, and they stay around long enough for me to get what I want."

Teething often takes away a child's appetite, especially when the first molars are on their way. He may eat only half his usual amount for days, or occasionally refuse an entire meal. Finally, and perhaps most important, there is the fact that appetite **naturally** varies from day to day and week to week. We grownups know that one day we grab a big glass of tomato juice and another day split-pea soup looks better. It is the same way with children and babies. But the reason you don't see this variation more often in infants under a year is that most of the time they are too hungry to turn anything down.

409. Dr. Davis's experiments in appetite. Dr. Clara Davis wanted to find out what children would eat if left to their own desires and given a variety of wholesome foods to choose from. She didn't start with older children for fear they would have already developed prejudices about food. So she picked three babies, 8 to 10 months old, who had never had anything to eat but breast milk. She took them to live at a place where they could be watched carefully. And this is how they were fed: At each meal a nurse would place before them six or eight serving dishes containing a variety of wholesome, unrefined foods. There were vegetables, fruits, eggs, cereals, meats, whole-grain bread, milk, water, and fruit juices. The nurse was told, "Don't help the baby till he shows you what he wants." The 8-month-old baby would lean forward and dip his fist into a dish of beets and then try to eat it off his hand. Now the nurse was permitted to give him a teaspoonful of beets. Then she must wait until he showed his choice again. Another spoonful of beets or maybe applesauce.

Dr. Davis discovered three important things. First, babies who chose their own diet from a variety of natural foods developed very well; none of them got too fat or too thin. Second, every baby, over a period of time, chose what any scientist would agree was a well-balanced diet. Third, from meal to meal and day to day, the appetite varied a lot. Each separate meal wasn't well-balanced. For several meals in a row a baby might feed largely on greens. Then he would change about and go more heavily for starches. Sometimes he would go on a real jag and, for instance, make a whole meal of nothing but beets, perhaps four times as much beets as a grownup would consider a polite amount. And after this spree he wouldn't vomit, he wouldn't have a bellyache or diarrhea. A baby would sometimes drink as much as a quart of milk in addition to his full meal, and at the next meal want very little milk at all. One baby, on several occasions, ate as many as six hard-boiled eggs in addition to a full meal. Dr. Davis kept track of the beef intake of a baby over a period of many days. He would go along for a while eating an average portion of beef, and then his appetite for beef would begin to increase. He might work up to four times as much beef as we would ordinarily think proper, keep up that rate for several days, and then taper off. The way this craving for beef gradually increased and then decreased suggested to Dr. Davis that there was a real bodily need for something in that beef that influenced the appetite for days. Dr. Davis eventually carried out the experiment with many older children, too, even hospital patients, and found that the results were just as good.

410. What parents can learn from Dr. Davis. The good results from this experimental method of feeding don't prove that a mother ought to serve her child six or eight dishes at each meal, like the hors d'œuvres in a Swedish restaurant. But it does show that she can trust an unspoiled child's appetite to choose a wholesome diet if she serves him a reasonable variety and balance of those natural, unrefined foods **that he enjoys eating at present.** It means that she can let him eat larger amounts than usual of a food his appetite craves without worrying about the consequences. Even more important, it means that she doesn't have to worry when he develops a temporary dislike of a vegetable.

It is hard for us moderns to have this kind of confidence in our children's appetites. We have heard so much about what the scientists say we **ought** to eat that we have forgotten that our bodies have known a lot about this for millions of years. Each kind of caterpillar knows for sure what sort of leaves it can eat and refuses all others. The deer travels for miles to the salt lick when his body craves salt. The robin knows what is good for him without ever attending a lecture. It is not surprising that man should also have some instinctive knowledge of what is good for him. I don't mean that a child or grownup will **always** eat what's best for him, and I don't mean that parents don't need to know what makes a balanced diet. If a mother doesn't know any better than to offer her child only doughnuts and coffee at every meal, there is no chance for him to pick a well-balanced diet out of this selection, no matter how sound his instincts are. It is important for a mother to know the value of vegetables, fruits, milk, meat, eggs, whole-grain cereal, so that she can offer her child a variety that covers all his needs. But it is just as important for her to know that her child's instincts are sound to start with, that his appetite naturally varies, that he will probably try to pick a well-balanced diet in the long run if he isn't given too many prejudices.

411. Let him give up certain vegetables for a while. If he suddenly turns against the vegetable that he loved last week, **let** him turn against it. If you don't make a fuss today, he will probably come back to it next week or next month. But if you insist on his taking it when he seems to dislike it, you only make him set in his mind that that particular food is his enemy. You turn a temporary dislike into a permanent hate. If he turns down the same vegetable twice in succession, leave it out for a couple of weeks. It is naturally irritating to a mother to buy a food, prepare it, serve it, and then have it turned down by an opinionated wretch who loved the same thing a few days ago. It is hard for her not to be cross and bossy at such a time. But it is worse for the child's feeling about food to try to force or urge it. If he turns down half his vegetables for a while, as is common in the second year, serve him the ones that he does like. This is the wise and pleasant way to take advantage of the great variety of fresh and canned vegetables that we have. If he turns against all vegetables for a while but loves his fruit, let him have extra fruit. If he is taking enough fruit, milk, and his vitamin drops, he is not missing anything that's in vegetables. (See Section 436 for vegetable substitutes.)

412. What to do if he is tired of cereal. Many babies get fed up with cereal sometime in the second year, especially for supper. Don't try to push it in. There are many substitutes you can offer, which are discussed in Sections 438 and 439. Even if he gives up **all** starches for a few weeks, it won't hurt him.

413. Don't be alarmed if he wants less milk at times. Milk is a very valuable food. It provides good amounts of most of the elements that are important for a child's diet, as is explained in Section 430. But it is helpful to remember that in the parts of the world where there are no cows or goats, children get these substances from other foods after their nursing period is over. It's also good to know that an average of a pint and a half (24 ounces) a day safely covers the needs of almost every child between 1 and 3 who is taking a reasonable diet otherwise. Many children between the ages of 1 and 2 want to cut down to this amount or less, at least temporarily. If a parent worries and sets to work to urge or force a larger amount, the child is apt to become steadily more disgusted. In the long run, he takes less milk than if he had been let alone.

Don't keep offering the cup again after he has shown that he's not interested. Every time he has to decline it makes him more determined he doesn't want it. If he drops down to an average of 8 ounces, wait a few days and see if he doesn't increase again.

If he goes on drinking less than a pint and a half, there are many other ways that milk can be used in the diet; these are discussed in Section 431. Milk in any of these forms is just as nutritious as when it comes straight from the cow.

If a child goes on for a month averaging less than a pint and a half of milk **in all forms,** the mother should report it to the doctor. He may prescribe calcium in some other form until the child's appetite for milk comes back.

414. Be wary of feeding problems now. The reason for discussing the natural variations in a child's appetite at this age is an important one. Feeding problems start more commonly between 1 and 2 years than at any other period. Once a child becomes balky, once a mother becomes worried and angry, the fat's in the fire. The more the mother frets and urges, the less the child eats. And the less he takes, the more anxious the mother is. Meals become agonizing. The problem may last for years. The tension that grows up between parent and child causes other behavior problems, too.

The best way to keep your child eating well is to let him go on thinking of food as something he wants. Allow him to eat a larger than usual amount of one wholesome food, less or none of another, if that's the way he feels. When making up his meals, select a well-balanced diet, but select it from among the wholesome foods that he really enjoys. Expect his taste to change from month to month. If you cannot consult a doctor about additions to his diet, look ahead to Sections 430 to 440 for new foods and those to substitute for the ones he is leaving out temporarily.

The chances are great that if you don't make a battle of it, your child will eat a reasonably balanced diet from week to week, though it may be somewhat lopsided from meal to meal or day to day. If it stays unbalanced for weeks, you should discuss the problem with a doctor, even if it is difficult to reach him.

415. Standing and playing at meals. This may be quite a problem even before the age of a year. It comes about because the baby is less ravenous for his food, more interested in all kinds of new activities, like climbing, handling the spoon, messing in the food, tipping the cup upside down, dropping things on the floor. I've seen a 1-year-old fed a whole meal standing up backward in the high chair, or even being followed around the house by a long-suffering mother with a spoon and dish in her hands.

Fooling at meals is only a sign that a child is growing up and that his mother is sometimes more keen about his eating than he is. It's inconvenient and irritating, and it's apt to lead to feeding problems, too. I wouldn't let it go on. You'll notice that the child climbs and plays when he's partly or completely satisfied, not when he's really hungry. So whenever he loses interest in his food, assume he's had enough, let him down from his chair, and take the food away. It's right to be firm, but you don't

Time to finish the meal.

need to get mad. If he immediately whimpers for his meal, as if to say he didn't mean he wasn't hungry, give him one more chance. But if he shows no regret, don't try to give him the meal a little later. If he gets extra hungry between meals, give him a little more than usual at his between-meal feeding, or give him his next regular meal early. If you **always** stop the meal casually when he loses interest, he does his part by paying attention when he is hungry.

Now I want to make a reservation. A baby around a year has a powerful urge to dip his fingers into the vegetable, or squeeze a little cereal in his hand, or stir a drop of milk around on the tray. This isn't fooling. He may be opening his mouth eagerly for food at the same time. I wouldn't try to stop the meal for this alone, and I wouldn't try to stop him from experimenting with the feel of his food. If he tries to turn the dish over, hold it down firmly. If he insists, keep it out of reach for a while or stop the meal.

416. Let him feed himself early. The age at which a baby feeds himself depends largely on the adult's attitude. Dr. Davis, in her experiments on what diets babies choose, found that some infants were efficiently spoon-feeding themselves **before the age of a year.** At the other extreme, an overprotective mother swears that her 2-year-old couldn't possibly feed himself at all. It all depends on when you give him a chance.

Most babies show an ambition to manage the spoon by a year, and if they have opportunity to practice, a lot of them can do a good job without help by 15 months.

A baby gets some preparation for spoon-feeding way back at 6 months, when he holds his own zwieback and other finger foods. Then at around 9 months, when he gets chopped foods, he wants to pick up the pieces and put them in his mouth. The baby who has never been allowed to feed himself with his fingers is apt to be delayed in taking to spoon-feeding.

Feeling is learning.

A polite baby of 10 or 12 months may just want to rest his hand on his mother's when she's feeding him. But most babies, when the urge comes, try to yank the spoon out of their mother's hand. A mother may think this has to be a tug of war, but she can give the baby that spoon and get another to use herself. The baby soon discovers that it's more complicated than just getting possession of the spoon. It takes him weeks to learn how to get a speck of food on the spoon, and weeks more to learn not to turn it upside down between the dish and his mouth. He becomes bored with trying to eat, and stirs or slops the food instead. Then it's time to move the dish out of reach, perhaps leaving a few crumbs of meat in front of him for him to experiment with.

Even when he's trying very hard to feed himself correctly, he makes plenty of accidental messes, and this you've got to put up with. If you're worried about the rug, put a big plastic tablecloth under his chair. It helps to use a hot-water plate with partitions. This keeps his food warm, is harder for him to pick up, and has straight sides to push the food against. Baby spoons with looped handles are meant to be easy to hold, but I think they are more difficult than small spoons with straight handles.

Recently some baby spoons have been made with thick plastic handles so shaped that they stay in the right position in the baby's hands.

If he can feed himself, let him take over completely. Now we come to the most important point. It isn't enough to let the baby have a spoon and a chance to use it; you've got to gradually give him more **reason** to use it. At first he tries because he wants to do things for himself. But after he sees how complicated it is, he's apt to give up the whole business **if you keep on rapidly feeding him, anyway.** In other words, when he begins to be able to get a speck to his mouth, you ought to let him have a few minutes alone with the food, at the beginning of the meal when he's hungriest. Then his appetite urges him on. The better he gets at feeding himself, the longer he should have at each meal to do it.

By the time he can polish off his favorite dish in ten minutes, it's time for you to be out of the picture. This is where mothers often go wrong. They say, "He can eat his own meat and fruit all right now, but I have to feed him his vegetable, potato, and cereal still." That's a little risky. If he's able to manage one food, he has skill enough to manage the others. If you go on feeding him the ones he doesn't bother with, you build up a sharper and sharper distinction between the foods **he** wants and the foods **you** want him to take. In the long run, this takes away his appetite for **your** foods. But if you put thought into serving as well-balanced a diet as possible from among the foods he is presently enjoying and let him feed himself entirely, the chances are great that he will strike a good balance from week to week, even though he may slight this or that food at certain meals.

Don't worry about table manners. A baby wants to eat more expertly, more neatly, all by himself. He wants to graduate from fingers to spoon and from spoon to fork, as soon as he feels equal to the challenge, just as he wants to try everything else difficult that he sees others doing. Dr. Davis noticed this in the babies she was observing, and they weren't coached at all. She pointed out that puppies show the same urge to learn eating manners without teaching. In the beginning, they stand in a pan of milk and dip their faces. First, they learn to keep their feet out; next, to lap the milk without dipping their faces; finally, to lick their whiskers politely at the end.

I have been making quite a point about letting a child learn to feed himself somewhere between the ages of 12 and 15 months, because that is the age when he wants to try. Suppose a mother keeps a baby from doing it at this age, and then at 21 months declares, "You big lummox, it's time for you to feed yourself." Then the child is apt to take the attitude, "Oh no! It's my custom and my privilege to be fed." He's now reached a more advanced stage, when trying to manage a spoon is no longer exciting. In fact, his whole sense of what's proper rebels against it. His mother has lost the golden opportunity.

Don't take this all so seriously that you think there is only one right age, or worry because your baby is not making sufficient progress, or try to force him to feed himself when he's not ready or not eager. That would only create other problems. I'm only making the point that babies want to learn this skill earlier than many mothers realize, and that it is important for the parent to gradually give up feeding as the child is able to take over.

Elements in the Diet

Before we talk about the everyday foods that children can eat, we ought to discuss the more important chemical substances that foods are composed of, and what the body uses them for.

You can compare a child's body, in one way, to a building under construction. A lot of different materials are needed to build it and to keep it in repair. But a human being is also a machine that's running. It requires fuel for energy, and other substances to make it work properly, just as an automobile needs gasoline, oil, grease, water.

PROTEIN

417. Protein is the main building material of the body. The muscles, heart, brain, kidneys, for instance, are largely made of protein (aside from water). The structure of bones is protein, filled in with minerals, much the way a collar is made stiff with starch. The child needs good food protein to continually increase the size of every part of his body, and also to repair wear and tear.

Most natural foods contain protein, some much, some little. Meat, poultry, fish, eggs, milk, are the foods richest in it. They are the only foods that supply "complete proteins"—that is to say, they contain the complete variety of protein elements the human body needs. That is why a child should be averaging a pint and a half of milk daily and also receiving either meat (or poultry or fish) or eggs daily, preferably both. Next in importance are the proteins in whole-grain cereals, nuts, and mealy vegetables (soy and other beans, peas). These grain and vegetable proteins are only fair in amount and are "incomplete." Whole wheat, for example, contains some essential protein elements; beans contain others. If a child is eating a variety of whole grains and vegetables, they will supplement the proteins from his meats, fish, eggs, milk, but will not take their place.

MINERALS

418. Minerals of many kinds play a vital part in the structure and in the working of every part of the body. The hardness of bones and teeth depends on calcium and phosphorus. The substance in red blood cells that carries the oxygen to all regions of the body is made partly of iron and copper. Iodine is necessary in the functioning of the thyroid gland.

All natural unrefined foods (fruits, vegetables, meats, whole grains, eggs, milk) contain a variety of valuable minerals. But the refining of grains and the prolonged cooking of vegetables in a lot of water removes a great deal. The minerals most likely to be insufficient in the diet are calcium, iron, and in certain areas, iodine. Calcium occurs in small amounts in vegetables and some fruits, but plentifully in milk (and cheese). Iron is supplied by green, leafy vegetables, meats, fruits, whole grains, but more abundantly by egg yolk and liver. Iodine is missing in some inland regions where the drinking water, vegetables, and fruits lack it, and sea food is not available. Table salt is iodized for people in those areas, to prevent goiter.

VITAMINS

Vitamins are special substances that the body needs in minute amounts in order to work right, somewhat the way any machine needs a few drops of oil, or a gasoline motor depends on a tiny electric spark.

419. Vitamin A is necessary to keep healthy the linings of the bronchial, intestinal, and urinary systems, and various parts of the eyes, including that which enables us to see in dim light. The body gets it plentifully from milk fat, egg yolk, green and yellow vegetables, vitamin drops. Probably the only people who receive too little are those on really bad diets or those who cannot absorb it because of serious intestinal disease. These people may be subject to bad colds because of the deficiency. There is no reason to believe, though, that the person on a decent diet will catch fewer colds by taking more and more vitamin A.

420. Vitamin B complex. Scientists used to think that there was just one vitamin B, which had several actions in the body. But when they studied "it," it turned out to be at least ten different vitamins. However, these mostly occur in the same foods. Since the B vitamins are not yet all known or understood, it is more important for people to eat plenty of the natural foods they mostly occur in than to take them separately in pill form. The three known to be most important for human beings are called by their chemical names now: thiamin, riboflavin, niacin. Every tissue in the body needs these three vitamins.

Thiamin (B_1) occurs in fair amounts in whole grains, milk, eggs, liver, meat, and certain vegetables and fruits. It is destroyed by long cooking, especially when soda is used. People are apt to receive an insufficient supply of it when they eat a lot of refined starches and sugars. Lack of thiamin can cause poor appetite, slow growth, fatigue, stomach and intestinal troubles, neuritis. (However, there are many different causes of all these symptoms, and thiamin deficiency is not the most common one.)

Riboflavin (also known as B_2 or G) occurs abundantly in liver, meat, milk, eggs, green vegetables, whole grains, yeast, so a reasonable diet should provide plenty. Deficiency causes cracks in the corners of the mouth and other lip, skin, mouth, and eye troubles.

Niacin (nicotinic acid) occurs abundantly in about the same foods as riboflavin (except milk). Deficiency causes mouth, intestinal, and skin troubles, which are part of the disease called pellagra.

421. Vitamin C (ascorbic acid) occurs most abundantly in oranges, lemons, grapefruit, raw and properly canned tomatoes and tomato juice, raw cabbage. It occurs in fair amounts in several other fruits and vegetables, including potatoes. It is included in many vitamin preparations. It is easily destroyed in cooking. It is necessary for the development of bones, teeth, blood vessels, and other tissues, and plays a part in the functioning of most of the cells in the body. Deficiency is commonest in babies living on cow's milk without orange or tomato juice or vitamin C medicine, and shows itself in painful hemorrhages around the bones and in swollen, bleeding gums. This condition is called scurvy.

422. Vitamin D is needed in large amounts for growth, particularly of the bones and teeth. It helps get calcium and phosphorus, which are in the food in the intestines, absorbed into the blood and deposited in the growing parts of the bones. That's why it should be added to the diet of children, especially in the period of rapid growth in infancy. Ordinary foods contain only a small amount. The sun's rays' shining on the fat in people's skins manufactures vitamin D right there, and that's how they naturally get it when they live outdoors and wear few clothes. When they live in colder climates, they cover up their bodies with clothes and live indoors. The sun's rays in these regions are more slanting and are shut off by soot in the air and by window glass. Various fish-liver oils and synthetic preparations are then the best source of vitamin D. (Fish store it in their livers by eating minute plants that float on the surface of the ocean. Sunshine manufactures it in these plants.) Vitamin D deficiency results in soft, bent bones, poor teeth, weak muscles and ligaments. This is called rickets.

Fully grown people probably receive enough vitamin D from the small amounts in eggs, butter, fish, and from a little sunshine. But the child who is not getting lots of sunshine should take a special preparation of vitamin D, summer and winter, until he has reached his full height in adolescence. Mothers need extra vitamin D during pregnancy and breast feeding.

WATER AND ROUGHAGE

423. Water provides no calories or vitamins, but it is vitally important in the make-up and working of the body. (A baby's body is 60 per cent water.) A child should have a chance to drink water once or twice in each between-meal period, more often in hot weather. Most foods are largely composed of water, too, and that is how people receive part of their daily needs.

424. Roughage means the fibers in vegetables, fruits, and grains (bran, for instance) that our intestines can't digest and absorb. The roughage passes on in the bowel movement, unused in one sense but useful in another. It provides part of the bulk in the bowel contents that helps to stimulate the intestines to function. If a person stays on a bland diet, let's say milk and broth and eggs, he is apt to become constipated from having too little substance left in his lower intestines.

FATS, STARCHES, SUGARS

425. Fuel. So far we have discussed the building materials of the body and the other substances that are necessary to make the system work right. But we haven't considered fuel. The body, being a sort of engine, requires constant fueling just as an automobile needs gasoline. When a person is asleep, the heart still beats, the intestines contract, the liver, kidneys, and other organs keep working. This is like an automobile in neutral with the motor idling. When the person wakes up, moves around, works, runs, he burns more fuel just as the automobile does. Most of the food a child eats is used up daily for fuel, even when he is growing rapidly.

The fuel substances are starch, sugar, fat (and to a slight degree, protein). A starch is composed of a chemical combination of sugars. In the intestines, it is broken up into sugars before it is absorbed into the body. Because starches and sugars are so closely related, they are lumped together under the term **carbohydrates.**

426. The body's fat. When a person eats more fat, sugar, starch, and protein than he needs for fuel, the extra is converted into fat and stored under his skin. When he is eating too little "fuel," he uses up some of his own fat and becomes thinner. This "fat pad," which all people have to a greater or lesser degree, serves not only as a storehouse of fuel but helps, like a blanket, to keep a person warm.

427. Calories. The fuel value of food is measured in calories. Water and minerals have no calories—that is, they have no fuel or energy in them. Fat is rich in calories; an ounce of it has twice as many as an ounce of starch, sugar, or protein. Butter, margarine, vegetable oil, which are almost entirely fat, and cream and salad dressings that contain a lot of it, are therefore very high in calories.

Sugars and syrups are also very high in calories, because they are wholly carbohydrates and contain no water or undigestible roughage.

Grains (which we eat as cereals, breads, crackers, macaroni, puddings, etc.) and starchy vegetables (such as potatoes, beans, corn) are high in calories because of the large proportion of starch in their make-up.

Meats, poultry, fish, eggs, cheese, are high in calories because of their combination of protein and fat. Most of us do not receive as many daily calories from these foods as we do from grains and starchy vegetables, because we eat them in smaller amounts. Milk is a fine source of calories because of its sugar, fat, and protein and because it is easily taken in good amounts.

Fresh and stewed fruits in general provide a fair number of calories because of the natural sugar they contain. Bananas and dried fruit are richer (comparable to potatoes).

Vegetables vary from moderately high to low in calories (mostly in the form of starch and sugar). The vegetables with a moderately high number of calories are white and sweet potatoes, corn, and such beans as soy, navy, baked, and lima. The vegetables that provide a fair number of calories are peas, beets, carrots, onions, parsnips, squash, beet greens. Vegetables low in calories are string beans, cabbage, cauliflower, celery, eggplant, spinach, tomatoes, lettuce, Swiss chard, broccoli, asparagus.

SENSIBLE DIET

428. Keep a balanced attitude. You don't judge foods on calories alone, or on vitamins alone, or on minerals alone. Everybody in the long run needs a balance of low- and high-calorie foods as he needs a balance in other respects in his diet. If a person takes one aspect of diet too seriously and forgets the others, it's apt to lead to trouble. An adolescent girl acquires a fanatical zeal to reduce, leaves out all the foods in which she has heard there are more than a few calories, tries to live on vegetable juices, fruit, and coffee. She is bound to be sick if she keeps on. A serious-minded mother who has the mistaken idea that vitamins are the whole show and that starches are inferior serves her child carrot salad and grapefruit for supper. The poor fellow can't get enough calories out of that to satisfy a rabbit. A plump mother from a plump family, ashamed of her child's scrawniness, serves him only rich foods. These depress his appetite further. Taking them in small amounts, he is apt to to be deprived of minerals and vitamins.

429. A simple guide to diet. The whole business of diet sounds complicated, but it needn't be. Fortunately, a mother doesn't have to figure out the perfect diet for her child. The experiments of Dr. Davis and others have shown that the child's own appetite seeks a well-balanced diet in the long run (Section 409), **provided** he hasn't been urged or given prejudices against foods. and provided he is offered a reasonable variety of wholesome, natural. unrefined foods. The parents' job is to have a general idea of the kinds of foods that combine to make a good diet, and which ones can be substituted for those that the child has lost his taste for. Roughly speaking, the following are required every day:

(1) Milk (in any form), preferably 1½ to 2 pints.
(2) Meat or poultry or fish.

(3) Egg (extra egg can partially substitute for meat and vice versa, though it is desirable to give both).

(4) Vegetable, green or yellow, 1 or 2 times, some of it raw.

(5) Fruit, 2 to 3 times, at least half of it raw, including orange juice (extra fruit can substitute for vegetable and vice versa).

(6) Starchy vegetable, 1 or 2 times.

(7) Whole-grain bread, crackers, cereals, 1 to 3 times (enriched starches can be substituted occasionally).

(8) Vitamin D (in milk or in drops).

Now we are ready to discuss actual foods.

Foods and Meals

What foods should be added to a child's diet and at what age are individual matters that his doctor should decide. It depends on how his digestion has handled various foods in the past, which ones he is refusing, which ones are available in the market.

This chapter is for the benefit of parents who are unable to consult a doctor regularly and have to depend on their own knowledge over long periods of time. If you are in this situation, use all your common sense. Avoid the idea that there is an exact age for a certain food. Start new foods gradually even in the second year. Go slow and play safe with the child who has bowel upsets easily.

Feeding Your Baby and Child, by Benjamin M. Spock, M.D. and Miriam E. Lowenberg, Ph.D.,[1] has many recipes and practical suggestions.

MILK

430. Milk after a year. Milk contains almost all the food elements that a human being needs: protein, fat, sugar, minerals, and most of the vitamins. Children who are taking a well-balanced diet except for milk are likely to get enough of **most** of these elements from other foods. The exception is calcium. Milk is the only food that contains a lot of it. That

[1] Duell, Sloan & Pearce, New York, 1955, $3.75. Pocket Books, Inc., New York, 1956, 25c.

is why you would like a child to average between 1½ and 2 pints a day, in some form.

Remember, though, that many children want less one day or one week, more the next, and that the surest way to keep them liking it is to let them take less temporarily when they feel that way. If your child cuts down, don't urge him. If he isn't back to a pint and a half in a few weeks, think of all the other ways you can serve milk.

431. Substitutes for plain milk. Precooked and dry cereals absorb a lot of milk in preparing. There are all the milk puddings from junket to rice pudding. Vegetable and chicken soups can be mixed with milk instead of water. Baked macaroni, scalloped and mashed potatoes, and many other cooked dishes can be made with milk.

What about flavoring milk? It is better to avoid flavoring if the child takes a reasonable amount of milk in other forms. But if necessary, milk can be made into cocoa or hot chocolate, or served cold, flavored with a little chocolate syrup. However, chocolate upsets some small children, so it is preferable to delay it until the age of 2, and to start very gradually. Milk can be flavored with vanilla or any of the commercial cereal-and-malt preparations sold for this purpose. With any flavoring, avoid making the milk really sweet, for fear of spoiling the appetite. Sipping a drink through a straw or glass tube may make it seem like a treat.

A flavored drink is likely to lose some of its appeal, anyway, when the novelty wears off. This is especially apt to happen if the mother begins to urge it the first time the child takes less than a glassful. It can't be repeated too often that when a parent says, "Drink a little more of your chocolate milk" (or anything else), it begins to take away a child's appetite.

Cheese is a useful form of milk. An ounce of most varieties contains about the same amount of calcium as 8 ounces of milk. But there are two important exceptions. You need three times as much cream cheese (3 ounces) to supply the amount of calcium in an 8-ounce glass of milk. Cottage cheese provides still less; in fact, it takes 10 ounces of cottage cheese to supply the calcium in 8 ounces of milk.

Cottage cheese, having little fat, is the most easily digested, and so it can be eaten in larger amounts, salted or mixed with grated raw vegetables or a little jelly. Other cheeses, being rich in fat, should be started gradually, and the child will probably want only small amounts. They can be served as spreads, or grated into other foods, or in pieces.

If a child doesn't want to take milk in any form (or is allergic to it), he should be receiving calcium in some other form that the doctor prescribes.

Butter or fortified margarine should be added very gradually to vegetables and to bread around the age of a year. Top milk can also be introduced slowly on cereal, puddings, fruits, for the child who is hungry. The digestive system needs time to adjust to increased amounts of fat.

MEATS, FISH, EGGS

432. Meats. Most babies by the age of a year will be eating ground or fine-minced beef, chicken, lamb, liver, bacon, veal, pork when these are served to the rest of the family, or they can continue having them as junior foods from jars or cans. Bacon contains little protein so should not be counted on regularly as a meat. Most of the fat should be trimmed off pork. Pork is an excellent source of vitamins. It should be thoroughly cooked, so that it is white all through, not pink. Incompletely cooked pork is the source of the dangerous disease trichinosis. Better wait until 2 before beginning ham (not fried) or beef frankfurters.

Many young children who love the taste of meat turn against it if it isn't cut up or ground finely enough. They become a little frightened and gag easily at lumps that don't easily turn to mush. So continue to mince fine or grind your child's meats until he is 5 or 6.

433. Fish of the white, nonoily varieties, such as cod, haddock, halibut, flounder, can be started cautiously at the age of a year, baked, boiled, or broiled. It should be carefully crumbled with the fingers to remove bones. The more oily fish and canned fish may be added gradually at 2. Some children love fish, and then it makes a fine substitute for meat once or twice a week. But many others stay firmly opposed even after several trials. Don't urge it.

434. Eggs. Eggs are equally valuable hard-boiled, soft-boiled, scrambled, fried, cooked into foods, or served in drinks. It is desirable for a child to have an egg a day if he likes them. He can have 2 eggs a day if desired.

If a child dislikes most meats and fish, or you cannot get them, his protein needs will probably be covered by 1½ to 2 pints of milk and 2 eggs a day, since he is getting some protein in his whole grains and vegetables.

If a child dislikes eggs or is allergic to them, it is more important for him to have meat regularly.

VEGETABLES

435. Varieties of vegetables. The baby during his first year has probably had most of the following vegetables: spinach, peas, onions, carrots, asparagus, chard, squash, tomatoes, beets, celery, potatoes.

Before a year the change should have been made gradually from puréed to a coarser, lumpy consistency. (Naturally, some puréed and finely mashed vegetables can still be served.) Peas should be mashed slightly to avoid their being swallowed whole.

Sweet potatoes or yams can be used at times instead of white potatoes, beginning at a year. If you have been sticking to the easily digested vegetables up to the age of a year, you can try gradually the less popular and sometimes less digestible ones, such as lima beans (mashed), broccoli, cabbage, cauliflower, turnips, parsnips. Much of their strong taste can be removed by changing the cooking water twice. Some children like them and digest them well, but many won't touch them. Wait until 2 years to serve corn in the kernel. Young children don't chew it; it comes through unchanged. Use only tender corn. When cutting it off the cob, don't cut too close. Then each kernel will be cut open. At 3 or 4, when you start corn on the cob, slice down the center of each row of kernels, so that they are all open.

The more easily digested raw vegetables are usually started between 1 and 2 years for the child with a good digestion. The best are peeled tomatoes, lettuce, sliced string beans, shredded carrots, scraped chopped celery. They should be well scrubbed. Go slow at first and see how they are digested. Orange juice or sweetened lemon juice, with a little salt, can be used for dressing.

Raw vegetable juices can be started at the same time. Raw vegetables and vegetable juices are not only as good as cooked vegetables for the child who digests them well—they are better, because the vitamins have not been partly destroyed by heat, and minerals and vitamins have not been dissolved out in the cooking water.

If a child has temporarily turned against plain vegetables, remember vegetable soups: pea, tomato, celery, onion, spinach, beet, corn, and the soups that contain a large amount of mixed vegetables.

436. Temporary substitutes for vegetables. Suppose a child has refused vegetables in any form for weeks. Will his nutrition suffer? Vegetables are particularly valuable for various minerals and vitamins, and also for roughage. But a variety of fruits supply many of the minerals and vitamins, and the same amount of roughage. If the child is taking vitamin drops, milk, meat, and egg, he is getting the other salts and vitamins that fruits do not provide so well. In other words, if your child dislikes all vegetables but likes fruits, don't fuss about what he is missing. Serve him fruit 2 or 3 times a day and forget about vegetables for a few weeks or even months. If you don't make an issue of them, the chances are great that his appetite will swing around to them again in time.

FRUITS

437. Fruits. A baby during his first year has probably had stewed or canned applesauce, apricots, prunes, pears, peaches, pineapple, and raw, ripe banana, apple, pear, avocado. By a year some of these should be served in a lumpy consistency. Canned fruits, such as pears, peaches, pineapple, put up for adults are not so desirable for children because they are heavily sweetened with syrup. At least, pour the syrup off.

Raw fruits, such as oranges, peaches, apricots, plums, seedless grapes, are usually added between the ages of 1 and 2 years for children with a good digestion. They should be thoroughly ripe. Peel them until the child is 3 or 4 years old. When the peel is left on, the fruit should be washed to remove chemicals used in spraying.

It is usually recommended to wait until the age of 2 to add cherries and raw berries (strawberries, raspberries, blackberries, blueberries, huckleberries, loganberries). Strawberries sometimes cause a rash. Small children swallow berries whole and pass them that way, so mash them until your child chews well. Remove cherry pits until he can separate them in his mouth. At whatever age you start berries, start gradually and stop if they cause upsets.

Cantaloupe, honeydew melon, watermelon, can be started cautiously at 2. Begin with small amounts, mashed.

Dried fruits, such as prunes, apricots, figs, dates, can be given unstewed at 2, chopped in salads or whole for nibbling. They should be well washed unless the package states they are ready for eating raw. These dried fruits stick to the teeth for a long time, so they should not be used frequently.

CEREALS AND SUPPERS

438. Cereals. A baby at a year can be, and probably is, taking one or a variety of the precooked cereals, and also cooked oatmeal and cooked whole-wheat cereals that the rest of the family eats. If he likes these, continue to serve them once or twice a day indefinitely.

Remember that young children like their foods either firm or else quite soft and runny. They are apt to dislike pasty consistencies. So keep cereal mixtures thin.

If your child gets bored with one, try another that he may not have been so keen about before. You can also serve occasionally boiled unpolished rice, hominy, or one of the refined wheat cereals.

There are also all the dry cereals, which offer variety and may be appealing because older children are eating them. Whole-wheat and oat cereals are the most valuable ones, because they are rich in vitamins and minerals. (Corn and rice are less valuable.)

439. Breads are cereals. If a child is sick of his ordinary cereal for breakfast, you can give him bread, toast, roll, or bun made of whole, cracked, or enriched wheat, rye, oatmeal, or banana bread. A cereal in baked form is just as valuable as in boiled form. The fact that it is not hot makes no difference in its food value or digestibility. Spread with butter or margarine (starting with a small amount for the 1-year-old). You can also spread with puréed fruit or a light touch of marmalade if it makes the bread more appealing.

The problem of substitutes for cereal comes up more often at suppertime and brings up the larger question of what that meal should consist of, anyway.

440. Suppers. "He's getting bored with his supper of cereal and fruit, and I can't think what to give him," mothers often complain during the second year. Supper should be an easy meal to plan and to vary. It doesn't need to be so conventional as breakfast or lunch.

If you are going to branch out at suppertime, it's good to have a simple rule to guide you, so that you won't serve two filling dishes one night and two skimpy ones another night. A good rough rule is to serve:

(1) Either a fruit or vegetable, **and**

(2) A filling dish with plenty of calories.

Let's discuss the filling dish. Cooked, precooked, or dry cereal can be made more appealing by adding sliced raw fruit, stewed fruit, chopped dried fruit, or a little brown sugar, honey, or molasses.

Breads and sandwiches of several kinds can be substituted for cereal as the baby grows older. When he's only a year old, he makes slow work of bread, and he always pulls a sandwich apart to get at the filling. But nearer to 2 years, he can handle these well. You can use rye bread, whole-wheat bread, oatmeal bread, enriched white bread, banana bread, to start with, and by the age of 2 add pumpernickel, nut bread. Spread with a little butter, margarine, cottage or creamed cheese. You can add a touch of jam, jelly, marmalade, honey, or a few grains of brown sugar for flavor if this is necessary to make the sandwich appealing, but I wouldn't put on a thick layer of any of these sugary substances. Sandwiches can be made with a wide variety of other foods, plain or in combination: raw vegetable (lettuce, tomato, grated carrot or cabbage), stewed fruit, chopped dried fruit, peanut butter, egg, canned fish, minced poultry and meats. Cheese can be used as a spread or grated, and later in thin slices. Creamed cheese or, after the age of 3, a little mayonnaise can be combined with many of the substances listed above.

A fairly substantial dish for occasional use is a broth or soup containing lots of barley, rice, or noodles; or a vegetable soup, plain or creamed, with a couple of handfuls of toast cut into small cubes to toss in.

A poached or coddled or scrambled egg can be given (in addition to or instead of the breakfast egg) on toast or with toast crumbled into it.

Simple crackers, preferably whole wheat or graham, can be served plain, or with a spread, or in a bowl of hot or cold milk. (Graham crackers have few calories, however.) Bread and toast in slices or pieces, salted, can also be served in a bowl of cold or hot milk.

Potato is a good filling supper dish if the child is fond of it. Macaroni, spaghetti, or noodles can be used occasionally.

Instead of a filling first course followed by stewed or raw fruit, you can occasionally serve first a cooked green or yellow vegetable, or a vegetable or fruit salad. Then follow with a milk-pudding dessert: custard, baked or boiled; rice, tapioca, bread, or cornstarch pudding; occasionally ice cream for the older child.

A banana makes an excellent filling dessert at supper and can also be used as a cereal substitute for breakfast.

Junket and gelatin desserts, preferably with fruit included, can also be served occasionally, but they don't contain enough calories to act as the appetite-satisfying dish of the meal.

There are some children who never want and never seem to need much starch. They are able to get enough calories from milk, meats, fruits, vegetables, to gain weight reasonably. They also get their B-complex vitamins from these foods. In other words, grains and other starches are the things you least need to worry about in your child's diet. Let him go without them for weeks if he is doing well otherwise.

Parents who have supper early may prefer to let the child have his main meal of the day, with meat, potato, vegetable, at that time with them. There is no harm to this arrangement if the child gets to bed and to sleep at a good hour. Then lunch becomes a light meal like the suppers that have been suggested in this section.

LESS VALUABLE AND UNDESIRABLE FOODS

441. Cookies, cakes, rich crackers, pastries. The main objection to these foods is that they are largely composed of refined starch, sugar, and fat. Being rich in calories, they quickly satisfy a child's appetite, but give him practically no salts, vitamins, roughage, or protein. They are sometimes called "deprived" foods. They cheat a child by making him feel well fed when he is being partly starved, and by spoiling his appetite for better foods.

You don't have to be so suspicious of rich, refined foods that you stop your child from eating cake at a birthday party. It's the steady diet of such foods that deprives him of nutrition. But there's no sense starting them at home when there is no need.

Filled pastries, such as custard and cream pies, éclairs, cream puffs, have an additional danger. Harmful bacteria grow readily in these fillings if they are not kept well refrigerated. They are a frequent cause of food poisoning.

442. Highly sweetened foods are also undesirable in the diet. They quickly satisfy the appetite, take it away for better foods, and favor decay of the teeth. If a child likes his cereal and fruits without extra sugar, by all means leave it off. If a thin sprinkle of sugar or a few drops of honey or molasses make a big difference, let him have it without an argument. But be cheerfully firm about not letting him pour it on thick. **Jellies, jams, most canned fruits** (except those put up for babies) contain excessive amounts of sugar, and it's best not to get in the habit of serving them. If a child enjoys his bread and butter only when there is jam on it, put on just enough to flavor it. If occasionally it is convenient to give him canned peaches because the rest of the family is having them, pour off the syrup. Raisins, dates, dried prunes and figs are also believed to be hard on the teeth when eaten regularly because they stick to the teeth for such a long time.

443. Candy, sodas, sundaes, being sweet, "deprived" foods, bring up special problems because they are often eaten between meals, when they have their worst effect on appetite and teeth, and because so many other children are eating them. There is no reason why a child of 2 years or more shouldn't occasionally have a serving of good ice cream or a piece of candy at the end of a meal when the rest of the family is enjoying it. But it's better to avoid sweets between meals as much as possible, and to avoid candy regularly even at the end of meals. Candy, particularly, is suspected of favoring decay of the teeth because it keeps the mouth syrupy for some time.

It's easy enough to keep **young** children from the candy habit by not having it around the home, and to avoid sodas and sundaes by not buying them. It is more difficult with the school-age child who has found out all about these delights. A mother hates to make her own child an exception or a sissy. If he has the desire only once in a while, it's probably best to let him be one of the boys. But if he craves sweets, and especially if he has teeth that decay easily, it's better for the parents to limit him strictly to special occasions.

444. Craving for sweets is often caused by parents. Children like sweets, for one reason, because their hungry, growing bodies recognize the extra calories in them. But it is not certain that unspoiled children want a lot of them. A few small children actually dislike all sweet foods. Dr. Clara Davis in her experiments in letting children choose their own diets from a variety of **natural** foods found that in the long run they wanted only a reasonable amount of the sweeter foods.

I think much of the exaggerated craving for sweets is caused unwittingly by parents. A mother, trying to get her child to finish his vegetable, says, "You can't have your ice cream until you've finished your spinach," or, "If you eat up all your cereal, I'll give you a piece of candy." When you hold back on food (or a prize of any kind), it whets the desire. This has exactly the opposite effect from what the mother wants: the child gets to despise spinach and cereal, and to want ice cream and candy more and more. I'd say jokingly that the only safe way to bribe a child about food is to say, "You can't have your spinach until you've eaten your ice cream." Seriously, though, **never** hold back on one food until another is eaten. Let your child go on thinking his plain foods are just as good as his sweet ones. If one day he catches sight of his dessert first and asks for it, let him have it right away, willingly.

445. Corn, rice, and refined wheat are less valuable than whole wheat and oats. Corn and rice are relatively low in vitamins and valuable proteins (even before they are refined) compared with oats, rye, and whole wheat. And when any grain is refined, much of its vitamins, minerals, and roughage are removed in the process. Therefore, the foods to serve less frequently are refined (white) wheat cereals, white bread that is not enriched, macaroni, spaghetti, noodles, crackers (aside from whole-wheat crackers), rice, corn meal, corn cereals, hominy. Then there are the desserts made from these grains: cornstarch, rice, tapioca puddings. When rice is used for cereal, puddings, and as a substitute for potato, it is better to use the unpolished brown rice. Enriched white bread has had some of the original B-complex vitamins restored, but it does not contain all the values in whole-wheat bread.

You may think that I am exaggerating the dangers of refined sweets and starches. I certainly don't want to turn you into a food crank who scolds his friends for serving white bread or who haunts the health-food stores looking for raw and coarse substances to munch. But there are plenty of children who get their daily carbohydrates somewhat as follows: Breakfast—a white cooked cereal (with lots of sugar) and a slice of white toast with jam. Lunch—macaroni, white bread and jam. Mid-afternoon—ice cream soda. Supper—corn flakes, cake, and a cornstarch pudding. Even if such a child is also taking vegetable, fruit, meat, and milk, he is still getting two thirds of his nourishment in a "deprived" form.

446. Coffee and tea are not good drinks for children because they take the place of milk and because they contain the stimulant caffeine. Most children are stimulated enough already. Flavoring a child's milk with a tablespoonful of coffee or tea may be justified if he likes it only in that pretend grown-up way. But in the case of most children, it's easier and safer not to get started with these beverages.

FROZEN FOODS

447. Frozen foods are just as good for children as fresh and canned foods, if used correctly. Freezing a food breaks it down chemically, just as cooking it does. It is then in a state in which both people and germs can digest it better. In other words, a cooked or a frozen food spoils more rapidly than an ordinary raw food because poisonous bacteria can live and multiply in it more easily.

Foods that spoil easily when kept long out of the refrigerator are milk, foods made with milk (puddings, pastry, fillings), vegetables, poultry, stuffing.

FEEDING BETWEEN MEALS

448. Use common sense between meals. Many young children, and some older ones, too, need a snack between meals. If it's the right kind of food, given at a sensible hour, presented in the right way, it shouldn't interfere with meals or lead to feeding problems.

Fruit juice, fruit, and vegetable juice are easily and quickly digested and are least likely to favor tooth decay. Milk stays in the stomach much longer and is therefore more apt to take away appetite for the next meal. Occasionally, though, you see a child who never can eat very much at one meal and gets,excessively hungry and tired before the next; he may thrive when given milk between meals. Its slow digestibility is what keeps him going, and he has a better appetite for the next meal because he's not exhausted.

Cakes, cookies, and pastry have three disadvantages; they are rich in calories, poor in other food values, and hard on the teeth. Even crackers and bread stick to the teeth for some time, and so are not ideal for a regular between meal diet.

For most children the snack is best given midway between meals, or not closer than 1 ½ hours bef6re the next one. Even here there are exceptions. There are children who receive juice in the middle of the morning but still get so hungry and cross before lunch is ready that they pick fights and refuse to eat. Getting a glass of orange or tomato juice the minute they get home, even though it is 20 minutes before lunch, improves their disposition and their appetite. So you see that what and when to feed between meals is a matter of common sense and doing what suits the individual child. Plenty of children can get along without any food between meals, and this is best of all for the teeth.

A mother may complain that her child eats badly at meals but is always begging for food between meals. This problem doesn't arise because a mother has been lenient about food between meals. Quite the contrary. In every case that I have seen, the mother has been urging or forcing the child to eat at mealtime and holding back on food at other times. It's the pushing that takes away his appetite at meals. After months of it the very sight of the dining room is enough to make his stomach revolt. But when the meal is safely over (though little has been eaten), his stomach feels natural again. Soon it's acting the way a healthy empty stomach is meant to act - it's asking for food. The treatment, then, is not to deny the child food between meals but to let mealtime be so enjoyable that his mouth waters then, too. What is a meal? It's food specially prepared to be appetizing. When a child finds it less appealing than snacks, something has gone wrong.

MEALS

449. Suggested guide for meals

Breakfast

>   (1) Fruit or fruit juice

>   (2) Cereal

>   (3) Egg

>   (4) Milk

Lunch (or supper)

>   (1) Meat or Fish or poultry (or extra. egg)

>   (2) Green or yellow vegetable (cooked or raw)

>   (3) Potato

>   (4) Raw fruit, occasionally a pudding

>   (5) Milk

Supper (or lunch)

>   (1) A filling dish, such as:

>>   cereal

>>   or bread or sandwiches

>>   or Potato

or soup with crackers toast barley rice noodles'
etc.

or an egg dish with toast

or (less frequently) a pudding, macaroni, or
spaghetti

(2) Vegetable or fruit, raw or cooked

(3) Milk

Vitamin Preparation daily

Fruit, or tomato juice between meals if needed

Bread (whole-grain) at meals if desired

Managing Young Children

PLAY AND OUTGOINGNESS

450. **Play is serious business.** When we see children building with blocks, pretending to be airplanes, learning to skip rope, we're apt to think, in our mixed-up, adult way, that these are just amusements, quite different from serious occupations such as doing lessons and holding a job. We are mixed up because most of us were taught in our own childhood that play was fun but that school work was a duty and a job was a grind.

The baby passing a rattle from one hand to the other or learning to crawl downstairs, the small boy pushing a block along a crack on the floor, pretending it's a train, are hard at work learning about the world. They are training themselves for useful work later, just as much as the high-school student studying geometry. A child loves his play, not because it's easy, but because it's hard. He is striving every hour of every day to graduate to more difficult achievements and to do what the older kids and grownups do.

The mother of a 1-year-old complains that he gets bored with hollow blocks and only wants to fit pots and pans together. One reason is that he knows already that his mother plays with pots and pans and not with blocks. That makes pots and pans more fun. It must be for this reason that 1-year-olds are fascinated with cigarettes.

451. **Simple toys are best.** Children usually love simple toys best and play with them longest. This isn't because children are simple - it's because they have so much imagination. There are two very different kinds of toy trains. One is made of metal painted to look real, and it is meant to run on a track. The other is made of plain, flat wooden blocks that link together easily. All that the young child can do with the realistic train is push one car along the floor. It is too hard to put the cars on the track or

hitch them together. He can't even put anything in the passenger coach until the top breaks off. After a while he gets bored. The wooden block cars are different. He can link a string of them together and admire his long train. Two make a trailer truck. He can pile small blocks on top, call it a freight train, and make deliveries. When he is bored with dry land, the blocks become separate boats or a string of barges with a tug. He can go on like this forever.

Sometimes parents with little money to spend feel sad that they can't buy a shiny automobile for their youngster to pedal or a playhouse. But think what a child can do with a packing box. By turns it's a bed, a house, a truck, a tank, a fort, a dolls house, a garage. Don't take this idea so seriously that you never get your child a really fine plaything.

The time will come when he wants a three-wheel bike or an express cart with all his heart, and you will want to buy it for him if you can. I only mean that simple things come first. Add the fancier toys as you can afford them as you find out what he really enjoys.

The baby, before he can use his hands, loves to watch bright-colored objects that hang on a string tied across the sides of his crib and that move slightly in the draft. In the last half of the first year, he loves objects to handle and rattle and chew, such as the newer plastic toys (small rings on a big ring, for example). There's no paint to come off, and there is no .danger from chips, as there is with thin celluloid toys.

Around a year to a year and a half, the child is fascinated with putting one thing into another, and pushing or pulling it around. The block that runs on four wheels ind has holes for pegs is a favorite-, but a plain box with a string is as good. As a matter of fact, pushing comes before pulling, and that's why the bell on wheels, pushed with a stick, is so popular. Hollow blocks don't interest him so long as pots, pans, strainers, and spoons.

Soft dolls and woolly animals are loved by most children throughout the early years. Others see no sense in them.

As the child gets toward the age of 2, he,s more interested in copying. First, it's the immediate things that his mother and father do, like sweeping, washing dishes, and shaving.

As he grows beyond 2, his imagination becomes more creative. This is the period for dolls and dolls, furniture, trucks and cars, and above all, blocks. Blocks piled on top of each other are..the Empire-State Building; from end to end are a train. They can be laid out on the floor in the outline of a house or boat to sit in, and so on indefinitely. A bag of wooden blocks of -different shapes is worth ten toys to any child up to 6 or 8.

452. Let children play at their own level. A grownup playing with

a child often is tempted to make the play too complicated. A mother who has brought her daughter a small doll with a whole wardrobe of clothes would like to dress the doll just right, beginning with the underclothes. But the little girl may want to start with the red overcoat. A mother buys her small, sick boy a box of crayons and a book of outline pictures to color. He picks up an orange crayon and rubs it back and forth across the page, not trying to keep within _the lines, not worrying that he is orange for sky and grass. It's hard for a parent not to say, "Oh, no, not like that. - See, you do it this way. Or a father. who' has never had enough chance to play with trains produces a whole set for his 3-year-old at Christmas. The father can't wait to get started. He fits the tracks together. But the boy has grabbed one of the cars and has shot it across the room, smack against the wall. "No, no!", says Father. "You put the car on the track like this". The child gives the car a push along the track, and it falls off at the curve. "No, no", says the Father. "You have to wind up the engine and let the engine pull the car." But the poor child hasn't the strength to wind up the engine or the skill to put the cars on the track. He doesn't care about realism yet. After his father has been impatient with him for fifteen minutes, he gets a strong dislike for tin trains and an uncomfortable feeling he can't measure up to his father's expectations. He wanders off to do something that he can enjoy.

A child becomes interested in dressing dolls properly, coloring carefully, playing trains realistically, each at a certain stage of his development. You can't hurry him. When you try, you only make him feel incompetent. This does more harm than good. Your child loves to have you play with him if you are willing to play at his level. Let him show your how. Help him if he asks for it. If you've brought him a toy that is too complicated, either let him misuse it in his own way or tactfully hid it until he is older.

453. Generosity can't be forced. When children begin to play around each other at 1 ½ , 2, 2 ½ , they are apt to grab things from each other without much ceremony. The small child who has a possession never gives it up to be nice. He either hangs on like grim death, perhaps whacking at the attacker, or he gives it up in bewilderment. Mothers, seeing these goings on, are sometimes horrified.

If your child, around 2, always seems to be the grabber, it doesn't mean that he's going to be a bully. He's too young to have much feeling for others. Let him grab sometimes. If he's doing it constantly, it may help to let him play part of the time with slightly older children who stand up for their rights. If he always intimidates a certain child, better keep them separated for a while. If your child is hurting another or looks as if he were planning murder, pull him away in a matter-of-fact manner and get him interested in something else. It's better not to heap shame on him—that only makes him feel abandoned, and more aggressive.

If a child goes on being unusually aggressive when he's 3 or older and doesn't seem to be learning anything about cooperative play, it's time to look into his adjustment at home. It's in these early, less serious problems that a good children's psychiatrist (either a private doctor or one in a child-guidance clinic) can help a parent and child most easily and most thoroughly (Section 570).

If your child at 2 doesn't give up his possessions, he is behaving normally for this age. He will come around to generosity **very** gradually, as his spirit grows up and as he learns to enjoy and love other children. If you make him give up his treasured cart whenever another child wants it, you only give him the feeling that the whole world is out to get his things away from him—not just the children but the grownups, too. This makes him **more** possessive, instead of less. When a child is reaching the stage when he's beginning to enjoy playing with others, somewhere around 3, you can help to make a game of sharing. "First Johnny has a turn pulling the cart and Catherine rides in it. Then Catherine pulls the cart and Johnny has a turn to ride in it." This makes sharing fun instead of an unpleasant duty. Timidity is discussed in Section 457.

454. Helping a first child to be outgoing. Most first children grow up happy and well adjusted like most second and third and fourth children in a family. But a few of them have a harder time adjusting to the outside world.

A mother is apt to say, "The second baby is so easy. He doesn't cry. He is rarely a serious problem. He plays contentedly by himself, and yet he is so friendly if you go near him." When he's several years older, the mother says, "The second is such a friendly, outgoing child that everybody just naturally loves him. When we're walking down the street, strangers smile at him and stop us to ask how old he is. They only notice the older one afterward, to be polite. You can see that it hurts the older one's feelings. He craves attention much more than the second."

What makes the difference? One trouble is that the first baby in some families gets more fussing over than is good for him, especially after the age of 6 months, when he begins to be able to amuse himself. The parents may be noticing him, suggesting things to him, picking him up, more than is necessary. This gives him too little chance to develop his own interests. He too seldom makes the first greeting, because the parents are speaking to him first. He may be shown off to other grownups too much. A little of this is harmless; a steady diet of it makes him self-conscious. When the first child is sick, the parents naturally hang over his bed with more concern and anxiety than they will after they have had longer experience. When he is naughty, they are more apt to take it seriously and to make a fuss about it.

A steady flow of fussy attention toward a child tends to spoil him somewhat for the outside world in two ways. He grows up assuming that he is the hub of the universe and that everyone should automatically admire him whether he is being attractive or not. On the other hand, he hasn't been practicing how to make his own fun or how to be outgoing and appealing to people.

Of course, the answer is not to ignore a first child. He needs affection and responsiveness in good measure. But let him play his own games as long as he is interested and happy, with the least possible interference, bossing, scolding, and anxious concern. Give him a chance to start the conversation sometimes. When visitors come, let him make up to them himself. When he comes to you for play or for affection, be warm and friendly, but let him go when he turns back to his own pursuits.

Another factor that sometimes seems to make a first child unsociable is too serious an attitude on the parents' part. It isn't that the parents are grim people; they can be easygoing with their friends and their later children. They are just trying too hard with the first.

You know what I mean if you have ever seen a tense person trying to ride a horse for the first time. He sits stiff as a china doll, doesn't know how to accommodate to the horse's movements, and is apt to be unnecessarily bossy. It's hard work for the horse and the rider. The experienced rider knows how to relax, how to give in and conform to some of the horse's motions without losing his seat, how to direct the horse gently. Bringing up a child isn't much like riding a horse, but the same spirit works in both jobs.

A similar example is the young officer or executive who is put in charge of other people for the first time. If he isn't too sure of himself, he may be unnecessarily solemn and strict in the beginning, for fear he won't keep control. The more experienced person isn't afraid to be friendly and reasonable.

You may say, "The trouble is that I **am** inexperienced." But you don't have to have experience to do a wonderful job with a baby—all you need to start with is a friendly spirit. A child won't throw you the way a horse might (at least not until he's much older), and he won't laugh at you the way a squad of men might. Don't be afraid to relax, to be agreeable. Better too easygoing than too stiff.

AGGRESSIVENESS AND TIMIDITY

455. Children learn to control their own aggressive feelings. Do you worry when your 2-year-old pulls another's hair, or your 4-year-old plays with a toy pistol? Some parents think that these aggressive actions ought to be squelched right away. There's no question that our civilized life couldn't last at all if people didn't learn to control their violent feelings. But parents don't have to worry about this job too much. A normal child learns these controls bit by bit as he develops, through the unfolding of his own nature and the good relationship he has with his parents.

Think of the transformations of the child's aggressive feelings at different age periods. The little baby who is hungry feels furious at the whole world. The 1-year-old sometimes slaps at his mother's face when he feels cross if she lets him. By a year and a half, if he has been treated gently but firmly, he's more apt to refrain from attack but he takes out his rage by kicking the floor.

A 2-year-old, when someone grabs his toy, may bat him over the head with a shovel without a moment's hesitation. Much more civilized is the 4-year-old. He's likely to argue with the grabber, at least some of the time.

And meanwhile he's been learning to take out his violent feelings in **play** form. First it's very simple. He points his pretend gun and says, "Bang! I'm shooting you dead." He's having fun with the **idea** of killing. But he doesn't need to be scolded or "taught better." He already knows that it's unthinkable to harm friendly people seriously but all right to let off steam pretending. (This is one reason children love stories of violence.) You can really go a step further and say that the child who can **play** at hurting and killing is able, as a result, to be more friendly than the child who bottles up his hostile feelings.

As boys get into the 6-to-10-year-old period, their games of make-believe violence are better organized. A crowd that wants to play war divides itself into teams, makes rules of the game. At the high-school and college level, make-believe no longer satisfies. Organized athletics, games, debates, and competitions for school jobs take its place. All these call for aggressiveness. But the fierce feelings are strictly controlled by dozens of rules and conventions.

And when a person goes out into the world and takes a job, he still needs his aggressive instincts, but they are further refined and civilized. He competes for a better position in the organization. He works to make his business concern the most successful. On a farm he fights the elements and the insects, and competes with other farmers at the county fair.

In other words, when your child at 2 bangs another over the head, or at 4 plays at shooting, or at 9 enjoys blood-and-thunder comic books, he is just passing through the necessary stages in the taming of his aggressive instincts that will make him a worth-while citizen.

I don't mean by all this that you should let your young child be unusually mean to others or that you should think nothing of it if your older child is preoccupied with violence much more than other boys his age. Extra aggressiveness needs curbing, and if it can't be easily controlled it needs looking into. (Section 570.)

456. Naughty words. Sometimes at 3, more often at 4, children go through a phase of reveling in bathroom words. They gaily insult each other with expressions like "You great big duty" and "I'll flush you down the toilet," and think they are very witty and bold. You should consider this a normal development. You can tell your child to stop it if you don't like it, or you can let him have his fun until you've had enough.

As they grow older, all normal children who have a chance (as they should) to be around other children, learn swear words and "dirty" words. Long before they know what the words mean, they know that they are naughty. Being human, they repeat them to show that they are worldly-wise and not afraid to be a little bad. It's usually quite a shock to conscientious parents to hear these words coming from the mouths of their supposedly sweet innocents. What's a good parent to do? It's better not to jump out of your skin or act horribly shocked. For the timid child this has too strong an effect; it worries him, makes him afraid to be around children who use bad words. But most children who find they have shocked their parents are delighted, at least secretly. Some of them go on cussing endlessly at home, hoping to get the same rise. Others, stopped at home by threats, use all their bad language elsewhere. The point is that when you tell a child that just by making certain sounds he has the power to scandalize the whole world, it's like handing him a full-sized cannon and telling him, "For goodness' sake, don't set it off." On the other hand, I don't think that you have to sit mute and just take it. You can just tell him firmly that you and most people don't like to hear those words and you don't want him to use them.

457. Timidity and sissiness. A first child who has not had much chance to play with other children is apt, at 2 years of age, to let them take his toys away from him and push him around. He may just look perplexed or he may run crying to his mother each time. This is apt to worry the father and mother. In most cases it is a temporary state of affairs caused by inexperience. If he continues to play near children regularly, the chances are great that as the months go by he will learn how to get mad and stand up for his rights. It's wise for his mother not to show too much concern or sympathy, not to fight his battles for him, not to tell him he must share, but to suggest casually that he go and get the toy back.

The second or third child in a family rarely has this problem, probably because he's had to stand up for his rights from the age of 1 year.

If there is one aggressive child who regularly bullies your child and your child is becoming more intimidated rather than less as the weeks go by, it may be wise for a couple of months to take him somewhere else to play, where he will have more chance of finding his courage.

If a child goes on past 3 or 4 being easily picked on, it's a good idea to consult a child-guidance clinic or a family social agency to try to find out what's wrong.

A father may be upset if his son at 2 likes to play occasionally with dolls and doll carriages. This is too early to start worrying. Children at 2 don't make much distinction between masculine and feminine activities. By 3 they are usually beginning to show a preference for the conventional activities of their own sex a **majority** of the time, and by 4 this preference is likely to be stronger still. It is perfectly natural for a regular boy of 3 or 4 to play with girls part of the time, the more so if there aren't boys of his own age available, but if they are playing house he should usually be wanting to play father or son.

If a boy of 3 or 4 or 5 is avoiding boys or is regularly preferring to take the part of a mother or girl in house play, he is probably afraid of being a boy and needs child-guidance help. He also needs a friendlier relationship with his father. Sometimes the mother is being too protective and enveloping.

458. Biting humans. It's natural for a baby around 1 year to take a bite out of his parent's cheek. His teething makes him want to bite, anyway, and when he feels tired he's even more in the mood for it. I don't think it means much, either, when a child between 1 and 2 bites another child, whether it's in a friendly or angry spirit.

After 2 or 2½ it depends on how often the biting occurs and how the child is getting along otherwise. If he is generally happy and outgoing but occasionally takes a bite when he gets in a fight, it's of no great importance. But if he is tense or unhappy much of the time and keeps biting other children for no good reason, it's a sign that something is wrong. Perhaps he is being bossed and disciplined too much at home and is in a frantic, high-strung state. Perhaps he has had too little chance to get used to other children and imagines they are dangerous and threatening to him. Perhaps he is jealous of a baby at home and carries over the fear and resentment to all other small children, as if they were competitors, too. If the cause and the cure are not easy to see, a children's psychiatrist will be able to help (Section 570).

Some mothers who have been bitten ask if they should bite back. A mother can control her child better by staying in charge as a friendly boss than by descending to his age level to battle with bites, slaps, or shouts. Besides, when you bite or slap a 1-year-old, he's apt to keep it up, either as a fight or a game. And if you just look reproachful, you bring out his meanness. The only thing you need to do is to keep from being bitten again, by drawing back when he gets that gleam in his eye, showing him clearly that you don't like it and won't let it happen.

459. Comforting a hurt child. When a child is hurt he wants to be comforted and his parent feels like comforting him. This is natural and right.

Sometimes a parent who is particularly anxious for his child to grow up brave and uncomplaining fears that comforting him will make him a sissy. But a secure child isn't made dependent by ordinary comforting. As he grows older, especially as he gets into the period beyond 6 years, he makes a great effort all by himself to be brave and not to run to his mother.

The child who is a cry-baby over small hurts and aches has had a more complicated past. He may have been made **generally** dependent by all kinds of fussing and overprotection. Sometimes the mother is a person who, without realizing it, has a rather severe, critical attitude toward him at most times and shows her tender side mainly when he is hurt or ill. Her move here is not to be more severe when he's in trouble but to show that she enjoys and loves him when he's all right. In another case a parent has an exaggerated horror of injuries, and the child has caught some of this anxiety.

You don't need to be afraid to comfort your child while he is miserable. Merely avoid emphasizing the injury, and distract him back to his regular activities as soon as he is able.

THE FATHER AS COMPANION

460. A boy needs a friendly, accepting father. Boys and girls need chances to be around their father, to be enjoyed by him, and if possible, to do things with him. Unfortunately, the father is apt to come home wanting most of all to slump down and read the paper. If he understands how valuable his companionship is, he will feel more like making a reasonable effort. I say **reasonable** because I don't think the conscientious father (or mother, either) should force himself beyond his endurance. Better to play for fifteen minutes enjoyably and then say, "Now I'm going to read my paper," than to spend all day at the zoo, crossly.

Sometimes a father is so eager to have his son turn out perfect that it gets in the way of their having a good time together. The man who is eager for his son to become an athlete may take him out at an early age to play catch. Naturally, every throw, every catch, has its faults. If the father is constantly criticizing, even in a friendly tone, the boy becomes uncomfortable inside. It isn't any fun. Also, it gives him the feeling of being no good, in his father's eyes and in his own. A boy comes around to an interest in sports in good time if he's naturally self-confident and outgoing. Feeling approved of by his father helps him more than being coached by him. A game of catch is fine if it's the son's idea and if it's for fun.

A boy doesn't grow spiritually to be a man just because he's born with a male body. The thing that makes him feel and act like a man is being able to copy, to pattern himself after, men and older boys with whom he feels friendly. He can't pattern himself after a person unless he feels that this person likes him and approves of him. If a father is always impatient or irritated with him, the boy is likely to feel uncomfortable not only when he's around his father but when he's around other men and boys, too. He is apt to draw closer to his mother and take on her manners and interests.

So a father who wants to help his small son grow up to be manly shouldn't jump on him too hard when he cries, scorn him when he's playing a girlish game, or force him to practice athletics. He should enjoy him when he's around, give him the feeling he's a chip off the old block, share a secret with him, take him alone on excursions sometimes.

The boy who hasn't got a father, temporarily or permanently, is discussed in Sections 778 and 779.

The father's part in discipline is discussed in Section 477.

There's more on the father's relations with son and daughter in Sections 507–509.

461. A girl needs a friendly father, too. It's easy to see that a boy needs a father to pattern himself after, but many people don't realize that a friendly father plays a different but equally important part in the development of a girl. She doesn't exactly pattern herself after him, but she gains confidence in herself as a girl and a woman from feeling his approval. I'm thinking of little things he can do, like complimenting her on her dress, or hair-do, or the cookies she's made. When she is older, he can show her that he's interested in her opinions and let her in on some of his. Later, when she has boy friends, it's important for him to welcome them, even if he secretly doesn't think they are quite good enough for her.

By learning to enjoy the qualities in her father that are particularly masculine, a girl is getting ready for her adult life in a world that is half made up of men. The way she makes friendships with boys and men later, the kind of man she eventually falls in love with, the kind of married life she makes, are all influenced strongly by the kind of relationship she has had with her father throughout her childhood.

462. A little rough-housing goes a long way. Lots of fathers enjoy rough-housing with their young children, and most children love it, too. But children easily become overexcited by it, and this sometimes leads to nightmares. It's good to remember that at 2 and 3 and 4, children's loves and hates and fears get out of control easily. And young children can't distinguish too clearly between real and pretend. For them, a father who is pretending to be a bear or a prize fighter really becomes one for the time being. This is usually too much for a small child to take. So rough-housing should be mild and good-natured and brief— even when the child begs for more. Most important is that it shouldn't be a pretend fight or a pretend chase. Let it just be simple acrobatics. Stop, anyway, if a child gets worked up.

463. A father should go light on kidding. On the average, men seem to have more fierceness in them than women do. In civilized life, they have to keep this under control. When a man feels irritated at a friend or a business associate, he can't simply hit him or insult him. But according to the rules, it's all right to kid him a little. So men learn to be kidders. Then when a father feels mildly irritated at his son, he may try to work it off as kidding. A child feels humiliated when he's laughed at, and he doesn't know how to kid back. Kidding is too strong for young children.

GOING TO BED

464. Keeping bedtime happy. Three or four factors can make the difference between the child who goes to bed willingly and the one who stalls and argues.

Keep bedtime agreeable and happy. Remember that it is delicious and inviting to the tired child if you don't turn it into an unpleasant duty. Have an air of cheerful certainty about it. Expect him to turn in at the hour you decide as surely as you expect him to breathe. It's good for a child to be able to persuade his mother (or father) to change her mind once in a while about bedtime (Fourth of July, for instance). But bedtime comes too often for regular argument. It usually works best to have the nap come right after lunch, before he has had time to become absorbed in play. The relationship between supper and bedtime is usually more complicated because of the bath and the father's coming home.

Until the child is at least 3 or 4, and in any case until he is responsible enough to like to get himself to bed, lead him rather than push him with words. Carry the very small child to bed affectionately. Lead the 3- or 4-year-old by the hand, both of you still chatting about what was last on his mind.

Small children are comforted by having a certain amount of ritual about going to bed. For example, the dolly is put in her bed and tucked in. Then the teddy bear is put in the child's bed. Then the child is tucked in and kissed. Then the mother pulls down the shade or puts out the light. Try not to rush going to bed, no matter how much of a hurry you are in. (On the other hand, it isn't wise to let the child keep lengthening the rituals.) Keep it peaceful. Tell or read a story regularly if you have time. It shouldn't be scary. Most children are helped in going to bed by having a cozy toy animal or doll for company in bed.

465. Taking things to bed. Is there any harm in letting a child get used to taking a cozy toy like a woolly animal to bed with him? Definitely not. If a toy gives him a sense of comfort and companionship, it's good for him. Human beings are born sociable. In civilizations that are simpler than ours, children and grownups, too, go to sleep curled up together. It's not surprising that a child, particularly an only one, feels a little lonesome going to sleep in a room by himself. If he can breathe life into a stuffed doll or animal, so much the better. Don't worry if the toy gets dirty or ragged. You can have it washed or cleaned, but don't dispose of it for hygienic reasons.

The same goes for a special woolly blanket, an old bed pad, a gray tattered diaper, or any of the odds and ends that a small child may become attached to. The only problem comes when the beloved object finally crumbles to dust. Sometimes a child is willing to let bygones be bygones when this happens. But if he wants to shift his devotion to a new object, don't try too forcibly to interfere. He will outgrow the need eventually, at his own rate. You may be able to hasten the process a bit by reminding him occasionally, in an encouraging tone, that someday he'll be grown-up and won't need it any more. What about hard toys? Parents sometimes fear that a child will hurt himself or disturb his sleep by rolling onto these. You don't need to worry. Children can sleep peacefully in a bed piled high with prize possessions.

466. How much sleep does a child need, anyway? You can usually trust an infant to take what rest he needs. By the time a child is 2 or more, you can't leave it all to him to decide. He may need more sleep but be kept from getting it by tenseness of different kinds: loneliness, fear of being left alone, fear of the dark, fear of nightmares, fear of wetting his bed, excitement from stimulating experiences. He may be all keyed up from competing with an older brother, or "burned up" with

jealousy of a younger sister. He may be on edge each evening because there is always a tug of war with his mother about when he is to go to bed or because he is worrying about his schoolwork or the radio thriller he has been listening to. The prevention of these various troubles is discussed elsewhere. I bring them up here only to point out at the start that you can't say that the child doesn't need more sleep just because he won't take it.

The average 2-year-old needs 12 hours sleep at night and 1 to 2 hours of nap. The nap or rest usually shortens as he grows from 2 to 6, and bedtime at night stays the same. Between the ages of 6 and 9, the average child can usually give up an hour of his night's sleep, half an hour at a time, and for instance, go to bed at 8 if he's getting up at 7. By the age of 12, he will probably have been able to clip off two more half hours and go to bed at 9. These are average figures. Some children need more, others less.

Many children stop going to sleep at naptime around the age of 3 or 4, but most of them still need a real rest or at least a quiet play period indoors after lunch until they are 5 or 6. Many wise schools provide a rest period through the sixth grade. It all depends on the individual child's temperament and activity.

Going-to-bed problems and sleep problems in infancy are discussed in Sections 284 and 285; around 2 years of age, in Sections 494 and 496; after 3, in Section 510.

DUTIES

467. Let him enjoy his duties. How does a child learn to perform various duties? By his very nature, he starts out feeling that dressing himself, brushing his teeth, sweeping, putting things away, are exciting and grown-up things to do. If his parents succeed in keeping on good terms with him as he grows older, he enjoys going on errands, carrying wood, beating rugs, because he still wants to have a part in important jobs and to please his mother and father. Most of us (including the author) aren't able to bring up our children so well that we get cooperation all the time, but if we realize that children prefer to be helpful, we are less likely to make household tasks sound like unpleasant duties or to assign them when we're irritable.

A child can't be expected to continue indefinitely to be responsible about his duties—even at 15 years. (Most adults lapse into irresponsibility at times, too.) He has to be reminded. If you can find the patience, try to make the reminder matter-of-fact, polite, as if you were speaking to an adult. It's the nagging, belittling tone that kills all pride in a job. It also helps a lot to assign a child tasks that he can do in the company of other members of the family, whether it's dish-drying or lawn-mowing. Then the grownupness of the task and the fun of helping spur the child on.

468. Dressing himself. Between the ages of 1 and 1½ years, a child begins to try to undress himself. (He pulls the toe of his sock directly toward his stomach, which makes it stick.) By about 2, he can do a pretty good job of stripping himself. Now he tries hard to put on his clothes, but gets all tangled up. It probably takes him another year to learn to put the easier garments on right, and another year still (till about 4 or 5) to handle the trickier jobs, like laces and buttons.

This period from 1½ to 4 years requires a lot of tact. If you don't let him do the parts he is able to, or interfere too much, it's apt to make him angry. If he never has a chance to learn at the age when it appeals to him, he may lose the desire. Yet if you don't help him at all, he'll never be dressed and he may get frustrated at his own failure. You can help him tactfully in the jobs that are possible. Pull the socks part way off so that the rest is easy. Lay out the garment that he's going to want to put on, so that he'll start straight. Interest him in the easier jobs while you do the hard ones. When he gets tangled up, don't insist on taking over but straighten him out so that he can carry on. If he feels that you are with him and not against him, he is much more cooperative. It takes patience, though.

469. Putting things away. When your child is very young and you still expect to pick up and put things away after he is through playing, you can do it as part of the game, with enthusiasm. "The square blocks go here, in big piles, and the long blocks go there. Over here let's pretend there's a garage, and all the cars go here to sleep at night." By the time he is 4 or 5, he has fallen into the habit of putting things away and enjoying it. Many times he does it without any reminder. But if he still needs help at times, join in sociably.

If you say to a 3-year-old, "Now put your things away," it sounds unpleasant. Even if he enjoys doing it, you are handing him a job that practically no 3-year-old has the perseverance to carry through. Furthermore, he's still at a very balky age.

Cheerfully helping a child to put things away not only develops a good attitude in him but is easier for the mother than long arguments.

470. Dawdling. If you ever see a mother trying to get a dawdling child going in the morning, urging him, warning him, scolding him, to get out of bed, to get washed, to get dressed, to eat his breakfast, to start for school, you will vow that you will never get in that fix. The dawdling child wasn't born that way. He was made that way gradually, in most cases, by constant pushing. "Hurry up and finish your lunch." "How many times do I have to tell you to get ready for bed?" It's easy to fall into the habit of prodding children, and it builds up an absent-minded balkiness in them. Parents say they have to nag or the child won't get anywhere. It's a vicious circle, but the parent starts it. More often it's the mother. She may be a somewhat impatient person with an itch to manage—especially males. She usually doesn't even realize how much initiative she tends to take away from her son.

In the early years, before a child is capable of carrying out directions, lead him through his various routines. As he gets old enough to want to take over responsibilities, step out of the picture as fast as you can. When he slips back and forgets, lead him again. When he goes to school, let him think of it as his job to get there on time. It may be better to quietly allow him to be late to school once or twice, or to miss the bus and school altogether and find out for himself how sorry he feels. A child hates to miss things even more than his mother hates to have him miss them. That's the best mainspring to move him along.

You may have the impression that I think a child should not be held to any obligation. On the contrary. I think he should sit down at table when a meal is ready and get up in the morning at the proper time. I'm only making the point that if he's allowed to use his own initiative most of the time, reminded in a matter-of-fact way when he's clearly failed to do something on his own, not prodded unnecessarily in advance, not pushed too much, he usually wants to do these things.

471. Let him get dirty sometimes. A small child wants to do a lot of things that get him dirty, and they are good for him, too. He loves to dig in earth and sand, wade in mud puddles, splash in water in the washstand. He wants to roll in the grass, squeeze mud in his hand. When he has chances to do these delightful things, it enriches his spirit, makes him a warmer person, just the way beautiful music or falling in love improves an adult.

The small child who is always sternly warned against getting his clothes dirty or making a mess, and who takes it to heart, will be cramped. If he becomes really timid about dirt, it makes him too cautious in other ways also, and keeps him from developing into the free, warm, life-loving person he was meant to be.

I don't mean to give the impression that you must always hold yourself back and let your child make any kind of mess that strikes his fancy. But when you do have to stop him, don't try to scare him or disgust him; just substitute something else a little more practical. If he wants to make mud pies when he has his Sunday clothes on, have him change into old clothes first. If he gets hold of an old brush and wants to paint the house, set him to work (with a pail of water for "paint") on the woodshed or the tiled floor of the bathroom.

472. Good manners come naturally. Teaching a child to say "How d'do" or "Thank you" is really not the first step. The most important thing is to have him like people. If he doesn't, it's hard to teach him even surface manners.

The second step is to avoid making him self-conscious with strangers. We're apt, especially with our first child, to introduce him right away to a new grownup and make him say something. But when you do that to a 2-year-old, you get him all embarrassed. He learns to feel uncomfortable just as soon as he sees you greeting somebody, because he knows he's about to be put on the spot. It's much better in the first 3 or 4 years, when a child needs time to size a stranger up, to draw the newcomer's conversation **away** from him, not **toward** him. A child of 3 or 4 is likely to watch a stranger talking to his mother for a few minutes and then suddenly break into the conversation with a remark like,

"The water came out of the toilet all over the floor." This isn't Lord Chesterfield's kind of manners, but it's real manners because he feels like sharing a fascinating experience. If that spirit toward strangers keeps up, he'll learn how to be friendly in a more conventional way soon enough.

The third, and probably most important, step is for a child to grow up in a family whose members are considerate of each other. Then he absorbs kindliness. He wants to say "Thank you" because the rest of the family say it and mean it. He enjoys tipping his hat to a lady when his father does, because he craves being like his father.

Certainly it is also necessary to teach a child just how to be polite and considerate. If it's done in a friendly spirit, he is proud to learn. More important, everybody likes a child with sensibly good manners and resents one who is rude or thoughtless. So the parents owe it to the child to make him likable. The appreciation he gets makes him more friendly in turn.

When you coach a child about manners, try to do it when you're alone with him rather than in the embarrassing presence of outsiders.

DISCIPLINE

473. Some common misunderstandings about discipline. A great deal of study has been given to the psychology of children in the past half century by educators, psychoanalysts, child psychiatrists, psychologists, and pediatricians. Parents have been eager to read the results; newspapers and magazines have obliged by publishing them. We have learned a great deal bit by bit: that children need the love of good parents more than anything else; that they work hard, all by themselves, to be more grown-up and responsible; that many of the ones who get into the most trouble are suffering from lack of affection rather than from lack of punishment; that children are eager to learn if they are given school projects that are right for their age and are taught by understanding teachers; that some jealous feelings toward brothers and sisters and occasional angry feelings toward parents are natural and that a child does not need to feel deeply ashamed of them; that a childish interest in the facts of life and in some aspects of sex is quite normal; that too harsh a repression of aggressive feelings and sexual interest may lead to neurosis; that unconscious thoughts are as influential as conscious ones; that each child is an individual and should be allowed to be so.

All these ideas sound commonplace today, but when they were first expressed they were very startling. Many of them ran counter to beliefs that had been held for centuries. It is not possible to change so many ideas about the nature and needs of children without mixing up a lot of parents. Parents who have had a very comfortable childhood and who are very stable people have been least confused. They may have been interested in hearing about these new ideas, and they may have agreed. But when it came to actually managing their children, they did it in much the same way they were brought up themselves. And it has been successful with their children, as it had been with them. This is the natural way to learn child care—from having been a child in a reasonably happy family.

The parents who have had more trouble with the new ideas are usually those who haven't been too happy about their own upbringing. Many of them have felt both resentful and guilty about the strained relations that existed at times between themselves and their parents. They haven't wanted their own children to feel that way about them. So they have welcomed new theories. They have often read meanings into them that went beyond what the scientists intended—for instance, that **all** that children need is love; that they shouldn't be made to conform; that they should be allowed to carry out their aggressive feelings against parents and others; that whenever anything goes wrong it's the parents' fault; that when children misbehave the parents shouldn't become angry or punish them but should try to show more love. All of these misconceptions are unworkable if carried very far. They encourage children to become demanding and disagreeable. They make children feel guilty about their excessive misbehavior. They make parents strive to be superhuman. When the bad behavior comes, the parents try to suppress their anger for a while. But eventually they have to explode. Then they feel guilty and bewildered. This leads to more misbehavior on the child's part. (See Section 474.)

Some parents who are very polite people themselves allow their children to be surprisingly obnoxious, not only to themselves but to outsiders as well. They don't seem to see what is going on. Some of these situations, when studied carefully, reveal that the parents had always been compelled to be much too good in their own childhood and to suppress all their natural resentments. Now they get a subtle glee from letting their own flesh and blood act out all the disagreeableness they themselves had to bottle up, pretending all the time that this is all according to the best modern theories of child rearing.

474. How feelings of guilt in the parents lead to discipline problems. There are many situations in which parents may always feel a bit guilty toward one child, or another. Some of them were mentioned in Sections 13 and 14. There are other obvious cases: the mother who goes to work without first settling in her own mind whether she will be neglecting her child; parents who have a child with a physical or mental handicap; parents who have adopted a baby and can't get over the feeling that they have to do a superhuman job to justify themselves in taking over someone else's child; parents who have been brought up with so much disapproval that they always feel guilty until they are proved innocent; parents who have studied child psychology in college or a professional school, who know about all the pitfalls, and who yet expect to have to do a superior job because of their training.

Whatever the cause of the feeling of guilt, it tends to get in the way of easy management of a child. The parent is inclined to expect too little from the child, too much from himself or herself. (It's more practical here to speak of the mother because she's usually so much more involved in child care, but the same things may apply just as well to the father.) The mother is often still trying to be patient and sweet-tempered when her overworked patience is really exhausted and the child is, in fact, getting out of hand and needs some definite correction. Or she is vacillating when the child needs firmness.

A child, like an adult, knows when he is getting away with too much naughtiness or rudeness even when his mother is trying to close her eyes to it. He feels guilty inside. He would like to be stopped. But if he isn't corrected, he's likely to behave worse and worse. It's as if he were saying, "How bad do I have to be before somebody stops me?"

Eventually his behavior becomes so provoking that his mother's patience snaps. She scolds him or punishes him. Peace is restored. But the trouble with the parent who feels guilty is that she is too ashamed of losing her temper. So instead of letting well enough alone, she tries to undo the correction or lets the child punish her in return. Perhaps she permits the child to be rude to her right in the middle of the punishment. Or she takes back the penalty before it has been half paid. Or she pretends not to notice when the child begins misbehaving again. In some situations if the child does not retaliate at all, a mother begins to subtly provoke him to do so—without realizing, of course, what she is up to.

All of this may sound too complicated or unnatural to you. If you can't imagine a parent letting a child get away with murder or, worse still, encouraging it, it only shows that you don't have the problem of guilt feelings. Actually, it isn't a rare problem. A majority of conscientious parents let a child get out of hand occasionally when they feel they have been unfair or neglectful. But they soon recover their balance. However, when a parent says, "Everything this child does or says rubs me the wrong way," it's a pretty good sign that the parent feels overly guilty and is chronically submissive and permissive, and that the child is reacting to this with constant provocation. No child can be that irritating by accident. If the parent can determine in which respects she may be too permissive and can firm up her discipline, she may, if she is on the right track, be delighted to find that her child becomes not only better behaved but much happier. Then she can really love him better, and he in turn responds to this.

475. You can be both firm and friendly. A child needs to feel that his mother and father, however agreeable, have their own rights, know how to be firm, won't let him be unreasonable or rude. He likes them better that way. It trains him from the beginning to get along reasonably with other people. The spoiled child is not a happy creature even in his own home. And when he gets out into the world, whether it's at 2 or 4 or 6, he is in for a rude shock. He finds that nobody is willing to kowtow to him; in fact, everybody dislikes him for his selfishness. Either he must go through life being unpopular, or he must learn the hard way how to be agreeable.

Conscientious parents often let a child take advantage of them for a while—until their patience is exhausted—and then turn on him crossly. But neither of these stages is really necessary. If parents have a healthy self-respect, they can stand up for themselves while they are still feeling friendly. For instance, if your child is insisting that you continue to play a game after you are exhausted, don't be afraid to say cheerfully but definitely, "I'm all tired out. I'm going to read a book now, and you can read **your** book, too."

If he is being very balky about getting out of the express wagon of another child who has to take it home now, though you have tried to interest him in something else, don't feel that you must go on being sweetly reasonable forever. Lift him out, even if he yells for a minute.

476. Let the child know that his angry feelings are normal. When a child is being rude to a parent—perhaps because he has had to be frustrated or because he's jealous of his brother or sister—the parent should promptly stop him and insist on politeness. But at the same time the parent can say that he knows his child is cross at him sometimes—all children get mad at their parents sometimes. This may sound contradictory to you; it sounds like undoing the correction. Child-guidance work teaches us in case after case that a child is happier as well as better-behaved if his parents insist on reasonably good **behavior.** But at the same time it helps a child to realize that his parents know he has angry **feelings** and that his parents are not enraged at him or alienated from him on account of them. This realization helps him get over his anger and keeps him from feeling too guilty or frightened because of it. Making this distinction between hostile feelings and hostile actions works out well in actual practice.

477. A father should share in discipline. A father who feels that in his own childhood his father was too severe with him may say, "I don't want my son to resent me as I sometimes resented my father." So he leans over backward to avoid any unpleasantness with his son and leaves all the disciplining to the mother. If the boy is doing something that makes him cross, the father tries to conceal his feelings and says nothing. This is trying too hard to be agreeable (or to pretend to be agreeable). A child knows when he has displeased a parent or broken a rule, and he expects to be corrected. If his parent tries to hide his disapproval or irritation, it only makes the child uneasy. He imagines that all this suppressed anger is piling up somewhere (which isn't too far from the truth) and worries about what will happen if it ever breaks out. Child-guidance clinic studies show clearly that the boy whose father declines to do his share in maintaining discipline is much more apt to be afraid of him than the one whose father has no hesitation in controlling his child and showing indignation when it is justified. In the latter case the boy pays the price of his misbehavior, learns that though it isn't pleasant it isn't fatal, either, and the air is cleared. So a boy needs a father who's a pal at times but who's a parent all the time.

478. Don't say, "Do you want to—?"; just do what's necessary. It's easy to fall into the habit of saying to a small child, "Do you want to sit down and have your lunch?" "Shall we get dressed now?" "Do you want to do wee wee?" The trouble is that the natural response of the child, particularly between 1 and 3, is No. Then the poor mother has to persuade him to give in to something that was necessary, anyway. The arguments use up thousands of words. It is better not to give him a choice. When it's time for lunch, lead him or carry him to the table, still chatting with him about the thing that was on his mind before. When you see signs that he needs to go to the bathroom, lead him there or bring the potty chair to him. Start undoing him without even mentioning what you're up to.

You might get the idea that I am advising you to swoop down on him and give him the "bum's rush." I don't mean exactly that. In fact, every time you take a child away from something he's absorbed in, it helps to be tactful. If your 15-month-old is busy fitting one hollow block inside another at suppertime, you can carry him to the table still holding his blocks and take them away when you hand him his spoon. If your 2-year-old is playing with a toy dog at bedtime, you can say, "Let's put doggie to bed now." If your 3-year-old is chugging a toy automobile along the floor when it's time for the bath, you can suggest that the car make a long, long trip to the bathroom. When you show interest in what he's doing, it puts him in a cooperative mood.

As your child grows older, he'll be less distractible, have more concentration. Then it works better to give him a little friendly warning. If a 4-year-old has spent half an hour building a battleship of blocks, you can say, "Put the guns on soon now; I want to see them shooting before you go to bed." This works better than pouncing on him without warning when the most exciting part of the play is still to come, or giving him a cross warning as if you never did see anything in battleships except the mess they make on the floor. All this takes patience, though, and naturally you won't always have it.

479. Don't give the small child too many reasons. You sometimes see a child between the ages of 1 and 3 who becomes worried by too many warnings. The mother of a certain boy 2 years old always tries to control him with ideas. "Jackie, you mustn't touch the doctor's lamp, because you will break it, and then the doctor won't be able to see." Jackie regards the lamp with a worried expression and mutters, "Doctor can't see." A minute later he is trying to open the door to the street. His mother warns him. "Don't go out the door. Jackie might get lost, and Mummie couldn't find him." Poor Jackie turns this new danger over in his mind and repeats, "Mummie can't find him." It's bad for him to be hearing about so many bad endings. It builds up a morbid imagination. A 2-year-old baby shouldn't be worrying about the consequences of his actions. This is the period when he is meant to learn by doing and having things happen. I'm not advising that you never warn your child in words, but only that you shouldn't always be leading him out beyond his depth with **ideas.**

I think of an overconscientious mother who feels she should give her 3-year-old a reasonable explanation of **everything.** When it's time to get ready to go outdoors, it never occurs to her to put the child's clothes on in a matter-of-fact way and get out. She begins, "Shall we put your coat on now?" "No," says the child. "Oh, but we want to get out and get some nice fresh air." He is used to the fact that she feels obliged to give a reason for everything, and this encourages him to make her argue for every point. So he says, "Why?" but not because he really wants to know. "Fresh air makes you strong and healthy so that you won't get sick." "Why?" says he. And so on and so forth, all day long. This kind of meaningless argument and explanation doesn't make him a more cooperative child or give him respect for his mother as a reasonable person.

He would be happier and get more security from her if she had an air of self-confidence and steered him in a friendly, automatic way through the routines of the day.

When your child is young, rely most heavily on physically removing him from dangerous or forbidden situations by distracting him to something interesting but harmless. As he grows a little older and learns the lesson, remind him by a matter-of-fact "No, no" and more distraction. If he wants an explanation or a reason, give it to him in simple terms. But don't assume that he wants an explanation for every direction you give. He knows inside that he is inexperienced. He counts on you to keep him out of danger. It makes him feel safe to have you guiding him, provided you do it tactfully and not too much.

480. Temper tantrums. Almost any baby has a few temper tantrums between 1 and 3 years. He's gotten a sense of his own desires and individuality. When he's thwarted he knows it and feels angry. Yet he doesn't usually attack the parent who has interfered with him. Perhaps the grownup is too important and too big. Also, his fighting instinct isn't very well developed yet.

When the feeling of fury boils up in him, he can't think of anything better to do than take it out on the floor and himself. He flops down, yelling, and pounds with his hands and feet and maybe his head.

A temper tantrum once in a while doesn't mean anything; there are bound to be some frustrations. If they are happening regularly, several times a day, it may mean that the child is getting overtired or has some chronic physical trouble. Frequent tantrums are more often due to the fact that the mother hasn't learned the knack of handling the child tactfully. There are several questions to ask: Does he have plenty of chance to play freely outdoors in a place where his mother doesn't have to keep chasing him, and are there things for him to push and pull and climb on there? Indoors, has he enough toys and household objects to play with, and is the house arranged so that his mother doesn't have to keep forbidding him to touch things? Is she, without realizing it, arousing his balking by **telling** him to come and get his shirt on instead of slipping it on without comment, **asking** him if he wants to go to the bathroom instead of leading him there or bringing the potty to him? When she has to interrupt his play to get him indoors or to meals, does she frustrate him directly, or get his mind on something pleasant? When she sees a storm brewing, does she meet it head-on, grimly, or does she distract him to something else?

You can't dodge all temper tantrums. A mother would be unnatural if she had that much patience and tact. When the storm breaks, you try to take it casually and help to get it over. You certainly don't give in and meekly let the child have his way; otherwise he'd be throwing tantrums all the time on purpose. You don't argue with him, because he's in no mood to see the error of his ways. Getting angry yourself only forces him to keep up his end of the row. Give him a graceful way out. One child cools off quickest if the parent fades away and goes about her own business, matter-of-factly, as if she couldn't be bothered. Another with more determination and pride sticks to his yelling and thrashing for an hour unless his mother makes a friendly gesture. She might pop in with a suggestion of something fun to do, and a hug to show she wants to make up, as soon as the worst of the storm has passed.

It's embarrassing to have a child put on a tantrum on a busy sidewalk. Pick him up, with a grin if you can force it, and lug him off to a quiet spot where you can both cool off in private.

Breath-holding spells, in which a child may turn blue and even lose consciousness momentarily, can be an expression of temper. They are alarming to a mother, but she should try to learn to manage them sensibly, as in the discussion above, in order to keep the child from deliberately using them more and more.

481. Is punishment necessary? The only sensible answer is that a great majority of good parents feel that they have to punish once in a while. On the other hand, a few parents find that they can successfully manage their children without ever having to punish. A lot depends on how the parents were brought up. If they were punished occasionally for good cause, they naturally expect to have to punish in similar situations. And if they were kept in line by positive guidance alone, they are apt to find that they can do the same with their children.

To keep the record straight, it should be realized that there are also a fair number of poorly behaved children. The parents of some of them punish a lot and the parents of others never do. So we can't say either that punishment always works or that lack of it always works. It all depends on the nature of the parents' discipline in general.

Before we go further with the subject of punishment, we ought to realize that it is **never** the main element in discipline—it's only a vigorous additional reminder that the parent feels strongly about what he says. We have all seen children who were slapped and spanked and deprived plenty, and yet remained ill-behaved. Many chronic criminals have spent half their adult years in jail, and yet each time they get out they promptly become involved in another crime.

The main source of good discipline is growing up in a loving family— being loved and learning to love in return. We want to be kind and cooperative (most of the time) because we like people and want them to like us. (Habitual criminals are people who in childhood were never loved enough to make much difference to them, and many of them were abused, besides.) A child gradually lessens his grabbing and begins to share, somewhere around the age of 3 years, not primarily because he is reminded by his mother (though that may help some) but because his feelings toward other children—of enjoyment and affection—have developed sufficiently.

Another vital element is the child's intense desire to be as much like the parent as possible. He works particularly hard at being polite and civilized and responsible in the 3-to-6-year-old period (see Sections 505 and 506). This is the time when the boy acquires much of his desire to be cooperative with men, brave in danger, courteous to women, faithful to a job, just as his father is. This is the age when a girl is inspired to be helpful in the home, devoted to babies (including dolls), tender to other members of the family, just as her mother is.

Though children do the major share in civilizing themselves, through love and imitation, it still leaves plenty for parents to do, as all of you know. In automobile terms, the child supplies the power but the parents have to do the steering. The child's motives are good (most of the time), but he doesn't have the experience or the stability to stay on the road. The parents have to be saying, "No, crossing the street is too dangerous," "You can't play with that, you'll hurt someone," "Say thank you to Mrs. Griffen," "You have to come in now because lunch is ready," "You can't take the wagon home because it belongs to Harry," "You have to go to bed to grow big," etc., etc. How well the guidance works depends on such factors as whether the parent is reasonably consistent (nobody can be completely consistent), whether she means what she says (is not just sounding off), and whether she is directing or prohibiting the child for a good reason (not just because she's feeling mean or bossy).

The everyday job of the parent, then, is to keep the child on the right track by means of firmness. (You don't sit by and watch a small child destroy something and then punish him afterward.) You come to punishment (if you use it at all) once in a while when your system of firmness breaks down. Maybe your child, sorely tempted, wonders whether you still mean the prohibition that you laid down a couple of months ago. Or maybe he is angry and misbehaves on purpose. Perhaps he breaks something that's very precious to you, by foolish carelessness. Or he's slightly rude to you at a moment when you are tense about another matter. Maybe he narrowly escapes being run over because he didn't look. Indignation or righteous anger wells up in you. At such a moment you punish, or at least you feel like punishing.

The best test of a punishment is whether it accomplishes what you are after, without having other serious effects. If it makes a child furious, defiant, and worse-behaved than before, then it certainly is missing fire. If it seems to break the child's heart, then it's probably too strong for him. Every child reacts somewhat differently.

There are times when a child breaks a plate or rips his clothes because of accident or carelessness. If he gets along well with his parents, he feels just as unhappy as they do, and no punishment is needed. (In fact, you sometimes have to comfort him.) Jumping on a child who feels sorry already sometimes banishes his remorse and makes him argue.

If you're dealing with an older child who is always fooling with the dishes and breaking them, it may be fair to make him buy replacements from his allowance. A child beyond the age of 6 is developing a sense of justice and sees the fairness of reasonable penalties. However, I'd go light on the legalistic, "take-the-consequences" kind of punishment before 6, and I wouldn't try to use it at all before 3. You don't want a small child to develop a **heavy** sense of guilt. The job of a parent is to keep him from getting into trouble rather than act as a severe judge after it's happened.

In the olden days children were spanked plenty, and nobody thought much about it. Then a reaction set in, and many parents decided that it was shameful. But that didn't settle everything. If an angry parent keeps himself from spanking, he may show his irritation in other ways, for instance, by nagging the child for half the day, or trying to make him feel deeply guilty. I'm not particularly advocating spanking, but I think it is less poisonous than lengthy disapproval, because it clears the air, for parent and child. You sometimes hear it recommended that you never spank a child in anger but wait until you have cooled off. That seems unnatural. It takes a pretty grim parent to whip a child when the anger is gone.

Some parents find that putting a child in his room works well. One theoretical disadvantage is that it may make his room seem like a prison. Having the young child sit in a special chair for a few minutes is an effective reminder in some families.

Avoid threats as much as possible. They tend to weaken discipline. It may sound reasonable to say, "If you don't keep out of the street with your bicycle, I'll take it away." But in a sense a threat is a dare—it admits that the child may disobey. It should impress him more to be firmly told he must keep out of the street, if he knows from experience that his mother means what she says. On the other hand, if you see that you may have to impose a drastic penalty like taking away a beloved bike for a few days, it's better to give fair warning. It certainly is silly, and quickly destroys all a parent's authority, to make threats that aren't ever carried out or that can't be carried out. Scary threats, such as of bogiemen and cops, are 100% wrong in all cases.

482. Parents who can't control their children or who have to punish frequently need help. A few parents have extreme difficulty controlling their children. They say their child "won't obey" or that he's "just bad." The first thing you see when you watch such a parent (let's say it's a mother, so we can refer to her as **she**) is that she doesn't appear to be really trying, even though she wants to and thinks she is. She threatens or scolds or punishes frequently. But one such mother almost never carries out a threat. Another, though she punishes, never in the end **makes** the child do what she said he had to do. And another makes him obey once, but five minutes later and ten minutes later she lets him get away with it. Another laughs in the middle of a scolding or punishment. Another just keeps shouting at the child that he's bad or asks a neighbor, right in front of the child, whether she ever saw a worse one. Parents like these unconsciously expect the child's bad behavior to go right on and can do nothing effective to stop it. They are inviting it, without realizing it. Their scolding and punishing is only an expression of frustration. In their complaints to neighbors they are only hoping to get some comforting agreement that the child is truly impossible. Frustrated parents like these have often had an unsatisfactory childhood during which they never received sufficient assurance that they were basically good and well-behaved. As a result they don't have enough confidence in themselves or in their children. They need a lot of help from a child-guidance clinic or from a family social agency (Sections 570 and 571).

JEALOUSY AND RIVALRY

483. Jealousy can be helpful as well as hurtful. It is a strong emotion even in grownups. It can be more disturbing to the very young child because he doesn't know just what has hit him.

If it is intense, it may sour his outlook on life for quite a while. But jealousy is one of the facts of life and can't be completely prevented, so parents shouldn't expect to accomplish the impossible. However, they can do a great deal to minimize it and to help the child convert it into other feelings that are painless and constructive. If he comes to realize that there is no reason to be so fearful of a rival, it strengthens his character so that he will be better able to cope with rivalry situations later in life, at work and at home.

484. Helping the child to feel more grown-up at this time. A great majority of young children react to a baby's arrival by yearning to be a baby again, at least part of the time, and this is quite normal. They want a bottle occasionally. They may wet their bed and pants, and they may soil themselves. They may relapse into baby talk and act helpless about doing things for themselves. I think a parent is wise to humor the craving to be a baby **at those moments** when it is very strong. They can even good-naturedly carry a child up to his room and undress him, as a friendly game. Then he can see that he is not being denied these experiences, which he imagines are delightful but which may prove disappointing.

However, I think the parents can help the child more by appealing, most of the time, to the side of him that wants to grow up. They can remind him of how big, strong, smart, or skillful he is. I don't mean that you should give him one big overenthusiastic sales talk but that you should hand him a sincere compliment whenever it is appropriate. From time to time the parent can refer to some aspect of the baby's helplessness in a tone of pity.

You'll notice that I'm not suggesting direct comparisons that imply that the parents definitely prefer the older child to the baby. To feel that he is the favored child may gratify a child temporarily. But in the long run he will feel insecure with parents who are partial—they might change their preference. The parents should, of course, let their love of the baby be evident. I'm only emphasizing the importance of giving the older child chances to feel proud of his maturity and to remember that there are lots of disadvantages to being a baby.

Encouraging the child to be grown-up should not be pushed too hard, however. If the parent is constantly calling all the things that the child temporarily yearns to do "babyish" and all the things that he's temporarily reluctant to do "grown-up," he can only come to the conclusion that he wants to be a baby for sure.

485. Turning rivalry into helpfulness. One of the ways in which a young child tries to get over the pain of having a younger rival is to act as if he himself were no longer a child, competing in the same league with the baby, but as if he were a third parent. Of course, when he's feeling very cross with the baby, he may act the disapproving parent. But if he's feeling more secure, he can be the kind of parent who teaches the baby how to do things, gives him toys, wants to assist in feeding and bathing and clothing him. comforts him when he's miserable. protects him from dangers. He tries to slip into the parental role even without much help from the parents. But the parents can assist him tremendously by suggesting how he can help them at times when it wouldn't occur to him, and by showing their real appreciation of his efforts. As a matter of fact, mothers of twins who were desperate for real help have told me they were amazed to find how much honest-to-goodness help they received from a daughter as young as 3 years, so it doesn't all have to be pretend. Even a young child can fetch a bath towel, a diaper, or a bottle from the refrigerator. He can pretend to help the baby, "watch" him while the mother is out of sight.

A small child almost always wants to hold the baby, and a mother is apt to hesitate for fear he may drop it. But if the child sits on the floor (on a carpet or blanket) or in a large stuffed chair or in the middle of a bed, there's little risk, even if the baby is dropped.

In such ways the parents can help a child to actually transform resentful feelings into cooperativeness and genuine altruism.

Usually the left-out feeling is more apt to be experienced by the first child when the second baby arrives, because he has been used to the spotlight and has had no practice in sharing the parents' love with others. A middle child doesn't have to decide between being a parent and being a baby, when a new one arrives. He can see that he's still just one of the children, as he has always been. I believe that the greater need of the average first child to think of himself as a parent helps to explain why so many first children later enjoy being parents and are so apt to go into professions like teaching, social work, nursing, medicine, which are concerned with caring for others.

486. Preparing the way for the baby. It is good for a child to know ahead of time that he is going to have a baby brother or sister, if he is old enough to understand such an idea at all, so that he can get used to the idea gradually. (Don't promise him it's going to be a girl or a boy; a child takes a promise like that seriously.) The question of where the baby is coming from is discussed more fully in the chapter called "The Facts of Life" (Sections 523–527). Most educators and child psychologists believe that it is wholesome for a child to know that the baby is growing inside his mother and to feel it move. It's hard to explain much to a child under 2.

The arrival of the baby should change a child's life as little as possible, especially if he has been the only child up to that time. It is better to make all possible changes several months ahead of time. If his room is to be given over to the baby, move him to his new room several months ahead, so that he feels that he is graduating because he is a big boy, not because the baby is pushing him out of his own place. The same applies to graduating to a big bed. If he is to go to nursery school, he should start a couple of months beforehand. Nothing sets a child's mind against nursery school so much as the feeling that he is being banished to it. But if he is already well established in nursery school, he goes on liking it, and his satisfying life there keeps him from being as much disturbed by what's going on at home.

How a child gets along while his mother is in the hospital makes a big difference in his feelings toward her and the baby when they come back. Most important is who takes care of him. This is discussed in Sections 495, 772, 777.

487. When the mother brings the baby home. It's usually a hectic moment when the mother comes back from the hospital. She is tired and preoccupied. The father scurries about, being helpful. If the older child is there, he stands around feeling troubled and left out. So this is the new baby!

If it's likely to be like this, it may be better for him to be away on an excursion if this can be arranged. An hour later, when the baby and the nurse and the luggage are all in their place and when his mother has at last relaxed on the bed, is time enough for the child to come in. His mother can hug him and talk to him and give him her undivided attention. Let him bring up the subject of the baby when he is ready to.

It's tactful to play down the new baby in the early weeks. Treat her casually. Don't act too excited about her. Don't gloat over her. Don't talk a lot about her. As far as is convenient, take care of her while the older one is not around. Fit in her bath and some of her feedings when he is outdoors or taking his nap. Many young children feel the greatest jealousy when they see the mother feeding the baby, especially at the breast. If he's around, he should be allowed in freely. But if he is downstairs playing happily, don't attract his attention to what's going on.

If he wants to drink from a bottle, too, I'd suggest cheerfully fixing him one. It's a little sad to see an older child trying a bottle out of envy of the baby. He thinks it's going to be heaven. When he gets up his courage to take a suck, disappointment spreads over his face. It's just milk, coming slowly, with a rubber taste. He may want a bottle off and on for a few weeks, but there's not much risk that he'll want to go on with it forever if his mother gives it to him willingly and if she is doing the other things she can to help him with his jealousy.

Other people play a part in jealousy, too. When the father comes home from work, he should suppress the impulse to ask the child, "How's the baby today?" Better to act as if he has forgotten there is a baby, sit down, and pass the time of day. Later he can drift on to have a look at her when the older one is interested in something else. Grandma, who used to make a big fuss over the child, can be a problem, too. If she meets him in the front hall with a big package tied up in satin ribbon, and says, "Where's that darling baby sister of yours? I've brought her a present," then his joy at seeing her turns to bitterness. If a mother doesn't know the visitor well enough to coach her in how to act, she can have a box of ten-cent-store presents on the shelf and produce one for the child every time a visitor comes with one for the baby.

Playing with dolls may be a great solace to the child, whether girl or boy, while his mother is caring for the baby. He wants to warm his doll's bottle just the way his mother does, and have a reasonable facsimile of the other pieces of clothing and equipment that his mother uses. But doll play shouldn't take the place of helping care for the real baby; it should only supplement it.

488. Jealousy takes many forms. If a child picks up a large block and swats the baby with it, the mother knows well enough that it's jealousy. But another child is more polite. He admires the baby for a couple of days without enthusiasm and then says, "Now take her back to the hos-

A child usually feels a mixture of love and jealousy of the baby.

pital." One child feels all his resentment against his mother, grimly digs the ashes out of the fireplace and sprinkles them over the living-room rug in a quiet businesslike way. One with a different make-up becomes mopey and dependent, loses his joy in the sand pile and his blocks, follows his mother around, holding onto the edge of her skirt and sucking his thumb. He may wet his bed again at night or even wet and soil in the daytime. Occasionally you see a small child whose jealousy is turned inside out. He becomes preoccupied with the baby sister. When he sees a dog, all he can think of to say is, "Baby likes the dog." When he sees his friends riding trikes, he says, "Baby has a tricycle, too." He's bothered, all right, but he doesn't admit it even to himself. This child needs help even more than the one who knows exactly what he resents.

A parent sometimes says, "We found that we didn't have to worry about jealousy at all. Johnny is **fond** of the new baby." It is fine when a child shows love for the baby, but this doesn't mean that jealousy should be ignored. It may show up in indirect ways or only in special circumstances. Perhaps he's fond of her indoors but is rude when strangers admire her on the street. A child may show no rivalry for months until one day the baby creeps over to one of his toys and grabs it. Sometimes this change of feeling comes on the day the baby begins to walk.

A mother may say, "Johnny seems very affectionate with the baby. In fact, he often hugs her so tight that she cries." This isn't really an accident. His feelings are mixed.

It's wise to go on the assumption that there is always some jealousy and some affection, whether they both show on the surface or not. The job is not to ignore the jealousy or to try to forcibly suppress it or to make the child feel deeply ashamed about it, but to help the feelings of affection to come out on top.

489. How to handle different kinds of jealousy. When the child attacks the baby, a mother's natural impulse is to act shocked and to shame him. This doesn't work out well for two reasons. He dislikes the baby because he's afraid that his mother is going to love her instead of him. When she threatens not to love him any more, it makes him feel more worried and cruel inside. Shaming also may make him bottle up his feelings of jealousy. Jealousy does more harm to his spirit and lasts longer if it is suppressed than if it is allowed to stay out in the open.

There are three jobs: to protect the baby, to show the child that his mother will not permit him to **carry out** his mean feelings in action, and to reassure him that his mother still loves him. When she sees him advancing on the baby with a grim look on his face and a weapon in his hand, she must jump and grab him, tell him firmly that he can't hurt the baby. (Whenever he succeeds in being cruel, it makes him feel guilty and more upset inside.) But she can occasionally turn the grab into a hug and say, "I know how you feel sometimes, Johnny. You wish there weren't any baby around here for Mother to take care of. But don't you worry, Mother loves you just the same." If he can realize at a moment like this that his mother accepts his angry feelings (not actions) and still loves him, it is the best proof that he doesn't need to worry.

As for the child who spreads the ashes around the living room, it's natural for his mother to feel exasperated and angry, and she will probably reprove him, anyway. But if she realizes that he did it from a deep sense of despair and bitterness, she may later feel like reassuring him, too, and try to remember what she did that he just couldn't take any longer.

The child who turns mopey in his jealousy, being of a more sensitive and in-turning nature, needs affection, reassurance, and drawing out even more than the child who eases his feelings by violence. With the child who doesn't dare show directly what's bothering him, it may actually help him to feel better if his mother can say understandingly, "I know that sometimes you feel cross at the baby, and cross at Mommy because I take care of her," and so on. If he doesn't respond after a while, his mother may want to get a temporary helper for the baby even though she decided beforehand that she couldn't afford it. If it works and helps him get back his old joy in life, it will have a permanent value far beyond the expense involved.

It is worth while consulting a children's psychiatrist about the child who has turned all his jealousy inside and been curdled by it, whether it takes the form of moping or of being obsessed with the baby. The psychiatrist may be able to draw the jealousy back to the surface again, so that the child can realize what's biting him and get it off his chest.

If the jealousy comes out strongly only after the baby is old enough to begin grabbing the older one's toys, it may help a great deal to give him a room of his own, where he can feel that he and his toys and his buildings are safe from interference. If a separate room is out of the question, his father or a carpenter can build him a big chest or cupboard for his things, with a mighty padlock. Not only does this protect his toys, but having a key of his own in his pocket and a grown-up lock to open gives him a great sense of being important.

Should he be urged or compelled to share his toys with the baby? Not compelled. A suggestion that he give the baby a plaything that he has outgrown may appeal to him a lot and foster his generosity. But gen-

The jealous one must be restrained, but he also needs reassurance.

erosity that has any meaning must come from inside, and a person must feel secure and loving first. Forcing a child to share his possessions when he is insecure and selfish makes those traits stronger and more lasting.

Generally speaking, jealousy of the baby is strongest in the child under 5, because he is much more dependent on his parents and has fewer interests outside the family circle. The child of 6 or more is drawing away a little from his parents and building a position for himself among his friends. Being pushed out of the limelight at home doesn't hurt so much. It would be a mistake, though, to think that jealousy doesn't exist in the older child. He, too, needs consideration and visible reminders of love from his mother, particularly in the beginning. The child who is unusually sensitive or who has not found his place in the outside world may need just as much protection as the average small child. Even the adolescent girl, with her growing desire to be a woman, may be unconsciously envious of her mother's new parenthood.

There's one caution that I'd like to add here that may sound contradictory. Conscientious parents sometimes worry so much about jealousy and try so hard to prevent it that they make the older child less secure rather than more so. They may reach the point where they feel positively guilty about having a new baby, feel ashamed to be caught paying any attention to it, fall all over themselves trying to appease the older child. If a child finds that his parents are uneasy and apologetic toward him, it makes him uneasy, too. It reinforces his own suspicion that there is dirty work afoot and inclines him to be more mean to both baby and parents. In other words, the parents should be as tactful as possible to the older child but should not be worried or apologetic.

490. Doesn't the new baby need some attention, too? We have certainly been thinking exclusively about the older child's jealousy of the baby and even talking about ignoring the baby at times for the sake of the other child. The new baby needs attention and affection, too. But in his early days and months, he sleeps three quarters of the time, and the minutes of the day when he's ready for fondling are few. This fits in with the needs of the older child. It's in the early days and months that he needs extra attention and demonstrations of affection. If the job is done well in the beginning, he gradually accustoms himself to the baby and loses his alarm. By the time the baby needs his full share of the family's attention, the older child should feel secure enough to permit it.

491. Jealousy between older children. There is almost bound to be some jealousy, and if it is not severe, it probably helps children to grow up more tolerant, independent, and generous.

In a general way, the more agreeably parents get along with the children, the less jealousy there is. When each child is satisfied with the warm affection he receives, he has less reason to begrudge attention to his brothers and sisters.

Basically, the thing that makes each child secure in the family is the feeling that his parents love him and accept him for himself, whether he is boy or girl, smart or dull, handsome or homely. If they are comparing him with his brothers or sisters, either openly or in their thoughts, he senses it, feels unhappy inside, resentful toward the other children and the parents.

A harassed mother who is trying hard to treat her jealous boys with perfect justice may say, "Now, Jackie, here is a little red fire engine for you. And Tommy, here is another, just exactly the same, for you." But each child, instead of being satisfied, suspiciously examines both toys to see if there is any difference. Her remark has called attention to their rivalry. It's as if she said, "I bought this for you so you wouldn't complain that I was favoring your brother," instead of implying, "I bought this for you because I knew you'd like it."

The fewer the comparisons, complimentary or uncomplimentary, between brothers and sisters the better. Saying to a child, "Why can't you be polite like your sister?" makes him dislike his sister, his mother, and the very idea of politeness. And if you say to an adolescent girl, "Never mind if you don't have dates like Barbara. You're much smarter than she is, and that's what counts," it doesn't help her feelings.

It generally works better if a mother keeps out of most of the fights between children who can stand up for themselves. When she concentrates on pinning the blame, it leaves one warrior, at least, feeling more jealous. To a greater or lesser degree, children squabble because of their jealousy, because each would like to be favored by the parents. When a parent is always ready to take sides, in the sense of trying to decide who is right and who is wrong, it encourages them to quarrel soon again. Each one hopes each time to win the parents' favor and to see the other scolded. If a mother has to break up a fight, to save life or to prevent rank injustice or to restore quiet for her own sake, it's better to simply demand an end to the hostilities, to refuse to listen to arguments, to act uninterested in discrimination (unless it is quite clear that one child was outrageously to blame), and to concentrate on what's to be done next and let bygones be bygones. In one case she can casually but firmly suggest a compromise, in another case distract them to a new occupation.

The Two-Year-Old

WHAT HE'S LIKE

492. The two-year-old learns by imitation. In a doctor's office he solemnly places the stethoscope bell in different spots on his chest. Then he pokes the ear light in his ear, and looks a little puzzled because he can't **see** anything. At home he follows his mother around, sweeping with a broom when she sweeps, dusting with a cloth when she dusts, brushing his teeth when she does. It's all done with great seriousness. He is making giant strides forward in skill and understanding by means of constant imitation.

He may be quite dependent around two. He seems to realize clearly who it is that gives him his sense of security, and shows it in different ways. A mother complains, "My 2-year-old seems to be turning into a mother's boy. He hangs onto my skirts when we're out of the house. When someone speaks to us, he hides behind me." It's a great age for whining, which is a kind of clinging. He may keep climbing out of bed in the evening to rejoin the family, or calling from his room. He may be timid about being left anywhere by his mother. He's apt to be upset if a parent or other member of the household goes away for a number of days or if the family moves to a new house. It's wise to take his sensitivity into account when changes in the household are being considered.

493. Two is the age to encourage sociability. At 2, children don't play much **with** each other, cooperatively. However, they love to watch each other's occupations, and enjoy playing alongside each other. It's worth a lot of trouble to bring a 2-year-old every day if possible, or at least

Playing near and watching come before playing together.

several times a week, to where other children are playing. A 2½- or 3-year-old child won't get the hang of sharing, of rough and tumble, unless he's already spent months becoming used to other children.

WORRIES AROUND TWO

494. Fear of separation. Here's what happens occasionally when a sensitive, dependent child of 1¾, 2, 2¼—particularly an only child—is separated abruptly from his mother. Perhaps she has to go out of town unexpectedly for a couple of weeks. Or she decides that she has to go to work, and arranges for a stranger to come in and take care of the child during the day. Usually the child makes no fuss while the mother is away, but when she returns, he hangs onto her like a leech and refuses to let the other woman come near. He becomes panicky whenever he thinks his mother may be leaving again. Separation anxiety is worst at bedtime. The terrified child fights against being put to bed. If his mother tears herself away, he may cry in fear for hours. If she sits by his crib, he lies down only as long as she sits still. Her slightest move toward the door brings him instantly to his feet.

In some of these cases there is also worry about urinating. The child keeps saying "Wee wee" (or whatever word he uses). His mother brings him to the bathroom, he does a few drops, and then cries "Wee wee" again just as soon as he is back in bed. You might say that he just uses this as an excuse to keep her there. This is true, but there is more to it. Children like this one are really worried that they might wet the bed. They sometimes wake every 2 hours during the night thinking about it. This is the age period when the mother is apt to be showing disapproval when there is an accident. Maybe the child figures that if he wets, his mother won't love him so much, and will therefore be more likely to go away. If so, he has two reasons for fearing to go to sleep.

495. Avoiding fears at this age. Children who from infancy have been around different people and who have been allowed to develop independence and outgoingness, are less apt to develop such fears.

If your child is around 2, be careful about drastic changes. If it's almost as easy to wait 6 months for a trip or to take a job, better wait, especially if it's your first child. If you have to go now, arrange for the child to get thoroughly used to the person who is going to take care of him, whether it's a friend, a relative, a maid, or a foster mother. (If the child is going to be staying at the other person's house, it's even more important for him to get used to the new person and the new place by gradual steps.) Allow 2 weeks, anyway. Let the new person just be around the child for a number of days without trying to take care of him, until he trusts and likes her. Then let her take over gradually. Don't leave him for a full day at first. Start with half an hour and work up. Your quick reappearance reassures him that you always come back soon. Don't go away for a month or so after you have moved or after another member of the household has left. A child at this age needs a long time to adjust to each of these changes separately.

In "The Working Mother", there is more discussion about what arrangements should be made by a mother who is going to be away from her child.

496. How to help a fearful two-year-old. If your child has become terrified about going to bed, the safest advice, but the hardest to carry out, is to sit by his crib in a relaxed way until he goes to sleep. Don't be in a hurry to sneak away before he is asleep. It alarms him again and makes him more wakeful. This campaign may take weeks, but it should work in the end. If he was frightened because you left town, try to avoid going away again for many weeks. If you **have** to go away each day to work, say good-by affectionately, but cheerfully and confidently. If you have an anguished, unsure-whether-you're-doing-the-right-thing expression, it adds to his uneasiness.

Making the child more tired by keeping him up later or omitting his nap, or having the doctor prescribe a sedative may help a little but usually won't do the whole job. A panicky child can keep himself awake for hours even though he's exhausted. You have to take away his worry, too.

If your child is worried about wetting, keep reassuring him that it doesn't matter if he does wee wee in his bed—that you'll love him just the same.

497. Overprotectiveness increases children's fears. A child who is frightened by separation—or anything else—is very sensitive to whether his mother feels the same way about it. If she acts hesitant or guilty every time she leaves his side, if she hurries into his room at night, her anxiety reinforces his fear that there really is great danger in being apart from her.

This may sound contradictory after I've said that a mother must reassure a frightened 2-year-old by sitting by his bed as he goes to sleep and by not going away on any more trips for a number of weeks. I mean that she must give him this special care the way she gives special consideration to a sick child. But she should try to be cheerful, confident, unafraid. She should be looking for signs of the child's readiness to give up his dependence, step by step, and encourage him and compliment him. This attitude of hers is the most powerful factor in getting him over his fear.

This connection between overprotective feelings in the parent and overdependence in the child applies to many other fear situations, sleep problems, and spoiling problems in infancy and childhood.

Overprotective feelings occur mostly in very devoted, tender-hearted parents who are too inclined to feel guilty when there is no realistic need for it (Sections 14 and 474). Most important of all, in a majority of cases, is the parent's inability to admit that he or she is sometimes resentful or angry toward the child (Section 8).

The parent and child who are afraid to recognize that there are naturally moments when they have mean feelings toward each other, when each wishes that something bad would happen to the other, have to imagine instead that **all** the dangers in the world come from somewhere else, and grossly exaggerate them. The child who is denying the meanness in his mother and in himself places it all in bogiemen or witches or robbers or dogs or dinosaurs or polio or lightning, depending on his age and experience. And he clings tightly to his mother—for protection for himself and to reassure himself that nothing is really happening to her. She suppresses her occasional mean thoughts and exaggerates the dangers of kidnapers or whooping cough or home accidents or inadequate diet. She has to stay close to the child to make sure the dangers don't strike, and her anxious expression convinces the child that his fears are well founded.

Of course, the answer is not for parents to take out all their angriest feelings on the child or to let him be abusive toward them. Neither of these would help. But it certainly is helpful for parents to recognize the inevitability of their occasional mean feelings toward their child and to admit them jokingly to each other. It helps to clear the air if a parent occasionally admits to a child how angry he felt—especially if the angriness was not quite fair—and it doesn't interfere with good discipline if it's done in a sensible way. It's good to say to a child once in a while, "I know how angry you feel toward me when I have to do this to you."

When it comes to the management of the child's fear, a lot depends on how important it is for him to get over it in a hurry, from a practical point of view. There's no great necessity for an anxious child to be hurried into making friends with dogs or going into deep water in the lake or taking a bus trip by himself. He'll want to do these things as soon as he dares. On the other hand, if he has already started in nursery school, I think it's better to insist that he go unless he's deeply terrified. At night a child should not be allowed to come into his parents' bed; he should be trained to stay in his own bed. A school-age child with a phobia must get back to school sooner or later; the longer it is put off the harder it is for him. In these various separation fears, it is wise for a mother to try to see whether her own protectiveness is playing a part and to overcome it. Both steps are difficult to accomplish alone, and the mother is certainly entitled to help from a child-guidance clinic or family agency (Sections 570 and 571).

498. Mild bedtime difficulties. I don't want to leave the impression that every 2-year-old who objects to being put to bed should be sat with. Far from it. Severe separation anxiety is rare, but mild reluctance to be separated is very common. There are two varieties. The first consists of trying to keep the mother in the room. The child urgently says, "Wee wee!" though he went to the bathroom just a few minutes ago. This puts the mother in a quandary. She knows it's an excuse, but on the other hand she wants to encourage cooperation from the child by being co-operative herself. So she says, "Once more." As soon as he's back in bed and she starts to leave, he cries, "Drink of water!" looking as pathetic as a man dying of thirst. If his mother complies he keeps alternating these two requests all evening. I think that such a child is feeling just **slightly** worried about being left alone. Usually the best and most practical way for his mother to reassure him is to remind him in a friendly, firm, and breezy tone that he's just had a drink and been to the bathroom, and then to say good night and leave his room without hesitation. If she allows herself to be detained or looks troubled and uncertain, it's as if she were saying, "Well, maybe there **is** something to be nervous about." Even if he whimpers or cries for a few minutes, I think it is wiser not to go back. It's much easier on him to learn the lesson right away with a little un-happiness than to have the struggle drag on for weeks.

The other type of mild bedtime anxiety is when a 2-year-old learns to climb out of his crib soon after being put to bed and appears at the parents' side. He's smart enough to be very charming at such a time. He's happy to chat or to be cuddled—things he has no time for during the day. This makes it very hard for the parents to be firm. But firm they have to be, and promptly, too. Otherwise repeated climbing out of bed may develop into an unpleasant battle lasting an hour or more every night.

When a climbing-out-of-bed problem in a 2-year-old has gotten com-pletely out of hand, parents sometimes ask if it is all right to lock the child's door. I don't like the idea of a child crying himself to sleep at a locked door. Less objectionable, I think, is to rig a string netting over the top of the crib. You can buy a badminton net at a sporting-goods store. It's too long and narrow, but it can be cut in half and the two pieces sewed together side by side. Then it can be bound with firm cord to the top rail of the side of the crib next to the wall, and also part way along the top of the head and foot of the crib. The front half of the net can be folded back to let the child in. Then the entire front edge can be tied firmly with several tapes or cords to the springs, way under the bed, out of reach.

I am not sure that such a net is harmless from a psychological point of view, but I think it is better than repeated angry scoldings every night. It should never be spoken of as a punishment or a threat. The mother can suggest it cheerfully as a top on the bed to make a cozy house for the child to stay in and sleep in, and ask the child's help in tying it on. Most children of 2 are intrigued with the idea, allow themselves to be put in willingly, do a little poking around to see if they can make an exit, and then go to sleep. I would not keep the child in this if he acted frightened, and I would not use it for a 3-year-old, who is more apt to develop claustrophobia.

I think it's sensible to keep a 2-year-old in his crib as long as he has not learned to climb out of it, even if another crib has to be bought for a new baby. I've heard too many stories of 2-year-olds who became evening wanderers just as soon as they were graduated to youth beds. By the time they can climb out of the crib, it doesn't make any difference.

If the child is afraid to go to bed, it sometimes solves the problem to have either an older or younger brother or sister sleep in his room.

CONTRARINESS

499. Balkiness between two and three. In the period between 2 and 3, children are apt to show signs of balkiness and other inner tensions. Babies begin to be balky and "negativistic" way back when they are 1 year old, so this is nothing new. But it reaches new heights and takes new forms after 2. The 1-year-old contradicts his mother. The 2½-year-old even contradicts himself. (Gesell and Ilg bring this out clearly in their discussion of the 2½-year-old in *Infant and Child in the Culture of Today*.) He has a hard time making up his mind, and then he wants to change it. He acts like a person who feels he is being bossed too much, even when no one is bothering him. He is quite bossy himself. He insists on doing things just so, doing them his own way, doing them exactly as he has always done them before. It makes him furious to have anyone interfere in one of his jobs, or rearrange his possessions.

It looks as though the child's nature between 2 and 3 is urging him to decide things for himself, and to resist pressure from other people. Trying to fight these two battles without much worldly experience seems to get him tightened up inside, especially if his parents are a little too bossy. It's similar to the 6-to-9-year-old period, when the child tries to throw off his dependence on his parents, takes over a lot of responsibility for his own behavior, becomes overfussy about how he does things, and shows his tenseness in various nervous habits.

It's often hard to get along with a child between 2 and 3. Parents have to be understanding. The job is to keep from interfering too much, from hurrying him. Let him help to dress and undress himself when he has the urge. Start his bath early enough so that he has time to dawdle and scrub the tub. At meals let him feed himself without urging. When he is stalled in his eating, let him leave the table. When it's time for bed, or going outdoors, or coming in, steer him while conversing about pleasant things. Get things done without raising issues. Don't be discouraged; there's smoother sailing ahead.

500. The child who can't stand two parents at once. Sometimes a child around 2½ or 3 can get along with either parent alone, but when the other one comes onto the scene he flies into a rage. It may be partly jealousy, but at an age when he's sensitive about being bossed and trying to do a little bossing himself, I imagine he feels outnumbered when he has to take on two important people at once. It's more often the father who is particularly unpopular at this period, and he sometimes gets the feeling he's pure poison. He shouldn't take it too seriously. It will help the child to play with his father alone, at times, so that he can know him as an enjoyable and loving person, not just an intruder. But the child must also learn that the parents love each other, want to be with each other, and will not be bullied by him.

STUTTERING

501. Stuttering is common between two and three. We don't entirely understand stuttering or stammering, but we know several things about it. It often runs in families, and it's much commoner in boys. This means that it is **easier** for certain individuals to develop it. Trying to change a left-handed child to right-handed sometimes appears to start it. The part of the brain that controls speech is closely connected to the part that controls the hand that a person naturally prefers. If you force him to use his wrong hand, it seems to confuse the nervous machinery for talking.

We know that a child's emotional state has a lot to do with stuttering. Most cases occur in somewhat tense children. Some stutter only when they are excited or when they are talking to one particular person. Here are some examples. One little boy began to stutter when a new baby sister was brought home from the hospital. He didn't show his jealousy outwardly. He never tried to hit or pinch her. He just became uneasy. A girl of 2½ began to stutter after the departure of a fond relative who had been with the family a long time. In 2 weeks the stuttering stopped for the time being. When the family moved to a new house, she was quite homesick and stuttered again for a period. Two months later the father was called into the Army. The family was upset, and the little girl started again. Mothers report that their children's stuttering is definitely worse when the mothers are tense. I think children who, during too much of the day, are being talked to and told stories, urged to talk and recite, shown off, are especially liable. Stuttering may start when a father decides to be stricter in his discipline.

Why is stuttering so common between 2 and 3? There are two possible explanations. This is the age period when a child is working very hard at his talking. When he was younger, he used short sentences that he didn't need to think out: "See the car," "Wan'na go out," etc. But when he gets past 2, he tries to make up longer sentences to express new ideas. He starts a sentence three or four times only to break off in the middle because he can't find the right words. His mother, worn out by his constant talking, doesn't pay too much attention. She says, "Uh huh," in an absent-minded way while she goes about her business. So the child is further frustrated by not being able to hold his audience.

It is also possible that the balkiness that is a part of this rather tense stage of development affects his speech, too.

502. What to do for stuttering. You may be especially distressed if you yourself or some relative has had a lifelong struggle to overcome stuttering. But there is no cause for alarm. I think nine out of ten of the children who start to stutter between 2 and 3 outgrow it in a few months' time if given half a chance. It's only the exceptional case that becomes chronic. Don't try to correct the child's speech or worry about speech training at 2½. Look around to see what might be making him tense. If he was upset by being separated from you for a number of days, try to avoid further separations for a couple of months. (See Sections 495 and 496.) If you think you have been talking at him or urging him to talk too much, try to train yourself out of it. Play with him by **doing** things instead of by always **talking** things. Is he having plenty of chance to play with other children with whom he gets along easily? Does he have toys and equipment enough, indoors and out, so that he can be inventing his own games without too much bossing? I don't mean that you should ignore or isolate him, but when you're with him be relaxed and let him take the lead. When he talks to you, give him your attention so that he doesn't get frantic. If jealousy is upsetting him, see whether you can do more to prevent it. Stuttering in most cases lasts a number of months, with ups and downs. Don't expect it to go right away; be content with gradual progress. If you can't figure what, if anything, is wrong, talk it over with a children's psychiatrist. A tongue-tie has nothing to do with stuttering, and should not be cut.

Some schools and hospitals have special speech classes or clinics, in which older children can receive special training. This is often helpful, but by no means always. It is most valuable for the school-age child who wants assistance. For the child who is of a distinctly nervous type, it might be better to consult a children's psychiatrist first to see if it's possible to discover and remove the causes of tenseness (Section 570).

NAIL-BITING

503. Nail-biting is a sign of tenseness. It is more common in relatively high-strung, worrisome children. They start to bite when they are anxious—for instance, while waiting to be called on in school, while watching a scary episode in a movie. It isn't necessarily a serious sign in a generally happy, successful child, but it is always worth thinking over.

Nagging or punishing a nail-biter usually doesn't stop him for longer than half a minute because he seldom realizes he is doing it. In the long run, it may increase his tension. Bitter medicine on the nails rarely helps.

The better course is to find out what some of the pressures on the child are and try to relieve them. Is he being urged or corrected or warned or scolded too much? Are the parents expecting too much in the way of lessons? Consult the teacher about his school adjustment. If movie, radio, and TV adventures make him much more jittery than the average child, he'd better be kept away from the worst programs.

A girl beyond the age of 3 may be helped by a manicure set, and perhaps some nail polish, if they are offered in a cooperative spirit.

Three to Six

DEVOTION TO THE PARENTS

504. Children at this age are usually easier to lead. Boys and girls around 3 have reached a stage in their emotional development when they feel that their father and mother are wonderful people. They pay their parents the compliment of wanting to be like them, do what they do, wear what they wear, use the same words. The 2-year-old girl who sees her mother sweeping wants to do it, too, but she's thinking mostly of the broom. The 5-year-old girl wants to dress up in her mother's clothes, but she's not thinking so much of the clothes as of looking and feeling like her mother. She is actually beginning to be like her mother, even when she isn't trying. This is called identification.

The automatic balkiness, the hostility that was just below the surface in the 2½-year-old period, seem to lessen after 3 in most children. The feelings toward the parents aren't just friendly; they are warm and tender. However, the child is not so devoted to his parents that he always obeys and behaves well. He is still a real person with ideas of his own. He wants to assert himself, even if it means going against his parents' wishes at times.

While I'm emphasizing how agreeable children usually are between 3 and 6, I ought to make a partial exception for 4-year-olds. There's a lot of assertiveness, cockiness, loud talk, and provoking that comes out around 4 years in many children and that requires a firm hand in the mother.

505. A boy now wants to be like his father. By the age of 3 a boy is beginning to realize more clearly that he **is** a boy and will grow up to be a man like his father. This gives him a special admiration for his father and other men and boys. He watches them carefully and works hard to be as much like them as he can, in appearance and behavior and interests. In his play he concentrates on propelling toy trucks, trains, and planes, pretending his tricycle is a car, being a policeman or fireman, making deliveries, building houses and bridges. He copies his father's remarks in his father's tone of voice. He takes on his father's attitude toward other males and toward women. He is preparing himself to play a man's part in the world, spiritually, occupationally, socially, by means of his love and admiration of his father and other men.

506. A girl wants to be like her mother. The girl at this age realizes that it is her destiny to be a woman, and this makes it particularly exciting and challenging for her to try to be like her mother and other women. She turns with more concentration to housework and baby (doll) care if these are her mother's occupations. In caring for her dolls, she takes on the very same attitudes and tone of voice her mother uses toward children. She absorbs her mother's point of view toward men and boys.

507. Boys become romantic toward their mother, girls toward their father. Up to this age, a boy's love for his mother has been predominantly of a dependent kind, like that of a baby. But now it also becomes increasingly romantic, like his father's. By the time he's 4, he's apt to insist that he's going to marry his mother when he grows up. He isn't clear just what marriage consists of, but he's absolutely sure who is the most important and appealing woman in the world. The little girl who is growing normally in her mother's pattern develops the same kind of love for her father.

These strong romantic attachments help children to grow spiritually and to acquire wholesome feelings toward the opposite sex that will later guide them into good marriages. But there is another side to the picture that creates a little tension in most children at this age and a lot of tension in a few. When a human male, old or young, loves a woman very much, he can't help wanting her all to himself. He can't help feeling jealous of the love that exists between her and some other man. And so, of course, the boy of 3 and 4 and 5, as he becomes more aware of his possessive devotion to his mother, also becomes aware of how much she already belongs to his father. This irritates him underneath, no matter how much he loves and admires his father. At times he secretly wishes his father would get lost, and then he feels guilty about such disloyal feelings. Reasoning as a child does, he imagines that his father has the same jealous and resentful feelings toward him. He tries to push these scary thoughts out of his mind since his father, after all, is so much bigger and stronger, but they are apt to come to the surface in his dreams. We believe that these mixed feelings—of love, jealousy, and fear —toward the father are the main cause of the bad dreams that little boys of this age are so apt to have—of being chased by giants, robbers, gorillas, and other frightening figures.

The little girl, if she is developing normally, also becomes more possessive in her love for her father. She wishes at times that something would happen to her mother (whom she loves so much in other respects) so that she could have her father for herself. She may even say to her mother, "You can go away for a long trip, and I'll take good care of Daddy." But then she imagines that her mother is jealous of her, too, and subconsciously worries about this.

These fears of children—that their parents are angry with them—get mixed up with their worries about why boys and men are shaped differently from girls and women. This will be discussed in Section 515.

Since all small children, we believe, go through this phase, it shouldn't make parents worry unless a child becomes excessively fearful or antagonistic to the parent of the same sex or much too close to the parent of the opposite sex. In that case, it's wise to get the help of a child-guidance clinic.

508. The attachment isn't meant to become too complete. This romantic attachment to the parent of the opposite sex in the years between 3 and 6 is what you might call Nature's way of molding a child's feelings in preparation for his eventual life as husband and father or wife and mother. But Nature doesn't want the attachment to go so far or get so strong that it lasts through life or even through childhood. Nature expects that the child by 5 or 6 will become quite discouraged about the possibility of having the parent all to himself, will stop trying, and will turn his interests increasingly to other activities, such as school, and to other children and adults outside the family. The intense attachment will then have served its constructive purpose (like creeping infancy) and will have been outgrown.

So a father who realizes that his young son sometimes has unconscious feelings of resentment and fear toward him does not help the boy by trying to be too gentle and permissive with him or by pretending that he, the father, doesn't really love his wife very much. In fact, if a boy was convinced that his father was afraid to be a strong man, a firm father, and a normally possessive husband, the boy would sense that he himself was having his mother too much to himself and would feel really guilty and frightened. And he would miss the inspiration of a manly father, which he must have in order to develop his own manliness and courage.

In the same way a mother, even though she knows that her young daughter is sometimes jealous of her, best helps her daughter to grow up by being a self-confident mother who doesn't let herself be pushed around, who knows how and when to be firm, and who isn't at all afraid to show her affection and devotion to her husband.

You can see why it complicates life for a boy if his mother is a great deal more permissive and affectionate toward him than his father is. The same is true if she seems to be closer and more sympathetic to her son than she is to her husband. Such attitudes have a tendency to alienate a boy from his father and to make him too fearful of him. In a corresponding manner, the father who is putty in his daughter's hands and is always undoing the mother's discipline, or the father who acts as if he enjoys his daughter's companionship more than his wife's, is being unhelpful not only to his wife but to his daughter. This interferes with the good relationship that a daughter should have with her mother in order to grow up to be a happy woman.

Incidentally, it is entirely normal for a father to be a bit more lenient toward his daughter and a mother toward her son, and for a son to feel a little more comfortable with his mother and a daughter with her father, because there is naturally less rivalry between male and female than between two males or two females.

I don't want to get fathers and mothers so concerned about these relationships that they become self-conscious or inhibited or worried. In the average family there is a healthy balance between the feelings of father, mother, sons, and daughters that guides them through these stages of development without any special effort or conscious thought. I bring these points up only to give some clues for those families whose relationships have gotten out of kilter—families in which, for instance, the parents are constantly at odds about disciplining the children, or a boy is becoming timid toward all boys and men, or a girl is excessively defiant of her mother.

509. Parents can help children through this romantic but jealous stage by gently keeping it clear that the parents do belong to each other, that a boy can't ever have his mother to himself or a girl have her father to herself, but that the parents aren't shocked to realize that their children are mad at them sometimes on this account.

When a boy declares that he is going to marry his mother, she can act pleased with the compliment but she can also explain that she's already married and that when he grows up he'll find another girl his own age to marry.

When parents are being companionable together, they needn't and shouldn't let a child break up their conversation. They can cheerfully but firmly remind him that they have things to talk over and suggest that he get busy, too. Their tactfulness will keep them from prolonged displays of affection in front of him (as it would if other people were present), but they don't need to spring apart guiltily if he comes into the room unexpectedly.

When a boy is being rude to his father because he's feeling jealous, or to his mother because she's the cause of his jealousy, the parent should insist on politeness. But at the same time the parent can ease the child's feelings of anger and guilt by saying that he knows that the child is cross at him. See Section 476.

510. Sleep problems at three, four, and five. Many of the sleep problems in 3-, 4-, and 5-year-old children that have been studied in child-guidance clinics are found to be caused by romantic jealousy. The child wanders into the parents' room in the middle of every night and wants to get into their bed because subconsciously he doesn't want them to be alone together. It's much better for him as well as for the parents if they promptly and firmly, but not angrily, take him back to his own bed.

CURIOSITY AND IMAGINATION

511. The child's curiosity at this age is intense. He wants to know the meaning of everything that meets his eye. His imagination is rich. He puts two and two together and draws conclusions. He connects everything with himself. When he hears about trains, he wants to know right away, "Will I go on a train someday?" When he hears about an illness, it makes him think, "Will I have that?"

512. A little imagination is a good thing. When a child of 3 or 4 tells a made-up story, he isn't lying in our grown-up sense. His imagination is vivid to him. He's not sure where the real ends and the unreal begins.

That is why he loves stories that are told or read to him. That is why he is scared at the movies and shouldn't go to them.

You don't need to jump on him for making up stories occasionally, or make him feel guilty, or even be concerned yourself, so long as he is outgoing in general and happy with other children. On the other hand, if he is spending a good part of each day telling about imaginary friends or adventures, not as a game but as if he believes in them, it raises the question whether his real life is satisfying enough. Part of the remedy may be finding him children his own age to play with and helping him to enjoy them. Another question is whether he is having enough easygoing companionship with his parents. A child needs hugging and piggyback rides. He needs to share in his parents' jokes and friendly conversations. If the adults around him are undemonstrative, he dreams of comfy, understanding playmates as the hungry man dreams of chocolate bars. If the parents are always disapproving, he invents a wicked companion whom he blames for the naughty things he has done or would like to do. If a child is living largely in his imagination and not adjusting well with other children, especially by the age of 4, a psychiatrist should be able to find what he is lacking.

Occasionally a mother who has always lived a great deal in her imagination and who is delighted to find how imaginative her child is overfills him with stories, and they both live for hours in fairyland. The games and stories that the other children make up are poor in comparison to hers. The child may be weaned away from his interest in real people and things and have a harder time later adjusting to the world. I don't mean that a mother should be afraid of fairy stories or of a little make-believe, but only that it should be in moderation.

513. Why does an older child lie? The older child who tells a lie to deceive is a different problem. The first question is, Why does he have to? Everyone, grownup or child, gets in a jam occasionally when the only tactful way out is a small lie, and this is no cause for alarm.

A child isn't naturally deceitful. When he lies regularly it means that he is under too much pressure of some kind. If he is failing in his schoolwork and lying about it, it isn't because he doesn't care. His lying shows that he does care. Is the work too hard for him? Is he confused in his mind by other worries so that he can't concentrate? Are his parents setting too high standards? The job is to find out what is wrong, with the help of the teacher, or the guidance teacher, or the school psychologist, or a psychiatrist (Section 570). You don't have to pretend that he has pulled the wool over your eyes. You might say gently, "You don't have to lie to me. Tell me what the trouble is and we'll see what we can do."

But he won't be able to tell you the answer right away because he probably doesn't know it himself. Even if he knows some of his worries, he can't break down all at once. It takes time and understanding.

FEARS AROUND THREE, FOUR, AND FIVE

514. Imaginary worries are common at this age. In earlier sections we discussed how anxieties are different at different age periods. New types of fear crop up fairly often around the age of 3 or 4—fear of the dark, of dogs, of fire engines, of death, of cripples. The child's imagination has now developed to the stage where he can put himself in other people's shoes and picture dangers that he hasn't actually experienced. His curiosity is pushing out in all directions. He wants to know not only the cause of everything but what these things have to do with him. He overhears something about dying. Quickly he wants to know what dying is, and as soon as he gets a dim idea he asks, "Do I have to die?"

These fears are commoner in children who have been made tense from battles over such matters as feeding and toilet training, children whose imaginations have been overstimulated by scary stories or too many warnings, children who haven't had enough chance to develop their independence and outgoingness, children whose parents are too protective (Section 497). The uneasiness that the child has accumulated before now seems to be crystallized by his new imagination into definite dreads. It sounds as if I mean that any child who develops a fear has been handled badly in the past, but I don't mean to go that far. I think that some children are born more sensitive than others; and all children, no matter how carefully they are brought up, are frightened by something. Read Section 507 about children's feelings about their parents.

If your child develops a fear of the dark, try to reassure him. This is more a matter of your manner than your words. Don't make fun of him, or be impatient with him, or try to argue him out of his fear. If he wants to talk about it, as a few children do, let him. Give him the feeling that you want to understand but that you are sure nothing bad will happen to him. This is the time for extra hugs and comforting reminders that you love him very much and will always protect him. Naturally you should never threaten a child with bogiemen or policemen or the devil. Avoid movies and scary TV programs and cruel fairy stories. The child is scared enough of his own mental creations. Call off any battle that you might be engaged in about feeding or staying dry at night. Keep him behaving well by firm guidance rather than by letting him misbehave and then making him feel guilty about it afterward. Threats about not approving of him or not loving him are the hardest of all for him to take when he is already insecure. Arrange to give him a full, outgoing life with other children every day. The more he is absorbed in games and plans, the less he will worry about his inner fears. Leave his door open at night if that is what he wants, or leave a dim light on in his room. It's a small price to pay to keep the goblins out of sight. The light, or the conversation from the living room, won't keep him awake so much as his fears will. When his fear subsides, he will be able to stand the dark again.

Realize ahead of time that questions about death are apt to come up at this age. Try to make the first explanation casual, not too scary. You might say, "Everybody has to die someday. Most people die when they get very old and tired and weak and they don't want to stay alive any more. They don't want to have to get up in the morning and work. They just stop being alive." Some parents like to express it in religious terms: "He was very, very sick, and God took him to Heaven to take care of him." If you think of death as something not to be dreaded, you will be able to give the same feeling about it to your child. Remember to hug him and smile at him and remind him that you're going to be together for years and years.

A fear of an animal is common at this period, even though the child has had no bad experiences. Don't drag him to a dog to reassure him. The more you pull him, the more you make him feel he has to pull in the opposite direction. As the months go by, he will try himself to get over his fear and approach a dog. He will do it faster by himself than you can ever persuade him. That reminds me of fear of the water. Don't ever pull a child, screaming, into the ocean or pool. It is true that occasionally a child who is forced in finds that it is fun and loses his fear abruptly, but in more cases it works the opposite way. Remember that the child is longing to go in even though he has a dread of it. Let him build up his own courage at his own speed.

With fears of dogs and fire engines and policemen and other concrete things, a child may try to get used to his worry and overcome it by playing games about it. This acting out of a fear is a great help if the child is able to. A fear is meant to make us act. Our bodies are flooded with adrenaline, which makes the heart beat faster and supplies sugar for quick energy. We are ready to run like the wind or to fight like wild animals. The running and the fighting burn up the anxiety. Sitting still does nothing to relieve it. If a child with a fear of a dog can play games in which he pounds the stuffing out of a toy dog, it partly relieves him. If your child develops an intense fear, or a number of fears, or frequent nightmares, or sleepwalking, you ought to get the help of a children's psychiatrist (Section 570).

515. Fear of injury. I'd like to discuss separately the fear of bodily injury in the age period between 2½ and 5, because there are special things you can do to prevent or relieve it. A child at this age wants to know the reason for everything, worries easily, and applies dangers to himself. If he sees a crippled or deformed person, he first wants to know what happened to him, then puts himself in the other's place and wonders if that injury might happen to himself. Children develop these fears not only about real injuries. They even get mixed up and worried about the natural differences between boys and girls. If a boy around the age of 3 sees a girl undressed, it may strike him as queer that she hasn't got a penis like his. He's apt to say, "Where is her wee wee?" If he doesn't receive a satisfactory answer right away, he may jump to the conclusion that some accident has happened to her. Next comes the anxious thought, "That might happen to me, too." The same misunderstanding may worry the little girl when she first realizes that boys are made differently. First she asks, "What's that?" Then she wants to know anxiously, "Why don't I have one? What happened to it?" That's the way a 3-year-old's mind works. He may be so upset right away that he's afraid to question his mother.

This worry about why boys are shaped differently from girls shows up in different ways. I remember a boy just under 3 who, with an anxious expression, kept watching his baby sister being bathed and telling his mother, "Baby is boo-boo." That was his word for hurt. His mother couldn't make out what he was talking about until he got bold enough to point. At about the same time he began to hold onto his own penis in a worried way. His mother was unhappy about this and assumed it was the beginning of a bad habit. It never occurred to her that there was a connection between these two developments. I remember a little girl who became worried after she found out about boys, and kept trying to undress different children to see how they were made, too. She didn't do this in a sly way; you could see she was fearful. Later she began to handle herself. A boy 3½ first became upset about his younger sister's body, and then began to worry about everything in the house that was broken. He would ask his mother nervously, "Why is this tin soldier broken?" There was no sense to this question, because he had broken it himself the day before. Everything that he saw damaged seemed to remind him of his fears about himself.

It's wise to realize ahead of time that a normal child is likely to be wondering about things like bodily differences between 2½ and 3½, and that if he isn't given a comforting explanation when he first gets curious, he's apt to come to worrisome conclusions. It's no use waiting for him to say, "I want to know why a girl isn't made like a boy," because he won't be that definite. He may ask some kind of question, or he may hint around, or he may just wait and get worried. Don't think of it as an unwholesome interest in sex. To him it's just like any other important question at first. You can see why it would be bad to shush him, or scold him, or blush and refuse to answer. That would give him the idea he was on dangerous ground, which is what you want to avoid. On the other hand, you don't need to be solemn as if you were giving a lecture. It's easier than that. It helps, first of all, to bring the child's fear out into the open by saying that he (or she) probably thinks a girl had a penis but something happened to it. Then you try to make it clear, in a matter-of-fact cheerful tone, that girls and women are **made** differently from boys and men; they are **meant** to be that way. A small child gets an idea more easily from examples. You can explain that Johnny is made just like Daddy, Uncle Harry, David, and so on, and that Mary is made like Mommy, Mrs. Jenkins, and Helen (listing all the individuals that the child knows best). A little girl needs extra reassurance because it's natural for her to want to have something that she can see. (I heard of a little girl who complained to her mother, "But he's so fancy and I'm so plain.") It will help her to know that her mother likes being made the way she is, that her mother loves her just the way she's made. This may also be a good time to explain that girls when they are older can grow babies of their own inside them and have breasts with which to nurse them. That's a thrilling idea at 3 or 4.

DIFFERENT CAUSES FOR HANDLING THE GENITALS

516. In the infant it's wholesome curiosity. Babies in the last half of the first year discover their genitals the way they discovered their fingers and toes, and handle them the same way, too. The 1¼-year-old baby, sitting on the potty, explores himself with definite curiosity for a few seconds at a time. This won't come to anything or start a bad habit. You can distract him with a toy if you want, but don't feel that you've **got** to. It's better not to give him the idea that he is bad or that his genitals are bad. You want him to go on having a wholesome, natural feeling about his entire body. If he is scared about any part of himself, it draws his attention to it, gets it on his mind, and may have bad results later. Furthermore, if you try to stop a year-old baby by saying, "No, no," or slapping his hand, or yanking it away, it's apt to make him more determined.

517. At three it's related to his feelings. Children between 3 and 6 are surprisingly grown-up in lots of ways. They love intensely and romantically those who are close to them, especially their parents.

We realize now that there is a childish kind of sexual feeling at this period, which is an essential part of normal development. (In former times people believed that nothing of this sort occurred until adolescence, probably because they themselves had been brought up worried about sex and they wanted to avoid recognizing it in their children as long as possible.) Children of 3, 4, and 5 are physically affectionate. They cling to their favorite grownups and lean against them. They are interested in each other's bodies, occasionally have the desire to see and touch each other. This is one reason why they like to play doctor.

If you realize that this early interest in sex is a natural part of the slow process of growing up and that it occurs to a degree in all wholesome children, you can take a sensible view of it. If a child is not preoccupied with sex, if he is generally outgoing, unworried, and has plenty of other interests and playmates. there is no cause for concern. If not, he needs to be helped.

If you discover your small child in some sort of sex play alone or with others, you'll probably be at least a little bit surprised and shocked. In expressing your disapproval it's better to be firmly matter-of-fact rather than very shocked or angry. You want him to know that you don't want him to do it, but you don't want him to feel that he's a criminal. You can say, for instance, "Mother doesn't want you to do that again," or "That isn't polite," and shoo the children out to some other activity. That's usually enough to stop sex play for a long time in normal children. It's sensible for a mother to keep some track of a group of small children who are in a period of occasional interest in sex, and make sure they have plenty of other things to do. The principal reason is that some children are upset and worried by what is done and said, especially if there is an older child with an exaggerated interest leading them on. Naturally, parents should not become suspicious snoopers or make accusations.

518. A lot at three may be due to worry. In Section 515 there were examples of children in the neighborhood of 3 years who handled themselves a great deal, in a preoccupied manner, after they became worried about why girls aren't made the same as boys. It's important for parents to know that the fear that something will happen or has happened to the genitals is one of the commonest causes of **excessive** handling or masturbation in young childhood.

To tell such a child that he'll injure himself makes matters worse.

To tell him that he's bad and that you won't love him any more gives him a new fear. The wise thing is to try to take away his fear as soon as you see it developing. If the mother of the little boy who said, "Baby is boo-boo," had known that this misunderstanding and this worry are common, she could have started to reassure him the first time he said it. The same thing applies to the mother of the little girl who anxiously tried to undress the other children.

519. After six there's a stronger effort to control it. Between the ages of 6 and puberty, it seems as if the child, by his own nature, makes an effort to suppress the impulse to masturbate or to become involved in sex play with others. Children get the idea that masturbation is considered wrong, whether their parents have told them so or not, and this is the period when their conscience is becoming strong. But it doesn't stop altogether in all children. Occasionally a child is drawn into it in the group because the others are doing it. It's a time in his life when he's striving with might and main to become a "regular guy."

520. It may be a sign of tenseness and worry at any age. At any age there are a few children who handle their genitals a great deal, sometimes in public. They hardly seem to be aware of what they are doing. They are usually tense or worried children. They aren't nervous because they are masturbating; they are masturbating because they are nervous. The job here is to find out what's causing the tenseness, instead of attacking the masturbation directly. An 8-year-old boy is terrified that his ill mother is going to die. He can't put his mind on schoolwork but absent-mindedly handles his genitals in school as he gazes out the window. Another child is thoroughly maladjusted, doesn't know how to get along with other children, has no close connection with the world around him. Cut off from the outside, he must live within himself. Such children and their parents need the help of a psychiatrist or child-guidance clinic (Section 570).

Many children hold their genitals when they need to urinate, especially the procrastinators, and this has no special significance.

521. Why threats are harmful. Most of us heard in childhood the threat that masturbation would lead to insanity. This belief is untrue. It grew up because certain adolescents and young adults who are becoming seriously ill mentally masturbate a great deal. But they aren't becoming insane because they are masturbating. The excessive masturbation is just one symptom of the nervous breakdown. This is an example of the fact that frequent masturbation is due to something else going wrong in the child's life or in his spirit. The job is to find the cause.

What's wrong with telling a child that masturbation will make him sick, or injure his genitals, or mark him as an evil person? First of all, none of these things is true. In the second place, and more important, it's risky and it's wrong to put deep fears into a child's mind. The self-confident, tough-minded child may not be much affected by these threats. But the sensitive child takes them to heart. He may develop such a morbid fear of anything sexual that he will grow up maladjusted, afraid, or unable to marry or have children.

Though masturbation doesn't lead to nervousness, excessive **worry** about it can certainly cause nervousness. I think of an adolescent boy whose parents were morbidly afraid of masturbation. They hired a companion for their son, whose job it was to stay close to him 24 hours a day to make sure he didn't do it. This reminded him of masturbation constantly, and at the same time gave him a monstrous fear of it. This is an exaggerated case, but it's an example of how unwise it is to attack the problem blindly. It's important that parents not only avoid serious threats but also avoid getting the child's mind on it.

All these reasons for avoiding severe methods of repression don't mean that a parent should try to ignore masturbation or other sex play. We were all brought up to be disturbed by it, and we can never unlearn that. We can't be comfortable with our children if they are doing things we dislike. Even if we could magically get over our disapproval (which I don't think would be desirable), the fact would remain that our children live in and must adapt to a society that disapproves. Furthermore, there is lots of evidence that all children feel guilty about masturbation whether or not their parents have found out about it or said anything about it. So I think it's quite appropriate when a mother discovers a child in sex play to give him the idea that she doesn't want him to do it any more, in a tone that implies that this will help him to stop. With the child who seems to need reassurance, the mother can explain that most boys and girls want to do it sometime or other but they can usually stop when they try.

522. Why there is more at adolescence. Among adolescents there tends to be an increased urge to masturbate for reasons that are easy to understand. Glandular changes are taking place that transform boy into man, girl into woman. The increased function of the glands doesn't affect just the body. It also affects the thoughts and emotions. The child becomes increasingly aware of his sexual and romantic feelings, not because he wants to but because his glands say he has to. Yet he is nowhere near ready, in the early part of adolescence, to express his feelings openly. When he is more grown-up, the same impulses find expression in dates, romantic companionship, dancing, and flirting. Later still, they lead to falling in love in earnest and marriage.

Some conscientious adolescents feel excessively guilty and worried about masturbation, even when it's just a thought, and need reassurance. If a child seems to be generally happy and successful, doing well in school, getting along with his friends, he can be told that all normal young people have these desires and do their best to control them. This won't take away all his feeling of guilt, but it will help. If, on the other hand, he is wrapped up in himself, or unable to enjoy friendships, or is getting into trouble with his schoolwork, then it is time to find help from someone who understands adolescents well. The best person would be a children's psychiatrist. If that's not possible, talk to the guidance teacher or counselor in the high school. In an unhappy child, frequent masturbation, or preoccupation with it, is only one symptom of a larger problem.

"THE FACTS OF LIFE"

523. Sex education starts early whether you plan it or not. It is common to think that sex education means a lecture at school or a solemn talk by a parent at home. This is taking too narrow a view of the subject. A child is learning about "the facts of life" all through his childhood, if not in a good way then in an unwholesome way. Sex is a lot broader than just how babies are made. It includes the whole matter of how men and women get along with each other, and what their respective places are in the world. Let me give you a couple of bad examples. Suppose a boy has a father who is disagreeable and abusive to the mother. You can't educate the boy with a lecture at school telling him that marriage is a relationship of mutual love and respect. His experience tells him differently. When he learns about the physical side of sex, whether it's from a teacher or from other children, he will fit it into the picture he has of a man being disagreeable to a woman. Or take the example of a girl who grows up feeling unwanted because she thinks her parents prefer her younger brother. She is going to resent men, because she believes that they get all the breaks—that women are always the victims. It won't matter how many books or talks you give her about sex and marriage. Whatever she hears or experiences she will fit into the pattern she has fixed in her mind: it's the man taking advantage of the woman. Even if she marries, she won't adjust to it.

So a child begins his sex education as soon as he can sense how his mother and father get along with each other in general, and how they feel about their sons and daughters.

524. A normal child asks questions around three. A child begins to get more exact ideas about the things that are connected with sex around the ages of 2½, 3, 3½. This is the "why" stage, when his curiosity branches out in all directions. He probably wants to know why boys are made differently from girls (which is discussed in Section 515). He doesn't think of it as a sex question. It's just an important question. But if he gains the wrong impression then, it will become mixed up with sex later and give him distorted ideas.

525. Where do babies come from? This question is also pretty sure to come up in the period around 3. It's easier and better to begin with the truth, rather than tell him a fairy story and have to change it later. Try to answer the question as simply as he asks it. For instance, you can say, "A baby grows in a special place inside his mother." You don't have to tell him more than that for the time being if it satisfies him. But maybe in a few minutes, maybe in a few months, he wants to know a couple of other things. How does the baby get in and how does he get out? The first question is apt to be embarrassing to the mother (or father). She may jump to the conclusion that he is now demanding to know about conception and sex relations. Of course, he has no such idea. He thinks of things getting into the stomach by being eaten and perhaps wonders if the baby gets in that way, too. A simple answer is that the baby grows from a tiny seed that was in the mother all the time. It will be months before he wants to know what part the father plays. Some people feel that the child should be told at the time of his earlier questions that the father contributes by putting his seed in the mother, too. Perhaps this is right, especially in the case of the little boy who feels that the man is left out of the picture. But most experts agree that at 3 or 4 years it is not necessary to try to give him an exact picture of the physical and emotional sides of intercourse. It's more than the child bargained for, you might say, when he asked his question. All that's necessary is to satisfy his curiosity at the level of his understanding.

To the question of how the baby gets out, a good answer is something to the effect that when he is big enough he comes out through a special opening that's just for that purpose. (It's just as well to make it clear that it is not the opening for bowel movements or for urine.)

526. Why not the stork? You may say, "Why isn't it easier and less embarrassing to tell him about the stork?" There are several reasons. We know that a child as young as 3, if he has a pregnant mother or aunt, may have a suspicion of where the baby is growing from observing the woman's figure and from bits of conversation that he overhears. It's apt to mystify and worry him to have his mother nervously telling him something different from what he suspects is the truth. Even if he doesn't suspect anything at 3, he is surely going to find out the truth or the half-truth when he's 5 or 7 or 9. It's better not to start him off wrong and have him later decide that you're something of a liar. And if he finds that for some reason you didn't dare tell him the truth, it puts a barrier between you, makes him uneasy. He's less likely to ask you other questions later, no matter how troubled he is. Another reason for telling the truth at 3 is that the child is satisfied with simple answers. You get practice for the harder questions that come later.

Sometimes a small child who has been told where the baby is growing confuses his parents by talking as if he also believed the stork theory. Or he may mix up two or three theories at the same time. This is natural. Small children believe part of everything they hear because they have such vivid imaginations. They don't try, like grownups, to find the one right answer and get rid of the wrong ones. You must also remember that a child can't learn anything from one telling. He learns a little at a time, and comes back with the same question until he feels sure that he has gotten it straight. Then at every new stage of development he's ready for a new slant.

527. A step at a time usually satisfies. Realize ahead of time that your child's questions will never come in exactly the form or at the moment you expect. A parent is apt to visualize the scene at bedtime when the child is in a confidential mood. Actually, the question is more apt to be popped in the middle of the grocery store or while you are talking on the street with a pregnant neighbor. If it does, try to curb that impulse to shush the child. Answer him on the spot if you can. If that is impossible, say casually, "I'll tell you later. These are things we like to talk about when other people aren't around." Don't make too solemn an occasion of it. When he asks you why the grass is green or why dogs have tails, you answer in an offhand way that gives him the feeling that it is the most natural thing in the world. Try to get the same spirit of naturalness into your answers about the facts of life. Remember that even if this subject is charged with feeling and embarrassment for you, it is a matter of simple curiosity to him. The question, Why don't babies come until you are married? or What does the father do about it? may not come until the child is 4 or 5 or older unless he observes animals. Then you can explain that the seed comes out of the father's penis and goes into the place where the baby will grow. It may be some time before he tries to visualize this situation. When he is ready for that, you can bring in something in your own words about loving and embracing.

A young child is very apt to stumble on some evidence of menstruation and to interpret this as a sign of injury. A mother should be ready to explain that all women have this discharge every month and that it doesn't come from a hurt. Something about the purpose of menstruation can be explained to a child of 4 or older.

The child who hasn't asked. What about the child who has reached the age of 4 or 5 or more and hasn't asked any questions at all? Parents sometimes assume that this means the child is very innocent and has never thought of these questions. Most people who have worked closely with children would be inclined to doubt this. It is more likely that the child has gotten the feeling, whether the parents mean to give it or not, that these matters are embarrassing. You can be on the lookout for indirect questions and hints and little jokes that a child uses to test out his parents' reaction. I think of several examples. A child of 7 who was not supposed to know anything about pregnancy kept calling attention to his mother's large abdomen in a half-embarrassed, half-joking way. Here was a good chance, better late than never, for the mother to explain. A little girl who is at the stage of wondering why she isn't made like a boy sometimes makes valiant efforts to urinate standing up. The mother then has an opportunity to give a reassuring explanation, even though the child hasn't asked a direct question. There are occasions almost every day, in a child's conversation about humans and animals and birds, when a mother on the lookout for indirect questions can help the child to ask what he wants to know.

528. How the school can help. If a child's mother and father have answered his earlier questions comfortably, he keeps on turning to them as he grows older and wants more exact knowledge. But the school has a chance to help out, too. Many schools make a point of letting children in kindergarten or first grade take care of animals, such as rabbits, guinea pigs, or white mice. This gives them an opportunity to become familiar with all sides of animal life—feeding, fighting, mating, birth, and suckling of the young. It is easier in some ways to learn these facts in an impersonal situation, and it supplements what the child has learned from his parents. But what he finds out in school he probably wants to discuss and clear up further at home.

By the fifth grade, it is good to have biology taught in a simple way, including a discussion of reproduction. At least some of the girls in the class are entering the puberty stage of development and need some accurate knowledge of what is happening. The discussion from a somewhat scientific point of view in school should help the child to bring it up more personally at home.

529. The right slant at adolescence. Girls. The puberty stage of development begins in most girls somewhere between 9 and 13, and in boys between 11 and 15. Whether or not the school helps with a course in biology, it is certainly important for a parent to have some discussion with a child by the time the puberty change begins. At this stage the parent usually needs to bring the subject up; the mixed feelings of most adolescents toward their parents are intense enough to make the topic embarrassing for them. The girl needs to be told that during the next 2 years her breasts will develop, hair will grow in the genital region and under the arms, that she will grow rapidly in stature and in weight, that her skin will change its texture and may become liable to pimples, that in about 2 years she will probably have her first menstrual period. How you tell her about her monthly periods makes a difference. Some mothers emphasize what a curse they are. But it is a mistake to stress that part to a child who is still immature and impressionable. Other mothers emphasize how delicate a girl becomes at such times and how careful she must be. This kind of talk makes a bad impression, particularly on those girls who have always been somewhat resentful that they weren't boys anyway and on those who are inclined to worry about their health. The more doctors and women's educators have learned about the periods, the more convinced they have become that most girls and women can live perfectly normal, healthy, vigorous lives right through them. It is only the occasional girl who has cramps severe enough to keep her out of activities. Incidentally, it's the girl who has developed a worried attitude about health and menstruation who is more apt to have severe cramps.

When a girl is on the threshold of womanhood, it's good for her to be looking forward to it happily, not feeling scared or resentful. The best thing to emphasize about menstruation is that the uterus is being prepared for the time she will be a mother.

It helps put the child in the right mood during the months she is waiting for her first period to give her a belt and a box of napkins. This makes her feel as if she is grown-up and ready to deal with life rather than waiting for life to do something to her.

530. Boys, by the time they are in the stage of puberty development, need to be told about the naturalness of erections and nocturnal emissions. Fathers who know that nocturnal emissions are certain to occur if a boy is normal, and that there will probably be a strong urge to masturbate at times, sometimes tell the boy that these things are not harmful if they don't happen too often. I think it's a mistake for a parent to set a limit, even though it may sound sensible. The trouble is that an adolescent easily becomes worried about his sexuality, easily imagines he is "different" or abnormal. Being told, "This much is normal, that much is abnormal," is apt to get his mind more preoccupied with sex.

531. Keep the tone wholesome. It's natural in most families for the father to talk to the son and the mother to the daughter. This shouldn't be considered an absolute rule, though, and if it comes much more easily to the other parent, then that's the best way. It's preferable, just as in earlier childhood, for talk about sex to come up easily from time to time rather than be one big solemn lecture. The parent has to be willing to bring it up early in puberty, though, since the child so often doesn't.

One mistake that is easy to make, especially if the parents themselves were brought up in fear of sex, is to concentrate on all the dangerous aspects of sex. A nervous mother may make her daughter so scared of becoming pregnant that the poor girl has a terror of boys under all circumstances. Or the father may overfill his son with dread of venereal disease. Of course, the child who is moving into adolescence should know how pregnancy takes place and that there is danger of disease in being promiscuous, but these disturbing aspects of sex shouldn't come first. The adolescent should think of it as primarily wholesome and natural and beautiful.

What worried parents find hard to believe, but what people who have studied young people know well, is that the happy, sensible, successful adolescent doesn't get into trouble with sex just because he hasn't been warned sternly enough. All the common sense, self-respect, and kindly feeling toward people that he has built up through the years keep him on an even keel even when he is sailing through an entirely new phase of development. To turn it around the other way, the adolescent who gets into trouble with the wrong kind of companions is usually a child who for years has been mixed up with himself and others.

The danger of scaring a sensitive child about sex is partly that you make him tense and apprehensive at the time, partly that you may destroy his or her ability to adjust to marriage later.

532. How much modesty in the home? In half a century, Americans have made a full swing from the excessive modesty of the Victorian period to the partial nudity of sports clothes and to complete nudity in quite a few homes today. Most people agree (and I certainly do) that today's casual attitude is a lot healthier. Nursery-school teachers, children's psychiatrists, and psychologists generally agree that it's wholesome for **young** children of both sexes to see each other undressed at times in the home and at the beach.

However, there's evidence that at least some young children get upset by regularly seeing their parents naked. The main reason is that young children's feelings for their parents are so intense. A boy loves his mother much more than he loves any little girl. He feels much more rivalrous with his father and more in awe of him than he feels toward any boy. So the sight of his mother may be a little too stimulating, and the chance to compare himself so unfavorably with his father every day may make him feel like doing something violent to his old man. (Nudist fathers have told me about snatching gestures their 3- and 4-year-old sons have made during morning shaving.) Then the boy feels guilty and fearful. A little girl who regularly sees her father nude may be too much stimulated.

I don't want to claim that all children are bothered by parental nudity. No study has been made of normal children. But since we know that it's a possibility, I think it's a little wiser for parents to give their children the benefit of the doubt and, as a general rule, keep reasonably covered and keep children out of the bathroom while a parent is bathing or using the toilet. This doesn't have to be carried to extremes. A parent is caught off guard occasionally, and he shouldn't then act shocked or angry. It's only necessary to say, "Will you wait outside until I get dressed?" After the age of 6 or 7, most children begin to want a little more privacy for themselves, at least at times, and I think it's good to respect this.

NURSERY SCHOOL

533. A good nursery school doesn't take the place of home; it adds to it. Most children would benefit from a good nursery school, but it certainly isn't necessary in every case. It is particularly valuable for the only child, for the child without much chance to play with others, for the child who lives in a small apartment, for the child whose mother finds him difficult to manage for any reason. Every young child by the age of 3 needs other children his own age, not just to have fun with but also to learn how to get along with. This is the most important job in his life. He also needs space to run and shout in, apparatus to climb on, blocks and boxes and boards to build with, trains and dolls to play with. He needs to learn how to get along with other grownups besides his parents. Few children nowadays have all these advantages in their own home. Nursery school doesn't take the place of home; it just adds to it.

534. What's the difference between the day nursery and a nursery school? For many years there have been day nurseries—good, bad, and indifferent—where mothers who have to work can leave their babies and small children. The good ones have been run by people who try to understand children's needs, love them, give them attention, affection, things to play with, freedom to develop. The poor ones have been run by people who think the main job is to discipline children into being good, or who think all a child needs in the way of care is cleanliness and enough food.

The people who started the nursery-school idea said, **"All** small children need a chance to be with other children, not just the ones whose mothers are working. **All** young children need space, music, paints, and clay to enrich their spirits." Furthermore, they said, "It isn't enough that a person who is going to take charge of young children should just love them; she must understand them, too; and that means going to a training school for nursery-school teachers."

But don't get the idea that any place that calls itself a nursery school is wonderful, for some of them are second-rate and just use the name because it's popular. And there are some day nurseries that have kept up with progress and are running excellent nursery schools with trained teachers under the old label. When you are thinking of placing your child in a nursery or nursery school, you want to know, What is the attitude of the teachers toward the children? Almost as important is the question, Have the teachers had real training? Next, How many children to a teacher? (It's hard to do a good job with more than 8 to 10 children to a teacher.) Finally, Is there enough play and rest space, indoors and out, enough equipment, toys, blocks, paints, clay, etc.?

You should be able to find out about nursery schools in your neighborhood by consulting a family social agency.

535. At what age to start nursery school? Most nursery schools begin with 3-year-olds, and this is a good age to start if your child seems ready for it. Some parents have the idea that the only good the child derives from school are skills like cutting out pictures and counting. I have heard mothers say, "I think I'll wait to put him in nursery school till he is 4 years old when he can get more out of it." This is a mistake. Skills are a very small part of what a good nursery school can give. Learning how to enjoy other children's company, to cooperate, to think up projects and work them out, and having the freedom to romp and dance and sing, are much more important. A child needs these experiences at 3 just as much as he needs them at 4. The longer they are postponed, the harder it is to pick them up easily.

A few nursery schools start with 2-year-olds. This may work very well **if** the child is fairly independent and outgoing (many are still quite dependent up to 2½ or 3), **if** the class is small (not more than 8), and **if** the teacher is so warm and understanding that she quickly makes children feel secure.

But lots of children are really too young to go to school regularly at

2. They are still dependent on their mothers, timid with other children and grownups. I don't mean that such children should be kept tied to their mothers' apron strings forever. They need every opportunity to be around where other children play so that they can become accustomed to them, interested in them, and wean themselves from their dependence. But this takes a little time. If you are in doubt about your child's readiness for nursery school, talk it over with a good nursery-school teacher.

There are a few children who are considered unready for steady schooling because they have been unusually sickly or because they easily become exhausted with a group. We have to admit that a child is apt to have more colds staying indoors with a group of children than if he just played outdoors with one or two regular friends. This is no reason for keeping a robust child out of nursery school, because he can stand a few more colds without any serious harm. All the other benefits from nursery school more than offset the disadvantage of the colds. It's a different proposition with the frail child whose colds are always severe. As for fatigue, a certain number of children are overstimulated and overtired at the beginning of nursery school in the fall. But in a few weeks **most** of them become adjusted to it and take it in their stride. The child who doesn't get used to it should try a shorter schedule.

536. The first days at school. The 4-year-old who is outgoing takes to nursery school like a duck to water. He doesn't need any gentle introduction. It may be quite different with a sensitive 3-year-old who still feels closely attached to his mother. If she leaves him at school the first day, he may not make a fuss right away, but after a while he may miss her. When he finds she isn't there, he may become frightened. The next day he may not want to leave home. With a dependent child like this, it's better to introduce him to school gradually. For several days his mother might stay near by while he plays, and then take him home again after a time. Each day the mother and child stay for a longer period. Meanwhile, he is building up attachments to the teacher and other children that will give him a sense of security when his mother no longer stays. Sometimes a child seems to be quite happy for several days, even after his mother has left him there. Then he gets hurt and suddenly wants her. In that case, the teacher can help the mother decide if she should come back for a number of days. When a mother is staying around the school, she ought to remain in the background. The idea is to let the child develop his **own** desire to enter the group, so that he forgets his need for his mother.

Sometimes the mother's anxiety is greater than the child's. If she says good-by three times over, with a worried expression, it gives him the idea, "She looks as if something awful might happen if I stay here without her. I'd better not let her go." It's natural for a tender-hearted mother to worry about how her small child will feel when she leaves him for the first time. Let the nursery-school teacher advise you. She's had a lot of experience.

When a child becomes reluctant or fearful about returning to a good school with understanding teachers, I think it is usually better for the parents to act quite confident and firm and explain that everybody goes to school every day. In the long run, it's better for the child to outgrow his dependence than to give in to it. When the child is having great difficulty separating from his mother at school, it often works better to have the father take him for a few weeks. If the child's terror is extreme, the situation should be discussed with a psychiatrist or child-guidance clinic. The connection between overprotectiveness and fears is discussed in Section 497.

537. Reactions at home. Some children make hard work of nursery school in the early days and weeks. The large group, the new friends, the new things to do, get them keyed up and worn out. If your child is too tired at first, it doesn't mean that he can't adjust to school, but only that you have to compromise for a while until he is used to it. Discuss with his teacher whether it would be wise to cut down his school time temporarily. In one case, coming to school in the middle of the morning is the best answer. Taking the easily tired child home before the end of the school day works less well because he hates to leave in the middle of the fun. The problem of fatigue in the early weeks is further complicated in the all-day school by the fact that a certain number of children are too stimulated or nervous to go to sleep at naptime at first. Keeping the child at home 1 or 2 days a week may be the answer to this temporary problem, too. Some small children starting nursery school preserve their self-control in school in spite of fatigue, but let loose on the family when they come home. This calls for extra patience and a discussion with the teacher.

A well-trained nursery-school teacher ought to be, and usually is, a very understanding person. A mother shouldn't hesitate to talk over the child's problems with her, whether or not they are connected with school. A teacher gets a different slant. She has probably faced the same problems before in other cases.

538. How to get nursery schools. You may say, "I believe in the importance of my child's going to nursery school, but there is none in my community." Nursery schools aren't easy to start. Well-trained teachers, plenty of equipment, indoor and outdoor space, are all necessary and all cost money. Good schools are never cheap, because a teacher can satisfactorily take care of only a small number of children. They have most commonly been formed on a private basis, with the parents paying the full expense; or by churches, which provide the space; or by women's colleges, for the training of students in child care. In many cities, groups of parents have formed cooperative nursery schools. They engage a trained head teacher and take turns in acting as assistant teachers under her supervision. In the long run, a sufficient number of nursery schools will be created, as a part of the public-school system, only if the citizens of the community convince the local government and school authorities that they want them, and vote for candidates for office who pledge themselves to work for them.

From Six to Eleven

FITTING INTO THE OUTSIDE WORLD

539. There are lots of changes after six. The child becomes more independent of his parents, even impatient with them. He's more concerned with what the other kids say and do. He develops a stronger sense of responsibility about matters that **he** thinks are important. His conscience may become so stern that it nags him about senseless things like stepping over cracks. He is interested in impersonal subjects like arithmetic and engines. In short, he's beginning the job of emancipating himself from his family and taking his place as a responsible citizen of the outside world.

For contrast, think what the younger child between 3 and 5 is like. He's openly devoted to his parents. He takes their word for it that certain things are right, wants to eat with the same table manners they have, likes to be dressed in clothes they choose. He uses their words even though he doesn't understand all of them.

Millions of years ago man's ancestors grew to adulthood in a few years, the way animals do. They developed full-sized bodies, but in their feelings they were probably a lot like our 5-year-olds whose lives are largely made up of copying their elders. It was only much later that men developed the ability to become more independent of their parents, learned to live by cooperation, rules, self-control, thinking things out.

It takes years for each individual to learn how to get along in this compli-cated, grown-up way. Probably that's the reason human beings are held up so long in their physical growth. The infant increases rapidly in size like an animal, and so does the older child in the puberty period. But in between he slows down more and more, particularly in the 2 years just before puberty development begins. It's as if his nature were saying, "Whoa! Before you can be trusted with a powerful body and full-grown instincts, you must first learn to think for yourself, control your wishes and instincts for the sake of others, learn how to get along with your fellows, understand the laws of conduct in the world outside your fam-ily, study the skills by which people live."

540. Independence of parents. The child after 6 goes on loving his parents deeply underneath, but he usually doesn't show it so much on the surface. He's apt not to enjoy being kissed, at least in public. He's cooler toward other adults, too, unless he's sure they're swell people. He no longer wants to be loved as a possession or as an appealing child. He's gaining a sense of dignity as an individual person, and he'd like to be treated as such.

From his need to be less dependent on his parents, he turns more to trusted adults outside his family for ideas and knowledge. If he mistak-enly gets the idea from his admired science teacher that red blood cells are larger than white blood cells, there's nothing his father can say that will change his mind.

The ideas of right and wrong that his parents taught him have not been forgotten. In fact, they have sunk in so deep that he now thinks of them as his ideas. He is impatient when his parents keep reminding him what he ought to do, because he knows already and wants to be con-sidered responsible.

541. Bad manners. The child drops the extra-grown-up words out of his vocabulary and picks up a little tough talk. He wants the style of clothes and haircut that the other kids have. He may leave his tie off and shoe laces untied with the same determination with which people wear party buttons during a political campaign. He may lose some of his table manners, come to meals with dirty hands, slump over his dish, and stuff more in his mouth. Perhaps he kicks the leg of the table absent-mindedly. He always throws his coat on the floor. He slams doors or leaves them open. Without realizing it, he is really accomplishing three things at once. He's shifting to his own age for his models of behavior. He's de-claring his right to be more independent of his parents. He's keeping square with his own conscience, because he's not doing anything that's morally wrong.

These "bad manners" and "bad habits" are apt to make good parents unhappy. They imagine that the child is forgetting all that they taught him so carefully. Actually, these changes are proof that he has learned for keeps what good behavior is—otherwise he wouldn't bother to rebel against it. It will come to the surface again when he feels he has established his independence. Meanwhile, understanding parents can be reassured that their child is growing up normally.

I don't mean that every child is a hellion during this age period. One who gets along happily with easygoing parents may show no open rebelliousness at all. Most girls show less than boys. But if you look carefully, you will see signs of a change of attitude.

What do you **do?** After all, the child must take a bath once in a while, get neatened up on Sunday. You may be able to overlook some of his

Manners may seem to be lost.

minor irritating ways, but you should stick to your guns in matters that are important to you. When you have to ask him to wash his hands, try to be matter-of-fact. It's the nagging tone, the bossiness, that he finds irritating and that spurs him on unconsciously to further balkiness.

542. Gangs and clubs. This is the age for the blossoming of clubs and gangs. A number of kids who are already friends decide to form a secret club. They work like beavers making membership buttons, fixing up a meeting place (preferably hidden), drawing up a list of rules. They may never figure out what the secret is. But the secrecy idea probably represents the need to prove they can govern themselves, unmolested by grownups, unhampered by other more dependent children.

It seems to help the child, when he's trying to be grown-up, to get together with others who feel the same way. Then the group tries to bring outsiders into line by making them feel left out or by picking on them. It sounds conceited and cruel to grownups, but that's because we are accustomed to using more refined methods of disapproving of each other. The children are only feeling the instinct to get community life organized. This is one of the forces that make our civilization click.

543. Helping a child to be sociable and popular. These are some of the early steps in bringing up a child to be sociable and popular: not fussing over him in his first years; letting him be around other children his size from the age of a year; allowing him freedom to develop independence; the fewest changes possible in where the family lives and where he goes to school; letting him, as far as possible, dress like, talk like, play like, have the same allowance and other privileges as the other average children in the neighborhood, even if you don't approve of the way they are brought up. (Of course, I don't mean letting him take after the town's worst scoundrel.)

How happily a person gets along as an adult in his job, in his family and social life, depends a great deal on how he got along with other children when he was young. If parents give a child high standards and high ideals at home, these form part of his character and show up in the long run, even though he goes through a period of bad English and rough manners in the middle period of childhood. But if parents are unhappy about the neighborhood they live in and the companions their child has, give him a feeling that he is different from the others, discourage him from making friends, the child may grow up unable to mix with any group or to make a happy life. Then his high standards won't be of any use to the world or to himself.

If a child is having trouble making friends, it helps most if he can be in a school and in a class where the program is flexible. Then the teacher can arrange things so that he has chances to use his abilities to contribute to class projects (Section 557). This is how the other children learn to appreciate his good qualities and to like him. A good teacher who is respected by the class can also raise a child's popularity in the group by showing that she appreciates him. It even helps to put him in a seat next to a very popular child, or to let him be partners with him in marching, going on errands around the school, etc.

There are things that the parents can do at home, too. Be friendly and hospitable when your child brings others home to play. Encourage him to invite them to meals and then serve the dishes that they consider "super." When you plan weekend trips, picnics, excursions, movies and other shows, invite another child with whom your child wants to be friends (not necessarily the one you would like him to be friendly with). Children, like adults, have a mercenary side, and they are more apt to see the good points in a child who provides treats for them. Naturally, you don't want your child to have only "bought" popularity; that kind won't last, anyway. But what you are after is to prime the pump, to give him a chance to break into a group that may be shutting him out because of the natural clannishness of this age. Then, if he has appealing qualities, he can take over from that start and build real friendships of his own.

SELF-CONTROL

544. He becomes strict about some things. Think of the games a child enjoys at this age. He's no longer so interested in make-believe without any plan. He wants games that have rules and require skill. In hopscotch, jacks, and mumblety-peg, you have to do things in a certain order, which becomes harder as you progress. If you miss, you must penalize yourself, go back to the beginning, and start over again. It's the very strictness that appeals. This is the age for starting collections, whether it's stamps or cards or stones. The pleasure of collecting is in achieving orderliness and completeness.

At this age the child has the desire **at times** to put his belongings in order. Suddenly he neatens his desk, puts labels on the drawers, or arranges his piles of comic books. He doesn't keep his things neat for long. But you can see that the urge must be strong just to get him started.

545. Compulsions. The tendency toward strictness becomes so strong in many children around 8, 9, and 10 that they develop nervous habits. You probably remember them from your own childhood. The commonest is stepping over cracks in the sidewalk. There's no sense to it, you just have a superstitious feeling that you ought to. It's what a psychiatrist calls a compulsion. Other examples are touching every third picket in a fence, making numbers come out even in some way, saying certain words before going through a door. If you think you have made a mistake, you must go way back to where you were absolutely sure that you were right, and start over again.

The hidden meaning of a compulsion pops out in the thoughtless childhood saying, "Step on a crack, break your grandmother's back." Everyone has hostile feelings at times toward the people who are close to him, but his conscience would be shocked at the idea of really harming them and warns him to keep such thoughts out of his mind. And if a person's conscience becomes **excessively** stern, it keeps nagging him

"Step on a crack, break your grandmother's back."

about such "bad" thoughts even after he has succeeded in hiding them away in his subconscious mind. He still feels guilty, though he doesn't know what for. It eases his conscience to be extra careful and proper about such a senseless thing as how to navigate a crack in the sidewalk.

The reason a child is apt to show compulsions around the age of 9 is not that his thoughts are more wicked than previously, but that his conscience is just naturally becoming stricter at this stage of development. He is now worrying, perhaps, about his suppressed desire to hurt his brother or father or grandmother when they irritate him. We know that this is an age when the child is also trying to suppress thoughts about sex, and these sometimes play a part in compulsions, too.

Mild compulsions are so common around the ages of 8, 9, and 10 years that it's a question whether they should be considered normal or a sign of nervousness. I wouldn't worry too much about a mild compulsion, like stepping over cracks, in a child around 9 years who is happy, outgoing, doing well in school. On the other hand, I'd call on a psychiatrist for help (Section 570) if a child has compulsions that occupy a lot of his time (for instance, excessive hand-washing, precautions against germs) or if he is tense, worried, unsociable.

546. Tics. Tics are nervous habits such as eye-blinking, shoulder-shrugging, facial grimacing, neck-twisting, throat-clearing, sniffing, dry coughing. Like compulsions, tics occur most commonly around the age of 9, but they can come at any age after 2. The motion is usually quick, and it is repeated regularly and always in the same form. It is more frequent when the child is under tension. A tic may last off and on for a number of weeks or months and go away for good, or a new one may take its place. Blinking, sniffing, throat-clearing, dry coughing, often start with a cold but continue after the cold is gone. Shoulder-shrugging may begin when a child has a new loose-fitting garment that feels as if it were falling off. A child may copy a tic from another child, but he wouldn't have picked it up if there hadn't been a tenseness already waiting in him.

Tics are more common in tense children, with fairly strict parents. There may be too much pressure at home. Sometimes the mother or father is going at the child too hard, directing him, correcting him, whenever he is in sight. Or the parents may be showing constant disapproval in a quieter way, or setting standards that are too high, or providing too many activities such as dancing, music, and athletic lessons. If the child were bold enough to fight back, he would probably be less tightened up inside. But being, in most cases, too well brought up for that, he bottles up his irritation, and it keeps backfiring in the tic.

The child should not be scolded or corrected on account of his tics. They are practically out of his control. The whole effort should go into making his home life relaxed and agreeable, with the least possible nagging, and making his school and social life satisfying. Tics must be distinguished from chorea and general restlessness (Section 678).

COMICS, RADIO, TELEVISION, AND MOVIES

547. The comics are serious business. Conscientious parents often dread the comic strips and comic books, thinking that they ruin their children's taste for good reading, fill their minds with morbid ideas, keep them indoors, interfere with homework, and waste good money. All these accusations have a bit of truth in them. But when children show a universal craving for something, whether it's comics or candy or jazz, we've got to assume that it has a positive, constructive value for them. It may be wise to try to give them what they want in a better form, but it does no good for us to cluck like nervous hens.

Children of all ages are filled with strivings to do great deeds of the kind they imagine adults performing. In their early years they are satisfied by copying the grown-up occupations that they see around them—driving trains, delivering groceries, playing doctor and nurse.

As they get into the age period beyond 6, their imaginary life is partly split off from their real life. They now spend long hours of the day applying themselves to schoolwork and the task of getting along with their fellows. When they have time to dream, their growing independence urges them to imagine deeds of their own that have nothing to do with their parents' and neighbors' humdrum pursuits. Feeling now that they know in themselves what is right and wrong, they delight in stories in which good is pitted against evil and always wins in the end. And since this is the stage when they feel from within the necessity to bottle up and control their aggressive impulses in daily life, there is all the more reason to dream of bold adventures and violent battles. You can see why the comics are meat and drink at this age. It's a mistake to think that these wild stories are put over on children. The people who write and draw them are only turning out what they have found that children want most. To educated adults they seem crude, lacking in any literary quality or fine idealism. This only shows that adults are at a different stage of development than 10-year-olds, which they should be. The child first must go through a period of blood-and-thunder adventure, where superhuman might **and** right always win at the last minute, before he can graduate to more sophisticated reading. There's no more reason to think it will ruin his taste than there is to fear that letting him creep on hands and knees in infancy will keep him from ever walking in the more elegant upright position.

548. Limits on comics. Certainly you have the right and the duty to forbid comics that are morally objectionable. And you don't want your child to be reading comics so constantly that he never goes outdoors and never has time to see his friends. You wouldn't want him to be that wrapped up in good literature, either. You may have to set limits: only so many comic books a week or only for a certain number of hours each day. Even a happy child who gets along well may have spells of being lost in the comics, but they don't last forever. If, on the other hand, a child lives entirely in his imagination, in stories, radio, and movies, he needs help, both from school and from parents, in finding the joy of friendships and games. (See Section 543.)

549. Do comics, TV, and movies contribute to delinquency? This is a frequent question of parents, and there is some difference of opinion among the professional people who ought to know the answer. A great majority of child psychiatrists believe that comics, TV, and movies do not play any important part in delinquency, and I agree with them. They believe that serious delinquency is a manifestation of a fundamental defect in a child's character. This may have been caused by growing up with parents who had delinquent tendencies themselves or who had no real love for the child. The child ends up with hostile feelings that are too strong and a conscience that is too weak. If a judge asks him where he got the idea for his crime, he may answer, "From a comic book" or "From a program." But the impulse to carry it out must have come from deep inside and from way back in his childhood.

However, this doesn't mean that a parent should be indifferent to the moral tone of the books and the shows that his child sees. Brutality and sexuality that are convincingly portrayed are not good for children of any age, and a parent has every right to forbid them. On the other hand, I wouldn't worry about a stable child of 6 or more watching the usual Western program on TV in which the good guys outride, outshoot, and outsmart the bad guys and in which the aggressiveness and killings are matter-of-fact in tone.

550. Radio and television programs. Children's fascination with radio and television brings up several problems for parents.

The first difficulty is with the child who is so scared by the tales of violence that he can't go to sleep at night or has nightmares. This is most apt to happen in the years before 6, and I don't think such programs are suitable in those early years. The danger is not that the child will be turned into a thug but that he will be upset. The sensitive child with a morbid imagination may be bothered until a much older age. If a child, whatever his age, is regularly upset in this way, his parents had better forbid the frightening programs, explaining their position reasonably to him.

Another problem is with the child who is glued to the set from the minute he comes in, in the afternoon, until he is forced to go to bed at night. He doesn't want to take time out for supper or for his homework or even to say hello to his family. It's better for the parents and child to come to a reasonable but definite understanding about which hours are for outdoors, for homework, for meals, and for programs, and then for everyone to stick to the bargain. Otherwise the parents are apt to be nagging him about his duties whenever they catch him at the set, and he is turning it on whenever he thinks they aren't paying attention. Some children and adults can work just as well with the radio on (they say better), though this is less likely with talking programs than with musical programs. There is no objection to this if the child is keeping up with his homework.

In general, if a child is taking care of his homework, staying outside with his friends in the afternoon, coming to supper, going to bed when it's time, and not being frightened, I would be inclined to let him spend as much of his evening with television or radio as he chooses. I wouldn't nag him about it or twit him about it. You won't take away his appetite for it by these methods—quite the reverse. Remember that these stories of amazing adventures, which sound like trash to you, may be deeply moving, even character-building experiences for him. Remember also that it's part of his social life to discuss them with his friends, just the way grownups discuss books and plays and the news. On the other hand, I wouldn't hesitate to forbid him to watch programs I considered truly objectionable.

If the rest of the family is driven mad by having to watch or listen to a child's programs and if they can afford the expense, it's worth while to get him a set for his room.

551. The movies. Adventure stories in the movies have the same appeal as the comics and television and radio stories. I think it is reasonable, if it is the custom in the neighborhood, to let a child of 7 see one suitable afternoon show over the week-end with friends. The child who lives out of town might be allowed to see a suitable early-evening show instead, if his only chance to go is with his parents. It is unwholesome to take younger children at night. I wouldn't let a child go to the movies more than once a week, because a theater is a poor place in which to spend hours, from the point of view of health.

Movies are a risky business under the age of 7. You hear of a program, let's say an animated cartoon, that sounds like perfect entertainment for a small child. But when you get there, you find, three out of four times, that there is some episode in the story that scares the wits out of little children. You have to remember that a child of 4 and 5 doesn't distinguish clearly between make-believe and real life. A witch on the screen is just as alive and terrifying to him as a flesh-and-blood burglar would be to you. The only safe rule that I know is not to take a child under 7 to a movie unless you, or someone else who knows small children well, has seen it and is **positive** that it contains nothing upsetting. Don't even take an older child to the movies if he gets frightened easily.

STEALING

552. Taking things in early childhood. Small children of 1, 2 and 3 take things that don't belong to them, but it isn't really stealing. They don't have any clear sense of what belongs to them and what doesn't. They just take things because they want them very much. It's better not to make a small child feel wicked. The mother needs only to remind him that the toy is Peter's, that Peter will want to play with it soon, and that he himself has lots of good toys at home.

553. What stealing means in the child who knows better. Stealing that means more occasionally crops up in the period between 6 and adolescence. When a child at this age takes something, he knows he is doing wrong. He is more apt to steal secretly, to hide what he has stolen, and to deny that he has done it.

When a parent or a teacher finds that a child has stolen something, she is pretty upset. Her impulse is to jump on him hard and fill him with a sense of shame. This is natural enough, since we have all been taught that stealing is a serious crime. It scares us to see it coming out in our child.

It is essential that a child know clearly that his parents disapprove of any stealing and insist on immediate restitution. On the other hand, it isn't wise to scare the daylights out of him or act as if his parents will never love him again.

Let's take first the child around 7 who has been carefully brought up by conscientious parents, who has a reasonable number of toys and other possessions, and who gets an allowance. If he steals something, it's apt to be small amounts of money from his mother or from classmates, or his teacher's pen, or a pack of trading cards from another child's locker. Often there's no sense to the stealing because he may own these things, anyway. We can see that he's mixed up in his feelings. He seems to have a blind craving for something, and tries to satisfy it by taking an object he doesn't really need. What does he really want?

In most cases, the child is unhappy and lonesome to some degree. He doesn't have a sufficiently warm relationship with his parents, or he doesn't feel completely successful in making friends with children his own age. (He may feel this way even though he is actually quite popular.) I think the reason that stealing occurs more often around 7 is that the child at this age may be feeling particularly distant from his parents. Then, if he hasn't the knack of making equally warm and satisfying friendships, he gets into no-man's land and feels isolated. This explains why some children who steal money use it all to try to buy friendship. One passes out dimes and nickels to his classmates. Another uses it to buy candy for the class. It's not just that the child is drawing away a little from the parents. The parents are apt to be more disapproving of him at this less appealing age.

The early part of adolescence is another period when some children become more lonely, because of increased self-consciousness, sensitiveness, and desire for independence.

A craving for more affection probably plays some part in stealing at all ages, but there are usually other individual factors, too, such as fears, jealousies, resentments. A girl who is deeply envious of her brother may repeatedly steal objects that are linked in her unconscious mind with boys.

554. What to do for the child who steals. If you are pretty sure that your child (or pupil) has stolen something, tell him so, be firm about knowing where he got it, insist on restitution. In other words, don't make it easy for him to lie. (If a parent accepts lies too easily, it's as if he were condoning the theft.) The child should take the object back to the child or store from which he took it. If it's a store, it may be tactful for the parent to go along to explain to the salesman that the child took it without paying and wants to return it. A teacher can return an article to its owner to spare the child from public shame. In other words, it's not necessary to humiliate the child who steals, only to make it crystal-clear that it can't be permitted.

It is time to think over whether the child needs more affection and approval at home, and help in making closer friendships outside (see Section 543). This is the time to give him, if possible, an allowance of about the same size as that of the other children he knows. It helps him to establish himself as "one of the boys." The parents should get help from a child-guidance clinic or a children's psychiatrist if the stealing persists or if the child seems maladjusted in other ways (Section 570).

The next type of stealing is entirely different. There are plenty of neighborhoods where the kids think of swiping things as the daring and manly thing to do. It's not proper, but it's not vicious and it's not a sign of maladjustment. The boy of conscientious parents who lives in such a neighborhood may need an understanding talk, but should not be treated as a criminal because he joined in one of these adventures. He was only obeying a normal instinct to make his place in the group. The cure lies in better economic conditions, better schools, better recreational facilities.

Finally, there is the stealing of the aggressive child or adult who has little conscience or sense of responsibility. A person gets this way only through a childhood quite lacking in love and security. His only hope is in good psychiatric treatment and being able to live with kind, affectionate people.

Schools

WHAT A SCHOOL IS FOR

555. The main lesson in school is how to get along in the world. Different subjects are merely means to this end. In the olden days, it used to be thought that all a school had to do was make children learn to read, write, figure, and memorize a certain number of facts about the world. I heard a great teacher tell how, in his own school days, he had to memorize a definition of a preposition that went something like this: "A preposition is a word, generally with some meaning of position, direction, time, or other abstract relation, used to connect a noun or pronoun, in an adjectival or adverbial sense, with some other word." Of course, he didn't learn anything when he memorized that. You learn only when things **mean** something to you. One job of a school is to make subjects so interesting and real that the children want to learn and remember.

You can go only so far with books and talk. You learn better from actually living the things you are studying. Children pick up more arithmetic in a week from running a school store, making change, and keeping the books than they learn in a month out of a book of cold figures.

There's no use knowing a lot if you can't be happy, can't get along with people, can't hold the kind of job you want. The good teacher tries to understand each child so that she can help him overcome his weak points and develop into a well-rounded person. The child who lacks self-confidence needs chances to succeed. The trouble-making show-off has to learn how to gain the recognition he craves through doing good work. The child who doesn't know how to make friends needs help in becoming sociable and appealing. The child who seems to be lazy has to have his enthusiasms discovered.

A school can go only so far with a cut-and-dried program in which everyone in the class reads from page 17 to page 23 in the reader at the same time and then does the examples on page 128 of the arithmetic book. It works well enough for the average child who is adjusted, any-way. But it's too dull for the bright pupils, too speedy for the slow ones. It gives the boy who hates books a chance to stick paper clips in the pigtails of the girl in front. It does nothing to help the girl who is lonely or the boy who needs to learn cooperation.

556. How schoolwork is made real and interesting. If you start with a topic that is real and interesting, you can use it to teach all manner of subjects. Take the case of a third-grade class in which the work of the year revolves around Indians. The more the children find out about In-dians, the more they want to know. The reader is a story of the Indians, and they really want to know what it says. For arithmetic they study how the Indians counted and what they used for money. Then arithmetic isn't a separate subject at all but a useful part of life. Geography isn't spots on a map; it's where the Indians lived and traveled, and how life on the plains is different from forest life. In science study the children make dyes from berries and dye cloth, or grow corn. They can make bows and arrows and Indian costumes.

People are sometimes uneasy about schoolwork's being too interest-ing, feeling that a child needs to learn, most of all, how to do what's un-pleasant and difficult. But if you stop to think of the people you know who are unusually successful, you'll see that in most cases they are the ones who love their work. In any job there's plenty of drudgery, but you do the drudgery because you see its connection with the fascinating side of the work. Darwin was a wretched student in all his subjects in school. But in later life he became interested in natural history, performed one of the most painstaking jobs of research that the world has ever known, and worked out the theory of evolution. A boy in high school may see no sense in geometry, hate it, and do badly in it. But if he is in the Air Force and sees what geometry is for, realizes that it may save the lives of the whole crew, he works at it like a demon. The teachers in a good school know well that every child needs to develop self-discipline to be a useful adult. But they have learned that you can't snap discipline onto him from the outside, like handcuffs; it's something that he has to de-velop inside, like a backbone, by first understanding the purpose of his work and feeling a sense of responsibility to others in how he performs it.

557. How a school helps a difficult child. A flexible, interesting pro-gram does more than just make schoolwork appealing. It can be ad-justed for the individual pupil. Take the case of a boy who had spent his first two years in a school where teaching was done by separate subjects. He was a boy who had great difficulty in learning to read and write. He had fallen behind the rest of the class. Inside, he felt ashamed about being a failure. Outwardly he wouldn't admit anything except that he hated school. He had never gotten along too easily with other kids, anyway, even before his school troubles began. Feeling that he was a dumbbell in the eyes of the others made matters worse. He had a chip on his shoulder. Once in a while he would show off to the class in a smarty way. His teacher used to think that he was just trying to be bad. Of course, he was really attempting, in this unfortunate way, to gain some kind of attention from the group. It was a healthy impulse to keep himself from being shut out.

He transferred to a school that was interested in helping him not only to read and write but to find his place in the group. The teacher learned in a conference with his mother that he used tools well and loved to paint and draw. She saw ways to use his strong points in the class. The children were all painting together a large picture of Indian life to hang on the wall. They were also working cooperatively on a model of an Indian village. The teacher arranged for the boy to have a part in both these jobs. Here were things he could do well without nervousness. As the days went by, he became more and more fascinated with Indians. In order to paint his part of the picture well, in order to make his part of the model correctly, he needed to find out more from the books about Indians. He **wanted** to learn to read. He tried harder. His new classmates didn't think of him as a dope because he couldn't read. They thought more about what a help he was on the painting and the model. They occasionally commented on how good his work was and asked him to help them on their parts. He began to warm up. After all, he had been aching for recognition and friendliness for a long while. As he felt more accepted, he became more friendly and outgoing.

558. Linking school with the world. A school wants its pupils to learn at firsthand about the outside world, about the jobs of the local farmers and businessmen and workers, so that they will see the connection between their schoolwork and real life. It arranges trips to near-by industries, asks people from the outside to come in and talk, encourages classroom discussion. A class that is studying food may have an opportunity, for example, to observe some of the steps in the collecting, pasteurizing, bottling, and delivery of milk, or in the transportation and marketing of vegetables.

High-school and college students have further opportunities to learn about the world by attending summer work camps. A group of students and teachers may work in a factory or in a farming area, discuss together, and come to understand better, the problems of various occupations and industries and how they are solved.

559. Democracy builds discipline. Another thing that a good school wants to teach is democracy, not just as a patriotic motto but as a way of living and getting things done. A good teacher knows that she can't teach democracy out of a book if she's acting like a dictator in person. She encourages her pupils to help decide how they are going to tackle certain projects and the difficulties they later run into, lets them help figure out among themselves which one is to do this part of the job and which one that. That's how they learn to appreciate each other. That's how they learn to get things done, not just in school but in the outside world, too.

Actual experiments have shown that children with a teacher who tells them what to do at every step of the way do a good job while she is in the room, but when she goes out a lot of them stop working, start fooling. They figure that lessons are the teacher's responsibility, not theirs, and that now they have a chance to be themselves. But these experiments showed that children who have helped choose and plan their own work, and have cooperated with each other in carrying it out, accomplish almost as much when the teacher is out of the room as in. Why? They know the purpose of the job they are on and the steps ahead in accomplishing it. They feel that it is their job, not the teacher's. Each one wants to do his share because he is proud to be a respected member of the group and feels a sense of responsibility to the others.

This is the very highest kind of discipline. This training, this spirit, is what makes the best citizens, the most valuable workers, and even the finest soldiers.

560. Cooperating with other child specialists. Even the best of teachers can't solve all the problems of their pupils alone. They need the cooperation of the parents through parent-teacher-association meetings and individual conferences. Then parent and teacher will understand what the other is doing, share what they know about the child. The teacher should even be able to get in touch with the child's scoutmaster, minister, doctor, and vice versa. Each can do a better job by working with the other. It's particularly important in the case of a child with a chronic ailment that the teacher know just what it is, how it's being treated, what she can do or watch for in school. It's just as important for the doctor to know how the disease is affecting the child in school hours, how the school can help, and how he can prescribe treatment so as not to work against what the school is trying to accomplish with the child.

There are children who have problems that the regular teacher and the parents, no matter how understanding, can solve better with the help of specialists in child guidance. Few schools as yet have a psychiatrist.

Some, though, have guidance counselors, psychologists, or visiting teachers, trained to help children, parents, and classroom teachers in understanding and overcoming a child's school difficulties. Where there is no guidance counselor or psychologist, or when the teacher finds that the problem is deep-rooted, it is wise to turn to a private children's psychiatrist or to a child-guidance clinic, if such is available.

561. How to work for good schools. Parents sometimes say, "It's all very well to talk about an ideal school that makes the work interesting and finds a way to bring out the best in every child. But the school that my child goes to is pretty cut-and-dried, and there's nothing I can do about it." That isn't true. Every town and city has the kind of schools its citizens want. If they know what good schools are and insist on having them, they can get them. That's how democracy works.

Parents can join their local parent-teacher association, go to meetings regularly, show the teachers and principals and superintendents that they are interested and will back them up when they are using sound methods. They can also vote for local officials who will work for constant improvement in the schools. No school system is ever perfect, and even the best of schools will go downhill unless the citizens stay interested.

There are lots of people who don't realize how much fine schools can accomplish in developing useful, happy citizens. They object to increasing the school budget for smaller classes, better-paid teachers, carpentry shops, laboratories, and afternoon recreation programs. Not understanding the purpose or value of these proposals, they naturally think of them as "unnecessary frills" just to amuse children or make jobs for more teachers. Even from a strictly cash point of view, that's penny-wise and dollar-foolish. Money spent **wisely** for better child care pays back the community a hundredfold. First-rate schools that succeed in making each child feels he really **belongs,** as a useful and respected member of the group, reduce drastically the number of individuals who grow up irresponsible or criminal. The value of such schools shows even more in all the other children (who would never be criminals, anyway), who take their places in the community as better workers at their jobs, more cooperative citizens, happier individuals in their own lives. How better can a community spend its money?

TROUBLE WITH LESSONS

562. There are many causes for failure in schoolwork. Individual problems are more common when a school is using rigid teaching methods, when the attitude toward the children is regimenting and harsh, when the classes are too large for individual attention.

In children themselves there are various reasons for poor adjustment. On the physical side, there are eye defects, deafness, occasionally fatigue or chronic illness. On the psychological side, there is the child unable to read because of a special difficulty in recognizing words, the child who is too nervous and worried about other things, the one who can't get along with teacher or pupils. There is the child who is too smart and the one who can't do the work because his intelligence isn't up to it. (The slow child is discussed in Section 798.)

Don't scold or punish the child who is having difficulties. Try to find out where the trouble lies. Consult with the principal or teacher. Get the help of the school guidance counselor if there is one. Have the child tested by the school psychologist if that seems the next step. Consult a child-guidance clinic or a private psychiatrist or psychologist if no specialists are available at the school (Section 570). Have him examined physically, including his vision and hearing.

563. The extra-bright child. In a class in which everyone does exactly the same lessons, the child who is smarter than others of his age may be bored because the work is too easy. The only solution seems to be to skip a grade. This may not work out too badly if the child is large for his age and advanced socially. But if not, he's apt to become socially isolated and lost, especially when his classmates get to the adolescent years. He may be too small to compete in games or be popular at dances. He's apt to have younger interests than the other members of his class, which keep him from mixing easily. What good is it for him to enter high school or college at a very young age if he is going to turn into a lonely person?

It is much better in most cases for the bright child to stay in a class that is close to him in age, provided the school has a flexible program that can be "enriched" for the pupils who are more advanced. He, for instance, is the one to read the more difficult reference books in the library. When a bright child is working for marks and to please the teacher, the other kids are quick to call him "Smarty" and "Teacher's Pet." But if he is working on group projects, they appreciate him all the more because of the extra help he can provide.

Even if you think your child is extra-smart, never try to get him into a more advanced grade than the school advises. Usually a teacher knows best about placement. It's cruel for a child to be placed beyond his capacities. In the end he does poorly or is left back again later.

That brings up the question of teaching a bright child to read and figure at home before he starts first grade. A parent may say that the child is asking questions about letters and numbers and practically insisting on being taught. This is true to a degree with some children, and there is no harm in casually answering their questions.

But there is another side to it in many such cases. It often turns out that the parents themselves are more ambitious for their child than they perhaps realize, more eager to have him excel. When he is playing childish games or rough-housing, they pay only a normal amount of attention. But when he shows an interest in reading at an early age, their eyes light up and they help him enthusiastically. The child senses their delight and responds with greater interest. He may be weaned away from the natural occupations of his age and turned into something of a scholar before his time.

Parents wouldn't be good parents if they weren't delighted with their children's fine qualities. But it's necessary to distinguish between which are the children's interests and which are the parents' eager hopes. If parents who are naturally ambitious can honestly admit this to themselves and be on guard against using their ambition to run their children's lives, the children will grow up to be happier, abler, and more of a credit to their parents. This applies not only to early reading and writing but to putting pressure on a child at any age, whether it's in schoolwork, music lessons, dancing lessons, athletics, or social life.

564. Poor schoolwork because of "nervousness." All kinds of worries and troubles and family frictions can interfere with a child's schoolwork. Here are some examples, though they don't cover all the possibilities by any means:

A 6-year-old girl who is burned up with jealousy of a younger brother may be tense, "distracted," unable to pay attention, and make sudden attacks on other children for no good reason.

A child may be worried about illness at home or a threatened separation of the parents or misunderstandings about sex. In the early grades especially, he may be afraid of a bully or a barking dog on the way to school, of the school janitor, of a severe-looking teacher, of asking permission to go to the toilet, of reciting before the class. These seem like small matters to an adult, but to a timid 6- or 7-year-old they may be terrifying enough to paralyze his thinking.

The child around 9 years old who is nagged and corrected excessively at home may become so restless and tense that he can't keep his mind on anything.

The "lazy" child who won't try to do his lessons usually isn't lazy at all. The young animal of all species is born to be curious and enthusiastic. If he loses that, it's because it's been trained out of him. Children **appear** to be lazy in school for a number of reasons. One is balky from having been pushed too much all his life. You'll find him eager enough about his own private hobbies. Sometimes a child is afraid to try in school (or anywhere) for fear of failing. This may be because his family has always been critical of his accomplishments or set too high standards.

Strange as it may seem, an occasional child may do poor schoolwork from being overconscientious. He keeps going over the lesson that he's already learned or the exercises that he's already finished for fear that something is incomplete or incorrect. He's always behind, fussing.

The child who has been severely deprived of love and security in his early years typically reaches school age as a tense, restless, irresponsible creature with little ability to get interested in schoolwork or to get along with teachers or pupils.

Whatever the cause of a child's difficulty in school, the problem should be attacked from two directions. Try to find the underlying cause, as suggested in Section 562. But whether or not you can discover what's bothering him inside, it should be possible for teacher and parents, by sharing their knowledge of a child, to use his interests and good qualities to draw him gradually into the group and the things they are working on.

565. Poor reading because of slow development of visual memory. To you and me the word *dog* looks entirely different from the word *god*. Most young children, when they are just beginning to read, think these words look much the same because each spells the other backward. They occasionally read *was* for *saw* and *on* for *no*. In writing they sometimes reverse letters, especially those like small *b* and small *p* which are confused with *d* and *q*. But as the months go by, they learn to perceive and remember more accurately and these mistakes become infrequent by the end of second grade.

But there are about 10% of children—most of them boys—who have much more than the average difficulty recognizing and remembering the appearance of words. They continue to reverse many words and letters for several years. It takes them a lot longer to learn to read reasonably well and some of them remain poor spellers for life, no matter how much they are drilled.

Such children quickly get the idea they are *dumb* and often come to hate school because they cannot keep up with the others. They need to be reassured by parents and teachers that this is a special memory problem (just the way some children can't carry a tune); that they are not stupid and not lazy; that they will learn to read and write and spell as soon as they are able.

Most of these children can be helped by extra practice in *phonics*, in which they *sound* the letters and the syllables of words, and point at them with their fingers at the same time. In this way, they can make up for some of their weakness in recognizing words. If the school can't provide extra help, the parents should consult the teacher or principal about whether it would be desirable to try tutoring outside of school hours, either with a tactful tutor or a very patient parent. It is also sensible to consider a check-up by a child psychiatrist or guidance clinic; especially if the child has other emotional problems, since these can play a large part in a reading disability.

566. Helping a child in his lessons. Sometimes a teacher advises that a child needs extra tutoring in a subject that he's falling behind in, or the parent has the idea himself. This is something to be careful about. If the school can recommend a good tutor that you can afford, go ahead. Too often a parent makes a poor tutor, not because he (or she) doesn't know enough, not because he doesn't try hard enough, but because he cares too much, is too upset when his child doesn't understand. If a child is already mixed up in lessons, a tense parent is the last straw. Another trouble is that the parent's method may be different from that being used in the class. If a child is already baffled by the subject in school, the chances are that he will be **more** baffled when it's presented in a different way at home.

I don't want to go so far as to say that a parent should **never** tutor a child because in an occasional case it works very well. I'd only advise a parent to talk it over thoroughly with the teacher first, and then quit right away if it isn't a success.

What should you do if your child asks for help with his homework? If he is puzzled once in a great while and turns to you for clarification, there's no harm in straightening him out. (Nothing pleases a parent more than to have a chance occasionally to prove to his child that he really knows something.) But if a child is asking you to do his work for him because he can't understand it, better consult the teacher. A good school prefers to help the child understand, and then let him rely on himself. If the teacher is too busy to straighten him out, you may have to lend a hand; but even then help him to understand his work, don't do it for him.

567. School phobia. Occasionally a child develops a sudden and unexplainable fear of going to school. This often happens after he has been absent for a few days because of an illness or accident, especially if the illness began or the accident happened at school. Typically, the child hasn't any idea of what it is he fears at school. Child-guidance studies of such cases show that often the real cause has little to do with school. The child has become more dependent on his mother because of his feelings of guilt over his unconscious antagonistic feelings toward her (Section 497). The illness at school and staying at home with her have brought this nearer the surface. If the child is freely allowed to stay home, his dread of returning to school usually gets stronger. It's increased by his fear that he is behind in his work and that the teacher and other children will criticize him for his absence. So it usually works best for the parents to be very firm about getting him back to school promptly and to refuse to be dissuaded by his physical complaints or to try to get the doctor to excuse him. (Of course, he needs to be checked by the doctor.) The child and parent should have child-guidance help if this can possibly be arranged. The child-guidance clinic usually considers such a case an emergency, knowing how time makes it worse (Section 570).

568. The child who can't eat breakfast before going to school. This problem comes up occasionally, especially with first- and second-graders, at the beginning of school in the fall. It's the conscientious child who is so overawed by the big class and the sovereign teacher that he can't eat the first thing in the morning. If his mother forces him to, he is only too likely to vomit on the way to school or after he's there. This adds a feeling of disgrace to his other troubles.

The best way to handle this is to let the child alone at breakfast time; let him take only his fruit juice and milk if that is all he can comfortably swallow. If he can't drink, let him go to school empty. It's not ideal for a child to start the day hungry, but he'll become relaxed and able to eat breakfast sooner if you leave him alone. Such a child usually eats fairly well at lunch, and then makes up for all he has missed with a huge supper. As he gets used to school and his new teacher, his stomach gradually becomes hungrier at breakfast time, provided he doesn't have to struggle against his mother, too.

Even more important for the child who is timid at the beginning of school is for the mother to talk things over with the teacher so that the latter can understand and work to overcome the difficulty at school. The teacher can make a special effort to be friendly with the child, and help him, in the projects they are working on, to find a comfortable place in the group.

569. Parent and teacher. It's easy to get along with a teacher if your child is her pride and joy and doing perfectly in class. But if he is having trouble, the situation is more delicate. The best parent and the best teacher are both very human. Each has pride in the job she is doing. Each has a possessive feeling toward the child. Each secretly feels, no matter how reasonable she is, that the child would be doing better if the other would only handle him a little differently. It's helpful for the parents to realize at the start that the teacher is just as sensitive as they are, and that they will get further in a conference by being friendly and cooperative. Some parents realize that they are scared of facing a teacher, but they forget that just as often the teacher is afraid of them. The parents' main job is to give a clear history of the child's past, what his interests are, what he responds to well, what badly, and leave it to the teacher how best to apply this information in school. Don't forget to compliment her on the parts of the class program that are a great success with the child.

CHILD GUIDANCE

570. Psychiatrists, psychologists, and child-guidance clinics. Parents are apt to be confused about what psychiatrists and psychologists are for and what the difference between them is. A children's psychiatrist is a physician trained to understand and treat all kinds of behavior problems and emotional problems of children. Back in the nineteenth century, psychiatrists were mainly concerned with taking care of the insane, and for that reason some people are still reluctant to consult them. But as psychiatrists have learned how serious troubles usually develop out of mild ones, they have turned more and more attention to everyday problems. In this way they do the most good in the shortest time. There's no more reason to wait to see a psychiatrist until a child is severely upset than to wait until he is in a desperate condition from pneumonia before calling the regular doctor. In larger cities there are child psychiatrists in private practice. Ask your family doctor.

Psychologist is a very general title used for people, not physicians, who specialize in one of the many branches of psychology. Psychologists who work with children are trained in such subjects as intelligence testing and aptitude testing, and the causes and treatment of learning problems in school.

In a **child-guidance clinic** (or children's psychiatric clinic) the psychiatrist is the doctor who takes charge of the case, gets to know the child and where his worries are coming from, helps him to understand and outgrow them. He may call on the psychologist for mental tests to see what the child's weak points and strong points are, or to give the child remedial teaching if, for instance, he has a reading problem. A psychiatric social worker may be asked to visit the school to find out from the teachers more exactly what difficulties the child is having there, and to give the teacher the benefit of the understanding of the problem that has been gained in the clinic. Either the social worker or the doctor has interviews with the parents to find out more about the child and to help the parents in managing him. Some child-guidance clinics are connected with hospitals; others are independent.

In a few cities there are child-guidance clinics connected with the board of education, staffed with psychiatrists, psychologists, social workers, to deal with all kinds of behavior problems. Some states have traveling clinics that visit different communities. Many other school systems, local and state, have psychologists for the testing and remedial teaching of children who are having school problems.

In a city you can inquire about a child-guidance clinic, or a private children's psychiatrist, or a psychologist for testing, through your regular doctor or a large hospital, through the school principal or superintendent, through a social service agency. Or you can look in the telephone book to see if there is a local Mental Hygiene Committee or Society. If you have no luck or live in a smaller place, you can write to the National Association for Mental Health, 1790 Broadway, New York City, and they will tell you the nearest place you can get help. If there is no child-guidance clinic, a family social agency may be able to give you the guidance you need.

Someday I hope there will be psychiatrists and psychologists connected with all school systems, so that children, parents, and teachers will be able to ask for advice on all kinds of minor problems as easily and as naturally as they can now inquire about inoculations and diet and the prevention of physical disease.

571. Family social agency. Most cities have at least one family social agency, and some large cities have Catholic, Jewish, and Protestant agencies. They are staffed by social workers trained to help parents with all the usual family problems—child management, marital adjustment, budgeting, chronic illness, housing, finding jobs, finding medical care.

Many parents have grown up with the idea that a social agency is for destitute people only and mainly provides charity. This is the opposite of the truth today. The modern family agency is just as glad to help solve small problems as large ones (they're easier), as glad to assist families who can afford to pay a fee as those who can't (that way they can expand their services).

If you have a problem with a child and you can make an appointment soon with a private child psychiatrist or a child-guidance clinic, that may be the most direct approach. But if there is no clinic available or if there is a long waiting list, it may be wiser to consult a family agency. If the problem is one that they can deal with satisfactorily, they will continue with your case. If they think it requires child-guidance treatment, they may be able to expedite an appointment.

Inquire at the Community Chest or, in a rural area, at County Welfare.

Puberty Development

PHYSICAL CHANGES

572. Puberty development in girls. By **puberty development** I mean the 2 years of very rapid growth and development that come before "maturing." A girl is said to mature at her first monthly period. In the boy there is no such clear-cut event. So let's discuss puberty development in the girl first.

The first thing to realize is that there is no regular age at which puberty begins. The largest number of girls begin their development at around the age of 11 and have their first period about 2 years later, at 13. But a fair number begin their development as young as 9. Late developers may not even begin until 13. There are extreme cases of girls starting as early as 7 or as late as 15.

The fact that a girl starts her puberty development much earlier or later than average usually doesn't mean that her glands aren't working right. It only means that she is working on what you might call a faster or slower timetable. This individual timetable seems to be an inborn trait. Parents who were late developers are more apt to have children who are late developers, and vice versa.

Let's trace what happens in the case of the average girl who starts her puberty development at 11. When she was 7 or 8 years old, she was growing 2 to 2½ inches a year. When she was 9 years old, her rate of growing slowed down to perhaps 1¾ inches a year. Nature seemed to be putting on the brakes. Suddenly, at about 11, the brakes let go. She begins to shoot up at the rate of 3 or 3½ inches a year for the next 2 years. Instead of putting on 5 to 8 pounds a year as she used to, she now gains between 10 and 20 pounds a year, without becoming fatter. Her appetite becomes enormous to make this gain possible.

But other things are happening, too. At the beginning of this period her breasts begin to develop. First the areola (the dark area around the nipple) enlarges and gets slightly puffed out. Then the whole breast begins to take shape. For the first year and a half it has a conical shape, but as her first menstrual period nears, it rounds out into more nearly a hemisphere. Soon after the breasts begin to develop, the pubic hair starts to grow. Later, hair appears in the armpits. The hips widen. The skin changes its texture.

At 13 the average girl has her first menstrual period. By now she has a woman's body. She has acquired most of the height and weight she will ever have. From this time on, her growing slows down rapidly. In the year after her first period she will grow perhaps 1½ inches, and in the year after that perhaps ¾ of an inch. In many girls the periods are irregular and infrequent for the first year or two. This is not a sign that something is wrong; it seems only to represent the body's inexperience.

573. Puberty begins at different ages. We have been talking about the average girl, but only a certain number of girls come near the average in any one particular. Many start their puberty development earlier than the average and many later. The child who begins at 8 or 9 is naturally apt to feel awkward and self-conscious when she finds herself the only girl in her class shooting upward and acquiring the shape of a woman. This experience isn't painful to every early developer. It depends, of course, on how well adjusted she was before and on how ready and eager she is to grow up. The girl who gets along well with her mother and wants to be like her is inclined to be pleased when she sees she is growing up, whether or not she is ahead of her schoolmates. On the other hand, the girl who resents being a girl—for instance, because of jealousy of her brother—or the child who is afraid to grow up is apt to be resentful or alarmed by early signs of womanhood.

Also bothered is the girl on a slow timetable. The 13-year-old who has shown no signs of puberty development has seen practically all her classmates grow rapidly taller and develop into women. She herself is still in the period of extra-slow growth that precedes the puberty spurt. She feels like an underdeveloped runt. She thinks that she must be abnormal. She needs to be reassured, to be told that her growth in height and her bodily development will be coming along just as surely as the sun rises and sets. If her mother and other relatives were late developers, she needs to be told that, too, in explanation. She can be promised that when her time comes, she will have 7 or 8 more inches of height before she stops growing altogether.

There are other variations besides the age at which puberty development begins. In some girls the pubic-hair growth comes months before the breasts start to develop. And once in a while hair in the armpits is the earliest sign of change instead of a late one. The length of time between the first signs of puberty development and the coming of the first period is usually about 2 years, but the girls who begin developing young are apt to have a shorter, quicker period of development, occasionally less than a year and a half. On the other hand, the girls who begin their puberty development later than average are more apt to take longer than 2 years to reach their first menstrual period. Occasionally one breast begins to develop months before the other. This is fairly common and nothing to worry about. The earlier-developing breast tends to stay larger throughout the puberty stage of development.

574. The average boy starts two years later than the girl. The first thing to realize about puberty development in boys is that the **average** boy begins 2 years later than the average girl, at 13 in contrast to her 11. The earlier developers among boys begin as early as 11, a few younger still. Plenty of slow developers start as late as 15, and there are a few who wait longer. The boy may grow in height at double the rate he was growing before. The penis, the testicles, and the scrotum (the sac in which the testicles lie) all develop rapidly. Pubic hair begins to grow early. Later comes the hair in the armpits and on the face. The voice cracks and deepens.

At the end of about 2 years' time, the boy's body has fairly well completed its transition to that of a man. In the following 2 years, he will creep up 2 or 2½ inches altogether and then practically stop.

The boy, like the girl, may go through a period of some physical and emotional awkwardness as he tries to gain control of his new body and new feelings. The way his voice keeps breaking down and up is an example of how he is both boy and man and yet not either.

This is a good moment to mention the difficulties of social life in school during puberty development and adolescence. The boys and girls in a class are of approximately the same age. And yet between the ages of 11 and 15, particularly, the average girl is 2 full years ahead of the average boy in development—towering over him in size and more grown-up in interests. She's beginning to want to go to dances and be treated as if she were glamorous, while he is still an uncivilized little boy who thinks it would be shameful to pay attention to her. During this

Adolescence comes at different ages.

whole period it is better for social functions to include different age groups for a better fit.

The boy who is on a slow timetable of development, who is still a "shrimp" at 15 when most of his friends have turned into grown men, needs reassurance even more than the slow-developing girl. Size and physique and athletic ability count for a lot at this age. What happens sometimes is that the boy, instead of being reassured that he will start developing in time and grow something like 8 or 9 inches in the process, is taken by his worried parents on a hunt for a doctor who will give gland treatment. This helps to convince him that something is really wrong with him. There are glandular preparations that bring on the signs of puberty at whatever age they are given. But it seems wiser and safer, when the boy is normal, to let his inborn pattern unfold in its proper order.

575. Skin troubles in adolescence. Puberty changes the texture of the skin. The pores enlarge and secrete more oil. Blackheads are formed by the combination of oil and dust and dirt. These plugs enlarge the pores further. Then it is easy for ordinary germs to get in under a blackhead and cause a small infection or pimple.

Adolescent children have a tendency to be self-conscious, anyway, and to worry about any defects in their appearance. They fret about pimples and are apt to finger them and squeeze them. The trouble is that when a pimple is broken, the germs are spread in large numbers onto the the surrounding skin and onto the fingers. Then when the child touches another part of his face, he inoculates the germs into other blackheads and starts new pimples. Squeezing a pimple often makes it larger and deeper and therefore more likely to leave a scar. Some adolescents, worried about sex, imagine that their pimples are caused by guilty thoughts or masturbation.

Parents commonly accept their children's pimples fatalistically, assuming that nothing but time will bring a cure. This is too pessimistic a view. With modern methods of treatment, great improvement can be made in many cases and some improvement in the others. A child is entitled to all the help he can get from his regular doctor or a skin specialist, for the sake of improving his present appearance and spirits, and to prevent the permanent scars that sometimes develop.

Whatever the specific methods are that the doctor prescribes, there are also general measures that are believed to be helpful. Vigorous daily exercise, fresh air, and direct sunshine seem to improve many complexions. The frequent eating of chocolate, candy, and other rich, sweet foods is suspected of favoring pimples, and it is worth while for the child to swear off these foods for a trial period, anyway. It has been the common practice to recommend thorough washing of the face twice a day, though skin specialists have doubts about it in some cases. The usual procedure is to thoroughly but gently clean the face with a hot, soapy washcloth, then rinse with hot and cold water. It is certainly important to make it clear to the child why he should keep his hands away from his face at all times except when he is washing it, and why he should never squeeze a pimple. If a whitehead has formed and is bothering him, he can soak it off with a piece of wet absorbent cotton, being careful not to spread the pus around when it breaks.

Another skin change at adolescence is a more profuse and strong-smelling perspiration in the armpits. Some children, and parents, too, are not aware of the odor, but it may cause unpopularity with schoolmates. It calls for thorough daily washing with soap and the regular use of a suitable deodorant, in all adolescents.

PSYCHOLOGICAL CHANGES

576. Self-consciousness and touchiness. As a result of all the physical, glandular, and emotional changes, a boy's or girl's attention is apt to be drawn to himself. He becomes more self-conscious. He may exaggerate and worry about any defect. (If a girl has freckles, she may think they make her look "horrible.") A slight peculiarity in the adolescent's body or how it functions easily convinces him that he is different or abnormal. He is changing so fast that he hardly knows who or what he is. He may not manage his new body as gracefully as he used to, and the same applies to his new feelings. He is apt to be touchy, easily hurt, when he's criticized. At one moment he feels like a grown-up man-of-the-world and wants to have the world, including his family, treat him as such. The next moment he feels like a child again and expects to be protected and mothered. His increased sexual feelings may bother him. He doesn't know at all clearly where they belong. The boy, but even more so the girl, becomes intense and romantic in attitudes toward people. But he is probably nowhere near the period where he can show these feelings toward a person of the same age and opposite sex. A boy may develop a great admiration for a man teacher. A girl may develop a crush on a woman teacher or a heroine of fiction. This is partly because for years the boys and girls have lived a way of life in which they stuck to their own sex and considered the opposite sex their natural enemies. It's only gradually that these old antagonisms and barriers are broken down. Perhaps the adolescent first dares to think romantically of someone in Hollywood. Eventually boys and girls in the same school can dream about each other, but even then it may take some time before the shy ones can show their interest face to face.

577. Demands for more freedom often express a fear of freedom. A common reproach of adolescents is that their parents don't allow them enough freedom. It's natural for a child who is approaching adulthood rapidly to insist on rights and dignities that belong to each step, and the parents need to be reminded by him that he is less and less a child. But parents don't have to take every claim at its face value or to give in without consideration. The fact is that the adolescent is also scared of growing up. He is very unsure about his capacity to be as knowledgeable, masterful, sophisticated, and charming as he would like. But he will never admit his doubts, least of all to his parents or to himself. Instead of seeing that it's he who's afraid of more freedom, he indignantly decides that it's the parents who are holding him back.

578. Adolescents appreciate reasonable rules. Teachers, psychiatrists, and other counselors who work with adolescents have heard some of them confess that they wished their parents would be a little stricter, like some of their friends' parents, and tell them more definitely what to do and what not to do. This is not to say that parents can be arbitrary. Parents need to talk to other parents and teachers of adolescents to get an idea of what is customary in the community, and they certainly need to discuss rules in a reasonable spirit with their child. But in the end they must make up their minds what is right and stick to it. If the decision is reasonable, the adolescent accepts it and is grateful for it underneath. In these decisions the parents have a narrow road to follow. In a sense they must say, "We know best," and yet they must feel and express a basic trust in their child's judgment and morality. It's mainly the child's sound upbringing and his belief that his parents have confidence in him —not their rules—that keep him on the right track. But he still needs the rules, and the realization that his parents care enough about him to give him the rules, in order to fill in the gaps in his experience.

579. Rivalry with parents and old attachments. Some of the tension that often shows at this stage between father and son or mother and daughter is due to a natural rivalry. The adolescent realizes that it's now his turn to be the grownup, the one who tackles the world, the one who fascinates the opposite sex, the one who will be the father or mother. So he feels like elbowing the has-been parent off the seat of power. Subconsciously the parent senses this and, understandably, doesn't feel too gracious about it.

But there is also apt to be tension between mother and son and between father and daughter. Back in the 3-to-6-year-old period, the boy was intensely attached to his mother and the daughter to her father. In the period between 6 and adolescence, the child tried to forget and deny all that. But when the rush of strong feelings wells up in adolescence, it first starts, like a spring flood, down the long-disused, dry riverbed toward the parent. Yet the adolescent realizes subconsciously that this is not right, at all. So his first big job at this age period is to steer his feelings away from his parent and toward someone outside the family. He covers up the positive feelings with negative ones. This is at least a partial explanation of why a boy so often picks fights with his mother and why a daughter may be surprisingly antagonistic to her father at times. In our kind of civilization it seems to be more necessary for the boy to cover up his positive feelings for his mother than it is for the girl to cover up her positive feelings for her father. Many adolescent girls can be quite comfortably and openly affectionate with their father.

The parents, of course, have more or less strong attachments for their adolescent children, and this helps us to understand why a mother may be secretly or openly disappointed with all the girls her son becomes interested in and why a father may take violent objection to the boys who court his daughter.

Problems of Feeding and Development

THIN CHILDREN

580. Thinness has various causes. Some children seem to be thin by heredity. They come from thin stock on one or both sides of the family. From the time they were babies they have been offered plenty to eat. They aren't sickly, and they aren't nervous. They just never want to eat a great deal, especially of the rich foods.

Some children are thin because their appetites have been taken away by too much parental urging (Section 583). Other children can't eat for other nervous reasons. The child who is worrying about bogiemen, or death, or his mother's going away and leaving him, may lose a lot of his appetite. The jealous younger sister who is driving herself all day long to keep up with her older sister burns up a lot of energy and gives herself no peace at mealtime, either. As you can see, the tense child is thinned out by a two-way process. His appetite is kept down, and his restlessness uses up extra energy.

There are many children throughout the world who are malnourished because their parents can't find or afford the proper food. There are a few chronic physical diseases that cause malnutrition. But children who become thin during an acute illness usually recover their weight promptly if during convalescence they are not urged to eat until their appetite recovers.

581. Care of a thin child. A thin child should, of course, have regular medical check-ups. This is more important if he acts tired or if he has lost weight or if he has failed to gain a reasonable amount.

Thinness, failure to gain weight, and fatigue come more often from emotional troubles than from physical causes. If your child is nervous or depressed, try to consult a child-guidance clinic or a child psychiatrist. Talk over his situation with his schoolteacher. In any case, it's wise to think over again his relations with parents, brothers, sisters, friends, and school. If you have gotten involved in a feeding problem, try to undo it.

Eating between meals is helpful for those thin children whose stomachs never seem to want to take much at a time but are quite willing to be fed often.

A healthy child may stay thin despite a large appetite, and this is probably the way he was meant to be. In many of these cases, the child prefers relatively low-calorie foods, like meat, vegetables, and fruit, and shies away from rich desserts. But some of these children, despite their aversion to rich foods, are quite agreeable to cream and butter. You can try substituting first thin cream and then thicker cream for the milk on cereal and add a little real cream to cream soups. You can put more butter on vegetables and bread. These changes should be made gradually, because it takes time for the digestive system to adjust to more fat in the diet. Don't make these changes if the child objects at all; you'll only take away his appetite.

Adding cream or butter to the diet of a child with a **small** appetite sometimes helps to put on weight, but not very often. The trouble is that it usually reduces his appetite still further.

Finally, if your child doesn't seem to be any kind of problem, has been slender since infancy, but gains a reasonable amount of weight every year, relax and let him alone. He is probably meant to be that way.

582. Extra rest. If a young child has become thinner, tenser, or more easily fatigued than usual, the doctor may recommend extra rest for a month or two.

What rests one child makes another frantic, so you have to fit the program to the individual. A school-age child is likely to fight any program that makes him different from the others.

An evening routine can often be arranged so that the child is kept quiet after supper, by means of television, radio, story-telling, working on a project with his father, reading.

In the case of a preschool child, it should be possible to put him to bed for supper and the evening. This will seem like a treat, at least for a few weeks, if it's presented as a privilege, not a punishment. Even if he hops out of bed from time to time, he is getting more rest than if he were tearing around constantly. If you have time, read to him after supper to keep him anchored.

Another variation for the young child is staying in bed for breakfast and perhaps an hour afterward. Or this can be combined with supper in bed.

The child who doesn't have to go to school in the afternoon and who is only more restless if made to lie down after lunch, may be perfectly willing to stay indoors for an hour playing quietly or helping his mother do housework or take care of the baby.

FEEDING PROBLEMS

583. Where feeding problems begin. Why do so many children eat poorly? Most commonly because so many mothers are conscientious about trying to make them eat well. You don't see many feeding problems in puppies, or among young humans in places where mothers don't know enough about diet to worry. You might say jokingly that it takes knowledge and many months of hard work to make a feeding problem.

One child seems to be born with a wolf's appetite that stays big even when he's unhappy or sick. Another's appetite is more moderate and is easily affected by his health and spirits. The first child seems to be cut out to be plump; the second is apparently intended to stay on the slender side. But **every** baby is born with enough appetite to keep him healthy, keep him gaining at the proper rate for him.

The trouble is that a child is also born with an instinct to get balky if he is pushed too hard, and an instinct to get disgusted with food that he's had unpleasant experiences with. There's one further complication: a person's appetite doesn't always go out to the same things. For a while he feels like eating a lot of spinach or a new breakfast cereal. Next month it may not appeal to him. Some people always go in heavily for starches and sweets; others are fed up with a little bit. If you understand these points, you can see how feeding problems begin at different stages in a child's development. The baby becomes balky in his early months if his mother often tries to make him finish more of his bottle than he wants, or, when the first solid food is introduced, he isn't given a chance to get used to it gradually. Many become more picky and choosy after the age of a year because they aren't meant to be gaining so fast, because they are more opinionated, and perhaps because of teething. Urging them reduces the appetite further and more permanently. A very common time for feeding problems to begin is at the end of an illness. If an anxious mother begins pushing food before the child's appetite returns, it quickly increases his disgust and gets it firmly fixed.

All feeding problems don't start from urging. A child may stop eating because of jealousy of a new baby or worries of many kinds. But whatever the original cause, the mother's anxiety and urging usually make it worse and keep the appetite from returning.

Put yourself in the child's place for a minute. To get in the mood, think back to the last time you weren't very hungry. Perhaps it was a muggy day, or you were worried, or you had a stomach upset. (The child with a feeding problem feels that way most of the time.) Now imagine that a nervous giantess is sitting beside you, watching every mouthful. You have eaten a little of the foods that appeal to you most and have put your fork down, feeling plenty full. But she looks worried and says, "You haven't touched your turnips." You explain that you don't want any, but she doesn't seem to understand how you feel, acts as if you are being bad on purpose. When she says you can't get up from the table until you've cleaned your plate, you try a bit of turnip, but it makes you feel slightly sick to your stomach. She scoops up a tablespoonful and pokes it at your mouth, which makes you gag.

584. A cure takes time and patience. Once a feeding problem is established, it takes time and understanding and patience to undo. The mother has become anxious. She finds it hard to relax again as long as the child is eating poorly. And yet her concern and insistence are the main things that are keeping his appetite down. Even when she reforms, by a supreme effort, it may take weeks for the child's timid appetite to come back. He has to have a chance to slowly forget all the unpleasant associations with mealtime.

His appetite is like a mouse and the mother's anxious urging is the cat that has been scaring him back into his hole. You can't persuade the mouse to be bold just because the cat looks the other way. The cat must leave him alone for a long time.

Dr. Clara Davis found that babies who hadn't built up any prejudices about foods naturally picked well-balanced diets in the long run when offered a variety of natural foods. But you can't expect a child who has been fighting against certain foods—vegetables, for example—for months or years to suddenly turn to those foods just because his mother gives him a free choice. He might at a camp where everyone else is eating the vegetables, where he's hungry, and where no one cares whether he eats them or not. But at home those vegetables have too many associations in his mind. Just as soon as he sees them, his spirit and his stomach say, "No!"

585. A mother has feelings, too. And they are strong feelings by the time she has a chronic feeding problem on her hands. The most obvious one is anxiety—that the child will develop some nutritional deficiency or lose his resistance to ordinary infections. Her doctor tries to reassure her again and again that children with feeding problems are not more susceptible to diseases, but this is hard for her to believe.

She is apt to feel guilty, imagining that her relatives, her husband's relatives, the neighbors, the doctor, consider her a neglectful mother. Of course, they don't. It's more likely that they understand because they have at least one child in the family who's a poor eater, too.

Then there's the inevitable feeling of frustration and angriness at a whippersnapper who can completely foil all his mother's efforts to do right by him. This is the most uncomfortable feeling of all, because it makes the conscientious mother feel ashamed of herself.

It's an interesting fact that many parents who have feeding problems in their children recall having been a feeding problem themselves in their own childhood. They remember only too well that urging and forcing work in the wrong direction, but they find themselves power-less to do otherwise. In such cases, the parent's strong feelings of anxiety, guilt, and irritation are partly leftovers from the same feelings implanted in him in childhood.

586. There's rarely danger for the child. It's important to remember that children have a remarkable inborn mechanism that lets them know how much food and which types of food they need for normal growth and development. It is extremely rare to see serious malnutrition or vita-min deficiency or infectious disease result from a feeding problem.

But the child who is eating poorly needs a doctor's expert help: to check him from time to time, to evaluate the diet he is taking for what it provides and what it lacks, to recommend substitute foods or medical preparations to make up for what the child is missing, to advise on the handling not only of the feeding but of the child generally, and to reas-sure the mother.

587. Make mealtime pleasant. The aim is not to **make** the child eat but to let his natural appetite come to the surface so that he wants to eat.

Try hard not to talk about his eating, either with threats or with en-couragement. I wouldn't praise him for taking an unusually large amount or look disappointed when he takes little. With practice, you should be able to stop thinking about it, and that's real progress. When he feels no more pressure, he can begin to pay attention to his own ap-petite.

You sometimes hear the advice, "Put the food before the child, say nothing, take it away in 30 minutes, no matter how much or little has been eaten. Give nothing else until the next meal." This is fine if it's carried out in the right spirit—that is to say, if the mother is really trying not to fuss or worry about the child's eating and remains agreeable. But an angry mother sometimes applies the advice this way. She slaps the plate of dinner in front of the child, saying grimly, "Now, if you don't eat this in 30 minutes, I'm going to take it away and you won't get a thing to eat until supper!" Then she stands glaring at him, waiting. This threatening hardens his heart and takes away any trace of appetite. The balky child who is challenged to a feeding battle can **always** outlast his mother.

You don't want your child to eat because he has been beaten in a fight, whether you have been forcing him or taking his food away. You want him to eat because he feels like eating.

Start with the foods he likes best. You want his mouth to water when he comes to meals so that he can hardly wait to begin. The first step in building up that attitude is to serve for **2 or 3 months** the wholesome foods he likes best (offering as balanced a diet as possible), and to omit all the foods that he actively dislikes.

If your child has a limited feeding problem, dislikes only one or another group of foods but eats most kinds fairly well, read Sections 430 to 440. They explain how one food can be substituted for another until a child's appetite swings around or until he loses his suspiciousness and tenseness at meals.

588. The child who likes few foods. A mother might say, "Those children who dislike just one type of food aren't real problems. Why, my child likes only hamburgers, bananas, oranges, and soda pop. Once in a while he'll take a slice of white bread or a couple of teaspoonfuls of peas. He refuses to touch anything else."

This is an unusually severe feeding problem, but the principle is the same. You could serve him sliced bananas and a slice of enriched bread for breakfast; hamburger, 2 teaspoonfuls of peas, and an orange for lunch; a slice of enriched bread and more banana for supper. Let him have seconds or thirds of any of the foods if he asks for them and you have them. Serve different combinations of this diet for days. Hold down firmly on his soda pop. If his stomach is awash with syrup, it takes away what little appetite he has for more valuable foods.

If at the end of a couple of months he is looking forward to his meals, add a couple of teaspoonfuls (not more) of some food that he sometimes used to eat—not one he hated. Don't mention the new addition.

Don't comment if he leaves it. Try this one again in a couple of weeks, and meanwhile try another. How fast you go on adding new foods depends on how his appetite is improving and how he's taking to the new foods.

589. Make no distinctions between foods. Let him eat four helpings of one food and none of another if that's the way he feels (as long as the food is wholesome). If he wants none of the main course but wants his dessert, let him have his dessert in a perfectly matter-of-fact way. If you say, "No seconds on meat until you've eaten your vegetable," or "No dessert until you've cleaned your plate," you further take away his appetite for the vegetable or the main course and you increase his desire for meat or dessert. These results are the exact opposite of what you want.

It's not that you want your child to go on eating lopsided meals forever. But if he has a feeding problem and is already suspicious of some foods, your best chance of his coming back to a reasonable balance is to let him feel that you do not care.

I think it's a great mistake for the parent to insist that a child who is a feeding problem eat "just a taste" of a food he is suspicious of, as a matter of duty. If he has to eat anything that disgusts him, even slightly, it lessens the chance that he will ever change his mind and like it. And it lowers his enjoyment of mealtimes and his general appetite for all foods by one more degree.

Certainly, never make him eat at the next meal food that he refused at the last meal. That's looking for trouble.

590. Serve less than he will eat, not more. For any child who is eating poorly, serve small portions. If you heap his plate high, you remind him of how much he is going to refuse and you depress his appetite. But if you give him a first helping that is less than he is willing to take, you encourage him to think, "That isn't enough." You want him to have that attitude. You want him to get to think of food as something he is eager for. If he has a **really** small appetite, serve him miniature portions: 1 teaspoonful of meat, 1 teaspoonful of vegetable, 1 teaspoonful of starch. When he finishes, don't say eagerly, "Do you want some more?" Let him ask, even if it takes several days of miniature portions to give him the idea.

591. Getting him to feed himself. Should the mother feed a poor eater? A child who is given proper encouragement (Section 416) takes over his own feeding somewhere between 12 and 18 months. But if an overworried mother has continued to feed him until the age of 2 or 3 or 4 (probably with a lot of urging), it won't solve the problem simply to tell her, "Stop!" The child now has no desire to feed himself; he takes being fed for granted. To him it's now an important sign of his mother's love and concern. If she stops suddenly, it hurts his feelings, makes him resentful. He is liable to stop eating altogether for 2 or 3 days—and that's longer than any mother can sit by doing nothing. When she feeds him again, he has a new grudge against her. When she tries another time to give up feeding him, he knows his strength and her weakness.

A child of 2 or more should be feeding himself as soon as possible. But getting him to do it is a delicate matter that takes several weeks. You mustn't give him the impression that you are trying to take a privilege away. You want him to take over because he wants to.

Serve him his favorite foods meal after meal and day after day. When you set the dish before him, go back to the kitchen or into the next room for a minute or two, as if you had forgotten something. Be away a little longer each day. Come back and feed him cheerfully with no comments. whether or not he has taken anything himself. If he gets impatient while you are in the next room and calls you to come and feed him, come right away, with a friendly apology. He probably won't progress steadily. In a week or two he may get to the point of eating one meal almost entirely himself, and the next meal want to be fed from the beginning. Don't argue at all during this process. If he eats one food, don't urge him to try another, too. If he seems pleased with himself for doing a good job of self-feeding, compliment him on being a big boy, but don't be so enthusiastic that he smells a rat.

Suppose for a week or so you have left him alone with good food for as long as 10 or 15 minutes and he's eaten nothing. Then you ought to make him hungrier. Gradually, in 3 or 4 days, cut down to half what you customarily feed him. This should make him so eager that he can't help starting in himself, provided you are being tactful and friendly.

By the time the child is regularly feeding himself as much as half a meal, I think it's time to encourage him to leave the table rather than feed him the rest of the meal. Never mind if he has left out some of his foods. The hunger will pile up and soon make him eat more. If you go on feeding him the last half of the meal, he may never take over the whole job. Just say, "I guess you've had enough." If he asks you to feed him some more, give him two or three more mouthfuls to be agreeable and then suggest casually that he's through.

After he has taken over completely for a couple of weeks, don't slip back into the habit of feeding him again. If some day he's very tired and says. "Feed me," give him a few spoonfuls absent-mindedly, and then say something about his not being very hungry. I make this point because I know that a mother who has worried for months or years about a child's eating, who spoon-fed him much too long, and finally let him feed himself, has a great temptation to go back to feeding him again the first time he loses his appetite or the first time he is sick. Then the job has to be done all over again.

592. Should the mother stay in the room while he is eating? This depends on what the child is used to and wants, and how well the mother can control her worry. If she has always sat there, she can't suddenly disappear without upsetting him. If she can be sociable, relaxed, and get her mind off the food, it's fine for her to stay (whether or not she is eating her own meal). If she finds that even with practice she can't get her mind off the child's eating, or stop urging him, it may be better for her to retire from the picture at mealtime, not crossly, not suddenly, but tactfully and gradually, a little more each day, so that he doesn't notice the change.

593. No acts or bribes. Certainly the parents shouldn't put on acts to bribe the child to eat, such as a little story for every mouthful or a promise from Father to stand on his head if the spinach is finished. All this kind of persuasion seems at the moment to be making the child eat a few more mouthfuls. But in the long run it takes his appetite away more and more. The parents have to keep raising the bribe to get the same results. They end up putting on an hour's exhausting vaudeville for five mouthfuls.

Don't ask a child to eat to earn his dessert, or a piece of candy, or a gold star, or any other prize. Don't ask him to eat for Aunt Minnie, or to make his mother happy, or to grow big and strong, or to keep from getting sick, or to clean his plate. Let's state the rule more briefly: Don't ask a child to eat.

There is no great harm in a mother's telling a story at suppertime, or playing the radio if that has been the custom, so long as it is not connected in any way with whether the child is eating or not.

594. It isn't necessary to be a doormat. I have said so much about letting a child eat because he wants to, that I may have given the wrong impression to some parents. I remember a mother who had been snarled up for years in a feeding problem involving her 7-year-old daughter, urging, arguing, forcing. When she understood the idea that the child probably had, underneath, a normal appetite and a desire for a well-balanced diet, and that the best way to revive it was to stop battling over meals, she swung to the opposite extreme and became apologetic. The daughter by this age had a lot of resentment in her from the long struggle. As soon as she realized that her mother was all meekness, she took advantage of her. She would pour the whole sugar bowl on her cereal, watching out of the corner of her eye to see her mother's silent horror. The mother would ask her before each meal what she wanted. If the child said, "Hamburger," she obediently bought and served it. Then the child, as like as not, would say, "I don't want hamburger. I want frankfurters," and the mother would run over to the butcher's to get it.

There's a middle ground. It's reasonable for a child to be expected to come to meals on time, to be pleasant to other diners, to refrain from making unpleasant remarks about the food or declaring what he doesn't like, to eat with the table manners that are reasonable for his age. It's fine for the mother to take his preferences into account as much as is possible (considering the rest of the family) in planning meals, or to ask him occasionally what he would like, as a treat. But it's bad for him to get the idea that he's the only one to be considered. It's sensible and right for the mother to put a limit on sugar, candy, sodas, cakes, and the other less wholesome foods. All this can be done without argument as long as the mother acts as if she knows what she is doing.

595. Gagging. The child beyond the age of a year who can't tolerate anything but puréed food has usually been fed forcibly, or at least urged vigorously. It isn't so much that he can't stand lumps. What makes him gag is having them pushed into him. The mothers of gagging children usually say, "It's a funny thing. He can swallow lumps all right if it's something he likes very much. He can even swallow big chunks of meat that he bites off the bone." There are three steps in curing a gagger. The first is to encourage him to feed himself completely. (See Section 416.) The second is to get him over his suspiciousness about foods in general. (See Sections 587 to 593.) The third is to go unusually slowly in coarsening the consistency of his food. Let him go for weeks—or even months if necessary—on puréed foods, until he has lost all fear of eating and is really enjoying it. Don't even serve him meats, for instance, during this time if he cannot enjoy them finely ground.

In other words, go only as fast as the child can comfortably take it.

A few babies have such sensitive throats that they gag even on puréed foods. In some of these cases, the cause seems to be the pasty consistency of the food. Try diluting it a little with milk or water. Or try chopping vegetables and fruits fine without mashing them.

FAT CHILDREN

596. The treatment depends on the cause. Many people think the cause is gland trouble, but actually this is rarely the case. There are several factors that make for overweight, including heredity, temperament, appetite, happiness. If a child comes from a stocky line on both sides of the family, there is a greater chance of his being overweight. The placid child who takes little exercise has more food calories left over to store in the form of fat. The most important factor of all is appetite. The child who has a tremendous appetite that runs to rich food like cake, cookies, and pastry is naturally going to be heavier than the child whose taste runs principally to vegetables and fruits and meats. But this only raises the question of why one child **does** crave large amounts of rich foods. We don't understand all the causes of this, but we recognize the child who seems to be born ("constitutionally") to be a big eater. He starts with a huge appetite at birth and never loses it afterward, whether he's well or sick, calm or worried, whether the food he's offered is appetizing or not. He's fat by the time he's 2 or 3 months old and stays that way at least through childhood.

597. Unhappiness is sometimes a factor. Of the excessive appetites that develop later in childhood, some at least are due to unhappiness. This happens, for instance, around the age of 7 in children who are somewhat unhappy and lonely. It is the period when the child is drawing away from his close emotional dependence on his parents. If he doesn't have the knack of making equally close friendships with other children, he feels left out in the cold. Eating sweet and rich food seems to serve him as a partial substitute. Worries about schoolwork or other matters sometimes make a child seek comfort in overeating, too. Overweight often develops during the puberty stage of development. The appetite normally increases at this time to take care of the increased rate of growth, but it's probable that loneliness plays a part in some cases, too. It is the period when the child may become more turned-in and self-conscious because of all the changes he is experiencing, and this may lessen his ability to get along enjoyably with his fellows.

598. Mild overweight is common between 7 and 12. But I don't want to leave the impression that every child who turns plump is unhappy. There seems to be a normal tendency for many children, including the cheerful and successful ones, to put on extra weight in the 7-to-12-year-old period. Very few of these become excessively obese. They are just slightly overpadded. Most of them stay plump during the 2 years of very rapid puberty development and then slender down as they get further into adolescence. Many girls, for instance, become slimmer around 15 years of age without great effort. It's good for parents to know that this mild school-age obesity is common and that it often goes away later, so that they won't make too much of an issue about it.

Obesity may become a vicious circle, no matter which factor caused

Fatness is complicated.

it in the beginning. The fatter the child, the harder it is for him to enjoy exercise and games. And the quieter he is, the more energy his body has to store as fat. It's a vicious circle in another way, too. The fat child who can't comfortably enter into games may come to feel more of an outsider, and he is liable to be kidded and ridiculed.

599. Dieting is difficult. What is there to do about a fat child? Right away you would say, "Diet him." It sounds easy, but it isn't. Think of the grownups you know who are unhappy because of their weight and who still aren't able to stick to a diet. A child has less will power than an adult. If the mother serves the child the less fattening foods, it means either that the whole family must go without the richer dishes or that the fat child must be kept from eating the very things his heart craves most while the rest of the family enjoys them. There are very few fat children reasonable enough to think that that's fair. The feeling of being treated unfairly may further increase the craving for sweets. Whatever is accomplished in the dining room may be undone at the refrigerator or candy-store between meals.

But the prospects of dieting are not so black as I have made out. A tactful mother can do a good deal to keep temptation away from her fat child without making an issue of it. She can serve rich desserts less frequently. She can stop having cakes and cookies always around in the kitchen, and provide fresh fruit for between-meals nibbling. She can serve frequently the less fattening foods that are his favorites. If the child shows any willingness to cooperate in his diet, he should certainly be encouraged to visit the doctor, preferably alone. Talking to the doctor, man to man, may give him the feeling of running his own life like a grownup. Anyone can take dietary advice better from an outsider. A child should never take any medicine for reducing without a doctor's recommendation, and unless he can return at **regular** intervals for checkup.

Since overeating is often a symptom of loneliness or maladjustment, the most constructive thing is to make sure that the child's home life, schoolwork, and social life are as happy and satisfying as possible (Section 543).

If despite your efforts to help him, a child's obesity is more than mild or if he is gaining weight too rapidly, you should certainly get medical and psychiatric assistance. Obesity is a serious problem for any child.

600. Dieting should be supervised by a doctor. Self-dieting sometimes becomes a problem and a danger in the adolescent period. A group of girls excitedly work themselves up to going on some wild diet that they have heard about. Within a few days, hunger makes most of them break their resolutions, but one or two may persist with fanatical zeal. Occasionally a girl loses alarming amounts of weight and can't resume a normal diet even when she wants to. The group hysteria about dieting seems to have awakened in her a deep revulsion against food, which is usually a hangover from some unsolved worry of early childhood. Another girl in the early stages of puberty declares hectically, "I'm getting **much** too fat," even though she is so slender that her ribs are showing. She may be emotionally unready to grow up and secretly disturbed by the development of her breasts. The child who becomes obsessed with dieting should have the help of a children's psychiatrist.

If either your child or you think he should be on a diet, the first step, for a number of reasons, is to consult a doctor. First, he will determine whether dieting is necessary or wise. Secondly, the adolescent is more apt to accept the doctor's advice than his parents'. If it is agreed that a diet is wise, it should certainly be prescribed by the doctor. He will take into account the child's food tastes, the family's usual menus, in order to work out a diet that is not only sound nutritionally but practical in that particular home. Finally, since weight loss puts some strain on health, anyone who is planning to reduce should be examined at regular intervals to make sure that the rate is not too fast and that he remains strong and healthy.

If it is not possible to have the supervision of a doctor, the parents should insist that a child who has the bit in his teeth must take at least the following foods daily: a pint and a half of milk, meat or poultry or fish, an egg, a green or yellow vegetable, fruit twice. The child can be assured that these foods in reasonable servings do not cause weight gaining and that they are essential to prevent the muscles, bones, and organs of his body from being dangerously depleted.

Rich desserts can be omitted without risk, and should be, by anyone who is obese and trying to reduce. The amount of plain, starchy foods (cereals, breads, potatoes) taken is what determines, in the case of most people, how much they gain or lose. Any growing child needs **some,** even though he is trying to lose weight. It is not wise for even a fat person to lose more than a pound a week, unless a doctor is carefully supervising.

GLANDS

601. Glandular disturbances. There are several definite glandular diseases, and there are a few glandular medicines that have a definite effect on human beings. For example, when the thyroid gland is not secreting sufficiently, a child's physical growth and mental development are definitely slowed down. He is sluggish, has a dry skin, coarse hair, and a low voice. His face may appear puffy. (Insufficient thyroid secretion does not cause obesity.) His basal metabolism, which means the rate at which his body burns fuel when resting, is below normal. The proper dose of thyroid medication brings about remarkable improvement.

Some people who have read popular articles on glands assume that every short person, every slow pupil, every nervous girl, every fat boy with small genitals, is merely a glandular problem who can be cured by the proper tablet or injection. This enthusiasm is not justified by what is known scientifically at the present time. It takes more than one symptom to make a glandular disease.

In many cases when a boy is heavy during the years before puberty development, his penis **appears** smaller than it really is because his plump thighs are so large in comparison and because the layer of fat at the base of his penis may hide three quarters of its length. Most of these boys have a normal sexual development at puberty, and many of them lose their excess weight at that time. See Sections 515 and 602 on the harm of worrying a boy about his genitals.

Certainly every child who is not growing at the usual rate or in the usual shape, or who appears dull or nervous or out of line in any other way, should be examined by a competent physician. But if the doctor finds that the child's stature is only his inborn constitutional pattern, or that his mental state is due to real troubles in his daily life, then what he needs is assistance in his adjustment to life, not a further search for magic.

UNDESCENDED TESTICLES

602. Undescended testicles. In a certain number of newborn boys, one or both testicles are not in the scrotum (the pouch in which the testicles normally lie) but are farther up in the groin or inside the abdomen. Most of these undescended testicles come down into the scrotum soon after birth. A great majority of the rest of them descend during the stage of puberty development, which begins in the average boy at about 13. There are only a very few cases in which the testicles don't ever come down by themselves, and in these there is some obstruction or abnormality.

The testicles are originally formed inside the abdomen and move down into the scrotum only shortly before birth. There are muscles attached to the testicles that can jerk them back up into the groin, or even back into the abdomen. This is to protect the testicles from injury when this region of the body is struck or scratched. There are lots of boys whose testicles withdraw on slight provocation. Even chilling of the skin from being undressed may be enough to make them disappear into the abdomen. Handling the scrotum in an examination frequently makes them disappear. Therefore, a parent shouldn't decide that the testicles are undescended just because they are not usually in sight. A good time to look for them is when the boy is in a hot bath, without handling his body.

Testicles that have been seen at any time in the scrotum, even if only rarely, need no treatment because they will surely settle down in the scrotum by the time puberty development is under way.

Sometimes just one testicle is definitely undescended. Though this may require treatment, there is no cause for great concern because one testicle is sufficient to make a boy develop properly and become a father, even in the unusual case in which the other one doesn't appear later.

If one or both testicles have never been seen in the scrotum by the time a boy is 2 years old, this should be discussed with the doctor.

If your child appears to have undescended testicles, try not to worry yourself and don't worry him. It is important not to make the child self-conscious by anxious looks and frequent examinations. It is really harmful to a boy's emotional development for him to get the idea that he is not formed properly. If glandular injections are recommended, the parents should speak of this treatment casually, in a way that is least likely to raise doubts in the boy's mind.

POSTURE

603. The treatment of bad posture depends on the cause. Good or bad posture is made up of a number of factors. One—perhaps the most important—is the skeleton the child is born with. You see individuals who have been round-shouldered from babyhood, like their fathers before them. Some children seem to be born with a relaxed set of muscles and ligaments. They run to knock-knees no matter how much vitamin D you give them. Another child looks tightly knit, in action or at rest. It's hard for him to slump. There are diseases that affect posture, such as rickets, infantile paralysis, and tuberculosis of the bones. Chronic illness and chronic fatigue, from any cause, that keep a child under par may make him slump and sag. Overweight sometimes produces swayback, knock-knees, and flat feet. Unusual tallness makes the self-conscious adolescent duck his head. A child with poor posture needs regular examinations to make sure that there is no physical disease.

Many children slouch because of lack of self-confidence. It may result from too much criticism at home, or from difficulties in school, or from an unsatisfactory social life. The person who is buoyant and sure of himself shows it in the way he sits and stands and walks. When parents realize how much feelings have to do with posture, they can handle it more wisely.

The natural impulse of a parent, eager to have his child appear well, is to keep after his posture: "Remember the shoulders," "For goodness' sake, stand up straight." But the child who is stooped over because his parents have always kept after him too much won't be improved by more nagging. Generally speaking, the best results come when he receives posture work at school, or in a posture clinic, or in a doctor's office. In these places the atmosphere is more businesslike than at home. The parents may be able to help him greatly in carrying out his exercises at home, if he wants help and if they can give it in a friendly way. But the main job for them is to help the child's spirit by aiding his school adjustment, fostering a happy social life, and making him feel adequate and self-respecting at home.

Illness

FEVER

604. What's fever and what isn't? Taking the temperature is a bugaboo to many mothers. They find a thermometer hard to read. They are confused by the difference between mouth and rectal temperatures.

It might be easier for you to get someone else to show you how to read one, but here goes. Most thermometers are engraved the same. They have a long mark for each degree and a short mark for each fifth of a degree. Only the even degrees—94, 96, 98, 100, 102, 104—are numbered on the thermometer, because of lack of space. There is an arrow pointing to the "normal" mark, 98⅗. Many thermometers are marked in red above the normal point.

The first thing to realize is that a healthy child's body temperature doesn't stay fixed at 98⅗. It is always going up and down a little, depending on the time of day and what the child is doing. It's usually lowest in the early morning and highest in the late afternoon. This change during the day is only a slight one, however. The change between rest and activity is greater. The temperature of a perfectly healthy small child may be 99⅗ or even 100° right after he has been running around. (On the other hand, a temperature of 101° probably means illness whether the child has been exercising or not.) The older child's temperature is less affected by activity. All this means that if you want to know whether your child has a slight fever due to illness, you must take his temperature after he has been really quiet for an hour or more.

In most feverish illnesses the temperature is apt to be highest in the late afternoon and lowest in the morning. But there is nothing to be surprised at if a fever is high in the morning and low in the afternoon.

There are a few diseases in which the fever, instead of climbing and falling, stays high steadily. The commonest of these are pneumonia and roseola infantum. A below-normal temperature (as low as 97°) sometimes occurs at the end of an illness, and also in healthy babies and small children on winter nights. This is no cause for concern so long as the child is feeling well.

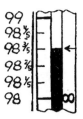

Now about the difference between mouth and rectal temperatures. Every part of the body has a different temperature. The trunk is warmest, because it is thick throughout and protected by clothing. A child's temperature is taken by rectum until about the age of 5 or 6, because he can't keep a thermometer under his tongue and because he might bite it. The rectal temperature is a little higher than the mouth temperature, but it's usually not a full degree higher. It's nearer half a degree.

605. The thermometer. The only difference between a mouth and a rectal thermometer is in the shape of the bulb. The bulb of the rectal thermometer is round so that it won't be so sharp. A mouth thermometer has a long slender bulb so that the mercury can be warmed more quickly by the mouth. The markings on the two thermometers are exactly the same and mean the same thing. (In other words, they are not marked differently to allow for the difference of temperature between the mouth and rectum.) You can use a clean rectal thermometer perfectly well in the mouth, and a mouth thermometer in the rectum, if inserted gently.

Most thermometers register well enough in a minute in the rectum. If you watch a thermometer sometime when it is in a baby's rectum, you can see that it goes up very rapidly at first. It gets within a degree of where it is going to stop in the first 20 seconds. After that it barely creeps up. This means that if you are nervous taking the temperature of a struggling baby, you can take the thermometer out in less than a minute and have a rough idea what the temperature is.

It takes longer to register the correct temperature in the mouth—1½ to 2 minutes. This is because it takes the mouth a while to warm up after being open and because the bulb is partly surrounded by air.

606. Taking the temperature. Before taking a temperature, shake the thermometer down. You hold the upper end of the thermometer (the opposite end from the bulb) firmly between your thumb and finger. Now shake the thermometer vigorously, with a sharp, snapping motion. You want to drive the mercury down at least as far as 97°. If it doesn't

go down, you aren't snapping hard enough. Until you get the hang of it, shake the thermometer over a bed or couch. Then if it slips out of your hand, it won't be broken. The bathroom is the worst place of all to shake a thermometer because of the hard surfaces.

If you are taking a rectal temperature, dip the bulb of the thermometer into petroleum jelly or cold cream. The best position for a baby is on his stomach across your knees. He can't squirm out of this position very easily, and his legs hang down out of the way. Insert the thermometer gently into his rectum. Push it in with a light touch, letting the thermometer find its own direction. If you hold it stiffly, it may poke him inside. Once the thermometer is in, it is better to shift your grip off the end of the thermometer, because if the baby struggles, the twisting might hurt him. Instead, lay the palm of your hand across his buttocks, lightly holding the thermometer between two of the fingers, the way you'd hold a cigarette.

You can also take the temperature easily, especially when the child is old enough to lie still, with him lying on his side on a bed with his knees drawn up a little. It is harder to find the rectum when a child is lying flat on his stomach. The worst position is with the child lying on his back. It is hard to get to his rectum, and his feet are in position to kick your hand accidentally or on purpose.

Reading the thermometer is very easy, once you get the knack. Most thermometers are somewhat triangular in shape, with one edge sharper than the rest. This sharp edge should point toward you. In this position the marks of the degrees are above and the numbers are below. Between them is the space in which the mercury shows. Roll the thermometer very slightly until you see the band of mercury. Don't worry too much

over the fractions of degrees. It makes little difference if the temperature is 99⅘ or 99⅗°. What the doctor will be interested in is **about** what the temperature is. When you report the temperature to the doctor tell him what the thermometer actually says, and then add "by mouth" or "by rectum." I say this because sometimes a mother who has the mistaken idea that the mouth temperature is the only correct one takes a temperature by rectum and then tells the doctor what she figures the mouth temperature would be. Usually the best times to take the temperature are in the first part of the morning and late in the afternoon.

The next question is how many days to go on taking the temperature. Here is what happens occasionally. A child has a bad cold with fever. The doctor visits regularly and has the mother take the temperature twice a day. Finally the fever is gone, the child is convalescing well, has only a mild cough and running nose. The doctor finds everything satisfactory at his last examination, tells the mother to let the child outdoors as soon as the cold is gone completely. Two weeks later the mother telephones to say that she and the child are getting desperate staying indoors, that the running nose and cough have been completely gone for ten days, that the child looks wonderful and eats well, but the "fever" is still going to 99.6° each afternoon. As I explained earlier, this is not necessarily a fever in an active child. The ten days of staying indoors and of worrying over the temperature have all been a waste and a mistake. When the temperature has stayed under 101° for a couple of days, it's a good general rule to forget about the thermometer unless the doctor asks you to continue or unless the child seems sicker in any way. Don't get in the habit of taking a child's temperature when he is well.

607. Emergency treatment of high fever. Between the ages of 1 and 5 years, children may develop fever as high as 104° (sometimes even higher) at the onset of mild infections, such as colds, sore throats, grippe, just as often as with serious infections. On the other hand, a dangerous illness may never have a temperature higher than 101°. So don't be influenced too much, one way or the other, by the height of the fever, but get in touch with the doctor whenever your child appears sick in any way.

If on the first day of an illness a child's temperature is 104° or higher, and if it will be an hour or more before you can speak to the doctor, even on the telephone, it's wise, as an emergency measure, to bring the fever down a little with a wet rub and aspirin—1 tablet of "baby" aspirin (1¼ grains) under a year; 2 baby tablets (2½ grains) between 1 and 5 years. (Be sure to keep aspirin out of your child's reach.)

The purpose of the wet rub is to bring the blood to the surface by rubbing and to cool it by the evaporation of the water off the skin. (Alcohol has traditionally been used in a wet rub, but if it is applied very freely in a small room, too much may be inhaled. Anyway, water is just as good even if it doesn't smell so important.)

Undress the child and cover him with only a sheet or light blanket. Wet your hand in a basin of water. Expose one of his arms and rub it gently for a couple of minutes, wetting it again any time it becomes too dry. Then put it back under the sheet. Proceed, in turn, to the other arm, each leg, the chest, the back. Take the temperature again in half an hour, and if it isn't under 104° give another rub. You prefer to keep the temperature under 104° until the doctor comes because a small child who develops a sudden high fever the first day of an illness may become trembly or even have a convulsion (see Section 700). When a child's fever is very high and he is flushed, use only light covers at ordinary room temperature, perhaps as little as a sheet. You can't get his temperature down very well if he's heavily covered. Naturally, if he feels chilly, he needs more covers.

Many parents assume that the fever itself is bad and want to give medicine to bring it way down, no matter what degree it is. But it's well to remember that the fever is not the disease. The fever is one of the methods the body uses to help overcome the infection. It is also a help in keeping track of how the illness is progressing. In one case the doctor wants to bring the fever down because it is interfering with the child's sleep or exhausting him. In another case he is quite willing to leave the fever alone, and concentrate on curing the infection.

GIVING MEDICINES AND ENEMAS

608. Giving medicine. It's sometimes quite a trick getting a child to take his medicine. The first rule is to slip it into him in a matter-of-fact way, as if it has never occurred to you that he won't take it. If you go at it apologetically, with a lot of explanation, you convince him that he's expected to dislike it. Be talking about something else when you put the spoon in his mouth. Most young children open their mouths automatically, like birds in their nest.

Tablets that don't dissolve can be crushed to a fine powder and mixed with a coarse, good-tasting food like applesauce. Mix the medicine with only 1 teaspoonful of the applesauce, in case he decides he doesn't want very much. Bitter pills can be mixed in a teaspoonful of sugar and water, or honey, or maple syrup, or jam. Eye ointments and drops can sometimes be applied during sleep.

When giving medicine in a drink, it's safer to choose an unusual fluid that the child does not take regularly, such as grape juice or prune juice. If you give a queer taste to his milk or his orange juice, you may make him suspicious of it for months.

Getting a small child to swallow a whole tablet or a capsule is difficult. Try putting it in something lumpy and sticky like banana and follow the teaspoonful quickly with a drink of something he likes.

609. Don't give medicine without a doctor's advice and don't continue it without keeping in touch with him. Here are some examples of why not. A child has a cough with his cold, and the doctor prescribes a certain cough medicine. Two months later he develops a new cough, and the mother has the prescription renewed without consulting the doctor. It seems to help for a week, but then the cough becomes so bad that she has to call the doctor, anyway. He realizes right away that the disease this time is not a cold but whooping cough. He would have suspected it a week before if he had been consulted. In that case the child could have been isolated immediately and would not have exposed unnecessarily a lot of other children.

A mother who has treated colds or headaches or stomach-aches a few times in the same way comes to feel like an expert, which she is in a limited way. But she's not trained, as a doctor is, to first consider carefully what the diagnosis is. To her, two different headaches (or two stomach-aches) seem about the same. To the doctor, one has an entirely different meaning from the other and calls for different treatment. People who have been treated by a doctor with one of the sulfa drugs or one of the antibiotics (such as penicillin) are sometimes tempted to use it again for similar symptoms. They figure that it produces wonderful results, is easy to take, and they know the dosage from the last time —so why not?

Serious reactions occasionally develop from the use of these drugs— fevers, rashes, anemia, bleeding from the kidney, obstruction to the flow of urine. These complications, fortunately, are rare, but they are more liable to occur the more often the drugs are used, especially if they are used improperly. That is why they should be given only when a doctor has decided that the danger from the disease and the likelihood of benefit from the medicine outweigh the risks of treatment.

Cathartics (drugs to make the bowels move) should not be used for any reason—especially not for stomach-ache—without consulting a doctor. Some people have the mistaken idea that stomach-ache is frequently caused by constipation, and want to give a cathartic first of all. There are many causes of stomach-ache (see Sections 689 to 691). Some, such as appendicitis and obstruction of the intestines, are made worse by a cathartic. Therefore, since you don't know for sure what is causing your child's stomach-ache, it is dangerous to give a cathartic.

610. Enemas and Suppositories. A doctor sometimes prescribes an enema or suppository when a child becomes suddenly constipated, particularly if he is sick. During some illnesses these are safer than a cathartic given by mouth because they will not cause vomiting or irritate the small intestines. He may prescribe an enema for severe gas pains, as in 3-month colic or after an operation.

A parent should not give an enema or suppository for constipation or illness or pains until the doctor has made the diagnosis and prescribed the treatment. It's particularly important not to give enemas or suppositories repeatedly for a tendency to constipation, because eventually they focus a child's mind on his anus and bowels.

A suppository for constipation is slipped all the way into the rectum where it dissolves. It contains a mildly irritating material which draws moisture into the rectum and encourages a movement. A baby can sometimes be stimulated to move his bowels if you merely insert a lubricated thermometer or ear syringe tip or small enema tip into his anus and hold it there for a couple of minutes. This is an emergency treatment, on the doctor's advice. It is unwholesome to use it repeatedly for constipation or toilet training.

The doctor will tell you what to put in the enema. A soapy enema is made by stirring a piece of mild toilet soap in the water until it is slightly milky. This is a little irritating and is less often given to an infant. Enemas can also be made wth a half teaspoonful of table salt, or a teaspoonful of bicarbonate of soda, added to an 8-ounce cup of water. The water should be at about body temperature. You can give 4 ounces to a small infant, 8 ounces to a 1-year-old, a pint to a 5-year-old.

Place a waterproof sheet on a bed and lay a bath towel over it. Have the child lie on this on his side with his legs pulled up. Have a potty close at hand.

For an infant or small child, it is easiest and safest to use a rubber ear syringe with a soft tip of the same material. Fill the bulb completely, so that you won't be injecting air. Grease the tip with petroleum jelly, cold cream, or soap; gently insert it an inch or two. Squeeze the bulb slowly and not too forcibly. The slower you put it in, the less liable it is to make the baby feel uncomfortable and expel it. The bowel contracts and relaxes in waves. If you feel a strong resistance wait until it "gives" rather than push harder. Unfortunately, a baby is apt to push as soon as he feels something in his anus, so you may not get much in.

As you pull the tip out, press his buttocks together to try to hold the water in a few minutes to do its job of softening the movement. If the water has not come out in 15 or 20 minutes, or if it has come out without much movement, you can repeat the enema. There is no danger from an enema's staying in.

With an older child who will cooperate, you can use a syringe or enema bag or enema can with a rubber tube and a small, hard-rubber tip. Don't hang the bag higher than 1 to 2 feet above the level of the rectum (the height determines the pressure). The lowest height that makes the water run in slowly causes the least discomfort and brings the best results.

HANDLING AN INVALID

611. Spoiling is easy. When a child is really sick, you give him lots of special care and consideration, not only for practical medical reasons but also because you feel sorry for him. You don't mind preparing drinks and foods for him at frequent intervals or even putting aside a drink he refuses and making another kind right away. You are glad to get him new playthings to keep him happy and quiet. You ask him often how he feels, in a solicitous manner.

A child quickly adjusts to this new position in the household. If he has a disease that makes him cranky, he may be calling and bossing his mother like an old tyrant.

Fortunately, at least 90% of children's illnesses are on the way to recovery within a few days. As soon as the mother stops worrying, she stops kowtowing to the child when he is unreasonable. After a couple of days of minor clashes, everyone is back to normal.

But if a child develops a long illness or one that threatens to come back, and if the parents have a tendency to be worriers, the continued atmosphere of overconcern may have a bad effect on his spirit. He absorbs some of the anxiousness of those around him. He's apt to be demanding. If he's too polite for that, he may just become excitable and temperamental, like a spoiled actor. It's easy for him to learn to enjoy being sick and receiving pity. Some of his ability to make his own way agreeably may grow weaker, like a muscle that isn't being used.

612. Keep him busy and polite. So it's wise for parents to encourage themselves to get back into normal balance with the sick child as soon as possible. This means such little things as having a friendly, matter-of-fact expression when entering his room rather than a worried one; asking him how he feels today in a tone of voice that expects good news rather than bad (and perhaps asking him only once a day). When you find out by experience what he feels like drinking and eating, serve it up casually. Don't ask him timidly if he likes it or act as if he were wonderful to take a little. Keep strictly away from urging unless the doctor feels that it is necessary. A sick child's appetite is more quickly ruined by pushing and forcing than a well child's.

When he's leaping around in bed, it's better to tell him to lie still so that he can get well soon, rather than warn him of how much worse the disease might become. Better still to go light on the talk except for a firm reminder, and put the effort into getting him busy with something else.

If you are buying new playthings, look particularly for the ones that make him do all the work and give him a chance to use his imagination (blocks, sets for building, sewing, weaving, bead-stringing, painting, modeling, stamp collecting). These make demands on him and occupy him for long periods, whereas toys that are merely beautiful possessions quickly pall and only whet his appetite for more presents. Deal out one

Help an invalid to remain independent and outgoing.

new plaything at a time. There are lots of homemade occupations, like cutting pictures out of old magazines, making a scrapbook, sewing, whittling, building a farm or town or doll's house of cardboard and glue.

If a child is going to be laid up for a long time, but is well enough, get a teacher or a tutor or the best teacher in the family to start him on his schoolwork again for a regular period each day, just as soon as possible.

If he's human, he wants company part of the time, and you can join in some of his occupations or read to him. But if he wants more and more attention, try to avoid arguments and bargaining. Have regular times when he can count on your being with him and others when he knows you are going to be busy elsewhere. If he has a disease that isn't catching and the doctor lets him have company, invite other children in regularly to play and for meals.

It all adds up to letting the child lead just as normal a life as is possible under the circumstances, expecting from him reasonable behavior toward the rest of the family, and avoiding worried talk, looks, and thoughts.

GOING TO THE HOSPITAL

613. How to help the child. There's no perfect way to handle the business of taking a child to a hospital. There's usually some disease or risk that worries the parents.

Between the ages of 1 and 3 years, the child is most worried about being separated from his parents. He feels as if he is losing them forever when they first leave him and at the end of each hospital visit. Between visits he may remain anxious and depressed. When the parents come to see him, he may silently reproach them by refusing to greet them at first.

After the age of 3 the child is apt to be more fearful about what's going to be done to him, the injury to his body and the pain. It won't do for the parents to promise that the hospital will be a bed of roses, because if unpleasant things happen, the child loses confidence in his parents. On the other hand, if he is told **everything** bad that might happen, he is apt to suffer more in anticipation than he will when he is there.

The most important thing is for the parents to show all the calm, matter-of-fact confidence they are capable of, without forcing it so much that it sounds false. Unless the child has been a hospital patient before, he tries anxiously to imagine what it will be like, perhaps fearing the worst. The parents can set his mind at rest better by describing hospital life in general than by arguing with him whether it's going to hurt a lot or a little. You can tell him how the nurse will wake him in the morning and give him a bath right in bed, how the meals will come on trays and be eaten in his own bed, how there will be time to play, how he may use the bedpan or urinal instead of the bathroom, how he can call the nurse if he needs someone. You can tell him about visiting days and about all the other children to keep him company in the ward.

If he's going to be in a private room, you can plan together what favorite toys and books he's going to bring, and see whether there is a small radio to take from home or to borrow from a friend. He'll be interested in the electric button for calling the nurse.

It's fair to dwell on these everyday, pleasanter aspects of hospital life because even at the worst the child will spend most of his time amusing himself. I wouldn't keep away from the medical program altogether, but let the child see that it's a small part of hospital life.

If he is going to have his tonsils out, you can tell him about the mask they will put up to his nose, and how he will breathe and breathe until he goes to sleep; how he will wake up in an hour and find that his throat is sore (the way it was last winter when he had tonsillitis); that you will be there when he wakes up (if that is true), or that you will come to get him the next day.

614. Let him tell you his worries. More important than telling your child what occurs to you is giving him chances to ask questions and tell you what he imagines. Young children view these things in ways that never occur to adults. In the first place, they often think they have to be operated on or taken to the hospital because they have been bad—because they haven't worn their rubbers or haven't stayed in bed when sick or have been angry with other members of the family. They may imagine that their necks have to be cut open to remove their tonsils or their noses removed to get at the adenoids. Because of their worries and misunderstandings about the physical differences between boys and girls, children—particularly between 3 and 6—often fear subconsciously that an additional operation may be performed on the genitals, especially if they feel guilty about masturbation. So make it easy for your child to raise questions, be ready for strange fears, and try to reassure him about these.

615. Let him know ahead of time. If you know days or weeks ahead of time that a child will be hospitalized, it brings up the question of when to tell him. If there is no chance of his finding out, I think it is kinder to wait to tell a small child until a few days before it's time to leave. It won't do him any good to worry for weeks. It may be fairer to tell a 7-year-old some weeks ahead if he's the kind who can face things reasonably, especially if he has some suspicions. Certainly, don't lie to a child of any age if he asks questions, and never lure a child to a hospital pretending it's something else.

If your child is going to have an operation and you have a choice in the arrangements, you can discuss the matter of anesthetists and anesthesia with the doctor. How a child accepts the anesthesia is apt to make the biggest difference in whether he is emotionally upset by an operation or whether he goes through it with flying colors. Often in a hospital there is one or another anesthetist who is particularly good at inspiring confidence in children and getting them under without fright. It is worth a great deal to obtain the services of such an anesthetist if you have a choice. In some cases, there is also a choice in the kind of anesthetic that the doctor is considering, and this also makes a difference to the child psychologically. Generally speaking, it is less frightening to the child to start with gas than to start with ether, which is uncomfortable to breathe. The type of anesthetic that is given by a small enema (into the rectum)—even before the child starts for the operating room—is least likely to frighten him, but it is not suitable medically in all cases. Naturally, the doctor is the one who knows the factors and has to make the final decision. It's when he feels that there is an equal choice medically that the psychological factor should be considered carefully.

616. Visiting time in the hospital brings up special problems in the small child. The sight of the parents reminds him how much he has missed them. He may cry heartbreakingly when they leave or even cry through the entire visiting period. The parents are apt to get the impression that he is miserable there all the time. Actually, young children adjust surprisingly well to hospital life when the parents are out of sight, even though they are feeling sick or having uncomfortable treatments. I don't mean that the parents should stay away. The child is getting security of a kind from the visits even though they upset him, too. The best the parents can do is to act as cheerful and unworried as possible. If the parents have an anguished expression, it makes the child more anxious.

The chance that a child will be emotionally upset by an operation is greatest in the first 5 years of life. This is a reason for postponing an operation if the doctor feels that there is no particular hurry, especially if the child is already dependent or worrisome or subject to nightmares.

DIET DURING ILLNESS

Diet during diarrhea is discussed in Section 299.

617. Diet for a cold without fever. Your doctor will tell you what diet to use in each of your child's illnesses, taking into account the nature of the disease and the child's taste. What follows are some general principles to guide you in emergencies when you are unable to get medical help.

The diet during a mild cold without fever can be entirely normal. However, a child may lose some of his appetite even with a mild cold because he's indoors, because he's not taking his usual amount of exercise, because he's a little uncomfortable, and because he's swallowing mucus. Don't urge him to take more than he wants. If he is eating less than usual, offer him extra fluids between meals. There is no harm letting a child drink all that he feels like drinking. People sometimes have the idea that the more fluid, the better the treatment. Excessive amounts of fluid don't do any more good than reasonable amounts.

618. Diet during fever (emergency advice until you can consult the doctor). When a child has fever above 102° with a cold, grippe, sore throat, or one of the contagious diseases, he usually loses most of his appetite in the beginning, especially for solids. In the first day or two of such a fever, don't offer him solid food at all, but offer fluids every half-hour or hour when he's awake. Orange juice, pineapple juice, and water are most popular. Don't forget water. It has no nourishment, but that's unimportant for the time being. It's for this very reason that it often appeals to the sick child most. Other fluids depend on the child's taste and his illness. Some children love grapefruit juice, prune juice, lemonade, pear juice, grape juice, weak tea with sugar. Older children like carbonated drinks, like ginger ale, sarsaparilla, fruit-flavored sodas, and the cola drinks. Some cola drinks contain small amounts of caffeine, a stimulant, so should preferably not be given within a couple of hours before sleep time.

Milk is hard to make a rule about. The sick baby usually takes more milk than anything else. If he takes it without vomiting, it is the right thing. The older child may reject or vomit it. Offer it if it is desired and held down. With fever of over 102°, milk is digested more easily when it is skimmed (the top cream poured off). It's the butter fat that is hardest to digest.

When a fever continues, a child is apt to have a little more appetite after the first day or two. If your child is hungry in spite of a high fever, he may be able to take simple soft solids like toast, crackers, cereal, custard, gelatin, junket, ice cream, applesauce, soft-boiled egg.

The foods that are usually not wanted and not well digested during fever are vegetables (cooked or raw), meats, poultry, fish, fats (such as butter, margarine, cream). However, Dr. Clara Davis in her experiments on diet found that children often crave meats and vegetables during **convalescence**—after the fever is gone—and digest them well.

One rule more important than any other is not to urge a sick child to eat anything that he doesn't want unless the doctor has a special reason for urging it. It's only too likely to be vomited, or to cause an intestinal upset, or to start a feeding problem.

619. Diet when there is vomiting (emergency advice until you can consult the doctor). Of course, vomiting occurs in many different diseases, especially at the beginning when there is fever. The diet depends on many factors and should be prescribed by the doctor. However, if you cannot reach the doctor immediately, you can follow these suggestions. Vomiting occurs because the stomach is upset by the disease and is not able to handle the food.

It's a good idea to give the stomach a complete rest for at least a couple of hours after vomiting. Then **if the child is asking for it,** give him a sip of water, not more than half an ounce at first. If this stays down and he begs for more, let him have a little more, say 1 ounce in 15 or 20 minutes. Increase gradually up to 4 ounces (half a glass) if he craves it. If he has gone this far all right, you can try a little orange juice or pineapple juice or a carbonated drink. It is better not to go beyond 4 ounces at a time the first day. If several hours have gone by since the vomiting and the child is begging for solid food, give something simple like a cracker, or a tablespoonful of cereal or applesauce. If he is asking for milk, skim it.

If he vomits again, be more strict. Give nothing at all for 2 hours, and then start with a teaspoonful of water or cracked ice. In 20 minutes let him have 2 teaspoonfuls. Work up cautiously again. **If a child who has previously vomited doesn't want anything to drink even several hours later, don't offer anything.** It would almost certainly be vomited. The reason you play safe is that every time he vomits he is apt to lose more than he has drunk.

The vomiting that goes with a feverish illness is most apt to occur on the first day and may not continue even if the fever goes on.

Small specks or streaks of blood sometimes show in the vomited material when a child is retching violently. This is not serious in itself.

620. Avoiding feeding problems at the end of illness. If a child has a fever for several days and wants little to eat, he naturally loses weight rapidly. This worries a mother the first time or two that it happens. When the fever is finally gone and the doctor says it's all right to begin working back to a regular diet, she is impatient to feed him up again. But it often happens that the child turns away from the foods that are first offered. If the mother urges, meal after meal and day after day, his appetite may never pick up.

Such a child has not forgotten how to eat or become too weak to eat. At the time his temperature went back to normal there was still enough infection in his body to affect his stomach and intestines. Just as soon as he saw those first foods, his digestive system warned him that it was not ready for them yet.

When food is pushed or forced onto a child who already feels nauseated because of illness, his disgust is built up more easily and rapidly than if he had a normal appetite to start with. He can acquire a long-lasting feeding problem in a few days' time.

Just as soon as the stomach and intestines have recovered from the effects of most illnesses and are in condition to digest food again, a child's hunger comes back with a bang—and not just to what it used to be. He usually is ravenous for a week or two in order to make up for lost time. You sometimes see such a child whimpering for more, 2 hours after a large meal. By the age of 3, he may demand the specific foods that his starved system craves most.

The parent's course at the end of illness is to offer the child only the drinks and solids he wants, without any urging, and to wait patiently, but confidently, for signals that he is ready for more. If his appetite has not recovered in a week, the doctor should be consulted again.

COLDS

621. The cold virus, and the germs that make complications. Your child will probably be sick with colds ten times as much as with all his other illnesses combined. We only partly understand colds at the present time. A cold is started by a "filtrable virus." This is a germ so small that it can pass ("filter") through unglazed porcelain, so small that it cannot be seen through an ordinary microscope. It is believed that the virus can cause only a mild cold with a clear nasal discharge and perhaps a slight scratchy feeling in the throat. If nothing else happens, the virus cold goes away in about 3 days. But something else often does happen. The cold virus lowers the resistance of the nose and throat, so that other germs that cause more trouble get going, germs such as the streptococcus, the pneumococcus, and the influenza bacillus. They are called "secondary invaders." These regular bacteria are often living in healthy people's throats during the winter and spring months, but do no harm because they are held at bay by the body's resistance. It's only after the cold virus has lowered the resistance that these other germs get their chance to multiply and spread, causing bronchitis, pneumonia, ear infections, and sinusitis. That's why it is a good idea to take care of a child who has just a cold.

The best thing that you can do to avoid a cold is to keep away from anyone who has one.

622. Resistance to colds. Many people believe that they are more susceptible to colds when tired or chilled, but this has never been proved. A person is less apt to be chilled if he has built up his resistance by regularly going out in cold weather. A bank clerk is more easily chilled when he gets outdoors than a lumberjack. That is why children of all ages should be outdoors several hours a day in winter and sleep in cold rooms. It's also the reason they shouldn't be overdressed outdoors or too heavily covered in bed.

Houses and apartments that are kept too hot and dry during the winter season parch the nose and throat, and this may lower resistance to germs. The air in a room that's 75° is excessively dry. Many people hopefully try to moisten the air by putting pans of water on the radiators, but this method is almost completely worthless. The right way to keep enough moisture in the air in winter is to keep the room temperature down to 70° or below (68° is a good figure to aim at); then you won't need to worry about the humidity. Buy a reliable indoor thermometer. (See if it corresponds with several of the best thermometers your dealer has—an inexpensive one may be 4 degrees off, which makes it useless.) Then train yourself to glance at the thermometer several times a day. Turn the heat off every time the temperature goes above 68°. It will seem like a chore at first, but after living for a few weeks in a temperature below 70°, you will be trained to it and will feel uncomfortable in a hotter room.

What is the effect of diet on resistance to colds? Naturally, every child should be offered a well-balanced diet. But there is no proof that a child who is already receiving a reasonable variety will have fewer colds if he gets a little more of one kind of food or less of another.

What about vitamins? It is true that a person who is receiving a shockingly small amount of vitamin A in his diet may be more liable to colds and other infections. But this danger doesn't apply to children who are taking a decent diet because vitamin A is plentiful in milk, butter, eggs, vegetables.

It is believed that a child who is suffering from rickets (because of too little vitamin D) is more susceptible to the complications of colds, such as bronchitis. But if a child has no rickets and is receiving a satisfactory dose of vitamin D, there is no reason to believe that he will have fewer colds if **more** vitamin D is stuffed into him. There should be a sufficient amount of vitamin C in the diet. (See Section 421.)

623. Age is a factor in colds. Children between 2 and 6 get more colds, have them longer and with more complications. (The average is 7 a year in northern cities in the United States—more if there are children in the family attending school.) After the age of 6 years, the frequency and the severity grow less. A 9-year-old is apt to be laid up only half as much as he was at 6, and the 12-year-old only half as much as at 9. This should comfort the parents of a small child who seems to be forever sick.

624. The psychological factor in colds. Psychiatrists feel quite sure that **certain** children and grownups are much more susceptible to colds when they are tense or unhappy. I think of a boy 6 years old who was nervous about school because he couldn't keep up with the class in reading. Every Monday morning for several months he had a cough. You may think he was putting it on. It wasn't so simple as that. It wasn't a dry, forced cough. It was a real, thick one. The cough would improve as the week went by and by Friday it would be all gone, only to reappear again Sunday night or Monday morning. There's nothing mysterious about this. We know that one person has cold, clammy hands when he is nervous; an athlete may have diarrhea before a race. So it's perfectly possible that nervousness may interfere with the circulation of the nose or throat so that germs have a better chance to flourish there.

625. Exposure to other children. There is another factor that influences the number of colds a child has. That's the number of children he plays with, especially indoors. The **average** single child living on an isolated farm has few colds because he is exposed to few cold germs. On the other hand, the **average** child in a nursery or elementary school has plenty, even though the school is careful to exclude every child who has symptoms. A person can probably give his infection to others for at least a day before he shows signs of it himself, and at times he can carry cold germs and pass them on to others without ever showing symptoms himself. There are some lucky children who rarely catch cold, no matter how many colds there are around them.

626. Can the spread of infection in a family be checked? Most colds that are brought into a family are caught by the younger children in at least a mild form, especially if the house is small and everyone has to use the same rooms. Not only do the germs of colds and other infections get passed from one person to another in large doses on the spray of sneezes and coughs, but they also float around in the air of the room in fair numbers just from being breathed into the air. Tests have shown that a gauze mask worn over the nose and mouth doesn't keep most germs from getting into the air. All of this means that there's no great advantage in the mother's wearing a mask or in trying half-heartedly to keep young children apart. Babies catch fewer colds, and it may be worth while for the mother—especially if she has a sore throat—to avoid sneezing, coughing, or breathing directly into a baby's face and to wash her hands with soap before handling things that will go into the baby's mouth—the bowl of the spoon, the mouth part of a nipple, a teething ring, finger foods—to prevent the transfer of large numbers of bacteria.

Under special circumstances, it may be worth while to go to extra lengths to protect a baby or small child who is frail or particularly susceptible to infections—if the house is large enough so that the baby can be kept in a separate room with the door closed and if there is one adult without symptoms who can care for him. It is probably preferable that this adult, who is also mixing with the rest of the family and who is therefore carrying some germs, not sleep in the baby's room or stay there when the baby doesn't need attention.

If an outsider has any suspicion of a cold or any other illness, be very firm about not letting him in the same house with the baby, or within a couple of yards of the carriage outdoors. Say that the doctor told you to keep people with colds away.

What about chronic nose colds or sinusitis? If a person has had such an infection for 2 weeks or more, it's probably no longer important to keep him out of the same room. I would still suggest the other precautions: hand-washing, keeping his face turned away when doing anything for the baby.

627. X ray for anyone with a chronic cough. Anyone in a household who has a chronic cough should be examined by a doctor and X-rayed to be sure it is not tuberculosis. This rule is particularly important if there is a baby or small child in the home, or if one is expected. If you have a baby or child and are hiring a maid or nurse, she should be examined and have a chest X ray before becoming a member of the household.

628. Colds in the infant. If your baby has a cold during his first year, the chances are that it will be mild. He may sneeze in the beginning; his nose will be runny or bubbly or stuffy. He may cough a little. He is not likely to have any fever. When his nose is bubbly, you wish you could blow it for him. But it doesn't seem to bother him. On the other hand, if his nose is obstructed with thick mucus, it may make him frantic. He keeps trying to close his mouth and is angry when he can't breathe. The stuffiness may bother him most when he tries to nurse at the breast or bottle, so much so that he refuses altogether at times.

Bubbling and obstruction can often be relieved by sucking the mucus out with a soft-rubber ear syringe with a soft-rubber tip. Compress the bulb, insert the tip into his nose, and release the bulb.

Extra moisture in his room (Section 632) helps prevent stuffiness. If it is severe, the doctor may prescribe the shrinking kind of nose drops for use just before nursing. In other respects the baby may not lose much of his appetite. Usually the cold is gone in a week. Sometimes, though, a small baby's cold can last an unbelievably long time even though it stays mild.

Of course, a baby's cold **can** become severe. He can have bronchitis and other complications, but these are less common during the first year than later. If he has a frequent cough or a deep cough or a wheezy cough, he should be examined by a doctor, even if he has no fever. The same rule applies if he **looks** sick with a cold. In other words, a baby can be quite sick and not have fever.

629. Colds and fever after infancy. Some children go on having the same mild colds, without fever or complications, that they had during infancy. It's more common, though, when a child gets to be 1 or 2 years old, for his colds and throat infections to act differently. Here is a common story. A child of 2 is well during the morning. At lunchtime he seems a little tired and has less appetite than usual. When he wakes up from his nap he is cranky and his mother notices that he is hot. She takes his temperature, and it's 102°. By the time the doctor comes, the temperature is 104°. The child's cheeks are flushed and his eyes are dull, but otherwise he doesn't seem particularly sick. He may want no supper at all, or he may want a fair amount. He has no cold symptoms, and the doctor hasn't found anything definite except that his throat is perhaps a little red. The next day he may have little fever, but now his nose may begin to run. Perhaps he coughs occasionally. From this point on, it's just a regular mild cold that lasts anywhere from 2 days to 2 weeks.

There are several variations of this typical story. Sometimes the child vomits at the time his fever is shooting up. This is particularly apt to happen if his mother has unwisely tried to get him to eat more of his lunch than he wanted. (Always take a child's word for it when he loses his appetite.) Sometimes the fever lasts several days in the beginning, before the cold symptoms appear. One reason that the nose doesn't run at first is that fever dries it up. Sometimes the fever lasts for a day or two and then goes away without any running nose or cough taking its place. In this case, the doctor may call it grippe or flu. These terms are commonly used for infections that have no **local** symptoms (like running nose or diarrhea), only **generalized** symptoms (such as fever or a sick-all-over feeling). You suspect that this kind of 1-day fever is sometimes a cold that was stopped in its tracks: the child seems perfectly well for a day or two after his fever is gone, and then promptly starts a running nose or cough when he is taken out in cold weather.

I am making the point that children over the age of 1 year often start their colds with sudden high fever so that you won't be too alarmed if this happens. You should, of course, always consult the doctor whenever your child falls ill with a fever because it occasionally means a more serious infection.

When a child is 5 or 6, he's more apt to be starting his colds without much fever again.

Fever that begins after a cold is well under way has a different meaning entirely from the fever that comes on the first day. It usually indicates that the cold has spread or become worse. This isn't necessarily serious or alarming. It only means that the doctor should see the child again to make sure that the ears, bronchial tubes, and urinary system are still healthy.

THE HANDLING OF A CHILD WITH A COLD

630. Calling the doctor. You should call the doctor when your child's first cold appears. He will decide whether he needs to make a visit, and outline the treatment. You may not need to call him every time another mild cold begins, but you certainly should call him every time an unusual symptom appears, every time there is fever of 101° or more, and every time the cold is more than just a mild one. (If you happen to find in the middle of the night that your child has a temperature of 101°, you don't have to call the doctor then, as long as the cold is mild. Call him in the morning.)

631. Keep him evenly warm. Chilling often makes a cold worse. That is why it is generally recommended that a child stay indoors and away from drafts until the cold is over. It's not quite so important in warm weather, but it is still advisable, especially for the young child. Wind cools one part of the body more than another, and it's this uneven coolness that seems to make the cold worse.

A mother is usually anxious to get her child outdoors again, and a doctor hears the following story many times each winter. The mother says, "His cold was so much better, and it was such a beautiful day, that I decided it would do him good to be outdoors. But tonight his cough is much worse, and he is complaining of an earache." There is no proof that sunshine does a cold any good, and there's plenty of evidence that chilling does harm.

There are lots of children who are never kept in when they have a cold, and nothing serious seems to happen. But this doesn't cover all the cases. A doctor sees the ones that become worse. Perhaps that makes him overcautious. It is safer to keep a young, susceptible child indoors for 1 or 2 full days after the last signs of the cold are gone, then let him out for 20 or 30 minutes in a sheltered spot. If the cold doesn't come back after the first day out, let him out for his usual length of time the second day. You don't have to be so fussy with an older child.

Whether a child has to stay in bed depends on whether he has fever, how old he is, and how much trouble he has, so your own doctor is the one to answer this. Generally speaking, it isn't necessary for him to be in bed unless he is running a fever. But I think it's preferable to keep a **small** child in bed at first, especially if his colds tend to be bad ones. If by the end of 2 days the cold is still mild and without fever, it is usually safe to let him up. However, some small children raise the devil if they are kept in bed, crying and raging for hours. Others who are always jumping around outside the covers can be kept warmer if they are up and dressed. In either of these cases it may be better to let the child stay up from the beginning if he has no fever; certainly keep him indoors and busy with quiet activities. A child of 5 or more who has only mild colds certainly doesn't need to be kept in bed if he has no fever.

Clothing during a cold is important. Aim to keep your child evenly, comfortably warm. If he is sitting up in bed, he should wear a light sweater or warm bathrobe over his pajamas to keep the upper half of his body as warm as the lower. Don't put too many blankets over his legs. In a warm room one is sufficient. You don't want him to be in a warm perspiration below and a cool perspiration above. The same principle of even warmth applies if he is up and around the house. He should have as much on his legs as on his chest. (The air is coolest and draftiest near the floor.) The best way to achieve this is with long overalls. A pair of long stockings or long underwear also does the job.

The temperature of the room in which the child plays might be kept around 72° (compared with the 68° that is ideal when he is healthy). It's better to keep the room comfortably warm during the night, too. This means keeping the windows closed. Then there is no danger of drafts or of chilling if he gets uncovered. Cold air is health-giving when a person is well, but when he has a cold it is somewhat risky. If you're worried about the stuffiness of the room, leave the door open into the hall, or give the room an airing by opening the window for a couple of minutes.

632. Keeping the air moist in an overheated room. The doctor sometimes recommends humidifying or steaming the room during a cold. It counteracts the dryness of the air and soothes the inflamed nose and throat. It is particularly valuable in the treatment of a tight, dry cough or croup. It is not necessary in warm weather when the heat is off.

There are several ways to get extra moisture into a room. You can buy an electric vaporizer ("croup kettle") at the drugstore. Get a large size that holds several quarts of water and evaporates at least a pint an hour. (A small vaporizer doesn't produce enough steam to moisten the air of a whole room. It requires the patient to sit close and breathe the steam as it emerges, but a small child won't do this.) Some vaporizers are designed to shut off the current when the water is low, which is an added safety factor. The vaporizer should be in a safe place where the child can't touch it or pull it over by the electric cord.

If you can't get a vaporizer, you can boil water in a pan or kettle on a small electric stove or hot plate. The bottom of the pan should be large enough to cover the coil (so that the heat mostly goes to make steam). **Precaution:** Be sure to have the boiling water in a place where a small child cannot get into it or pull it over on himself. It's unsafe to use this arrangement if a child can climb out of his crib unless you are going to be in his room constantly or unless he is old enough to be really responsible. An electric burner should never be left on after the family have gone to sleep. Such stoves can catch fire.

Sometimes the doctor recommends including a soothing medication in the vaporizer. But the moisture is the main factor.

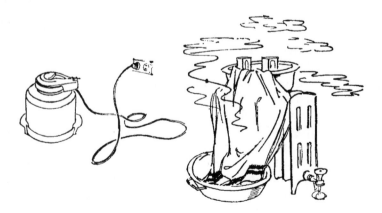

Another method for getting extra moisture into the air is keeping the radiator covered by a wet bath towel. It needs to be wrung out in water every 20 minutes. Or you can keep both ends of the towel constantly in water. Put a pan full of water on top of the radiator and a dishpan of water on the floor. Hang the bath towel from one into the other. Spread it out to cover as much of the front of the radiator as possible. Anchor the towel in the top pan with two bricks or clothespins.

You can also humidify a room by hanging a wet sheet on a line, but it gets in the way and drips on the floor.

633. Nose drops. The doctor may prescribe nose drops. Generally speaking, they fall into two groups. There are the mild antiseptics to kill germs. Their usefulness is limited because they can't kill the germs that are below the surface. The other general class of nose drops are the solutions that shrink the tissues in the nose. This opens up more space for breathing and gives the mucus and pus a better chance to drain. The main drawback is that after the tissues have been shrunk a reaction sets in and they expand again. This may leave the nose more stuffy than ever and may be irritating to the delicate membranes if it's done too often. There are three situations in which the shrinking kind of nose drops are useful. The first is when a baby is so stuffed up that he is frantic. He can't nurse without suffocating, and his sleep is interrupted. (This condition may be relieved by suction with an ear syringe alone.) The second is in the late stages of a bad cold or sinusitis, when the nose is filled with a thick yellow secretion that does not discharge by itself. The third is when the doctor wants to open up the Eustachian tube, which connects the ear with the throat, during an ear infection.

Nose drops do a lot more good if they get back into the inner and upper passages of the nose. Suck out the mucus in the front of the nose with an ear syringe. Then have the child lie on his back across a bed with his head hanging **well** down over the side. Insert the drops and try to keep him in this position for half a minute while the drops work back and up.

Nose drops should be used only on a doctor's recommendation, no more often than every 4 hours. Don't use them for more than a week unless the doctor says to go on. One disadvantage of all nose drops is that many small children fight them. There are only a few conditions in which nose drops do enough good to be worth getting the child all upset.

There are a number of commercial ointments for rubbing on the chest. The idea is to stimulate the skin of the chest to relieve a cough, or to help the nose with the aromatic oils that are wafted upward. There is no proof of the benefit of this kind of treatment, but if it seems to help, there is no harm in its use.

634. Cough medicines. No cough medicine can cure a cold, in the sense of killing the germs. It can only make the windpipe less ticklish, so that coughing is less frequent, or loosen up the mucus. A person who has an infection in his windpipe or his bronchial tubes **should** cough once in a while to bring up the mucus and pus. The doctor prescribes a cough medicine to keep the cough from being so frequent that it tires the person out or interferes with his sleep or irritates his throat. Any child or grownup who has a cough that is that frequent should be under the care of a doctor, and he is the one to prescribe the right cough medicine.

EAR INFECTIONS

635. Mild ear infections are common in young children. Some children have inflammation of the ears with most of their colds, and others never do. The ears are much more apt to be infected in the first 3 or 4 years of life. In fact, there is a slight ear inflammation in a majority of colds at this age, but it usually never comes to anything, and the child has no symptoms.

Usually the ear doesn't become inflamed enough to cause pain until after a cold has been going for several days. The child over 2 tells what is the matter. A baby may keep rubbing his ear or just cry piercingly for several hours. There may or may not be fever. The doctor is apt to find at this stage that there is only a mild inflammation of the upper part of the eardrum. This is not an abscess. Many ear infections of this degree get well again in a few days with bed rest in a warm room, whether or not other treatment is used. A few, however, especially those in which there is fever from the beginning, get worse and develop into abscesses in a few days if treatment is not started. Incidentally, many early mild inflammations of the ear cause pain and tenderness behind the ear, in the mastoid region, but this does not mean an infection of the mastoid bone and is not a serious sign at this stage. I mention these points so that you will not begin worrying about an abscess or a mastoid infection the first time an earache develops.

With prompt treatment with modern drugs, few ear infections get even as far as an abscess, and mastoiditis is rare.

Any time that your child has an earache, you should get in touch with the doctor that same day, particularly if there is any fever. The drugs that are used when necessary work much better in the early stages of ear infections.

Suppose it will be several hours before you can reach the doctor. What can you do to relieve the pain? A hot-water bottle or an electric heating pad helps some. Small children are impatient with them. Aspirin relieves a certain amount of pain—for an infant, 1 tablet of baby aspirin (1¼ grains); for a 1-to-5-year-old, 2 tablets of baby aspirin (2½ grains); for a 6-to-12-year-old, 3 tablets of baby aspirin (3¾ grains). What will help even more, if you happen to have it on hand, is a dose of a cough medicine containing codeine that the doctor has prescribed for that particular child. (A medicine prescribed for an older child or adult might contain too much of the drug.) Codeine is an efficient pain killer as well as cough remedy. If the earache is severe, you can use all these remedies together.

Once in a while an eardrum breaks very early in an infection and discharges a thin pus. You may find the discharge on the child's pillow in the morning without his ever having complained of pain or fever. Usually, however, the drum breaks only after an abscess has been developing for several days, with fever and pain. In any case, if you find your child's ear discharging, the most that you should do is to tuck a loose plug of sterile absorbent cotton into the opening to collect the pus, wash the pus off the outside of the ear with soap and water, and get in touch with the doctor. If the discharge leaks out anyway and irritates the skin, wash the pus off and protect the skin with petroleum jelly.

It is quite common for a child to become deaf after a few days of even a moderate ear infection. In practically all cases, this deafness clears up if the infection is promptly and correctly treated.

BRONCHITIS AND PNEUMONIA

636. Bronchitis. There are all degrees of bronchitis, from very mild with no fever, to severe. Bronchitis simply means that a cold has spread down to the bronchial tubes. There is usually plenty of cough. Sometimes you can hear faraway squeaky noises as the child breathes, and feel the vibration of the mucus as you touch his chest.

A very mild bronchitis, without fever, without much cough, without loss of appetite, is only a little more serious than a nose cold. However, if the child acts sick, or coughs frequently, or has a fever of 101°, the doctor should be reached that same day, because modern drugs are of great benefit in cases that require them.

The young infant who has a frequent cough should be examined whether he has a fever or not, because in the first month or two of life there can be serious infections without fever. In the meantime, you don't need to worry if his appetite and general appearance are satisfactory.

637. Pneumonia. Pneumonia usually comes on after a child has had a cold for several days, but it may start without any previous warning. You suspect it when the temperature climbs up to 103 or 104°, the breathing becomes rapid, and there is a cough. Vomiting often occurs at the beginning, and there may even be a convulsion in a small child. Modern drugs bring about a prompt cure of the ordinary types of pneumonia if treatment is started early. Naturally, you call the doctor if your child develops a fever and cough.

There are also unusual types of pneumonia, most of which are probably caused by filtrable viruses. In many of these "atypical" pneumonias, the child is less sick, though the disease may last a long time.

CROUP

638. Spasmodic croup without fever. Croup is the word commonly used for various kinds of laryngitis in children. There is usually a hoarse, ringing, barking cough (croupy cough) and some tightness in the breathing.

The commonest and mildest type, **spasmodic croup without fever,** comes on suddenly during the evening. The child may have been perfectly healthy during the day or have had the mildest kind of cold without cough. Suddenly he wakes up with a violent fit of croupy coughing, is quite hoarse, and is having difficulty breathing. He struggles and heaves to get his breath in. It's quite a scary picture when you see it the first time, but it's not so serious as it looks. You should call the doctor promptly for any kind of croup.

The emergency treatment of croup, until the doctor can be reached, is moist air. A small room is preferable because you can steam it up faster. If the water runs hot, take the child into the bathroom and run hot water into the tub (to make steam, not to put the child in). If there is a shower, that will work best of all. If the water is not hot, make steam with an electric vaporizer ("croup kettle") or by boiling a pan of water on an electric stove or hot plate. Hold him close to the steam until the whole room gets steamy. If you have no hot water in the pipes and no electric vaporizer or hot plate, take him to the kitchen and hold him close while you boil water on the stove. An umbrella covering both the child's head and the boiling saucepan will keep the moist air around him. See Section 632.

When the child breathes the moist air, the croup usually begins to improve rapidly. Meanwhile, the air in the room where he will go back to bed should be moistened. An adult should stay awake as long as there are any symptoms of croup, sleep in the same room with the child for

3 nights, and wake herself 2 or 3 hours after the croup is over to make sure that the child is breathing comfortably.

Spasmodic croup without fever sometimes comes back the next night or two. To avoid this, have the child sleep in a room in which the air has been moistened for 3 nights. This form of croup is apparently caused by the combination of a cold infection, a child with a sensitive larynx, and dry air.

639. Severe croup with fever (laryngo-bronchitis). This is a more severe form of croup that is usually accompanied by a real chest cold. The croupy cough and the tight breathing may come on gradually or suddenly at any time of the day or night. Steaming only partly relieves it. **If your child has hoarseness with fever or tightness of breathing with fever, he must be put under the close, continuous supervision of a doctor without delay.** If you cannot reach your doctor right away, find another doctor. If a doctor cannot reach you, you should take the child to a hospital.

640. Diphtheria of the larynx is still another cause of croup. There is a gradually increasing hoarseness, cough, difficulty in breathing, and moderate fever. There is practically no danger of this form of croup developing if a child has received diphtheria inoculations.

However, with any form of croup, a child should be seen promptly by a doctor. The urgency is greatest when hoarseness and tight breathing are persisting, even mildly, and when there is fever of 101° or more.

SINUSITIS, TONSILLITIS, AND SWOLLEN GLANDS

641. Sinusitis. The sinuses are cavities in the bones surrounding the nose. Each sinus cavity connects with the interior of the nose through a small opening. The maxillary sinuses are in the cheekbones. The frontal sinuses are in the forehead, just above the eyebrows. The ethmoid sinuses are up above the inner passages of the nose. The sphenoids are farther back, behind the nasal passages. The maxillary and the ethmoid sinuses are the only ones that are well enough developed in the early years of childhood to be infected then. The frontals and sphenoids develop gradually after the age of 6. When there is a severe or prolonged cold in the nose, the infection may spread from the nose into these various sinus cavities. Sinus infections usually last longer than simple nose colds, because they are more closed in, can't drain so well. A sinus infection may be very mild and show itself only by a chronic discharge of pus from the back of the nose into the throat (called a postnasal drip). This sometimes causes a chronic cough when the child lies down in bed or when he first gets up in the morning. On the other hand, sinusitis may be severe, with high fever and pain. When a doctor suspects sinusitis, he sometimes investigates further by X-ray pictures or by shining a light through the sinuses in a dark room. He uses various treatments, such as nose drops, nose packs, suction, drugs, depending on the case.

Whatever specific method the doctor is using, remember that the general care of the child is important, too. A sinus infection is, after all, only a more advanced and persistent form of a cold. Like a cold, it is helped by keeping a child indoors, in a warm, even-temperatured room with moist air. The child should be evenly clothed, the windows should be kept closed at night.

642. Tonsillitis. Real tonsillitis is a definite disease, caused by the streptococcus. The child usually has high fever for a number of days and feels sick. Headache and vomiting are common. His tonsils become fiery red and swollen. After a day or two, white spots or white patches appear on them. An older child may complain of such a sore throat that he can hardly swallow. Young children may be bothered surprisingly little by the sore throat.

You should have the doctor for a case of tonsillitis. It is important to treat it promptly and thoroughly with one of the drugs that is so effective in overcoming the infection and preventing complications. (The action of the drug should continue for at least 10 days.) Convalescence is often slow. If the neck glands become swollen, if the child continues to look washed out or to run a low fever, treat him as an invalid and keep in touch with the doctor.

643. Other throat infections. There are all kinds and degrees of throat infections, caused by a variety of germs. The medical term for them is pharyngitis. Many people feel a slight sore throat at the beginning of every cold. Often the doctor, in examining a child with a fever, finds a slightly red throat as the only sign of disease. The child may or may not notice any soreness. Most of these are soon over. The child should stay indoors until the sore throat is all gone. The doctor should be called if there is any fever, or if the child looks sick, or if the throat is more than slightly sore (even if there is no fever). If the doctor suspects a streptococcal infection, he may take a throat culture or treat it anyway with one of the effective drugs, to prevent possible complications.

644. Swollen glands. The lymph glands that are scattered up and down the sides of the neck sometimes become infected and swollen as a result of any disease in the throat, mild or severe. The commonest cause is tonsillitis. It can develop in the middle of the tonsillitis or a week or two later. If the glands are swollen enough to be visible, or if there is fever of 101° or more, the doctor should certainly be called. Treatment with drugs may be called for in certain cases and is most valuable if begun early.

Slightly enlarged neck glands may last for weeks or even months after some throat infections. They can come from other causes, too, such as infected teeth, scalp infections, and general diseases, like German measles. You should consult your doctor about them. But if he finds the child generally healthy, don't worry about slightly swollen glands.

TONSILS AND ADENOIDS

645. The tonsils and adenoids are meant to be there unless they are causing trouble. Tonsils and adenoids have been blamed for so many things in the last half century that many people think of them as villains that have to be removed eventually, and the sooner the better. This is the wrong way to look at them. They are there presumably for the purpose of helping to overcome infection and build up the body's resistance to germs. The trouble is, particularly in cities, that there are so many infections around that the tonsils sometimes are overwhelmed and become storehouses of the very germs they are meant to destroy. And the adenoids, when overworked, become so large that they block the back of the nose. This obstructs the breathing and keeps infections in the nose from discharging properly.

The tonsils and adenoids are made of what is called lymphoid tissue, and are similar to the glands in the sides of the neck, the armpits, and the groin. Any of these glands, including the tonsils and adenoids, become swollen when there is infection near by, as they labor to kill germs and build resistance.

646. The tonsils. In normal, healthy children, the tonsils gradually become larger until the age of 7 or 8 or 9, and then gradually decrease in size. In former years it was believed that all abnormally enlarged tonsils were diseased and should be removed. Nowadays it is believed that the size alone is relatively unimportant. The real question is how the tonsils work and whether they are chronically diseased. In any case, the doctor doesn't try to judge their size during or right after a throat infection, because they are probably swollen at this time. If the tonsils and the surrounding folds of skin are always inflamed, week in and week out, they are under suspicion. Sometimes chronically infected tonsils are the cause of a generally run-down state, or of a chronic fever, or of prolonged swollen glands in the neck, or of other disturbances. The doctor is the one to decide whether the tonsils are chronically infected.

Another reason for considering removal of the tonsils is repeated at tacks of severe tonsillitis. The same question is usually raised if the child has an attack of quinsy sore throat (an abscess behind the tonsil).

The tonsils are sometimes removed for other reasons—for instance, because of frequent colds, ear infections, rheumatism, and chorea—even though they do not appear definitely diseased. But the likelihood of improvement in these conditions is not great. There is no need to remove the tonsils, even when they are large, in a child who is perfectly healthy and has few nose and throat infections. There is no reason to operate because of a feeding problem, or stuttering, or nervousness; in fact, the operation may make the child worse.

647. The adenoids. The adenoids are clusters of lymphoid tissue up behind the soft palate, where the nose passages join the throat. When they become too enlarged they block this passageway from the nose. This causes mouth breathing and snoring. It may prevent the free discharge of mucus and pus from the nose, and thus help to keep bad colds and sinus infections going. Enlarged adenoids may also block the passages leading from the nose to the ears and favor ear infections.

So the adenoids are most often removed because of mouth breathing, chronic nose and sinus infection, repeated or persistent ear abscesses. Removing them does not necessarily make a child breathe through his nose. Some children are mouth-breathers because of habit (they seem to be born that way) and not because of obstruction. And some children's noses are obstructed not by adenoids but by swollen tissues in the front of the nose (for instance, by hay fever or other forms of allergy). Removing the adenoids decreases only moderately the chances of more ear infections.

When the tonsils are removed, the adenoids are practically always cut out, too, because the latter is much the easiest part of the job. On the other hand, there is often good reason to take out the adenoids alone if they are causing obstruction, and to leave the tonsils if they look healthy and are causing no trouble.

The adenoids always grow back to some extent, and the body always tries to grow new lumps of lymphoid tissue where the tonsils used to be. This isn't a sign that the operation was done incompletely or that it has to be done again. It shows only that the body means to have lymphoid tissue in that region and tries hard to replace it. If the adenoids grow large enough again to cause serious obstruction, the operation may have to be repeated. The new growth in the tonsil region seldom needs to be removed a second time because it is rarely the seat of chronic infection or a true tonsillitis.

Doctors generally try to postpone operations on the tonsils and adenoids, if there is any doubt about it, until the child is in the neighborhood of 7 years old. There are several reasons. After 7 there is a tendency for the tonsils and adenoids to become smaller at the same time that the throat structure is growing larger. Another reason is that the adenoid and tonsil tissue grows back more vigorously before the age of 7. A third and important reason is that the young child may be frightened by the operation and remain nervous for a long while afterward. In general, it is the timid and sensitive children who are more apt to take it hard. However, if there are urgent reasons for performing the operation in the early years, it should be done.

If there is no great rush about the operation, it is better to do it in the late spring or fall, when throat infections are less common. The operation is usually postponed several weeks after a fresh cold or sore throat for fear of stirring up the infection again. The operation is also avoided during the poliomyelitis season, since it makes a child susceptible to the disease in its most dangerous form.

In Sections 613 to 616 there are suggestions about handling operations.

ALLERGIES

648. Allergic nose troubles, including hay fever. You probably know someone who has ragweed hay fever. When ragweed pollen gets in the wind in mid-August, he starts to sneeze and his nose begins to be stuffed up and itch and run. This means that his nose is **allergic,** or oversensitive, to the pollen, which doesn't bother other people at all. Some people have hay fever in spring because they are allergic to certain tree pollens, and others have it in early summer from certain grasses. If your child develops a running, itching nose that lasts for weeks, at the same time every year, you should take it up with your doctor. From the appearance of the nose in the season and from skin tests with the suspected pollens, he can tell whether it's hay fever. The treatment often consists of frequent injections carried out over a long period. The doctor can usually give temporary relief with medicine.

But there are nose allergies aside from seasonal hay fevers that may be less dramatic but more troublesome. There are noses that are sensitive to the feathers in pillows, or to dog hair, or to house dust, or to any number of other substances. Such year-round allergies as these may keep a child stuffy or running at the nose, breathing through his mouth, month in and month out. The chronic obstruction may make him more susceptible to sinus infections. If your child is much bothered this way, your doctor, or an allergy specialist whom he recommends, may be able to find the cause. The treatment is different in each case and depends on the causes. If it's goose feathers, you change the pillow. If it's dog hair, you may have to give away the dog and substitute some other plaything. If it's something hard to avoid, like house dust, the doctor may give injections of the offending substance over a long period. He is likely to recommend "stripping the room" to lessen the dust there, especially if the symptoms occur mainly at night or the first thing in the morning. You remove the rugs and curtains for good and give the room a wet-mopping every day. You eliminate all wool from the room and also the stuffed toys. You either buy dustproof coverings for the mattress and pillow, specially made for this purpose, or get a canvas cot with no pillow at all.

Allergy symptoms usually can't be eliminated completely. You have to be satisfied with partial improvement.

649. Asthma. Asthma is another kind of allergy. Instead of the sensitive organ being the nose, as in hay fever, it is the bronchial tubes. When the irritating substance reaches the small bronchial tubes, they swell, thick mucus is secreted, and the passageways for air are so narrowed that breathing becomes difficult, labored, and wheezing. Coughing occurs.

When an older child has chronic asthma, it's apt to be due to substances that float in the air, such as horse dander, dog hair, molds, etc. Allergists call these "inhalants." In a very young child, allergy to foods is more likely to be the cause or to play a part.

The child who has chronic asthma of more than slight degree is usually tested to discover the offending substances, and then treated. If the disease is neglected, the repeated attacks may have a harmful effect on the structure of the lungs and chest. The treatment depends on the cause and is different in each case. Foods that the child is sensitive to are eliminated from the diet. When inhalants are the cause, the treatment is much the same as in year-round allergies of the nose (Section 648).

Asthma is not simply a matter of allergy to certain substances. A person has an attack at one time and not at another, even though he's in the same place leading the same life. Attacks are more common at night. Season of year, climate, temperature, exercise, state of mind, play a part in different cases. Colds often start an attack. Certain children are apt to have attacks of asthma (or other allergies) at the times they are nervous or upset and may be greatly improved when their troubles are straightened out, perhaps with a psychiatrist's help. In other words, you try to treat the whole child, not just the asthma.

The treatment of the individual attack of asthma depends a lot on how severe it is, and on what the doctor finds is helpful for that case.

There are drugs given by mouth or injection for temporary relief when the child is having real difficulty breathing.

If your child develops asthma for the first time when you are out of reach of a doctor, don't be alarmed. The condition is rarely as dangerous as it looks. Keep him in bed if the breathing is very difficult. If it's winter and the house is heated, have the room comfortably warm and get extra moisture into the air (Section 632). If he is coughing much and you have cough medicine that was prescribed for him before, you can give him a dose. Get him occupied in play or reading while you go about your own work, or read to him yourself. If you hover over him anxiously, it keeps him more frightened and may actually make the asthma worse. If he continues to have spells, you can try stripping his room (Section 648), until you are able to consult a doctor.

It is impossible to predict about asthma. Cases that start early in childhood are more apt to clear up in a few years than those that start later. A certain number go away by the age of puberty. But sometimes hay fever takes the place of the asthma.

650. Asthmatic bronchitis should be mentioned separately. An occasional baby or small child has spells of wheezing, difficult breathing, not at any old time, as in typical chronic asthma, but only when he has a real cold. This tendency is most common in the first 3 years of life. It's discouraging to have a baby who regularly has this much trouble with his colds, but there is a brighter side to the picture. The tendency to asthmatic bronchitis is usually well on its way to disappearing in a couple of years. The doctor should be called, of course. The infection and the cough may need treating as much as the wheezing. If the house is heated, it may help to get extra moisture in the air (Section 632). The injections and medicines to open up the bronchial tubes, that are often helpful in ordinary asthma, have little effect in asthmatic bronchitis.

651. Hives. Hives are considered, at least in some cases, to be due to allergy of the skin. The commonest kind consists of raised welts. They are often pale in the raised part, because the blood has been pressed out by the swelling. They itch, sometimes unbearably. A few individuals get hives repeatedly, or even most of the time. But many people have them only once or twice in a lifetime. They are occasionally found to be caused by sensitivity to some food. They also come from serum injections and at the end of certain infections. In many cases the cause cannot be discovered.

A household remedy for itching hives is a hot bath to which has been added bicarbonate of soda (baking soda). Use a cupful for a small tub,

2 cupfuls for a large one. The doctor can usually relieve the attack of hives with medicine or an injection.

652. Eczema. Eczema is a rough, red rash that comes in patches. It is caused by allergy, like hay fever and asthma. In hay fever the nose is allergic (sensitive) to a pollen, like ragweed. In eczema the skin may be allergic to some food in the diet. When that food gets into the blood and reaches the skin, the skin becomes inflamed. In another case the skin may be allergic to some material, like wool, silk, rabbit's hair, or some substance, like orrisroot in powder, that comes in direct contact with the skin. A baby is more likely to have eczema if he has relatives who have asthma, hay fever, hives, or eczema.

Even when eczema is primarily due to allergy to foods, two other factors may play a secondary part. The first is irritation of the skin from the outside. One baby has eczema only when his skin is irritated by cold weather, another only in hot weather from the irritation of perspiration, still another only in the diaper region from the irritation of the urine. If a baby has eczema only where wool comes in contact with his skin, it may be that he is really allergic to wool directly, or it may be that he is allergic to some food and the wool merely acts as a simple irritant.

Another factor in eczema is the baby's fatness and rate of gaining weight. There is much more eczema in fat babies than in medium-weight babies. Thin babies rarely get it.

You need a doctor, of course, to diagnose and treat the condition. The easiest eczema to describe is the kind that comes in patches of rough, red, thick, scaly skin. When eczema is mild or just starting, the color is apt to be a light red or tannish pink, but if it becomes severe, it turns a deeper red, usually itches, and the baby scratches and rubs it. This causes scratch marks and "weeping" (oozing). When the oozing serum dries, it forms crusts. When a patch of eczema is healing, even after the redness has all faded away, you can still feel the roughness and thickness of the skin.

The commonest place for eczema to begin in a young baby is on the cheeks or the forehead. From there it may spread back to the ears and neck. The scaliness looks from a distance as if salt has dried there, especially on the ears. Near a year of age, eczema may start almost anywhere—the shoulders, the diaper region, the arms, the chest. Between 1 and 3, the most typical spots are the creases in the elbows and behind the knees. Severe eczema can be a very trying disease to take care of. The baby is wild with the itching. The mother is wild trying to keep him from scratching. It can last for months.

653. There are several angles to the treatment. What a doctor does in studying and treating a case depends on many factors, including the baby's age, the location and character of the rash, his fatness and the rate at which he is gaining, the history of what new foods were introduced before the rash began, and how he responds to different forms of treatment. Some mild cases can be cured by lotions and ointments alone. In the more persistent ones, an effort is made to find what food or foods the child is allergic to. In the young infant, fresh cow's milk is often found to be the cause. Then a shift to evaporated milk sometimes helps, because any food is less likely to cause allergy when it is thoroughly cooked. Evaporated goat's milk occasionally succeeds when cow's milk fails. A few babies can be cured only by giving up real milk altogether and shifting to one of the artificial milks, such as those made from soybeans. Eliminating orange juice often helps.

In severe eczema in older babies and children who are eating a number of foods, the doctor experiments carefully by eliminating various ones from the diet. In severe and persistent cases he may do "skin testing" by injecting samples of different foods. Hives develop around the injections of foods to which the child is sensitive. If a baby is fat or gaining rapidly, it may help to remove much of the sugar starches from the diet.

When an external irritant seems to be playing a part, that needs attention, too. Wool is very commonly irritating to eczema, and it is usually eliminated from the clothing. If the eczema is all in the diaper region, it is worth while to take all the precautions discussed in Section 302 on diaper rashes. If cold, windy weather brings out the eczema, find a sheltered place for outings. Soap and water are sometimes irritating to eczema, in which case the baby can be cleaned with mineral oil on absorbent cotton.

If for the time being you are out of reach of a doctor and your young baby develops a severe itching eczema, it will do no harm, and it may help, to shift from a fresh-milk to an evaporated-milk formula. You can also eliminate the sugar from his formula and limit his cereal, so that he won't gain so rapidly. If you are in the same situation with an older baby who, for instance, develops a severe eczema after starting on egg, leave out the egg until you can get advice. It may take 2 weeks or more for the improvement to show. Wheat is another common offender. It is a mistake, though, for a parent to begin eliminating a **number** of foods from the diet, and not even one food should be eliminated by the parent if it is possible to get a doctor's help. The reason is this: a case of eczema varies from week to week even with the same diet. When you are changing the diet around yourself you are apt to think that first one food, then another, is the cause. Every time the eczema becomes worse again, you become more confused. The danger is that you will make the diet so lopsided that the child's nutrition will suffer. If the eczema is not bothering the baby much, don't try any changes in the diet until you can get help.

The thing to remember about eczema is that it's a tendency inside the child, not an infection, like impetigo, that you can get rid of completely. In most cases you have to be satisfied if you can just keep the rash mild. A majority of the eczemas that start early in infancy clear up completely, or at least become much milder, in the following year or two.

SKIN DISEASES

654. Distinguishing the common rashes. This section isn't meant to make you a diagnostician. If your child has a rash, you need your doctor's help. Rashes due to the same cause vary so in different individuals that even a skin specialist sometimes has a job diagnosing them. They confuse less expert people very easily. The purpose of this section is only to give you a few general pointers about the commoner rashes of children to relieve your mind until you can reach your doctor.

Measles. Fever and cold symptoms appear 3 or 4 days before the rash begins. It consists of flat, pink spots that begin around the ears and work down. The fever is high when the rash begins (Section 663).

German measles. Flat, pink spots, often faint, that rapidly spread all over the whole body. Little or no fever. No cold symptoms, but swollen glands on the back of the head and neck (Section 664).

Chicken pox. Separate raised pimples. Some of these develop tiny, delicate blisters on top, which break within a few hours, leaving a small crust. The pimples come out a few at a time, beginning on the body or face or scalp. The doctor, to make the diagnosis, searches among all the crusted pimples for a few fresh tiny blisters (Section 666).

Scarlet fever. The child is sick for a day before the rash comes out, usually with headache, fever, vomiting, and sore throat. The rash, which is a red blush, starts in the warm, moist parts of the body, armpits, groin, and back (Section 669).

Prickly heat. Comes in babies in the beginning of hot weather. Starts around the shoulders and neck. It is made up of patches of many small tan-pink pimples, some of which develop tiny blisters (Section 304).

Diaper rash. All in the area that is wet with urine. Pink or red pimples of various sizes, or patches of rough, red skin (Section 302).

Eczema. Patches of red, rough skin, which in the beginning come and go. If it is bad, it becomes scaly, itchy, and crusted. Apt to start on cheeks in the very young infant, later in the first year on the trunk. Common spots after a year are behind the knees and in the elbow folds (Section 652).

Hives. Welts scattered pretty evenly over the entire body. They itch (Section 651).

655. Insect bites. There are many different kinds, from big, puffy swellings, the size of a half dollar, down to a simple blood-crusted spot without any swelling. But there are two common characteristics of most bites. There is a tiny hole or tiny bump in the center where the stinger went in. And the bites are located on the exposed parts of the skin, in most cases.

Any insect bite that is itching (mosquito bite, for instance) or stinging may be partly relieved by applying a paste made by running a few drops of water into a teaspoonful of bicarbonate of soda. For a **bee sting,** remove the stinger, if visible, with tweezers and apply bicarbonate of soda. More effective for a **wasp** or **hornet sting** is to rub a drop of vinegar into the spot.

656. Scabies. Groups of pimples topped with scabs, and a lot of scratch marks from the incessant itching. Located on parts of the body that are frequently handled: backs of hands, wrists, penis, abdomen. Not on the back. It is contagious, needs treatment.

657. Ringworm. Circular patches of rough skin, most commonly about nickel size. The outer rim is made up of little bumps. In ringworm of the scalp, there are round patches of scaly skin in which the hair is broken off short. Ringworm is a fungus infection that is contagious, has nothing to do with worms, requires treatment.

658. Impetigo. In a child past infancy there are scabs or crusts, partly brown, partly honey-colored. In fact, any scabs on the face should first be suspected of being impetigo. The infection is apt to start with a pimple with a yellowish or white blister on top, most often on the face, but this soon gets rubbed off and the scab takes its place. Other spots develop on the face and on any part of the body that the hands can carry the infection to. You should have the doctor see it promptly for diagnosis and treatment. It spreads easily if neglected, and is contagious to others.

In the newborn infant, impetigo is different. It starts with a very delicate small blister that contains yellowish fluid or white pus and is surrounded by reddened skin. The blister is easily broken and leaves a small raw spot. It does not develop a thick crust as in the older child. It's apt to start in a moist place, such as the edge of the diaper or in the groin or armpit. New spots may develop. It should be treated promptly by a doctor. If you cannot reach a doctor, the best method is to carefully wipe off the blister with a piece of cotton (so as not to spread the pus onto the surrounding skin), and then leave the raw spot exposed to the air. Arrange the clothing and bedclothes so that they do not cover the spot or spots, and keep the room warmer than usual if necessary. During impetigo, boil the diapers, sheets, underclothing, nighties, towels, and washcloth every day.

659. Poison ivy. Clusters of small blisters of various sizes, on reddened, shiny skin. It itches, comes on the exposed parts of the body, in spring and summer. Consult your doctor about treatment if it is extensive.

660. Head lice. It's easier to find the eggs than the lice. They are tiny, pearly-white, egg-shaped objects, each one firmly cemented to a hair. There may be itching red pimples where the hair meets the back of the neck.

661. Birthmarks. Most babies have a collection of red, mottled spots on the backs of their necks when they are born. These also commonly occur in two other places: between the eyebrows and on the upper eyelids. These blotches disappear gradually in most cases, and nothing needs to be done for them.

"Port-wine stains" are areas of skin that have a deep-red coloring but are flat and otherwise normal. They are similar to the red spots on the neck and eyelids, mentioned in the first paragraph, but they occur on other parts of the body, are apt to be larger, deeper-colored, and more permanent. Some of them do fade, particularly the lighter-colored ones. There is no easy treatment for them.

"Strawberry marks" are fairly common. These are raised and are of an intense, deep-crimson color. They look very much like a piece of the outside of a shiny strawberry. They may be small at birth and later increase in size, or they may not appear at all until after birth. They are apt to grow for a while and then stop. As the years go by, most of them shrink back to nothing without treatment. They can be treated if the doctor thinks it necessary.

"Cavernous hemangiomas" are fairly large blue-and-red marks caused by collection of distended veins deep in the skin. Sometimes they can be removed if they are disfiguring.

Moles can be of all sizes, smooth or hairy. They can be removed surgically if they are disfiguring or irritated by the clothing.

662. Warts. There are different types of ordinary warts that develop on the hands, soles of the feet, face. They are mildly contagious and should be seen by a doctor. In addition, there is a special type known as "contagious warts." At first they are round, smooth, waxy, the size of a pinhead, and white or pink in color. They multiply, enlarge, and become concave in the center. They should be treated to avoid spreading.

MEASLES, GERMAN MEASLES, ROSEOLA

663. Measles. Measles for the first 3 or 4 days has no rash. It looks like a bad cold that is becoming worse. The eyes are red and watery. If you pull the lower lid down, you see that it is angry red. There is a hard, dry cough that becomes frequent. The fever usually goes higher each day. The rash comes out about the fourth day, when the fever is high, as indefinite pink spots behind the ears. They spread gradually over the face and body, becoming bigger and darker-colored. The day before the rash comes out, "Koplik's spots" appear on the inside of the cheeks, next to the lower molar teeth. They are minute white spots surrounded by redness, but are hard to recognize unless you know them.

The fever stays high, the cough frequent (in spite of medicine), and the child feels pretty sick while the rash comes out full, which takes 1 to 2 days. Then everything should improve rapidly.

You suspect a complication if the fever stays high more than 2 days from the time the rash begins, or if the fever goes down for a day or more and then comes back again. The commonest complications are ear abscesses, bronchitis, and pneumonia. You will be sending for a doctor at least once during a case of measles, whether you suspect the disease or not, because of the cough and fever. You must call him back promptly or bring the child to a hospital if the fever stays up or comes back after 2 days of the rash. The complications can be serious, and unlike the measles itself, can be successfully treated by modern drugs.

During the feverish part of the disease, the child almost completely loses his appetite. The most he usually takes is fluids, which should be offered frequently. The mouth needs to be gently cleaned three times a day. It used to be thought necessary to keep the room very dark to protect the eyes. But now it is known that there is little danger. All that is necessary is to darken the room somewhat if the light makes the child uncomfortable. The room should be kept comfortably warm to prevent chilling. The child is usually let out of bed 2 days after the fever is gone. It is safe to let him outdoors and to play with other children a week after the rash began, provided all cough and other cold symptoms are completely gone.

The first symptoms of measles begin anywhere from 9 to 16 days after exposure. It is contagious to others from the very beginning of the cold symptoms. No one with a cold or sore throat should come anywhere near a child with measles, since it is cold germs that cause the complications. It is unusual for a person to catch real measles twice.

An attack of measles can be prevented or made milder if gamma globulin is given in time. It's a good idea to prevent measles before the age of 3 or 4, because that is the time when complications are more frequent and more severe. It is also wise to prevent it in an older child who is run-down or ill. Get in touch with your doctor immediately to discuss globulin while it will still be effective. The protection of globulin lasts for only a couple of weeks. There's no point preventing measles in a healthy older child because he'll probably catch it again some other time, anyway, but it is sometimes considered desirable to make the case milder with globulin.

664. German measles. The rash of German measles looks much like the rash of real measles, but the two diseases are entirely separate. In German measles there are no cold symptoms (running nose or cough). There may be a little sore throat. The fever is usually low (under 102°). The person may hardly feel sick at all. The rash consists of flat, pink spots, which usually cover the body the first day. The second day they are apt to fade and run together, so that the body looks flushed instead of spotty. The most characteristic sign is swollen, tender glands on the back of the skull, behind the ears, and on the sides of the neck, toward the back. These glands may swell before the rash comes out, and the swelling is apt to last some time after the disease is over.

German measles usually develops from 12 to 21 days after exposure. The child is usually kept in bed while rash and fever exist. A doctor should make the diagnosis because German measles is easily confused with real measles and scarlet fever.

It is bad for a woman to have German measles during the first 3 months of pregnancy because of the chance of her baby acquiring some defect from the disease. If she is exposed at this time, she should promptly discuss with her doctor the advisability of gamma globulin. Many doctors feel that girls should be deliberately exposed to this disease so that they have it before marriage.

665. Roseola. The proper name for this disease is exanthem subitum, but it's easier to call it roseola, short for roseola infantum. It is a less well-known contagious disease. It usually occurs between the ages of 1 and 3, rarely afterward. The child has a steady high fever for 3 or 4 days without any cold symptoms, and usually without seeming to be very sick. (Occasionally there is a convulsion on the first day because of the fever.) Suddenly the fever falls to normal, and a pinkish flat rash, something like the rash in measles, comes out on the body. By this time the child no longer looks ill but may be cranky. The rash is gone in a day or two, and there are no complications to worry about.

CHICKEN POX, WHOOPING COUGH, MUMPS

666. Chicken pox. The first sign of chicken pox is usually a few of the characteristic pimples on the body and face. These pox are raised up like ordinary small pimples, but some of them have tiny, yellow water blisters on top. The base of the pimple and the skin around it are reddened. The delicate blister head breaks within a few hours and dries into a crust. When a doctor is trying to make the diagnosis, he searches among all the crusted pimples to find a fresh one that still has the blister. New pox continue to appear for 3 or 4 days.

An older child or adult may feel sick and have headache the day before the pox appear, but a small child doesn't notice these symptoms. The fever is usually slight at the beginning, but may go higher the next day or two. Some children never feel sick, never have a temperature of more than 101°. Others feel quite sick and have high fever. The pox usually itch.

You should call a physician to diagnose and treat your child if he has a rash, certainly if he has a fever or feels sick. (Chicken pox, for instance, can be confused with smallpox and other diseases.) The child is usually kept in bed as long as new pox are appearing. The itching can be relieved by placing him in a warm starch or soda bath for 10 minutes 2 or 3 times a day. Use a starch that dissolves in water, or bicarbonate of soda (1 cupful for a small tub, 2 for a large one). Do not rub the scabs off. The only common complication is boils, which come from infecting the pox by scratching. Wash his hands with soap 3 times a day, and keep his fingernails very short.

Chicken pox usually develops between 11 and 19 days after exposure. The usual rule is to let a child out and back to school a week after the disease began, or 2 days after new pox have stopped appearing. The dried scabs are not contagious and should not be a reason for keeping the child quarantined. However, some schools insist that he stay away until all the scabs have fallen off.

667. Whooping cough. There's nothing about whooping cough in the first week to make you suspect that disease. It's just like an ordinary cold with a little running nose and a little dry cough. Toward the end of the week the mother usually thinks that the cold is about over and sends the child back to school. "There was just a little dry cough left." It is during the second week that the first suspicion arises. Now it's noticed that the child is beginning to have long spells of coughing at night. He coughs 8 or 10 times **on one breath.** One night, after several of these long spells, he gags and vomits. Or maybe he whoops. The whoop is the crowing noise he makes trying to get his breath back after a spell of coughs. In these days, when whooping-cough shots are so widely used, many cases never are bad enough to reach the whooping stage, and in some there isn't even vomiting. The diagnosis is then based on the character of the cough in the second week (cough, cough, cough, cough, cough, cough, cough, cough—a string of coughs in rapid succession, without a breath in between) and on the fact that there are other cases in the neighborhood.

You should never jump to the conclusion that your child has whooping cough because he develops a bad cough in the first few days of a cold. In fact, a bad cough in the beginning of a cold argues against the diagnosis of whooping cough.

Whooping cough lasts for weeks and weeks. In an average case, the whooping stage lasts 4 weeks, in a severe case 2 or 3 months. A doctor thinks of whooping cough whenever a dry cough lasts a month.

When there is a doubtful case and it is important to make the diagnosis, there are two laboratory tests that sometimes help. The first is a "cough plate." The doctor has the child cough into a laboratory plate containing a special gelatin on which whooping-cough germs grow easily. If he finds the germs, he is sure it is whooping cough. But if he doesn't find the germs, it doesn't prove that it isn't whooping cough. This test is most reliable in the first week or two of the disease. The other test is a blood count. In some cases the result is definite, especially in the third and fourth week; in others it is no help.

Whooping cough can be a serious disease, especially in a baby under 2. It's a disease to avoid like the plague if you have a baby in the household. The main danger at this age is exhaustion and pneumonia.

Your doctor will prescribe treatment, based on the age of the child and the severity of the case. Cough medicines are always used but often have only a small influence. Most cases do better when in cold air, day and night, but naturally the child must be protected against chilling. Robust children are sometimes allowed to play outdoors throughout the disease as long as they have no fever. Naturally, they should not play with other children. Some children have many fewer coughing spells when they are kept in bed. When vomiting is a problem, frequent small meals stay down better than the regular three full meals. The safest time of all to feed a child is right after he has vomited, since he usually won't have another bad spell for some time. A tight abdominal binder may give relief to the exhausted abdominal muscles.

Since whooping cough is sometimes a serious disease, especially in babies and young children, it is important to call a doctor promptly where there is a suspicion. There are two main reasons: to make sure of the diagnosis, if possible; and to prescribe the right treatment. Special treatment is called for and is valuable in infants.

Quarantine regulations are different in different communities. Usually a child is kept out of school until 5 weeks after the beginning of the disease and until he has stopped vomiting. The contagiousness of whooping cough does not cease suddenly after a certain number of weeks. It gradually diminishes, sooner in a light case. For home purposes, you can count a child as being no longer much danger to others when his cough has been much improved for 2 weeks. Whooping cough takes from 5 to 14 days to develop after exposure. If an infant who has not yet had his whooping-cough shots is exposed to the disease, a serum can be given to prevent the disease or make it lighter.

668. Mumps. Mumps is principally a disease of the saliva glands, most commonly the parotid glands, which lie in the hollow just under the lobe of the ear. First the gland fills in the hollow, then it swells the whole side of the face. It pushes the lobe of the ear upward. If you run your fingers up and down the back part of the jawbone, you can feel that the hard swelling runs forward, covering part of the jawbone.

When a child has a swelling in the side of the neck, the question always comes up, Is it mumps (a specific infection of the parotid saliva gland), or is it one of the other, rarer diseases of the parotid gland (which may recur repeatedly), or is it an ordinary swollen gland (one of the lymph glands in the side of the neck)? The ordinary lymph glands that sometimes swell after a sore throat are lower down on the neck, not tucked up under the ear lobe. The hard swelling does not cross the jawbone.

When a small child develops mumps, the swelling under the ear is usually the first thing noticed. An older child may complain of pain around his ear or in the side of his throat, especially on swallowing or chewing, for a day before the swelling begins. He may feel generally sick. There is often little fever in the beginning, but it may go higher on the second or third day. Most commonly the swelling begins on one side first, but spreads to the other side in a day or two. Sometimes it takes a week or more to spread to the other side, and of course, in some cases the second side never swells.

There are other saliva glands besides the parotids, and mumps sometimes spreads to these, too. There are the submaxillary glands tucked up under the lower part of the jawbone. The sublinguals are just behind the point of the chin. Occasionally a person gets one of the complications of mumps without having had a swelling in any of the saliva glands.

A very mild mumps swelling may go away in 3 or 4 days. The average swelling lasts a week to 10 days.

Mumps can spread to the testicles in men and boys who have reached the age of puberty. This usually involves only one testicle. But even when both are inflamed, it is rare for this to cause sterility (inability to have children). However, it is preferable for boys to have mumps before puberty, and some doctors recommend deliberate exposure. Adolescent boys and men should avoid exposure. Mumps sometimes causes a special kind of mumps meningitis. The child has high fever, a stiff neck, and is delirious. This is seldom dangerous. Infection of the pancreas gland in the abdomen may cause severe abdominal pain and vomiting.

Mumps is one contagious disease that some doctors, including myself, think you can catch a second time, so don't do any unnecessary exposing. The fact that a person has had it on both sides doesn't make any difference; he can still get it again.

You should call the doctor for a suspected case of mumps. It is important to be certain of the diagnosis. If it turns out to be a swollen lymph gland, the treatment is quite different.

The child is usually kept in bed until the swelling is gone. Some people can't take tart-tasting foods like lemon juice during mumps (it hurts the inflamed glands), but others continue to enjoy them. So a lemon or pickle is no test of mumps.

Mumps takes 2 to 3 weeks to develop after exposure.

SCARLET FEVER, DIPHTHERIA, POLIOMYELITIS

669. Scarlet fever. Scarlet fever usually begins with some of these symptoms: sore throat, vomiting, fever, headache. The rash is not apt to appear for a day or two. It begins on the warm, moist parts of the body, such as the sides of the chest, the groin, the back where the child has been lying. From a distance it looks like a uniform, red flush, but if you look at it more closely, you can see that it is made up of tiny red spots on a flushed skin. It may spread over the whole body and the sides of the face, but the region around the mouth stays pale. The throat is red, sometimes very angry, and after a while the tongue usually gets red, first around the edge. You should, of course, call the doctor if your child has fever and sore throat.

Nowadays scarlet fever is not apt to be so severe as it used to be. It is not an entirely separate disease with a germ of its own, like measles. It is caused by one type of the common streptococcus, which produces sore throats, swollen glands, ear abscesses, in other people. Scarlet fever is just one form that a streptococcus infection can take, most commonly between 2 and 8 years of age. In the olden days, before it was known to be a form of streptococcus infection, scarlet fever was dreaded because cases developed far away in time and distance from other cases. Thinking that one case must come from another, people would blame the contagion on a toy that had been played with by another scarlet-fever patient a year before. Now we understand that a child who develops scarlet fever probably picked up a germ from someone who just had a sore throat or was carrying the streptococcus without feeling its effect at all.

Scarlet fever should be treated promptly and carefully with one of the modern drugs that shorten the disease and greatly lessen the chances of complications. The common complications are ear infections, swollen glands in the neck, nephritis (which produces blood in the urine), rheumatic fever. Chilling is suspected of bringing on complications. They may begin any time in the disease, but most commonly 10 to 15 days after the fever has come down, when the child seems to be completely recovered. That is why a scarlet-fever case is watched carefully for a full 3 weeks. The child should be examined regularly, and you should keep in close touch with the doctor until he is really well. Report promptly any new symptoms, such as ear pain, swelling of the neck, redness or scantiness of the urine, arthritis, any return of the fever.

Though scarlet fever may spread easily in an institution, it is not very contagious in ordinary day schools. You should not be alarmed if you receive a notice from your child's school that he has been exposed. His chances of catching it are small. When it does develop, it is usually within a week after exposure. Quarantine regulations vary a great deal in different localities.

670. Diphtheria. Diphtheria is a serious but completely unnecessary disease. If your child is given 3 injections in infancy and booster shots at 1 year and then every 3 years, there's practically no chance of his catching it. It begins with feeling sick, sore throat, and fever. Dirty-white patches develop on the tonsils and may spread to the rest of the throat. Occasionally it begins in the larynx, with hoarseness and barking cough; the breathing becomes tight and difficult. In any case, you should have a doctor promptly when your child has sore throat and fever, or when he has any croupy symptoms. The treatment of any case of suspected diphtheria is the immediate use of serum along with other drugs. The disease develops within a week after exposure.

671. Infantile paralysis (anterior poliomyelitis). In the summer and early fall, when most epidemics of infantile paralysis occur, parents naturally think of this disease whenever a child becomes sick. It begins, like many other infections, with a general sick feeling, fever, and headache. There may be vomiting, constipation, or a little diarrhea. But even if your child has all these symptoms and pains in his legs in addition, it's a mistake to jump to conclusions. The chances are still great that it's just grippe or a throat infection. Of course, you will be getting a doctor, anyway. If it's a long time before he comes, you can reassure yourself this way: If the child can put his head between his knees or bend his neck forward so that his chin touches his chest, he probably hasn't got it. (Even if he can't do these tests, it doesn't prove that he has the disease.)

When there are cases of infantile paralysis in their part of the country, parents are troubled about how strict to be with their children. Your doctor, who knows local conditions, can advise you best. There's no point in being panicky or shutting your children away from all human contact. If there are cases in your community, it is sensible to keep your child away from crowds, especially in closed places like stores and movies, and away from swimming places that many people use. On the other hand, it's out of proportion, from what we know at present, to keep him from seeing his regular friends. If you were going to be that careful with him the rest of his life, you wouldn't ever let him cross a street. Doctors suspect that chilling and exhaustion make a person more susceptible to the disease, but it's sensible to avoid these at any time. Of course, the commonest cause of chilling in summer is staying in the water too long. A child should be called out when he begins to lose color—before his teeth chatter.

The Salk vaccine, which is made from the polio virus, is of great value in building a child's resistance to the paralytic form of the disease. It stimulates his body to develop its own protection, but this takes a number of weeks to accomplish. The vaccine can't help in a hurry if he has already been exposed. On the other hand, gamma globulin (which is made from the blood of adults who have some protection) can provide a partial protection for a few weeks. It doesn't last because the child didn't build it himself.

So far there has not been sufficient experience to decide how many years the protection from the Salk vaccine can be expected to last and what is the best time schedule for inoculations and booster shots. Your doctor can advise you. At the present time (1957), the second shot is commonly given 2 to 6 weeks after the first, and the third preferably 7 or more months later.

As yet, there is no known way to stop the infection in a case after it has started. On the other hand, a majority of the children who catch it don't have any paralysis at any time. A fair number of those who are paralyzed for a while recover completely. Most of those who don't recover completely improve considerably.

If there is any paralysis after the acute stage of the infection is over, it is vitally important that the child continue to have regular medical attention from a competent doctor. How a limb is to be treated so that it will be most efficient in the long run depends on many factors. The doctor has to judge at each stage, and there are no general rules. Many ingenious operations can be performed to increase the usefulness of limbs and to prevent deformities, when some paralysis remains. The National Foundation for Infantile Paralysis stands ready to help families obtain medical care for this disease. You can write to the foundation in any large city.

QUARANTINE

672. Quarantine or isolation for contagious diseases. On general principles, it's a good idea to keep a child with a contagious disease away from all other members of the household except the one person who is taking care of him. This is, first of all, to prevent others—either adults or children—who have not had the disease from catching it unnecessarily. If your other children were exposed before you knew what the disease was, they will most likely catch it, anyway, but it is just as well for them not to be continually overexposed. Another reason is so that they will not carry the germs to others outside the home. To be sure, the risk of a healthy person's carrying the germs to other outsiders is slight in measles, chicken pox, and whooping cough, though it occasionally occurs if less than half an hour elapses. In the case of scarlet fever, it is more important for only one adult to be in the child's room because the streptococcus that causes it can be carried in the throat for long periods. The fewer people who pick it up from the child, the less chance of its being spread around the community. Another reason for keeping the sick child isolated is so that he will not be picking up new germs from others to complicate his illness.

How do you maintain a good quarantine? You keep the child in one room and keep everyone else out except the one grownup who is taking care of him. She slips on a smock that is kept hanging in the room just for this purpose. This keeps her regular clothes from collecting germs. She takes it off every time she leaves the room. She washes her hands every time she leaves the room. All the drinking and eating utensils that leave the room should be carried to the kitchen in a dishpan and boiled in it before being handled or washed or mixed with the utensils for the rest of the family.

In the case of scarlet fever, diphtheria, and some other serious diseases, further precautions are required by some health departments.

In most places, grownups in the family—except those who are schoolteachers or food handlers—are not restricted about leaving the home or going to business in **any** of the diseases. You have to use your own good sense, though, about visiting families who have susceptible children. The chances of your carrying the germs to other children are practically zero as long as you keep away from them. Just the same, you're not going to be very welcome if the mother is fussy, especially if the disease is one that is dreaded, such as mumps for a man, whooping cough for a baby, scarlet fever. She'll blame you if anyone in her family catches that disease any time in the next year. On the other hand, don't hesitate to go if the disease is one of the less feared ones, like measles, chicken pox, and German measles, and if you have had the disease, and if a friend who doesn't worry and whose children are out of the way asks you over for the evening.

Other children in the home who have had the disease in question are practically always allowed to go to school during the quarantine period if it is one of the less serious diseases. The rules about brothers and sisters may be stricter for such diseases as scarlet fever, diphtheria, meningitis, poliomyelitis, etc. The rules about other children in the family who **haven't** yet had the disease vary in different localities and in different schools. For the sake of other small children and your own conscience, keep your child away from the neighbor's small children at the time when he is due to come down with a disease.

TUBERCULOSIS

673. Tuberculosis is different in infants, children, and adults. Most people think of tuberculosis as it occurs typically in adults. A "spot," or cavity, develops in the lung, and produces such symptoms as fatigue, loss of appetite, loss of weight, fever, cough, sputum.

Tuberculosis in childhood usually takes other forms. In the first 2 years of life, resistance is not so good as in later years, and there is more chance of the infection's spreading to other parts of the body. That is why you never take the slightest chance of exposing a baby to a known case of tuberculosis unless the doctor and the X ray guarantee that the person has been completely cured. It's a reason also why anyone in a household who has a chronic cough should be examined and X-rayed, and why it's wise to have a new maid or nurse examined and X-rayed.

In later childhood, tuberculous infection is fairly common and less likely to cause serious trouble. This is not a reason to treat it lightly or take any chances. Tuberculin tests show that in some cities as many as 50% of all children have had a slight infection with tuberculosis by the time they are 10 years old. Most of these cases have been so mild that no one suspected that anything was wrong at the time. An X ray shows at most a little scar where the infection healed in the lung or in the lymph glands at the roots of the lungs.

Sometimes, however, a childhood type of tuberculosis is active enough to cause symptoms, such as fever, poor appetite, poor color, irritability, fatigue, and perhaps a cough. (There isn't much sputum, and what there is, is swallowed, of course.) The infection may be in other parts of the body, such as the bones or the neck glands, but most commonly it's in the lungs and in the lymph glands at the roots of the lungs. In most of these active cases, healing gradually takes place over a period of 1 to 2 years if the child is well cared for, and only a scar is left. With proper treatment with special drugs, healing is fostered and a serious spread of infection is prevented.

As the child reaches adolescence, he becomes more liable to develop the serious, adult type of tuberculosis. This should be kept in mind whenever an adolescent or young adult is run-down, tired, loses appetite or weight, whether or not there is any cough.

674. The tuberculin test. A few weeks after tubercle bacilli have gotten into a person's body, he becomes "sensitized" to them. After that, if the doctor injects a drop of tuberculin (material from dead tuberculosis germs) into his skin, a red spot develops. This is a positive tuberculin test. (There is another method called the tuberculin patch test. This involves applying what looks like a prepared bandage and requires no injection.) The red spot shows that the body has already had experience with tuberculosis germs and reacts against them. If no red spot develops, it shows that the body has not contained the germs before. Generally speaking, if a person has ever had a tuberculous infection, he will react with a positive test the rest of his life, even though the infection was healed long ago.

Doctors often give tuberculin tests in routine examinations—for instance, when a child comes to the office or to a clinic for the first time.

The test is also made when a child isn't doing well, or has a chronic cough, or when tuberculosis is discovered in another member of the family.

If your child is ever found to have a positive tuberculin test (which is not impossible when you consider how many children are positive). you have to keep a sense of balance. There's no need to be alarmed, since a great majority of the cases discovered throughout middle childhood have either healed already or will heal gradually with care. On the other hand, you don't want to neglect any precautions.

The first step is the doctor's investigation of the child's case. X ray of the lungs is essential in all cases to see if there are any signs of active infection or of healed scars. Sometimes the doctor orders other tests: X rays of other parts of the body, washing out of the stomach to see if there are tubercle bacilli in sputum the child has swallowed, taking of temperatures for a period. If the doctor is convinced that the infection is already well healed, he may recommend that the child lead an entirely normal life. However, he will want to take further X rays at regular intervals to be sure. He advises also taking precautions to avoid measles and whooping cough for several years if possible, since these diseases sometimes stir up recently healed tuberculosis.

If there is any suspicion of **active** tuberculosis or if the child is less than 2 years old, the doctor may start treatment with special drugs and continue it for at least a year.

Aside from the child himself, the doctor checks every other member of the household (and any other adult that the child regularly comes in contact with) to discover, if possible, where the tuberculosis germs came from, and to find out if other children in the household have been infected, too. Other children should all have tuberculin tests. Any child with a positive test should be examined and have his lungs X-rayed. It doesn't matter how healthy the other members of the household feel or how unnecessary they think all the fuss is. Many times no disease is found in any adult in the household, and it has to be assumed that the child picked up the germs from some source outside the home. On the other hand, an active case of tuberculosis is sometimes found in the least suspected adult in the house. It's a lucky thing for him to have his disease discovered at an early stage, and it's lucky for the rest of the family to have the danger removed. No person with active tuberculosis should stay in a house with children; he should go promptly to a sanitarium, where he has the greatest chance of being cured and the least chance of infecting others.

RHEUMATIC FEVER

675. It takes many forms. Rheumatic fever is a disease that affects the joints, the heart, and other parts of the body. The liability to it runs in certain families. Doctors believe that it is a reaction in some part of the body (a joint or the heart, for instance) to a streptococcus infection in the throat. When not treated promptly and adequately, an attack is apt to last for weeks or months. Furthermore, it is a disease that has a tendency to recur again and again throughout childhood, whenever the child has another streptococcal throat infection.

Sometimes it takes a very acute form with high fever. In other cases, it smolders along for weeks with only a little fever. When there is severe arthritis, it travels around from joint to joint, causing them to become swollen, red, and exquisitely tender. In other cases, the arthritis may be mild—just an aching off and on in one joint or another. If the heart is being affected severely, the child is visibly prostrated, pale, and breathless. In another case, it is discovered that the heart has been damaged by some past attack that was so mild it was not noticed at the time.

In other words, rheumatic fever is an exceedingly variable disease. Naturally, you consult your doctor if your child develops any of the symptoms in a severe form. But it's just as important to have a child examined who has vague symptoms, like paleness, tiredness, slight fever, mild joint pains.

Nowadays we have several drugs that are effective in clearing up streptococcal infection in the throat—the root of the disease—and in hastening the end of the rheumatic inflammation in the joints or the heart. As a result, heart valves are no longer so likely to be damaged in the first attack. More important still, the child who has had one attack of rheumatic fever can usually be kept from having further attacks—and further heart damage. He must continue indefinitely, under the doctor's continuing supervision, to take medication by mouth or by injection (to prevent new streptococcal infections) **absolutely regularly.**

676. Joint and "growing pains." In the olden days, it was thought natural for children to complain of "growing pains" in their legs and arms, and nobody worried about them. Ever since it was discovered that rheumatic fever pains could be very mild, doctors have had to consider them as a possibility in every case of pains in the limbs. But parents sometimes assume that rheumatic fever is the only cause for all of them, and worry unnecessarily.

There are, for instance, leg pains caused by flat feet and weak ankles, which occur most commonly toward the end of the day when the child is tired. Then there is the child between the ages of 2 and 5 who wakes up crying, complaining of pain around his knee or his calf. It happens only during the evening, but may recur each night for weeks on end. On investigation, it usually proves not to be due to rheumatic fever. It is often believed to be caused by cramps in the calf muscles.

There are many other causes for pains in the arms and legs, and you can see that you need a doctor to examine, test, and decide in every case.

677. Heart murmurs. The words **heart murmur** have an alarming sound to parents. It's important to realize that a great majority of heart murmurs don't mean anything serious. Generally speaking, there are three kinds, called acquired, congenital, and functional (or "innocent").

Most **acquired** murmurs in childhood come from rheumatic fever, which inflames the valves and may leave scars on them afterward. This causes them either to "leak" or to obstruct the proper flow of blood. When a doctor hears a murmur in a child's heart that wasn't there before, it may mean, on the one hand, that **active** rheumatic inflammation is going on. In this case, there are other signs of infection, such as fever, rapid pulse, elevated blood count and sedimentation rate. The doctor treats such a child with drugs and keeps him at complete bed rest until all signs of inflammation go away—even if it takes months. On the other hand, if there have been no signs of active infection for some time, the murmur may be due to old scars left over from a previous attack.

In former years, the child with an old murmur was sometimes treated as a semi-invalid for years, forbidden to play active games or sports, even though there were no signs of active infection. A doctor's tendency nowadays is to let the child who is **completely** over the stage of active inflammation go back gradually to as normal a life as possible (including the games and sports that he can do easily), if the healed scars do not noticeably interfere with the efficient working of the heart. There are two reasons for this. The muscles of the heart, as long as they are not inflamed, are strengthened by ordinary activity. Even more important is keeping the child's spirit healthy—preventing him from feeling sorry for himself, from feeling that he is a hopeless case, that he's different from everyone else. Such a child should be receiving **absolutely regular medication,** however, to prevent further streptococcus infection.

A murmur caused by **congenital heart disease** is usually discovered at birth or within a few months afterward (occasionally not till several years later). Such a murmur is usually not caused by inflammation but means that the heart was improperly formed in the first place. The important thing is not so much the murmur itself but whether the malformation interferes with the efficiency of the heart. If it does, the baby may have blue spells, or breathe too hard, or grow too slowly.

A baby or child with a congenital heart murmur needs a careful investigation by specialists. Some cases that are serious can be cured by operation.

If a child with a congenital murmur can exercise without turning blue and without becoming abnormally out of breath, and grows at the normal rate, it is important for his emotional development that he not be thought of or treated as an invalid but that he be allowed to lead a normal life. He does need to avoid unnecessary infections and to be well cared for during illnesses, but so do all children.

The term **functional** or **innocent murmur** is just a clumsy way of saying that a child has a murmur that doesn't come from a congenital malformation or from rheumatic fever. These innocent murmurs are **very** common in the early years of childhood. They tend to fade out as the child reaches adolescence. Your doctor tells you about an innocent murmur in your child so that if it is discovered later in childhood by a new doctor, you can explain that it has been there all along.

678. Chorea. Chorea, or St. Vitus' dance, is a nervous disease in which there are twitching or writhing movements of different parts of the body, which may last for months. They may be very obvious or so slight as to be hardly noticeable. Twitches of the muscles of the face produce irregular grimacing. A shoulder may shrug, first in one direction and then in another. Twitchings of the trunk muscles make the body lurch slightly. The hands and fingers may twitch or writhe. The child's handwriting may become poor, and he may drop things. The movements come **irregularly,** first in one muscle, then in another. No two movements are exactly the same.

Some children who have attacks of chorea also have definite attacks of rheumatic fever in the sense of heart disease and arthritis. This has made many doctors assume that chorea is just another form of rheumatic fever. But other children have one or more attacks of chorea without ever having another symptom of rheumatic fever. Therefore some doctors believe that these are two separate kinds of chorea—one rheumatic and the other not.

Most attacks of chorea occur between the age of 7 years and the beginning of adolescence. Other nervous traits, such as **tics and general restlessness,** are common in this age period, too, and are often confused with chorea. A child with a tic nervously and repeatedly makes exactly the same motion, such as eye-blinking, throat-clearing, shoulder-shrugging (Section 546), whereas the movements of chorea are skipping around and always different. General restlessness is something else again. By that I mean the activity of a child who is constantly squirming in his chair, shuffling his feet around, fiddling with his hands, etc.

During an attack of chorea, a child is apt to be unstable. He cries easily, laughs easily, flies off the handle on slight provocation. You have to make allowances for this in handling him at home because he can't help it. A child with chorea should be under a doctor's care. The chorea will surely go away in time, even if there are several attacks. But the child must be examined regularly to make sure that no other signs of rheumatic fever develop. If they do, they should be carefully treated.

URINARY DISTURBANCES

679. Late bed-wetting (enuresis). There are a number of different causes. A very few cases are due to physical disease. In these there are usually symptoms, such as inability to control the urine in the daytime, that make the doctor suspicious. The great majority of cases are due to tenseness of various sorts in a child's feelings.

There are situations that upset a **young** child in such a way that unconsciously he wants to retreat into babyhood again. A 3-year-old who has been dry for 6 months may begin to wet again when he moves to a new house for the summer. Even though he is happy in his new surroundings, he evidently feels homesick underneath. When the children of London were removed to the country at the beginning of the war, away from family, friends, and familiar surroundings, bed-wetting was common, even in adolescent children. It is frequent in some orphanages. Children are also apt to wet after an exciting experience, like a birthday party or an afternoon at the circus.

The commonest occasion in early childhood is the arrival of a new baby in the home.

It's important to realize that in these situations children are not wetting deliberately. After all, they are sound asleep. It is their unconscious feelings that take over at night and that express themselves in dreams. Bed-wetting often occurs during dreams in which the child is in a distressing situation and feels powerless to do anything. The child who wets when he is homesick or upset by the new baby may be dreaming that he is a lost baby himself, looking for the mother who will care for all his bodily needs without complaint, the way she used to.

In the case of the homesick small child, the parent's job is to be around him a little more for a few days to ease his loneliness and help him find the joys of the new place. If there is a new baby, the job is to reassure the child that he doesn't have to feel displaced (Sections 483 to 489). There is no need to scold or shame him for wetting; he usually feels bad about it. It helps him if you express confidence that he will soon be staying dry again.

What about the child of 3 or 4 or 5 who has never become dry in the first place? (A majority of children become dry at night somewhere between 2 and 3 years of age.) In some of these cases, there has been tension over daytime toilet training. The child resisted for a long while, and the mother became more impatient. He eventually accepted daytime training, but it looks as if his resistance is continuing in his unconscious mind at night, along with a guilty feeling that he is still a naughty baby. It's wise to try to eliminate any conflict about daytime training if it still exists, and any shaming about bed-wetting. In most cases, it is advisable to stop picking the child up in the evening because he is apt to interpret this as a reminder that he's only a baby. What he needs is the confidence of his parents and himself that he's growing up and that someday he will be able to stay dry all by himself.

680. A common type in boys. Some psychiatrists who have studied bed-wetting in children believe that one of the commonest types in boys (and 80% of enuretics are boys) is the following: The boy is somewhat insecure and too easily convinced that he's inadequate. He may be afraid to compete with other boys or to stand up to them. He's inclined to feel dominated by his mother. She is devoted to him, but for his particular personality she is at times too impatient, too interfering. He is too strictly brought up to fight back openly. He resists passively by procrastinating or by just being irritating. Then his mother can't help feeling more dissatisfied with him. Often in these cases the father is not giving the boy enough moral support. See Sections 460 and 477.

The measures that parents sometimes use for enuretics of this type may work in the wrong direction. To pull a groggy child out of bed (enuretics seem to be particularly heavy sleepers) and push him into the bathroom each night only convinces him further that he is a baby. Restricting a child's fluids after 5 o'clock usually makes him imagine he is thirsty right away (it would be the same with you and me) and almost guarantees a running argument between him and his mother all evening, which isn't good for either of them. Making a boy wash and hang out his sheets fills him with dread that other boys will learn of his disgrace. It isn't lack of shame that causes his enuresis. Any boy over 5 would give a million dollars to overcome the problem. He wants to cooperate, but he has little control over the unconscious feelings that produce the wetting in his sleep.

What the enuretic boy needs is more confidence that he is a competent person, and this can be gained only gradually, with help. The most direct way is through a child-guidance clinic or a child psychiatrist, especially if the child has a variety of troubles. But if this is not possible, there are a number of things the parents can do, depending on circumstances. Their general attitude should be one of encouragement. They can explain that they have learned that quite a few boys have this problem but that practically all of them overcome it in time. They can express their confidence that he will, too.

I think it is preferable in most cases to give up such methods as getting the boy up at night and restricting fluids.

Pasting gold stars on a chart is occasionally helpful for a 5-, 6-, or 7-year-old but usually not for an older boy. A reward that has great appeal—skates, bicycle, sports equipment—may be worth a trial. Even better, I think, though it may not sound sensible to you, is to give the boy, right away, a possession that he has yearned for but that his parents have been withholding until he becomes dry. The idea is to make him begin to feel equal with other boys as soon as possible.

If the father has been too self-effacing at home, it helps a lot for him to take a more active part in managing the child and, if possible, to find some hobby that he can enjoy with the boy occasionally. If his mother has been pushing and prodding him in other areas, such as homework, or getting dressed in the morning (Section 470), she can try to ease up. A conference with the teacher should produce a useful comparing of notes.

681. Enuresis in girls. The commonest picture in enuresis in girls is quite different from that in most boys. The girl is more apt to be a spunky sort, perhaps a tomboy who is competing with a brother and also competing with her mother. (She may feel, for instance, that she can take care of her father and keep him company better than her mother can.) In such cases, the job is to help her feel more comfortable about being a girl, to lessen the causes of rivalry with her brother, for her parents to show her they love her most as a girl, for her father to demonstrate that he loves her as a daughter but that he shares his concerns and interests primarily with his wife. Child-guidance or psychiatric help is most valuable in these cases, too, not just to get the girl over her enuresis but to get her ready to enjoy her life as a woman.

682. Daytime wetting. Late daytime wetting (say after the age of 3) is, once in a great while, due to physical disease. In such a case, the child usually just dribbles a small amount at frequent intervals. He needs a thorough check-up by the doctor. The urine should be examined in **all** cases of late wetting.

In most cases of daytime wetting, there is bed-wetting, too, and much that was said in Sections 679 to 681 about the importance of various kinds of nervousness could be repeated here.

But there are two factors that ought to be emphasized. Most of the children who go on wetting in the daytime have a tendency to balk and to procrastinate. Watching such a child, you can see that one half of him knows perfectly well that his bladder is uncomfortable—he's prancing around restlessly and crossing his legs. But the other half of him is absorbed in play and refuses to do anything about it. There's nothing to be concerned about if a slight "accident" occurs once in a while with a small child when he's deeply absorbed. But if he's stalling and procrastinating all the time, about everything, it's usually a sign that he's being pushed and bossed too much. It's become such a habit to resist that he does it not just when his parents but when his own insides tell him there is something he ought to be doing. This is often called laziness, but actually it requires a lot of effort. It's like a car being driven with the brakes on.

A few children, even happy, well-adjusted ones, have trouble controlling the bladder when they are excited or frightened or laugh suddenly. At these times, they find themselves wetting without any warning. This is not a disease, and it's not an entirely strange thing. Many animals automatically empty the bladder when they are alarmed. The child needs only to be reassured that he has done nothing to be ashamed of.

683. Frequent urinating. Frequent urinating has several possible causes. When it develops in a child who was not frequent before, it may mean some disease, such as an infection of the urinary system or diabetes. The child and a urine specimen should be examined promptly by the doctor.

A few individuals, even calm ones, seem to have bladders that never hold as much as the average, and this may be the way they were made. But most of the children (and adults, too) who regularly have to urinate frequently are somewhat high-strung or worried. In one case it's due to a temporary strain; in another it's a chronic tendency. Even the healthy, normal athlete is apt to have to go to the toilet every fifteen minutes just before a race. The parents' job, then, is to find out what, if anything, is making the child tense. In one case it's the handling at home, in another it's his relations with other children, in another still it's school. Most often it's a combination of these. A common story involves the timid child and the teacher who seems severe. To begin with, the child's apprehensiveness keeps his bladder from relaxing sufficiently to hold much urine. Then he worries about asking permission to be excused. If the teacher makes a fuss about his leaving the room, it's worse still. It's wise to get a note from the doctor, not simply requesting that the child be excused, but explaining the child's nature and why his bladder works that way. If the teacher is approachable and the parent is tactful, a personal visit will help, too.

684. Difficult urination. Once in a great while a baby, usually a boy, is born with such a small urinary passage or opening that he has to push hard to pass his urine, or the urine comes only in a small stream or dribble. The urinary passage needs to be enlarged promptly by a doctor. It is harmful to the inner passages and the kidneys to have the urine obstructed.

Occasionally in hot weather, when a child is perspiring a great deal and not drinking enough, he may pass his urine infrequently, perhaps not for 12 hours or more. What does come is scanty and dark and it may burn. The same thing may happen during a fever. A child in hot weather or when feverish needs plenty of chances and occasional reminders to drink between meals, especially when he is too small to tell what he wants.

A fairly frequent cause of painful urination in girls is an infection of the vagina that inflames the lower urinary passage, too. This may make her feel as if she has to urinate frequently, though she may be unable or too scared to do anything, or pass only a few drops. The doctor should be consulted and a urine specimen examined. Until he can be reached, she can be relieved by sitting several times a day in a shallow warm bath to which has been added a cup of bicarbonate of soda. After gently blotting dry the urinary region, a thick dab of petroleum jelly, boric-acid ointment, zinc ointment, or plain cold cream can be applied to it to soothe and protect it.

685. Sore on the end of the penis. Sometimes a small raw area appears around the opening, or "meatus," of the penis. There may be enough swelling of the tissues here to close up the meatus and make it difficult for the boy to pass his urine. This little sore is a localized diaper rash, caused by ammonia (which can be smelled in the bed in the morning). The ammonia is not passed in the urine but is manufactured from urine by bacteria in the diaper, night clothes, and bedclothes. This ammonia sore occurs most often when the baby is over a year old and the mother has stopped using the diaper service. The bacteria have accumulated in the pajamas, sheets, and pads, and they set to work making ammonia just as soon as the child wets himself in the evening. The important thing in treatment is to boil the diapers, pajamas, sheets, and pads every day or treat them with a diaper antiseptic (Section 302) as long as any sore exists. Meanwhile, the sore can be soothed and protected by frequent application of zinc ointment or other ointment, especially before going to bed. If the child is in pain from being unable to urinate for many hours, he can be sat in a warm bath for half an hour. If this doesn't make him urinate, the doctor should be called.

686. Infections of the urinary tract (pyuria, pyelitis, pyelonephritis, cystitis). Infections in the kidneys or the bladder may cause a stormy illness with a high, irregular fever. On the other hand, infection is sometimes discovered by accident in a routine urine examination in a child who hasn't felt sick at all. An older child may complain of frequent, burning urination, but most often there are no signs pointing to the urinary tract. These infections are commoner in girls, and in the first 2 years of life. Prompt medical treatment is necessary, and usually is successful.

A urine specimen should be examined any time a child has a fever without a known cause. It should also be examined any time a fever lasts more than a few days, even if there is a cold or sore throat to explain the temperature, since an infection elsewhere in the body may spread to the urinary system and keep the fever going.

If there is a lot of pus, the urine may be hazy or cloudy, but a little may not show to the naked eye. On the other hand, a normal child's urine may be cloudy, especially when it cools, due to ordinary minerals in it. So you can't tell definitely from looking at the urine whether it is infected or not.

If a urinary infection does not clear up satisfactorily, or if the child ever has a second urinary infection, his whole urinary system should be investigated thoroughly with special examinations. Urinary infections are more common in children who have abnormally formed urinary passages. If there is anything pointing to such an abnormality, it should be corrected before permanent harm is done to the kidneys. For this reason it is wise, after a child has had a urinary infection, to check his urine again 1 and 2 months later to make sure the infection has not come back, even though he appears well.

687. Pus in a girl's urine may not mean urinary infection. There is always the possibility that pus in a girl's urine is coming from a vaginal infection, even one so mild that there is no visible inflammation or discharge. For this reason, it should never be assumed, without further investigation, that pus in an ordinary specimen means an infection of her urinary system. The first step is to secure a "clean" urine specimen. That means to separate the labia, sponge the genital region briefly and gently with a piece of wet absorbent cotton, and blot dry with a soft towel or a piece of dry absorbent cotton, before letting her pass urine for the specimen. If the clean specimen also shows pus, then the doctor, to be absolutely sure, can pass a catheter (a small rubber tube) into her bladder to obtain a specimen that has not touched her skin outside at all.

VAGINAL DISCHARGE

688. Treat it considerately. It is fairly common for young girls to develop slight vaginal discharges. A majority of these are caused by unimportant germs and clear up in a short time. A thick, profuse discharge that is irritating may be caused by a more serious infection and needs prompt medical treatment. A mild one that persists for days should be examined, too. A discharge that is partly pus and partly blood is sometimes caused by a small girl's having pushed some object into her vagina, which remains there, causing irritation. If this is discovered to be the case, don't try to make her feel guilty or give her the idea that she has injured herself. She hasn't shown any vicious tendency, only a natural desire to explore and experiment.

As explained in Section 515, the girl, particularly between the ages of 3 and 5, may be upset because her body is not shaped like a boy's. This sometimes leads to handling of the genitals, which in turn may cause mild vaginal irritation. If the grownups show anxiety about her genitals, it may make her more alarmed. The burning sensation from a slight discharge can often be relieved without fuss by sitting her, twice a day, in a bath to which bicarbonate of soda has been added; then a dab of petroleum jelly or boric-acid ointment can be applied after the bath. The main thing is to cheerfully assure her that nothing's wrong— that it's just a little sore.

STOMACH-ACHES AND UPSETS

Diarrhea is also discussed in Sections 298–300, vomiting in Sections 288, 289, and 619.

689. Call the doctor. Don't give cathartics. You certainly should get in touch with the doctor for any stomach-ache that lasts as long as 1 hour, whether it is severe or not. There are dozens of causes. A few of them are serious; most are not. A doctor is trained to distinguish between them and prescribe the right treatment. People are apt to jump to the conclusion that a stomach-ache is due either to something that has been eaten or to appendicitis. Actually, neither of these is a common cause. Children can usually eat strange foods or an unusual amount of a regular food without any indigestion.

It is wrong to give a cathartic before the doctor has seen the child because there are some stomach-aches for which a cathartic is dangerous. Before you call the doctor, take the child's temperature so that you can tell him what it is. The treatment, until you reach him, should consist of putting the child to bed and giving him nothing to eat. If he's thirsty, give him small sips of water.

690. Common causes of stomach-ache. In the early weeks of life, stomach-ache is common in **indigestion** and **colic.** These are discussed in Sections 275, 276 and 290.

There is a rare condition called **intussusception,** in which the intestine telescopes into itself and becomes obstructed. It causes sudden severe cramps in a baby or child who has seemed otherwise healthy. The cramps come a number of minutes apart, and between them the baby may be fairly comfortable. Vomiting is apt to occur and be repeated. After a number of hours (during which there may be normal or loose movements), a movement is passed containing mucus and blood—a "currant jelly" or "prune juice" stool. This condition occurs most commonly between the ages of 4 months and 2 years, though it may occur outside this age period. It is rare, but it requires emergency medical treatment, without delay, and that is why it is mentioned here.

Also rare but serious are other types of **intestinal obstructions.** A part of the intestine gets kinked and stuck in a pocket in the abdomen —most frequently in an inguinal hernia (Section 695). There are usually sharp cramps and vomiting.

After the age of a year, one of the commonest causes of stomach-ache is the onset of a simple **cold** or **sore throat** or **grippe,** especially when there is fever. It is just a sign that the infection is disturbing the intestines as well as other parts of the body. In the same way, almost any infection may cause vomiting and constipation, especially in the beginning. A small child is apt to complain that his tummy hurts when he really means that he feels nauseated. He often vomits soon after this complaint.

There are many different kinds of **stomach** and **intestinal infections** that cause stomach-ache, sometimes with vomiting, sometimes with diarrhea, sometimes with both. These are often loosely called "intestinal flu" or "intestinal grippe," meaning a contagious disease caused by an unknown germ. These infections often pass through several members of a family, one after the other. Some epidemics of "intestinal flu" turn out to be dysentery or paratyphoid infections. There may or may not be fever with any of them.

"Food poisoning" is caused by eating food that is heavily contaminated with poisonous bacteria. The food may or may not taste queer. Food poisoning seldom occurs from food that has been thoroughly and recently cooked, because the cooking kills these germs. It's caused most often by pastries filled with custard or whipped cream, and poultry stuffing. Germs multiply readily in these substances if they remain out of the refrigerator for many hours. Another cause is improperly home-canned foods.

The symptoms of food poisoning are usually vomiting, diarrhea, and stomach-ache. Sometimes there are chills and sometimes fever. Everyone who eats the contaminated food is apt to be affected by it to some degree at about the same time, in contrast to an "intestinal flu." which usually spreads through a family over a number of days.

Children with **feeding problems** often have stomach-aches when they sit down to a meal or after they have eaten a little. The parents are apt to think the child has made up the stomach-ache as an excuse not to eat. I think that it's more likely that his poor stomach is all tightened up by his tense feeling at mealtimes, and that the stomach-ache is real. The treatment here is for the parents to handle mealtimes in such a way that the child enjoys his food. (See Sections 587 to 594.)

Children who have never been feeding problems but who have other **worries** can have stomach-aches, too, especially around mealtime. Think of the child who is nervous about starting school in the fall and has a stomach-ache instead of an appetite for breakfast, or the child who feels guilty about something that hasn't been found out yet. All kinds of emotions, from fears to pleasant excitement, can affect the stomach and intestines. They can cause not only pains and lack of appetite, but vomiting and diarrhea and constipation.

A few children who have **worms** seem to have stomach-aches from them, but most aren't affected that way.

There are other infrequent causes of stomach-ache, too: chronic indigestion with gas, intestinal allergies, inflamed lymph glands in the abdomen, rheumatic fever, kidney disturbances, and so on. As you can well see, a child who has pains—whether they are acute and severe, or mild and chronic—needs a thorough check-up by the doctor.

691. Appendicitis. Let me at the start contradict some common notions about appendicitis. There isn't necessarily any fever. The pain isn't necessarily severe. The pain doesn't usually settle in the lower right side of the abdomen until the attack has been going on for some time. Vomiting doesn't always occur. A blood count doesn't prove that a stomach-ache is or isn't due to appendicitis.

The appendix is a little offshoot from the large intestine, about the size of a short earthworm. It usually lies in the central part of the right lower quarter of the abdomen. But it can be lower down. or over toward the middle of the abdomen, or as far up as the ribs. When it becomes inflamed, it's a gradual process, like the formation of a boil. That's why a sudden severe pain in the abdomen that lasts a few minutes and then goes away for good isn't appendicitis. The worst danger is that the inflamed appendix will burst, very much as a boil bursts, and spread the infection all through the abdomen. This is called peritonitis. An appendicitis that is developing very rapidly can reach the point of bursting in less than 24 hours. That's why any stomach-ache that persists for as long as 1 hour should be seen by a doctor, even though nine out of ten cases prove to be something else.

In the most typical cases, there is pain around the navel for several hours. Only later does it shift to the lower right side. There is apt to be vomiting once or twice, but it doesn't always occur. The appetite is usually diminished, but not always. The bowels may be normal or constipated, rarely loose. After it's gone on a few hours, the temperature is apt to be elevated to 100 or 101°, more or less, but it's possible to have real appendicitis without any fever at all. The person may feel more pain when he pulls his right knee up, or when he stretches it way back, or when he walks around. You can see that the symptoms of appendicitis vary a lot in different cases and that you need a doctor to make the diagnosis. The doctor is guided most by whether he finds a tender area in the right side, as he feels deeply but gently into every part of the abdomen. You will notice that he doesn't ask whether it hurts every time he pokes, but on the contrary tries to distract the child from what he is doing. This is because many children with a pain in the stomach, especially young ones, are delighted to say, "Yes, that hurts," every time they are asked. When the doctor finds a tender spot in the right side of the abdomen, he is suspicious of appendicitis, but he sometimes likes to have a blood count to help him decide. A raised blood count just says there is infection somewhere. It doesn't say where.

It's often impossible for the most expert of doctors to be absolutely sure whether or not a child has appendicitis. When there is much suspicion he advises operation, and for a very good reason. If it is appendicitis, it is dangerous to delay; but if it is not, no great harm has been done by the operation.

692. Celiac disease. This condition should be thought of when there is a chronic tendency to frequent, large, loose, smelly bowel movements. It usually becomes definite during the second year, but looking back, it's often possible to see that it occurred off and on during the last half of the first year. The tendency lasts several years.

The intestines are unable to handle fats and starches, especially the gluten in wheat and rye.

When the condition is severe, the child becomes malnourished but has a pot belly, is irritable, usually has a poor appetite. The movements are generally loose, foul, and foamy (they float), but there may be spells of constipation.

A first step in treatment may consist simply in eliminating all gluten from the diet (any foods containing wheat or rye). If this does not bring about marked improvement, the child may be tried on a diet containing at first only skimmed or "protein" milk, cottage cheese, and ripe banana. When the movements and appetite are much improved, other foods are added cautiously, one by one, over a period of months: lean meats, fruit juices and fruits, nonstarchy vegetables. A good dose of a multivitamin preparation is important from the start.

This condition is mentioned here only so that you will be aware of it in case you are far from medical care. You need to get the help of a competent doctor and to keep in close touch with him. The condition lasts a long time and has many ups and downs even when treatment is going well.

693. Pancreatic fibrosis. This is another uncommon disease in which the bowel movements become chronically loose, large, foul-smelling. It differs from celiac disease in that there is also a persistent cough and bronchitis, and that these symptoms develop in the earliest months of life. The sweat is excessively salty.

694. Worms are no disgrace, but need treatment. It horrifies a mother to find worms in her child's movement, but there is no reason to be distressed or to decide that the child has not been properly cared for.

Pinworms, or threadworms, are the commonest variety. They look like white threads, a third of an inch long. They live in the lower intestine, but come out between the buttocks at night to lay their eggs. They can be found there at night or in the bowel movement. They cause itching around the anus, which may disturb the child's sleep. In former days worms were thought to be the chief cause for children's grinding their teeth at night, but this is probably not so. Save a specimen of the worms to show the doctor. There is an efficient treatment for pinworms, which a doctor should supervise.

Roundworms look very much like earthworms. The first suspicion comes when one is discovered in the bowel movement. They usually don't cause symptoms unless the child has a great number of them. The doctor will prescribe treatment.

Hookworms are common in some parts of the southern United

States. They may cause malnutrition and anemia. The disease is contracted by going barefoot in soil that is infested. A doctor can prescribe treatment.

HERNIAS, RUPTURES, HYDROCELE

695. Hernias, or ruptures. The commonest hernia of all, protruding navel, is taken up in Section 236.

The next commonest is what doctors call inguinal hernia. There is meant to be a small passage from inside the abdomen, down along the groin, into the scrotum (in the case of a boy), for the blood vessels and nerves that go to the testicles. This passageway has to pass through the layers of muscle that make up the wall of the abdomen. If these openings in the muscles are larger than average, a piece of intestine may be squeezed out of the abdomen and down the passageway when the child strains or cries. If the intestine goes only part way down, it makes a bulging in the groin. If it goes all the way down into the scrotum (the pouch for the testicles behind the penis), the scrotum looks very enlarged for the time being. Inguinal hernia does occur, though less commonly, in girls. It appears as a protrusion in the groin.

Rupture is a bad name for a condition like this, because it sounds as though something breaks when the intestine is pushed down during straining. This idea makes a mother worry unnecessarily about her baby's crying. Actually, nothing breaks. The overlarge passageway is present at the time the baby is born; it is the way he is made.

In most hernias the intestine slips back up into the abdomen when the baby or child is lying down quietly. It may push down every time he stands up, or it may go down only once in a great while when he strains hard.

Occasionally an inguinal hernia becomes "strangulated." This means that the intestine has stuck in the passage and that the blood vessels have been kinked and shut off. It is a form of intestinal obstruction. This causes abdominal pain and vomiting. It calls for emergency surgical care.

Strangulation of an inguinal hernia occurs most often in the first 6 months of life. Usually it is a hernia that has not been noticed before. The mother changes the baby because he is crying so hard and notices the lump in his groin for the first time. (The groin is the groove between the abdomen and the thigh.) It is not wise to try to push the lump down with the fingers. However, while waiting for the doctor or while driving the baby to the hospital, you can elevate his hips on a pillow, give him a bottle to stop his crying, and apply an ice bag (or crushed ice in a sock) to the hernia. These procedures together may make the intestine slip back into the abdomen.

If you suspect a hernia in your child, you should, of course, report it to the doctor right away. Nowadays inguinal hernias are usually repaired promptly by surgery. It is not a serious operation, it is almost always successful, and the child is soon out of bed.

696. Hydrocele, or swelling around the testicle. Hydrocele is often confused with hernia or rupture because it also causes a swelling in the scrotum. Each testicle in the scrotum is surrounded by a delicate sac that contains a few drops of fluid. This helps to protect the testicle. Quite often in newborn babies there is an extra amount of fluid in the sac that surrounds the testicle, and this makes it appear to be several times its normal size. Sometimes this swelling takes place at a later period.

A hydrocele is nothing to worry about. The fluid in most cases diminishes as the baby gets older, and then nothing needs to be done for it. Occasionally an older boy has a chronic hydrocele, which should be operated on if it is uncomfortably large. You should not try to make the diagnosis yourself. Let the doctor decide whether it's hernia or hydrocele.

EYE TROUBLES

697. Reasons for seeing the eye doctor. A child needs to go to an eye doctor if his eyes turn in (cross-eyes) or out (wall-eyes) at any age; if he is having **any** trouble with his schoolwork; if he is complaining of aching, smarting, or tired eyes; if his eyes are inflamed; if he is having headaches; if he holds his book too close; if he cocks his head to one side when looking at something carefully; or if his vision is found to be defective by the chart test at school. However, just because a child can read a chart satisfactorily in school does not mean for sure that his eyes are all right. If he is having symptoms of eyestrain, he should be examined anyway. To be completely sure, it is a good idea to take a child to the oculist when he starts school. It is not absolutely necessary, however, if the school tests his vision yearly, and he has no symptoms. Chart testing, at school or the doctor's, should be done each year after 6.

Nearsightedness, which is the commonest eye trouble that interferes with schoolwork, develops most often in the age period between 6 and 10. It can come on quite rapidly, so don't ignore the signs of it (holding the book closer, having trouble seeing the blackboard at school) just because the child's vision was all right a few months before.

Inflammation of the eye (conjunctivitis) can be caused by many different infections. Most of the mild cases are caused by ordinary cold germs, and accompany colds in the nose. You should be more suspicious of inflammation when there is no nose cold. It is a good idea to get in touch with your doctor, anyway, but particularly when the white of the eye becomes reddened or when there is pus.

698. Specks. Specks in the eye should be removed promptly. It is always preferable to let a doctor do this if possible. It is absolutely necessary to go to a doctor if the speck has not been removed in half an hour. A speck that stays imbedded over the pupil or iris for several hours may cause a serious infection. There are three methods you can try if it is difficult to reach the doctor. The first is to draw the upper eyelid down and away from the eye, holding it by the lashes. This gives the tears a chance to wash the speck out. Next, you can use an eyecup, containing a sterile 2% solution of boric acid (2 level teaspoonfuls of boric-acid powder in a cupful of boiled water). The child tips his head down, applies the filled eyecup to his eye, straightens his head up, blinks several times with the cup against the eye. The third method is to examine the inside of the upper lid. This is where most specks lodge. You need a clean cotton swab (made on a toothpick or matchstick) and a plain match or toothpick. Tell the child to look down and **keep** looking down. This relaxes the upper lid. Take hold of the eyelashes of the upper lid, pull the lid down as far as it goes, lay the matchstick horizontally across the middle of the lid, and fold the eyelid back over the matchstick. While you hold the lid firmly folded back, reach for the cotton swab. If you see the speck on the lid, gently wipe it off with the swab. You need a good strong light. If you can't find the speck and the pain goes on, or if the speck is lodged on the eyeball, go to an eye doctor promptly. Don't try to remove a speck from the eyeball yourself.

699. Styes. A stye is an infection in a hair follicle of the eyelashes, and is similar to a pimple anywhere else. A stye is caused by ordinary pus germs that happen to be rubbed onto the eyelid. The stye usually comes to a head and breaks. The doctor may prescribe an ointment to promote healing and prevent spreading. An adult with a stye feels more comfortable if he puts on hot applications, and this may hasten its coming to a head and breaking, but it makes no great difference. A child doesn't want to be bothered. The main trouble with a stye is that one often leads to another, probably because when the first one breaks the germs are spread to other hair follicles. This is a reason for trying to keep a child from rubbing or fingering his eyelid at the time a stye is coming to a head or discharging. If a child has several styes in succession, he should be examined by his doctor and have a urine analysis. Styes occasionally mean that a person has some condition that lowers his resistance.

A mother with a stye should wash her hands thoroughly before doing things for a baby or small child, especially if she has touched her stye, because the germs are easily passed from person to person. A father or brother with a stye had better not handle the baby temporarily.

CONVULSIONS

700. A convulsion is a frightening thing to see in a child, but in most cases it is not dangerous in itself. Most convulsions stop in a short time, whether or not any treatment is used.

Telephone for the doctor. If you cannot reach him immediately, don't worry. The convulsion is usually over, anyway, and the child asleep by the time the doctor can get there.

Keep the child from hurting himself. If he is biting his tongue, you can try to keep his jaws separated with a clothespin or with the small end of a fountain pen or with a pencil.

Don't try to get him into a tepid bath; it won't make that much difference.

If the child has a high fever, give him a wet rub to get his temperature down. Take off his clothes. Wet your hand in water and rub one arm for a couple of minutes, then the other arm, each leg, the chest, the back. Keep wetting your hand as necessary. The gentle rubbing brings the blood to the surface, and the evaporation helps in the cooling. If the convulsions continue or if the temperature stays above 103°, you can continue to rub. Don't cover him with blankets when you are trying to get the temperature down.

In most convulsions, the child loses consciousness, the eyes roll up, the teeth are clenched, and the body or parts of the body are shaken by twitching movements. The breathing is heavy, and there may be a little frothing at the lips. Sometimes the urine and bowel movement are passed.

Convulsions are brought on by irritation of the brain from a number of different causes. The causes are different at different age periods. In the newborn baby they are usually due to injury to the brain.

701. In the young child, between 1 and 5, the commonest cause is sudden fever at the onset of colds, sore throats, and grippe. Fever coming on so quickly seems to make the nervous system irritable. Lots of children of this age are trembly at the start of their fevers, even though they don't have convulsions. So if your child around 2 or 3 has a convulsion at the onset of a fever, it doesn't necessarily mean that he has a serious disease, and it doesn't mean that he's going to have more convulsions in later life. Convulsions are rare after the first day of fever.

702. Epilepsy is the name given to convulsions that occur repeatedly in the older child, without any fever or other disease. Nobody knows the real cause. There are two different forms of epilepsy. In "grand mal" attacks, the person loses consciousness completely and has convulsions. In "petit mal," the attack is so brief that the person doesn't fall or lose control of himself; he may just stare or stiffen momentarily.

Every case of epilepsy should be investigated by a doctor familiar with the disease. Though the condition is usually a chronic one, there are several drugs that are helpful in stopping or reducing the frequency of the spells.

There are other causes of convulsions less common than these that have been mentioned.

First Aid

CUTS, HEMORRHAGE, AND BURNS

703. Soap and pure water for cuts and scratches. The best treatment for scratches and small cuts is to wash them with soap and pure water on a piece of absorbent cotton or clean cloth. Then rinse the soap off with plenty of clear water. Ask your doctor whether the water you use is pure enough to wash wounds with. If not, you can keep a bottle of hydrogen peroxide to use for this soaping and rinsing.

An antiseptic is less important than careful washing, and some doctors prefer that none be used. Don't use iodine. Cover with a bandage. The only purpose of the bandage is to keep the cut reasonably clean.

For large cuts that gape open, you should, of course, consult your doctor. It is good to have expert care for cuts on the face, even when they are small, since scars are more noticeable there, and also for cuts on the hand and wrist, because of the danger of cut nerves and tendons.

Wounds that might be contaminated by any street dirt or soil that contains manure should be reported to your doctor. Manure frequently carries the germs of tetanus (lockjaw). The doctor may recommend a tetanus toxoid booster shot or antitoxin, especially for deep cuts or puncture wounds.

Animal bites. Get in touch with the doctor promptly. Meanwhile, first aid is the same as for cuts. The important thing is to keep track of the animal to be sure he is not developing rabies. If the animal does develop rabies or if he cannot be traced, the doctor gives rabies inoculations.

704. Bandaging. What you use for bandaging depends on the size and location of the scratch or cut. Small prepared sterile bandages are good for most small wounds. They won't stick on the palm. For larger cuts and scratches, use a gauze square that comes sterile in an envelope, or a folded piece of clean cotton cloth. It can be held in place by narrow strips of adhesive. (A small child can loosen a bandage in no time at all.) Any bandaging has to be snug to do any good.

Don't wrap adhesive all the way around the arm or leg (so that it overlaps itself) because this might shut off the circulation. If the foot or hand becomes at all swollen or darker in color after the leg or arm has been bandaged, it means that the bandage is too tight. It should be loosened right away. It's all right to wrap a small prepared bandage around a finger if it's not too tight. Strips of adhesive to hold a bandage in place have more chance of staying if you make them plenty long.

A wound heals quicker and is less apt to become infected if you don't disturb the bandaging too often. If it becomes too loose or dirty-looking, apply a new layer on top of the old. Take a bandage off very gently. Peel the inner layer back in the same direction as the cut runs. (For instance, if the line of the cut runs up and down the arm, peel the bandage up or down the arm.) In this way there is less likelihood of pulling the edges of the cut apart. A cut may throb the first day and night, and this doesn't mean much. If it becomes increasingly painful later, it may be due to infection. Then the bandage should be removed to see what is happening. If there is swelling or redness, the doctor should see it.

Barked knees, after being washed, are best left unbandaged until a dry scab is formed. Otherwise the bandage gets stuck and pulls off the scab when it is changed.

If a small child has a cut near the mouth, it may stay cleaner without any bandage (to catch food and saliva).

705. Bandaging a finger. A child's finger is the part most frequently bandaged and the most difficult to bandage. Use a prepared bandage wrapped around the finger if this will cover the cut. If not, wrap the finger with a sterile gauze square or a strip of clean cloth. Hold this in place with a couple of strips of adhesive that circle the finger.

Now take a narrow strip of adhesive tape about a foot long, apply one end to the base of the bandage on the palm side, run to the end of the finger, over the end, up the back side of the bandage, up the back of the hand, and halfway up the arm. When you are sticking the adhesive to the back of the hand and arm, have the child's finger and wrist partly bent over; otherwise the adhesive acts as a halter holding the finger up straight. With another piece of adhesive, circle the middle of the bandage once more, snugly, to hold it together and to keep the lengthwise strip of adhesive from coming loose.

706. Bleeding (hemorrhage). Most wounds bleed a little for a few minutes, and this is good because it washes out some of the germs that were introduced. It's only profuse or persistent hemorrhage that needs special treatment.

Bleeding of the hand, arm, foot, or leg stops sooner if the part is elevated. Have the child lie down, and put a pillow or two under the limb. If the wound continues to bleed freely, press on it with a sterile gauze square or any clean cloth, until it stops or until you decide to bandage it. Clean and bandage the wound while the limb is still elevated.

If the wound was made in a clean way (with a knife, for instance) and bled freely, don't try to wash the cut but clean around it gently (soap and water, or soap and hydrogen peroxide on sterile cotton). If the wound still contains dirt, clean inside the cut, too.

When bandaging a cut that has bled a lot or is still bleeding, use a number of gauze squares (or folded pieces of clean cloth) on top of each other so that you have a thick pad over the cut. Then, when you snugly apply the adhesive or gauze roll bandage, it exerts more pressure on the cut and makes it less likely to bleed again. This is the principle of the "pressure bandage."

707. Severe bleeding. If a wound is bleeding at an alarming rate, don't wait to find the right bandages. Stop the bleeding with pressure immediately and wait for someone else to bring the bandages. Elevate a limb if possible. Make a pad of the cleanest material you have handy, whether it's gauze squares, a clean handkerchief, or the cleanest piece of clothing on the child or yourself. Press the pad against the wound, and keep pressing until help arrives or until the bleeding stops. Don't remove your original pad. As it is soaked through, add new material on top. If the bleeding is easing up and you have suitable material, apply a pressure bandage. The pad over the wound, made of a number of gauze squares or folded material of the cleanest available, should be thick enough so that when it is bandaged it presses on the wound. A small pad is enough for a finger, but a thick dressing is necessary for a thigh or abdominal wound. Bandage snugly with gauze bandage or adhesive tape or long strips of any kind of material. If the pressure bandage doesn't control the bleeding, continue hand pressure directly over the wound. If you have no cloth or material of any kind to press against a wound that is bleeding alarmingly, press with your hands on the edges of the wound, or even in the wound.

A great majority of even serious hemorrhages can be stopped by simple direct pressure. If you are dealing with one that can't and if you have learned in a first-aid class how to apply a tourniquet, then go ahead. It's seldom necessary, though, and it's nothing that a novice should try to learn for the first time in an emergency. It **must** be loosened every 30 minutes.

708. Nose bleeds. There are a number of simple remedies for nosebleed. Just having a child sit still for a few minutes is often sufficient. To avoid his swallowing a lot of blood, have him sit up with his head bent forward, or if he's lying down, turn his head to the side so that his nose points slightly down. Keep him from blowing his nose or from pressing and squeezing it with his handkerchief. It's all right to hold the handkerchief gently against the nostril to catch the blood, but moving the nose around helps to keep up the bleeding.

Cold applied to any part of the head constricts the blood vessels and helps to stop a hemorrhage. Place something cold against the back of the neck, or the forehead, or the upper lip. A cloth wrung out in cold water, an ice bag, or a cold bottle from the refrigerator will do.

If the nosebleed continues for 10 minutes in spite of these measures, get in touch with the doctor. If you have a bottle of nose drops of the kind that shrink the tissues, wet a small, loose wad of cotton with the nose drops and tuck it into the front part of the nostril. Nosebleeds usually occur from the front part of the nose. You can sometimes stop a severe hemorrhage by gently pinching the lower part of the nose for 10 minutes. Let go slowly and gently.

Nosebleeds occur most frequently from blows on the nose, from picking the nose, and from colds and other infections. If a child has repeated hemorrhages from no apparent cause, he needs to be examined by a doctor to make sure he has none of the general diseases that sometimes cause nosebleeds. If no disease is found, it may be necessary to cauterize (burn) the exposed blood vessel that is always breaking. The proper blood vessel to cauterize can be discovered only right after a hemorrhage.

709. Burns. The treatment of burns has changed a lot in recent years and is continuing to change. It is a good idea to ask your doctor ahead of time what he recommends in case of emergency.

In case of a burn, call the doctor for instructions before doing anything else. If he is not there, ask the office to reach him and have him call you as soon as possible. Meanwhile, give first-aid treatment. Then, if the burn is severe and it looks as though you can reach a hospital sooner than you will hear from the doctor, start for the hospital.

One satisfactory first-aid treatment for a small burn is to apply plain petroleum jelly (petrolatum) and cover loosely with a clean bandage. If you have no petrolatum, you can use clean vegetable fat (shortening) or even butter.

Another method, clumsier than ointment, is to cover the burn with clean gauze pads wet with bicarbonate of soda solution (a level teaspoonful to a cup of water). Hold them in place with loose bandaging and moisten from time to time with more of the solution, until you can get ointment for a small burn or get a doctor for a larger one.

It is much safer to consult a doctor for any burns that cause blisters or raw spots. Some of the blisters are apt to break, and infection easily occurs under the edges of a broken blister.

If you have to deal with one or two small, unbroken blisters without the help of a doctor, don't open them or try to puncture them with a needle. There is less danger of infection if you leave them alone. Small blisters sometimes reabsorb without ever breaking; or if they break after several days, the new skin is pretty well formed underneath. When a blister does break, it is better to cut all the loose skin off. Use a pair of nail scissors and a pair of tweezers, both of which have been boiled for 10 minutes. Then cover with a sterile bandage coated with petroleum jelly. If a blister becomes infected, as shown by pus in the blister and redness around the edge, you should certainly consult your doctor. If this is impossible, cut away the blister and use wet dressings (Section 711).

Never put iodine or any similar antiseptic on a burn of any degree. It makes matters worse.

710. Sunburn. The best thing for sunburn is not to get it. Severe sunburn is painful, dangerous, and unnecessary. A half hour of direct sunshine at a beach in summer is enough to cause a burn on a fair-skinned person who is unused to exposure.

Better to take too little sun the first days on the beach or in the country than too much. You can't tell when the skin's had enough from looking at it or feeling it. It takes hours for a burn to show. A good rule for the first few days at the beach is to keep the child's face, body, and legs covered or shaded except when he is actually going into the water. That means a hat to shade the forehead and nose, a shirt to cover the shoulders, and overalls to protect the legs, especially the back of the knees while lying on the stomach.

"Tanning" lotions that promise to make a nice tan without burning may help a little, but they can't protect against a large amount of sunshine.

For relief of sunburn, you can apply plain cold cream or petroleum jelly. With a moderately severe burn, a person may have chills and fever and feel sick. Then you should consult a doctor, because sunburn can be just as serious as a heat burn. Keep sunburned areas completely protected from sunshine until the redness is gone.

711. Wet dressings for skin infections until you can reach the doctor. If a child has a boil, or an infection of the end of his finger, or around his finger nail or toenail, or an infected cut, or any similar type of infection under his skin, it should be seen by the doctor. Meanwhile, the child should be quiet, preferably in bed, with the limb elevated on a pillow.

If there is an unavoidable delay in reaching the doctor, the best first-aid treatment is to apply a continuous wet dressing. This softens the skin, hastens the time when it breaks to allow the pus to escape, and keeps the opening from closing over again too soon.

You can make a solution by boiling a cupful of water and adding a tablespoonful of Epsom salts, or magnesium sulfate, or table salt.

Make a fairly thick bandage over the infection and pour enough of the salt solution into the bandage to make all of it wet. Every few hours, when it begins to dry, add more solution.

You can keep it wet longer, especially at night, and keep the child's clothes and bedclothes dry, by covering the whole dressing with a piece of waterproof material, such as the plastic bags that are used in refrigerators, or plastic wrapping. Use a large enough piece to extend beyond the edges of the bandaging, and hold it in place with strips of adhesive tape. (Don't run adhesive tape tightly around an arm or leg—it may cut off the circulation.)

If a child has fever with a skin infection, or if there are red streaks running up his arm or leg, or if he has tender lymph glands in his armpit or groin, the infection is spreading seriously and should be considered a real emergency. Get the child to a doctor or a hospital, even if you have to drive all night. Modern drugs are vitally important in combating serious infections.

SPRAINS, FRACTURES, HEAD INJURIES

712. Sprains usually need examination and treatment. If your child sprains his ankle, have him lie down for a half hour or so and elevate the foot on a pillow. This keeps the deep hemorrhage and swelling to a minimum. If swelling occurs, you ought to consult your doctor, because it is possible that a bone has been cracked or broken.

A sprained knee should always be seen by a doctor and treated carefully. A neglected knee sprain in which a cartilage has been injured may not heal properly and may give trouble for years. If a child has fallen on his wrist and it remains painful, either when it is still or when it is moved, you have to suspect a fracture, even though there is no crookedness or swelling.

You can say, then, that any sprain that continues to be painful or that swells should be examined. This is not only because of the possibility of fracture, but also because most sprains are much more comfortable if they are splinted or bandaged correctly. Many sprains and partial fractures are numb for an hour or so and then become more and more painful.

713. Fractures. The brittle bones of adults really break. The softer bones of children are more apt to bend and splinter a little ("greenstick" fractures). Another type of fracture in a child is loosening or breaking off of the growing end of a bone. This is particularly apt to happen at the wrist. When a child has had a severe fracture, it is easy enough for anyone to see. But there are some common fractures that don't look especially deformed. A broken ankle can look straight enough, but there is considerable swelling and pain. A black-and-blue spot appears after a number of hours. Only a doctor can distinguish between an ankle that is severely sprained and one that is broken, and he often needs an X ray to tell. A wrist can be broken without being out of line enough for you to realize it. Finger bones are often chipped when a ball is caught on the end of a finger. There is only swelling and later some blueness. A vertebra (one of the bones in the spine) is sometimes slightly crushed when a child falls on his behind. Nothing shows outside, but he complains of pain when he curves his body forward or when he jumps and runs. In a general way, suspect a fracture if pain in a limb continues, or if there is swelling, or if a black-and-blue mark appears.

Avoid further injury in a suspected fracture. Don't move the injured limb around. Don't let the child move it. If he's in a halfway comfortable place and you can get a doctor soon, keep him quiet where he is. If he has to be moved, put some kind of splint on first.

A splint to do any good must extend far enough up and down the limb. For an ankle injury, the splint should reach to the knee; for a break in the lower leg, it should go up to the hip; for a break in the thigh, you need a board that goes from the foot to the armpit. For a broken wrist, the splint should go from the finger tips to the elbow; for a broken lower or upper arm, it should go from the finger tips to the armpit. You need a board to make a long splint. A short one for a small child can be made by folding a piece of cardboard. Move the limb with extreme gentleness when you are applying the splint to it, and try to avoid any movement where the break is. Tie the limb to the splint snugly in 4 to 6 places, using handkerchiefs, strips of clothing, or bandages. Two of the ties should be close to the break, on either side of it, and there should be one at each end of the splint. For a back injury, it is even more important to leave the patient where he is if he can possibly be made comfortable there. If he must be moved, use a stretcher or a door. In picking up a person with a back injury, keep his back straight or arched inward (so that it is "hollow"). Never let his back curve outward. That means that when he is picked up, or if he has to be carried on a mattress or other makeshift stretcher that sags, he should be on his stomach. In case of a neck injury, the neck should be kept straight or, if curved at all, curved backward. (His head should not bend forward.) For a broken collarbone (at the top of the chest in front), make a sling out of a large triangle of cloth and tie it behind the neck, so that it supports the lower arm across the chest.

If a person with a serious injury has to be kept for some time in a cold place, protect him reasonably with blankets or with other clothing. Put a blanket under him. It is no longer considered wise to try to make a person in shock really warm with many hot blankets or hot-water bottles.

714. Head injuries. A fall on the head is a common injury from the age when a baby can roll over (and thereby roll himself off a bed). A parent usually feels guilty the first time this happens. But if a child is so carefully watched that he **never** has an accident, he is being fussed over too much. His bones may be saved, but his character will be ruined.

If, after a fall on the head, a baby stops crying within 15 minutes, keeps a good color, and doesn't vomit, there is little chance that he has injured his brain. He can be allowed to resume his normal life right away.

When a blow on the head is more severe, the child is apt to vomit, lose his appetite, be pale for a number of hours, show signs of headache, fall asleep easily but be able to be roused. If a child has any of these symptoms, you should get in touch with your doctor. He may want to examine the child or have his skull X-rayed. The child should be kept as quiet as possible for 2 or 3 days and any new symptoms reported to the doctor immediately. It's a good idea to rouse the child once during the first night after the fall to make sure that he's not unconscious. If he is not feeling his usual self the next day, the doctor should be notified again.

If a child loses consciousness either right after a fall or later, he should certainly be examined by a doctor immediately. The same rule applies even without unconsciousness if the child continues to complain of headache, trouble with his vision, or if he vomits later.

A swelling that puffs out quickly on a child's skull after a fall doesn't mean anything serious in itself if there are no other symptoms. It is caused by a broken blood vessel just under the skin.

SWALLOWED OBJECTS AND CHOKING

715. Swallowed objects. Babies and small children swallow prune pits, coins, safety pins, beads, buttons—in fact, anything you can mention. They seem to be able to pass most of these things through their stomachs and intestines with the greatest of ease, even open safety pins or a little broken glass. The objects that are more dangerous are needles and common pins.

If your child has swallowed without discomfort a smooth object, like a prune pit or a button, you don't have to worry or give him bread to push it along. Just watch the movements for a few days to reassure yourself that it has come out. Naturally, if he develops vomiting or pains in the stomach, or if an object gets painfully stuck in his gullet, or if he has swallowed a sharp object such as an open safety pin or a needle, you should consult the doctor immediately.

Never give a cathartic to a child who has swallowed an object. It won't do any good and it may do harm.

716. Choking. When a child breathes or coughs something into his windpipe and is choking, hold him upside down and slap him vigorously on the back of his chest. If he keeps on choking and begins to turn blue, rush him to the nearest hospital or doctor's office. Let someone else telephone ahead. Don't wait for anything.

A sharp object stuck in the throat, like a fishbone, though very uncomfortable and gagging, is not dangerous like an object that is obstructing the breathing. You should reach the doctor as soon as possible, but it isn't a matter of life or death. Lots of times the object can't be found when the doctor examines the throat, though the child keeps saying it's there. In these cases the fishbone, or whatever it is, has been swallowed, but the child is still feeling the scratches left in his throat.

ARTIFICIAL RESPIRATION
717. Artificial respiration.

If person has drowned, first drain water from lungs by laying him on stomach for 10 seconds with hips a foot higher than head (over your knee, a box, etc.).

A person may stop breathing because of smothering, drowning, electric shock, inhaling gas. Start artificial respiration promptly. Keep it up until he continues to breathe by himself or until help comes, as long as two hours. **Never give it to a person who is breathing.**

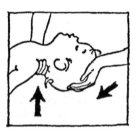

It is vital to open the air passages by raising neck, tilting head **way** back.

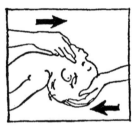

Then keep victim's **chin pressed upward all the time,** to keep the passages open.

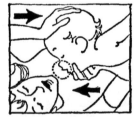

With a child's small face you can breathe into nose **and** mouth together. (With adult, breathe into mouth **or** nose, and keep the other pinched shut.)

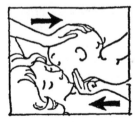

Breathe into victim, using only mild force. (A small child's lungs cannot contain your entire exhalation.) Remove your lips, allowing his chest to contract while you inhale your next breath. Breathe into victim again.

Each of your breaths goes into the victim. With an adult, breathe at your natural speed. With a child use slightly quicker, shorter breaths.

OBJECTS IN THE NOSE AND EARS

718. Objects in the nose and ears. Small children often stuff things like beads and wads of paper into their nose or ears. The important thing is not to push the object any farther in, in your efforts to take it out. Don't try to go after a smooth, hard thing. You are almost certain to push it in farther. You may be able to grasp a soft object that isn't too far in, with a pair of tweezers.

With objects in the nose, have the child blow his nose. (Don't try this if he is so young that he sniffs in when told to blow.) He may sneeze the object out in a little while. If the object stays in, take him to your doctor or a nose specialist. Foreign objects that stay in the nose for several days usually cause a bad-smelling discharge tinged with blood. A discharge of this kind from one nostril should always make you think of this possibility.

POISONS

719. Doctor or emergency ward. If your child has swallowed something that you think might be poisonous, telephone your doctor for advice.

If you can't reach him immediately, ask his secretary or the telephone operator to find him or some other doctor. While you are waiting to hear from the doctor, **keep off the phone** and **read the next section (720)** about whether you should try to make the child vomit.

If you haven't heard in ten minutes, it may be more sensible to **start for a hospital emergency room.** You or someone should phone the doctor's secretary again so that he can meet you at the hospital when he has been located. Ask the secretary to phone the hospital that you are coming and what the poison is, so that they can be ready. Take the container of the poison with you, and any vomitus you may have caught.

If you have no phone, read the next section about whether or not you should make your child vomit, and then start for the hospital or a physician's office. Bring the container of the poison, and the vomitus if possible.

720. Whether or not to make a child vomit. Vomiting is the best first-aid treatment for suspected poisoning with most substances but **not** the following:

Do **not** induce vomiting for these:

kerosene	liquid auto polish	lye
gasoline	liquid furniture polish	ammonia
benzene	insect sprays	drain cleaners
cleaning fluids	phenol	caustic lime

strong acids (sulfuric, nitric, hydrochloric, carbolic)

Kerosene, gasoline, benzene, are most harmful when breathed or choked into the lungs, and vomiting might cause more to be breathed in. Acids, lye, and other caustics would burn the throat again coming up, so it is not wise to induce vomiting.

721. The simplest method to cause vomiting, not always successful, is to slip your finger down the child's throat to make him gag. Have him lie on his stomach across a bed with his head hanging over the edge. Keep him there until he stops vomiting. Try to catch the vomitus in a basin or dishpan, for the doctor to analyze. Run your finger down the back of his throat in an unhesitating way, and don't be afraid to **keep it there a few seconds, in motion, to make him gag thoroughly.** A brief gag probably won't be enough. If you hesitate on the way in or out, you may be bitten. He can't bite while he's actually gagging. If it's some time since he's eaten, he will vomit more easily if you **give him a glass of water or milk first.**

After he has vomited, give him another drink and make him vomit again.

722. Other ways to cause vomiting. If your child is old enough or cooperative enough to do something unpleasant, you can probably make him vomit by having him drink a glassful of water to which has been added a tablespoonful of salt, or a teaspoonful of mustard, or enough soap to make suds. This is called an **emetic.** After the child has vomited once, try to get him to take another glassful of the emetic and make him vomit again.

There is one further emergency measure you can take for a young child if you are quite sure he has taken a dangerous amount of poison, and if you are unable to make him vomit by the methods above, and if it's going to take half an hour or more to get to the doctor or hospital. Give him a dose of **syrup of ipecac** (2 teaspoonfuls for a child of 2 or more, 1½ teaspoonfuls for one under 2 years) if you have it in the medicine cabinet or can pick it up at the drugstore without delay. If vomiting has not occurred, give an additional teaspoonful every 10 minutes, up to a total of 6 teaspoonfuls. Do not repeat after vomiting occurs.

723. Do not neglect to get medical attention just because a child seems all right an hour or two after taking a poison. Some poisons (such as aspirin) have a delayed reaction. Close continuous medical observation is necessary for at least 12 hours in some cases.

724. List of common poisons. Induce vomiting unless otherwise stated. But get in touch with the doctor in **all** cases.

Allonal. (See Barbiturates.)

Ammonia. Do not induce vomiting. (See Lye.)

Amytal. (See Barbiturates.)

Antifreeze solutions. Induce vomiting.

Ant powder. Induce vomiting.

Arsenic. Small amounts are dangerous. Give milk and induce vomiting.

Aspirin. This is one of the commonest causes of serious poisoning. The reaction is slow to appear. Induce vomiting. Close medical observation should be continued for 12 hours.

Atropine in drops or tablets. Small amounts are dangerous. Induce vomiting.

Automobile polish (liquid). Do not induce vomiting.

Barbiturates. These include many of the sleeping tablets and capsules given to adults. Three sleeping tablets or capsules intended for an adult is a dangerous dose for a 1-year-old. Induce vomiting.

Belladonna. (See Atropine.)

Benzene. Do not induce vomiting. One teaspoonful is a dangerous dose for a 1-year-old.

Bichloride of mercury. (It usually comes in blue tablets to make antiseptic solutions.) Induce vomiting repeatedly. Speed is vital. Eggs and milk are of some help as antidotes.

Boric acid. An ounce of the solution or a quarter teaspoonful of the powder is dangerous for a 1-year-old. Induce vomiting.

Camphorated oil. Induce vomiting.

Carbolic acid. Do not induce vomiting. Eggs and milk are of some help as antidotes. Wash face and mouth with lots of water. Half a teaspoonful of a concentrated solution would be a dangerous dose for a 1-year-old.

Carbon tetrachloride. Do not induce vomiting.

Cathartics. "Compound cathartic" pills contain strychnine. Three such pills are dangerous for a 1-year-old. Induce vomiting promptly.

Cascara alone, phenolphthalein alone, milk of magnesia, are not very poisonous.

Caustic lime, potash, soda. (See Lye.)

Cigarettes. One swallowed cigarette may be dangerous for a 1-year-old. Induce vomiting promptly.

Cleaning fluids. Do not induce vomiting.

Codeine tablets, or cough syrups containing codeine, in doses prescribed for adults, may be serious for a 1-year-old. Induce vomiting.

Cough syrups. Patent cough syrups may contain, in a teaspoonful, an amount of codeine that is a full-sized dose for a 1-year-old. Therefore 3 or 4 teaspoonfuls may be poisonous. Induce vomiting. Brown's Mixture contains no codeine.

Cresol. (See Carbolic acid.)

D.D.T. Induce vomiting.

Drain cleaners. (See Lye.)

Fly poisons. (See Arsenic.)

Fowler's solution. (See Arsenic.)

Furniture polishes. Do not induce vomiting.

Gasoline. A teaspoonful is a dangerous dose for a 1-year-old. Do not induce vomiting.

Hydrochloric acid. Dangerous when not dilute. Do not induce vomiting. Give a teaspoonful of bicarbonate of soda in a glass of water. "Dilute hydrochloric acid" used in prescriptions for stomach ailments is not very dangerous.

Ink. Some inks contain a poisonous chemical. Induce vomiting if more than a taste has been swallowed.

Insect sprays. Do not induce vomiting.

Iodine. A few drops of tincture of iodine are not dangerous; they produce only an uncomfortable burn of the mouth, throat, and stomach. A teaspoonful might be a serious dose for a 1-year-old. Give bread or precooked cereal, and induce vomiting.

"Iron, quinine, and strychnine" tonic pills are a frequent cause of poisoning. Three pills are dangerous for a 1-year-old. Do not induce vomiting.

Iron tablets with candy coating may be taken in large quantities and are dangerous. Induce vomiting.

Kerosene. A tablespoonful is a dangerous dose for a 1-year-old. Do not induce vomiting.

Lighter fluid. Do not induce vomiting.

Luminal. (See Barbiturates.)

Lye. Dangerous in small amounts. Do not induce vomiting. Wash face and mouth freely with water. Give as much grapefruit juice, or lemon juice (can be sweetened), or dilute vinegar (1 part to 3 parts of water) as the child will drink. Same treatment for ammonia, washing soda, potash, caustic lime, quicklime, caustic soda, drain cleaners.

Matches of any kind and the place to strike them are no longer made of dangerous chemicals. (Don't let children eat them, however.)

Mercury in metal form from a broken thermometer is usually not very dangerous. Consult the doctor, however. (For other forms of mercury, see Bichloride of mercury.)

Mothballs. Induce vomiting.

Mushrooms and toadstools. Some of the nonedible varieties are poisonous. Induce vomiting.

Nembutal. (See Barbiturates.)

Nicotine. One swallowed cigarette or a few drops of a plant spray containing nicotine are dangerous for a 1-year-old. Induce vomiting immediately.

Nitric acid. (See Sulfuric acid.)

Phenobarbital. (See Barbiturates.)

Phenol. (See Carbolic acid.)

Phosphorus. (See Rat and Roach poisons.)

Plant sprays are apt to contain nicotine or arsenic and are dangerous in small amounts. Induce vomiting.

Potash. (See Lye.)

Quicklime. (See Lye.)

Rat poisons usually contain arsenic or phosphorus. An amount the size of a small pea may be dangerous. Induce vomiting.

Roach powder may contain concentrated sodium fluoride. A half teaspoonful may be dangerous for a 1-year-old. Induce vomiting.

Seconal. (See Barbiturates.)

Shoe polish. Some black shoe polishes and dyes contain poisonous chemicals. Induce vomiting.

Sleeping medicines. (See Barbiturates.)

Soda bicarbonate. Not serious.

Soda, caustic. Dangerous. (See Lye.)

Soda, washing. (See Lye.)

Strychnine. Two tablets prescribed for an adult may be dangerous for a 1-year-old. Induce vomiting.

Sulfuric acid. Do not induce vomiting. Wash face and mouth freely with water. Give 1 teaspoonful of bicarbonate of soda in a glass of water.

Thallium preparations. Induce vomiting.
Turpentine oil. Induce vomiting.
Washing soda. (See Lye.)
Weed killers. Induce vomiting.
Wintergreen oil. A teaspoonful is a dangerous dose for a 1-year-old. Induce vomiting.

Special Problems

TRAVELING WITH A BABY

There are several methods of preparing and carrying formula when traveling. Which one is most convenient for you depends on the facilities you will have and on how long you will be away from a kitchen and refrigerator.

725. Adding the milk to each bottle. If you are going to be traveling 24 hours or less with a baby on an evaporated-milk formula, you can bring the required number of bottles, containing only the water and sugar, all sterilized in the usual manner. You carry the evaporated milk in small, 6-ounce cans, 1 can for each feeding. At each feeding you open a fresh can of milk, pour the required amount into the bottle containing the water and sugar, put the nipple on, shake, and warm. When you make up the sugar water, you use the usual amounts of sugar and water, but you have to figure the amount of sugar water that goes into each bottle and the amount of evaporated milk that later goes into each. (Divide the total water and the total milk by the number of bottles.) For example, suppose your usual total formula is 13 ounces evaporated milk, 19 ounces water, and 3 tablespoons corn syrup, divided into 5 bottles. Mix your water and syrup, put 4 ounces into each of 5 bottles, and sterilize. When ready to feed, add 2½ ounces evaporated milk to a bottle (up to the 6½-ounce mark) and discard the rest of the can. With this method, the milk stays safe, despite the lack of refrigeration, because it remains sterile in the cans until feeding time.

726. Using a traveling ice box. Another method, for 24 hours or less, is to prepare and refrigerate the required number of bottles of regular formula just as you do for home use, and keep them cold in a picnic ice box or in the pail you use for sterilizing the bottles. This method can be used for an evaporated-milk or pasteurized-milk formula or for plain pasteurized milk. All you need is room in the car for the ice box or sterilizing pail. Wrap the entire outer surface of your sterilizing pail, and line the lid inside, with about 10 layers of newspaper, tied on with string, in such a way that you can remove the top without undoing it. When it's time to go, place the bottles in the bottle rack in the pail and pack in all the ice, in chunks or cubes (chipped ice melts too fast), that the pail will hold. The milk will stay cold for many hours, depending on the temperature of the place where you keep it.

727. Refrigerating the quart bottle. Another method, which will save space, is to put the entire formula for 24 hours in a sterilized quart bottle, which is kept in the picnic ice box or iced sterilizing pail in the car. If the baby is on plain pasteurized milk, just bring the dairy bottle on ice. For a train or plane trip, consult the ticket agent ahead of time about the accommodations for keeping such a bottle refrigerated. At each feeding you fill a nursing bottle, through a funnel, from the large bottle. After feeding, wash the bottle, nipple, and funnel, with soap and brush, before using them again, or bring enough clean bottles and nipples to last the trip.

728. Insulating one or two bottles. If you are going to be traveling through only 1 or 2 feedings, wrap 1 or 2 bottles, well refrigerated, in 10 or 15 layers of newspaper, or carry them in an insulated bag made to keep things cold. A dining-car waiter will keep a bottle or two in the refrigerator. Some planes have ice boxes.

729. Making up each bottle, on a longer trip. If you are going to be traveling several days, it's more complicated. You should talk it over with the doctor, taking into account the nature of the travel, the baby's diet and digestion. Call the air line or railroad to find what conveniences they can promise you. If your baby is on an evaporated-milk formula, the easiest method is to prepare each bottle just before feeding, using the small, 6-ounce cans of evaporated milk. Then nothing has to be refrigerated. You carry as many of these cans as there will be feedings during the trip. Bring a jar of sugar or a bottle of corn syrup. The most convenient way to carry water for formula is to buy a half-gallon bottle of sterile distilled water at the drugstore. Another bottle can be bought wherever you go, and it will be sterile and the same composition. (It's tasteless to drink!) Or you can boil your own water at home and bring it in bottles or a jug. (It's better not to use water from the train or from faucets along the route. It will have to be boiled. Also, changes of water may upset a baby's bowels temporarily.) You'll need your funnel, measuring spoon, can opener, bottle brush, enough clean bottles and nipples to last until you can wash them again.

At each feeding pour into a clean bottle the proper amount of syrup or sugar, water, and evaporated milk from a freshly opened can. Put on the nipple and shake until well mixed. Your doctor can tell you the proportions for each bottle. For instance, if the usual total formula is 13 ounces evaporated milk, 19 ounces water, and 3 tablespoonfuls corn syrup, divided into 5 bottles, then each bottle would be made with 2 teaspoonfuls of corn syrup, 4 ounces water, 2½ ounces evaporated milk.

You can warm the bottle of formula in a washstand in a train. The waiter on a railroad diner, the stewardess on a plane, the waitress or cook in a roadside diner or restaurant, will warm the bottle for you. If you will be traveling by car, you can buy a bottle warmer made to plug into the cigarette lighter or you can bring a Sterno burner along.

Since you probably won't be able to boil the bottles and nipples, you should wash them and the funnel carefully—as soon as you get a chance —with soap and a bottle brush. Rinse and drain dry. The reason you can use a clean but unboiled bottle again is that there is no formula in it between feedings, for bacteria to multiply in.

730. Solid foods. Most solid foods should be in jars. These can be warmed before opening, and the baby can be fed directly from them. Don't worry about providing everything that the baby usually gets (potatoes, for example). Just bring enough of the things he likes best and digests most easily. Many traveling babies do not want so much as they would be taking at home. Don't urge anything that he doesn't want even if he is taking much less than usual. He may want to be fed small amounts at more frequent intervals.

731. Foods for a child. It's better to keep a small child from drinking train water (bring some in a bottle) and eating unusual foods. When buying food for him in public places, avoid particularly cakes and pastries with moist fillings, milk puddings, cold meats, cold fish, and cold eggs, creamy salad dressings (including sandwiches and salads that contain them). These are the foods that are most easily contaminated with poisonous bacteria if carelessly handled or not properly refrigerated. Better stick to hot foods, fruit that you peel yourself, milk in separate containers. (Of course, you can put up your own sandwiches at home, such as peanut butter, jelly, tomato.) Even if you are expecting to feed a child at roadside restaurants, or in the diner, or on the meals provided in a plane, bring a bag of food for snacks or in case meals are delayed—a box of salted crackers (said to be helpful for car sickness), cookies and lollipops (even though you avoid these at home), cheese and hard-boiled eggs in the shell (if enjoyed), fruit, a Thermos bottle of milk, a jar of puréed prunes in case of constipation.

732. Other tips. It is worth while, with a baby, to travel by the best accommodations that you can afford. You will get more service on a first-class railroad ticket, and if you can afford it, you will feel a lot more comfortable in a compartment when the baby is fussing.

Disposable diapers are a great help, especially the type in which a disposable pad fits into a cover.

With a small child, don't forget to have handy the cuddly **toys** that he takes to bed. They will be an extra comfort in traveling. In addition to his favorite toys, it is wise to bring a few new playthings of the kind that take a lot of doing—miniature cars or trains, a small doll with several articles of clothing or other equipment, a coloring or cut-out book, a new picture book, cardboard houses or other objects to fold and assemble, a pad of paper, pencil and crayons. A child of 3 or over likes to pack his favorite toys in his own small suitcase.

A large box of **cleansing tissues** is essential. A couple of large **plastic tablecloths** are valuable, one for protecting the mattress from bed-wetting, another to cover the carpet if a small child is eating in a hotel room or a baby is sitting on the floor, or to cover a bed on which a baby is being changed.

In car travel, it is wise to stop, not only at regular mealtimes, but also in midmorning and midafternoon, for a snack and for a chance for children to run around for a few minutes in a place, perhaps a field or a playground in a city park, where they don't have to be constantly warned to keep off the road.

For a small child, it may be important to carry along the **toilet seat** he is used to.

The leg space for the back seat of a car can be filled with luggage and covered with a pad so that a crawling baby or small child has room in which to roam or fall asleep. If children insist on standing, they should stand on the floor, not on seats; the back of the front seat can be padded to lessen injury in case of a sudden stop.

A baby's **auto bed** or a basket made into a bed is extremely helpful for car, plane, or train. You can move the baby around in it without waking him up, and it's more comfortable for the mother, even if she has to hold it in her lap at times.

A good rule for car travel is to plan to always stop for the night by 4 P.M., so you'll have more chance of finding a motel room and avoid driving on for hours with tired children. Many a man gets the bit in his teeth about making a certain distance and refuses to stop even though it's getting very late. But if he solemnly agrees before the trip to a certain stopping hour, there's more chance of his being reasonable.

THE PREMATURE BABY

A baby weighing less than 5½ pounds at birth requires special care whether he was born early or not. He particularly needs a doctor's close supervision. If he weighs much under 5 pounds, he will probably be taken to a hospital where an incubator and expert care are available, if that is possible.

The information in this chapter is given only to cover those rare emergency situations in which a premature baby **has** to be cared for, temporarily, by the family until the doctor can be reached or the baby is taken to the hospital.

733. Keep the baby warm from the beginning. This is by far the most important emergency treatment for the family to attend to. A premature baby loses body heat rapidly when exposed to cool air, and his body's ability to make heat and to keep an even temperature is poor.

Wrap him in a warm cotton receiving blanket and then in a soft, wool baby blanket the minute he is born (even before the cord is cut) and keep him in a warm place. If he is born without a doctor's presence, the cord should not be tied and cut until it stops beating. This is to make sure he receives all the blood available from the placenta.

734. The room temperature should be 80° day and night. This means a very warm room. If the baby is born in a cool room, get him into the warmest room in the house as soon as the cord is cut. Then try to warm up one room to 80°. Other things being equal, it is easier to keep a small room warm than a large one—if you are using an electric or kerosene heater, for instance. If you have no special way to heat up a room, the kitchen may be best, temporarily.

735. The air should be somewhat moist. Except in summer, the air in a room that is 80° is exceedingly dry. If the baby is going to stay at home for more than a few hours, you should get extra moisture into the air by one of the methods described in Section 632. Pans of water placed in the room will not make enough difference.

It is not necessary or wise to keep the room steamy or dripping wet, as you try to do in the treatment of croup—only comfortably moist, so that it feels pleasant, unparched, to breathe.

736. Preparing the bed. (How to keep the bed warm will be taken up in the next section. Be warming his mattress near a fire or on a radiator while you are preparing his bed. You will need hot water for hot-water bottles, or warmed bricks or bags of sand, as soon as the bed is ready.)

His bed can be an ordinary bassinet, a wooden box, or a cardboard carton. A bureau drawer is too shallow to keep the outer covering off his body. A crib is too large to enclose and keep warm. If you have no baby's mattress, you can use a pile of folded newspapers topped with a folded pad or small blanket. It should not be a pillow; it's too soft.

Here is one way to arrange the bed. Line it with a wool blanket, crib or adult size. You can let the ends hang down outside. (A lining of 10 thicknesses of newspaper will do just as well, when you have the time. Line the bottom as well as the sides.)

Replace the mattress. Cover it with a piece of waterproof sheeting (or a few thicknesses of newspaper). This should be cut small or folded so that it doesn't have to be tucked in—you want to be able to change it easily without undoing the whole bed. Use a folded diaper for a sheet—it shouldn't be tucked in, either.

Place the baby, still loosely wrapped in only the blankets, in the bed, on his back. Now an ordinary wool blanket, crib or adult size, should be stretched over the top of the bed in such a way that it does not lie on the baby's body and does not cover his head. The edge of the blanket toward his head should dip down to his neck (to close in his body and leave his head out).

737. Heating his bed. If a baby weighs 4½ pounds or more, and if his room can be kept at 80°, his bed may not need to be heated additionally. But if he weighs less, or his room is cooler, it will probably be necessary.

The bed should be kept between 80 and 90°—checked constantly with a thermometer (see Section 739). Experience will show what is the right bed temperature in order to keep the baby's body temperature between 95 and 99°.

The easiest way to heat the bed, until the baby can be in an incubator, is with two or more ordinary rubber hot-water bottles tucked in along the edges of the mattress. If these are not available, you can use any bottles that can be well stoppered and that hold a pint or more—for example, quart vinegar, wine, or whisky bottles with tight corks or screw-on caps, or preserve jars with washers and screw-on or clamp-on tops. It is necessary to have bottles that cannot leak or become unstoppered by accident.

Bricks, bags of sand, or even small boulders can be heated in the oven to provide warmth.

Whatever heated objects are used should not be put into the baby's bed until they are cool enough to be held in the bare hand. Even then, they should be covered with cloth to prevent the baby's tender skin from being burned in case of accidental contact. One thickness of bath toweling or knitted blanket, or 2 layers of diaper, should be enough. (If the covering is too thick, it prevents the heat from getting into the bed properly.) The blanket that the baby is wrapped in is another protection. Even so, his body should not be up against the hot objects.

On the other hand, you can't be so worried about burning the baby that you use the hot-water bottles or bricks only barely warm. They must be hotter than the body to do any good. If you have a bath thermometer, use water at 115° for hot-water bottles. This is about the hottest water most people can put their hands in.

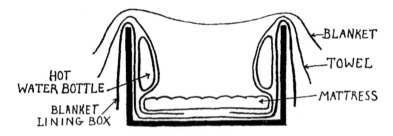

One way to cover the hot-water bottles or bricks, and hold them in place, is with bath towels. Hang a bath towel over the side of the bed. The end which is inside is tucked well under the mattress. The other end hangs down outside the bassinet. Then there is a pocket inside the bed, between the bath towel and the blanket lining the bassinet, which will hold the hot-water bottle in a fairly upright position. One large bath towel on each side of the bed may make a pocket large enough to hold two hot-water bottles on each side. A bottle can be removed without opening the bed by slipping the hand up under the loose edge of the bath towel.

How many bottles or bricks must be used and how often they must be changed depends on several factors. You are trying to keep the bed temperature steady at a point that keeps the baby's body temperature between 95 and 99°. If it varies more than this, you must change the bottles more frequently. If it tends to stay below 95°, you must use more bottles or other warm objects. Start with two hot-water bottles for a trial.

You should change one object at a time, otherwise they will all be hot or cool at the same time. Remove a bottle or brick that has become lukewarm. If it is cooler than the baby's body, it is cooling him and his bed. You'll probably have to change each one every hour, anyway.

738. Taking the baby's temperature is very important. Get a clinical thermometer as soon as you can, either a rectal or mouth thermometer. You take the temperature in his armpit. Place the bulb end of the thermometer in his armpit, hold it in place by pressing his arm against his side, for 1½ minutes. You do all this without letting cool air into his bed by slipping your hand in under the covering blanket.

How often you take the temperature at first depends on how successful you are in keeping his temperature between 95 and 99°. Take it half an hour after birth and an hour after he has been put in the heated bed. If it is satisfactory, wait 2 hours the next time, 4 hours the next. When everything is well regulated, every 6 hours is often enough. But if you find his temperature under 95°, add more heated objects and take his temperature every hour until it has stayed between 95 and 99° for a couple of hours. If it is above 99°, remove all the heated objects and take the temperature every hour until it is staying at the right level. Then lengthen the interval to 2, 4, and 6 hours.

I have been using the figures 95 to 99°, and this is the level to aim for. But with a very small baby in the first few days of life, you may not be able to get his temperature above 93°, and this is good enough.

Don't remove the baby from the heated bed. You change his special diaper and the sheet and waterproof sheeting under him, take his temperature, feed him, while he is in the heated bed. Don't open the top cover more often, or wider, or for longer than is absolutely necessary.

739. One house thermometer is necessary. It is better to use two, if you have them or can borrow or buy them. You can use a house thermometer or an outdoor thermometer or a bath thermometer. One is to lay in the covered part of the bed beside the baby's body, the other is to hang in his room near the bed. If you have only one, lay it beside the baby's body most of the time, and take it out into the room occasionally for 20 minutes to check the room temperature.

It is ideal if you can keep the bed temperature from varying more than 2 or 3 degrees. For a baby under 3 pounds, it is usually necessary to keep the bed temperature up around 85 to 90°. A larger baby may stay warm enough with a bed temperature between 80 and 85°.

740. Going to the hospital. When you can reach the doctor, he will decide when and how the baby will go to the hospital.

Even if you are in a very remote place, you should make every effort to get the baby to a good hospital that is equipped to care for premature babies, especially if the baby is under 4 pounds.

If you are not able to get in touch with the doctor right away, don't take the baby to the hospital until you can get a traveling incubator or until you have arranged a heated bed that is working right, until the baby's temperature is being held between 95 and 99°, and until you have a heated car (unless it is summer). It is much safer for the baby to stay warm at home for a few hours or even a couple of days than to get chilled on the way to even the best hospital in the world.

He should travel to the hospital preferably in an incubator (which is available in some hospitals and health departments) or in a heated bed. You have to be extra careful, with the jouncing, that the hot-water bottles stay in position and that the baby does not lie against them.

A premature baby is usually kept in the hospital until he weighs about 5½ pounds.

741. Clothing and diapering the premature. Since the premature baby is in a warm room (80°) and in a bed that is further warmed (between 80 and 90°), it isn't necessary to bundle him up in a lot of clothes. You don't want to move him from his warmed bed to dress or diaper him, and you don't even want to open up the bed more than you have to. The simpler the clothing, the easier it is to change. Just keep him wrapped in the receiving blanket and wool baby blanket. You can cut them to make them small enough. Later you can get or make soft wool flannel gowns that open down the back (no hurry about this). You can cut small diapers for him, or you can lay a piece of absorbent cotton covered by a layer of gauze under his buttocks (inside the blanket or gown) to absorb urine and bowel movements, and throw it away when it is soiled.

742. A homemade incubator. If a baby can't possibly get to a hospital and if there is electricity in the home, someone may be able to build a peaked wooden hood to fit over the bed (instead of the blanket cover) to cover the baby's body up to his neck. An electric light bulb of 25 or 40 watts, protected by wire screen (so that there is no chance that the baby or the clothing will come in contact with it), fixed to the underside of the hood in its highest part provides even heat. The head end of the hood, which is open, is fitted with a curtain of flannel that hangs down to the bed (and over the baby's neck) to keep the warm air in.

743. Daily care. Handle him little and don't remove him from the heated bed, except possibly to weigh him speedily every third day.

Since it is wise to bother a premature as little as possible, don't try to give him a sponge or oil bath all over. After each bowel movement, wipe his buttocks with warm water on absorbent cotton.

You daily change his waterproof sheeting and the diaper used as a sheet by lifting him up and slipping the used ones out and the fresh ones in.

After 2 or 3 days, when you have learned how to keep his body temperature level, you need to take his temperature only twice a day.

By the time he is 1 or 2 weeks old, and if he weighs 4 pounds, you may not have to keep his bed temperature above 80°. If you can keep the room at that temperature, you may be able to stop using heat in the bed. It all depends on what his body temperature does. By 5 pounds you can probably cut the room temperature to 75°, and by 6 pounds to 70°. Then you use regular baby clothes and bedclothes, and his blanket-lined and blanket-covered bed isn't necessary.

Since a premature baby catches skin infections, colds, diarrhea, easily, it is preferable that only 1 or 2 people take care of him, if possible, and that no one else come into his room until he weighs 6 pounds. If a person caring for him develops the slightest feeling of a cold, sore throat, or other illness, she should be replaced immediately, if possible.

If you have scales, weigh him twice a week. Weigh him quickly, wrapped in his baby blanket. Later weigh the blanket and anything else that was on him, and subtract from the total weight to get the baby's actual weight.

A small baby is slower to start gaining weight than a large one. A small premature may lose weight for a week and then pause for as long as another week before starting to gain. It may well take him 3 weeks to get back to birth weight. For a while he's apt to average between half an ounce and an ounce a day in gain. By the time he weighs 6 or 7 pounds, he'll probably be gaining 1 to 2 ounces a day.

744. Feeding the premature baby when it is impossible to have a doctor's advice. The feeding of a premature baby is the most difficult part of his care. It is also the most dangerous because he is so apt to choke and stop breathing in his first few days. If there is a chance of getting a baby to a hospital by the time he is 5 days old, it is safer **not to feed him anything** at home.

If you have to continue to care for your baby at home, **you should not begin to feed him until he is 72 hours old,** which is the beginning of his fourth day of life. This gives him a chance to get used to breathing well first.

If he still sounds as if he has mucus in his bronchial tubes or is having any other trouble breathing, wait another day, or even 2 days, before starting to feed him.

The following rough guide is only for the rare case in which it is absolutely impossible to get a doctor's help.

The premature baby can take only small amounts at first, chokes easily, and yet, in most cases, needs a good intake of milk to gain weight. Until he weighs about 5 pounds, he is usually too weak to suck at a nipple so must be fed by **medicine dropper.** It is wise to slip a piece of small soft-rubber tubing over the end of the dropper to avoid scratching his mouth. The medicine dropper should be boiled each time before it is used again.

Breast milk is much safer and better, if it can be procured. The mother's breasts should be carefully emptied every 3 or 4 hours (Sections 136–139). At feeding time, the correct amount of breast milk can be poured from the bottle in which it has been kept in the refrigerator, into a clean cup.

If no milk has been obtained by the fourth day, it will be necessary to use a cow's-milk formula until the breast milk comes in. Don't give up trying to get breast milk until the tenth day, anyway. Keep it up then if as much as half an ounce is obtained at a time. That will help even though it has to be combined with formula.

The best cow's-milk formula to use is:

half-skimmed milk	12 ounces
water	6 ounces
corn syrup	2 tablespoonfuls

You can use pasteurized half-skimmed milk or a mixture of equal parts pasteurized whole milk and skimmed milk. But if you are far from medical care, you are probably far from a good dairy, too.

Powdered half-skimmed milk can be bought in cans in some stores. To make the above formula, you would use:

powdered half-skimmed milk	6 level tablespoonfuls
water	18 ounces
corn syrup	2 tablespoonfuls

If you can't get powdered half-skimmed milk, you may be able to get powdered whole milk and powdered skimmed milk:

powdered whole milk	3 level tablespoonfuls
powdered skimmed milk	3 level tablespoonfuls
water	18 ounces
corn syrup	2 tablespoonfuls

If you can't get any kind of half-skimmed milk, use:

evaporated milk	6 ounces
water	12 ounces
corn syrup	2 tablespoonfuls

The directions for making a formula are in Sections 168 to 170, and for liquefying powdered milk in Section 156.

Prepare your formula daily and put 6 ounces in each of 3 bottles. At each feeding, measure out the amount you need with a measuring teaspoon into a small cup. Throw away what you do not need at the end of 24 hours. Prop the baby's head and shoulders up with a small pillow at feeding time. For the first 2 or 3 days of feedings, particularly with a baby under 4 pounds, go **very** slowly in dropping the milk into his mouth. Put in only a couple of drops at a time, and wait until he swallows. Don't worry if each feeding takes the better part of an hour at first. As he gets more used to it, he will swallow sooner and you can go faster.

745. Using the feeding chart (when it is impossible to have a doctor's advice). The amounts given in the chart are meant to be only a very rough guide. One baby will want to increase faster than another, but don't increase too fast the first 2 or 3 days—that is the period when the baby is most likely to choke.

The chart shows increases of ½ teaspoonful or 1 teaspoonful from one day to another, but you should make these changes more gradual from one feeding to the next. For example, if you are going to increase from 2 teaspoonfuls to 3 teaspoonfuls over a 24-hour period, give 2¼ teaspoonfuls for a couple of feedings, then 2½ teaspoonfuls, next 2¾ teaspoonfuls, finally 3 teaspoonfuls. Don't increase faster than the baby can take it comfortably. It's better to be several days behind schedule than to get in trouble.

The bottom part of the chart does not list the days of the baby's age, since by this time one baby wants an increase in 2 or 3 days, another not until 10 days.

How do you know when to increase? A premature baby is less likely to show his hunger by waking early and crying than a full-sized baby. But if he has been taking his last increase well for 2 or 3 days, it's a good time to increase again. If he stops gaining weight for several days, it may be a sign he needs an increase, provided he is willing to take more.

The formula is given every 3 hours, day and night. The usual hours are 6 A.M., 9 A.M., 12 noon, 3 P.M., 6 P.M., 9 P.M., 12 midnight, 3 A.M.

When your baby gets to the bottom of one column of the chart, go to the next column, 1 line up. The bottom part of the last column (the 5-pound baby) changes from teaspoonfuls to ounces. At somewhere between 5 and 6 pounds, the baby is able to go for 4 hours at a stretch at night (3 hours still in the daytime), which means that the total formula is then divided into 7 bottles instead of 8. When you need more than a total of 18 ounces, change to the formula in Section 164.

Day of Life	About 2 pounds	About 3 pounds	About 4 pounds	About 5 pounds
	Teaspoonfuls each feeding	Teaspoonfuls each feeding	Teaspoonfuls each feeding	Teaspoonfuls each feeding
4th	½	½	1	2
5th	1	1	2	4
6th	1½	2	4	6
7th	2	3	5	7
8th	2½	4	6	8
9th	3	5	7	9
10th	3½	5	7	10
Next increase in 2–10 days	4	6	8	1¾ ounces in each of 8 bottles or 2 ounces in 7 bottles
Next increase in 2–10 days	5 Next increase, to 6 teaspoonfuls, is in next column, 1 line up.	7 Next increase is in next column, 1 line up.	9 Next increase is in next column, 1 line up.	2½ ounces in 7 bottles

When he is over 5 pounds, it is time to try putting him to breast or giving him his formula from the bottle.

746. Other needs of the premature baby. He needs a full dose of vitamins D and C by the time he is 10 days old. Give 0.6 cc. a day of an A, C, and D combination.

By the age of a month he may need an iron prescription to prevent anemia.

He has to wait until a later age than the full-term baby to have cool air in his room and to go outdoors, but you can follow the guide in Section 244, which is based on weight.

Most premature babies develop quite normally, allowing for their prematurity. They usually gain and grow more rapidly for a while to make up for the slow gaining at first. Naturally, they cannot make up for their youngness. The baby who was born 2 months early and has become "1 year old" should be thought of as really a 10-month-old.

747. Taking the premature home. The riskiest time for a premature, especially the small one, is the first few days of life. The danger is that he will just stop breathing, or choke a little and stop, which is simply another way of saying he was not sufficiently developed to make the grade. If he has the stuff to keep breathing those first days, he won't give up easily later. Until he is 5 or 6 pounds he is still more susceptible to colds and intestinal infections than a full-term baby, and that is why the hospital is so fussy about visitors. By the time he is 6 pounds there is no reason to fuss over him. He's not only as able as the average baby to take the world as it comes; he's proved that he has extra vitality.

In previous years parents had to worry about the possibility of blindness from retrolental fibroplasia. This condition baffled doctors for many years. They were keeping more premature babies alive with improved methods—incubators, oxygen, careful feeding—and yet more of the smallest ones became blind. It was finally discovered that it was the large amount of oxygen used in efforts to keep the smallest babies alive that was causing the blindness. Nowadays some babies still have to have oxygen to survive, but doctors know better how to keep the oxygen to the absolute minimum, and as a result the development of blindness has become rare, indeed.

748. It's hard to get over your anxiety. By the time a premature baby weighs 6 pounds, he needs no more coddling or worrying than any baby, but this is very hard for the parents to believe. In the beginning the doctor himself cautioned them against being too optimistic, and he only gradually became more reassuring. The baby probably had to be in an incubator, watched constantly by nurses and doctors, and probably had to be fed by tube. The parents weren't able to get near him most of that time. The mother had to go home from the hospital without him, and both parents then lived a strange kind of parental life for a number of weeks, knowing in a theoretical way that they had a baby but not feeling as if they did. As such parents say, "It was the hospital's baby, not ours."

It's no wonder that when the doctor finally says, "Now you can take him home," the parents feel quite frightened and unready. They find that they don't yet have all the clothing and equipment (the mother had counted on more time at the end of her pregnancy). They find that one or the other has a slight cold. All kinds of small reasons seem terribly important reasons why they can't take him yet.

When the baby at last comes home, all the worries that all new parents experience—about room temperature, baby temperature, breathing, hiccups, burps, bowel movements, formula-making, schedule, crying, colic, spoiling—hit the parents of a premature with triple force. It may take weeks before they gain self-confidence and months before they are convinced that the baby is as healthy, husky, and advanced as any other conceived at the same time.

749. Worrisome neighbors. Meanwhile, other troubles may come from the outside. Neighbors and relatives often act more anxious, more awe-struck, more preoccupied, than the parents. They question, they exclaim, they fuss, until the parents can hardly stand it any longer. A few of them insist on telling the parents all the wild stories they have heard about how frail and susceptible prematures remain. This kind of talk would be bad enough for the parents to hear if it were true. It's particularly unfortunate for them to be subjected to untruths of this sort at a time when they are trying to overcome their own anxiety.

I don't know what to tell parents of a premature except that they should keep reminding themselves that all other parents in the same situation have felt the same way and that if they continue to try hard to treat their baby as normal they will finally become convinced that he is.

750. Feeding. If your baby is about 5½ pounds when you bring him home, he probably wants feedings about every 3 hours in the daytime and every 4 hours at night. The average amount desired per feeding is about 2½ ounces, but there is considerable variation. By the time he weighs 7 or 8 pounds he probably doesn't want to be fed that often. If you are feeding him when he wakes, the interval will sometimes be 4 hours, sometimes 3 or 3½. If he is on a regular schedule, I'd change him to 4 hours by the time he weighs 8 to 9 pounds.

Somewhere between 7 and 10 pounds, most babies are ready to give up one of the night bottles. They show it by sleeping through at 10 P.M. and waking at 11 or 12.

I would encourage the mother of a premature to be looking for this readiness and to take advantage of it by waking and feeding the baby just before she retires, hoping that he will then sleep through till 4 or 5 A.M. By helping him to give up this feeding, she will be convinced in one more respect that he is growing up normally. Each time a feeding is dropped, the same total formula is then divided into fewer bottles.

The main thing to be on guard against in the beginning is attempting to get the baby to take more milk (and, later, more solids) than he wants. This is a great temptation because he looks so slender. You feel that if you could squeeze a little more in, he would fatten up faster and thus be better able to throw off any germs. But resistance to disease has nothing to do with fatness. Your baby, like every other, has his individual pattern of growth and an appetite to take care of it. If you push food beyond what he is eager for, you only take away his appetite and slow up his weight gaining.

A premature particularly needs his vitamins with regularity. The doctor has to watch him for anemia because he has inherited little iron from his mother. Solids can be started by the time he's been home 6 to 8 weeks. Because of the parents' anxiety about growth, it's important here, too, to be tactful, to give him plenty of time to get to like solids, and to increase them only as he shows his enthusiasm. In other words, avoid feeding problems.

751. No other precautions. He can have a tub bath as soon as he weighs 6 or 7 pounds, and I'd encourage the mother to start them by 7 pounds. He, like any baby, can go for outings and have his window open when he weighs 8 pounds if the temperature is 60°, and he can be out in cold weather as soon as he weighs 10 pounds.

The parents certainly don't need to wear masks even when he first comes home. He has to get used to the ordinary family germs. He shouldn't be exposed to outsiders with colds or other infections any more than any baby or child should, but otherwise no special precautions are necessary or wise.

THE RH FACTOR

752. If you have an Rh problem in the family, you need the help of your doctor in understanding how it applies to your particular situation. This is just a very abbreviated discussion of a complicated subject for general information.

A majority of people have the "Rh positive factor" in their blood. A minority have the "Rh negative factor." There is no problem if a man and wife are both Rh positive or both Rh negative or if the wife is positive and the husband is negative.

But difficulty sometimes arises if the man is positive and the wife is negative. In this situation, which occurs in about 1 marriage in 8 in the United States, some of the children inherit the Rh positive factor from their father. Then if an Rh-positive baby is growing in the uterus of an Rh-negative mother, a little of his blood may get into the mother's blood through the placenta, especially during labor. The mother's system may then develop protective antibodies that destroy these alien blood cells— just as we all develop antibodies against the germs of measles to destroy them if they try to attack us a second time. But if the mother develops antibodies against her baby's Rh-positive cells, her antibodies go back through the placenta into the baby's circulation and destroy some of his own blood cells there. If a lot are destroyed, the baby becomes anemic soon after birth, and the material from the destroyed cells makes him jaundiced and sick.

A mother's blood won't develop antibodies in time to destroy blood cells in her first Rh-positive baby, but each such baby may sensitize her blood to a greater degree, so there may be increasing difficulty after the first. However, the mother may have developed antibodies even before her first pregnancy if she has had transfusions with Rh-positive blood.

The important things to keep in mind are that only 1 marriage in 8 is between an Rh-positive man and an Rh-negative mother, and even in such a marriage there is only 1 chance in 20 that a baby's blood will be destroyed to a serious degree. In other words, it's the exception rather than the rule.

TWINS

I once made an appeal to mothers of twins to tell me what solutions they had found for their problems, so that I could pass them on. I got 200 wonderfully helpful letters. As you might expect, they showed sharp differences of opinion in some respects, great unanimity in others.

753. Help! All mothers of twins agree that the work is terrific, especially at first, but that the rewards are great.

You need all the help you can get, for as long as you can get it. If possible, hire somebody, even though you have to go into debt. Or beg your mother or another relative to come for a month or two. When there is no room and no privacy in the house, parents have even turned the garage into a bedroom for the helper, in suitable climates. Part-time assistance is a lot better than none at all: a high-school student after school, a cleaning woman or a sitter once or twice a week. Encourage the neighbors to help regularly with certain feedings. It's surprising how much assistance can be gotten from even a 3-year-old sister of the twins.

Of course, the most important helper by far is the father of the twins —in spelling the mother in giving night feedings (alternate feedings or alternate nights) or suppertime baths, making formula, doing some of the household chores that the mother never finds the time for during the day. Even more important to the mother than the practical help is her husband's moral support—patience, appreciation, sympathy, affection. The father of twins has the greatest opportunity that ever comes to a husband to show his devotion and his caliber.

754. Laundry. Mechanical aids become triply valuable. Now is the time, if at all possible, to get an automatic washer and dryer, especially if no diaper service is available. They save hours of work and produce dozens of clean, dry diapers, sheets, pads, shirts, nighties, even in rainy weather.

The babies' wash can be done daily or every other day, depending on what suits the mother's wishes. Frequency of change of sheets and pads can be decreased by placing a small additional waterproof sheet under the baby's hips.

Diaper service is a greater bargain than ever. Laundry service, complete or partial, for the rest of the family is also an important saver of time and energy.

The diaper load can be reduced by changing diapers only once at each feeding, either before or after.

755. Short cuts. Any mother of twins simply has to find short cuts in housework. She can go through her house, room by room, stripping it of unessential furnishings and furniture that prolong housecleaning. Furthermore, she should clean only half as often as before. She can select clothes for the family that don't muss and soil quickly, that launder easily, and that, as far as possible, don't need ironing. She can select foods that require the minimum of preparation and attention, let dishes soak clean in suds, let them drain dry.

756. The right equipment for the twins can be enormously helpful. Many mothers find a single crib, with a partition across the middle designed by the father, very practical for the first couple of months until the twins become too large and active. Cribs with springs that can be elevated save parents' backs and energy, can serve as diapering and dressing tables. An extra bassinet in which one fussing baby can be wheeled into another room helps to keep the other baby asleep. A great convenience in a two-story house is extra cribs and stores of clothing downstairs for the daytime, eliminating constant stair climbing. Much of the equipment can be borrowed or bought second-hand.

A hospital table on wheels or a tea table on wheels may be convenient, with certain room layouts, for holding stacks of diapers, clothing, sheets, etc. It can be wheeled from crib to crib or room to room.

A double baby carriage is too wide for most doors, and two babies sleeping that close together begin to disturb each other within a few months. On the other hand, a double stroller usually proves valuable for many months. Two car beds are useful.

757. Bathing can be skimped a great deal, if care is taken. Faces can be kept clean with plain water on a washcloth. The diaper area can be washed daily with a soapy washcloth and the soap wiped off twice with a rinsed washcloth. Then, as long as the skin stays in good condition, the all-over bath can be cut down to every other day, twice a week, or even once a week. The complete bath can be given with a washcloth on a waterproof sheet (a sponge bath) if more convenient. It's hard to finish baths for two babies soon enough to avoid a lot of crying from one or both. There are several solutions: a helper to feed the baby who is bathed first; baths in the evening so that the father can help; different bath days or bath hours for different babies. If a tub bath is given (in sink, washstand, or fabric tub) and if the babies can wait long enough, it's time-saving to bathe one right after the other in the same water. All bath equipment, clothing, crib, and bottles warming in a pan must be ready and close at hand before the bath is started.

758. Breast feeding is practical and possible. From letters I received, I believe that twins are breast-fed for a number of months as often as single babies. (This proves again that there is no set limit to the amount of milk a mother can produce. The breasts supply whatever the baby or babies demand if the mother is going about it with the right method and attitude.) If the babies are too small to nurse well or if they stay in the hospital longer than the mother, then it is a job to establish the breast-milk supply by means of manual expression. But as soon as the babies can nurse at the breast, they can both be put to breast together. The mother must have a comfortable chair with good arm support. There are at least three possible positions. If the mother can half recline, or recline, a twin can lie along each of her arms. If she sits up fairly straight, with pillows at each side, the babies can lie along each side, feet toward her back, heads held up to her breasts with her hands. It's also possible to lay the babies across the mother's lap, one more or less on top of the other, but with heads at opposite sides of the mother. The underdog doesn't object in these circumstances.

759. The making and storing of formula for two is cumbersome. Twins are usually small at birth and may need feedings every 3 hours, which adds up to 16 bottles every 24 hours. Two sterilizing pails are necessary to avoid doing that job twice. If refrigerator space is a real problem, the formulas can be sterilized in two dairy milk bottles (quart size), which are stored in the refrigerator. Then at each feeding, 2 sterilized nursing bottles are filled with the correct amount of formula. The nursing bottles can be sterilized once a day by boiling or, if more convenient, by baking (see Section 175). The nipples should be boiled, not baked.

Some mothers swear by the disposable thin plastic "bottles." They come in long strips already sterilized, occupy less refrigerator space, warm up easily. Only the nipples need to be sterilized.

760. Feeding schedule. A great majority of mothers of twins have found that it is essential to get onto a regular schedule as soon as possible and to feed both babies at once, or one right after the other. Otherwise feeding is going on at all hours of the day and night. (A few mothers find a modified demand schedule is practical. They wait for the first baby to wake and cry, but they wake up the second baby as soon as the first is finished.) Most babies can be accustomed to regularity within a few days. If a baby wakes and fusses before feeding time, you stall for a while, hoping he will go back to sleep. If he gets crying hard, you may have to compromise and feed ahead of schedule, but each day you get stricter, counting on the baby's digestive system to become habituated to the schedule. A pacifier is usually a great help in keeping a baby happy until feeding time. In a few cases, with very irregular, fretful babies, scheduling doesn't work. Then it's easier to feed on demand for a few weeks, however irregularly, rather than have to listen to crying for long periods.

Twins are often premature and small. Then they may require a 3-hour schedule, at least in the daytime, until they weigh 6 or 7 pounds. If one twin is much smaller, he may require a 3-hour schedule for a few weeks while the other is fed every 4 hours, but the smaller one may still be able to go 4 hours at night.

761. How to give bottles. How do you feed bottles to two babies at the same hour? There are several methods. If you have a regular helper, you can each feed a baby. A few mothers have trained one cooperative baby to wake half an hour after the other. But most mothers find that both babies wake together and that there is nothing more nerve-racking than to feed one while the other howls. One solution in the early weeks is to lay the twins on a sofa or bed on either side of the mother, their feet toward her back; in this position she can give two bottles at the same time. Another method is to use a bottle holder for one while she holds the other, alternating babies each feeding.

But some mothers find that a bottle holder (or propping a bottle on a folded diaper) doesn't work that well, at least in the early weeks. Either the baby loses the nipple and cries, or he chokes. Then the mother has to hurriedly drop the other baby, who cries, while she rescues the first. These mothers find it more practical to use bottle holders or propping for both babies simultaneously. They sit close by or between the babies, with both hands free to give whatever help is needed. As these mothers correctly point out, they save enough time with bottle holders to be able to give the twins more and better cuddling at less hectic times.

If there is much irregularity in the early weeks in the amounts or times of feedings, it is necessary to keep a record of how much formula each baby has taken at what hour, and also data on weights and baths. Otherwise you forget too much or try to feed one twin twice and burp the one with the empty stomach. A notebook or a blackboard serves the purpose, or a cardboard clock face for each crib, with elastic bands for minute and hour hands.

Many twins, like single babies, burp themselves if laid on their stomachs after feeding. Remember, too, that though some babies will be uncomfortable unless the bubble is gotten up, others don't seem to feel any difference and then there is no need to make the effort.

762. Feeding of solid food has to be done efficiently, too. When it's all new to the twins, many mothers spoon-feed one baby while the other takes the bottle, and then reverse the process. Additional time can be saved in two others ways: You can bunch the solids so that they are all given in 2 feedings a day instead of 3. You can also give the solids (cereal and fruit, for instance) at one of the daily feedings in the bottle of formula, with a nipple hole as large as the head of a pin. This leaves the other feeding each day in which the babies learn how to swallow solids from a spoon. By the time the twins are skillful at taking solids, they can be propped up in the corners of bassinet, crib, or arm chair, and spoon-fed together. Or there is an infant feeding table that comes in twin size, with seats that can be adjusted to a semireclining position for babies who can't sit up yet; mothers find it extremely useful.

It is a great time-saver to spoon-feed twins simultaneously. One has just time enough to swallow his mouthful while the mother is loading the spoon and offering it to the other. It may not seem hygienic or polite to use one dish and one spoon, but it's so much more practical.

With twins, there's extra reason for an early start with finger foods (zwieback, bread, wholesome crackers, chopped cooked vegetables, chopped meats) and for relying on them heavily. There's also reason to encourage self-feeding by spoon at least by the age of 12 months.

763. A play pen is particularly valuable for twins (it's impossible to watch two crawling babies at once), and fortunately they are happy in it for longer hours and until a later age than single babies because of each other's company. (It can even be used as a double crib in traveling.) They should be put in it for play periods by 2 or 3 months, so that they won't become accustomed to freedom first. Heavy or sharp toys must be avoided because twin babies whack each other without realizing that it hurts. Later, if they begin to be bored in the pen together, one can be moved to a jouncing chair, then the other. Such variations interest even the one in the crib.

After the age of a year it's a great convenience to have a separate room for the twins to play in, with a gate at the door. It can be furnished so that the children can't easily hurt it or themselves (twins are ingenious, cooperative and lightning fast in getting into mischief), and they will play happily in it much longer than a single child would.

764. Clothes and toys: similar or dissimilar? Some mothers point out that since there is usually only one kind of playsuit, for instance, in a store that appeals to the mother in terms of design, warmth, price, it is difficult if not impossible to dress twins differently. And their twins, they say, usually insist on wearing similar clothes at the same time. Other mothers emphasize—about dresses, for instance—that it's usually impossible to buy two of a kind, so twins are compelled to dress differently. Still other mothers say that since the twins have to wear mostly hand-me-down clothes, they have to dress differently from the start and enjoy having their own distinctly different clothes.

Some mothers report that they have had to buy identical toys from the start, or their twins would be rivalrous and miserable. Others say that they usually buy different toys (except for particularly precious possessions like tricycles, dolls), and that twins learn to share happily from an early age.

I suspect that the attitude of the parent makes the biggest difference. If the parent takes it for granted that twins must wear different clothes most of the time and share some of their playthings, either by necessity or on principle, the twins will generally accept this. But if the parent encourages the expectation of identical clothes and toys, and especially if she gives in every time the twins insist, they may well become more insistent with time. Of course, this same principle applies to single children: if parents are firm, children accept; if parents are hesitant, children argue.

It helps twins develop a sense of individuality about their own clothes and a liking for them if each has separate drawer and closet space and if similar garments are marked with names or other markings. Similar garments of different colors preserve some of the advantages of being both twins and individuals. When one twin always has green and the other yellow, this helps everybody keep them straight.

765. Individuality. This brings us finally to the philosophical question of how much to emphasize the twinness of twins and how much to encourage the individuality, especially with identical twins. The whole world is fascinated with twins, makes a fuss over them, likes them to look alike and be dressed alike, asks the parents silly questions about them ("Which is smarter?" "Which do you love best?"). It's hard for the parents not to play up to the world's sentimental or morbid interest. Why not? The trouble is that this may give the twins the feeling that their only source of attraction is their cuteness as a look-alike, dress-alike pair. This may seem appealing at 3 years of age. But if it ends up, as it occasionally does, in two women still trying to attract attention by dressing alike at 30, so dependent on each other that they can't fall in love or marry, the result is not cute but sad.

Now, this doesn't mean that the parents should be afraid of ever dressing the twins alike or should be ashamed to enjoy the world's attention to their children. Twinness is fun for the twins **and** for the parents.

Twins, in fact, develop special strength of personality from being twins: early independence of parental attention, unusual capacity for cooperative play, great loyalty and generosity toward each other.

But to avoid overemphasis on twinness, it's wise for parents, particularly with identical or very similar twins, to keep away from very similar names (it's hard enough to call the right twin even when the names are dissimilar), to refer to them by their names rather than as "the twins," to dress them alike only part of the time, to introduce them early and regularly to other children before they become used to each other's company exclusively, to let them make separate friends to the degree they wish, to encourage the neighbors to feel free to invite one of them over to play or to a party occasionally (while the other twin has a chance to have his parents all to himself for a change).

In an occasional case, one twin becomes so dependent on the other in schoolwork that it is wise to separate them. But it seems foolish and cruel to have an arbitrary rule about separation when there is no need.

766. Don't worry about favoritism. One further word of advice. Some conscientious parents become too worried at the start that they may give a bit more attention to one baby or always serve him first—because he's smaller, for instance, or more responsive. Such strict impartiality is not necessary—in fact, it encourages a too mechanical, too forced, kind of attention. Every child wants and needs to be loved naturally for his own lovable qualities. He is satisfied if he knows that he has a good niche of his own in his parents' hearts and does not worry then about what love his brother or sister is getting. But in the long run he will sense the hollowness of forced attention. A legalistically equal treatment will focus his attention on his rights and make him argue for them like a lawyer. Avoid systems like (Mother puts A's shirt on first, then B's pants on first," or "Today is A's chance to sit next to Daddy."

767. Twin language. Twins often develop a private language between themselves—glances, grunts, foreign-sounding words—which may lead to delay in speaking the family's language and may even cause temporary backwardness in school. Some parents have had to insist that the twins' demands not be met unless they were expressed in English.

SEPARATED PARENTS

768. Is separation necessary? Parents who are considering separation sometimes ask a doctor whether it is better for the children if the parents separate for the sake of peace, or if they hold the family together in spite of friction. Of course, there is no general answer to this. It all depends on why the parents don't get along and the chances of their working out their differences.

It's usually true that when a couple are disagreeing, each one feels that the other is mostly to blame. Yet an outsider can often see that the trouble is not that one or the other is a villain but that neither seems to realize how he or she is acting. In one case, each spouse unconsciously wants to be pampered by the other, like an adored child, instead of being willing to contribute his or her share in a partnership. In another case, a bossy spouse has no idea how much he or she is trying to dominate the other; and the one who is being nagged may be asking for it. Very often in the case of unfaithfulness, the faithless one is not really falling in love with an outsider but, rather, running away from a hidden fear or unconsciously trying to make the spouse jealous. If husband, wife, or both are willing to make a real effort to save the marriage, a good psychiatrist or social worker or a wise and tolerant minister should be able to help them to analyze where the trouble lies.

769. Let the child stay loyal to both. How much a separation will damage the child's security depends very largely on how the whole matter is handled. The children should certainly be told soon after the parents have made their decision. Children are always disturbed by a family crisis anyway, and more so if it is kept a mystery. The important things to let the children understand are: 1. Even though the parents separate, the children will still belong to both and will always be able to see both regularly. 2. That neither parent is the good one or the bad one. This is the hardest rule for the parents to abide by. It is only human for each to feel that the other is at fault and to want to get the children to agree with him. It's terrible for a child to become convinced that one of his parents is bad. The child of a divided home needs to believe in both of his parents just as much as the child of a happy family. But there is another danger, even for the parent who has won the child over to his side. When the child reaches a later stage of development, most often in adolescence, when his feelings toward the people who are close to him are going through all kinds of upheavals, he may suddenly turn against the parent he has been loyal to all along and switch sides completely. In other words, each parent has a better chance of keeping a child's love and respect if the child is never encouraged to take sides.

In what words can you explain the separation to a child? It depends on the age of the child and what he wants to know. The mother of a small child might say, "Your Daddy and I argue and fight too much, just the way you and Peter Jenkins do. So we've decided that we'll all have a better time if we don't try to live in the same house. But Daddy will still be your Daddy and I'll still be your Mummy." This is explaining it at the level of the small child who knows well what arguing and fighting are. The older child will want to see the reasons a little more clearly than this. I would try to give him answers that satisfy him, but steer away from pinning blame.

Arguments aren't shameful. Parents who are disagreeing often make a great point of trying to conceal their arguments from their children and even imagine that they don't suspect that anything is up. It is certainly better to carry on heated fights when the children are out of the way, but it's a mistake to think that they aren't aware of family tensions. When a child stumbles in unexpectedly on a scene, I think it's much better for the parents to admit humanly that they have been having an argument than to suddenly become silent and severe and order the child out of the room. It helps to clear the air for everyone to admit that fights are one of the facts of life, even among grownups, that people can fight at times and still love and respect each other, that a fight doesn't mean the end of the world.

770. Living arrangements for the child's benefit. What arrangements are made for the children's spending time with each parent depends on circumstances. If the parents live within a reasonable distance of each other and if the children spend most of the time with their mother, the best arrangement may be to have them visit their father on week ends and during those vacations that he can share with them. Whether the visits occur once a week or once a year, it's better for them to be regular, and it's very important for the father not to miss or postpone them.

An arrangement whereby the children stay 6 months of the year with one parent and then 6 months with the other usually works out badly. It breaks up their schooling, separates them for too long a time from the other parent, and gives them a feeling that their lives are chopped in two in a very arbitrary way.

It's a mistake for either parent to pump the child about what happened while he was visiting the other parent, or to criticize the other parent. This only makes the child uneasy when he's with either parent. In the end, it may backfire and make him resent the suspicious parent.

In all cases, but especially if the parents can't agree on a reasonable sharing of the child or if he himself dislikes visiting one of them, it is better for the parents to consult a children's psychiatrist (Section 570) about what will work out best for the child, instead of fighting for his custody, like dogs fighting for a bone.

THE WORKING MOTHER

771. To work or not to work? Some mothers **have** to work to make a living. Usually their children turn out all right, because some reasonably good arrangement is made for their care. But others grow up neglected and maladjusted. It would save money in the end if the government paid a comfortable allowance to all mothers of young children who would otherwise be compelled to work. You can think of it this way: useful, well-adjusted citizens are the most valuable possessions a country has, and good mother care during early childhood is the surest way to produce them. It doesn't make sense to let mothers go to work making dresses in a factory or tapping typewriters in an office, and have them pay other people to do a poorer job of bringing up their children.

A few mothers, particularly those with professional training, feel that they must work because they wouldn't be happy otherwise. I wouldn't disagree if a mother felt strongly about it, provided she had an ideal arrangement for her children's care. After all, an unhappy mother can't bring up very happy children.

What about the mothers who don't absolutely have to work but would prefer to, either to supplement the family income or because they think they will be more satisfied and therefore get along better at home? That's harder to answer.

The important thing for a mother to realize is that the younger the child the more necessary it is for him to have a steady, loving person taking care of him. In most cases, the mother is the best one to give him this feeling of "belonging," safely and surely. She doesn't quit on the job, she doesn't turn against him, she isn't indifferent to him, she takes care of him always in the same familiar house. If a mother realizes clearly how vital this kind of care is to a small child, it may make it easier for her to decide that the extra money she might earn, or the satisfaction she might receive from an outside job, is not so important, after all.

772. What children need most from parents or substitutes. The things that are most vital in the care of a child are a little bit different at different age periods. During the first year, a baby needs a **lot** of motherly care. He has to be fed everything he eats, he eats often, and his food is usually different from the adults'. He makes a great deal of laundry work. In cities he usually has to be pushed in his carriage for outings. For his spirit to grow normally, he needs someone to dote on him, to think he's the most wonderful baby in the world, to make noises and baby talk at him, to hug him and smile at him, to keep him company during wakeful periods.

A day nursery or a "baby farm" is no good for an infant. There's nowhere near enough attention or affection to go around. In many cases, what care there is is matter-of-fact or mechanical rather than warm-hearted. Besides, there's too much risk of epidemics of colds and diarrhea.

773. Individual care at least until three. The infant whose mother can't take care of him during the daytime needs **individual care,** whether it's in his own home or someone else's. It may be a relative, neighbor, or friend whom the mother knows and has confidence in. If a new maid or nurse is to come into the home, the mother should know her well before she leaves the baby in her care. Or the mother may decide to leave him in a foster home for "foster day care," that is to say, in the care of a woman who makes a profession of caring for children. But the foster mother should be doing it more because she loves children than for the income it brings. The only safe way to choose a foster home is through a first-rate, conscientious child-placing agency that investigates and supervises the individual homes it recommends. But whoever the mother chooses should be a woman who is gentle and loving, and who is not trying to take care of more than two or, at the very most, three babies or small children.

Between the ages of 1 and 3, the care of a child requires a little less time but a lot more understanding. It's good for him to have other children around. He's a person now, with ideas of his own. He needs more and more opportunity to be independent, has to be steered tactfully. An adult who is too bossy makes him balky and frantic. One who lacks self-confidence may be helpless to control him. One who smothers him with too much attention hampers his development. Furthermore, this is the age when he comes to depend for security on one or two familiar, devoted people, and is upset if they disappear or keep changing. This is the least advisable period for the mother who has always taken care of him to go off to work for the first time, or to make changes in the person who takes her place. Many day nurseries do not have enough nurses or attendants to give each child the feeling of really belonging to someone. And the staff may not have had the expert training in understanding small children to be able to foster their fullest development, spiritually, socially, and physically.

So if you have to go off to work when your baby is about a year old, the best solution is individual care, just as it is for the younger infant. But for this age it is particularly important to find a person who has the ability to understand a child and get along with him easily, and who is not likely to quit the job in a few months.

How to get a small child used to a new grownup is discussed in Section 495.

774. Possibly a nursery school at three. A good nursery school or day nursery (Section 533), staffed by trained teachers, may become the best solution somewhere between 2 and 3 years of age. If a first-rate school that takes 2-year-olds is available, and the mother can take over for part of the afternoon, I think it is all right to start a 2-year-old who is quite independent, especially if individual care has not worked out well or if the child has had no chance to play with other children. It might be better to wait until 2½ or even 3, if he is a timid, dependent child (though he should be getting used to other children in the meantime) or his mother's working hours mean his staying in school all day long.

But if there is no good nursery school, if the individual care is satisfactory, if the child is having a chance to play with other children, anyway, then there is every reason to continue with individual care right up until he starts first grade.

If you live in a city, get the help of a child-guidance clinic or of the best child-care agency or family agency in town, in deciding about a nursery school or foster day care. Even the best of nursery schools is apt to have two disadvantages for the working mother. The school day may not last until she can take over, and there is the problem of who is to take care of the child when he is sick.

Whatever the age of the child, it is much better for him and for his mother if she can possibly find a job that leaves her part of the afternoon (or any other part of the day) to be with him.

Between 3 and 6, a child still needs plenty of affectionate, understanding care from adults. If his mother is working most of the day and he goes to a nursery school, he must feel he belongs to his teacher, too. This is why she ought not to be taking care of more than 8 or 10 children. However, at this age he is able to adjust to a teacher, and get a sense of security from her, more easily and completely than at 2. He still should find someone dear to him when he comes home from school, whether at noon, or 3 or 6 P.M.

775. The school child should belong somewhere after school. After 6 years, and particularly after 8, the child seeks and enjoys independence, turns more to outside adults (especially to good teachers) and children for his ideals and companionship. He can get along comfortably for hours at a time without having to turn to a close adult for support. After school he still ought to have a feeling he belongs somewhere, even if he forgets to go there. A motherly neighbor may be able to substitute for a working mother until the latter comes home. After-school play centers are valuable for all children, but particularly for those whose mothers work.

776. The temptation to spoil. A working mother may find that because she is starved for her child's company (and perhaps because she feels guilty about seeing him so little), she is inclined to shower him with presents and treats, bow to all his wishes regardless of her own, and generally let him get away with murder. When a child finds that his mother is an appeaser, it doesn't satisfy him—it's apt to make him more greedy. It's fine for a working mother to show her child as much agreeableness and affection as comes naturally, but she should feel free to stop when she's tired, consider her own desires, spend only what money is sensible, expect reasonable politeness and consideration—in other words, act like a self-confident, all-day parent. He will not only turn out better, he'll enjoy her company more.

777. What to look for in a nurse or foster mother. It's easy to make a list of all the virtues you would like the person who is to take care of your child to have. But when it comes down to choosing among the actual human beings available, you have to decide which qualities are more valuable.

Far and away the most important is the woman's disposition. Toward the child she should be affectionate, understanding, comfortable, sensible, self-confident. She should love and enjoy him without smothering him with attention. She should be able to control him without nagging or severity. In other words, she should get along with him happily. It is a help when interviewing a prospective maid, nurse, or foster mother to have your child with you. You can tell how she responds to a child better by her actions than by what she says. Avoid the person who is cross, reproving, fussy, humorless, or full of theories.

I think the commonest mistake that parents make is to look first of all for a person with a lot of experience. It's natural that they should feel more comfortable leaving a child with someone who knows what to do for the colic or the croup. But illnesses and accidents are a very small part of a child's life. It's the minutes and hours of every day that count. Experience is fine when it's combined with the right personality. With the wrong personality, it's worth hardly anything.

Cleanliness and carefulness are a little more important than experience. You can't let someone make the baby's formula who refuses to do it correctly. Still, there are many rather untidy people who are careful when it's important. Better a nurse who is too casual than one who is too fussy. One who can't keep a child clean is a poor nurse.

Some parents feel that the education of a nurse or foster mother has an influence on the child, but I think it's unimportant compared with other qualities, especially for a young child. Even if he learns to say "ain't," he'll surely drop it later if it's not used by his parents and friends.

A nurse or maid who has to have several nights off a week for social life may be a more balanced person and a better nurse than the one who has no interests but the child. However, the fact that a woman is an old maid doesn't prove that she can't be a wonderful, sensible nurse.

A common problem is that a relative or maid may favor the youngest child in the family, especially one who was born after she joined the household. She calls him **her** baby. If this is a joke and she really is just as devoted to the older children and they know it, there's no harm. But if the older children feel discriminated against and show it in their spirits, it's a bad business and she should not stay. It does irreparable harm to leave a child in the care of a person who does not give him security.

THE FATHERLESS CHILD

778. When the father's away. If a father is far away when his baby is born and growing up, it doesn't mean he can't have a feeling of taking part in the baby's care, or that the child will be seriously deprived. Far from it. The father needs lots of news and pictures. When a mother is writing, she's apt to think of the facts that are important to her: The baby is healthy, he's gaining weight at a good rate, he has two teeth, the doctor says he's normal—in fact, very advanced. The father wants to know these things, but even more he wants to know the little details that the mother takes for granted. Tell him how loud the bubble burp is and how dignified the baby looks when he lets it out. Jot down all the things he does for ten minutes: how he scrambles for a magazine, settles back on his behind, tastes the cover, puckers his face and shudders at the bitter taste, leans way forward to gaze at a picture as if he recognized something, tears it apart, rubs the shreds in his hair, crawls off with a piece in his hand, stops at the radio to bat it solemnly. You'll be amazed at how much there is to tell, and the father will grin all over when he pictures it. With a little practice you can remember some of a small child's remarks word for word until you get a chance to write them down. The most skilled author can't make up a child's conversation that's half as amusing or heart-warming as what any small child says any old time.

Take as many snapshots as you can, and send along any that don't look like midnight. A proud mother feels like holding back on the pictures that make the baby or her look homely or silly or cross. But a father trying to imagine his family doesn't want all smiling faces any more than a hungry man wants all candy. Keep sending a few pictures regularly, rather than a big bunch infrequently.

There's another point that's a little more serious and important. A father (like a mother) wants to feel that he's necessary and that he's helping. If the mother, to keep him from worrying, tells him only about how easily she has settled all the questions that have come up and how she has everything under control, he can't help feeling unnecessary. On the other hand, it won't help him to hear all the mother's secret worries about the baby that he can't do anything about. But there are always plenty of reasonable questions in a mother's mind: Should she spend the money to take him to the country on a holiday? Should he go to nursery school next fall? Should he be allowed to tear his clothes and endanger his limbs by climbing trees? These are questions that a father would naturally help to decide if he were at home. He may see them from new, helpful angles that haven't occurred to the mother, and it gives him a real sense of closeness if he is given a chance to share in deciding them.

A mother may feel that she's having a hard enough time as it is, making wise decisions—that it would only complicate matters to get opinions from her husband. But for better or worse, the bringing up of a child has to be shared by both parents in the long run. If a father, during a long absence, comes to feel that the mother is getting off the beam, that there is a lot he will have to undo when he gets home, it will complicate things for a long time after he arrives. It **sometimes** works out better in the long run if the mother (or father) agrees to a decision that she doesn't think is the right one.

779. Making it up to the child. It would be foolish to say that his father's absence or death makes no difference to a child, or that it's easy for a mother to make it up to him in other ways. But if the job is well handled, the child, either boy or girl, can continue to grow up normal and well adjusted.

The mother's spirit is most important. She may feel lonely, imprisoned, or cross at times, and she will sometimes take it out on the child. This is all natural and won't hurt him too much. The important thing is for her to go on being a normal human being, keeping up her friendships, her recreations, her outside activities, as far as she can. This is hard if she has a baby or child to take care of and no one to help her. But she can ask people in, and take the baby to a friend's house for an evening if he can adjust to sleeping in strange places. It's more valuable to him to have his mother cheerful and outgoing than to have his routine perfect. It won't do him any good to have her wrap **all** her activity and thoughts and affection around him.

A child, whether he's young or old, boy or girl, needs to be friendly with other men if the father is not there. With the baby up to the age of a year or two, a good deal is accomplished if he can just be reminded frequently that there **are** such creatures as agreeable men, with lower voices, different clothes, and different manners than women. A kindly grocer or milkman who just grins and says hello helps even if there are no closer friends. As the child goes on toward 3 and over, the kind of companionship with men is increasingly important. Whether he is boy or girl, he needs chances to be with and feel close to other men and older boys. Grandfathers, uncles, cousins, scoutmasters, men teachers at school, the minister, old family friends, or a combination of these can serve as substitute fathers if they enjoy the child's company and see him fairly regularly. Any child of 3 or over builds up an image of his father that is his ideal and inspiration, whether he remembers him or not. The other friendly men he sees and plays with give substance to the image, influence his conception of his father, make his father mean more to him. The mother can help by being extra hospitable to male relatives, sending her son or daughter to a camp that has some men counselors, picking a school, if she has a choice, that has some men teachers, encouraging a child to join clubs and other organizations that have men leaders.

The boy without a father particularly needs opportunity and encouragement to play with other boys, every day if possible, by the age of 2, and to be mainly occupied with boyish pursuits. The temptation of the mother who has no other equally strong ties is to make him her closest spiritual companion, getting him interested in clothes and interior decoration, in her opinions and feelngs about people, in the books and other recreations she enjoys. If she succeeds in making her world more appealing to him, easier to get along in, than the world of boys (where he has to make his own way), then he may grow up precocious, with feminine interests. It's all to the good if a mother can spend time and have plenty of fun with her boy, provided she also lets him go his own way, provided she shares in his interests rather than having him share too many of hers. It helps to invite other boys to the house regularly and to take them along on treats and trips.

THE HANDICAPPED CHILD

780. Treat him naturally. A child with a handicap may need treatment of the defect. But even more he needs to be treated naturally, whether the handicap is mental slowness, crossed eyes, epilepsy, deafness, shortness, a disfiguring birthmark, or a deformity of any other part of the body. This is easier said than done. A defect quite naturally upsets the parents to some degree. Here are examples of different reactions they may have.

781. His happiness depends on his attitude, not on his defect. A boy has been born with only a thumb and one finger on his left hand. At 2½ years he is happy and can do almost as much with his left hand as with his right. His 6-year-old sister is fond and proud of him, wants to take him with her everywhere she goes, never seems to worry about his hand. The mother, however, is very conscious of the missing fingers. She winces when she sees a strange child catch sight of his hand and stare. She thinks it is fairer to the child to keep him at home where he won't be subjected to curiosity and remarks, makes excuses when he wants to go shopping with her. Which attitude is better for him, the mother's or the sister's? We first have to answer another question. Does a defect in itself make a child seriously self-conscious and ashamed? Generally speaking, No.

Of course, all of us are slightly self-conscious, and we all focus on what we think are our weakest features. Those with defects naturally worry about them some. But anybody who has known many cripples, for example, realizes that some of those with the worst handicaps are just as outgoing, happy, and unworried as anyone with sound limbs. And at the other extreme, you can probably think of one acquaintance who is miserably self-conscious, for instance, about the prominence of her ears, when actually they are not noticeable at all.

In other words, the seriousness of a defect has little to do with whether a person grows up feeling self-conscious, ashamed, unhappy.

The important factors that make a person **(with or without defects)** grow up happy and outgoing are having parents who thoroughly enjoy and approve of him, who do little worrying, urging, fussing, criticizing; having opportunities to learn the fun of give and take with other children from an early age. If the parents from the beginning are unhappy or ashamed about a child's appearance, always wishing he were different, overprotecting him, keeping him from mingling with others, he is apt to grow up turned in on himself, dissatisfied, feeling that he is queer. But if they take his disfiguring birthmark or deformed ear as of no great importance, act as if they consider him a normal child, let him go places like anyone else, don't worry about stares and whispered remarks—then the child gets the idea he is a regular guy and thinks little of his peculiarity.

As for the stares and pointing and whispered remarks, the child with a noticeable defect has to get used to them, and the younger the easier. If he is hidden most of the week and gets one stare on Sunday, it is more disturbing than ten stares every day, because he is not accustomed to them.

782. He'll be happier without pity. A 6-year-old boy has a birthmark that covers half his face. His mother has taken this hard and feels a lot of pity for him. She is strict with her two older daughters but excuses the boy from household tasks, lets him get away with rudeness to her and meanness to his sisters. He's not too popular with his sisters or other children.

It's understandable why parents of a handicapped child are inclined to feel too sorry for him for his own good and to expect too little of him. Pity is like a drug. Even if it's distasteful to a person at first, he's likely to come to depend on it. Naturally, a child with a defect needs understanding, and he often needs special handling. The slow child should never be expected to do a job that is beyond his mental development, and one with stiff hands shouldn't be criticized for poor penmanship. But the child with a defect can be reasonably polite, take turns, do his share of the chores. Everyone is happier and more pleasant when he knows he's expected to be considerate. The child with a handicap wants to be treated the same, held to the same rules as other children.

783. Fairness to the whole family. A 4-year-old child has been found to be very slow in his mental and physical development. The parents have taken him from doctor to doctor and clinic to clinic. Each time they hear the same story. It is not a mental defect for which there is any curative treatment, though there are many things to be done to bring him up happy and useful. The parents naturally want more than this, and they end up traveling long distances and paying exorbitant fees to a quack who promises a magical cure. As a result, the other children in the family receive less than their share of attention. The parents, however, feel much happier spending the money and making the effort.

It certainly is right and normal for parents to want to do whatever has a reasonable chance of helping a child with a handicap. But there's another hidden factor. It's human nature for them to feel, underneath, that they are somehow to blame—even though all the doctors and books explain that the condition is a pure accident of nature. All of us in our upbringing have been made to feel guilty about things we did and things we ought to have done. If we have a handicapped child, this guiltiness left over from youth is apt to get focused on the handicap.

This unreasonable sense of guilt often drives parents, especially if they are very conscientious people, to **do something** even if it's not sensible. It's a kind of penance, though they don't think of it that way.

If parents are on the lookout for this tendency, they are better able to choose the right treatment for the child and, incidentally, spare their other children (and themselves) unnecessary deprivation.

784. Love him for himself. A certain child at the age of 10 is distinctly shorter than average, even shorter than his 8-year-old sister. The parents feel that this is a real tragedy and keep taking him to new doctors, all of whom agree that there is no deficiency disease—he is merely a child who seems to have been born with a small pattern. The parents show their concern in other ways, too. They frequently urge him to eat more so that he will grow faster. When there is any allusion to his size compared to his sister's or to other boys', they eagerly remind him how much smarter he is.

There is enough rivalry among boys so that an individual who is short feels some disappointment, anyway. But the two factors that make the biggest difference are the boy's general happiness and self-confidence, and how easily the parents accept his shortness.

Being told to eat reminds him of how worried his parents are and is more likely to take his appetite away than to improve it. Being compared favorably to his sister and friends in other qualities doesn't make him feel better about being short, and it only emphasizes the idea of competition and rivalry. There are times when the parents sense that a short child, or a homely one, or a nearsighted one wants to be told how unimportant his handicap is. Confident reassurance is then a great help. But if the parents are the uneasy ones, always bringing up the subject, it convinces the child that he must be in a bad way.

785. Brothers and sisters take their attitude from the parents. A child, now 7 years old, was born with cerebral palsy. His intelligence has not been affected at all, but his speech is hard to understand and his face and limbs are constantly making strange contortions over which he has little control.

His mother has a sensible attitude toward his handicaps. She treats him the same as her younger boy except that she takes him several times a week to a special clinic, where he receives massage, exercises, and training in control of his limbs and speech. His younger brother and the children in the neighborhood are all devoted to him because of his friendly nature and enthusiasm. He gets in all their games and, though he often can't keep up, they make allowances. He goes to the regular neighborhood school. He is naturally handicapped in some ways, but since the program is flexible and the children take a part in planning and working out their projects, his good ideas and cooperative spirit make him a popular member of the class. His father, who is more of a worrier, thinks the boy might be happier in the long run if he were sent away to a special boarding school, among others with similar handicaps. He also fears that when the younger boy grows older, he will be embarrassed by the other's peculiar appearance.

If the parents accept a handicapped child wholeheartedly and matter-of-factly, the brothers and sisters are apt to do so also. They are not too upset by the remarks of other children. But if the parents feel embarrassed and tend to conceal him, he will be on the minds of the brothers and sisters just as much as if he were in sight.

786. Changes in the parents' feelings. Many parents who discover that they have a child with a serious handicap go through much the same stages of feelings. First is the painful shock and the natural resentment. "Why does this have to happen to our family?" Then so often comes the guiltiness (discussed in Section 783). "What did I do wrong or what did I not do that I should have done?" The doctor keeps explaining, "You could not have prevented this condition." But it takes a long time for the parents to begin to feel convinced on the inside.

A difficulty that arises now and later is that various relatives and acquaintances keep coming forward with tales they have heard of experts and new treatments all over the world. They insist that the parents consult each in turn. They act shocked when their advice is not followed. They are well-meaning, but they keep the parents troubled.

The next stage is often one in which the parents become so preoccupied with the handicap and its treatment that they partly lose sight of the child as a person. They fail to enjoy all his other good qualities, which are quite unimpaired. Then as they gradually get back into focus and begin to think of him as another nice human being who just happens to have a particular difficulty, they can't help being irritated by those relatives and friends who still can't talk about anything but the child's handicap.

It helps parents in going through these painful stages to know that hundreds of thousands of other good parents have had the same experience.

787. Most parents need some help, too. Caring for a child with a handicap usually means extra effort and extra strain. To make the best plans for him requires real wisdom, which is hard to come by when you are upset and have little experience. All this adds up to the fact that you who are parents of handicapped children often need guidance and you are certainly entitled to it. I am thinking not just of medical advice.

I'm thinking of opportunities to discuss the management of the child at home, the problems created for the other members of the family, the pros and cons of the local school compared with schools farther away, the frustrations and resentment of the parents themselves. To get such matters clarified usually takes many long talks, over a period of years, with a counselor who is experienced in the field and is comforting to deal with.

There are usually social workers in state bureaus for the blind, deaf, crippled, and retarded, and also on the staffs of the schools and clinics that care for such children. In a rural district there may be a county welfare worker. In cities there are social workers in family and children's social agencies. To find the right person to help you with your problems, write, if you live in the country or a small town, to the department of welfare in your state capital. If you live in the city, call the Community Chest. They can tell you the right agency.

In recent years, the parents of children with various handicaps have organized themselves into local chapters and national associations. There are several purposes, all worth while. They share their special problems and solutions. They hear talks by professionals in the field. They exert their influence to get better facilities for their children. They raise funds for research and treatment.

You may be able to get information from the following national organizations:

The National Nephrosis Foundation, Inc.
143 E. 35th Street, New York 16, N. Y.

United Cerebral Palsy Association, Inc.
369 Lexington Avenue, New York 17, N. Y.

Muscular Dystrophy Associations of America, Inc.
1790 Broadway, New York 19, N. Y.

Cystic Fibrosis Foundation
2300 Westmoreland Street, Philadelphia, Pa.

United Epilepsy Association, Inc.
113 W. 57th Street, New York 19, N. Y.

National Association for Retarded Children, Inc.
99 University Place, New York 3, N. Y.

788. Where to live, where to go to school, where to get special training. Suppose a child has a defect that does not interfere with his getting to the regular neighborhood school and does not handicap him in learning in a regular class. Examples would be minor crippling, healed heart disease that does not seriously limit a child's activity, peculiarities of appearance such as birthmarks. It's best for such a child to go to the regular neighborhood school. He will be living the rest of his life among average people, and it's best for him to start out that way, thinking of himself as average in almost all respects.

789. Regular school when possible. In previous times it was believed that children with handicaps that interfere with ordinary classroom learning—such as impaired hearing or vision, for instance—should be sent from the start to specialized day schools in their own community or, if none were available, to specialized boarding schools. In more recent years it has been realized that though the education of the handicapped child is extremely important, even more important is his adjustment and his happiness. This means keeping in mind the sociability he will acquire from being with unhandicapped as well as handicapped children, the wholesome view he will take of the world and of himself if he grows up thinking of himself as a regular guy in most respects, the security he will gain from being part of his family. It is certainly preferable that a child live at home if possible. The younger a child is (especially up to the age of 6 or 8), the more he needs the close, loving, understanding kind of care, the sense of really belonging, that he is more likely to get at home than in even the best of boarding schools. So there has been an increasing effort to provide for handicapped children in regular neighborhood day schools wherever that is possible and, when appropriate, to keep them in regular classes as much of each day as is possible. This means increasing school budgets and training more specialized teachers so that local schools can have such facilities. It means in one case that the handicapped child may spend part of each day in a special class and other periods in the regular classroom with unhandicapped children. In some cases a specialized teacher can coach the regular classroom teacher in how to teach a subject so that the handicapped child can comprehend and participate.

How the philosophy works out in any community or school depends on many factors: the number and skill of the special teachers, the size of classes and classrooms, the kind of handicap, the severity of the handicap, the age and the previous training of the handicapped child.

790. The hard-of-hearing child. The child who is slightly hard of hearing needs lip-reading instruction and perhaps speech correction. The child who is more severely hard of hearing needs a hearing aid, lip-reading instruction, auditory training, and speech correction. When these special needs have been supplied, he can usually take his place in regular local schools.

791. The totally or nearly deaf child, on the other hand, can get little from a regular class until he has learned well how to communicate with others. This requires a long and very special training in speech and language, with the help of a hearing aid and intensive lip-reading practice.

In general, such training exists only in the larger cities. It is important for a deaf child to start between the ages of 2 and 3, if he can live near such a school. If not, he should, in most cases, be in a special boarding school by the age of 4, but one that understands and provides for the special emotional needs of the young child. The Volta Bureau, 1537 35th Street, N.W., Washington 7, D.C., will supply information on special schools for the deaf, and instruction for mothers of preschool children.

792. A blind child may be able to get a great deal from the regular school class (or regular nursery school) even though he needs some special instruction at the same time. It is amazing and inspiring to see how well even a 3- or 4-year-old blind child can get along in a class of seeing children. The inexperienced teacher, just like the parent, tends to be anxiously overprotective at first, but gradually comes to realize that overprotection is not necessary and only gets in the child's way. Of course, sensible precautions have to be taken and allowances made. The other children accept the handicapped one easily after a little questioning. They usually make allowances and give help in a very sensible manner. Information about special classes and schools for blind children can be obtained from your State Board of Education or State Commission for the Blind.

793. Some children with cerebral palsy or infantile paralysis require not special classes but highly skilled muscle treatment and training that is available in only a few places. Information about classes, schools, and other facilities for crippled children can be secured from your State Department of Health, Division of Crippled Children. The very special training that is needed for children with cerebral palsy cannot yet be secured in every part of the country. You can consult the National Society for Crippled Children and Adults, Inc., 11 South LaSalle Street, Chicago 3, Ill.

If no satisfactory training and treatment can be received where a family lives, they may consider moving.

794. Steady medical care. The parents of a child with any defect should, of course, get expert advice, from a private doctor or from a good hospital clinic. If they don't feel satisfied or if the suggested treatment sounds drastic, they are entitled to request another opinion, in consultation with the first doctor. Occasionally parents who have received what sounds like good advice from one doctor will go to one or two more "just to be sure," but they are apt to be confused by minor differences in treatment or terminology, and end up with more doubts than they started with.

If you have found a skillful doctor who understands your child's problem, stay with him, consult him regularly. The doctor who has known the child and family over a period of time is in a better position to prescribe wisely than the doctor who has just been called in. Psychologically, it is apt to be upsetting to the child with a defect to be taken to one new doctor after another. If you read of a new discovery in the condition your child has, ask your own doctor about it rather than rush to the discoverer. If it has been proved to be beneficial, your own doctor will know or can find out whether it has any promise in your child's case.

795. Mental slowness. You can roughly divide cases of real mental slowness into three groups: organic, glandular, and "natural." Organic cases are those in which there is physical brain damage, caused, for example, by insufficient oxygen reaching the brain during birth or by encephalitis. Glandular cases are due to deficient functioning of the thyroid gland; if they are diagnosed early and treated correctly, the mental deficiency may be kept to a minimum.

The majority of cases of mental slowness are "natural," in the sense that they are not caused by disease or injury or by anything that the parents did wrong or failed to do right. The child merely has less than the average degree of intelligence, just the way other children are brighter, shorter, or taller than average. His intelligence continues to develop steadily but at a slower rate than average. If a particular child at the age of 4 years has the intelligence of the average 3-year-old, then at 16 he will probably have the intelligence of an average 12-year-old. He is said to have an intelligence quotient (I.Q.) of 75 ($3/4 = 12/16 = 75/100$). Though there is lots to be done for the naturally slow child, there is no cure, any more than there is a cure for blue eyes or large feet.

796. Being accepted enables him to make the most of his abilities. The behavior problems that a few slow children develop are usually due not to low intelligence but to mistaken methods of handling. If the parents feel that the child is queer or shameful, for instance, their love may not go out to him in sufficiently full measure to give him security and happiness. If they mistakenly believe that they are to blame for his condition, they may insist on unwise "treatment" of all kinds that disturbs him without benefiting him. If they jump to the conclusion that he is a hopeless case who will never be "normal," they may neglect to provide him with the playthings, the companions, the proper schooling, that are needed by **all** children to bring out their best abilities. The greatest danger of all is that the parents, trying to ignore the signs that he is slow, trying to prove to themselves and the world that he is just as bright as the next child, will push him all along the line—try to teach him skills and manners before he is ready, hurry his toilet training, get him into a school class that he isn't up to, coach him at home in his lessons. The constant pressure makes him balky and irritable. Being frequently in situations in which he can't possibly succeed robs him of self-confidence.

Sadly enough, the slow child whose parents have had only an average amount of schooling and are living happily on a modest scale often makes out better than the child who is born into a college-educated family or one that has high ambitions for worldly success. The latter are more likely to assume that it's vital to get good marks at school, to go to college, to go into a profession.

There are many useful and dignified jobs that are best performed by people who have less than average intelligence. It's the right of every individual to grow up well enough adjusted and well enough trained to be able to handle the best job that he has the intelligence for.

The slow child must be allowed to develop in his own pattern, to have eating habits, toilet habits, that are suitable for his stage of mental growth rather than suitable for his age. He needs opportunities to dig and climb and build and make-believe at the periods when he is ready for these activities, playthings that appeal to him, chances to play with children that he can enjoy and keep up with (even if they are a year or more younger in age). When he goes to school, he must go into a class where he can feel that he belongs and is accomplishing something. He needs to be loved warmly and enjoyed for his appealing qualities.

Anyone who has observed groups of slow children knows how natural and friendly and appealing most of them are—particularly the ones who have been accepted naturally at home. And when they are busy at play or schoolwork that is right for them, they have the same eager, interested attitude that average and superior children do. In other words, the "dumb" look comes more from feeling out of place than from having a low I.Q. Most of us would have a stupid look in an advanced lecture on relativity.

The child who is only mildly or moderately slow is, of course, usually cared for at home. This is the place where he, like the average child, gets the most security. It will be good for him to go to nursery school, if possible, where the teachers can decide whether he should be with his own age or younger children.

797. The care of a slow child at home. Parents, when they become convinced that a child is slow in his mental development, are apt to ask the doctor or social worker what special playthings and educational material they should buy and what special instruction they should give the child at home. This is due to people's natural tendency to think, at first, that a handicapped child is very different from other children. To be sure, a retarded child has interests and capabilities that are not up to his chronological age; they correspond to his mental age. He is apt to want to play with children younger than himself, and with toys suitable for that younger age. He won't begin to try to tie his shoe laces or to pick out letters at 5 or 6, but he probably will become interested in these activities several years later when his mental age is 5 or 6.

The mother of a child of average intelligence doesn't have to ask a doctor or read a book to find out his interests. Mostly she watches him playing with his own possessions and with the possessions of neighbors and senses what else might appeal to him. She observes what he is trying to learn and helps him tactfully.

It's really just the same with a retarded child. You watch to see what he enjoys. You get him the playthings, indoors and out, that are sensible. You help him locate the children he has fun with, every day if possible. You teach him the skills he wants assistance with.

798. The right school placement is vital. It is wise to get the opinion and guidance of a psychiatrist or psychologist, privately or through a child-guidance clinic or through the school system, when it is suspected that a child is slow (Section 570). It is important that he be tested by the time he is 5 or 6 years old, before he enters kindergarten or first grade. He should not get into a class that is beyond him. Every day that he is unable to keep up, his self-confidence is destroyed a little, and being left back a grade or demoted hurts him a lot. If he is only slightly slow and the school program is one in which every child can contribute according to his ability, he may be able to move along with children his own age. But if he is moderately slow, or if the schoolwork is the same for all children in the class, then he should not start first grade until his mental ability is up to it. This may mean waiting 1 or more years. If there is a kindergarten, it may be wise to wait to start this until the year before he is ready for first grade, so that he won't be disappointed if he does not move on to the grades with his class. On the other hand, if the kindergarten is very flexible, it may be better for him to plan to be there for 2 years, especially if he has few children to play with at home.

In a large school system there may be special "opportunity" classes for children who are moderately slow. They start in the special class at 6 or 7 or 8, but postpone book work for several years, depending on what they are ready for.

If the family have determined in advance, with the help of a psychologist, that a child needs to be in a special class, they may be able to move into a neighborhood where such classes exist by the time the child is of school age.

If it is impossible to get the help of a psychologist, discuss the child thoroughly with the teacher or principal, giving her all the facts. If there is any doubt of his readiness, it is better to wait too long than to start too soon.

799. Boarding school if it offers more. The situation can always be reviewed again later to see whether the day school is meeting the needs of the child, in either a regular or special class. If the child is not up to the work in the class that is available and is not happy there, or if his handicap is too upsetting to other members of the family, it may be better for all concerned, at some future stage, to take advantage of the opportunities offered by a state or private boarding school. At least the parents will want to look into this carefully. The waiting list at most state schools is long and there may be a delay of several years between the time that application is made and the child is accepted. Better to get on a waiting list early and then give up the place later if it is not needed than to delay applying because you are undecided.

800. The more seriously retarded child. The child who at 1½ or 2 years, for instance, is still unable to sit up, who shows little interest in people or things, presents more complicated problems. He will have to be cared for as a baby for a long time. Because of his very limited awareness, he receives less benefit from the family and they find less to respond to in him. Of course, there is no one right answer. It depends on the degree of retardation, the temperament of the child, how he affects other children in the family, whether by the time he is active he can find playmates and activities to keep him happy, whether there is a special class in one of the local schools that will accept him and suit him, the availability and quality of boarding schools. Most of all, it depends on how much his mother can enjoy caring for him or how much he exhausts her physically and emotionally. Some of these questions can't be answered until the child is several years older.

One mother is so constituted that she can take a retarded child in her stride. She can find ways to care for him that don't exhaust her. She is able to enjoy his agreeable qualities, not be upset by the difficulties he presents, and not become too wrapped up in his care. The other children in the family take their cue mainly from her in these respects. The acceptance by the rest of the family brings out the best in the retarded child and gives him a good start in life. He may be able to benefit most by living at home indefinitely.

Another mother who is equally devoted finds herself becoming increasingly tense and impatient in caring for a child with such special needs. This may impair her relationship with her husband and other children, and the children may be upset by the presence of the handicapped child. The mother needs a lot of help from a social worker. This should lead either to a more comfortable attitude or to making some other provision for the child that will be better for all concerned.

Still another mother finds that she can throw herself into the care of a seriously handicapped child without a feeling of undue strain, even with an enjoyable devotion. But an outsider can see that her sense of obligation to the child is so intense that she is not thinking enough of her husband, her other children, or her own normal interests. In the long run, this is not healthy for the family as a whole or even for the retarded child. The mother needs help in gaining a sense of proportion and in easing up in her preoccupation (Section 787).

801. Mongolism. There is a special type of organic mental deficiency called Mongolism. This is a disturbance of bodily as well as mental development. The eyes slant upward like an Oriental's, and this is how the condition received its name. There are other distinctive characteristics. Physical growth is slow, and the child does not reach full size. Intelligence develops very slowly in most cases, but in a few it develops to a fair degree. In disposition, these children are characteristically sweet-natured.

The chances of having a Mongolian baby increase toward the end of the childbearing period. A young woman whose first baby is Mongolian can be reassured that there is very little chance of her having another at this stage of life.

Mongolism can usually be diagnosed at birth, but in a few cases there is uncertainty until the child's development has been observed for a number of months.

As in other forms of mental slowness, the best course for the future depends on how the child develops, the local opportunities for classes and playmates, how difficult or how comfortable it proves for the mother to carry out her other jobs and this special one, too. Some Mongolian children are reared at home enjoyably and without undue strain on parents and children. In other cases, it turns out as the child grows older that he and the rest of the family would be happier if he were cared for in a state or private boarding school. With this possibility in mind, it is wise to make tentative application early, because there is usually a waiting list of several years' duration. The application can always be canceled later if it is not wanted. Continued counseling is helpful in arriving at the best decision.

Some doctors recommend to parents who can afford it that the baby be cared for in a private nursing home from birth so that they will not become overattached to a child who is not likely to develop far and so that they can devote all their care to the other children. This may be the better plan in some families, not in others. I think parents should take their time in coming to a decision and that if they are in doubt, it is helpful to get counsel from a family social agency or a psychiatrist. Very few families, however, can afford such private care, year after year. Very few state schools can accept such children before they are 5 years or older because of policy or because of lack of facilities.

ADOPTING A CHILD

802. Both parents should want him very much. A couple should decide to adopt a child only if both of them love children and feel that they just can't get along without them. All children, "own" or adopted, need to feel that they belong to and are loved by both father and mother, deeply and "forever," if they are to grow up secure. It's worse for an adopted child to sense a lack of devotion in one or both parents because he's not quite so secure to begin with. He knows that he was given up for some reason by his true parents, and he may fear secretly that his adopted parents might someday give him up, too. You can see, then, why it's a mistake to adopt when only one parent wants to, or when both parents are thinking of it only for practical reasons, such as to have extra help on the farm or to have someone to take care of them in their old age. Occasionally a woman who is afraid that she's losing her husband wants to adopt a child with the futile hope that this will hold his love. Adoption for reasons like this is not just unfair to the child. It usually proves to be wrong from the parents' point of view, too. All too often the adopted child who is not deeply loved becomes a serious behavior problem.

It's usually unwise for a single person to adopt a child. This is because boys and girls both need the influence of father and mother in their upbringing, and because the single person may become too wrapped up in the child.

A couple should not wait until they are too old to adopt a child. They are liable to become too set in their ways. They've dreamed so long of a little girl with golden curls filling the house with song as she goes about her daily tasks that even the best of children turns out to be a rude shock. How old is "too old"? It's not a matter of years alone. It's something to discuss with a child-placing agency.

Parents who have a child of their own who is not very happy or sociable sometimes consider adopting another to keep him company. It's a good idea to talk this over with a children's psychiatrist or the child-placing agency before thinking of this very seriously. The adopted child is apt to feel like an outsider compared to the "own" child. If the parents lean over backward to show affection for the newcomer, it may upset rather than help their own child. It's a risky business.

There's sometimes danger, too, in adopting to "replace" a child who has died. If there are other "own" children in the family, an adopted child may feel at a disadvantage. But even if the parents have no other children, they should adopt only because they want a child to love for himself. There is no harm in adopting one who is similar in age and sex and appearance to the child who died, but the comparison should stop there. It is unfair and unsound to want to make one individual play the part of another. He is bound to fail at the job of being a ghost, and he will disappoint the parents and become unhappy. He should not be reminded of what the other child did, or be compared with him out loud or in the parents' minds. Let him be himself. (Some of this applies also to the "own" child who is born after an older one dies.)

803. Adopt through a good agency. Probably the most important rule of all about adoption is to arrange it through a first-rate child-placing agency. It is always risky for the adopting parents to deal directly with the true parents or through an inexperienced third person. It leaves the way open for the true parents to change their minds and to try to get their child back. Even when the law stands in the way of this, the unpleasantness can ruin the happiness of the adopting family and the security of the child. The good agency stands like an impenetrable wall between the two sets of parents, keeps them from ever knowing each other, keeps them from ever making trouble for each other, and thereby protects the child. The agency helps the natural mother and relatives to make the right decision in the first place as to whether to give the baby up or not. It uses its judgment and experience in deciding which couples should be dissuaded from adopting. The agency also watches the child during the probationary period in the new family to make sure that the arrangement is working out well for all concerned. Wise agencies and wise state laws require a probationary period before the adoption becomes final.

At what age should a child be adopted? In a general way, the younger the better. The adopting parents feel that they are starting with a clean slate and can get used to the baby through the same easy stages as if he were their own. However, plenty of successful adoptions have been made later in childhood.

Adopting parents usually wonder about the baby's heredity and how it will affect his future. The more we have learned about personality development, including intelligence, the clearer it becomes that the most important factor by far is the environment in which the child grows up, especially the love he receives and the feeling of belonging that he acquires. There is no evidence that specific social abnormalities like alcoholism, immorality, delinquency, or irresponsibility are inherited.

804. Let him find out naturally. Should an adopted child be told he is adopted? All the experienced people in this field agree that the child should know. He's **sure** to find out sooner or later from someone or other, no matter how carefully the parents think they are keeping the secret. It is practically always a very disturbing experience for an older child, or even an adult, to discover **suddenly** that he is adopted. It may disturb his sense of security for years. Supposing a baby has been adopted during his first year, when should he be told? The news shouldn't be saved for **any** definite age. The parents should, from the beginning, let the fact that he's adopted come openly, but casually, into their conversations with each other, with the child, and with their acquaintances. This creates an atmosphere in which the child can ask questions whenever he is at a stage of development in which the subject interests him. He finds out what adoption means bit by bit, as he gains understanding.

Some adopting parents make the mistake of trying to keep the adoption secret; others err in the opposite direction by stressing it too much. Most adopting parents have, quite naturally, an exaggerated sense of responsibility at first—as if they have to be letter-perfect to justify the fact that someone else's child has been entrusted to their care. If they go too earnestly at the job of explaining to the child that he's adopted, he begins to wonder, "What's wrong with being adopted, anyway?" But if they accept the adoption as naturally as they accept the color of the child's hair, they won't have to make a secret of it, or keep reminding him of it. They should remind themselves that, having been selected by the agency, they're probably darned good parents and the child is lucky to have found them.

Let's say that a child around 3 hears his mother explaining to a new acquaintance that he is adopted, and asks, "What's **adopted,** Mommy?" She might answer, "A long time ago I wanted very much to have a little baby boy to love and take care of. So I went to a place where there were a lot of babies, and I told the lady, 'I want a little boy with brown hair and brown eyes.' So she brought me a baby, and it was you. And I said, 'Oh, this is just exactly the baby that I want. I want to adopt him and take him home to keep forever.' And that's how I adopted you." This makes a good beginning because it emphasizes the positive side of the adoption, the fact that the mother received just what she wanted. The story will delight him, and he'll want to hear it many times.

But somewhere between the ages of 3 and 4, if he is like most children, he wants to know where babies come from in the beginning. The answer is discussed in Section 525. It is best to answer truthfully, but simply enough so that the 3-year-old can understand easily. But when his adopted mother explains that babies grow inside the mother's abdomen, it makes him wonder how this fits in with the story of picking him out from all the other babies at the institution. Maybe then, or months later, he asks, "Did I grow inside you?" Then the adopting mother can explain, simply and casually, that he grew inside another mother before he was adopted. This is apt to confuse him for a while, but he will get it clear later.

Eventually he raises the more difficult question of why his own mother gave him up. To imply that his mother didn't want him would shake his confidence in all mothers. Any sort of made-up reason may bother him later in some unexpected way. Perhaps the best answer and nearest to the truth might be, "I don't know why she couldn't take care of you, but I'm sure she wanted to." During the period when the child is digesting this idea, he needs to be reminded, along with a hug, that he's **always** going to be yours now.

805. He must belong completely. The secret fear that the adopted child may have is that his adopting parents will someday give him up as his true parents did, if they change their minds or if he is bad. Adopting parents should always remember this and vow that they will **never,** under any circumstances, say or hint that the idea of giving him up has ever crossed their minds. One threat uttered in a thoughtless or angry moment might be enough to destroy the child's confidence in them forever. They should be ready to let him know that he is theirs forever at any time the question seems to enter his mind; for instance, when he is talking about his adoption. I'd like to add, though, that it's a mistake for the adopting parents to worry so about the child's security that they over-emphasize their talk of loving him. Basically, the thing that gives the adopted child the greatest security is **being** loved, wholeheartedly and naturally. It's not the words but the music that counts.

INDEX

3

EMERGENCIES

Index

H

Made in the USA
Columbia, SC
20 December 2018